CLAUDIAN

PANEGYRICVS
DE SEXTO CONSVLATV
HONORII AVGVSTI

CLAUDIAN

PANEGYRICVS DE SEXTO CONSVLATV HONORII AVGVSTI

EDITED WITH
INTRODUCTION, TRANSLATION, AND
LITERARY COMMENTARY BY

MICHAEL DEWAR

CLARENDON PRESS · OXFORD
1996

Oxford University Press, Great Clarendon Street, Oxford OX2 6DP

Oxford   New York

Athens   Auckland   Bangkok   Bogota   Bombay
Buenos Aires   Calcutta   Cape Town   Dar es Salaam
Delhi   Florence   Hong Kong   Istanbul   Karachi
Kuala Lumpur   Madras   Madrid   Melbourne
Mexico City   Nairobi   Paris   Singapore
Taipei   Tokyo   Toronto

and associated companies in
Berlin   Ibadan

Oxford is a trade mark of Oxford University Press

Published in the United States
by Oxford University Press Inc., New York

British Library Cataloguing in Publication Data

Data available

Library of Congress Cataloging in Publication Data
[Panegyricus de sexto consulatu Honorii Augusti. English & Latin]
Panegyricus de sexto consulatu Honorii Augusti / Claudian: edited
with introduction, translation, and literary commentary by Michael Dewar.
Includes bibliographical references and indexes.
1. Laudatory poetry, Latin—Translations into English.   2. Rome—
—History—Honorius, 395-423—Poetry.   3. Honorius, Flavius, 384-423—
—Poetry.   4. Kings and rulers—Poetry.   5. Laudatory poetry, Latin.
I. Dewar, Michael (Michael J.)   II. Title.
PA6373.E5P34   1996   873'.01—dc20   96-1460

ISBN 0-19-814964-6

1 3 5 7 9 10 8 6 4 2

Typeset by Regent Typesetting, London
Printed in Great Britain on acid-free paper by
Bookcraft (Bath) Ltd., Midsomer Norton

PREFACE

THIS book has been a long time in the making. It owes its distant genesis to a graduate seminar given by Professor R. G. M. Nisbet on *De Sexto Consulatu Honorii* some time near the very beginning of the last decade. This seminar I was privileged to attend, despite being at the time a singularly ill-informed, inarticulate, and unlettered undergraduate. It proved to be one of my first inductions into the pursuit of rigorous philology and textual criticism, and I have never forgotten it. My study of Claudian was of necessity laid aside while I applied myself to the business of jumping through various fiery hoops held out by the members of the Faculty of Literae Humaniores in the University of Oxford to test the mettle of the young and eager. Duly singed and scorched, I here attempt to show that in the intervening years I have at least learned a little of what I ought to have known at the start of that Trinity Term so long ago.

The innocent eye sees nothing, as a famous art critic once said; the same maxim surely applies to those who dare to explicate texts for others. I therefore make no pretence of innocence, and I am quite sure that my own views on Claudian's literary processes and on how to interpret this, his last (and, to my mind, his finest) poem will be clear enough to all but the least attentive readers. But, although the tropes of objectivity that characterize this traditional form of scholarly writing smack, perhaps, of authoritarianism, I should like to think that the present edition is more of a mushy liberal in many respects. I have, that is, done my level best to offer all the information and guidance I could to those whose readings of the poem will be shaped by scholarly and critical discourses other than those usually permitted to assume all the prestige and privilege traditionally conferred by distinguished bindings of gold and dark blue.

The introduction to this book lays out as succinctly as I could manage such basic information as I thought essential to an understanding of the background to the poem. The text presented has largely been compiled from published sources, most notably the Teubner text of J. B. Hall. From this it none the less differs in

some half a dozen places; hunting these down I leave to the dili-
gence of reviewers, while advising other readers to be sceptical of
any would-be judge who proves unable to identify and evaluate,
let us say, three or more. This task I cheerfully impose upon
reviewers in order to keep them humble when they turn their
attention to the apparatus criticus; that essential tool of scholarship here employs the unorthodox, but, I believe, helpfully lucid
system of manuscript citation pioneered by Dr Claire Gruzelier in
her edition of Claudian's *De Raptu Proserpinae* (Oxford, 1993). In
conformity with current practice, I have attached an English
translation—or, rather, an English prose paraphrase, since it aims
at nothing nobler than a reasonable degree of brutally literal
accuracy. The Latinless—and, still more, the lazy—are warned
that its function is only to serve as an aid to the comprehension of
Claudian's original text, not as a substitute for it. The heart of the
book, however, remains the commentary, in which the focus is on
literary and linguistic matters, above all Claudian's panegyrical
techniques, his narrative structure, his language and metre, and
his use of allusion to a vast range of other poets, both Latin and
Greek. In addition to being a splendid literary construct, *VI Cons.*
is also one of the very few surviving contemporary records of
Alaric's first incursion on to Italian soil, albeit one with a forceful
agenda of its own. I hope that what I have to say on such matters
as the chronology of the campaign or Stilicho's relations with the
Senate will provide something of interest for historians of the
period, but I must stress that any discussion of this kind offered
below is subservient to the purpose of literary evaluation.

Professor Nisbet kindly read every word of the draft of the commentary and made more suggestions for its improvement than I
could count: I can only hope that the finished version is not one
with which he will be sorry to see his name associated. My
colleague Dr John Vanderspoel also read the whole of the
typescript in its early stages, and in addition to making many
acute individual observations helped me to avoid exposing too
blatantly my ignorance of the bibliography on the historical
problems presented by the poem. Dr Claire Gruzelier generously
gave me her permission to make use of the system of manuscript
citation mentioned above. For various references, and for the loan
of books and other materials, I am indebted to Professor Martin

Cropp, Mr Adrian Hollis, Dr John Humphrey, and Dr Mary Walbank. In this regard my life was also made much easier by Prof. Dr. Heinz Hofmann, who provided me with a personal copy of Karl Müller's hard-to-obtain 1938 commentary on the poem. Conversations with Dr Eric Savoy regularly sharpened my brain, though not yet, I fear, to his daunting standards. And I have learned much more from my graduate students Christina Vester and Andrew Zissos than they realize, or will readily believe.

For financial help I am grateful to the University Research Grants Committee here at the University of Calgary, who twice dug deep into their institutional pockets to let me spend part of the summer reading in the Bodleian and British Libraries. The award of a Killam Resident Fellowship in the autumn of 1993 gave me the relative leisure I needed to move from making piles of chaotic notes to the composition of ordered text. In general, I have been lucky in belonging to a department and to a faculty which have been willing to do all in their power to aid my research. Indeed, in every way I have been happier in these last six years in Calgary than at any other time in my life, and I am glad to have found the opportunity to say so publicly.

Lillian Kogawa showed far more patience in answering my endless cranky questions on technical matters than I was ever able to find for my word-processor, splendid machine though it undoubtedly is. And my brother Stephen Jenkin ducked a few fiery hoops of his own to check for me in the Bodleian Library a number of references I had been too disorganized to find for myself the previous summer. At the Oxford University Press, Hilary O'Shea has always been blessedly unruffled, however false my promises concerning deadlines turned out to be.

In editing the original typescript Dr Leofranc Holford-Strevens removed a great deal that was erroneous, superfluous, or misleading, and also taught me more in twenty-four pages of closely argued comments than I usually succeed in learning from entire books.

Lastly, to more friends than I could conveniently name in these pages I am grateful for their unstinting encouragement and support. But I should like to record my particular gratitude to Miss Sarah Graham, Dr David Herrmann, Nageeb Kassim, Dr Sophie Mills, Dr Ingrid Rowland, and—the sweetest debt of all—

Edgardo Silva: *Ficava-nos também na amada terra* | *O coração, que as mágoas lá deixavam.* | *E já despois que toda se escondeu,* | *Não vimos mais emfim que mar e céu.* My heartfelt thanks to them all.

MICHAEL DEWAR

Calgary
August, 1995

CONTENTS

ABBREVIATIONS

Axelson	B. Axelson, *Unpoetische Wörter* (Lund, 1945)
Barr	William Barr, *Claudian's Panegyric on the Fourth Consulship of Honorius* (Liverpool, 1981)
Barth	K. von Barth, *Claudii Claudiani quae exstant* (Hanover, 1612; 2nd edn. Frankfurt, 1650)
Birt	T. D. Birt, *Claudii Claudiani Carmina* (*MGH AA* 10; Berlin, 1892)
Bury, *LRE*	J. B. Bury, *History of the Later Roman Empire*, i (London, 1889, repr. New York, 1958)
Cameron	Alan Cameron, *Claudian: Poetry and Propaganda at the Court of Honorius* (Oxford, 1970)
Christiansen	Peder G. Christiansen, *The Use of Images by Claudius Claudianus* (The Hague, 1969)
CIL	*Corpus Inscriptionum Latinarum* (Berlin, 1862–)
Coleman	K. M. Coleman, *Statius. Siluae IV. Edited with an English Translation and Commentary* (Oxford, 1988)
Courtney, *FLP*	Edward Courtney, *The Fragmentary Latin Poets, Edited with Commentary* (Oxford, 1993)
Crees	J. H. E. Crees, *Claudian as an Historical Authority* (Cambridge, 1908)
Daremberg–Saglio	C. Daremberg and E. Saglio, *Dictionnaire des antiquités grecques et romaines d'après les textes et les monuments*, 5 vols. (Paris, 1877–1919)
Der Kleine Pauly	Konrat Ziegler and Walther Sontheimer (edd.), *Der Kleine Pauly. Lexikon der Antike in fünf Bänden*, adapted from Pauly's *Realencyclopädie* (Munich, 1979)
Döpp	Siegmar Döpp, *Zeitgeschichte in Dichtungen Claudians* (Hermes Einzelschriften, 43; Wiesbaden, 1980)
Fargues	Pierre Fargues, *Claudien: études sur sa poésie et son temps* (diss. Paris, 1933)
Fargues on *Eutr.*	Pierre Fargues, *Invectives contre Eutrope* (Paris, 1933)

xiii

Gesner	J. M. Gesner, *Claudii Claudiani quae exstant* (Leipzig, 1759)
Griffin	Jasper Griffin, *Homer on Life and Death* (Oxford, 1980)
Gruzelier	Claire Gruzelier, *Claudian, De Raptu Proserpinae, Edited with Translation, Introduction, and Commentary* (Oxford, 1993)
Gualandri	I. Gualandri, *Aspetti della tecnica compositiva in Claudiano* (Milan, 1968)
Hall	J. B. Hall, *Claudii Claudiani Carmina* (Leipzig, 1985)
Heather	P. J. Heather, *Goths and Romans 332–489* (Oxford, 1991)
Jones, *LRE*	A. H. M. Jones, *The Later Roman Empire 284–602: A Social, Economic and Administrative Survey*, 2 vols. (Guildford/London, 1964, repr. 1973)
KG	R. Kühner, *Ausführliche Grammatik der griechischen Sprache: Satzlehre*, 3rd edn. by B. Gerth (Hanover, 1898–1904)
Kromayer– Vieth	J. Kromayer and G. Veith, *Heerwesen und Kriegführung der Griechen und Römer* (Munich, 1928)
KS	R. Kühner, *Ausführliche Grammatik der lateinischen Sprache: Satzlehre*, 2nd edn. by K. Stegmann (Hanover, 1912)
Levy	Harry L. Levy, *Claudian's* In Rufinum: *An Exegetical Commentary* (American Philological Association, Monograph 30; Case Western Reserve University, 1935; repr. 1971)
LHS	M. Leumann, J. B. Hofmann, A. Szantyr, *Lateinische Grammatik* (Munich, 1977)
Liebeschuetz	J. H. W. G. Liebeschuetz, *Barbarians and Bishops: Army, Church, and State in the Age of Arcadius and Chrysostom* (Oxford, 1990)
Löfstedt, *Syntactica*	Einar Löfstedt, *Syntactica: Studien und Beiträge zur historischen Syntax des Lateins*, 2nd edn. (Malmö, 1956)
MacCormack	Sabine MacCormack, *Art and Ceremony in Late*

Antiquity (Berkeley and Los Angeles, 1981)

McCormick — Michael McCormick, *Eternal Victory: Triumphal Rulership in Late Antiquity, Byzantium and the Early Medieval West* (Cambridge, 1986)

Matthews — John Matthews, *Western Aristocracies and Imperial Court A.D. 364–425* (Oxford, 1975)

Millar — Fergus Millar, *The Emperor in the Roman World*, 2nd edn. (London, 1992)

Müller — Karl Albert Müller, *Claudians Festgedicht auf das sechste Konsulat des Kaisers Honorius* (diss. Heidelberg; Berlin, 1938)

Nisbet–Hubbard — R. G. M. Nisbet and Margaret Hubbard, *A Commentary on Horace: Odes, Book I* (Oxford, 1970); *A Commentary on Horace: Odes, Book II* (Oxford, 1978)

Ogilvie — R. M. Ogilvie, *Livy 1–5* (Oxford, 1965)

O'Flynn — John Michael O'Flynn, *Generalissimos of the Western Empire* (Edmonton, Alta. 1983)

OLD — *The Oxford Latin Dictionary*, ed. P. G. W. Glare (Oxford, 1968–82)

Olechowska — Elżbieta M. Olechowska, *Claudii Claudiani De Bello Gildonico, texte établi, traduit et commenté* (Leiden, 1978)

Palmer — L. R. Palmer, *The Latin Language* (London, 1954; repr. Bristol, 1988)

Platnauer — Maurice Platnauer (ed., tr.) *Claudian* (Loeb Classical Library, 2 vols.; New York and London, 1928)

PLRE — A. H. M. Jones, J. R. Martindale, and J. Morris (eds.), *The Prosopography of the Later Roman Empire*, 3 vols. (Cambridge, 1971–92)

RE — *Real-Encyclopädie der classischen Altertumswissenschaft* (Stuttgart, 1893–1980)

Richardson — L. Richardson, Jr., *A New Topographical Dictionary of Ancient Rome* (Baltimore and London, 1992)

Roberts — Michael Roberts, *The Jeweled Style. Poetry and Poetics in Late Antiquity* (Ithaca, 1989)

Schmidt — Peter L. Schmidt, *Politik und Dichtung in der*

	Panegyrik Claudians (Konstanzer Universitäts-reden, 55; Konstanz, 1976)
Schroff	Helmut Schroff, *Claudians Gedicht vom Gotenkrieg* (Klassisch-philologische Studien, Heft 8; Berlin, 1927)
Simon	Werner Simon, *Claudiani Panegyricus de Consulatu Manlii Theodori* (Berlin, 1975)
TLL	*Thesaurus Linguae Latinae* (Leipzig, 1900–)
Trump	F. Trump, *Observationes ad genus dicendi Claudiani eiusque imitationem Virgilianam spectantes* (Halle, 1887)
Weinstock	Stefan Weinstock, *Divus Julius* (Oxford, 1971)
Wolfram	Herwig Wolfram, *History of the Goths*, tr. Thomas J. Dunlap (Berkeley and Los Angeles, 1988)
Woodcock	E. C. Woodcock, *A New Latin Syntax* (London, 1959; repr. Bristol, 1985) [cited by section]

INTRODUCTION

I. CLAUDIAN'S LIFE AND WORKS

THE lives and characters of numerous authors of the Late Roman Empire, most notably Symmachus and Augustine, are as well known as those of almost any of the famous writers of the Republic or of the time of Augustus.[1] But Claudian, like Prudentius, the other great poet of his day, is in many ways a mystery. We know neither the place nor the date of his birth, though Alexandria and c.370 seem reasonable suppositions.[2] We know nothing at all of his family, and practically nothing of his education other than what can be deduced from our knowledge of the general forms of instruction that fourth-century Egypt had to offer. And for all that he lived in an age often regarded by both his contemporaries and ours as one in which the new faith battled to the death with the old, even his views on religion are a matter of some dispute.

It seems, however, tolerably clear that Claudian is only one example, albeit an exceptionally talented one, of an entire 'school' of professional poets of Egyptian background who flourished in the fourth and fifth centuries. The general nature of this group, which includes such erstwhile famous names as Olympiodorus, Nonnus, Cyrus of Panopolis, and Pamprepius, has been firmly established by Alan Cameron.[3] Their shared characteristics include paganism, great learning, an involvement in politics and Imperial administration, and the fact that, although some also wrote on mythological or other more self-consciously 'literary' themes, the bulk of their poetic output was on contemporary politics. These writings took the form of encomia delivered to prominent officials of the Empire or to Emperors themselves and, more rarely, invectives against their enemies: for such compositions the poets were paid, whether in the form of government posts, in kind, or in hard cash. To that extent, they are the

[1] For a full general discussion of Claudian's life and background, see Cameron 1 ff.; also *PLRE* ii. 299 f., Barr 7 ff.   [2] Note esp. *c.m.* 19. 3 '*nostro* cognite Nilo'.
[3] 'Wandering Poets: A Literary Movement in Byzantine Egypt', *Historia*, 14 (1965), 470–509.

successors of those professional poets of the Early Empire who made their living from a combination of prizes won in the literary contests of the great games of the Greek world, from careers as *grammatici*, and from the generosity of grateful patrons.[4]

Until, probably, the year 394, Claudian's career is likely to have followed much the same lines as those of his peers. It can be reasonably surmised that, while in the East, he composed mainly in Greek, and a quantity of poetry attributed to him and written in that language, including fragments of a *Gigantomachia*, may belong to his early years.[5] What is certain, however, is that by the beginning of 395 he was in Rome, already celebrating in highly polished and faultlessly classical Latin hexameters the joint consulship of the young sons of the great Petronius Probus, Olybrius and Probinus. Probus was himself a former consul and four-time praetorian prefect, and his family, the Anicii, were the undoubted doyens of Rome's Christian aristocracy, a class that was growing ever more powerful under the patronage of the stoutly Catholic house of Theodosius the Great. How long by this point Claudian had been in the Western half of the Empire is a matter of mere conjecture, but unless he was a young man given an extraordinary break by Fortune, he must surely have already established a formidable reputation for his poetry and an equally remarkable command of Latin. In this he has been rightly compared with Ammianus, another native Greek-speaker who made his home in the West and his fame in Latin. It may have been an exceptional ability in the language that persuaded Claudian to try his luck in Rome, or perhaps the main attraction was the unparalleled wealth of the senatorial aristocracy, a wealth which far surpassed that of their Eastern counterparts.[6] Even in this, however, he is less of an anomaly than is often assumed. There is plenty of evidence that Latin literature was widely studied, at least in some circles, in Egypt at this period, and a knowledge of the language was a decided recommendation in those who hoped to hold posts in the administration even of the Eastern Empire.[7]

[4] This phenomenon is admirably discussed in Alex Hardie, *Statius and the Silvae: Poets, Patrons and Epideixis in the Graeco-Roman World* (Liverpool, 1983).

[5] Claudian's Greek poems may be most conveniently consulted on pp. 429 ff. of J. B. Hall's edition (Leipzig, 1985).

[6] See e.g. Matthews 1 ff., 277 f., Peter Brown, *The World of Late Antiquity* (London, 1971), 115 ff.   [7] See Cameron, 494 ff.

Barely a year after his encomium of the young Anicii, Claudian had left Rome and taken up residence with the court in Milan. Somehow praise of his skill had come to the ears of Stilicho, husband of Serena, Theodosius the Great's niece and daughter by adoption. Theodosius had died on 17 January 395, leaving Stilicho as guardian of his son and successor in the West, Honorius. In Stilicho Claudian acquired the most powerful and influential patron available to him in the Western Empire. For the next decade he served him loyally as his chief apologist, attacking his enemies and glorifying his wars, his connections by marriage with the Imperial family, and his consulship in 400. Even those of his poems which nominally offer their praise directly to the ineffectual Emperor, or to other luminaries, including Serena and the philosopher-statesman Mallius Theodorus, none the less give much prominence to the real source of power in the state, and Stilicho is the true hero of *De Sexto Consulatu Honorii* just as much as of *De Bello Getico*, the unfinished epic on his victories over Alaric.[8]

Most of what has been said above is deduced from Claudian's own writings, but a few other pieces of contemporary evidence survive for us. The Senate had a bronze statue erected in his honour in the Forum of Trajan, probably in 400. The inscription survives and informs us that Claudian held the ranks of *uir clarissimus* and *tribunus et notarius*: he was thus formally a senator himself.[9] Augustine knew his poetry, and, quoting his account of the battle of the Frigidus, describes him in an aside as 'a Christi nomine alienus', while his disciple Orosius is more blunt, calling him a 'paganus peruicacissimus.'[10] But even these uncompromising statements can hardly be taken as incontrovertible fact. They may be deductions based on a miscomprehension, or hostile misrepresentation, of the literary paganism of his poetry, or else they may originate in anti-Stilichonian rumour; the same charge, after all, was levelled against Stilicho's own son Eucherius, on grounds that seem very weak. Claudian's writing itself is not conclusive at all. His lesser poems include an Easter hymn (*c.m.* 22) which may

---

[8] See in general Cameron 46 ff.

[9] See *CIL* vi. 1710. The statue is mentioned by Claudian at *pr. Get.* 7 f., and is associated there with his poem on the consulship of Stilicho. That it was erected in 400 is thus a reasonable bet.

[10] Augustine, *Ciu. Dei* 5. 26 (citing *III Cons.* 96 f.), and Orosius 7. 35.

be regarded either as a confession of personal faith, or else as a literary exercise written to satisfy a commission from the pious Christian court.[11] And on the other hand they also offer us a bitter epigram against one *dux Iacobus* who is seemingly mocked for his excessive devotion to the cult of the saints (*c.m.* 50). In particular, this latter poem has been interpreted in strikingly different ways. Cameron offers the strongest scepticism: 'According to Fargues . . . the poem proves beyond doubt that Claudian viewed Christianity with disfavour. In fact all it proves is that Claudian viewed Jacob with disfavour.'[12] But more recently, John Vanderspoel has attempted a careful reading of the poem's allusions and concludes that it suggests that 'at best, [Claudian] was tolerant of Christianity.'[13] As for Claudian's panegyrics and epics, they are wholly pagan in their conception and in their traditional literary form, but not one whit more so than those of Sidonius Apollinaris, who enjoyed the status of bishop and saint. Christian poetry, after all, was still in the making; it may not yet have seemed wholly respectable to a graduate of the schools of Alexandria. Indeed, outside of his *magnum opus*, the mythological epic *De Raptu Proserpinae*, Claudian tends to avoid the traditional Graeco-Roman pantheon and prefers instead more abstract and less offensive personifications, such as Roma, the only deity given a speaking role in *VI Cons.* And nowhere in his panegyrics can Claudian be conclusively shown to be taking an aggressively pro-pagan stand. *VI Cons.*, for example, touches upon two issues that were the subject of religious controversy in his day, but the nearest he gets in either case to pagan propaganda is in suggesting that the rain-miracle in Marcus Aurelius' campaign against the Quadi might possibly be attributed to the intervention of 'the Thunderer'; and this traditional epithet of Jupiter is in any case applied by his contemporary Prudentius to the Christian God.[14] His Egyptian background and the evidence of Augustine do, on

---

[11] See Cameron 215 ff., and cf. Peter L. Schmidt, *Politik und Dichtung in der Panegyrik Claudians* (Konstanz, 1976), 12.　　　　　　　　　　　　　　　　　　　　[12] Cameron 225.

[13] 'Claudian, Christ and the Cult of the Saints', *CQ*, NS 36 (1986), 244–55, esp. 252. One might compare Thomas Hodgkin, *Claudian: The Last of the Roman Poets* (London, 1875), 4, 49: 'heathen in the midst of triumphant Christianity, like some grey old boulder-stone, memorial of the glacial epoch, left in a smooth and verdant valley'.

[14] See 339–50 and 597–602 nn. *Tonans*: compare *VI Cons.* 349 with e.g. Prud. *Pe.* 6. 98, *Ham.* 376, 669.

balance, imply that Claudian was most likely a pagan. But if so, his faith is unlikely to have been of the abrasive or controversial kind, since his Western patrons were staunch Catholics. Quite simply, he appears not to have written anything that Stilicho, at any rate, 'found . . . either compromising or offensive'.[15]

Claudian's death is perhaps even more mysterious than his origins. After ten years in which he brought out major poems at an average rate of one a year, nothing is heard of him after *VI Cons.* was recited in January 404. At Stilicho's command his poems, which might otherwise have proved as ephemeral as those of the majority of his peers, were gathered into an omnibus edition. His death may thus be dated to the period between early 404 and Stilicho's fall from grace and execution in late 408, and no doubt occurred sooner rather than later in that period; indeed, 406 is a likely *terminus ante quem*, given that we have no poem by him celebrating Stilicho's victory over Radagaisus at Faesulae that year. The present poem is thus his last major work, and it shows him, appropriately enough, at the height of his powers.

2. LATIN PANEGYRIC

A full history of panegyrical Greek and Latin literature, both prose and verse, is something which could hardly be encompassed within the bounds of a book such as this, nor is it strictly necessary for the general understanding of Claudian's poetry. It is clear enough that the praise of patrons, political and social superiors, or friends was regarded as a major function of literary compositions from the earliest times, and that encomium might be worked into any genre conceivable. Even within the practice of a single genre a poet might choose between a number of ways in which to glorify a particular honorand. A whole epic, for example, might essentially be devoted to praising the military achievements of a single living man. The works of Choerilus of Iasos on Alexander, the *De Bello Germanico* of Statius, and the *Iohannis* of Corippus can be cited to show the resilience of panegyrical epic over a millennium. Alternatively, within an epic, an honorand might be directly praised only in the proem or the epilogue, as is the case with the *Thebaid* of Statius. In the most complex form of all, an

---

[15] Cameron 227.

entire epic might be capable of interpretation as an extended encomiastic allegory replete with cameo appearances by the honorand: the most prominent example of this technique is, of course, the *Aeneid* itself.

The point seems worth stressing because formal prose and verse panegyric as genres are still so often, and so misleadingly, seen as monolithic. In fact, the history of panegyric is inseparable from the history of many other genres, not least epic; and, though there is a continual bleeding of Greek traditions into the Latin West from the third century BC until the very end of classical antiquity, none the less Latin panegyric remained in some ways distinct. Claudian came from one tradition and inserted himself into another. His work shows the influence of both, and he in his turn affected the development of Latin panegyric in ways that set the pattern for the fifth and sixth centuries.[16]

It is reasonable to suppose that in the native Latin tradition poetry was an important vehicle for the circulation of encomium, and perhaps also invective. Indigenous Latin bards may well have functioned much as their counterparts in other oral Indo-European cultures, glorifying nobles and ridiculing their enemies in return for material reward and status much like the *filid* of ancient Ireland.[17] But such suppositions cannot be tested directly, and the earliest formal panegyrics in Latin known to us were prose speeches in honour of the dead, the *laudationes funebres*. It is perhaps because of the continued influence of this rite, so particularly associated with the traditions of the Roman patrician *gentes*, that prose as a medium for praise was never wholly usurped in the classical period by verse. Instead the two continued side by side, each revered and each no doubt deemed appropriate to particular circumstances. It is not easy to say when formal verse panegyrics as a literary phenomenon distinct from epic appeared

---

[16] For useful general discussions of the history of Latin panegyric see Sabine MacCormack, 'Latin Prose Panegyrics: Tradition and Discontinuity in the Later Roman Empire', *Revue des études augustiniennes*, 22 (1976), 29–77; G. A. Kennedy, *Classical Rhetoric and its Christian and Secular Tradition from Ancient to Modern Times* (London, 1980), 3–181; Barr, 17 ff.; D. A. Russell and N. G. Wilson, *Menander Rhetor* (Oxford, 1981), esp. pp. xi–xxxiv; Peter Godman, *Poets and Emperors: Frankish Politics and Carolingian Poetry* (Oxford, 1987), 10 ff.; Coleman on Stat. *Silu.* 4. 1 (pp. 62 ff.); Judith W. George, *Venantius Fortunatus: A Poet in Merovingian Gaul* (Oxford, 1992), 35 ff.

[17] See e.g. Myles Dillon, *Early Irish Literature* (Chicago, 1948).

for the first time in Latin.[18] The earliest known example, however, appears to be Varius' hexameter poem in praise of Augustus, though at least one prominent scholar is sceptical about the very existence of this poem.[19] There can, at any rate, be no such doubts about another poem of the Augustan Age, the *Panegyricus Messallae*, composed in a little over two hundred hexameters and attached to the Corpus Tibullianum.[20] Its place there serves to remind us that prominent citizens other than the Emperor could receive the adulation of aspiring poets in search of a patron; so also, for example, does the *Laus Pisonis*. By the time of Domitian we find an individual poet, the Neapolitan Statius—a native Greek-speaker writing in Latin like Claudian—composing in a number of metres, and on all kinds of occasions, for both the Emperor and a fairly wide range of minor aristocrats and important public servants and freedmen.[21] It is not always clear under what circumstances even surviving poems were performed. Statius' poem on the seventeenth consulship of Domitian, for example, was eventually 'published' and circulated, but there is no conclusive evidence to show whether it was offered spontaneously in the hope of winning Imperial favour, directly commissioned for private consumption, or actually performed publicly as part of the consular ceremonies.[22] But as a very loose rule of thumb, it could perhaps be said that encomiastic Latin poetry might be written in any of a number of metres and recited in all kinds of settings, but that such poems tended to be short, to contain a personal element associating the poet in some way with the honorand, and to be more or less 'private' in character.

For great formal occasions, above all consulships and Imperial anniversaries, the preferred medium remained prose. The tradition of formal prose encomium can be traced back, unsurprisingly, to the Hellenistic kingdoms.[23] In the Greek East this tradition was

[18] Barr 18 cites Lucilius 620 M 'percrepa pugnam Popili, facta Corneli cane', Hor. *S.* 2. 1. 10ff. But the language used in these passages seems more suited to formal epic (cf. Hor. *Ars* 73f.) and cannot, as he acknowledges, be taken as sure evidence for the existence of formal Latin verse panegyrics.
[19] See Varius fr. 5 Büchner (p. 131). Courtney, *FLP* 275, believes that 'the odds are that Horace made up the quotation'. [20] [Tib.] 4. 1.
[21] See in general David Vessey, *Statius and the Thebaid* (Cambridge, 1973), 15ff.; Coleman, pp. xv ff.; and Hardie (n. 4), *passim*. [22] See Barr 19f., Coleman 63f.
[23] See Russell–Wilson, (n. 16), pp. xvi ff.

in time schematized and codified in rhetorical handbooks such as the works of Menander Rhetor, and reaches its apogee in the dazzling rhetoric of Libanius, Julian, and Themistius. In the Latin world it will no doubt have been reinforced by the primacy given in political debate to the Senate floor and the Rostra. The path that leads in the field of literature from such a work as the *De Imperio Cn. Pompeii* of Cicero to the orations of Pacatus and Symmachus broadly parallels the course of Roman politics from a Republican oligarchy to an Imperial monarchy. The practice by which a new consul delivered a *gratiarum actio* thanking the Emperor for his appointment was in time established as a regular opportunity for encomium of the ruler, the great model for later generations in this area being Pliny the Younger's refined and all-embracing panegyric to Trajan. Pliny's speech, delivered in AD 100, stands at the head of our major surviving body of Latin panegyrical prose, the *XII Panegyrici Latini*. This collection is largely the work of a 'school' of Gallic orators of the Tetrarchy and the reign of Constantine, though it seems to have been assembled in its present form much later; Pacatus' panegyric, the second in the corpus, is addressed to Theodosius the Great. The speeches contained in it celebrate the most important elements of Imperial ceremonial, such as consulships, visits to Rome and elsewhere, anniversaries, and military victories. Outside the corpus we can point to speeches that must have been very similar, such as Fronto's *gratiarum actio* to Marcus Aurelius[24] or Symmachus' orations on the quinquennium of Valentinian I in 369 and on his third consulship in 370.[25] We can assume, then, that the *Panegyrici Latini* allow us to see pretty clearly how the Latin tradition stood when Claudian made his way from Alexandria to Rome at the close of the fourth century.

The Greek and Latin traditions had much in common, and there were in general so many well-established topoi of encomium scattered through literature of all kinds that an aspiring orator or poet could draw upon many models. None the less, the Latin tradition may be said to have been distinguished from the Greek in that, in the absence of schematic handbooks outlining the ideal

[24] See Fronto 161. 13 van den Hout².
[25] Valentinian's *quinquennium*: *Or.* 1 (= pp. 318ff. Seeck). His third consulship: *Or.* 2 (= pp. 323ff. Seeck).

structure and character of panegyrics, the Latin forms seem to have been open to freer interpretation.[26] Claudian's great innovation within the genre was to extend the range of verse panegyric at the expense of prose, thus gaining the benefits of still greater freedom. Verse thereafter became acceptable for consular panegyric just as much as for more private occasions such as weddings, while the looser structural conventions of Latin prose panegyric were simultaneously enhanced by the greater freedom of invention generally permitted the poet. This alternative tradition, exemplified by Sidonius Apollinaris, Flavius Merobaudes, Corippus, and Venantius Fortunatus, gave a new and vigorous lease of life to ceremonial Latin literature that lasted throughout the tumultuous period that saw the disappearance of the Western Empire and the establishment of the new 'barbarian' kingdoms. Claudian's achievement on the broad canvas of Latin literary history is often attributed to his 'classical purity' and his status as a historical anomaly of whom we could say that he 'placed himself, after an interval of three hundred years, among the poets of ancient Rome.'[27] It may be more useful to see that, like Ennius, Virgil, and Horace, albeit on a lesser scale, he is part of an ancient process by which Roman literature was renewed by innovation from the Greek East.[28]

In the broad structure of his consular panegyrics it is true that Claudian adheres quite closely to the kind of instruction which Menander Rhetor offers the budding prose orator in his description of the Imperial oration, or βασιλικὸς λόγος (*laudatio*).[29] Indeed, *De Quarto Consulatu Honorii* in particular has sometimes been presented as a perfect example of the schematically constructed encomium.[30] Such claims tend to exaggerate the parallels, and do scant justice to the reality of Claudian's hybrid rhetorical tech-

[26] See Godman (n. 16), 11f.

[27] Edward Gibbon, *The Decline and Fall of the Roman Empire*, ed. J. B. Bury (London, 1909–14), iii. 299.

[28] For the kind of compositions written in Greek by the 'wandering poets' of Egypt see Cameron (n. 3), 477ff. That they included ἐγκώμια is, at any rate, indisputable, but it is not clear that consular panegyrics were composed in verse. If they were not, then perhaps Claudian took his cue from Statius, *Siluae* 4. 1; his own poems, which are vastly longer and more elaborate, would represent a correspondingly more original contribution to the history of Latin literature.

[29] See Menander Rhetor 368ff. (pp. 76ff. Russell–Wilson) for the βασιλικὸς λόγος.

[30] Cameron, (n. 3), 478 with n. 50, judiciously draws attention to this fact.

nique and his imaginative flexibility. There had long been a kind of contamination of one form of writing with another, and Fronto, for example, talks of the same speech to Marcus Aurelius both as a *gratiarum actio* and, more loosely, as a *laudatio*.[31] In all truth, any speech which was addressed to, or directly dealt with the Emperor, could hardly fail to take on something of the character of a Menandrean βασιλικὸς λόγος, and, as was remarked above, the individual topoi of praise could be drawn from a wide range of different poetic sources and genres. Menander himself is insistent on the need for the orator to be flexible, expanding one topic when it is appropriate to do so in the light of the particular honorand's accomplishments, and aiming at discreet brevity when he in some way falls short of the ideal.[32] Even *IV Cons.*, for all its supposed rigidity of form, is admirably flexible in the kind of ways that Menander probably envisages. To be precise, it shows great ingenuity in compensating for the teenage Emperor's lack of military and political accomplishments (πράξεις, or 'deeds', avowedly the most important part of the βασιλικὸς λόγος[33]) by vastly extending the section on γένος ('birth') and incorporating a subsection on ἀνατροφή ('upbringing') in which Theodosius is imagined as instructing his young son in the nature and duties of the ideal philosopher-emperor.[34]

The present poem, *De Sexto Consulatu Honorii*, is still more flexible and is in fact an amalgam of several different strands of panegyrical writing. Its title designates it clearly enough as a consular oration, a verse equivalent of Symmachus' speech to Valentinian. But the consular oration is not a separate category in Menander, and if we must attach a label to it we are obliged to call it a βασιλικὸς λόγος, like *IV Cons.* And so, for example, Fargues thought it possible to identify a structure for the poem that follows fairly closely the Menandrean classification: προοίμιον

---

[31] That Fronto calls the same speech a *laudatio* and a *gratiarum actio* is noted by Coleman 63.

[32] Among numerous possible examples consider Menander Rhetor 370. 9ff. (p. 81 Russell–Wilson), on the Emperor's native city: ἐὰν δὲ μήτε ἡ πατρὶς μήτε τὸ ἔθνος τυγχάνῃ περίβλεπτον, ἀφήσεις μὲν τοῦτο, θεωρήσεις δὲ πάλιν, πότερον ἔνδοξον αὐτοῦ τὸ γένος ἢ οὔ. κἂν μὲν ἔνδοξον ᾖ, ἐξεργάσῃ τὰ περὶ τούτου, ἐὰν δὲ ἄδοξον ᾖ ἢ εὐτελές, μεθεὶς καὶ τοῦτο ἀπ᾽ αὐτοῦ τοῦ βασιλέως τὴν ἀρχὴν ποιήσῃ.

[33] See Menander Rhetor 372. 30f. (p. 84 Russell–Wilson) for the central importance of πράξεις, noting esp. γνωρίζει γὰρ βασιλέα πλέον ἡ ἀνδρεία.   [34] See Barr 21f.

(1–25), γένος/γένεσις (25–64), ἀνατροφή (65–100), πράξεις (101–648, subdivided into 'virtues', esp. 'courage', 101–330 and 'Fortune', 331–648), and ἐπίλογος (649–60).[35]

This classification, however, is far too neat; first of all, note that Claudian draws, in both his proem and his epilogue, not only on the traditions of prose oratory, but also on Statius' verse encomium on the seventeenth consulship of Domitian.[36] Strictly speaking, however, *VI cons.* is clearly not a pure βασιλικὸς λόγος even on these conditions, but can also be classified as an 'arrival poem' or ἐπιβατήριος (*aduentus*), since it recounts Honorius' visit to Rome in 403–4.[37] This much is made clear in the text of the poem itself: '*aduentus* nunc *sacra tui* libet edere Musis' (*VI Cons.* 125), and as confirmation we can point in particular to Claudian's use of the star-imagery recommended by Menander for the ἐπιβατήριος and to the insistence on an atmosphere of joy which the handbook declares to be its characteristic note.[38]

These two categories are clearly distinguished from each other by Menander, who thinks of the ἐπιβατήριος primarily in terms of a speech delivered to the Emperor's representative, a governor, rather than to the Emperor himself.[39] Still, Menander is concerned with the day-to-day practicalities of the orator's life, in which an Imperial *aduentus* in his home town would surely be a relative rarity. Claudian's case, on the other hand, is somewhat special—the first visit of Honorius in well over a decade to the ancient capital of the Empire in order to celebrate his consulship—and it is therefore only natural that the *De Sexto* should show affinities with both types of speech. But even there we are not finished. Immediately after declaring his pleasure in singing of Honorius' *aduentus*, Claudian goes on to link the Imperial visit explicitly with the re-establishment of peace after the conclusion of the Gothic war: 'libet . . . | grata . . . patratis exordia sumere bellis' (*VI Cons.* 125–6). For Honorius' visit to Rome was also a

---

[35] See Fargues 195 ff., esp. 214. Even this schema omits a whole section highlighted by Menander (ἐπιτηδεύματα, 'accomplishments'), and he accepts that another (συγκρίσεις, 'comparisons') is scattered all through the poem rather than presented neatly in unified form just before the ἐπίλογος. Readers are invited to attempt their own schema.

[36] Cf. n. 22.

[37] See Menander Rhetor 378 ff. (pp. 94 ff. Russell–Wilson) for the ἐπιβατήριος.

[38] Star imagery: 23 n. (*imperii sidus*). Joy: 500 n. *laetior*; 640 n. *fastis . . . felicibus*.

[39] Menander Rhetor 378.

triumphal occasion, celebrating Stilicho's victories over Alaric and the Visigoths at the battles of Pollentia and Verona, and *VI Cons.* has many of the characteristics of an epic. This too is broadly in step with Menander's instructions, since, as we saw above, he makes it clear that the central and much the most important part of the βασιλικὸς λόγος is the πράξεις, the celebration of the Emperor's mighty deeds, both in war and in peace, but especially in war.[40] Menander stresses the opportunities offered by this section of a speech for pleasurable and attractive digressions. As examples, he shows how the orator can enliven his work by quotations from Homer and by such flights of poetic fancy as talking river-gods, or else moralizing passages on the humanity and mercy shown by the Emperor in battle: both of these ideas are taken up in the poem.[41] But the influence of epic poetry on *VI Cons.* is not a matter of a few minor decorative additions. About half the poem could in fact, in isolation, easily be taken for an extract from a full-scale epic.[42] This is true of the account of the aftermath of Pollentia which Claudian gives *in extenso* in the voice of an omniscient narrator (vv. 127–330), and of the flashback to the siege of Milan the previous winter, narrated by Honorius to the goddess Roma (vv. 440–90). In fact, the theory has even been advanced that vv. 127–330 are an accidental interpolation from a never-completed second book of his epic *De Bello Getico*, or else a deliberate recycling of material prepared earlier for an epic.[43] The integrity of the poem as it has been transmitted to us should certainly be maintained. None the less, the doubts raised in the minds of some scholars on this issue serve to remind us how Claudian has exploited to the full the freedoms that both the panegyrical tradition and the choice of verse over prose permitted his imagination and his ingenuity.

This ability to adapt generic form in the structure and disposition of his various topoi goes hand in hand with a similar resourcefulness in an area still more important. For *De Sexto Consulatu Honorii* is at least as much concerned with Claudian's patron proper and the real source of power in the Western

[40] See n. 33.

[41] Talking river-gods: see 146–209nn. The victor's *clementia*: see 228 *i, nostrum uiue tropaeum* n.

[42] For the difficulty in deciding whether a papyrus fragment of verse on military themes is to be attributed to a panegyric or an epic see Cameron (n. 3), 480.   [43] See 331–55n.

Empire as it is with a nondescript *roi fainéant* not yet out of his teens. Indeed, although Honorius as official honorand is given what is denied Stilicho, namely a speaking role, he uses his chance to remind Roma of his own relative passivity in the Gothic War. He tells her how he was imprisoned behind the walls of Milan by the barbarian hosts until, in the dead of winter and thinking nothing of the danger to himself, the noble Stilicho crossed the swollen waters of the Addua and burst through the enemy ranks to come to his rescue.[44] And it is Stilicho who is praised for his piety and his devotion in taking the dead Theodosius' place as father and conscientiously carrying out the regency entrusted to him. Above all, it is Stilicho who is credited with the glorious defeat of the Goths through both force of arms and battle-cunning, and Stilicho whose name, coupled with that of Italy, torments the humiliated Alaric:

> quaeue arua requiram
> in quibus haud umquam Stilicho nimiumque potentis
> Italiae nomen nostras circumsonet aures?

> (*VI Cons.* 317–19)

3. ALARIC'S FIRST INVASION OF ITALY

The opening years of the fifth century saw the first major incursion of barbarian troops on to Italian soil since Marius had defeated the Cimbri half a millennium before.[45] Alaric had led a band of Goths on Theodosius' side at the Frigidus in 394, but, denied the formal Roman command he longed for, had clashed with the Imperial forces, led by Stilicho, in 395 and, after the wholesale devastation of the Balkans, again in 397.[46] Unable to defeat him, the Romans, not for the first time, bought him off, and

---

[44] *VI Cons.* 440–90.

[45] For general accounts of Alaric's first invasion of Italy see Cameron 180 ff., O'Flynn 37 ff., Liebeschuetz 48 ff. (esp. 61–4), Heather 208 ff. For Stilicho's career in general see also *PLRE* I. 853 ff. Marius defeated the Cimbri at Campi Raudii near Vercellae in the Po Valley in 101 BC. Claudian explicitly draws the parallel between the Cimbri and the Visigoths, and plays on the proximity of Vercellae and Pollentia, in the stirring climax of his poem on the Gothic war: *Get.* 645 ff. 'hic Cimbros fortesque Getas, Stilichone peremptos | et Mario, claris ducibus, tegit Itala tellus. | discite, uaesanae, Romam non temnere, gentes.'

[46] For detailed accounts of Stilicho's first two campaigns against Alaric see Cameron 59 ff., O'Flynn 28 ff., and Heather 199 ff.

Eutropius, chief minister of the Eastern Emperor Arcadius, appears to have appointed him *magister militum per Illyricum* soon after the débâcle of the 397 campaign.[47] Alaric would thus seem to have won both the legitimacy and the Gothic homeland within the Empire that he craved, and his motives for once more risking war remain obscure. Possibly the resources of Illyricum had been exhausted, or else the Goths may have been feeling pressure to move westwards as a result of a massive Hunnic invasion of the eastern part of the Prefecture in 400/1. Opportunism will also have played a part. Italy's defences were laid wide open by unrest in Raetia and Noricum, where, as a result, Stilicho was obliged to concentrate his troops.[48] But the primary impulse that drove the Goths westwards was most probably the collapse of the *entente* that Alaric had come to with Eutropius. The unfortunate eunuch-courtier had been toppled abruptly from power in 399, and influence over Arcadius passed into the hands of an aggressively 'anti-barbarian' faction headed first by Aurelianus and then by his brother Caesarius. Though allied with the Gothic commander Gainas in his struggle for ascendancy, Caesarius turned on Gainas and massacred his supporters in July 400. Perhaps Alaric waited a little to see what way the wind of change was blowing, but his decision to head west in the following year strongly suggests that no acceptable arrangement with Caesarius had proved possible.[49]

It seems likely that Alaric's main aim was to force the Imperial court to grant the Goths formal recognition and land for settlement in the Western Empire. Since the path the Goths took was a westward one through northern Italy and along the Po, the plan was probably to enter Gaul and settle there or still further west.[50]

[47] Such is the implication of *Eutr.* 2. 214 ff. 'uastator Achiuae | gentis et Epirum nuper populatus inultam | *praesidet Illyrico;* iam, quos obsedit, amicus | ingreditur muros illis *responsa daturus,* | quorum coniugibus potitur natosque peremit', and of *Get.* 535–6 'at nunc Illyrici postquam mihi tradita iura | meque suum fecere ducem.' See further *PLRE* ii. 44 f.; Crees 156 f.; Cameron 176; Heather 199 ff., 204 f.

[48] For the Hunnic invasion see G. Wirth, 'Zur Frage der föderierten Staaten in der späteren römischen Kaiserzeit', *Historia,* 16 (1967), 242; Maria Cesa and Hagith Sivan, 'Alarico in Italia: Pollenza e Verona', *Historia,* 39 (1990), 361–74, esp. 367. For the revolt in Raetia see *Get.* 278 ff. 'perfidia nacti penetrabile tempus | inrupere Getae, nostras dum Raetia uires | occupat atque alio desudant Marte cohortes'.

[49] See the very persuasive discussion at Heather 206 ff.

[50] See esp. Wolfram 151; Cameron 184; Cesa and Sivan (n. 48), 373; Heather 208 f., 215 ff. The language used by such authors as Orosius and Zosimus in recording Alaric's later negotiating terms is ambiguous, and leaves room for considerable difference of

His Roman contemporaries, however, paint a lurid picture of a savage driven by a demonic impulse to sack and destroy Rome itself:

> temptauit Geticus nuper delere tyrannus
> Italiam patrio ueniens iuratus ab Histro
> has arces aequare solo, tecta aurea flammis
> soluere, mastrucis proceres uestire togatos
>
> (Prudentius, *C. Symm.* 2. 696 ff.)

Indeed, Claudian portrays Alaric as being haunted by a prophecy apparently encouraging him with the promise that he would reach Rome:

> rumpe omnes, Alarice, moras; hoc inpiger anno
> Alpibus Italiae ruptis penetrabis ad Vrbem.
>
> (*Get.* 546 f.)

Who, asks Alaric, would hesitate to obey Heaven's express summons? But, in the traditional manner, the prophecy proves deceptively ambiguous and Alaric reaches not 'the city' (*Vrbs*), but only the river Urbs (Orba) hard by the walls of Pollentia (*Get.* 554 ff.). Needless to say, for neither Claudian's prophecy nor Prudentius' picture of a psychopath with a grudge against Roman civilization itself is there any evidence. Both accounts are presumably inspired by a desire to magnify the danger threatened by Alaric in order correspondingly to heighten the panegyric of Stilicho and, in Prudentius' case, of the Catholic faith.[51]

---

opinion. But whereas Liebeschuetz 68 ff. argues that the Goths sought land not for farming but for 'billeting' (*hospitalitas*), Heather, locc. citt., makes a compelling case for the likelihood that the Goths did indeed require land for permanent agricultural settlement. *VI Cons.* 446 ff. apparently alludes to attempts by Alaric to force concessions from Honorius, and it may be that Alaric hoped for grants of land in Italy itself. Other possibilities, however, deserve attention: note e.g. that after the sack of Rome in 410 the Goths tried to cross over to Africa (e.g. Wolfram 159). But on balance it seems that they may very well have intended to settle in Gaul from the very beginning of their trek. Pollentia, where Alaric's advance was first checked, is a long way west, on the road to Provence, and *VI Cons.* 230 ff. asserts that, even after Verona, Alaric was still trying to find a mountain route 'in Raetos Gallosque'. Eventually the Goths were given permission to settle in Aquitaine in 418, whence they later migrated to Spain.

[51] Claudian's aims are connected with other propaganda-related and panegyrical concerns, not least the relationship between the Senate and the court: below, § 4. As Cameron puts it (p. 184), 'It is surely no accident that Claudian, reciting his poem in Rome, so carefully fosters the myth.'

Whatever his motives, Alaric crossed over the Julian Alps into Italy towards the end of autumn 401.[52] He met with little resistance, though Claudian mentions a Roman defeat on the Timavus and an ignominious rout in the Alps (*Get.* 562 f.). Venetia was overrun and Aquileia besieged.[53] Panic seized Italy. Claudian offers a powerful description based on Lucan's account of the terror that ensued in Rome when Caesar crossed the Rubicon, tricked out with the traditional prodigies of history and historical epic.[54] Claudian even portrays the inhabitants of Italy, and Honorius' own court, preparing in their terror to flee to Corsica or Sardinia or Gaul, until reassured by Stilicho in a lofty speech of encouragement.[55] This done, Stilicho, unable to face Alaric until the revolt in Raetia was crushed, issued orders for the recall of troops from Britain and Gaul,[56] and then, leaving Honorius in safety behind the walls of Milan, applied himself to a hard winter's campaigning against the insurgents.

Over the winter the towns of Italy prepared to defend themselves. In Rome the Aurelian walls, with Stilicho's encouragement, were extensively and hastily repaired, and rendered more formidable by the narrowing or blocking-up of gates and the raising of impressive new towers.[57] The Senate, no doubt anxious for their estates up and down the country as well as for the safety of the City, sent Symmachus as their ambassador to the court at Milan. A letter to his son reveals that he arrived, after a lengthy detour through Ticinum, on 24 February. After he had had an audience with the Emperor, he was obliged to await the return of Stilicho, who was expected to arrive shortly 'cum praesidiis valen-

[52] Most scholars accept the date given by the *Fasti Vindobonenses priores*, 18 Nov. The *Addit. ad Prosperi Chron.* give 23 Aug., but are generally less reliable: see Cesa–Sivan (n. 48), 371 n. 28.

[53] Venetia overrun: Prud. *C. Symm.* 2. 700. Aquileia besieged: Jerome, *In Rufinum* 3. 21. See Wolfram 436 n. 200 for the state of the Roman defences in NE Italy at this time. It is not clear whether Aquileia fell, though 'deploratumque Timauo | uulnus' (*Get.* 562 f.) perhaps implies so. [54] *Get.* 213 ff.; Luc. 1. 466 ff.

[55] *Get.* 217 ff., 296 f. 'quid turpes iam mente fugas, quid Gallica rura | respicitis?', 314 f. 'his dictis pauidi firmauit inertia uulgi | pectora migrantisque fugam conpescuit aulae'. The detail of the planned flight of the court itself, surely too discreditable to be the poet's invention, is especially telling. Compare the diaspora of refugees, particularly to Africa, after the sack of Rome in 410 (Matthews 300).

[56] With, eventually, disastrous results, namely the collapse of the Rhine frontier in 406/7, leading in time to Stilicho's own downfall.

[57] See below, p. xl, and 531–6 n.

tissimis'.[58] That Symmachus' primary mission was to canvass Imperial aid for the Senate and for Rome is made clear by his explanation in another letter, to Helpidius:

Mediolanum sum missus a patribus ad exorandam diuini principis opem quam communis patriae sollicitudo poscebat. (*Ep.* 5. 95.)

Agitation in Rome was clearly extreme, serious enough, certainly, to necessitate the Senate's most famous spokesman and orator undertaking a difficult journey in winter, with a highly mobile enemy at large, and at the cost of ill-health.[59] It is, given the grave danger of military defeat, at the very least possible that Symmachus also used this mission as an opportunity to restate the case for the restoration of the Altar of Victory in the Senate.[60]

Shortly thereafter Alaric laid siege to Milan, intending, as Claudian makes Honorius tell the goddess Roma, to frighten the timid Emperor into making concessions (*VI Cons.* 441 ff.). But Stilicho, who had successfully quashed the Raetian revolt, advanced rapidly with the vanguard of his army, forced the crossing of the Addua, relieved the city and compelled Alaric to give up the siege.[61] Shortly thereafter the court moved permanently to the safe haven of Ravenna, guarded by the marshes and the sea.

Alaric now crossed the Po in the direction of the Ligurian Apennines, heading perhaps for the coastal road westwards into Gaul. Along the way he apparently made an unsuccessful attempt to take Hasta, or else clashed with Roman troops near the city.[62] The beginning of April found him still further to the south-west, in the vicinity of Pollentia, with Stilicho in close pursuit.

Battle was joined on Easter Day, 6 April 402, violating the holiest feast of the Christian calendar and occasioning a great deal

---

[58] Symmachus, *Ep.* 7. 13; the information is repeated in another letter, 7. 14. See further Matthews 273 f.

[59] *Ep.* 5. 96. Symmachus seems to have died soon after this mission.

[60] A cogent argument for this possibility is presented by T. D. Barnes, 'The Historical Setting of Prudentius' *Contra Symmachum*', *AJP* 97 (1976), 373–86, esp. 381 ff. *VI Cons.* 597 ff. may be tentatively interpreted as offering support for this view: see n. ad loc.

[61] Claudian, who was apparently besieged along with the rest of the court, describes the relief of the city first in brief but stirring lines at *Get.* 450 ff., and later, with the panoply of epic and historical comparisons at *VI Cons.* 441 ff. (Honorius' speech to Roma). See further 440–93 n. Claudian's striking description of Stilicho's sudden arrival (*Get.* 459 f. 'emicuit Stilichonis apex et cognita fulsit | canities') was quoted by Disraeli in his obituary of the Duke of Wellington: see Cameron 450.

[62] See 203 *moenia uindicis Hastae* n.

of religious polemic.[63] No doubt to keep his distance from an impiety of his own devising, Stilicho handed over command to Saul, a pagan, who was in charge of the unruly Alan contingent in the army. The Goths, who were pious Arians, had withdrawn, presumably to keep a feast on which they will have thought themselves immune from attack by a Christian army, but Saul suddenly assailed them 'cedentique hosti propter religionem, ut pugnaret, extortum est.'[64] Claudian gives much space to speeches of exhortation supposedly delivered by Alaric and Stilicho, but the course of the battle itself is allocated barely seventeen lines (*Get.* 581–97). The details that emerge are few, but significant. A *gentis praefectus Alanae*—probably Saul himself—died heroically in battle, wiping out, asserts Claudian stoutly, the unjust suspicions of disloyalty held against the Alans before the engagement. The fear will no doubt have been that they would defect, enticed by bribes from Alaric, and Claudian's protestations serve largely to alert us to the reality of the danger. In the battle itself they do appear to have let Stilicho down. When their commander fell, the Alan cavalry were driven back in confusion and Claudian expressly states that the battle would have been lost had not Stilicho (who may have wanted to keep his hands clean entirely) come to the rescue with infantry (*Get.* 594 ff.). Moreover, precipitate action by the Alans is expressly said elsewhere to have been responsible for Alaric's managing to escape after Verona.[65]

Claudian portrays Pollentia as a resounding Roman victory. His contemporary Prudentius is even more emphatic: under the banner of Christ the Imperial forces exacted the penalty for thirty years of Gothic outrages against Rome, and left the fields piled high with corpses (*C. Symm.* 2. 715 ff.). But later sources favourable to the Goths paint a different picture, and for Cassiodorus (*Chron. Min.* ii. 154) and Jordanes (*Get.* 155) it was a Gothic victory. Alaric's advance was certainly checked, and he was forced to turn upon

[63] Orosius 7. 37. 2 'sanctum pascha uiolatum est.' For general accounts of Pollentia, its outcome, and the polemic surrounding it, see Cameron 180 ff., Crees 164 ff., Cesa–Sivan (n. 48), 366 f., Döpp 212 ff.; J. Vanderspoel (n. 13), esp. 253 ff. who suggests (p. 253) the intriguing possibility that Stilicho may have taken his cue from an incident related by Amm. Marc. 27. 10. 1.　　　　　　　　　　　　　　　　　　　　　　　[64] Orosius ibid.

[65] See 224 n. It seems best to take 'incauti . . . Alani' as a collective singular (with Cameron 186). If an individual is meant, it will be either Saul (supposing he survived Pollentia) or his successor.

his heels and head back, eventually, for Illyricum, apparently under a promise of safe conduct from Stilicho.[66] His camp too was overrun and much booty from earlier campaigns taken, along with a large number of captives including his wife.[67] But his military losses were not crushing, as Claudian, twenty months later, himself admits:

> non me Pollentia tantum
> nec captae cruciastis opes; hoc aspera fati
> sors tulerit Martisque uices. non funditus armis
> concideram; stipatus adhuc equitumque cateruis
> integer ad montes reliquo cum robore cessi.
>
> (*VI Cons.* 281 ff.; Alaric speaking)

In short, the battle appears to have given the Romans the tactical edge; halting Alaric in his tracks was no small achievement in the circumstances.[68] But Stilicho was prevented from enjoying more than a partial victory by his inability fully to control the barbarian elements in his own army. Far from being the decisive conflict Claudian and Prudentius claim, Pollentia left the enemy quite powerful enough to strike another blow if the opportunity presented itself.

Anxieties about a future in which Alaric was left still at large, anxieties which in the event proved justified, will have therefore been widespread, and addressing them was surely part of the court panegyricist's job. Critics and opponents of Stilicho will have wanted to know why, especially if the victory was so decisive, Alaric, as in 395 and 397, was allowed to escape. Something of the suspicion that fell on Stilicho can be sensed from the sarcasm of Orosius, who was later to comment grimly 'taceo de Alarico rege cum Gothis suis saepe uicto, saepe concluso semperque dimisso' (7. 37. 2). In answer to such criticism, the first reason furnished by Stilicho's apologist is *clementia*: the most satisfying form of revenge is to see the enemy bend the knee (*Get.* 90 ff.). But to this he adds a more specific and politically more significant motive:

> sed magis ex aliis fluxit clementia causis,
> consulitur dum, Roma, tibi: tua cura coegit

[66] See further 204 *pacta movet* n.
[67] See further 127 *tenuatus*, 128 f., 210–28, 281–5 nn.
[68] See Cameron 181 f.

inclusis aperire fugam, ne peior in arto
saeuiret rabies uenturae conscia mortis.

(*Get.* 95 ff.)

Stilicho feared that, if driven to despair, Alaric might prefer to take down into ruin with himself the Eternal City, and so, out of *pietas* and presumably with great reluctance, allowed him to leave unmolested.[69] *De Bello Getico* was delivered in Rome, no doubt before the Senate, whose great estates were most exposed to Alaric's marauding armies. It is clearly their ill will that Stilicho, through Claudian, is attempting to conciliate, and the special pleading involved surely allows us to identify the senatorial aristocracy as the most vocal critics of Stilicho's handling of the battle. The truth was undoubtedly that Stilicho simply did not have the resources to annihilate the Goths, and was surely satisfied to have them withdraw back into Illyricum, where they would be the Eastern Empire's headache, not his. As we saw, after Pollentia Alaric first moved south to the Ligurian Apennines (*VI Cons.* 284 ff.), probably in the hope of continuing his trek westwards by the coastal road into Gaul. But if so, Stilicho blocked his path and it was perhaps then that he made his agreement with the Romans to leave Italy. We next hear of him at Verona, far to the northeast on the way back over the Julian Alps.

The traditional chronology of the first invasion and of Pollentia followed above has been occasionally challenged, most notably, in recent years, by J. Barrie Hall.[70] Hall has attempted to show not only that the invasion began earlier than is usually assumed, with advance parties arriving as early as 400, but also that the battle of Pollentia and the later clash of arms at Verona *both* took place in 403. Maria Cesa and Hagith Sivan, however, have satisfactorily shown all the arguments advanced to be either mistaken or else based on data perfectly easy to reconcile with the standard chronology.[71]

---

[69] The propaganda is well thought out and consistent. This particular claim fits nicely with the similar statements of Prudentius (*C. Symm.* 2. 696 ff., cit. above) and with Claudian's assertion that Alaric was motivated by a prophecy to attack the city itself (*Get.* 546 f.). Claudian also incorporates it into Alaric's speech at *VI Cons.* 293 ff. The desire to involve the whole world in one's own destruction, as a solace for one's death, is said to be Rufinus' aim too (*Ruf.* 2. 206 ff., esp. 212 f.): see the commentary, 292–7, 293 f. nn.

[70] J. B. Hall, 'Pollentia, Verona, and the Chronology of Alaric's First Invasion of Italy', *Philologus*, 132 (1988), 245–57.   [71] Art. cit. (n. 48).

Understandably dissatisfied with a certain degree of confusion among the ancient chroniclers, Hall seeks hard evidence first in the account given by Claudian of the celestial portents that heralded the catastrophe (*Get.* 233 ff.). Hall argues that not all the portents are expressly attributed to the year that directly preceded the invasion, and that 'they invite a retrospect over a wider span of time than just one preceding year' compatible with 'a vantage point of 402 . . . and with the view that Pollentia and Verona took place in 403.'[72] This is on the face of it fair enough, but as Cesa and Sivan point out,[73] it is not in itself decisive or indeed very cogent, precisely because Claudian's phrasing is so very vague. Indeed the most natural, if not the only, reading of *Get.* 238 ff. ('tunc anni signa prioris, | et si quod fortasse quies neclexerat omen, | addit cura nouis') is to associate the portents that directly follow primarily with the year before the invasion. Since the most prominent of these is a comet (*Get.* 243 ff.) clearly to be identified with that dated by Chinese astronomers to 19 March 400, it seems most sensible to argue that the passage in question supports, if not quite guarantees, a date in 401 for Alaric's crossing of the Alps.[74]

More persuasively, Hall further argues that the appointment of Flavius Rumoridus, a known pagan, to the Western consulship of 403, was an attempt to secure the loyalty of the large pagan element in the Senate at a time of military insecurity.[75] This would fit well with the striking attempts made by the court to build bridges with the Senate, Christians and pagans alike, at a time when its loyalty, and, no less, the manpower its estates would provide for the army, were so badly needed. It accords particularly well with the morale-boosting visits to Rome by Stilicho just after Pollentia, and by Honorius to celebrate his triumph and sixth

---

[72] Art. cit. (n. 70), 249.   [73] Art. cit. (n. 48), 362.

[74] It seems strange that Hall (loc. cit.) should assert that 'it is noteworthy that the comet . . . is not given special prominence'. On the contrary it receives a fuller treatment—no fewer than six lines—than any of the other celestial phenomena and, more importantly, marks the climax of that particular list. All are naturally overshadowed by the portent of the wolves (*Get.* 249 ff.) which, whatever its factual base (see Döpp 220 ff.), is given the greatest attention because it directly involves Stilicho and the Emperor.

[75] Hall (n. 70), 249 f. Rumoridus and the Frankish general Bauto, another pagan, were present when Ambrose's reply to Symmachus' *relatio* on the altar of Victory was read out (Ambrose, *Ep.* 57): see Cesa–Sivan (n. 48), 368. It is not known how far in advance the nomination was made.

consulship in the winter of 403/4.[76] Cesa and Sivan reply that rela-
tionships between the Senate and the court were more concerned
with the need to ensure the loyalty of the barbarian elements in
the army and, after Pollentia, to reorganize the military structure
of the Western Empire in case of future attacks by Alaric. In this
capacity, Rumoridus' own German extraction and experience as
magister utriusque militiae under Valentinian II in 384 will have been
invaluable.[77] In reality the two arguments are not incompatible:
Rumoridus' appointment could have fulfilled both requirements
with admirable neatness. What is, for our present purposes, most
significant is Cesa and Sivan's demonstration that the military
concerns that may have motivated Rumoridus' consulship are just
as relevant to the still precarious situation after Alaric's repulse at
Pollentia as before the battle. It follows that the same applies to
any perceived need to ensure the co-operation of the Senate.

A similar but clearer case can be made against Hall's deductions concerning a series of laws issued between December 402
and October 403 from Ravenna.[78] These laws deal largely with
the questions of recruitment and, especially, the treatment of
deserters. *C. Th.* 7. 18. 11 (24 Feb. 403, Ravenna), for example,
arranges for the apprehension of deserters and their referral to
Hadrian, the praetorian prefect of Italy, and *C. Th.* 7. 18. 12 (25
July 403, Ravenna) imposes the penalty of land confiscation on
those harbouring deserters. As Cesa and Sivan show, such legisla-
tion is perfectly appropriate to the situation obtaining *after* a campaign, when indeed, brigandage by runaways from both armies
may well have been a problem. Moreover, *C. Th.* 7. 13. 15 (6 Dec.
402, Ravenna) excuses from the furnishing of recruits all *honorati*
who had won this rank through the holding of a magistracy, a
provision which is surely best seen as an indication of a partial
relaxation of recruiting requirements compatible with the waning
of the Gothic menace.[79] To this add the consideration that *C. Th.*
7. 18. 12 will have had implications for senators eager to recover
land-workers conscripted for the compaigs of the spring. Such
measures will have seemed to some unnecessarily Draconian if,
by this time, Alaric had been out of Italy for about a year, and

---

[76] The relationship between the court and the Senate is discussed in full below,
pp. xliv–lii.

[77] Art. cit. (n. 48), 365 ff.   [78] Art. cit. (n. 70), 250 f.   [79] Art. cit. (n. 48), 370 f.

Rumoridus' assistance in reconciling the senatorial aristocracy to the necessity of maintaining the strength of the army as a guarantee against future attacks will have been invaluable. Harder evidence, however, comes from the fact that these laws, all securely dated, were issued from Ravenna. The question is a critical one. If the court had moved to Ravenna by December 402, then the siege of Milan must be dated to the spring of that year and Pollentia, in accordance with the traditional chronology, to the month of April. Hall asserts that nothing can be proved from the place of issue, that Stilicho could have issued them on his authority as commander-in-chief and the Emperor's guardian, and that only part of the court had moved to Milan. This is clearly erroneous. As Cesa and Sivan remind us, *constitutiones* could only be issued by the Emperor himself and there is absolutely no evidence to show that Stilicho would have violated the law in so high-handed a fashion. The unmistakable conclusion is that Honorius was indeed in residence in Ravenna by December 402.

By far the weakest part of Hall's argument is his attempt to prove that the Gothic hordes, a people on the march including non-combatants among their number, will have moved with extreme slowness and 'not have progressed more than a few miles a day on average'.[80] This hypothesis is used to back up a chronology which contradicts the impression of a *Blitzkrieg* given by the sources. Hall does not believe that Claudian's explicit claim that the invasion and the campaign of Pollentia lasted no longer than a single winter (*Get.* 151ff.) is literally true. Instead he stretches out the whole tale of the invasion over a period of some three years (late 400 to summer 403). Cesa and Sivan make short work of this, demonstrating that Hall's data, based as they are on the experience of the pioneers of the rugged American West and of the Voortrekkers in the rough country of South Africa, are simply not applicable to north Italy. Not only is the climate quite different, but this area possessed a still largely intact system of roads which obviously did not exist in the territory taken for comparison. The Gothic host could, in fact, move very fast, as was later seen when, in 408, less than a month sufficed for them to cover the distance from Noricum to Rome.[81]

[80] Art. cit. (n. 70), 255.   [81] Art. cit. (n. 48), 371ff.

In short, Hall's suggested chronology is wholly indefensible. It offers much evidence that is plainly mistaken and none that cannot be made without much difficulty to square with the traditional dating. True, the chroniclers do not agree, and it is at least possible that Hall is right in attributing the claim of Prosper, Cassiodorus, and Jordanes that Alaric's troops invaded in 400 to the presence of advance parties. But it looks more like a simple mistake, easily made. The dates given by the *Fasti Vindobonenses* (18 Nov. 401) and the *Addit. ad Prosperi Chron.* (23 Aug. 401) agree tolerably well with each other. Add to them Claudian's firm statement that the campaign up to Pollentia took only a single winter and the clear evidence of the court's removal from Milan to Ravenna by the end of 402, and the traditional chronology looks largely unassailable. The clinching argument is provided by the three inscriptions preserved from the Honorian restoration of the walls of Rome, as preparation against attack by Alaric.[82] These inscriptions, identical apart from trivial differences in lettering and method of abbreviation, declare that the restoration, initiated by Stilicho, took place in the reigns of Arcadius and Honorius. None mentions Theodosius II, who was proclaimed Augustus in January 402: allowing time for a messenger to reach Rome from Constantinople, this clearly establishes as a *terminus ante quem* for the restoration some date in March of the same year.[83]

After the check received at Pollentia, and, possibly, another attempt to break into Gaul, the Goths withdrew towards the Alps. Somewhere near Verona, which commands the passes back into Illyricum, they again clashed with the Imperial forces. Why the agreement with Stilicho was broken is not known. Claudian's explanation—plain bad faith on Alaric's part—cannot be wholly ruled out as simplistic propaganda. Alaric did indeed have a poor record when it came to keeping his word, and he may have thought himself well placed for another attempt to scare the Imperial court into conceding land. There will also surely have been those within his own army who were unhappy with the

---

[82] *CIL* vi. 1188–90. See further the commentary, 531–6n.

[83] Hall (n. 70), 249 is not the first scholar to have been led astray by an unfortunate error on the part of O. Seeck, who in his edn. of Symmachus (*MGH AA* 61; Berlin, 1883), p. clxxxviii, dated Theodosius II's elevation to the purple to 10 Jan. 403. Seeck retracted this error in *Die Regesten der Kaiser und Päpste* (Stuttgart, 1919), 305.

apparent failure of the expedition and who may have encouraged him to attack again. But quite possibly the breach of faith was caused by factors outside his personal control, by unauthorized looting or by the intemperate action of hostile elements among his men dissatisfied with his leadership.[84] Another possibility is that he was deliberately provoked by Stilicho, who perhaps thought he was now in a better position to win a decisive victory, or was feeling the pressure of criticism concerning his apparent weakness. Nor is it much easier to estimate the magnitude or the significance of the battle of Verona, since no mention of it survives in the chroniclers and we are obliged to rely wholly on Claudian's account (*VI Cons.* 201–9). This account is painfully short, one-sided, and obscured by rhetorical hyperbole and the traditional features of epic. None the less it should be made clear that the fact that Claudian alone records the battle need not mean that it was unimportant. It would not be unreasonable that Pollentia, given both its significance as the first real brake applied to Alaric's advance and, above all, the furore of religious polemic that surrounded it, should have totally eclipsed Verona in the eyes of later writers. On the other hand, Verona may have been given greater prominence than its real significance warranted for the simple fact that Claudian had already celebrated Pollentia in *De Bello Getico* and needed new material.[85] Certainly, Claudian's description of Gothic corpses feeding carrion birds or being swept down to the sea by the river Athesis cannot be taken literally. Equally clearly, however, it must imply a clash of arms where blood really was spilt, a real battle and not a skirmish, since otherwise Claudian's propaganda would have stood no chance of persuading his contemporaries.[86] Whatever the details, it seems best to assume that a substantial clash of arms took place and that its real significance was that it put paid to whatever plans or hopes Alaric still entertained after Pollentia of continuing his Italian campaign; that it was, in a word, decisive in so far as it finally sent him packing back into Illyricum.

As after Pollentia, Stilicho seems to have been embarrassed about how to explain why, if Alaric had been so thoroughly defeated, he had been allowed yet again to escape with his life.

[84] See 204 n. (*pacta movet*).   [85] Döpp 236.
[86] Cf. Cameron 169, on the campaign against Alaric in Greece in 397.

Claudian answers these criticisms by refining the case given in *De Bello Getico*. There, Alaric was said to have been spared out of *clementia* and out of *cura* for Rome. Now Claudian asserts that, all along, Stilicho was using cunning and that his aim was to lure Alaric back over the Po, relying all the time on the Goth's habitually treacherous nature to provide him with an excuse, once Rome was secure, to attack and defeat him completely. To drive the point home, this explanation is first put forward by the poet (*VI Cons.* 210ff.) and then dramatically repeated by Alaric himself, who is made to declare that he has been properly ensnared by his own deceitfulness (ibid. 300ff.).[87] Why, then, was Alaric not killed and taken at Verona? The answer offered is that he almost was, but escaped because Stilicho's carefully laid plan was spoiled by precipitate action, or else plain bungling, or perhaps treachery glossed over by Claudian as such, on the part once more of the unreliable Alans. Claudian puts a brave face on it by claiming a greater pleasure in seeing Alaric survive, a living trophy of Roman victory:

> ipsum te caperet letoque, Alarice, dedisset,
> ni calor incauti male festinatus Alani
> dispositum turbasset opus; prope captus anhelum
> uerbere cogis equum, nec te uitasse dolemus.
> i potius genti reliquus tantisque superstes
> Danubii populis, i, nostrum uiue tropaeum.
>
> (*VI Cons.* 223ff.)

This follows quickly on the heels of Claudian's explanation for Stilicho's unpopular use of barbarian mercenaries: Stilicho cunningly employed barbarians to kill barbarians, with double gain for Rome as the grim Danubian tribesmen fell on either side (*VI Cons.* 218ff., esp. 221f.). Clearly, the aim in general was to make the barbarian mercenaries a scapegoat, a promising ploy given the prejudices of the senatorial audience.[88]

The date of Verona, like that of Pollentia, has been repeatedly disputed. It was once common to follow Birt in assuming that Alaric in effect invaded Italy twice, and that while *De Bello Getico* describes an invasion of 401/2 thwarted at Pollentia, *VI Cons.* recounts another, belonging to 402/3 and stopped at Verona. As

---

[87] See further Cameron 184ff., Döpp 226ff.   [88] See Cameron 186.

is generally accepted, Birt was wrong in thinking the two poems dealt with different campaigns, and such apparent minor discrepancies as he claimed to find are the result of the selection of different details motivated by the different concerns and points of view of the two works.[89] In particular the narrative of the events put into Alaric's mouth at *VI Cons.* 281 ff. (Pollentia, retreat to the Ligurian Apennines, Stilicho's 'trick', Verona) is perfectly seamless and reads most naturally as the account of a single campaign. Hence Cameron confidently declares: 'No one is likely to maintain Birt's once fashionable dating of Verona to 403.'[90] The case for Birt's chronology, though on different grounds, has, however, been restated in recent years with considerable force by T. D. Barnes, who lays much emphasis on Claudian's explicit statement that *De Bello Getico* was recited in Rome (*pr.* 1 ff.) in Stilicho's presence (*VI Cons.* 123 f. 'arma Getarum | nuper apud socerum plectro celebrata recenti').[91] If Pollentia was fought in early April and Verona in the scorching heat of summer as Claudian tells us (*VI Cons.* 215), this leaves very little time for a triumphant visit by Stilicho to Rome, and Barnes therefore dates Verona to about June 403.[92]

Barnes's case is by no means rock-solid. Cesa and Sivan argue that the success at Pollentia, the subsequent pact with Alaric, and not least their possession of numerous hostages including Alaric's own wife, will have made the Romans feel relatively secure.[93] Stilicho may well have been happy to leave a subordinate in charge in the north to supervise the evacuation while he himself went south to put his case, partly through Claudian, to a Senate with whose hostility and cynicism he appears to have had to contend. We must also consider the unity of Claudian's narrative of the campaign in *VI Cons.* and indeed the total absence of anything

---

[89] See Birt, pp. lii ff., arguing that after Pollentia Alaric retreated as far as Histria and that, though he may not actually have returned to Illyricum, 'tamen pax ipsi Italiae aestate anni 402 reddita est' (p. lii). See N. H. Baynes, *JRS* 22 (1922), 207 ff. for the case against Birt, and also Barnes (n. 60), 374 f.

[90] Cameron 184 n. 3. Specialists on Prudentius, however, do seem frequently to follow Birt's chronology, perhaps indirectly under the influence of A. Kurfess's article on Prudentius at *RE* xxiii (1957), 1043. 10 ff. [91] Barnes (n. 60), 375 f.

[92] Many of Hall's arguments, discussed above, which were not conclusive for dating Pollentia to 403 might with greater cogency be used to support a date in that year for Verona, especially those concerning Rumoridus' consulship and the military concerns that dominate the Ravenna *constitutiones* of 402/3. [93] Art. cit. (n. 48), 361 n. 2.

in the poem to license the supposition that Alaric remained in Italy for as long as eighteen months or more. The time-frame Barnes understandably finds constricting can also be enlarged, indeed doubled. Claudian's vague wording ('accensos aestiuo puluere soles') could easily be interpreted as referring to, say, August rather than June, thus allowing as much as four months after Pollentia for the events concerned. In short, then, the bulk of the evidence supports a date in the summer of 402 for the battle of Verona, but is much too inconclusive wholly to rule out the possibility that it took place a year or so later.

However that may be, Honorius entered Rome in triumph in the autumn of 403, celebrated his sixth consulship to the tune of Claudian's praises in the following January, and remained there until at least July 404.[94] Claudian paints a triumphant picture of Alaric ingloriously retreating from Italy in terror, taunted by the river-god Eridanus, destined never to return, and of the body of Italy itself purified by Stilicho from his polluting touch (*VI Cons.* 127 ff., 324 ff.). In the following years no more is heard of Claudian, but concerning Alaric history has much to say.

4. STILICHO AND THE SENATE

In *VI Cons.* only three characters have speaking parts: Alaric, Honorius, and the goddess Roma. As we have seen, however, the presence of Stilicho is also practically tangible throughout the poem, and he dominates, in particular, both the account of Alaric's utter defeat in the aftermath of Verona (210–330) and Honorius' justification to Roma of his failure so far to visit her personally (426–90).[95] There is, in addition, yet another presence that can be discerned, both on the stage and off it.

The poem was recited as part of the celebrations for Honorius' sixth consulship, in Rome, and presumably on 1 Jan. 404. In accordance with tradition, Honorius had already addressed the Senate and the People himself (*VI Cons.* 587 ff.), and made his way back up the *uia sacra* to his 'ancestral home' ('patriis laribus', *VI Cons.* 603 f.: cf. 53, 71), the *Domus Augustana* on the Palatine. It was here, either in an audience chamber of the palace, or perhaps in the library of Augustus' temple of Apollo, that the poem was

[94] Döpp 229 f.   [95] See above, pp. xxviii–xxix.

recited.[96] In the preface Claudian compares his audience and their reception of Honorius after the victories of the Gothic war to the company of gods welcoming back the triumphant Jupiter:

> en princeps, en orbis apex aequatus Olympo,
> en, quales memini, turba uerenda, dei!
>
> (*pr. VI Cons.* 23 f.)

His eulogistic phrasing no doubt embraces both court and Senate; in any case, many of those normally resident with the Emperor in Milan, or now Ravenna, were naturally *ex officio* members of the Senate themselves. So it was that, in celebrating the consulship of Mallius Theodorus in Milan only a few years before, Claudian had been able to declare:

> culmina Romani maiestatemque senatus
> et, quibus exultat Gallia, cerne uiros.
>
> (*pr. Theod.* 7 f.)

But this time the audience will probably have included representatives of a particular element of the Senate, a group who only showed their faces in Milan relatively rarely: the 'Romans of Rome', a body of fabulously rich, deeply conservative, and, in many cases, aggressively pagan men to whom the character and policies of the upstart semi-barbarian general were anathema.

Emperors did not often visit the ancient capital of the Empire at this period, and Honorius himself had not been there in the eleven years since he had been raised to the rank of Augustus. But, in the right circumstances, a state visit could both enhance the prestige of a reigning Emperor and serve a useful political and propaganda purpose. To cite the most significant examples from the second half of the fourth century, the visits of Constantius in 357 and of Theodosius in 389 both functioned as a powerful symbolic reassertion of legitimate authority in the Latin-speaking West after the elimination of dangerous usurpers.[97] And similarly, when Stilicho made a visit to Rome some time after the inauguration of his consulship in 400, his purpose must surely have been to reinforce his support, weakened in recent years by the defection

---

[96] See *pr.* 23 n. *orbis apex aequatus Olympo*.
[97] Constantius: Amm. Marc. 16. 10, and 58–64, 392–406, 566–8, 569–77, 645–8 nn. Theodosius: 53–76, 65 f. nn.

of Gildo and the African provinces to the Eastern Empire, and by the ignominy of seeing himself declared *hostis publicus* by Eutropius, chief minister of the Eastern Emperor Arcadius. On this occasion too he had taken Claudian in tow, and his official spokesman, in an additional, third book of the *De Consulatu Stilichonis*, reminded the Senate of Stilicho's successes and of his claims on their loyalty.

Of course, no one could expect Claudian to be so crass as to make any explicit admission of political motive in *VI Cons.* Honorius' decision to celebrate his Gothic triumph and his sixth consulship in the City is presented as one prompted by proper *pietas* towards the goddess Roma herself: 'nec legum fas est occurrere matri', as the young Emperor is made to say in reply to her impassioned complaints in an exchange that dominates the central portion of the poem.[98] The remainder of the poem traces Honorius' path to Rome and recounts his rapturous welcome into the City, effortlessly—and unhistorically—blending together the language of *aduentus*, triumph, and consular inauguration ceremonies.[99]

Once within the walls of Rome the Emperor, even in these days of effective autocracy, was expected to honour the traditional *libertas* of her citizens, showing due respect to both the People and the Senate. More than one Emperor found the duties of *ciuilitas* onerous, but none the less Honorius was set the *exemplum* of the *optimus princeps*, Trajan himself.[100] Theodosius, in his visit of 389, was effusively praised by Pacatus for living up to this ideal, and in

---

[98] *VI Cons.* 356–493. The quotation is from v. 428.

[99] The consulship was, naturally, inaugurated on 1 Jan. 404, but Honorius and his entourage reached Rome in the middle of either Oct. or Nov. 403: see 541 *lunam . . . rudem* n. Whether or not a separate triumph was celebrated is not entirely clear, but the probability is against it. Instead, the consulship and the triumph are fused: consider esp. 647f. 'et sextas Getica praeuelans fronde secures | colla triumphati proculcat Honorius Histri', and see further Döpp 235f. Claudian's narrative, at any rate, is seamless. The Emperor arrives via the Flaminian Way at 520–2. The descriptions of the people enthusiastically welcoming him contain numerous topoi which are standardly associated in prose panegyrics with *aduentus* (see ad loc., *passim*) but which are also appropriate enough to a triumphal procession (523–77). By 578–80 the emphasis seems to be on the triumphal aspects ('curru cum uectus eodem | urbe triumphantem generum', 579f.). This, however, may be a figurative triumph only, since the language and imagery of victory were in any case inextricably bound up with *aduentus* celebrations: see in general the splendid analysis at MacCormack, 17–89, esp. the detailed discussion of *VI Cons.* at pp. 52–4. And only a few lines later we are unmistakably witnessing consular ceremonies as the Emperor addresses the Senate and People: see 587–602, and esp. 589f., 603–10, 603nn.   [100] *ciuilitas*: see 58–64n.

this poem too Claudian reminds his audience of the properly modest behaviour shown on the earlier occasion.[101] In 389 Honorius had accompanied his father and, though still a small boy, had been dutifully presented to the Senate for their approval as his heir.[102] The son now proves himself worthy of his father in his respect for tradition and the constitution. In the Circus the People and he make obeisance to each other, acknowledging the majesty and the sovereignty each possesses in law:

> o quantum populo secreti numinis addit
> imperii praesens genius, quantamque rependit
> maiestas alterna uicem, cum regia circi
> conexum gradibus ueneratur purpura uulgus
> adsensuque cauae sublatus in aethera uallis
> plebis adoratae reboat fragor unaque totis
> intonat Augustum septenis arcibus echo!
>
> (*VI Cons.* 611ff.)

For Claudian, however, it is in his modest demeanour before the third element in the constitution that Honorius most clearly reveals his *ciuilitas*. He was a *triumphator* as well as a new consul, and so he had by custom the right to see the Senate march on foot before his triumphal car. But this right he humbly forgoes, to universal approval:

> temnunt prisca senes et in hunc sibi prospera fati
> gratantur durasse diem moderataque laudant
> tempora, quod clemens aditu, quod pectore †solus†
> Romanos uetuit currum praecedere patres.
>
> (*VI Cons.* 548ff.)

As so often, praise of Honorius turns into praise of Stilicho; we discover that the privilege conceded to the senators of Rome was not granted by the general to his own son, and the Emperor's brother-in-law, Eucherius (*VI Cons.* 552–6). The honour done the Senate was thus all the greater, and, so Claudian tells us, wiser and older heads in the crowd reflected on the difference between the young prince and his predecessors:

> haec sibi cura senum maturaque conprobat aetas

---

[101] See 53–76nn. For Trajan as a role-model for Theodosius and his sons see 58–64, 333–8, 645–8nn., Cameron 382f. [102] See 65f.n.

idque inter ueteris speciem praesentis et aulae
iudicat, *hunc ciuem, dominos uenisse priores.*

(*VI Cons.* 557 ff.)

And in addition to this generous display of reverence, Honorius is seen scrupulously fulfilling the ancient custom whereby the new consul, after the oath-taking, addresses the Senate directly:

solio fultus genitoris eburno
gestarum patribus causas ex ordine rerum
euentusque refert ueterumque exempla secutus
digerit imperii sub iudice facta senatu.

(*VI Cons.* 588 ff.)[103]

Custom, of course, required the Senate to be treated with reverence, and in a poem delivered in their ancient seat and in the very presence of some of their most august members Claudian could hardly fail to omit encomium of some kind in their honour.[104] But it would be naïve to see the gestures of respect described above as being no more than empty courtesies, or the account of them as evidence of personal emotional attachment on Claudian's part to the Roman past.[105] Other such incidents are recorded by the poet as proof of Honorius', or more usually Stilicho's, humility with respect to that venerable body, but it has been convincingly demonstrated that in these cases the hard motives of *Realpolitik* are discernible beneath the smooth surface of protocol and courteous scrupulosity in the observance of ancient forms of constitutional procedure. In particular, Claudian lays great stress on the fact that, when Gildo transferred his allegiance from the Western Empire to Arcadius, Stilicho left it to the Senate to declare him *hostis publicus* and so give sanction to an expedition against him:

hoc quoque non parua fas est cum laude relinqui
quod non ante fretis exercitus adstitit ultor

---

[103] See further 587 *rostra Quirites* n., Cameron 382.

[104] See Cameron 381 f., citing *IV Cons.* 503 f. 'quae *denique* Romae | cura tibi! quam fixa manet reuerentia patrum!', at the end of a very long list of Imperial virtues. Note also the pieties of *Stil.* 2. 297 ff. and 3. 115 ff.

[105] Whether or not Claudian had any personal attachment to Rome cannot be deduced beyond all doubt from his poems, where he is writing to a brief and expressing, not his own views, but Stilicho's propaganda. For a masterly demolition of the rather romantic line taken on this issue by some earlier scholars see Cameron 349 ff.

ordine quam prisco censeret bella senatus.
neclectum Stilicho per tot iam saecula morem
rettulit, ut ducibus mandarent proelia patres
decretoque togae felix legionibus iret
tessera. Romuleas leges rediisse fatemur,
cum procerum iussis famulantia cernimus arma.

(*Stil.* 1. 325 ff.)

Cameron[106] shows that, far from being a demonstration of genuine respect or even, as Boissier thought, 'a mere formality', this superficially magnanimous action in fact lets us see a shrewd politician manipulating the Senate for his own ends. Stilicho had himself been declared *hostis publicus* by Eutropius, and Gildo could therefore claim to be upholding true legitimacy. In the circumstances Stilicho needed a public demonstration of support on the part of the Senate, while this senatorial decree also provided a cover of legality for his actions which will surely have been extremely welcome at such a moment of crisis. Moreover, war against Gildo could hardly fail to result in the disruption of the regular corn-supplies from Africa to Rome, and by transferring formal responsibility from himself to the Senate Stilicho was able to deflect much of the ill will felt by the populace. If this indeed was Stilicho's calculation, it proved to be a very shrewd one: such was the shortage of food in the City that the senators were obliged to distribute corn from their own warehouses, while the violence of the people was extreme enough to force Symmachus, who had moved the motion on the Senate floor, to flee to a villa in the suburbs.[107]

That political considerations are at the root of much of what Claudian says about the Senate in *VI Cons.* is thus a fair bet. True power certainly lay with the court and with whoever held sway over the army, but the Roman aristocracy formed an important constituency, far surpassing their Eastern counterparts in wealth, in the vastness of their estates, and in their potential for influence. Their support, especially in the form of contributions of conscripts from their lands or of money to the Imperial armies, or at the very

---

[106] See Cameron 230 f., 362 f. Similar considerations assuredly lay behind Stilicho's decision to let the Senate conduct the investigation into magistrates who had served in Africa under Gildo: see *Stil.* 3. 99 ff., Cameron 234, 379 f.

[107] See Cameron 231, Matthews 269.

least their acquiescence, was thus a political necessity.[108]
Claudian's consular panegyrics regularly boast of harmony
between court and Senate in terms which present them as the
military and civilian wings of the state respectively,[109] but an especially insistent note is perhaps to be heard in the present poem:

> agnoscunt proceres, habituque Gabino
> principis et ducibus circumstipata togatis
> iure paludatae iam curia militat aulae.

(VI Cons. 594 ff.)

In all truth, Alaric's invasion of Italy seems to have put Stilicho's
relations with the Senate under particular strain. We saw above
how, in both *De Bello Getico* and *VI Cons.*, Claudian uses every
scrap of his formidable ingenuity to explain the circumstances
of Alaric's escape and to defuse the suspicion of treasonable
collusion between him and Stilicho.[110] The diehard pagan and
nationalist senators of Old Rome will not have been easy men to
persuade. It is not difficult to see that the shock of barbarian
incursions on to the very soil of Italy must have been a scandal of
the greatest imaginable proportions, and many no doubt wanted
to know why the shame had not been wiped out in Alaric's own
blood. And side by side with the concerns of patriotism stood
others of a more material sort: it was the vast estates of this very
senatorial class, the source of their wealth and their prestige, that
were laid open to the Gothic advance. It is no doubt very much
with these considerations in mind that Claudian puts into Alaric's
mouth a speech expressing his despair that he could not bring
himself to drive his host as far as the walls of Rome and, burning
the very crops around him, die within sight of the City:

> haec ego continuum si per iuga tendere cursum,
> ut prior iratae fuerat sententia menti,

---

[108] For Stilicho's need for senatorial support, and the difficulty he experienced in obtaining it, see Cameron 232 ff., Matthews 276 ff.

[109] See e.g. *III Cons.* 5 f., *IV Cons.* 5 ff. 'cernis ut armorum proceres legumque potentes | patricios sumunt habitus et more Gabino | discolor incedit legio positisque parumper | bellorum signis sequitur uexilla Quirini?. . .', *Theod.* 257 ff. 'illumque habitum, quo iungitur aulae | curia, qui socio proceres cum principe nectit, | quem quater ipse gerit, perfecto detulit anno | deposuitque suas te succedente curules'.

[110] See above, Sect. 3. Claudian has ingeniously adapted to a particular set of political circumstances what Menander Rhetor gave as a general precept: see above, n. 41.

1

iam desperata uoluissem luce, quid ultra?
omnibus oppeterem fama maiore perustis!
et certe moriens propius te, Roma, uiderem,
ipsaque per cultas segetes mors nostra secuto
uictori damnosa foret! sed pignora nobis
Romanus carasque nurus praedamque tenebat.

(*VI Cons.* 291 ff.)

Alaric's avowed wish that he had involved the whole world in his own ruin is an epic topos entirely appropriate to a speech in such a context.[111] But here it serves also to give the senators a sobering picture of what they have been spared by Stilicho's policies: their farmland reduced to burnt stubble, and the Gothic host at the very gates of Rome while they themselves, one might imagine, cowered in terror in their luxurious but vulnerable city mansions.

For all Claudian's eloquence and his dazzling brilliance in the manipulation of rhetoric and political reality, the 'Romans of Rome' were never really convinced. The next year saw another Gothic invasion, this time under Radagaisus. This time, for once, Stilicho won a decisive victory, at Faesulae. But irreparable damage had been done to public confidence in his ability to keep the barbarians out of the heart of the Empire, and the suspicions of treachery grew ever stronger. On the very last day of 406 the Rhine frontier collapsed, and waves of Suebi, Vandals, and others flooded Gaul. In the ensuing chaos a number of adventurers decided to try their luck, and soon Britain and a large part of Gaul were in the hands of a usurper who gave himself the ominous name of Constantine. In desperate need of friends even among those who had formerly been his foes, Stilicho once more opened negotiations with Alaric. Early in 408 he pressed the Senate to approve the supply of large subsidies to the Goths. At first they refused, but he forced the motion through. One senator—Lampadius, the brother of Mallius Theodorus, himself the recipient of one of Claudian's consular panegyrics—protested by crying out in the authentic voice of the senatorial aristocracy, 'non est ista pax, sed pactio seruitutis'.[112] The death soon after this of Arcadius threw matters into further turmoil, and power slipped with stunning rapidity from Stilicho's hands. In the wake of unrest

---

[111] For the topos see 292–7, 293 f. nn.   [112] Zosimus 5. 29. 9.

stirred up by Olympius and of mutiny in the army, Stilicho was arrested at Bononia. Even then he was busy assembling troops for another grandiose scheme, a march to the East in order to assert his right to a regency over Arcadius' young son, Theodosius II. Deceived into leaving the church where he had taken sanctuary, he was dragged to his death.[113] As for Claudian, had he still been alive, we may assume that he would have met his end in the slaughter of Stilicho's associates that accompanied the general's own fall.

It had long been a privilege of the senators of Rome to record their country's history from their own viewpoint. Their short-sighted parsimony and their arrogance; their constant refusal to contribute recruits for the defence of the Empire; their rage at the very suggestion that, for the good of the state they claimed to embody, they should offer up on the altar of necessity the exemptions from tax they considered theirs by right of birth: all these have been identified as major contributory causes for the great disaster that finally overtook them in 410.[114] But as he made his way back from the shattered city to his estates in Gaul, one of their number was sure that he knew who was to blame:

> quo magis est facinus diri Stilichonis acerbum,
>   proditor arcani quod fuit imperii.
> Romano generi dum nititur esse superstes,
>   crudelis summis miscuit ima furor;
> dumque timet quicquid se fecerat ipse timeri,
>   inmisit Latiae barbara tela neci.
> uisceribus nudis armatum condidit hostem,
>   illatae cladis liberiore dolo.
>
> (Rutilius Namatianus, *De Reditu Suo* 2. 41 ff.)

Claudian, no doubt, would have been able to put the record straight.

5. METRE, GRAMMAR, DICTION

For those who wish to gain a proper understanding and appreciation of Claudian's verse there can, of course, be no substitute for

---

[113] For Stilicho's last days see Zosimus 5. 34, Bury, *LRE* 166 ff., Matthews 274 ff., O'Flynn 55 ff.   [114] See esp. Matthews 276 ff., 387.

the direct experience of reading. What follows, then, is intended to serve only as an identification of some of the more prominent characteristics of his metre and language; for more precise information readers should consult the notes in the commentary at the lines indicated.[115]

Perhaps the most striking feature of Claudian's verse is its extraordinary fluidity, a smoothness which his harsher critics go so far as to call monotonous.[116] This quality is the result of the repeated use of the same metrical patterns, the avoidance of elision, and the rigidly classical prosody. To this extent Claudian is merely following in the footsteps of the most prestigious post-Augustan hexameter poets, and in his metrics, as in his fondness for antithesis, word-play, and the eye-catching phrase, he is more the devotee of Ovid and Statius than the heir of Virgil.

Claudian's prosody is well discussed by Birt.[117] By comparison with, for example, his contemporary Prudentius, Claudian is practically faultless in his classical purity. Certainly there is very little in *VI Cons.* for the severest critic to complain of on this score. Indeed, the only generally agreed instance of a false quantity in his work was long thought to be *feritura*, where the *i* of the second syllable is scanned short (*Rapt.* 3. 359). Hall would remove even this by printing Scaliger's 'petit ira',[118] though two other probable errors, both in fairly rare proper names, can be identified (*Ăcin* at *Rapt.* 3. 332[119] and *Syphăcem* at *Gild.* 91). But to put it succinctly, Claudian's prosody is more accurately classical than that of any other Latin poet of the fourth and fifth centuries. For one whose native language was Greek this is a formidable achievement, and perhaps it should be attributed to his having learned Latin painstakingly as a foreign language, with scrupulous regard to the poets of the classical period.

---

[115] For Claudian's metre and language see in general F. Trump, *Observationes ad genus dicendi Claudiani eiusque imitationem Vergilianam spectantes* (Breslau, 1887); Birt, pp. ccxi–ccxix; A. Welzel, *De Claudiani et Corippi sermone epico* (Diss. Breslau, 1908), Fargues on *Eutr.*, 16 ff.; Cameron 287 ff.; Barr 24 ff.; Gruzelier, pp. xxviii f.

[116] See esp., Cameron 288: 'The fault of Claudian's versification is precisely that it is flawless—too flawless. He has weeded out almost all the "licences" which disfigure the pages of Vergil'; id. 290 f., citing Dryden: also Fargues on *Eutr.* 17, Barr 26.

[117] See Birt, p. ccxi.

[118] But see Gruzelier ad loc. for an argument in favour of retaining *feritura*.

[119] This too is disputed. Hall again wanted to remove the anomaly by emendation (from *flumen Acin* to *flauum Acin*), but Gruzelier ad loc. is rightly suspicious of the abrupt elision.

Like many Latin poets Claudian is fond of using a golden line to close a section of his poem in style. An example in *VI Cons.* is l. 469 'barbara fulmineo secuit tentoria cursu', which gives a resounding conclusion to Honorius' narrative of Stilicho's heroism in relieving the siege of Milan. Hexameters constructed out of only four words can be made to fulfil the same function, as at v. 177 'gurgite sidereo subterluit Oriona'. That line, however, also offers an instance of something relatively rare in Claudian, the spondaic fifth foot. Elision is avoided by Claudian, whose average is calculated by Cameron at about one every eighteen lines; contrast Virgil's rate of one every two lines, or even Ovid's one every three and a half lines.[120] And where elision does occur, it is almost always of a short syllable, usually a final *e*. Indeed, so rare is strong elision of terminal long vowels that Claudian's usual metrical practice must be taken into account in evaluating the conjectures *uigili* (Gesner, *pr.* 8) and *uenienti* (Heinsius, v. 107). The sense of flow that results is enhanced by Claudian's marked preference for the same metrical patterns: Duckworth calculates that over four-fifths of Claudian's lines follow one of eight out of sixteen possible combinations of dactyls and spondees in the first four feet. This regularity is increased still further by the relative frequency of what Duckworth calls 'repeat clusters', or the appearance of the same pattern six times or more within a space of sixteen lines.[121] One could say the same of Claudian's weakness for the type of line ending in which a dactylic word fills the fifth foot and a disyllable the sixth, in combination with double coincidence of ictus and accent. True, this type of line-ending had long been a favourite one in the Latin hexameter, but it is not easy to imagine Virgil, for example, being satisfied with using the same ending six times in seven lines, or four consecutively (vv. 229–35). And much the same could be said of Claudian's fondness for a trochaic caesura in the third foot, accompanied by strong breaks in the second and fourth: four consecutive examples can be found at vv. 253–6. The general effect, then, is of high technical competence and fluidity, at the price of a certain lack of variety.

---

[120] For these figures see Cameron 289. Barr attempts more precise figures at pp. 25f., noting that *VI Cons.* 'show[s] a higher than average incidence' of elision (6.7%).

[121] G. E. Duckworth, 'Five Centuries of Latin Hexameter Poetry: Silver Age and Late Empire', *TAPhA* 98 (1967), 77–150. See also Cameron 291.

Claudian's diction is, like his prosody, classical and conservative. His use of Graecisms is confined to those long sanctioned by tradition. In this class of linguistic feature we should probably include forms such as the 'retained accusative' of the type 'resoluta comam' (v. 153). This and the other so-called 'Greek accusatives' may well have native Latin roots, but they are avoided in classical prose, and in using them frequently Latin poets no doubt thought of themselves as adapting Greek syntax. Neologisms too tend to be few in number, and entirely in the mould of established forms. Fargues, on *Eutr.* 1. 429 *belliferam* (*belligeram* Hall) claims that Claudian's works offer only thirty-three hapax legomena. Even this figure almost certainly overstates the incidence of active verbal innovation, since many, if not all, of these words no doubt appeared in the works of other poets now lost to us. One distinctive feature of Claudian's diction worth commenting on is the fairly high incidence of prosaisms, particularly words and phrases primarily associated with history: examples are *patratis . . . bellis* (v. 126) and *transfuga* (v. 250). But such words are hardly inappropriate to contemporary military epic, and in any case 'historia . . . est . . . proxima poetis et quodam modo carmen solutum' (Quint. *Inst.* 10. 1. 31).

For Claudian's grammar readers are referred to the exhaustive discussion in Birt's preface (pp. ccxx–ccxxv). Departures from classical usage are very few, and where they occur they are not idiosyncratic, but easily paralleled in other texts from late antiquity. Examples include the use of *tanti* for *tot* (43n.) or the substitution of a reflexive form for a classical passive (40f. 'se . . . | aestimat', 502 'se perforat').

6. THE TEXT

The various poems of Claudian have come down to us in well over a hundred manuscripts, by more than one route of transmission, and in a vast turmoil of contamination. The stoutest of hearts have quailed before the prospect of extracting a stemma from the resulting confusion: none is attempted here. Indeed, the text and apparatus of *De Sexto Consulatu Honorii* offered in this volume have been constructed almost entirely on the strength of the manuscript readings reported by earlier editors, above all

INTRODUCTION

T. Birt (*MGH, AA* 10; Berlin, 1892) and J. B. Hall (Bibliotheca Teubneriana; Leipzig, 1985). Readers who wish to acquire a fuller understanding of the manuscript tradition are referred to the following works: J. B. Hall, *Prolegomena to Claudian* (*BICS*, Suppl. 45; London, 1986), Hall's own summary of this work at L. D. Reynolds (ed.), *Texts and Transmission* (Oxford, 1983), 143–5, and P. L. Schmidt, 'Die Überlieferungsgeschichte von Claudians Carmina Maiora', *Illinois Classical Studies*, 14 (1989), 391–415.

The degree of contamination between manuscripts is so severe that it is often difficult in the extreme, when faced with a choice between manuscripts of similar age, to judge one generally superior to another. In any case, despite the profusion of variants, it is relatively rare to find an intractable crux in the text of Claudian. Above all, as Housman observed with regard to the text of Lucan, '[t]here were no sequestered valleys through which streams of tradition might flow unmixed, and . . . the true line of division is between the variants themselves, not between the manuscripts which offer them.'[122] This dictum is perhaps even more applicable to the text of Claudian, and it was with considerations such as these in mind that Claire Gruzelier, for her recent edition of *De Raptu Proserpinae* (Oxford, 1993; pp. xxix–xxxi), devised the following simplified system of manuscript citation:

x indicates any reading with manuscript support sufficient to show that it has 'a reasonable chance of dating from antiquity'.[123]

ς indicates a reading found only in a few, or late, manuscripts and which is presumably a mistake or conjecture.

In addition, she uses the abbreviation *Is.* for readings taken from the edition of Michael Bentinus, printed by Michael Isengrin in Basle in 1534. This edition bears strong signs of having drawn on a manuscript which is now lost but which would appear to have been superior to all those that still survive. As in Gruzelier's edition of the *De Raptu*, 'the system of the "negative apparatus" is adopted: i.e. every reading printed in the text is an *x* reading, except where otherwise stated; other *x* readings recorded as such in the apparatus have roughly comparable authority. If a ς

---

[122] A. E. Housman, *M. Annaei Lucani Belli Ciuilis libri decem* (Oxford, 1926; repr. 1970), p. vii.　　　　[123] Gruzelier, p. xxx.

reading is adopted in the text, it is explicitly described as such in the apparatus and has little authority.'[124]

As Gruzelier acknowledges, her system is open to the charge that it is excessively arbitrary, since deciding whether to classify a particular reading as x or ς is by no means always a clear-cut matter. Moreover, where there is a crux, the apparatus may well end up presenting a string of undifferentiated readings in which all are designated x and which therefore may seem to claim that no meaningful distinction can be made between them at all. None the less the beautiful simplicity of Gruzelier's system seems much more likely to provide, with concision and efficiency, the kind of information most urgently required by those readers who are primarily interested in the text of Claudian's poems for their literary and historical value. It is therefore gratefully adopted in the present edition of *VI Cons.*, and readers who wish more precise information about the manuscript tradition are urged to avail themselves of the rich detail provided by the apparatus criticus to Hall's essential Teubner edition of Claudian's complete works.

[124] Gruzelier, p. xxx.

SIGLA

x   uaria lectio in satis multis et uetustioribus codicibus tradita

ς   uaria lectio in paucis uel tantum recentioribus codicibus tradita

Is.   uaria lectio ex editione Isengriniana citata (*marg.* indicat lectionem in margine huius editionis positam)

PANEGYRICVS
DE SEXTO CONSVLATV
HONORII AVGVSTI

PRAEFATIO

OMNIA quae sensu uoluuntur uota diurno
    pectore sopito reddit amica quies.
uenator defessa toro cum membra reponit,
    mens tamen ad siluas et sua lustra redit.
iudicibus lites, aurigae somnia currus   5
    uanaque nocturnis meta cauetur equis.
furto gaudet amans, permutat nauita merces
    et uigil elapsas quaerit auarus opes,
blandaque largitur frustra sitientibus aegris
    inriguus gelido pocula fonte sopor.   10
me quoque Musarum studium sub nocte silenti
    artibus adsuetis sollicitare solet.
namque poli media stellantis in arce uidebar
    ante pedes summi carmina ferre Iouis;
utque fauet somnus, plaudebant numina dictis   15
    et circumfusi sacra corona chori.
Enceladus mihi carmen erat uictusque Typhoeus
    (hic subit Inarimen, hunc grauis Aetna domat);
quam laetus post bella Iouem susceperit Aether
    Phlegraeae referens praemia militiae.   20
additur ecce fides nec me mea lusit imago,
    inrita nec falsum somnia misit ebur.
en princeps, en orbis apex aequatus Olympo,
    en quales memini, turba uerenda, dei!
fingere nil maius potuit sopor, altaque uati   25
    conuentum caelo praebuit aula parem.

2 tempore nocturno ς   3 cum membra toro defessa ς: dum (cum ς) fessa toro sua
membra ς   5 cursus ς   7 gaudet amans furto ς   8 peruigil elapsas ς: et
uigili elapsas *Gesnerus*: et uigili lapsas *Bücheler*   12 assiduis *x*   inuigilare iubet ς
13 axe ς: orbe ς   15 plauserunt ς   17 uinctusque *x*   18 hunc premit
inarimes ς   19 laetum *x*   suscepterat *x*   21 iam mea lusit ς: iam me lusit ς: me
iam lusit ς: me mea fallit ς: me delusit *Goodyear*   23 aequatur *x*: aequandus ς
24 dei *Scaliger*: deos *codd*.

A PANEGYRIC
ON THE SIXTH CONSULSHIP OF
THE EMPEROR HONORIUS

PREFACE

ALL the desires that our waking minds ponder by day, these does friendly sleep bring back to us when once our spirits are lulled in slumber. When the huntsman lays down his weary limbs upon his bed, all the same his mind returns to his familiar coverts and the woods. Judges dream of lawsuits, and the charioteer of his chariot as with his horses of the night he steers safely past a phantom turning-post. In stolen delights the lover finds his joy, the merchant barters his goods, and, on waking, the miser seeks in vain the riches that have slipped from his grasp, while to poor mortals stricken by thirst sleep streaming in lavishes—but all in vain—pleasing draughts from cool springs.

Me too in the silence of the night devotion to the Muses commonly troubles with my accustomed craft. For I seemed to find myself in the very heart of the citadel of the starry heavens, bringing my songs before the feet of Jupiter the Most High. And, such is the flattery of dreams, the gods applauded what I sang, and so also all the sacred throng that stood around. Enceladus was my theme, and Typhoeus conquered (one lies beneath Inarime, the other weighty Etna holds in subjection); and how joyful was Heaven when, the war concluded, it welcomed Jupiter, receiving the spoils of battle on the fields of Phlegra!

See how confirmation is now granted me, and my vision has not played me false, nor has the deceitful Gate of Ivory sent dreams that come to nothing. Behold our Prince, behold the world's pinnacle made level with Olympus! Behold the gods as I remember them, a venerable host! Sleep could imagine nothing greater, and this lofty hall has shown the bard a gathering that is the peer of heaven.

3

PANEGYRICVS

Aᴠʀᴇᴀ Fortunae Reduci si templa priores
ob reditum uouere ducum, non dignius umquam
haec dea pro meritis amplas sibi posceret aedes
quam sua cum pariter trabeis reparatur et urbi
maiestas; neque enim campus sollemnis et urna   5
luditur in morem, species nec dissona coetu
aut peregrina nitet simulati iuris imago.
indigenas habitus natiua Palatia sumunt,
et, patriis plebem castris sociante Quirino,
Mars Augusta sui renouat suffragia campi.   10
qualis erit terris, quem mons Euandrius offert
Romanis auibus, quem Thybris inaugurat, annus?
quamquam omnes, quicumque tui cognominis, anni
semper inoffensum dederint successibus omen
sintque tropaea tuas semper comitata secures,   15
hic tamen ante omnes miro promittitur ortu
urbis et Augusti geminato numine felix.
namque uelut stellas Babylonia cura salubres
optima tum spondet mortalibus edere fata,
caelicolae cum celsa tenent summoque feruntur   20
cardine nec radios humili statione retundunt,
haud aliter Latiae sublimis Signifer aulae,
imperii sidus propria cum sede locauit,
auget spes Italas; et certius omina surgunt
uictrici concepta solo.
               cum pulcher Apollo   25
lustrat Hyperboreas Delphis cessantibus aras,
nil tum Castaliae riuis communibus undae
dissimiles, uili nec discrepat arbore laurus
antraque maesta silent inconsultique recessus.

---

2 pro reditu ς non] num ς: nec ς   3 latas ς amplis . . . aedem *Jeep*
4 trabeis pariter ς reparetur ς: repetatur *x*   5 nec *x* campi . . . urnae *Scaliger*
6 non *x* cultu ς, *Schraderus*   9 patribus . . . sanctis *Paul*   10 reuocat ς
11 erat *x*: eat *Heinsius*   12 annum *x*   13 quoscumque ς: quotcumque *Heinsius*
14 dederant *x*: dederunt *Heinsius*   15 suntque *x*, *Heinsius*   17 urbis et] ter bis in
Scaliger nomine *x*   19 tum *Hall*: tunc *x*: nunc *x* facta *x*   20 fruuntur ς
21 retundunt ς, *Gesnerus*: recondunt *x*: recumbunt ς, *quo sumpto* radiis *Heinsius*
24 omnia *x*   26 auras *x*: arces ς: Arctos *Heinsius*

4

THE PANEGYRIC

IF those that went before us vowed to Fortuna of the Home-
coming golden temples for their leaders' safe return, never would
this goddess more deservedly demand a spacious mansion in pay-
ment for her services, than when the majesty that is theirs is
restored all at once to the consulship and the City. For the
annual election on the Field of Mars and the voting urn are not
made mock of in the usual way, nor is this a sham out of harmony
with such an assembly, nor is the glitter that of the alien imitation
of a feigned legitimacy. Our ancestral Palatine puts on its native
garb, and, as Quirinus unites the people in alliance with their
nation's army, Mars renews the imperial suffrage of his field.
What face will it show the world, a year bestowed by Evander's
mount with omens truly Roman, a year inaugurated by the
Tiber? Though all the years that bear your name have always
given omens of success that never stumble, and though trophies
have always been the companions of your fasces, yet this year,
born from so wonderful a source, promises to be blessed beyond
all others under the twinned divinity of the City and of the
Augustus. For just as Babylonian lore pledges that beneficent stars
proclaim the best fate for mortals at that time when the heaven-
dwellers hold the summit of the sky and are borne along at their
zenith, not hiding their rays in a lowly station; just so when the
Standard-Bearer of the Roman Palace has placed the Empire's
star in its own proper seat, he swells the hopes of Italy; and more
surely rise the omens conceived on victorious ground.

When fair Apollo, as Delphi lies idle, moves in procession
round the altars of the Hyperboreans, in no way then are
Castalia's waters different from common streams, nor is the bay
to be distinguished from any worthless tree, and the caves are
sorrowful and silent, and the inner hallows left unconsulted. But
if Phoebus is present and, seeking once more his tripods, with
his reins turns back his griffin team from the Riphaean pole, then
the woods, and then too the caves give utterance, then the

5

at si Phoebus adest et frenis grypa iugalem 30
Riphaeo tripodas repetens detorsit ab axe,
tum siluae, tunc antra loqui, tum uiuere fontes,
tum sacer horror aquis adytisque effunditur echo
clarior et doctae spirant praesagia rupes.
ecce Palatino creuit reuerentia monti 35
exultatque habitante deo potioraque Delphis
supplicibus late populis oracula pandit
atque suas ad signa iubet reuirescere laurus.
   non alium certe decuit rectoribus orbis
esse larem, nulloque magis se colle potestas 40
aestimat et summi sentit fastigia iuris.
attollens apicem subiectis regia rostris
tot circum delubra uidet tantisque deorum
cingitur excubiis! iuuat infra tecta Tonantis
cernere Tarpeia pendentes rupe Gigantas 45
caelatasque fores mediisque uolantia signa
nubibus et densum stipantibus aethera templis
aeraque uestitis numerosa puppe columnis
consita subnixasque iugis inmanibus aedes,
naturam cumulante manu, spoliisque micantes 50
innumeros arcus. acies stupet igne metalli
et circumfuso trepidans obtunditur auro.
   agnoscisne tuos, princeps uenerande, penates?
haec sunt quae primis olim miratus in annis
patre pio monstrante puer. nil optimus ille 55
diuorum toto meruit felicius aeuo
quam quod Romuleis uictor sub moenibus egit
te consorte dies, cum se melioribus addens
exemplis ciuem gereret terrore remoto,
alternos cum plebe iocos dilectaque passus 60
iurgia patriciasque domos priuataque passim
uisere deposito dignatus limina fastu.

31 ueniens ς   32 fontes] frondes *Delrius*   37 fundit *x*   41 sensit *x*:
sancit *Heinsius*: scandit *Birt*   fastigia] uestigia ς: suffragia ς   44 intra *x*: inter *Jeep*
templa *x*   46 elatasque ς   thoros ς   47 demptum *Birt*   48 aruaque
Koch   numerosa ueste *x*: numeroso uecte *Heinsius*   49 condita ς   51 innu-
meris *Barthius, Heinsius*   53 custos ς   54 miratur ς   ab annis *x*   55 puer
ς: petis *x*: uias *Camers marg.*   57 quod] quos *Heinsius*   59 gereret ciuem ς
61 seria *Schraderus*   62 limina . . . uisere ς

springs come alive, then the waters shudder with his holy presence and from the sanctuary the echo pours out louder, and the inspired cliffs breathe out their prophecies. See how the reverence owed to the Palatine mount has grown and how it exults in the god now dwelling there, and to suppliant nations far and wide reveals oracles more powerful than those of Delphi, and commands the bays that are its own to grow green again, for our standards.

In truth no other place was fitting to be the home of the rulers of the world, and on no hill can power's majesty better take its own measure or sense the pinnacle of highest authority. Raising its crown above the rostra far below, the palace sees around it so many shrines and such a company of gods keeping watch in their protective ring! Delight it is to see beneath the Thunderer's roof the Giants hanging from the Tarpeian Rock and the chiselled temple-doors and the statues soaring through the midst of the clouds, and the upper air dense-packed with crowding temples, and the forest of bronze beaks thick-planted on the columns clad with many a ship's prow, and the mansions resting on the massive hills—for the hand of man has added to the work of nature—and uncounted arches gleaming with the spoils of war. The eye is stunned by the blaze of metal and left trembling and dimmed by the gold that is scattered all around.

Do you recognize your home, my venerable Prince? These are the sights at which in time gone by, in your earliest years, you gazed in wonder, as a boy when your loving father showed them to you. Best as he was of all the gods, he never achieved anything more felicitous in all his life than that he spent his time as victor under the walls of Romulus with you at his side, when, adding his name to the roll-call of the nobler princes, he played the part of citizen, all terror far removed, enduring the exchange of jests with the people and the raillery that they love, enduring too to lay aside the haughtiness of rank and deign to visit in every quarter the houses of senators and the doors of ordinary subjects. And so the people's love burns fiercer, when moderation makes royal majesty bow in just humility to the people. And though the diadem

7

publicus hinc ardescit amor, cum moribus aequis
inclinat populo regale modestia culmen.
teque rudem uitae, quamuis diademate necdum   65
cingebare comas, socium sumebat honorum
purpureo fotum gremio, paruumque triumphis
imbuit et magnis docuit praeludere fatis.
te linguis uariae gentes missique rogatum
foedera Persarum proceres cum patre sedentem   70
hac quondam uidere domo positoque tiaran
summisere genu. tecum praelarga uocauit
ditandas ad dona tribus; fulgentia tecum
collecti trabeatus adit delubra senatus
Romano puerum gaudens offerre fauori,   75
ut nouus imperio iam tunc adsuesceret heres.
  hinc tibi concreta radice tenacius haesit
et penitus totis inoleuit Roma medullis,
dilectaeque urbis tenero conceptus ab ungue
tecum creuit amor; nec te mutare reuersum   80
eualuit propria nutritor Bosporos arce.
et quotiens optare tibi quae moenia malles
alludens genitor regni pro parte dedisset,
diuitis Aurorae solium sortemque paratam
sponte remittebas fratri:'regat ille uolentes   85
Assyrios; habeat Pharium cum Tigride Nilum;
contingat mea Roma mihi.' nec uota fefellit
euentus. Fortuna nouum molita tyrannum
iam tibi quaerebat Latium, belloque secundo
protinus, Eoa uelox accitus ab aula,   90
suscipis Hesperiam patrio bis Marte receptam.
ipsa per Illyricas urbes Oriente relicto
ire Serena comes nullo deterrita casu,
materna te mente fouens Latioque futurum
rectorem generumque sibi, seniore supernas   95
iam repetente plagas. illo sub cardine rerum
sedula seruatum per tot discrimina pignus

64 inclinet ς   65 nondum x   66 honoris ς   67 fetum x: secum x
trophaeis ς   68 induit x   fastis x   72 praeclara ς   74 collecto . . . senatu ς   75 afferre ς   77 hic ς   78 assueuit ς   79 tenero . . . ungue
ς: teneris . . . annis x   82 uelles x   91 retentam ς   93 perterrita ς
95 seniore] rectore ς: genitore Schraderus

was not yet bound around your hair, he took you, still in your
tenderest youth, as companion of his honours, nestling you on his
purple-clad bosom, and, small though you were, he gave you your
first taste of triumphs and taught you to play the prelude to your
mighty destiny. And peoples diverse in tongue, and the nobles of
Persia sent to sue for peace, once saw you sitting with your father
in this very house, and bending the knee they lowered their
crowns before you. With you he called forth the tribes to be
enriched by bounteous gifts; with you he made his way, clad in the
robes of victory, to the radiant shrine where the Senate was
assembled, rejoicing to present you while a boy to the favour of
the Romans, so that even then the new heir might grow accustomed to Imperial rule.

From this time Rome planted her roots firm within your heart,
and held you all the more firmly in her grip, wholly grafted on to
your being's inmost depths, and the love of City you adored, conceived in your first infancy, grew even as you did. Nor did the
Bosporus, who nourished you in his own palace, have the power
to change your feelings when you had returned. And whenever in
play your father had given you to choose for your share of the
kingdom the city that you preferred, freely you would yield to
your brother the rich East's throne and the lot that was reserved
for him: 'Let him rule over willing Assyrian slaves; let him keep
Pharian Nile and Tigris too; let my own dear Rome be my
portion.' Nor were your wishes disappointed by events. Fortune,
contriving a fresh usurper, was already seeking to make Latium
yours, and as soon as a second war broke out you were summoned
to come in haste from the Eastern Court, and you took up the
burden of Hesperia, recovered for a second time by your father in
war. Leaving the East and journeying through the cities of
Illyricum, Serena herself came as your companion, by every blow
of chance all undeterred, cherishing you with a mother's care, to
be both a ruler for Latium and a son-in-law for herself when the
Emperor, as age crept on, now returned to the world above. At
that moment on which history turned, steadfastly she restored the
child she had kept safe through so many dangers to her uncle's

restituit sceptris patrui castrisque mariti.
certauit pietate domus, fidaeque reductum
coniugis officio Stilichonis cura recepit.   100
    felix ille parens, qui te securus Olympum
succedente petit! quam laetus ab aethere cernit
se factis creuisse tuis! duo namque fuere
Europae Libyaeque hostes: Maurusius Atlans
Gildonis furias, Alaricum barbara Peuce   105
nutrierat, qui saepe tuum spreuere profana
mente patrem. Thracum uenientem e finibus alter
Hebri clausit aquis; alter praecepta uocantis
respuit auxiliisque ad proxima bella negatis
abiurata palam Libyae possederat arua.   110
quorum nunc meritam repetens non inmemor iram
suppliciis fruitur natoque ultore triumphat.
ense Thyestiaden poenas exegit Orestes,
sed mixtum pietate nefas dubitandaque caedis
gloria materno laudem cum crimine pensat;   115
pauit Iuleos inuiso sanguine Manes
Augustus, sed falsa pii praeconia sumpsit
in luctum patriae ciuili strage parentans:
at tibi causa patris rerum coniuncta saluti
bellorum duplicat laurus, isdemque tropaeis   120
reddita libertas orbi, uindicta parenti.
    sed mihi iam pridem captum Parnasia Maurum
Pieriis egit fidibus chelys; arma Getarum
nuper apud socerum plectro celebrata recenti.
aduentus nunc sacra tui libet edere Musis   125
grataque patratis exordia sumere bellis.
    iam Pollentini tenuatus funere campi,
concessaque sibi (rerum sic admonet usus)
luce, tot amissis sociis atque omnibus una
direptis opibus, Latio discedere iussus   130
hostis et inmensi reuolutus culmine fati

---

99 fidoque ς   100 officiis *x*   102 qui ς   103 fastis ς
107 uenientem e ς: uenientem *x*: euenientem ς: ueniens e *x*: ueniens a ς: uenienti (*cum*
aquas 108) *Heinsius*   108 aquas *x*   109 auxiliis *x*   110 adiurata ς   libyes
ς   112 triumphans ς   113 thyestiadae *x*   115 maternae *x*   120 triumphis ς   125 tuis libet edere muris *Heinsius*

sceptre and her husband's army. Man and wife were rivals in the display of family love, and when you were brought back to him through the offices of his faithful spouse Stilicho received you into his care.

Happy that father who, free of care since it is you who succeed him, makes his way to Olympus! With what joy he sees from Heaven his own glory made yet greater by your deeds! For two foes there were, from Europe and from Africa: Maurusian Atlas had reared the mad Gildo, and savage Peuce had reared Alaric, who many a time with impious hearts showed your own father scorn. One checked his path with Hebrus' waters as he advanced from the lands of Thrace; the other, when he summoned him, spurned his commands, and, denying him aid for wars that were pressing close, had seized for himself the fields of Libya, fields whose legitimate rule he had openly forsworn. And now, calling to mind once more the anger he justly felt and forgetting nothing, Theodosius takes joy in their punishment and triumphs in the vengeance exacted by his son. Orestes with the sword made Thyestes' son pay the price in full, but in him was sin confounded with the deeds of duty, and the glory that the slaughter brought was made doubtful, since in the scales he put his crime against his mother to match his weight of praise; Augustus sated Julius' ghost with the blood he hated, but false were his boasts of filial piety when the offerings he made to his father's shade were civil strife and his country's grief. But for you your father's cause was joined with the safety of the state, so doubling the laurels of your victory; and through the same triumphs freedom has been given back to the world, and his revenge to your father.

But long ago did my Parnassian lyre with its Pierian strings sing of how the Moor was taken; and only a little time has gone since it celebrated the wars against the Goths, in verse still fresh and with Stilicho there to hear me. Now it is my delight to record for the Muses the sacred rituals of your coming, and, now that war is ended, to begin a song of thanksgiving.

With his ranks now thinned by the carnage of Pollentia's field, and with his life conceded him (for so does policy advise), with so

turpe retexit iter. qualis piratica puppis,
quae cunctis infensa fretis scelerumque referta
diuitiis multasque diu populata carinas
incidit in magnam bellatricemque triremim,   135
dum praedam de more putat; uiduataque caesis
remigiis, scissis uelorum debilis alis,
orba gubernaclis, antemnis saucia fractis,
ludibrium pelagi uento iactatur et unda
uastato tandem poenas luitura profundo: 140
talis ab urbe minas retro flectebat inanes
Italiam fugiens, et quae uenientibus ante
prona fuit, iam difficilis, iam dura reuersis.
clausa putat sibi cuncta pauor, retroque relictos,
quos modo temnebat, rediens exhorruit amnes.   145
    undosa tum forte domo uitreisque sub antris
rerum ignarus adhuc ingentes pectore curas
uoluebat pater Eridanus: quis bella maneret
exitus, imperiumne Ioui legesque placerent
et uitae Romana quies, an iura perosus   150
ad priscos pecudum damnaret saecula ritus?
talia dum secum mouet anxius, aduolat una
Naiadum resoluta comam, conplexaque patrem,
'en Alaricus' ait, 'non qualem nuper ouantem
uidimus; exangues, genitor, mirabere uultus.   155
percensere manum tantaque ex gente iuuabit
reliquias numerasse breues. iam desine maesta
fronte queri, Nymphasque choris iam redde sorores.'
    dixerat; ille caput placidis sublime fluentis
extulit et totis lucem spargentia ripis   160
aurea roranti micuerunt cornua uultu.
non illi madidum uulgaris harundine crinem
uelat honos; rami caput umbrauere uirentes
Heliadum totisque fluunt electra capillis.
    palla tegit latos umeros, curruque paterno   165

---

132 retraxit ς   133 scelerisque *x*   refecta ς: repleta ς   136 parat *x*: petit *Heinsius*   137 remigiis ς: remigibus *x*: *an* caeso remigio?   142 italia *x*
143 diff. iam p. f. nec dura r. ς: diff. iam pena f. nec dura r. ς   145 terrebat *x*
146 domu *x*   147 ingenti *x*   149 legesne ς   151 rictus ς: uictus ς
156 manus ς   157 numerare ς   158 i redde *Heinsius*   sonoris *x*
159 placidum ς   164 ruunt ς

many of his comrades lost, and all his wealth plundered with them, our enemy, bidden to depart from Latium and tumbled from the peak of an incalculable destiny, retraced his steps in shame. As a pirate ship, the terror of every sea, which is stuffed with the spoils of its infamy and has ravaged ships, many in number, for many a day, falls upon a great and warlike trireme, thinking it plunder in the usual fashion: suddenly its oarsmen are slaughtered and stripped away, and, crippled by the tearing of the wings that bear its sails, bereft of its rudder, and stricken by the shattering of its yard-arms, it is tossed by wind and wave, a mere plaything of the sea, and on the waters of the deep that it has laid waste it will pay the penalty at last: just so did Alaric turn his empty threats backwards from the City, fleeing Italy, and the road that was easy for them when they came now is difficult, now is hard on their return. Fear believes all paths are closed to it, and the streams that only a short while since it left behind in contempt now in returning it has beheld in horror.

It happened that in his wave-lapped home deep in its glassy cavern father Eridanus, knowing nothing of what had befallen, was then pondering weighty cares within his heart: what would be the outcome of the war? did empire and law, and peaceful life beneath the sway of Rome find approval in the mind of Jove, or did he, in hatred of what is right, condemn future generations to the beast-like customs of ancient times? While his troubled heart considered matters such as these, one of the Naiads, her hair unbound, flew to his side, and embracing her father said: 'Behold now Alaric, not exultant as when we saw him a short while since; you will, my father, look in wonder at a face now drained of blood. You will take delight in reviewing his troops and in making the tally of what little remains from so populous a race. Now cease to lament with sorrowful brow, and now restore my sister Nymphs to their dances.'

So she spoke; Eridanus raised his head aloft from his calm stream, and his golden horns, scattering light over all the banks, flashed from his dripping face. For him no common decoration veiled his wet hair with reeds; green branches from the trees of

intextus Phaethon glaucos incendit amictus,
fultaque sub gremio caelatis nobilis astris
aetherium probat urna decus. namque omnia luctus
argumenta sui Titan signauit Olympo:
mutatumque senem plumis et fronde sorores,   170
et fluuium, nati qui uulnera lauit anheli;
stat gelidis Auriga plagis; uestigia fratris
germanae seruant Hyades, Cycnique sodalis
lacteus extentas aspergit circulus alas;
stelliger Eridanus sinuatis flexibus errans   175
clara Noti conuexa rigat gladioque tremendum
gurgite sidereo subterluit Oriona.
   hoc deus effulgens habitu prospexit euntes
deiecta ceruice Getas; tum talia fatur:
'sicine mutatis properas, Alarice, reuerti   180
consiliis? Italae sic te iam paenitet orae?
nec iam cornipedem Thybrino gramine pascis,
ut rebare, tuum, Tuscis nec figis aratrum
collibus? o cunctis Erebi dignissime poenis,
tune Giganteis urbem temptare deorum   185
adgressus furiis? nec te meus, inprobe, saltem
terruit exemplo Phaethon, qui fulmina praeceps
in nostris efflauit aquis, dum flammea caeli
flectere terrenis meditatur frena lacertis
mortalique diem sperat diffundere uultu?   190
crede mihi, simili bacchatur crimine, quisquis
adspirat Romae spoliis aut Solis habenis.'
   sic fatus Ligures Venetosque erectior amnes
magna uoce ciet. frondentibus umida ripis
colla leuant pulcher Ticinus et Addua uisu   195
caerulus et uelox Athesis tardusque meatu
Mincius inque nouem consurgens ora Timauus.
insultant omnes profugo pacataque laetum
inuitant ad prata pecus; iam Pana Lycaeum,

---

167 multaque ς: fuluaque *Is. marg.*: sculptaque ς: pulchraque *Jeep*   170 mutauitque
x   174 extensas *x*   aspersit ς: extendit ς   175 stellifer *x*: signifer ς   sinuosis
Heinsius   fluctibus *x*   177 subterfluit ς   178 prospectat *x*   181 iam te sic ς:
sic iam te ς: iam sic te ς   182–3 cornipedes . . . tuos ς: cornipedem . . . tuo *Burmannus*
183 frangis ς   187 fulmine ς, *Birt*: flamina ς   192 aut] ut ς, *Scaliger*   195 et]
atque *x*   ardua *x*   198 exultant ς   199 Lycaeo *Schraderus*

Helios' daughters shaded his head and from all his locks streamed amber. A cloak covered his broad shoulders, and woven on it was Phaethon in his father's chariot, setting the grey-green garment ablaze. And resting in the protection of his lap was an urn splendid with engraved stars, bearing witness to his heavenly glory. For the Titan-sun had placed upon the sky all the story of his grief: the old man transformed with feathers and the sisters with leaves, and the river that washed the wounds of his smouldering son; in the chill zones of Heaven stands the Charioteer; the sister Hyades follow close upon their brother's tracks, and the Milky Way sprinkles the outstretched wings of the Swan who bears him company; star-bearing Eridanus, wandering in winding curves, waters the South's bright vault and in a spangled stream flows beneath Orion, fearsome with his sword.

Brilliant in this garment the god looked out at the Goths as they went on by with their necks bowed down; then he spoke as follows: 'Is this how you hasten to return, Alaric, your plans all changed? Is this how you now show regret for the shores of Italy? And do you no longer feed your horse, as you thought you would, on Tiber's grassy banks? Nor plant your plough on Tuscany's hills? O most worthy as you are of all the torments of Erebus, did you with the madness of the Giants set out to make an attempt on the City of the Gods? And—you shameless man!—did not at the least my own Phaethon fill you with the fear of his own example, Phaethon, who, falling headlong, gasped out in these my waters the thunderbolt with his last breath, at that time when he thought to guide with earthly arms the reins of fire and hoped to spread the daylight from a mortal face? Believe me, no different is the crime raging in the heart of any man who aspires either to the spoils of Rome or the chariot of the Sun.'

So saying he rose up taller and summoned in a loud voice the rivers of Liguria and Venetia. From the leafy banks they raised their streaming necks: fair Ticinus and Addua blue of face, and swift Athesis, and slow-gliding Mincius, and Timavus swelling to his ninefold mouth. All hurl insults at the fugitive and invite the joyful cattle to their meadows, peaceful now; now they recall

iam Dryadas reuocant et, rustica numina, Faunos.　200
tu quoque non paruum Getico, Verona, triumpho
adiungis cumulum, nec plus Pollentia rebus
contulit Ausoniis aut moenia uindicis Hastae.
hic, rursus dum pacta mouet damnisque coactus
extremo mutare parat praesentia casu,　205
nil sibi periurum sensit prodesse furorem
conuerti nec fata loco, multisque suorum
diras pauit aues, inimicaque corpora uoluens
Ionios Athesis mutauit sanguine fluctus.
oblatum Stilicho uiolato foedere Martem　210
omnibus adripuit uotis, ubi Roma periclo
iam procul et belli medio Padus arbiter ibat.
iamque opportunam motu strepuisse rebelli
gaudet perfidiam praebensque exempla labori
sustinet accensos aestiuo puluere soles.　215
ipse manu metuendus adest inopinaque cunctis
instruit arma locis et, quo uocat usus, ab omni
parte uenit. fesso si deficit agmine miles,
utitur auxiliis damni securus, et astu
debilitat saeuum cognatis uiribus Histrum　220
et duplici lucro committens proelia uertit
in se barbariem nobis utrimque cadentem.
ipsum te caperet letoque, Alarice, dedisset,
ni calor incauti male festinatus Alani
dispositum turbasset opus; prope captus anhelum　225
uerbere cogis equum, nec te uitasse dolemus.
i potius genti reliquus tantisque superstes
Danubii populis, i, nostrum uiue tropaeum.
non tamen ingenium tantis se cladibus atrox
deicit: occulto temptabat tramite montes,　230
si qua per scopulos subitas exquirere posset
in Raetos Gallosque uias. sed fortior obstat

200 et]ac ς: iam ς　203 aut] nec ς　204 mouet] nouat *Heinsius*　damno-
que ς　206 sentit x　207 conuertit x　dolo *Birt*　membrisque *Goodyear*
212 belli medius x: medius belli ς, *Barthius*　213 importunam ς　214 praebens-
que] praebens x: praebent ς　laboris x: labores x: laborum ς　215 aestiuos
accenso *Heinsius*　216 certis ς　217 quo ς: qua x　223–8 *interpolatos esse
putat Jeep*　223 raperet ς　224 incautus (*cum* festinantis ς) *Heinsius*
227 gentis x　reliquum x　228 i] in ς: et x　229 nec ς　230 obliquo ς
uertice x　231 quas x　232 gallos rethosque ς　extat ς

Lycaean Pan, now the Dryads and the spirits of the countryside, the Fauns.

You also, Verona, to the Gothic triumph make no small addition, nor did Pollentia contribute more to Ausonia's affairs, nor did the walls of avenging Hasta. Here, while once more he disturbs the treaty and, forced by his losses, tries to change his present case by one last throw, he learnt that his perjury and his madness avail him nothing nor is his destiny changed by a change of place, and with many of his men he fed the carrion birds, and Athesis, rolling down his stream the bodies of our foes, dis-coloured the Ionian waves with blood.

When the treaty was violated, Stilicho seized the battle offered him in answer to his every prayer, where Rome now was far from danger's way and Padus flowed between as the arbiter of war. And now he rejoices to find that timely treachery has broken out in clamorous rebellion and, setting toil an example, he endures the heat of suns made hotter by the summer's dust. He himself, fearsome with his right arm, is present in the fray, and everywhere he draws up the battle-lines that no one thought to see, and wherever necessity calls him he is there, whatever the direction he must come from. If the troops are failing and their line is weary, then, caring nothing for the loss, he makes use of the auxiliaries, and cunningly weakens the savage Hister's tribes with their own kinsmen's strength, and in joining battle makes a twofold gain by turning the barbarians on themselves, as, to our advantage, they fall on either side. And you yourself he would have taken captive, Alaric, and given up to Death, had not the over-hurried zeal of the tempestuous Alan chief hurled into turmoil the plans that he had laid; all but captured, you use the lash to force onwards your breathless steed, and we do not grieve that you have escaped. Go rather, pitiful remnant of your race, sole survivor of so many Danube tribes, go, and live on as the trophy of our victory.

Yet even so his fierce spirit was not cast down by disasters great as these: still he tried to cross the mountains by way of secret paths, if only he could find some route to bring him suddenly over the cliffs into Raetia or Gaul. But our general's foresight was

cura ducis. quis enim diuinum fallere pectus
possit et excubiis uigilantia lumina regni?
cuius consilium non umquam repperit hostis 235
nec potuit texisse suum. secreta Getarum
nosse prior celerique dolis occurrere sensu.
  omnibus exclusus coeptis considit in uno
colle tremens; frondesque licet depastus amaras
arboreo figat sonipes in cortice morsus 240
et taetris collecta cibis annique uapore
saeuiat aucta lues et miles probra superbus
ingerat obsesso captiuaque pignora monstret,
non tamen aut morbi tabes aut omne periclum
docta subire fames aut praedae luctus ademptae 245
aut pudor aut dictis mouere procacibus irae,
ut male temptato totiens se credere campo
comminus auderet. nulla est uictoria maior
quam quae confessos animo quoque subiugat hostes.
iamque frequens rarum decerpere transfuga robur 250
coeperat inque dies numerus decrescere castris;
nec iam deditio paucis occulta parari,
sed cunei totaeque palam discedere turmae.
consequitur uanoque fremens clamore retentat
cumque suis iam bella gerit; mox nomina supplex 255
cum precibus fletuque ciet ueterumque laborum
admonet et frustra iugulum parcentibus offert,
defixoque malis animo sua membra suasque
cernit abire manus: qualis Cybeleia quassans
Hyblaeus procul aera senex reuocare fugaces 260
tinnitu conatur apes, quae sponte relictis
desciuere fauis, sonituque exhaustus inani
raptas mellis opes solitaeque oblita latebrae
perfida deplorat uacuis examina ceris.

233–4 possit | pectus ς   234 excubias *Heinsius*   numina *x*   235 huius ς
238 elusus *Bücheler*   consedit *x*   241 cibis] herbis ς   Austrique *Heinsius*: stag-
nique *Birt*   242 acta *x*: atra ς   244 nec ς   rabies ς   249 confertos
Heinsius   250 rerum *x*   252 iam nec ς: non iam ς   seditio *x*
253 descendere *x*: desciscere ς: decrescere ς   turbae ς   255 numina *x*: nomine
Burmannus   256 fletu precibusque *x*: precibus uotisque ς   261 conatus ς
261–2 relictis | destituere fauis ς: relictos | deseruere fauos ς   263 tenebrae ς

stronger and barred his way. For who could deceive that prescient mind and those ever-wakeful eyes that keep watch over the realm? His plans no enemy has ever yet found out, nor been able to conceal from him his own. He knew the secrets of the Goths before they themselves knew them, and with swift perception forestalled their treachery.

Debarred from his every undertaking, Alaric took up position—on a single hill, trembling with fear; and though his horses fed on bitter leaves and fastened their biting teeth on the bark of trees and despite the raging of a pestilence contracted from foul food and made worse by the season's heat, and though the presumptuous soldiers heaped abuse upon the besieged general, showing him his captive children: even so, neither the corruption of plague, nor hunger that is schooled to endure any danger, nor grief for the booty taken from him, nor shame nor anger at insulting words so moved him as to make him dare at close quarters to trust his fortunes to the battle-field he had so often tried before, without success. No victory is greater than the one that brings beneath the yoke enemies who acknowledge defeat in their hearts. And now deserters thick and fast had begun to pluck away a strength already thinned, and as the days went by the numbers in his camp had begun to sink away, nor was surrender planned only by a few and in secret, but squadrons and entire companies were openly deserting. He pursues them and, bellowing with useless shouts, he tries to hold them back, and it is with his own men that he now finds himself waging war; and soon with tears and prayers he calls on them by name, a suppliant, and reminds them of the shared sufferings of old, baring in vain his throat to men who spare him; his mind is transfixed by sorrow as he sees the troops who are his own limbs and hands abandon him. Just so in Hybla an old man, striking far off the cymbals of Cybele, strives with their tinkling to recall the runaway bees which have deserted him, leaving their hive of their own accord; himself exhausted by the unavailing noise the old man cries over the plundered stores of honey and over the treacherous swarms, forgetful as they are of their accustomed lair, their waxen cells all empty.

ergo ubi praeclusae uoci laxata remisit   265
frena dolor, notas oculis umentibus Alpes
aspicit et nimium diuerso stamine fati
praesentes reditus fortunatosque reuoluit
ingressus: solo peragens tum murmure bellum
protento leuiter frangebat moenia conto,   270
inridens scopulos; nunc desolatus et expes
debita pulsato reddit spectacula monti.
tum sic Ausonium respectans aethera fatur:
'heu regio funesta Getis, heu terra sinistris
auguriis calcata mihi, satiare nocentum   275
cladibus et tandem nostris inflectere poenis!
en ego, qui toto sublimior orbe ferebar
ante tuum felix aditum, ceu legibus exul
addictusque reus flatu propiore sequentum
terga premor. quae prima miser, quae funera dictis 280
posteriora querar? non me Pollentia tantum
nec captae cruciastis opes; hoc aspera fati
sors tulerit Martisque uices. non funditus armis
concideram; stipatus adhuc equitumque cateruis
integer ad montes reliquo cum robore cessi,   285
quos Appenninum perhibent (hunc esse ferebat
incola, qui Siculum porrectus ad usque Pelorum
finibus ab Ligurum populos conplectitur omnes
Italiae geminumque latus stringentia longe
utraque perpetuo discriminat aequora tractu).   290
haec ego continuum si per iuga tendere cursum,
ut prior iratae fuerat sententia menti,
iam desperata uoluissem luce, quid ultra?
omnibus oppeterem fama maiore perustis!
et certe moriens propius te, Roma, uiderem,   295

---

265 remittit ς   266 notasque ς   267 diuerso stamine ς, *Wakefield, Jeep*:
diuersi stamine *x*: diuersi stamina ς, *Hertel*   269 tunc *x*: cum *x*   270 praetento
Heinsius   271 expers *x*   273 dixit *x*   275 satiere ς   279 propriore *x*
frequentum ς: frementum *Heinsius*   281 nec me *x*: me non ς   282 non ς
captae] raptae ς   cruciatis *x*   haec *x*   prospera ς   283 fors ς,
Heinsius   nec ς   285 inpiger ς   288 a *x*: ad *x*   290 disterminat ς
291 haec *x*, *Scaliger*: huc ς: hic ς: hunc *x*: hinc ς   292 mentis ς   293 ualuissem
x   294 forma ς: flamma *Scaliger*   meliore ς   peremptis *x*: praeustis *Heinsius*:
peractis *Jeep*

And so when grief loosened and relaxed the reins from his imprisoned voice, he gazed with moistened eyes at the Alps he knew too well and pondered in his mind his present returning— all too different the thread of fate that it was spun upon—and the fortune that had attended his advance: then he concluded wars with nothing more than a whisper and broke down walls by lightly holding his cavalry-pole before him as he laughed the cliffs to scorn; now, wholly alone and in despair, he offered back to the mountains he had battered down the spectacle that was their due. Then, gazing behind him at the Ausonian sky, he spoke these words:

'Alas, land fated to bring disaster to the Goths, and earth I trod upon, alas!, with sinister auguries, be sated with the afflictions of those who did you wrong, and be appeased at last by this our punishment! See me now, who once was thought higher than all the world, fortune's darling before I came to you, now like a man condemned in law to exile and convicted of my crime, with the breath of my pursuers' horses hot upon my back. Which of my disasters shall I, in my speech, lament first, which last? Not so much did Pollentia, nor so much the capture of my treasures, torment me; I concede that destiny's cruel lot and the vicissitudes of Mars have brought me this. In battle I had not fallen wholly; men still thronged around me and my troops of cavalry remained intact, and with what of my strength was left to me I withdrew to those mountains that men call the Apennines. (This range it is, the people of this region say, that, stretching out as far as Sicilian Pelorus from the lands of the Ligurians, embraces all the nations of Italy and divides with its never-broken chain the two seas that graze the length of her twin coasts.) And if, as the thought in my enraged mind had prompted me before, I had been willing to follow my course uninterrupted over these crests, now despairing of the light of life, what was left to me? Burning everything in my path I should have met my doom with greater glory! And sure it is that with my dying eyes I should have looked on you, Rome, from closer by, and my very death amidst the fields of growing corn would have cost the conqueror who followed on my heels

ipsaque per cultas segetes mors nostra secuto
uictori damnosa foret! sed pignora nobis
Romanus carasque nurus praedamque tenebat:
hoc magis exertum raperem succinctior agmen!
   'heu, quibus insidiis, qua me circumdedit arte   300
fatalis semper Stilicho! dum parcere fingit,
rettudit hostiles animos bellumque remenso
eualuit transferre Pado. pro foedera saeuo
deteriora iugo! tum uis extincta Getarum;
tum mihi, tum letum pepigi. uiolentior armis   305
omnibus expugnat nostram clementia gentem,
Mars grauior sub pace latet, capiorque uicissim
fraudibus ipse meis. quis iam solacia fesso
consiliumue dabit? socius suspectior hoste.
atque utinam cunctos licuisset perdere bello!   310
nam quisquis duro cecidit certamine, numquam
desinit esse meus. melius mucrone perirent,
auferretque mihi luctu leuiore sodales
uicta manus quam laesa fides. nullusne clientum
permanet? offensi comites, odere propinqui!   315
quid moror inuisam lucem? qua sede recondam
naufragii fragmenta mei? quaeue arua requiram
in quibus haud umquam Stilicho nimiumque potentis
Italiae nomen nostras circumsonet aures?'
   haec memorans instante fugam Stilichone tetendit, 320
expertas horrens aquilas; comitatur euntem
Pallor et atra Fames et saucia liuidus ora
Luctus et inferno stridentes agmine Morbi.
lustralem sic rite facem, cui lumen odorum
sulpure caeruleo nigroque bitumine fumat,   325
circum membra rotat doctus purganda sacerdos,

---

296 sequenti ς   297 nobis] nostra x   299 excitum ς: extremum *Jeep*
301 feralis ς   302 ret(t)udit x, *Is. marg.*: ret(t)ulit x: contudit ς: obruit ς: reppulit ς
animas ς   303 per x   305 cum letum x: deletum *Goodyear*   306 mentem
ς: regem ς   308 quisnam ς   309 consiliumque ς   dabit] ferat x: feret x
hoste est ς   310 o utinam x   311 nusquam *Heinsius*   312 desinet x,
Mommsen: desiit x   314 laesa] lassa ς: lapsa *Heinsius olim*   nullusque x
315 infensi ς   317 quaue ς   319 nostras nomen x   circumsonat x: circum-
tonet *Wakefield*   320 retendit x   321 comitantur ς   322 languidus ς
323 ordine ς   324 sic] tum ς   rite] triste x

most dear! But the Roman held my children, my beloved womenfolk, and my plunder. More reason then that, with my loins girt up, I should have swept onwards my unencumbered host!

'Alas, in what a snare, and with what cunning did Stilicho entrap me, Stilicho now and ever my appointed doom! While feigning mercy he blunted the sharp edge of my hostile spirit and found the strength to carry the war back over the Po. Ah! treaty worse to me than the cruelty of the yoke! Then it was that the power of the Goths was extinguished; then for my own self, yes, then did I make a pledge for my own death. A clemency more forceful than any sword took our race by storm, Mars in a more grievous form lay hidden beneath that peace, and in my turn I was myself taken prisoner by my own deceits. Who now shall bring me comfort or advice in my weariness? My ally is more suspect than my foe.

'And would that it had been given me to lose them all in battle! For any man that has fallen in the bitter fight never ceases to be mine. It would be better that they had perished by the sword, and my grief would have been more bearable if not broken faith but only defeat in battle had taken my comrades from me. Does not one of my dependants remain to the end? My companions are turned against me, and my kin detest me! Why do I linger in a life I hate? In what place shall I hide the shattered remnants of my shipwrecked fortunes? What lands shall I seek, in which Stilicho and the name of Italy, all too powerful for me, is never to resound in my ears?'

So saying he turned in flight, for Stilicho pressed hard upon him and he dreaded the eagle-standards that he knew too well; his companions as he went were Pallor and black Hunger, and Grief with his face discoloured and torn, and a hellish company of shrieking Plagues. Just so, around a body that must be purged of sickness a skilled priest whirls the ritual purifying torch, its pungent light smoking with dark blue sulphur and black pitch, as he sprinkles the limbs with holy dew and the herbs that drive out polluting spirits, and, praying to Jupiter the Cleanser and to the

rore pio spargens et dira fugantibus herbis
numina, purificumque Iouem Triuiamque precatus
trans caput auersis manibus iaculatur in Austrum
secum rapturas cantata piacula taedas.   330
  acrior interea uisendi principis ardor
accendit cum plebe patres et saepe negatum
flagitat aduentum. nec tali publica uota
consensu tradunt ataui caluisse per urbem,
Dacica bellipotens cum fregerat Vlpius arma   335
atque indignantes in iura redegerat Arctos,
cum fasces cinxere Hypanin mirataque leges
Romanum stupuit Maeotia terra tribunal;
nec tantis patriae studiis ad templa uocatus,
clemens Marce, redis, cum gentibus undique cinctam 340
exuit Hesperiam paribus Fortuna periclis.
laus ibi nulla ducum; nam flammeus imber in hostem
decidit; hunc dorso trepidum fumante ferebat
ambustus sonipes; hic tabescente solutus
subsedit galea liquefactaque fulgure cuspis   345
canduit et subitis fluxere uaporibus enses.
tum, contenta polo, mortalis nescia teli
pugna fuit, Chaldaea mago seu carmina ritu
armauere deos, seu, quod reor, omne Tonantis
obsequium Marci mores potuere mereri.   350
nunc quoque praesidium Latio non desset Olympi,
deficeret si nostra manus; sed prouidus Aether
noluit humano titulos auferre labori,
ne tibi iam, princeps, soceri sudore paratam,
quam meruit uirtus, ambirent fulmina laurum.   355
  iam totiens missi proceres responsa morantis
rettulerant, donec differri longius urbis
communes non passa preces penetralibus altis
prosiluit uultusque palam confessa coruscos

328 t(h)urificumque *x*: terrificumque *x*: lustrificumque *Heinsius olim*   329 aduersis
x Austrum] altum ς   333 tali nec *Birt*   335 dacia *x*   fregerit *x*: frangeret ς
336 redegerit *x*   338 maeotica *x*   342 hostes ς   343 fumante ς, *Is. marg.*:
flammante *x*   345 subsidit *x*   sulphure ς   347 concepta ς   348 grami-
na ς: numina ς   350 mores marci ς: martis mores ς   351 subsidium ς
354 receptam ς   355 fulgura *Heinsius*   356 morantis *Paul*: moranti ς, *Heinsius*:
morandi *x*   357 attulerant ς: detulerant ς   orbis *Barthius*

Goddess of the Crossways, over his head and into the South Wind he hurls with back-turned hands the torches, for these will carry away with them the refuse of the atonement-rite.

Meanwhile the desire to see their Prince burns fiercer and inflames both senators and people, demanding the visit so often denied; it was not with harmony such as this, or so our ancestors relate, that the people's prayers grew fervent throughout the City, when Trajan, mighty in war, had broken the armies of Dacia and brought the indignant North beneath his sway, at that time when the rods of Roman power encircled Hypanis and when the land of Lake Maeotis gazed in wonderment at our laws and stood astounded by the sight of a Roman tribunal. Nor was it with zeal such as this on the part of your countrymen that you were summoned to return to thanksgiving in the temples, kindly Marcus, when Hesperia was surrounded by barbarians on every side and Fortune set her free from dangers that might match our own. Then was no glory owed the generals; for a shower of flame fell down upon the enemy; one man was carried away on the still-smoking back of his fire-scorched steed; another melted and sank to his knees as his helmet dissolved, and spear-tips glowed white-hot as lightning made the metal run while swords in sudden vapours poured away. On that day the battle was content with Heaven's aid, and felt no need of any mortal's spear: whether it was that Chaldaean spells with magic rites gave weapons to the gods, or, as I believe, all the Thunderer's compliance was earned by the power of Marcus' upright soul. Now too, if our sword-arms should prove too weak, the protection of Olympus would not fail the Roman world; but celestial providence was unwilling to steal their glory from the toils of men, lest the laurels won for you, my prince, by the sweat of Stilicho's brow, laurels won by prowess, should now be claimed by the lightning-bolt.

And up to now the ambassadors so often sent had brought back replies saying that he could not come, until, enduring no longer that what the City with one voice was praying for should be delayed, Roma herself leapt from the depth of her sanctuary and,

inpulit ipsa suis cunctantem Roma querellis: 360
'dissimulata diu tristes in amore repulsas
uestra parens, Auguste, queror. quonam usque tenebit
praelatus mea uota Ligus, uetitumque propinqua
luce frui, spatiis discernens gaudia paruis,
torquebit Rubicon uicino numine Thybrim? 365
nonne semel spreuisse satis, cum reddita bellis
Africa uenturi lusit spe principis urbem
nec duras tantis precibus permouimus aures?
ast ego frenabam geminos, quibus altior ires,
electi candoris equos, et nominis arcum 370
iam molita tui, per quem radiante decorus
ingrederere toga, pugnae monumenta dicabam
defensam titulo Libyam testata perenni.
iamque parabantur pompae simulacra futurae,
Tarpeio spectanda Ioui: caelata metallo 375
classis ut auratum sulcaret remige fluctum,
ut Massyla tuos anteirent oppida currus
Palladiaque comas innexus harundine Triton
edomitis ueheretur aquis et in aere trementem
succinctae famulum ferrent Atlanta cohortes, 380
ipse Iugurthinam subiturus carcere poenam
praeberet fera colla iugo, ui captus et armis,
non Bocchi Sullaeque dolis. sed prima remitto.
num praesens etiam Getici me laurea belli
declinare potest? sedesne capacior ulla 385
tantae laudis erit? tua te benefacta morantem
conueniunt, meritisque suis obnoxia uirtus
quos seruauit amat. iam flauescentia centum
messibus aestiuae detondent Gargara falces,
spectatosque iterum nulli celebrantia ludos 390

362 precor ς   363 ligur x   364 decernens x   364–5 hemistichia discernens . . . paruis et uicino . . . Thybrim inter se esse permutanda putat Jeep   365 uicino numine ς, Gesnerus: uicino nomine x: inuiso nomine Birt   366 satis ς: sat est x   367 spe lusit x   368 nec] non ς: num Heinsius   369 geminis x   altius x: aptior ς   372 parabam ς: ferebam Is. marg.   373 libiam titulo ς   per aeuum x   375 spectata x   376 auratum . . . pontum ς: auratos . . . fluctus ς: aurato . . . fluctus Gesnerus   379 equis x   trementi Heinsius   post 380 uersum excidisse suspicatur Goodyear   381 passurus ς   383 nec ς   384 nunc x   385 sedesue x   386 erat x   387 tuis ς, Camers marg.   388 quod x: quem ς   390 spectatos ς: spectandosque ς

26

openly revealing her flashing countenance, urged him on for all his hesitating with this complaint:

'Too long ignored, Augustus, I, mother of you all, complain of sorrow at my rejection in love. How long will the favoured Ligurians possess what I have prayed for? How long will Rubicon, separating Tiber from his delight by so small a distance, tantalize him with the nearness of your divinity while forbidding him to enjoy from close at hand the glory of your light? Surely it is enough to have spurned us once already, when the restoration of Africa through war deceived the City with the hope that her Emperor would come to her, and for all our prayers we could not make your obstinate ears listen to us? And I was already reining to the chariot twin horses of outstanding whiteness to make you more exalted in your progress, and had constructed an Arch that bore your name through which, resplendent in your shining toga, you might march into the City; and I was busy dedicating monuments to your battles that bore witness in everlasting inscriptions to Libya's defence. And for the procession that was to take place tableaux were already being prepared, for Tarpeian Jove to gaze upon: all this so that a fleet, engraved on metal, might cleave furrows with its oars in waves of gold, and Massylian towns march before your chariot, and Triton, his hair entwined with Pallas' reeds, be borne along, his waters now subdued, and the troops, their tunics girt up high, carry Atlas, now a slave and trembling in bronze, and Gildo himself stretch his savage neck out to the yoke, destined to endure in prison the punishment of Jugurtha, but captured by force of arms and not by the treachery of Bocchus and of Sulla.

'But this first injury I overlook. Surely the laurels for the Gothic War, fought before my very eyes, cannot also pass me by? And will any place prove more fitting to hold so much glory? While you linger, your own good offices crowd around you, and your virtue, indebted to its own good deeds, loves that which it has kept safe. Now for the hundredth time the sickles of summer shear the harvests of golden Gargara, and the hundredth consul hurries on the returning ages that celebrate the games no man has seen a

27

circumflexa rapit centenus saecula consul:
his annis, qui lustra mihi bis dena recensent,
nostra ter Augustos intra pomeria uidi,
temporibus uariis; eadem sed causa tropaei,
ciuilis dissensus, erat. uenere superbi,   395
scilicet ut Latio respersos sanguine currus
aspicerem. quisquamne piae laetanda parenti
natorum lamenta putet? periere tyranni,
sed nobis periere tamen. cum Gallica uulgo
proelia iactaret, tacuit Pharsalia Caesar.   400
namque inter socias acies cognataque signa
ut uinci miserum, numquam uicisse decorum.
restituat priscum per te iam gloria morem
uerior, et fructum sincerae laudis ab hoste
desuetum iam redde mihi iustisque furoris   405
externi spoliis sontes absolue triumphos.
    'quem, precor, ad finem laribus seiuncta potestas
exulat imperiumque suis a sedibus errat?
cur mea quae cunctis tribuere Palatia nomen
neclecto squalent senio, nec creditur orbis   410
illinc posse regi? medium non deserit umquam
caeli Phoebus iter, radiis tamen omnia lustrat.
segnius an ueteres Histrum Rhenumque tenebant,
qui nostram coluere domum? leuiusne timebant
Tigris et Euphrates, cum foedera Medus et Indus   415
hinc peteret pacemque mea speraret ab arce?
hic illi mansere uiri quos mutua uirtus
legit et in nomen Romanis rebus adoptans
iudicio pulchram seriem, non sanguine duxit;
hic proles atauum deducens Aelia Neruam   420

391 aperit *Goodyear*   392–3 his annis qui lustra sibi bis dena recenset, | nostra ter Augustos intra pomeria uidit *Birt*   392 recenset *x*   393 inter *x*   uidit *x*   394 trophaeis ς: triumphi ς   397 respicerem ς   pio ς   laetanda] laudanda ς: laudata ς: iactanda *Heinsius olim*   398 putat *x*   fauere *x*   tyrannis *x*   400 pharsalica *x*   401 iamque ς: nempe ς   402 decorum est *x*   403 iam per te ς   404 serior ς   405 des(s)uetae ς   sumptisque *x*: fultosque ς: fultusque *Gesnerus*   406 hesterni ς: extremi ς: interni *Jeep*   sontes spoliis ς: spoliis sontesque *Heinsius*   408 erret ς   410 neglecta *Bücheler*   non ς   411 nec ς   414 nostrum . . . larem ς   leuiusque ς: leuiusue ς: meliusne *x*   timebat ς: tremebant ς   416 spectaret ς   417 hinc ς   mutua] unica *uel* Martia *Heinsius*   420 hinc ς

second time: in all these years, which I number at twice ten lustres, three times have I seen an Emperor within my sacred boundary; the times were different, but the reason for their victory was the same, and it was civil war. In their arrogance they came, no doubt, that I might see their chariots bespattered with the blood of Romans. Could any man think that for a loving mother the lamentations of her sons were cause for joy? Usurpers they were who died, but when they died, still they were mine. Though he boasted at large of his battles against the Gauls, Caesar kept silent on Pharsalus. For when ally fights with ally and kindred raise their standards against each other, then, just as it is pitiful to lose, so also it never brings honour to have won. Through your deeds may a truer glory now restore the customs of antiquity, and do you give back to me now the long-unfamiliar fruits of unsullied praise won from the enemy, and, by means of spoils justly taken from the madness of foreigners, acquit me of those triumphs stained with guilt.

'Till when, I beg you, will power be an exile divided from its home, and imperial sway wander far from its own proper dwelling-place? Why do my Palaces, which gave their name to all the others, lie desolate in neglect and decay? And why is it thought that the world cannot be ruled from there? Phoebus never strays from the middle path through Heaven, and yet with his rays he illuminates all things. Was it with a looser grip that the men of old held the Danube and the Rhine, they who made me their home? Did Tigris and Euphrates tremble less, when from this place, and from my citadel, the Indian and the Mede begged for treaties that would give them peace? Here dwelt those heroes whom virtue, recognizing virtue, chose and by adoption giving them their name for the benefit of Rome continued a noble dynasty through judgement and not through blood; here lived the Aelian clan that traced its ancestry back to Nerva, here too the peace-loving family of Pius and the warrior scions of Severus. Citizen as you are, deign to enter this company and let us see once more the face we saw so long ago, so that, recalling in his mind that earlier triumph, Tiber, who had welcomed you as your father's com-

tranquillique Pii bellatoresque Seueri.
hunc ciuis dignare chorum conspectaque dudum
ora refer, pompam recolens ut mente priorem,
quem tenero patris comitem susceperat aeuo,
nunc duce cum socero iuuenem te Thybris adoret.'   425
    orantem medio princeps sermone refouit:
'numquam aliquid frustra per me uoluisse dolebis,
o dea, nec legum fas est occurrere matri.
sed nec post Libyam (falsis ne perge querellis
incusare tuos) patriae mandata uocantis   430
spreuimus: aduectae misso Stilichone curules,
ut nostras tibi, Roma, uices pro principe consul
inpleret generoque socer. uidistis in illo
me quoque; sic credit pietas, non sanguine solo,
sed claris potius factis experta parentem.   435
cuncta quidem centum nequeam perstringere linguis,
quae pro me mundoque gerit; sed ab omnibus unum,
si fama necdum patuit, te, Roma, docebo,
subiectum nostris oculis et cuius agendi
spectator uel causa fui.
                        'populator Achiuae   440
Bistoniaeque plagae, crebris successibus amens
et ruptas animis spirans inmanibus Alpes
iam Ligurum trepidis admouerat agmina muris,
tutior auxilio brumae (quo gentibus illis
sidere consueti fauet inclementia caeli),   445
meque minabatur calcato obsidere uallo,
spem uano terrore fouens, si forte remotis
praesidiis, urgente metu, qua uellet obirem
condicione fidem; nec me timor inpulit ullus
et duce uenturo fretum memoremque tuorum,   450
Roma, ducum, quibus haud umquam uel morte parata
foedus lucis amor pepigit dispendia famae.
    'nox erat et late stellarum more uidebam

422 hoc . . . forum *x*   423 refers ς   ut] et ς: sub *x*   priorum *x*   424 susceperit ς   425 hunc ς   427 per me frustra ς   428 obstare parenti ς
429 nec] neque ς: ne ς   ne] nec ς   431 secures ς   434 si *x*   nec *x*
437 quae romae *x*   438 nondum ς   442 sperans *x*: superans ς   444 quod
x: quia ς   445 frigore *x*   consuetis *x*   446 falcato *Heinsius*: calcatum *Schraderus*
447 si] ni *x*: nisi ς   450 hoc duce *Scaliger*   453 mox et per *x*   latium *x*

panion in the tender years of childhood, may now worship you as a young man under the guidance of your father-in-law.'

As she was still uttering this entreaty the Emperor soothed her spirits: 'Never will you grieve at any wish of yours left unfulfilled if I can prevent it, my goddess, nor is it right to stand against her who is the mother of our laws. But neither did I in the aftermath of victory in Africa—do not persist in accusing with these unjust complaints those who love you—spurn the commands of the fatherland that summoned me: the curule chair was brought before you when I sent you Stilicho, so that as consul in his Emperor's place and as father-in-law for his son-in-law he might, Roma, fill my part for you. Me also did you see in him; so does my love for him believe, knowing him for my father not through blood alone but rather through his glorious deeds. In truth, not with a hundred tongues could I so much as touch upon all that he achieves in my service and the world's; but one deed out of them all, if the report of it has not yet made it clear to you, shall I tell you, Roma, one that took place before my very eyes, and of its performance I was the witness, or indeed the cause.

'He that plundered the lands of Achaea and Bistonia, mad-dened by his many successes and exulting in his savage heart at the shattering of the Alps, had now brought his troops up to the terror-stricken walls of the Ligurians, safer now that he had winter to aid him (a season in which the forbidding skies they know so well favour these peoples), and, trampling down the ramparts, he threatened to blockade me in, cherishing the hope that perhaps, in vain terror, with the garrisons all gone and with fear pressing hard upon me, I might make terms with him on any conditions that he liked; but no fear shook my constancy, since I was both confident that my general was on his way and mindful, Roma, of *your* generals, who never, even though death awaited them, bartered the loss of their good name for base love of life.

'It was night, and far and wide I saw the barbarian campfires burning like the stars; now had the trumpets roused the men of the first watch from sleep, when from the snow-chilled North the

barbaricos ardere focos; iam classica primos
excierant uigiles, gelida cum pulcher ab Arcto   455
aduentat Stilicho. medius sed clauserat hostis
inter me socerumque uiam pontemque tenebat,
Addua quo scissas spumosior incitat undas.
quid faceret? differret iter? discrimina nullas
nostra dabant adeunda moras. perrumperet agmen?   460
sed paucis comitatus erat; nam plurima retro,
dum nobis properat succurrere, liquerat arma
extera uel nostras acies. hoc ille locatus
ancipiti, longum socias tardumque putauit
expectasse manus et nostra pericula tendit   465
posthabitis pulsare suis mediumque per hostem
flammatus uirtute pia propriaeque salutis
inmemor et stricto prosternens obuia ferro
barbara fulmineo secuit tentoria cursu.
   'nunc mihi Tydiden attollant carmina uatum,   470
quod iuncto fidens Ithaco patefacta Dolonis
indicio dapibusque simul religataque somno
Thracia sopiti penetrauerit agmina Rhesi
Graiaque rettulerit captos ad castra iugales,
quorum, si qua fides augentibus omnia Musis,   475
impetus excessit Zephyros candorque pruinas.
ecce uirum taciti nulla qui fraude soporis
ense palam sibi pandit iter remeatque cruentus
et Diomedeis tantum praeclarior ausis
quantum lux tenebris manifestaque proelia furtis!   480
adde quod et ripis steterat munitior hostis
et cui nec uigilem fas est conponere Rhesum:
Thrax erat, hic Thracum domitor. non tela retardant,
obice non haesit fluuii. sic ille minacem
Tyrrhenam labente manum pro ponte repellens   485

456 aduenit *x*   medium ς: mediam *Delrius*   457 socerum pontemque uiamque *x*
458 ardua *x*   quo] qua *x*   spumantior ς   459 faciat ς   460 arcenda *uel*
pellenda *Birt*   461–3 *uerba* nam plurima . . . nostras acies *damnauit Barthius*
466 mediosque . . . hostes ς   468 praesternens *Scaliger*   omnia *x*   470 nunc
tibi *x*   471 qui ς   iuncto] uincto ς   473 penetrauerat ς: penetrauit in ς: penetrauit ad ς, *Jeep*   474 grataque *x*   477 ecce uir, en *Koch*   qui nulla *x*
479–80 tanto . . . quanto *Heinsius*   482 fas sit *Heinsius*   483 Thrax ille, hic
Thracum *uel* Thrax erat is, Thracum hic *Heinsius*   nec *x*   485 Tyrrhenum *Barthius*
manu ς, *Barthius*

glorious Stilicho arrives. But the enemy stood between us, and had closed off the road that led from my father-in-law to me. They also held the bridge, which tore the waters of the Addua and churned them into fuller foam. What was he to do? Should he put off his march? But the dangers that I faced permitted no delay. Should he break through their ranks? But those who accompanied him were few in number, for in his haste to come to our relief he had left behind him both many companies of auxiliaries and our native troops. This was the dilemma in which he found himself, but he judged it too long and slow to wait for allied forces and, counting his own perils as of lesser weight, he struck out to hammer those that threatened me, and inflamed by a loving valour, forgetful too of his own safety, he drove through the midst of the enemy, and, cutting down with drawn sword all that lay in his path, he slashed in lightning-course through the tents of the barbarian host.

'Now, I say, let the songs of bards exalt the son of Tydeus, because, trusting to the Ithacan at his side, when the Thracian ranks had been betrayed by Dolon's deposition and were constrained at once by feasting and by slumber, he made his way, or so they tell, into their midst while Rhesus slept, and brought back to the Grecian camp the captured team of horses, whose speed, if we may trust the Muses in whose telling every story gains, surpassed the Zephyrs as their whiteness did the frosts. Here you may see a man who, not under any treacherous cover of silence and sleep, openly cut himself a path and came back smeared with gore, and was as much more glorious in his victory than was Diomedes in his deeds of daring as light is more glorious than darkness and open battle is than ambush! And add to this the fact that on the banks there was an enemy who had taken up a stronger position, an enemy with whom not even when awake can Rhesus be rightfully compared: for he was a Thracian, but Alaric a conqueror of Thracians. Spears did not slow down his course, nor was he halted by the river's barrier. Just so Horatius Cocles, driving back from the collapsing bridge the threatening Etruscan band, crossed the Tiber with that same shield with which he had

traiecit clipeo Thybrim, quo texerat urbem,
Tarquinio mirante Cocles mediisque superbus
Porsennam respexit aquis. celer Addua nostro
sulcatus socero; sed, cum tranaret, Etruscis
ille dabat tergum, Geticis hic pectora bellis.   490
'exere nunc doctos tantae certamina laudis,
Roma, choros et quanta tuis facundia pollet
ingeniis nostrum digno sonet ore parentem.'
    dixit, et antiquae muros egressa Rauennae
signa mouet; iamque ora Padi portusque relinquit   495
flumineos, certis ubi legibus aduena Nereus
aestuat et pronas puppes nunc amne secundo,
nunc redeunte uehit, nudataque litora fluctu
deserit, Oceani lunaribus aemula damnis.
laetior hinc Fano recipit Fortuna uetusto,   500
despiciturque uagus praerupta ualle Metaurus,
qua mons arte patens uiuo se perforat arcu
admisitque uiam sectae per uiscera rupis,
exuperans delubra Iouis saxoque minantes
Appenninigenis cultas pastoribus aras.   505
quin et Clitumni sacras uictoribus undas,
candida quae Latiis praebent armenta triumphis,
uisere cura fuit. nec te miracula fontis
praetereunt, tacito passu quem si quis adiret,
lentus erat; si uoce gradum maiore citasset,   510
commixtis feruebat aquis; cumque omnibus una
sit natura uadis similes ut corporis umbras
ostendant, haec sola nouam iactantia sortem
humanos properant imitari flumina mores.
celsa dehinc patulum prospectans Narnia campum   515
regali calcatur equo, rarique coloris
non procul amnis abest, urbi qui nominis auctor:

488 prospexit ς: despexit *Heinsius*   ardua *x*   489 sulcatur *x*   dum ς
transiret ς   490 bellis] telis *Scaliger*   491 tante doctos ς   certamine *x*: in
certamina ς: ad certamina *Wakefield*   493 digno nostrum ς   494 muris *x*
495 reliquit *x*   497 secundo] ret(r)uso *uel* refuso *x*   502 unco se *Heinsius*
503 admittitque *x*   504 minaces ς: micantes ς: minanti *Goodyear*   508 fuit]
trahunt ς: trahit *Heinsius*   510 si uoce gradum] se moxque gradu *Heinsius*. si forte
gradum *Burmannus*   511 cum mixtis *x*: commotis ς: cum motis ς: commissis *uel* admis-
sis *Heinsius*   514 motus *Burmannus*   516 albique ς: rauique *Heinsius*
517 iens *Goodyear*

defended the City, while Tarquin watched and marvelled, and triumphantly he looked back from the middle of the stream at Lars Porsenna. The swift Addua it was through whose waters my father-in-law cut his furrow: but Cocles, as he swam across, turned his back to the Etruscans, while Stilicho showed his face to the Goths and battle.

'Now, Roma, lead out your troupes skilled to sing of contests that win such glory, and let the finest eloquence with which your great writers excel sound out the praises of my father with such a song as he is worthy of.'

So he spoke, and led on his armies as they passed beyond the walls of ancient Ravenna; and now they leave behind them the mouths of the Po and the river-ports, where in obedience to fixed laws Nereus, a stranger here, surges and now carries the ships headlong on the following stream, and now down again as it returns back to the sea, abandoning the shores and stripping them of their waves, in emulation of the Ocean's moon-inflicted losses. Next Fortuna with a gladder heart receives him in her age-old Fane, and from the heights he looks down at the Metaurus wandering through a steep valley where the mountain is skilfully laid open, pierced by an arch of living stone, and has let in the road straight through the bowels of the cloven rock; then he climbs high above the shrine of Jupiter and the menacing altars on the cliff-ledge, altars worshipped by the shepherds of the Apennines. And it was even your desire to visit the waters of Clitumnus, sacred to victors, which offer their white cattle for the triumphs of Rome; nor did you fail to observe the miraculous nature of the spring, which, if any man approached with a silent tread, remained untroubled; but if he had quickened his steps and made a louder noise, its waters used to churn and seethe; and though all streams have but a single nature, so that they show us the body's reflection, this river alone, boasting a property unheard of, is swift to imitate men's very natures. Next your royal horse treads upon the streets of Narnia, lofty Narnia that looks out over the spreading plain, and not far off there is a river rare in colour, which gives the city its name: narrowed by the dark forests of

ilice sub densa siluis artatus opacis
inter utrumque iugum tortis anfractibus albet.
inde salutato libatis Thybride lymphis   520
excipiunt arcus operosaque semita uastis
molibus et quidquid tantae praemittitur urbi.
  ac uelut officiis trepidantibus ora puellae
spe propiore tori mater sollertior ornat
adueniente proco uestesque et cingula comit   525
saepe manu uiridique angustat iaspide pectus
substringitque comam gemmis et colla monili
circuit et bacis onerat candentibus aures,
sic oculis placitura tuis insignior auctis
collibus et nota maior se Roma uidendam   530
obtulit. addebant pulchrum noua moenia uultum
audito perfecta recens rumore Getarum,
profecitque opifex decori timor, et, uice mira,
quam pax intulerat bello discussa senectus
erexit subitas turres cinctosque coegit   535
septem continuo montes iuuenescere muro.
ipse fauens uotis solitoque decentior aer,
quamuis adsiduo noctem foedauerat imbre,
principis et solis radiis detersa remouit
nubila; namque ideo pluuiis turbauerat omnes   540
ante dies lunamque rudem madefecerat Auster
ut tibi seruatum scirent conuexa serenum.
  omne Palatino quod pons a colle recedit
Muluius et quantum licuit consurgere tectis,
una replet turbae facies: undare uideres   545
ima uiris, altas effulgere matribus aedes.
exultant iuuenes aequaeui principis annis;
temnunt prisca senes et in hunc sibi prospera fati
gratantur durasse diem moderataque laudant

---

518 artatur *x*   520 nymphis *x*   524 propriore *x*   526 ipsa manu
Marklandus   528 ornat ς   531 augebant *x*   532 rumore . . . perfecta ς
535 cunctosque *x*   536 colles ς   537 serenior *Heinsius*   538 noctes ς
foedauerit ς   imbri *x*   540 iamque ς   pluuiis ideo *x*   541 rudem] udo
Heinsius   austro *x*   543 qua ς   monte ς   recessit ς   544 miluius *x*   in ς
545 undare] uno ore *x*   546 altasque ς   548 fata ς

thick-packed holm-oaks it gleams white as it winds its tortuous way between the mountains on either side. Then, after he had hailed Tiber with a sprinkling of water, arches welcome him, and the massive structures of a road built with great labour, and all else that marks the approach to a mighty city.

And as a mother, with greater care than ever now that the groom draws near and her hopes of a marriage come closer to fulfilment, adorns a girl's face in trembling acts of attentiveness, and time and time again re-arranges with her own hand the bride's dress and girdle, tightening her breast with green jasper and binding back her hair with gems, putting a necklace around her throat and weighing down her ears with shining pearls: just so did Rome, destined to give pleasure to your eyes, more glorious since now her hills rise higher, and greater than the City that we knew, reveal herself to your vision. The new walls but recently completed at the rumour of the Goths' approach increased the beauty of her face, and fear was a craftsman working to her enhancement, and, by a strange reversal, the creeping age that peace had brought upon her was scattered by war, and raised towers all of a sudden and compelled the seven hills, now girt by one unbroken wall, to grow young again. And though the very air had made foul the night with continual showers, now, showing favour to our prayers and turning fairer than is usual, it wiped away the rain-clouds with the beams cast by the Emperor and the sun; for the South Wind had muddied all the days that went before with rain, and left the young moon dripping wet only so that Heaven's vault might know that the cloudless skies were kept for you.

All the space that extends from the Palatine hill as far as the Mulvian Bridge, and from the ground up as far as the roofs could soar, was filled by a crowd that wore a single face: you could see the ground flooded with waves of men and the high buildings ablaze with matrons. Young men rejoice in an Emperor as young as themselves; old men dismiss the distant past in scorn and congratulate themselves on a prosperous destiny that has lasted till this very day, and praise the moderation of the times, because, as

tempora, quod clemens aditu, quod pectore †solus†   550
Romanos uetuit currum praecedere patres,
cum tamen Eucherius, cui regius undique sanguis
atque Augusta soror, fratri praeberet ouanti
militis obsequium: sic illum dura parentis
instituit pietas in se uel pignora parci   555
quique neget nato procerum quod praestet honori.
haec sibi cura senum maturaque conprobat aetas
idque inter ueteris speciem praesentis et aulae
iudicat, hunc ciuem, dominos uenisse priores.

    conspicuas tum flore genas, diademate crinem   560
membraque gemmato trabeae uiridantia cinctu
et fortes umeros et certatura Lyaeo
inter Erythraeas surgentia colla smaragdos
mirari sine fine nurus; ignaraque uirgo,
cui simplex calet ore pudor, per singula cernens   565
nutricem consultat anum, quid fixa draconum
ora uelint, uentis fluitent an uera minentur
sibila suspensum rapturi faucibus hostem.
ut chalybe indutos equites et in aere latentes
uidit cornipedes, 'quanam de gente' rogabat   570
'ferrati uenere uiri? quae terra metallo
nascentes informat equos? num Lemnius auctor
indidit hinnitum ferro simulacraque belli
uiua dedit?' gaudet metuens et pollice monstrat,
quod picturatas galeae Iunonia cristas   575
ornet auis uel quod rigidos uibrata per armos
rubra sub aurato crispentur serica dorso.

    tum tibi magnorum mercem Fortuna laborum
persoluit, Stilicho, curru cum uectus eodem
urbe triumphantem generum florente iuuenta   580

---

550 quo ς   aditu] habitu ς, *Jeep*: actu *Koch*   quod] quo ς: pro *Barthius*   pectore]
tempore ς   solo ς: sollers ς   pectore, solus *distinxerunt Barthius et Heinsius*: quod
solus habitu quod pectore clemens *Jeep*: quod pectore solus | Romano *Goodyear*: quod
pectore mitis *uel* lenis *uel aliquid simile Hall*: quod pectore sanctus *Nisbet per litteras*
554 officium *x*   556 negat ς   praestat ς   557 hoc ς   cura] curua *Birt*
559 indicat *x*   560 conspicuo ς   cum ς   561 radiantia ς: uernantia *Wakefield*
cultu ς   565 sup(p)lex *x*   currens *Burmannus*   568 rapturis ς
569 chalybem *x*   inductos *x*   nitentes ς   572 informet ς   573 addidit *x*:
abdidit ς   bellis *x*   575 quot *Heinsius*   pennas ς   576 ornat ς   quot
Heinsius   577 aerato ς   crispantur ς   578 tum] nunc ς   mercem] sese ς

mild to approach as he is [mild?] of heart, he would not permit Rome's conscript fathers to march before his chariot, when even Eucherius, whose blood on either side is royal and whose sister is the Empress, did a common soldier's service for his triumphant brother-in-law; for so was he brought up by the stern love of a father who was sparing to himself and to his children, love such as would deny his son what he grants to the honour of the nobles. All this both old men burdened by care and those of robust years approve, and judge that this is what distinguishes the aspect of the old rule and the new: this man has come as fellow-citizen, but those before had come as the masters of slaves.

And then the women marvelled ceaselessly at the unmatched bloom upon his cheeks, at his hair crowned with the diadem, at limbs that reflected the green light from his jewel-studded consular robe, at his strong shoulders and at his neck which, soaring through oriental emeralds, could match in beauty that of Lyaeus; and the innocent maiden, the blush of simple modesty burning on her cheek, lets her eyes rove over every detail, plying her aged nurse with questions: what do the dragons attached to their standards signify? are they only fluttering in the winds, or is their menacing hissing real, ready as they are to seize some enemy in their jaws and hold him aloft? When she saw the horsemen clad in steel and the stallions hidden beneath their covering of bronze, she would ask 'From what race have these men of iron come? What land fashions horses born of metal? Surely it cannot be that the Smith of Lemnos has implanted in iron the power to neigh and given us living images of war?' Her heart is a mixture of delight and fear and with her finger she points out how Juno's bird adorns the helmets' coloured crests and how over the muscled shoulders the red silk shimmers and ripples beneath the covering of gilded metal on the horses' backs.

Then it was that Fortuna paid you back in full, Stilicho, the reward for your mighty labours, when, borne in the same chariot with him, you looked upon your son-in-law as he celebrated his triumph in the City, still in the bloom of his youth, and deep in your heart you recalled that day, when, with the world in a

conspiceres illumque diem sub corde referres
quo tibi confusa dubiis formidine rebus
infantem genitor moriens commisit alendum.
uirtutes uariae fructus sensere receptos:
depositum seruasse, Fides; Constantia, paruum   585
praefecisse orbi; Pietas, fouisse propinquum.
hic est ille puer, qui nunc ad rostra Quirites
euocat et solio fultus genitoris eburno
gestarum patribus causas ex ordine rerum
euentusque refert ueterumque exempla secutus   590
digerit imperii sub iudice facta senatu.
nil cumulat uerbisque nihil fiducia celat;
fucati sermonis opem mens conscia laudis
abnuit. agnoscunt proceres, habituque Gabino
principis et ducibus circumstipata togatis   595
iure paludatae iam curia militat aulae.
adfuit ipsa suis ales Victoria templis,
Romanae tutela togae, quae diuite pinna
patricii reuerenda fouet sacraria coetus
castrorumque eadem comes indefessa tuorum   600
nunc tandem fruitur iunctis, atque omne futurum
te Romae seseque tibi promittit in aeuum.
   hinc te iam patriis laribus Via nomine uero
Sacra refert. flagrat studiis concordia uulgi,
quam non inlecebris dispersi colligis auri,   605
nec tibi uenales captant aeraria plausus
corruptura fidem: meritis offertur inemptus
pura mente fauor. nam munere carior omni
obstringit sua quemque salus. procul ambitus erret:
non quaerit pretium, uitam qui debet, amori.   610
   o quantum populo secreti numinis addit
imperii praesens genius, quantamque rependit

581 aspiceres ς   illamque ς   referres]teneres ς   582 qua . . . confusis dubia
ς   583 moriens genitor ς   habendum ς   584 fructum . . . receptum ς
585 seruare ς   591 fata ς, *Heinsius*   592 quae nil *Birt*   593 fuscati *x*
conscia laudum ς: nescia fraudis *Heinsius*   594 cinctuque ς   597 ales *x, Is. marg.*:
talis *x*   598 pinna] pompa *x*: parma ς: palma *Heinsius*   599 ueneranda ς
601 iunctis] uotis *x*   603 patris ς   604 studiis flagrat ς   605 quem ς:
quod ς   608 clarior ς   609 obstrinxit ς: astringit *x*   610 quaeret *x*:
quaerat ς   non quaerat pretio uitam *Heinsius*   amoris *Semple*   611 nominis *x*:
muneris ς   612 genius] species *x*

turmoil of fear and confusion, a father near to death entrusted to your keeping his infant son to rear. Your manifold virtues have now known the harvest of their fruits; loyalty, in having kept safe what was given you in trust; firmness of purpose, in having set in dominion over the world one so small; family duty, in having cherished a kinsman. This is that very boy, he who now summons the Romans of Rome to the rostra and seated on his sire's throne of ivory reports in due order to the conscript fathers the causes and the outcome of his deeds and, following the precedent set by the men of old, submits to the Senate's judgement a full exposition of the achievements of his rule. Truthfulness exaggerates nothing, and hides nothing, in her words; a mind that is aware of true worth refuses the aid of false-hued speech. The nobles recognize him for their own, and with an Emperor dressed in the Gabine robe, and with generals clad in the toga thronging round, the Senate now does battle-service with the authority of a Court that wears the soldier's cloak. Winged Victory herself, protectress of the Roman peace, was present in her temple, she who with golden wing shelters the awesome sanctuary where the fathers assemble, she who is also the unwearied companion of your wars; now at last she takes her joy in your union, and for all eternity she promises that you will belong to Rome and she to you.

From here the Sacred Way, now truly named, brings you back to your ancestral home. The people are fired by a harmony of zeal, but this you do not gather with the lure of scattered gold; nor do the public coffers, seeking to bribe them into loyalty, try to win for you an applause put up for sale: to your merits is their favour presented, unpurchased and offered by untainted hearts. For their own deliverance, more dear than any gift, makes each beholden to you. Let corruption be banished far! The man who is indebted for his life puts no price upon the love he gives.

Oh how great the mysterious godhead that the presence of the Empire's guardian spirit bestows upon the people! How great the honour paid in turn by majesty to majesty when the purple of Imperial might does reverence to the masses crowded together on

maiestas alterna uicem, cum regia circi
conexum gradibus ueneratur purpura uulgus
adsensuque cauae sublatus in aethera uallis   615
plebis adoratae reboat fragor unaque totis
intonat Augustum septenis arcibus echo!
nec solis hic cursus equis: adsueta quadrigis
cingunt arua trabes, subitaeque †aspectus† harenae
diffundit Libycos aliena ualle cruores.   620
haec et belligeros exercuit area lusus,
armatos hic saepe choros certaque uagandi
textas lege fugas inconfususosque recursus
et pulchras errorum artes iucundaque Martis
cernimus. insonuit cum uerbere signa magister,   625
mutatos edunt pariter tot pectora motus
in latus allisis clipeis aut rursus in altum
uibratis; graue parma sonat, mucronis acutum
murmur, et umbonum pulsu modulante resultans
ferreus alterno concentus plauditur ense.   630
una omnis summissa phalanx tantaeque salutant
te, princeps, galeae. partitis inde cateruis
in uarios docto discurritur ordine gyros,
quos neque semiuiri Gortynia tecta iuuenci
flumina nec crebro uincant Maeandria flexu.   635
discreto reuoluta gradu torquentur in orbes
agmina, perpetuisque inmoto cardine claustris
Ianus Bella premens laeta sub imagine pugnae
armorum innocuos paci largitur honores.

    iamque nouum fastis aperit felicibus annum,   640
ore coronatus gemino; iam Thybris in uno
et Bruti cernit trabeas et sceptra Quirini.
consule laetatur post plurima saecula uiso
Pallanteus apex; agnoscunt rostra curules

---

615 consensuque *x*: consessuque ς   616 fauor ς   617 collibus ς: montibus ς
618 aduecta *x*: attrita ς   619 arma *x*   tigres *x*   adgestus *Nisbet per litteras*
620 diffudit *x*: effudit ς   621 hic et *x*   ludos *x*   622 hac sepe *Heinsius*: haec
saepe *Birt*   628 palma *x*   acutum *x*, *Is.*: acuti *x*   629 murmuret ς: murmure
et (*cum* mucronis acuti *siue* acuto) *uel* murmura et (*cum* mucronis acutum *sc.* sonant) *Heinsius*
resultat *x*   630 plauditur *Scaliger*: clauditur *codd.*   631 una animis ς: uni omnis
Heinsius: unanimis *Birt*   subnixa *x*   634 semiferi *x*   635 uel ς   uincant crebro ς   637 perpetuis (*om.* -que) ς   638 laetae ς   643 saecula plurima ς
644 cognoscunt ς

the Circus' tiers of steps, and when, in unison from the hollow of the valley, the roars of the populace so honoured are carried high into the heavens and there they sound and sound again, as all at once the echo thunders out the name of the Augustus from all the seven hills! Nor is this place witness only to the running of horses: a palisade surrounds the track that is better used to chariots, and the spectacle offered by an arena swiftly built pours out the blood of Libyan lions in a valley not their own. This ground has also practised exercises that are both war and sport, and here we often see armed formations, roving in accordance with unwavering laws, weave their retreating paths and then return again, keeping their order undisturbed, a fine display of disciplined confusion, war in the form of sheer delight. When the master of ceremonies has given the signal with the whiplash, all at once so many bodies execute new movements, clashing their shields against their sides or once more brandishing them on high; deep sounds the shield, sharp is the sword-blade's ring, and, echoing to the beat that the shield-bosses set, a harmony of steel is struck by the blows that the swords exchange. All at once the whole battalion sinks down in reverence as the helmets on so many heads bow, my Prince, before you. Next the companies divide and in skilled order wheel this way and that, in such paths as neither the Cretan palace of the half-human steer nor Maeander's stream with all its many windings could surpass. Flowing backwards in their separate courses the companies twist into circular formations, and so Janus, imprisoning Wars behind his never-opening doors on their unmoving hinges, lavishes on peace, in the joyful semblance of a battle, the homage of a combat that sheds no blood.

And now, with a garland crowning both his brows, he opens for the happy calendar a new year; now Tiber in a single man sees united both Brutus' consular robe and Quirinus' sceptre. The Pallantean hill rejoices in the sight, after so many ages gone, of a consul; the rostra recognize the curule chair our forefathers heard of so long ago, and, though this is a spectacle grown unfamiliar, the royal lictors with their gilded rods of office now surround the Forum of Trajan, and veiling with Gothic laurels the axes that are

auditas quondam proauis, desuetaque cingit 645
regius auratis fora fascibus Vlpia lictor,
et sextas Getica praeuelans fronde secures
colla triumphati proculcat Honorius Histri.
exeat in populos cunctis inlustrior annus,
natus fonte suo, quem non aliena per arua 650
induit hospes honos, cuius cunabula fouit
curia, quem primi tandem uidere Quirites,
quem domitis auspex peperit Victoria Bellis!
hunc et priuati titulis famulantibus anni
et quos armipotens genitor retroque priores 655
diuersis gessere locis, ceu numen adorent;
hunc et quinque tui, uel quos habiturus in urbe
post alios, Auguste, colant. licet unus in omnes
consul eas, magno sextus tamen iste superbit
nomine, praeteritis melior, uenientibus auctor. 660

649 annis *x*   650 sponte sua *Heinsius*   651 imbuit ς, *Scaliger*   honor *x*
655 regesque *x*   656 egere ς   659 ille ς: ipse ς, *Claverius*: ecce *Heinsius*

his for the sixth time, Honorius tramples underfoot the necks of the Danube's conquered tribes. Let this year of office go forth into the world more glorious than all the others, born from its own true source, an honour that no stranger assumes in the midst of foreign fields, one whose cradle the Senate House has cherished, one, at last, that the citizens of Rome were first to see, one born of auspicious Victory now that Wars are vanquished! Years named by commoners, their titles subject to yours, and those in which your father, mighty in battle, and all your predecessors before held consulships, here or in other places, let them all adore this year as one divine; let it be worshipped too by the five that are yours and by any others you will hold, Augustus, in the City in future days. And were you as sole consul to inaugurate them all, yet does that sixth glory in its mighty name, better than all that went before, a precedent for all that are to come.

COMMENTARY

PREFACE

LONG hexameter poems in Late Antiquity are often accompanied by detachable verse prefaces in a slighter metre, a custom which seems to have developed gradually from the introductory proems integrated into the beginnings of epics and didactic verse (e.g. *Il.* 1. 1 ff., Hes. *Th.* 1 ff., Virg. *A.* 1. 1 ff.). Further impulses towards the development of independent introductory pieces were no doubt contributed by the self-consciously personal *sphragis* found at the end of some long poems (e.g. Virg. *G.* 4. 559 ff., Ov. *Met.* 15. 871 ff., Stat. *Theb.* 12. 810 ff.) and by the use of the first poem of a collection to serve a programmatic purpose or make a dedication (e.g. Catul. 1, Mart. 5. 1, 6. 1). The polemical prologues that accompany some of Terence's comedies are also broadly comparable, as are perhaps the mysterious *praefationes* said to have headed the tragedies of Seneca and Pomponius (Quint. *Inst.* 8. 3. 31). As early as Catul. 65–6 we find a short dedicatory elegy introducing a longer poem in the same metre (a translation of Callimachus), while Persius' satires are prefaced by a prologue in scazons. For the important influence of contemporary rhetoric and of the custom of prefacing a declamation with προλαλιά see T. Viljamaa, *Studies in Greek Encomiastic Poetry of the Early Byzantine Period* (Helsinki, 1968), 68 ff.

Roughly half of Claudian's long poems have come down to us with prefaces attached, all in elegiacs, but no clear pattern can be discerned. Thus there are prefaces for the panegyrics on Honorius' third and sixth consulships but not his fourth, while *De Raptu Proserpinae* 1 and 2 have prefaces (a weighty 52 lines in the case of book 2), but book 3 does not. A singular case is *In Eutropium*, with no preface for the first book, but one of 76 lines accompanying the second: see Cameron, pp. 76 ff., 136 ff. for an ingenious attempt to account for this. It seems reasonable to assume at least the possibility that some have been lost, and that they may never have survived long enough to make it into the omnibus edition of Claudian's political works prepared on the orders of Stilicho after the poet's death (*pace* Cameron 457). This state of affairs can be attributed to their being even more ephemeral than the propaganda poems themselves, since they were very much directed at one particular audience on one particular occasion. By Claudian's time the topoi were highly traditional, and included programmatic or apologetic remarks on the nature of the poet's craft and his devotion to it (11 f.), the assumed modesty of the poet (15), allusive indications of the proposed themes of the poem to whet the appetite (17ff.), and, perhaps most important of all, encomium of the audience and addressee (23f.). Their essential function, then, was to act as a *captatio beneuolentiae* designed to put the audience into a receptive frame of mind. See further Viljamaa, loc. cit., Simon 119, Coleman on the preface to Stat. *Silu.* 4 (pp. 53ff.), Gruzelier 79f., and Grant Parker, *The Prose Prefaces of Martial and Statius: A Study in Literary Purpose* (MA thesis, Cape Town, 1991), chs. 1 and 9. Claudian's choice of metre for his prefaces is something of a surprise, since in Late Antiquity the general convention, at least in the Greek East, was that prefaces to hexameter poems were written in iambics: see Alan Cameron, *CQ* NS 20 (1970), 119–29, esp. 119f. It may be that in the Latin-speaking West a convention of using elegiacs in prefaces had established itself, and that Claudian wished to conform to it; this, however, is pure speculation. What does seem tolerably clear is that the Latin tradition permitted greater variety, and so an alternative explanation might be that Claudian opted for elegiacs because, like most educated non-native users of Latin, he was more at home with dactylic metres. After Claudian, at any rate, we find Latin hexameter panegyrics equipped with prefaces in either metre, iambics in the case of Priscian's encomium of Anastasius, for example, but elegiacs in that of Corippus' panegyric on Justin.

The preface to *VI Cons.* is also found attached in a large number of manuscripts to the third book of the *De Raptu Proserpinae*, and scholars inevitably disagree on the question of which poem it was originally composed for. As the following notes will show, however, the concerns of the preface correspond closely with those of the main body of the *VI Cons.*, in particular the conceit of Gigantomachy (17f.) and the insistence on the link between the court and the Senate which seems to lie behind 23f. The misattribution may have been motivated by a desire to provide a preface for the only book of the *De Raptu* that lacked one, and the choice of preface to be transferred made as a result of the perceived thematic association between Claudian's claim to have written a Gigantomachy in his dream and such passages as the description of the grove displaying the spoils of the Giants at *Rapt.* 3. 332ff.

1–10. The rationalizing belief that in dreams the sleeper continues mentally to carry out the activity that engrossed his attention in the hours of wakefulness can be traced as far back at least as Hdt. 7. 16 πεπλανῆσθαι αὗται μάλιστα ἐώθασι αἱ ὄψιες τῶν ὀνειράτων, τά τις ἡμέρης φροντίζει. Democritus and Epicurus developed an explanation for this in terms of atomic theory, arguing that in sleep the mind continued to perceive *simulacra* of the same things that had occupied it when awake: see further R. D. Brown, *Lucretius on Love and Sex* (Leiden, 1987), 171 ff. Cf. also Men. fr. 780 Körte–Thierfelder ἃ γὰρ μεθ' ἡμέραν τις ὑπερεσπούδασε, | ταῦτ' εἶδε καὶ νύκτωρ, Acc. *praet.* 28–30 Warmington = *Brut.* 663–5 Dangel 'rex, quae in uita usurpant homines, cogitant curant uident | quaeque agunt uigilantes agitantque, ea si cui in somno accidunt, | minus mirum est' (cited by Cicero at *Diu.* 1. 45, where see Pease), Ter. *An.* 971 f., [Sen.] *Oct.* 740 ff. 'quaecumque mentis agitat intentus uigor, | ea per quietem sacer et arcanus refert | ueloxque sensus', Fronto 233. 10–15 van den Hout[2] (note esp. 'ea somnia plerumque ad uerum conuertunt'). Lucan adapts the idea at *De Bello Ciuili* 7. 760 ff., where on the eve of Pharsalus the army dreams of the impious slaughter they will do on the *next* morning.

Claudian's version of this common topos bears a particularly close resemblance in its language and choice of examples to the long discussion on the nature of dreams given by Lucretius at *De Rerum Natura* 4. 962 ff. 'et quo quisque fere studio deuinctus adhaeret | aut quibus in rebus multum sumus ante morati | atque in ea ratione fuit contenta magis mens, | in somnis eadem plerumque uidemur obire; | causidici causas agere et componere leges, | induperatores pugnare ac proelia obire, | nautae contractum cum uentis degere duellum, | nos agere hoc autem et naturam quaerere rerum | semper et inuentam patriis exponere chartis. | cetera sic studia atque artis plerumque uidentur | in somnis animos hominum frustrata tenere.' Lucretius continues with a lengthy demonstration of this theory, elaborating a number of examples, both human and animal, such as games-enthusiasts, racehorses, hunting dogs, and men who dream of such activities as doing battle, drinking when thirsty or making love. Also very close are two passages from Petronius and Nonnus: Petr. *c.* 30 'somnia, quae mentes ludunt uolitantibus umbris, | non delubra deum nec ab aethere numina mittunt, | sed sibi quisque facit. nam cum prostrata sopore | urget membra quies et mens sine pondere ludit, | quidquid luce fuit tenebris agit. oppida bello | qui quatit et flammis miserandas eruit urbes, | tela uidet uersasque acies et funera regum | atque exundantes profuso sanguine campos. | qui causas orare solent, legesque forumque | et pauidi cernunt inclusum chorte tribunal. | condit auarus opes defossumque inuenit aurum. | uenator saltus canibus quatit. eripit undis | aut premit euersam periturus nauita puppem. | scribit amatori meretrix, dat adultera munus: | et canis in somnis leporis uestigia lustrat. | in noctis spatium miserorum uulnera durant', and Nonn. *D.* 42. 325 ff.: ἀντίτυπον γὰρ | ἔργον, ὅ περ τελέει τις ἐν ἤματι, νυκτὶ δοκεύει. | βουκόλος ὑπνώων κεραοὺς βόας εἰς νομὸν ἕλκει. | δίκτυα θηρητῆρι φαείνεται ὄψις ὀνείρου. | γειοπόνοι δ' εὔδοντες ἀροτρεύουσιν ἀρούρας, | αὔλακα δὲ σπείρουσι φερέσταχυν. ἀζαλέη δὲ | ἄνδρα μεσημβρίζοντα κατάσχετον αἴθοπι δίψῃ | εἰς ῥόον, εἰς ἀμάρην ἀπατήλιος ὕπνος ἐλαύνει. | οὕτω καὶ Διόνυσος, ἔχων ἰνδάλματα μόχθων, | μιμηλῷ πτερόεντα νόον πόμπευεν ὀνείρῳ, | καὶ σκιεροῖσι γάμοισιν ὁμίλεεν. The connection between Claudian and Petronius' poems was recognized at an early date: these ten lines appear as if they were an elegiac poem in their own right, accompanying the Petronian pieces, in a 9th-c. manuscript of Ausonius (Vossianus F. 111).

Claudian follows the same basic structural pattern as Lucretius in that he makes a generalization, offers a few succinct examples, and then observes that the same principle applies to his own dreams of writing poetry (11 ff. 'me quoque Musarum studium . . .': Lucr. 969f. 'nos agere hoc autem . . .'). His human hunter matches those of Petronius (12) and Nonnus (328), but also has his literary ancestor in Lucretius' description of the dreams of hunting dogs (991–1006). The lawyers and their suits go back to Lucretius (966) and Petronius (9f.), while the charioteer is another humanization of a Lucretian example, the racehorses of 987–90. For Claudian's transference of Lucretian ideas from animals to humans cf. also 8 *quaerit* n. The adulterous lover has his parallels in all three of these passages: see further 7 *furto gaudet amans* n. The sailor and the miser recall Petronius (12f., 11), while the sleepers plagued by thirst correspond to Lucr. 4. 1024f. 'flumen item sitiens aut fontem propter amoenum | adsidet et totum prope faucibus occupat amnem' and Nonnus 42. 330–2. To all this, however, Claudian has added another element, that of wish-fulfilment. The dreams presented are also *uota*: in his sleep each man's prayer for success in the business to which he devotes his waking hours is temporarily answered. This is signalled in l. 1, but does not begin to emerge with proper clarity until, perhaps, *cauetur* (5: the charioteer successfully manœuvres his chariot round the *meta*, no doubt thus winning his race) and, more clearly, *furto gaudet amans* (7). An extra twist is given to the idea in l. 8, where the miser on waking finds that the treasure he possessed in his dreams has slipped from his grasp: so too the illusory draughts of cooling water fail to refresh the thirsty sleepers outside their dream (*frustra* 9). Once this point is grasped, the significance of the generalization of ll. 1–10 for the poet's own circumstances can be more easily seen. Claudian spends his days in the composition and recitation of poetry, hoping for a favourable reception from a powerful and revered public: in his dream he writes a *Gigantomachy* and wins the applause of the most powerful audience of all, Jupiter and the Olympian gods. But yet a third element is added, drawing a powerful contrast between Claudian on the one hand and, in particular, the miser and the thirsty sufferers of ll. 8–10: his night-time vision also turns out to be a true prophetic dream and his triumph is granted him in reality after he wakes (21 ff.). The distinction which Claudian makes between himself and the other dreamers seems to reflect the division made in ancient treatises on interpreting dreams between an ἐνύπνιον, which correspond to the dreamer's present physical state (including desires), and an ὄνειρος, which provides true information about the future. See the discussion of Artemidorus' *Oneirocritica* in John J. Winkler, *The Constraints of Desire* (New York, 1990), 24 f.

1. **uoluuntur:** implying considered reflection: cf. 148, *Ruf.* 2. 330 f. 'quid plurima uoluis | anxius?' See also Korn on V. Fl. 4. 84.

2. **pectore sopito:** *pectore* = the seat of the intellectual faculties (*OLD* s.v. 3b, citing e.g. Ov. *Met.* 15. 63 f. 'quae natura negabat | uisibus humanis, oculis ea pectoris hausit'). For both the phrasing and the idea see Cic. *Diu.* 1. 115 'qui (sc. animus) . . . ita est adfectus ut sopito corpore ipse uigilet'. There is a slight paradox in that here the mind is conceived as still being active whereas more normally sleep slows down all intellectual activity (Acc. *trag.* 91 f. Warmington = 140 f. Dangel), or else cares and sorrows in the *pectus* prevent the onset of sleep (e.g. Virg. *A.* 4. 529 ff., Cor. *Ioh.* 7. 20 f.).

   reddit amica quies: *reddit* is to be taken closely with *uota* (1): sleep not only 'brings back' (Platnauer) to the slumbering mind the activities of the day but also 'discharges the vows' that mortals make during the daytime pursuit of their chosen occupations, thus allowing them in their dreams to obtain the success that was the object of their vow. The epithet *amica* is thus pointed: sleep is a true friend who does us a great *beneficium* by paying on our behalf this debt to the gods. There is also another touch of paradox in that sleep is usually 'kindly', a boon to mortals, because it provides rest from the troubles of the day, but here is so described because, in a delightful manner, it *prolongs* the concerns of the hours of wakefulness. For the choice of epithet cf. Ov. *Ep.* 19. 33 'noctis amicior hora', Tert. *Anim.* 43, Cor. *Ioh.* 7. 17 'noctis amica quies'.

3–8. The comparisons between dreamers and their differing preoccupations in both their dreams and their waking hours is strongly reminiscent of such sweeping poetic surveys of the variety of human activity and pleasures as Hor. *Carm.* 1. 1. See Nisbet–Hubbard's introduction (pp. 1–3) to that poem for the literary-historical background and its close links with philosophical writing. For the rhetorical exercise of the *comparatio* of differing professions, and its influence on poetry, see further J. C. McKeown, *Ovid: Amores. Text, Prolegomena and Commentary, Volume II. A Commentary on Book I* (Leeds, 1989), 259 f.

reponit: = *deponit*. For Claudian's fondness for verbs with the prefix *re-*, particularly at the end of the hexameter (cf. *redit* 4), see Birt, p. ccxxii. An especially clear example of this tendency can be found at 91–100, where three lines out of ten end with such verbs.

4. **ad siluas et sua lustra:** *sua* carries extra weight since *lustra* are usually thought of as belonging to the wild animals that inhabit them rather than to the huntsman: e.g. Virg. *G.* 2. 471 'saltus ac lustra ferarum', *A.* 3. 646 f., Luc. 3. 408, Stat. *Silu.* 3. 1. 169, *Rapt.* 3. 44 f., Cor. *Laud. Iust.* 4. 24 'horrescunt sua lustra ferae'. For the additional degree of emphasis carried by possessives when they precede their substantive see LHS ii. 408.

5. **iudicibus lites:** contrast Aus. *Ephem.* 8. 4 ff. Green, where *fora* and *lites* are material for nightmares, on a level with terrible dreams of war, of being torn to pieces by wild beasts in the amphitheatre, or of sexual pollution.

5 f. **auriga . . . equis:** the idea and phrasing recall Hor. *Carm.* 1. 1. 3 ff. 'sunt quos curriculo puluerem Olympicum | collegisse iuuat, metaque feruidis | euitata rotis palmaque nobilis | terrarum dominos euehit ad deos'. The charioteer faced a test of nerves every time he rounded a turning-post. The trick was to keep in as close as possible without actually bringing the wheel into contact with it. The over-cautious or cowardly charioteer who gave the post too wide a berth risked letting a competitor slip past him into pole position: e.g. Ov. *Am.* 3. 2. 69 f. 'me miserum, metam spatioso circuit orbe! | quid facis? admoto proxumus axe subit!', Stat. *Theb.* 6. 440 ff. But on the other hand, striking the post with the axle of the wheel could result in utter disaster, as Nestor warns Antilochus at *Il.* 23. 338 ff. A misjudgement of this type is imagined as causing the grisly death of Orestes in the *paedagogus'* fictional account at Soph. *El.* 720 ff. Lucan conveys the skill of a helmsman by comparing him to a charioteer who successfully executes this manœuvre: 8. 199 ff. 'non sic moderator equorum, | dexteriore rota laeuum cum circumit axem, | cogit inoffensae currus accedere metae'.

6. **uana:** i.e. 'not real', because it exists only in a dream. Cf. Ov. *Met.* 8. 824 ff. 'petit ille dapes sub imagine somni | oraque *uana* mouet, dentemque in dente fatigat | exercetque cibo delusum guttur *inani*', Sen. *Dial.* 2. 11. 1 'uanas species somniorum uisusque nocturnos nihil

52

habentis solidi atque ueri', Luc. 3. 38, 7. 8, Stat. *Theb.* 2. 126, *Rapt.* 3. 96. Note also *inania* in Lucr. 4. 995, cit. on 8 *quaerit*, and see *TLL* vii/1. 823. 24 ff.

7. **furto gaudet amans:** Ov. *Ep.* 15. 291 'Iuppiter his gaudet, gaudet Venus aurea furtis'. *furto* implies a secret, illicit liaison: for this sense of the word, first extant in Catullus (68. 136, 140) and thereafter common in love elegy, see *TLL* vi/1. 1649. 68 ff., Servius on *A.* 10. 91 'furtum est adulterium', *Nupt.* 81, *Rapt.* 1. 106. Cf. Petronius' picture of the *meretrix* and her lover continuing to play the usual roles of their affair in their sleep at *c.* 30. 14. *gaudeo,* and more particularly *gaudium,* often bear thinly veiled sexual connotations: see J. N. Adams, *The Latin Sexual Vocabulary* (London, 1982), pp. 196–8, citing Catul. 61. 110 ff. 'quanta gaudia, quae uaga | nocte, quae medio die | gaudeat', Hor. *Carm.* 3. 6. 27 ff. Such connotations are commonly attached to the word from Lucretius on (4. 1106 'iam cum praesagit gaudia corpus', 1196, 1206): a very clear example is furnished by Statius at *Ach.* 1. 640 ff. (Achilles raping Deidamia) 'densa noctis *gauisus* in umbra | tempestiua suis torpere silentia *furtis* | ui potitur uotis'. Lucretius' discussion of dreams ends with a description of the propensity of adolescent youths to release nocturnal emissions under the influence of sexually stimulating *simulacra* (4. 1030 ff.). We should therefore probably interpret *gaudet* as indicating that the lover reaches an orgasm: cf. the colloquial use of the Fr. *jouir.* The passage of Nonnus quoted above (1–10 n.) closes with Dionysus enjoying sexual congress with the beloved in his dream, 42. 325 καὶ σκιεροῖσι γάμοισιν ὁμίλεεν.

8. **uigil:** this, the reading of all the manuscripts, has given some difficulty: why is the miser alone imagined as being awake? Both Gesner and Bücheler conjectured *uigili,* which would yield tolerably good sense: the miser would then be seeking to recover in his dreams some treasure he has lost in his waking existence. But not only does this require the reader to supply the elements of a 'plot' that explains *elapsas,* it also rules out the more striking meaning for *quaerit* suggested in the next note. It is preferable to accept *uigil* and understand this as an example of the word being used rather freely, for the sake of vividness, as equivalent to *euigilans:* the miser has enjoyed a luxurious dream of possession, but is linguistically jolted awake to find his dream-treasure slip from his grasp. This also squares better with Petronius' picture of a miser discovering buried treasure in his dreams (*c.* 30. 11, cit. 1–10 n.) and, more clearly still, with his other treatment of this idea, *Satyrica* 128: 'nocte soporifera ueluti cum somnia ludunt | errantes oculos effossaque protulit aurum | in lucem tellus: uersat manus improba furtum | thesaurosque rapit, sudor quoque perluit

ora | et mentem timor altus habet, ne forte grauatum | excutiat gremium secreti conscius auri: | mox ubi fugerunt elusam gaudia mentem | ueraque forma redit, animus, quod perdidit, optat | atque in praeterita se totus imagine uersat.' Perhaps the difficulty presented by this line could even be attributed to Claudian's having consciously set about condensing the sense of these verses as succinctly as possible. It is true that this in one sense disturbs the pattern of examples of dreamers enjoying their night-time imaginations, particularly since this departure interrupts the sequence in that it appears in the penultimate example, and not the last, where it might be less anomalous. But it does so only by extending it in a meaningful way, which is continued by *frustra* (11) and which prepares the contrast with Claudian's own discovery on waking that his dream has come true. Another option, suggested to me by Professor Nisbet, is open to those who find the arguments offered here unconvincing: the miser is perhaps, in a neat paradox, to be imagined as 'dreaming of being vigilant'. In this case, perhaps in his 'vigilant dreams' the miser attempts to make up the profit that had slipped from his grasp during the day (*elapsas . . . opes*); for *quaero* with the sense 'to acquire, earn' or the like see *OLD* s.v. 7.

quaerit: i.e. in vain, the *opes* having been as substanceless as the *uana . . . meta* of l. 6. See *OLD* s.v. 2 and cf. esp. Stat. *Theb.* 9. 600f. (Atalanta waking from a nightmare) 'abrupere oculi noctem maestoque cubili | exilit et falsos quaerit per lumina fletus.' The idea can also be paralleled in Lucretius: 4. 995f. (the hunting dogs) 'expergefactique sequuntur inania saepe | ceruorum simulacra, fugae quasi dedita cernant'.

9 f. blanda . . . pocula: cf. V. Fl. 2. 416f. 'quin et Iouis armiger ipse | accipit a Phrygio iam pocula blanda ministro', where it refers to draughts of nectar. Note also Luxorius 320. 6 Ries = 34. 6 Rosenblum.

9. frustra: all the largesse of this imaginary stream cannot truly quench their thirst.

sitientibus aegris: irresistibly recalling, with all its concomitant pathos, the Homeric tag δειλοῖσι βροτοῖσιν (*Il.* 22. 31 etc.) and its standard Latin equivalent *mortalibus aegris* (e.g. Lucr. 6. 1, Virg. *G.* 1. 237, *A.* 10. 274, 12. 850). Cf. esp. Virg. *A.* 2. 268f. 'tempus erat quo prima mortalibus aegris | incipit et dono diuum gratissima serpit'.

10. inriguus . . . sopor: cf. esp. Pers. 5. 56 'hic satur inriguo mauult turgescere somno', and Cyr. Gall. *gen.* 34 'inriguo perfundit lumina somno', cited at *TLL* vii/2. 421. 66. Sleep is frequently described in poetry in terms of a flood sweeping over the body: cf. Lucr. 4. 907f.

'somnus per membra quietem | inriget', Virg. *A.* 1. 691f., 3. 511 'fessos sopor inrigat artus', Fronto 233. 1–4 van den Hout[2]. Williams, on *A.* 3. 511, comments 'it is not only the dampness of sleep but its diffusing power which is pictured metaphorically': here the idea of sleep as refreshing is uppermost, while the epithet also obviously contributes to the general idea of thirsty men receiving respite from their thirst through dreams.

gelido . . . fonte: a standard collocation: Virg. *Ecl.* 10. 42, *Nupt. pr.* 7, *c.m.* 25. 100. The epithet is often no more than padding, as can be seen from the way Cicero translates Homer's ἀμφὶ περὶ κρήνην (*Il.* 2. 305) as 'circum latices gelidos' (fr. 23. 8 Büchner). But here it is fully operative, since it is the coolness of the stream that relieves the sufferers' thirst (cf. e.g. Catul. 68. 57ff.).

11. **me quoque:** the abrupt shift, the sense of contrast between the poet and others, and the concentration on the poet's vocation recall Virg. *G.* 2. 475ff. 'me uero primum dulces ante omnia Musae . . .'.

Musarum studium: cf. *c.m.* 25. 46 'dedite Musarum studio' and contrast *Theod.* 138f. 'iam satis indultum studiis, Musaeque tot annos | eripuere mihi'. Behind these passages seems to lie Hor. *S.* 2. 3. 105 'nec studio citharae nec Musae deditus ulli': since that line appears in a diatribe against the folly of misers the train of thought that apparently led from Petronius to the miser of l. 8 may perhaps have prompted Claudian's memory of Horace by association.

nocte silenti: Lucretius too claimed to find himself writing his poem even in his sleep: 4. 969f., cit. 1–10n. Far more frequent is the topos of the learned poet being prevented from sleeping at night by the endless labour required of him in his devotion to his craft: see further Richard F. Thomas, *HSCPh* 83 (1979), 195ff., Michael Dewar, *Mnemosyne*[2], 46 (1993), 212ff.

12. **artibus adsuetis sollicitare:** in the context of dreams *sollicitare* would more usually imply a nightmare or dream of ill omen, as it does at Mart. 7. 54. 1f. 'semper mane mihi de me mera somnia narras, | quae moueant animum sollicitentque meum'. But here, though the dream turns out to be an auspicious one, the verb alludes to the traditional cares and labours of the poet's craft. For the collocation *artes adsuetae* cf. Ov. *Rem.* 287 'adsuetas Circe decurrit ad artes', *Pont.* 1. 5. 36.

13. **poli media stellantis in arce:** recalling in particular Virg. *A.* 7. 210f. 'aurea nunc solio stellantis regia caeli | accipit', of the deification of Dardanus. Cf. also e.g. V. Fl. 5. 622, Stat. *Theb.* 6. 579, *III Cons.* 33 'rex o stellantis Olympi'. Heaven regularly appears as a 'citadel' in heroic verse, the emphasis being more on height than on

impregnability: Virg. *A.* 1. 250 'caeli quibus adnuis arcem', Ov. *Met.* 1. 163 'quae pater ut summa uidit Saturnius arce', *III Cons.* 167, *IV Cons.* 198, *Rapt.* 1. 214. *media* thus draws attention to the astonishment Claudian feels at finding himself so elevated. MacCormack (pp. 138 ff., 332 n. 214, 334 n. 223) discusses the connection between these lines and the language of pagan *consecratio*, and compares them with Septimius Severus' dream of his own ascent to Heaven at SHA *Sept. Seu.* 22. 1 f.

uidebar: standard in first-person narratives of dreams from Enn. *Ann.* 40 ff. Skutsch 'postilla, germana soror, errare uidebar | tardaque uestigare et quaerere te neque posse | corde capessere.' Cf. also e.g. Virg. *A.* 2. 279, *Gild.* 356 f.

14. **ante pedes . . . ferre:** an act of homage, while the *carmina* are also in a sense part of the tribute or spoils of war. Cf. Ov. *Am.* 2. 13. 24 'ipse feram ante tuos munera uota pedes'.

summi . . . Iouis: such phrases are commonly used of Jupiter from Enn. *scen.* 176 'Iuppiter . . . supreme': Jocelyn ad loc. argues that they translate ὕπατος or ὕψιστος. Cf. Naev. fr. 16 Büchner, Pl. *Am.* 780, V. Fl. 1. 505, Sil. 2. 535 'summum . . . Iouem', *III Cons. pr.* 14 'gesturus summo tela trisulca Ioui', *Rapt.* 3. 174; also Virg. *A.* 7. 558.

15. **utque fauet somnus:** an indication of modesty.

plaudebant numina dictis: a prompt for the mixed audience of senators and courtiers, when the end of the poem comes? At *Get.* 452 Claudian uses *plaudo* with the accusative: for the dative cf. Hor. *S.* 1. 1. 66 f. 'populus me sibilat; at mihi plaudo | ipse domi', Tac. *Hist.* 2. 55.

16. **circumfusi:** Platnauer interprets as 'gathered about Jove's throne', but the emphasis is primarily on the poet, who is surrounded (*OLD* s.v. 6) by the applauding deities as he metaphorically places his poems at the feet of the king of the gods: cf. *c.m.* 31. 51 f. 'me iungeret auspex | purpura, me sancto cingeret aula choro', of an imagined recitation before the 'gods' of the Court.

sacra corona chori: similar phrases are used of the retinues of gods at e.g. Ov. *Fast.* 2. 156 'Callisto sacri pars fuit una chori (sc. Dianae)', 5. 352. The language is easily transferred to the court (*c.m.* 31. 51 f. cit. previous n.), and here includes the Senate (24 n.). For *corona* of a ring of bystanders forming an audience, cf. Cic. *Tusc.* 1. 10 'tibi ipsi pro te erit maxima corona causa dicenda', Catul. 53. 1, Ov. *Met.* 13. 1, Stat. *Theb.* 11. 422.

17 f. The subject of Claudian's song in his dream was a Gigantomachy, in honour above all of Jupiter: he can thus be considered as enjoying an association with such other distinguished exponents of this theme as Orpheus (*c.m.* 31. 23 ff.) and Apollo himself (Stat. *Theb.* 6. 355 ff.). Two unfinished or fragmentary Gigantomachies attributed to

Claudian in fact survive, one in Latin (*c.m.* 53) and one in Greek (*Carm. Graec.* 1f.), but references to the war between the Gods and Giants abound in his other works, in particular in *De Raptu Proserpinae* (see Gruzelier on 1. 43ff.). Here the implication is political, since the clear equation in l. 23 of Jupiter with Honorius requires the Giants to correspond with the recently defeated Goths, and the couplet thus prepares the way for the Gigantomachic allusions in the poem proper: see further 45 *Gigantas*, 185f.nn. This couplet is closely imitated by Sidonius, *Carm.* 6. 27f. (preface to a consular panegyric on Avitus) 'Enceladus patri iacuit fratrique Typhoeus; | Euboicam hic rupem sustinet, hic Siculam'.

17. Enceladus mihi carmen erat: cf. *Aetna* 1ff. 'Aetna mihi . . . carmen erit', Claud. *Ap.* 2. 10 'Alcides mihi carmen erit'.

uictusque Typhoeus: = 'the defeat of Typhoeus': the *ab urbe condita* construction, for which see LHS ii. 393f., Nisbet–Hubbard on Hor. *Carm.* 1. 37. 13, 2. 4. 10, Coleman on Stat. *Silu.* 4. 4. 40. Zeus' victory over Typhoeus, child of Earth and Tartarus and most fearsome of all the Titan and Giant opponents of the Olympians, is the final act that assures him mastery over all the universe: Hes. *Th.* 819ff. For the general confusion in poetry of the Titanomachy, the Gigantomachy, and the revolt of Typhoeus see Gruzelier on *Rapt.* 2. 22.

18. Hesiod consigns the vanquished Titans and Typhoeus to Tartarus (*Th.* 717ff., 868), but by Claudian's time poetic imagination, and no doubt common belief, had long presented the great mountains, and in particular the volcanoes, of the Mediterranean area as imprisoning the defeated Giants and those associated with them. The stages of the elaboration are practically palpable at Pind. *Pyth.* 1. 15ff., where it is said that ὅς (i.e. Τυφὼς) τ' ἐν αἰνᾷ Ταρτάρῳ κεῖται, θεῶν πολέμιος, but that Sicily lies on top of him, and then Etna too. The reasons given for this are various: Earth, as the mother of the Giants, is perhaps made to take them back into her womb or else hides them in her grief (Hor. *Carm.* 3. 4. 73f.), or the Giants are turned to stone by Pallas' use of the head of Medusa on the aegis (Luc. 9. 655ff., *c.m.* 53. 91ff.), while some poets express the idea that the Giants' bodies still smoke from being blasted by thunderbolts, or that volcanic eruptions are caused by the imprisoned Giant moving his bulk beneath the mountain (Ov. *Met.* 5. 354f., Stat. *Theb.* 3. 594ff., *Rapt.* 1. 153ff.). The author of the *Aetna* examines such tales in considerable detail, only to dismiss them sniffily (41ff., 74 'haec est mendosae uulgata licentia famae'). See also Strabo 5. 4. 9.

Which Giant is said to lie under which mountain is a matter of bewildering confusion among the poets. The oldest tradition seems to place Typhoeus under Sicily, and more specifically under Etna: Aesch. *PV* 353 f., Pind. *Pyth.* 1. 15 ff., Ov. *Fast.* 1. 573 f. 'spirare Typhoea credas | et rapidum Aetnaeo fulgur ab igne iaci', 4. 491 f., V. Fl. 2. 24 'Sicula pressus tellure Typhoeus', Nonn. *D.* 2. 623 f.: cf. Apollod. 1. 6. 3. Ovid offers a colourful development of this basic idea at *Met.* 5. 346 ff., esp. 350 ff. 'dextra sed Ausonio manus est subiecta Peloro, | laeua, Pachyne, tibi, Lilybaeo crura premuntur, | degrauat Aetna caput'. Another version, however, located him under Inarime, identified with Ischia in the Bay of Naples (see below). An alternative tradition, which can be traced to Callimachus, named the Giant under Etna as Enceladus, and this is the one that proved more popular among the Roman poets: see Call. *Aet.* fr. 1. 35 f. Pf. cit. on 18 *grauis Aetna*, Virg. *A.* 3. 578 ff. 'fama est Enceladi semustum fulmine corpus | urgeri mole hac, ingentemque insuper Aetnam | impositam', Luc. 6. 293 ff., Stat. *Theb.* 3. 594 ff., 11. 8, 12. 275, *Aetna* 71 f., Quint. Smyrn. 5. 641 ff., Orph. Arg. 1257: cf. Apollod. 1. 6. 2. Conversely, Servius on *A.* 9. 716 asserts that some authorities placed Enceladus under Inarime. Silius, whether deliberately playing with these various traditions or simply through carelessness, is strikingly inconsistent: at 14. 578 f. he has Etna cover Enceladus, and yet Typhoeus appears under Etna in the same book (14. 196) but elsewhere under Inarime (8. 540 f.) and, apparently, in Tartarus (12. 659 f.): as if that were not enough, Inarime imprisons neither Typhoeus nor Enceladus at 12. 148 ff., but Iapetus. See further Williams on Stat. *Theb.* 10. 917.

Which tradition is Claudian following here? Platnauer translates 'the first (= Enceladus) a prisoner beneath Inarime, the second (= Typhoeus) oppressed by the weight of Etna'. It is true that the *hic* . . . *hic* construction can mean 'the former . . . the latter': see *TLL* vi/3. 2717. 44 ff., citing e.g. Virg. *Ecl.* 4. 55 ff. 'non me carminibus uincet nec Thracius Orpheus | nec Linus, huic mater quamuis atque huic pater adsit, | Orphei Calliopea, Lino formosus Apollo', Stat. *Theb.* 8. 453 ff., Tac. *Hist.* 4. 55. But in fact, it is more common for *hic* . . . *hic* to mean 'the latter . . . the former', and this is accordingly the sense given priority by the *TLL*: see vi/3. 2717. 19 ff. ('a. primo loco significat posterius'), citing e.g. Ter. *Hau.* 275 ff. 'ubi uentum ad aedis est, Dromo pultat fores; | anu' quaedam prodit; haec ubi aperuit ostium, | continuo hic se coniecit intro', Stat. *Theb.* 10. 249 ff., 11. 114 f., *Rapt.* 2. 18 ff. 'candida Parrhasii post hanc regina Lycaei (sc. Diana) | et Pandionias quae cuspide protegit arces (sc. Pallas), | utraque uirgo, ruunt: haec (sc. Pallas) tristibus aspera bellis, | haec (sc. Diana) metuenda feris'. That it is Typhoeus (*hic*, 'the latter') who lies under Inarime here, and Enceladus (*hunc*, 'the former') under Etna is there-

fore likely on linguistic grounds. Moreover, confirmation of this interpretation is found in the practice followed in the rest of Claudian's
works. There we discover that Claudian associates Inarime once
with Typhoeus (*Rapt.* 3. 183f.) and Etna invariably with Enceladus
(*III Cons.* 161 'si furor Enceladi proiecta mugiat Aetna', *Rapt.* 1. 154f.
'Aetna . . . | Enceladi bustum', 3. 123, 186f., *c.m.* 17. 32ff.): this
Alexandrian poet working in the Latin West thus aligns himself with
the Callimachean–Virgilian tradition. To sum up, it is best to take *hic*
as referring to Typhoeus and *hunc* to Enceladus, but since the slight
possibility remains that Claudian is as capricious as Silius, the translation can be left as open as the Latin ('one . . . the other').

hic: for the scansion and pronunciation see 587n.

subit: i.e. 'supports', with no motion necessarily implied: cf. Virg.
A. 2. 708 'ipse subibo umeris', Apul. *Met.* 5. 1. 3 'summa laquearia . . .
subeunt aureae columnae'.

Inarimen: the poetic name for the volcanic island near the coast
of Campania now known as Ischia: in antiquity the name Aenaria was
also used. Williams on Stat. *Theb.* 10. 917 points out that the name
originated in a misunderstanding of Homer's lines describing the
blasting of Typhoeus with a thunderbolt, *Il.* 2. 782f. ὅτε τ' ἀμφὶ
Τυφωέι γαῖαν ἱμάσσῃ | εἰν Ἀρίμοις, ὅθι φασὶ Τυφωέος ἔμμεναι εὐνάς.
Cf. Virg. *A.* 9. 715f. 'tum sonitu Prochyta alta tremit durumque cubile
| Inarime Iouis imperiis imposta Typhoeo', Luc. 5. 101, *Rapt.* 3. 183f.

grauis Aetna: cf. Call. *Aet.* fr. 1. 35f. Pf. αὖθι τὸ δ' ἐκδύοιμι, τό μοι
βάρος ὅσσον ἔπεστι | τριγλώχιν ὀλοῷ νῆσος ἐπ' Ἐγκελάδῳ, Ov. *Met.*
5. 352 'degrauat Aetna caput (sc. Typhoei)'.

19f. The scene imagined recalls Statius' simile illustrating the joy and
relief of the gods at Jupiter's destruction of the Gigantomachic figure
Capaneus with a thunderbolt: *Theb.* 11. 7f. 'gratantur superi, Phlegrae
ceu fessus anhelet | proelia et Encelado fumantem impresserit
Aetnen.' Cf. also Nonn. *D.* 2. 700ff., describing Zeus' return to
Heaven after the defeat of Typhoeus, and the detailed elaboration of
Claudian's idea at Sid. *Carm.* 1. 1ff.

19. susceperit: paving the way for the account of Honorius' *aduentus* in
Rome at 523ff. Cf. also *Stil.* 3. 30f. 'non alium certe Romanae clarius
arces | suscepere ducem'.

20. Phlegraeae: Phlegra, the mythological battlefield of the Gods and
Giants, was later localized in Thrace, in particular in Pallene, the
most westerly of the three peninsulas of the Chalcidice (Hdt. 7. 123,
Strabo 7. fr. 27). A still later, variant tradition placed it in the so-called
'Phlegraean Fields' in Campania (Plin. *Nat.* 3. 5. 9): note, however, the
scepticism of Strabo (5. 4. 4). Claudian, like most poets, leaves it to the

reader to decide, but in a poem so passionately concerned with the
defence of Italy against a latter-day army of Giants patriotism no
doubt inclined the audience to think of Campania. Note also *Rapt.* 2.
255, 3. 201, 337.

21. **nec me mea lusit imago:** this, in combination with the next line,
can be thought of as answering an unvoiced question comparable to
Europa's at Hor. *Carm.* 3. 27. 37 ff. 'uigilansne ploro | turpe com-
missum, an uitiis carentem | ludit imago | uana, quae porta fugiens
eburna | somnium ducit?' Cf. further *Stil.* 2. 217 'aut monitos certa
dignantur imagine somnos', also of prophetic dreams that will come
true. Similar phrases abound in Latin literature: cf. Ov. *Met.* 13. 216
(Agamemnon) 'deceptus imagine somni', Luc. 7. 8 (night) 'sollicitos
uana decepit imagine somnos', Petr. 128. Cf. also Virg. *A.* 1. 407 f.
'falsis | ludis imaginibus', Ov. *Met.* 3. 463, 6. 103 f., where the same
language is used with different sense.

   imago here = 'dream' (*TLL* vii/1. 409. 3 ff.). The sense is clear
enough in the present context, but in general poets use the word in
combination with others that leave no room for ambiguity: see e.g.
Ov. *Met.* 8. 824 'petit ille dapes sub imagine somni', 9. 480, 11. 587 f.
'exstinctique iube Ceycis imagine mittat | somnia ad Alcyonen ueros
narrantia casus', Luc. 3. 38. Given the influence here of Lucretius'
thought and language, Claudian may have in mind the word's semi-
technical 'Epicurean' sense as a translation of εἴδωλον, i.e. any image
given off by an object and leaving a sense-impression on the eyes (*OLD*
s.v. 4, Lucr. 4. 739, 741, 782), including dreams (Lucr. 4. 770, 818).

22. Claudian naturally presumes that his audience is familiar with the
conceit whereby true dreams issue through a gate of horn and false
ones through a gate of ivory. At the root of this tradition lies Homer's
description of the Gates of Dreams at *Od.* 19. 562 ff., but in Latin
poetry the primary reference point is of course Virg. *A.* 6. 893 ff.
'sunt geminae Somni portae, quarum altera fertur | cornea, qua
ueris facilis datur exitus umbris, | altera candenti perfecta nitens
elephanto, | sed falsa ad caelum mittunt insomnia Manes.' See
further Austin ad loc., citing Hor. *Carm.* 3. 27. 37 ff., Stat. *Silu.* 5. 3. 288
f., Aus. *Cup.* 103 Green: add Tert. *Anim.* 46 'Homerus duas portas
diuisit somniis, corneam ueritatis, fallaciae eburneam. respicere est
enim, inquiunt, per cornu, ebur autem caecum est' (in fact, Homer's
reasoning is etymological, associating ἐλέφας with ἐλεφαίρομαι and
κέρας with κραίνω), Aus. *Ephem.* 8. 22 ff. Green. The metonymy present in Claudian's *falsum . . . ebur* may have been inspired directly from
Statius' *malignum . . . ebur* (*Silu.* 5. 3. 288 f.), but the epithet is transferred
from the dreams themselves in Virgil's lines (*falsa . . . insomnia*). For

falsus in such contexts cf. also Stat. *Theb.* 2. 350f. 'numquam mihi falsa per umbras | Iuno uenit'.

23f. A splendid *tricolon abundans* triumphantly expresses the confirmation in the reality of the present moment of Claudian's dream. *princeps* indicates Honorius, corresponding to the victorious Jupiter, the *orbis apex* is the Palatine (or perhaps more generally Rome), answering to Heaven, and the *turba uerenda* of earthly gods are the audience of courtiers and, more particularly, senators. The triple anaphora of *en* (the only example in Claudian, though double *en* is used at e.g. *Ruf.* 1. 51f., 357f., *Rapt.* 3. 425ff.) compels the visual as well as intellectual attention of the listener, and was perhaps accompanied in recitation by appropriate gestures. *en* may be followed by either the accusative (Virg. *Ecl.* 5. 65 'en quattuor aras', the preferred construction in prose) or the nominative (Virg. *A.* 5. 639 'en quattuor arae', Claudian's own usual preference: cf. 154 *en Alaricus*).

23. orbis apex aequatus Olympo: Birt quotes Optatus Afer *de schismat. Donatist.* 1. 13 'apices et principes omnium . . . episcopi', but, as Müller sees, the reference here is to a place, almost certainly the Palatine Hill, which figures so largely in the poem (8, 11f., 35ff., 53, 603f. nn). These indications in the text of the poem proper reveal that Claudian delivered *VI Cons* to an audience gathered in a building on the Palatine, but it is not entirely clear which one. Claudian several times refers to the Palatine in connection with the Emperor's ancestral house (*larem* 40; *tuos . . . penates* 53; *patriis laribus* 603), which can only be the Domus Augustana, the great complex of Imperial residences to which *aula* (26) would of course be appropriate. The direct question *agnoscisne tuos, princeps uenerande, penates?* (53: cf. *hac . . . domo* 71) is also most naturally taken as referring to the audience's immediate surroundings, and so a large audience chamber in the palace itself seems the most likely venue. This is not, however, absolutely certain, since such language could, at a stretch, be used to refer to the palace as viewed from another building in the vicinity, or even (less likely) in very general terms to Rome itself. One good alternative candidate for the scene of Claudian's original delivery of the panegyric might be the library of the temple of Palatine Apollo, a stone's throw from the Domus Augustana. This was in some sense the literary nerve-centre of the city and, moreover, a place where the Senate had been accustomed to meet since the days of Augustus (Suet. *Aug.* 29, Tac. *Ann.* 2. 37, Serv. on *A.* 11. 235; probably also Cass. Dio 58. 9, Tac. *Ann.* 13. 5). Indeed, the preface to *De Bello Getico*, delivered in Rome in Stilicho's presence in 402 (cf. 123f.n., Müller on 124 *apud socerum*), seems to indicate that the library was the scene for that performance: *Get. pr.* 3f.

'optatos renouant eadem mihi culmina coetus | personat et noto
Pythia uate *domus.*' Ammianus Marcellinus (23. 3, 3) records that the
temple was burnt down on the night of 18 Mar. 363, but does not
specifically mention whether the portico and library shared that fate:
H. Jordan (*Topographie der Stadt Rom im Altertum* (Rome, 1970), i. 3, p. 72)
remarks cautiously that the library 'fand seinen Untergang *vielleicht* i.
J. 363 zugleich mit dem Tempel', but Claudian's evidence might even
be regarded as decisive here. Such a setting would give further point
to the comparison between Apollo and Honorius (25 ff.). See further
Schroff on *Get. pr.* 4.

From seeing the Emperor as an earthly version of Jupiter, it is only
the next step to posit an equivalence between his house and the
dwellings of the gods on Olympus. Claudian cannot but have in mind
the most influential treatment of this idea in Latin poetry, Ov. *Met.* 1.
168 ff., where, by inversion, Olympus is imagined in terms of the
Palatine with its residence of Augustus: note esp. 175 f. 'hic locus est,
quem, si uerbis audacia detur, | haud timeam magni dixisse Palatia
caeli.' Cf. also Stat. *Silu.* 3. 4. 47 ff. (of the Palatine) 'iam Latii montes
ueterisque penates | Euandri, quos mole noua pater inclitus orbis |
excolit et summis aequat Germanicus astris', Cor. *Laud. Iust.* 3. 179 ff.
Claudian has incorporated into all this an echo of Virg. *A.* 6. 781 f. 'en
huius, nate, auspiciis illa incluta Roma | imperium terris, animos
aequabit Olympo' (of Romulus), but note the possible significance of
the tense-shift from *aequabit* to *aequatus*: in this day's celebration of
Honorius' consulship and of his victory over Alaric Anchises' pro-
phecy has been fulfilled. Cf. further *Stil.* 3. 67 f. 'aequataque templa |
nubibus', in a passage comparable to *VI Cons.* 42 ff. For *apex* in connection with the Palatine cf. 42 *attollens apicem . . . regia,* 644 *Pallanteus
apex.* The sense *apex* = 'hill' is fairly common in poetry: e.g. Virg. *A.* 4.
246 f. 'apicem et latera ardua cernit | Atlantis duri', Stat. *Silu.* 3. 5. 72,
Fesc. 2. 9, *Rapt.* 1. 160.

24. turba uerenda, dei: the audience was no doubt comprised of both
Court officials and senators, but, since these consular ceremonies
properly belong to the Senate, the emphasis is perhaps on the latter.
For the flattery cf. Themistius, *Or.* 13. 178 B σύγκλητος ἀγορὰ θεῶν καὶ
δῆμος ἡρώων, of the Senate and People of Rome. For *uerendus* of the
Senate cf. 599 *patricii reuerenda . . . sacraria coetus*: the Senate thus enjoys
the same respect given to the Emperor (53). It seems practically impossible to justify the change of case presented in the transmitted reading
turba uerenda, deos, and Scaliger's *dei* is therefore accepted here.

25. Cf. *Eutr.* 1. 172 'quod nec uota pati nec fingere somnia possent'.

26. conuentum: too technical-sounding a word to be common in high poetry. See Austin on Virg. *A.* 6. 753 'conuentus trahit in medios' (the only appearance in Virgil), and cf. Lucr. 4. 784, Catul. 64. 32 f., Hor. *S.* 1. 7. 23, *Ruf.* 1. 61.

aula: originally associated primarily with oriental royalty, but also long established as a term indicating the residence of Roman Emperors: [Sen.] *Oct.* 162, Suet. *Nero* 6. 2, Mart. 9. 16. 3; *VI Cons.* 90, 558, 596. In verse it is also used of temples, as at Mart. 7. 60. 1 (Jupiter) 'Tarpeiae uenerande rector aulae', Stat. *Silu.* 3. 1. 10.

THE PANEGYRIC

1–25. *In this year more than any other a temple is owed to Fortuna Redux, for with Honorius' return to Rome the consulship is a sham no more.*

Honorius, still only nineteen, inaugurated his sixth consulship in Rome on 1 Jan. 404: the beginning of his earlier ones had all found him in Constantinople or Milan. His Eastern colleague Aristaenetus appears not to have been recognized in the West: see Roger S. Bagnall, Alan Cameron, Seth R. Schwartz, and Klaas A. Worp, *Consuls of the Later Roman Empire* (Atlanta, 1987), 342 f. For a full discussion of the historical background to this event, and of the extreme rarity at this period of Imperial visits to Rome, see the Introd. §4.

1–3. The cult of Fortuna Redux was initiated on 12 Oct. 19 BC, when the Senate voted the consecration of an altar to the goddess, with annual sacrifices conducted by the Pontifices and the Vestals. It was built near the Porta Capena through which Augustus entered the City on his return from campaigns in Syria (*Res Gestae* 11). See Weinstock 126, and Courtney on Gallus fr. 2. 4 'reditum' *(FLP 266)*. The cult proved popular with later Emperors and, though literary references to it are scarce, it is abundantly attested on coins and in inscriptions: see *RE* vii. 37. 62 ff., citing the most significant epigraphical evidence (*CIL* i², p. 229, iii. 1422, vi. 196 = *Inscr. Ital.* xiii/2. 516, 519, 538).

1. aurea ... templa: Domitian built a temple to Fortuna Redux, probably soon after his triumphal return from the war with the Sarmatians in 93. It stood in the southern part of the Campus Martius near the Porta Triumphalis: see the *RE* article cited in the previous note, and Richardson, 157. The dedication is recorded in an epigram of Martial (8. 65).

aurea is best taken as referring to a gilded roof: cf. Mart. 8. 65. 1 f. 'hic ubi Fortunae Reducis *fulgentia* late | templa *nitent,* felix area nuper erat.' Perhaps Claudian also has in mind Stat. *Theb.* 2. 726 ff. (Tydeus vows a temple to Pallas) 'si patriis Parthaonis aruis | inferar et reduci pateat mihi Martia Pleuron, | *aurea* tunc mediis urbis tibi *templa* dicabo | collibus'. For *aurea templa* cf. further Prop. 4. 1. 5 'fictilibus creuere deis haec aurea templa', Ov. *Am.* 3. 9. 43, *Fast.* 1. 223f., and also Virg. *A.* 8. 347f. 'hinc ad Tarpeiam sedem et Capitolia ducit | aurea nunc, olim siluestribus horrida dumis'. The Augustan poets insist on the contrast between Rome's humble past and her magnificent present, but Claudian sees in the circumstances of the day good grounds for still further enhancement of Rome's glory and beauty.

Fortunae Reduci: Müller draws attention to the ironic word-play at *Eutr.* 2. 551 'et similes iterum luctus Fortuna reduxit'. In her more usual aspect Fortuna is an important protectress of Rome in this poem, saving Italy in the reign of Marcus Aurelius (341), joyously receiving Honorius at Fanum on his triumphal progress to Rome (500), and giving Stilicho the just reward for his *pietas* (578f.). Her one apparently hostile act is a blessing in disguise: see 88–91n. Cf. also *IV Cons.* 4 'exultant reduces Augusto consule fasces'; here the cause for joy is greater, because the consulship is returned to the Emperor and the Emperor to Rome. Honorius' Heaven-blessed return to Rome is in direct contrast to the fate of Alaric, who in defeat ruefully reflects on the difference between his *fortunatos ingressus* and his *praesentes reditus* (i.e. back to Illyricum, not forwards to Rome) at 268f.

2. **ob reditum uouere:** for the idea and phrasing cf. Juv. 12. 93f. 'Catullus, | pro cuius reditu tot pono altaria', Suet. *Cal.* 14. 2 'uota pro reditu suscepta sunt'. Perhaps the most common pledge offered in a vow for one's own return or for that of a loved one is a lock of hair, e.g. *Il.* 23. 144ff., Catul. 66. 33f., V. Fl. 1. 378f., though cf. Virg. *A.* 2. 17 'uotum pro reditu simulant', of the Trojan Horse. Claudian addresses a prayer to Serena as to a goddess who can grant him a safe return home at *c.m.* 31. 57f. 'saltem absens, regina, faue reditusque secundos | adnue sidereo laeta supercilio.' It seems that *ob* has a slightly archaic, perhaps legalistic tone: see *TLL* ix/2. 26. 60ff., citing e.g. Virg. *G.* 4. 455 'haudquaquam ob meritum poenas', Prop. 4. 5. 66.

3. **amplas . . . aedes:** cf. Virg. *A.* 1. 725f. 'ampla . . . | atria', *Ruf.* 1. 213 'turba salutantum latas ibi perstrepit aedes'.

4. **sua cum:** the postponement of *cum* lays heavy emphasis on the possessive. See further LHS ii. 399, Williams on Virg. *A.* 5. 22.

trabeis: the *trabea* was properly a short, striped garment, sometimes contrasted with the long *toga.* It was originally worn on ceremonial and state occasions by the kings and so was assumed as an emblem of venerable authority by their successors, the consuls, and by some of the *flamines.* Like the *fasces*, it was almost certainly of Etruscan origin: see Fordyce on Virg. *A.* 7. 187f. and cf. 15n. *secures.* It was especially associated with Romulus (Quirinus): see e.g. Virg. *A.* 7. 612 f. (the consul opening the gates of Janus) 'ipse Quirinali trabea cinctuque Gabino | insignis reserat stridentia limina consul', Ov. *Fast.* 1. 37, 2. 503 f., 6. 375, Juv. 8. 259. As Fordyce notes, Servius (on *A.* 7. 612) identifies three kinds of *trabea*: 'unum dis sacratum quod est tantum de purpura, aliud regum quod est purpureum, habet tamen album aliquid, tertium augurale de purpura et cocco.' Supposing these distinctions had been maintained in the fifth century Honorius' would have been of the second kind, partly purple and partly white, and no doubt made of silk. But in Late Antiquity ceremonial garments had come to be highly decorated with illustrative bands and patches of brilliant hues, enhanced with gold thread and even, in the case of Imperial consuls, gemstones. Poetic examples are the magnificent 'rigentia . . . dona, graues auro trabeas', offered by Roma to Stilicho and decorated with pictures illustrating his connection with the Imperial family (*Stil.* 2. 339 ff.) and the work woven by Araneola at Sid. *Carm.* 15. 150 ff. Particularly significant in the present connection is *IV Cons.* 585 ff., where the splendid consular robe (*uelamenta* 586) worn by Honorius is decorated with emeralds, amethysts, jasper, and pearls as well as gold, and has embroidered pictures and cameos (*segmenta*) sewn on it. Cf. also 561 *membra . . . gemmato trabeae uiridantia cinctu.*

Properly speaking, the *trabea* was appropriate for the celebration of consulships, and the *toga picta* for triumphs, but since the latter was more splendid Emperors had begun to extend the wearing of it to other ceremonies too. Some Late Antique poets accordingly use the technical terms loosely and often interchangeably: see W. B. Anderson's note on Sid. *Carm.* 15. 150 f. 'proaui trabeas imitata rigentes | palmatam parat ipsa patri' (Loeb edn. (Cambridge, Mass., 1936, repr. 1980), i, p. 236). Note also Aus. *Grat. Act.* 52 Green on the *toga palmata*: 'namque iste habitus, ut in pace consulis est, sic in uictoria triumphantis'. It should therefore be borne in mind that when Claudian employs the word *trabea* on any particular occasion, he most likely means a highly decorated and jewelled *toga picta*; alternatively, he may mean no more than 'consular robe(s)' in a very loose sense, and that is perhaps how we should translate the word to be on the safe side. At any rate, whatever actual garment he has in mind when he uses the term *trabea*, in Claudian's consular panegyrics it serves primarily as a symbol of the consulship itself, and not of Imperial rank. This is made quite explicit at 642 *et Bruti cernit trabeas et sceptra Quirini*. For the metonymy cf. e.g. *Ruf.* 1. 249 'post trabeas exul', *Eutr.* 1. 464 'adspirant trabeis', 2. 123, *Theod.* 338, *Stil.* 2. 258, 322, 407 'trabeis . . . secundis': also Symm. *Ep.* 9. 112 'redditae sunt mihi litterae, quae te

annalem trabeam meruisse loquerentur'. See further *RE* vi. 1860. 53
ff. (*trabea*) and viiA. 504. 62 ff. (*uestis triumphalis*), Coleman on Stat. *Silu.*
4. 2. 32 f., and also Roberts 111 ff. Note that while Honorius restores to
the *trabea* its proper dignity, Eutropius in his physical repulsiveness
had disfigured it (*Eutr.* 1. 119 ff.).

 reparatur: cf. *Get.* 571 (Stilicho to the army at Pollentia)
'Romanum reparate decus'. Honorius is now completing the process
begun on the battlefield.

5–10. The power of the Roman people to elect its own magistrates at the
comitia centuriata had withered in the last part of Augustus' long reign
with the introduction of *destinatio,* perhaps by the *lex Valeria Cornelia* in
AD 5. This was a preliminary voting procedure in which specially
appointed centuries of senators and *equites* marked individuals out for
office and the *comitia* in effect rubber-stamped the appointment.
Tacitus states that the process was completed by Tiberius, who transferred even the formality of the election to the Senate: this development met with little opposition from the People and was entirely
welcome to the Senate, which was relieved from the expense and
indignity of campaigning (*Ann.* 1. 15). As the principate became firmly
established the Emperor's right to nominate or recommend candidates to the Senate for approval (*nominatio/commendatio*) was more and
more commonly exercised, and the election of magistrates by the
comitia became purely a matter of memory and nostalgia. Although
Suetonius claims that Gaius 'attempted' to revive the old custom
('temptauit et comitiorum more reuocato suffragia populo reddere',
Cal. 16. 2), the Emperor's motives are unclear and Suetonius' own
wording draws attention to the fact that this was only a short-lived
measure.

 In these lines Claudian claims that Honorius has won his sixth consulship by a proper election, but quite what is meant by this is not easy
to establish. As commentators point out, he is adapting and reversing
Lucan's scathing denunciation of the sham elections which marked
the beginning of Caesar's tyranny, *De Bello Ciuili* 5. 392 ff. 'fingit
sollemnia Campus | et non admissae dirimit suffragia plebis |
decantatque tribus et uana uersat in urna'. In his poem on the civil
war Petronius likewise comments more generally on the corruption of
the late Republic in terms similar to Claudian's in the lines immediately preceding these: with 4 f. cf. 119 vv. 43 f. 'sparsisque opibus
conuersa potestas | ipsaque maiestas auro corrupta iacebat'. In
language very like that used by Claudian here Calpurnius Siculus had
also heralded the return of the Golden Age (under Nero?) with a pre-
diction of the restoration of real consular elections and the proper

constitutional process: *Ecl.* 1. 69 ff. 'iam nec adumbrati faciem mercatus honoris | nec uacuos tacitus fasces et inane tribunal | accipiet consul; sed legibus omne reductis | ius aderit, moremque fori uultumque priorem | reddet et afflictum melior deus auferet aeuum.' Calpurnius speaks generally of the restoration of consular elections, but a significant parallel for the claim that an Emperor was scrupulous in observing legal form when presenting *himself* as a candidate for the office can be found in Pliny's panegryric of Trajan (*Pan.* 63): 'in primis . . . comitiis tuis interfuisti candidatus, non consulatus tantum sed immortalitatis et gloriae, et exempli quod sequerentur boni principes, mali mirarentur. uidit te populus Romanus in illa uetere potestatis suae sede; perpessus es longum illud carmen comitiorum nec iam inridendam moram consulque sic factus es ut unus ex nobis, quos facis consules.' Pliny's insistence on Trajan's not only holding *comitia* but personally attending the vote authorizes us to imagine Honorius taking a similar course of action: a free vote and a choice between rival candidates seems hardly likely, but it is hard to see how Claudian could make the claim he does if at least the formalities of the election process had not been observed. Any revival of old election customs for the occasion will of course have been intended to do honour to the People of Rome by indicating respect for them as the ultimate source of legitimate authority in the state. Comparable acts are Stilicho's reinstitution, at the beginning of the campaign against Gildo, of the Senate's privilege of formally declaring war (*Stil.* 1. 325 ff., esp. 328 f. 'neclectum Stilicho per tot iam saecula morem | rettulit') and of the right of the Senate and People to review the actions of magistrates in Africa at the end of their year of office (*Stil.* 3. 99 ff.). See Introd. n. 106.

Panegyrists have to be flexible, and tailor their praise to suit their circumstances. The more usual situation, and no doubt also the more usual way of dealing with it, can be exemplified by a passage from Ausonius' *gratiarum actio* to Gratian for his consulship: *Grat. Act.* 13 Green 'consul ego, imperator Auguste, munere tuo non passus saepta neque campum, non suffragia, non puncta, non loculos, qui non pressauerim manus nec salutantium confusus occursu aut sua amicis nomina non reddiderim, aut aliena imposuerim, qui tribus non circumiui, centurias non adulaui, uocatis classibus non intremui, nihil cum sequestre deposui, cum diribitore nil pepigi. Romanus populus, Martius campus, equester ordo, rostra, ouilia, senatus, curia—unus mihi omnia Gratianus'.

5 f. campus sollemnis et urna | luditur in morem: in effect both metonymy and hendiadys are at work here: = 'the yearly elections'.

The *comitia centuriata* traditionally met on the Campus Martius outside the *pomerium*, because the People were technically under arms, which is why they voted by century. Plain *campus* for *comitia* is a standard metonymy, featuring in Cicero's list of common examples at *de Orat.* 3. 167 'Cererem pro frugibus, Liberum appellare pro uino, Neptunum pro mari, curiam pro senatu, campum pro comitiis': cf. *Pis.* 2, Hor. *Carm.* 3. 1. 10 f. The *urna* is the voting urn in which the ballots were cast (Luc. 5. 394, *Stil.* 2. 363 f.). *in morem* = 'in the usual way', a phrase pioneered by Virgil (*A.* 5. 556, 8. 282: cf. *Cat.* 14. 10) but which never really established itself very securely in poetic diction. Claudian also experiments with plain *de more* (136). For the general phrasing cf. *IV Cons.* 612 f. 'sollemnia ludit | omina libertas', though there *ludit* has no negative connotation. For the phrasing cf. also Plin. *Pan.* 64. 1 'sollemnia comitiorum'.

6 f. As Müller sees, *dissona* should be taken with *species*, and *peregrina* with *imago*: this observes the standard rule against multiple epithets (Quint. *Inst.* 8. 6. 43 'duo uero uni adposita ne uersum quidem decuerint') and provides a pleasing balance of phrases. With *species nec dissona coetu* understand *est*.

Though the general sense is clear enough—this is no false show, but a real Roman election—pinpointing the full meaning is difficult. Platnauer's translation ('nor see we a consul of other race than his electors nor a foreigner claiming pretended rights') seems to stretch *species* uncomfortably far. The emphasis is very much on words that convey the idea of false appearances (*species*), deceptive brilliance (*nitet*) and imitation (*simulati, imago*), and perhaps we should therefore understand these phrases primarily as an amplification of *luditur in morem*. That is, here we have a real election conducted at Rome, not, as is the usual case, a mere pretence (*species*) that looks good (*nitet*) but jars with the dignity of the Roman People gathered in assembly to vote (*dissona coetu*), and not a consulship which, as a result of having been inaugurated somewhere other than Rome (*peregrina*), possesses only the appearance of an authority it pretends to (*simulati iuris imago*).

6. species: i.e. 'semblance', as opposed to the reality, and so balancing *imago*: see *OLD* s.v. 6 'the semblance . . . , illusory appearance'. Müller cites Cic. *ND* 2. 9 'ueritas auspiciorum spreta est, species tamen retenta', Tac. *Ann.* 15. 48 'claro apud uulgum rumore erat per uirtutem aut species uirtutibus similes'. Cf. also Calp. *Ecl.* 1. 69 'adumbrati *faciem* . . . honoris', of a sham election for the consulship, and 72 f. *'uultumque* priorem | reddet' of the restoration of real ones. The sense is made harder to establish beyond doubt because of the lack of a clarifying genitive (e.g. *comitiorum*).

dissona: i.e. 'not in harmony with', 'inappropriate to' (*OLD* s.v. 2 b). *dissonus* in this sense is found with *ab* at Liv. 8. 8. 2 'nihil apud Latinos dissonum ab Romana re praeter animos erat', and so, as Müller argues, *coetu* here may be a plain ablative, used rather freely. But the dative seems at least as likely, since what we have here is a metaphorical development of the sense *OLD* s.v. 1b 'sounding different from': *OLD* cites Stat. *Theb.* 8. 620 'uoxque illa tamen non dissona uerbis' and, more clearly, Maur. 116 'uocula dissona priori'. For a similarly ambiguous case see *Eutr.* 2. 42 f. 'dissona partu | semina'. At *Theod.* 249 f. 'dissona ritu | barbaries' and *Stil.* 1. 152 ff. 'certe nec tantis dissona linguis | turba', however, we have the ablative of respect: cf. Sil. 16. 19 f. 'tot dissona lingua | agmina'.

7. **peregrina:** contrasting with *indigenas* and *natiua* (8). Significantly the only other appearance of this word in Claudian is 'peregrina piacula', of Eutropius polluting the consulship (*Eutr.* 1. 431). Müller rightly compares this line with 650 f. (*annus) natus fonte suo, quem non aliena per arua | induit hospes honos*: a 'Roman' consulship inaugurated in a city other than its true home is nothing more than a foreigner.

    simulati iuris imago: for the phrasing cf. Cic. *Agr.* 2. 88, *Off.* 3. 69 'nos ueri iuris . . . solidam et expressam effigiem nullam tenemus, umbra et imaginibus utimur', Liv. 41. 8. 11 'postea his quoque imaginibus iuris spretis', Vell. 2. 30, Tac. *Ann.* 13. 28.

8 f. Cf. particularly *IV Cons.* 5 ff. 'cernis ut armorum proceres legumque potentes | patricios sumunt habitus et more Gabino | discolor incedit legio positisque parumper | bellorum signis sequitur vexilla Quirini?': cf. also 594–6 n. The idea is developed at length by Merobaudes, at *Pan.* 2. 30 ff. 'sic tranquilla togae recipit dum praemia ductor | pacatamque iubet lituos nescire curulem, | ipsa triumphales habitus mirantia passim | Bella dedere locum . . .'. For the essentially urban and senatorial nature of the consular *aduentus*, and the resulting symbolic importance attached to the toga, see MacCormack 58, 162.

8. **indigenas habitus:** primarily the toga, but perhaps also the consular vestments: cf. Hor. *S.* 2. 7. 54 'Romano . . . habitu' and see 594 *habituque Gabino* n. Once again the contrast can be drawn between Honorius' truly Roman consulship and the false one of Eutropius: *Eutr.* 1. 461 ff. 'eunuchi *uestros habitus*, insignia sumunt | ambigui *Romana* mares; rapuere tremendas | Hannibali Pyrrhoque *togas*'.

    natiua Palatia: *natiua* cannot be taken literally, since Honorius was born in Constantinople (80 f.); the phrase is pretty much on a par with *patriis laribus*, of the Palatine, at 603. The plural *Palatia* of the hill goes back to Virg. *G.* 1. 499 'Romana Palatia', and of the Imperial residence at least to Stat. *Silu.* 4. 1. 8 (Domitian's seventeenth consulship) 'subiere noui Palatia fasces', and Mart. 7. 28. 5: cf. 409 below. Platnauer translates 'the palace now our own', taking the phrase to refer to the Court's return to Rome. *Palatia* of course does double duty here, but given the insistence in the poem on the central importance of the Palatine hill itself (see *pr.* 23n.) a translation along the lines of 'our ancestral Palatine puts on its native garb' would be a little closer the mark: Emperor and Court (the *Palatini*), once more in the ancestral house of the Caesars on the Palatine, don the toga.

9. Quirinus (the deified Romulus) is the natural choice of bridge-builder between the citizenry of Rome and the Imperial forces, being not only the founder of the city but also a king who was closely associated by tradition with the army as his successor Numa was with the arts of peace; Liv. 1. 21. 6 'ita duo . . . reges, . . . ille (sc. Romulus) bello, hic (sc. Numa) pace, ciuitatem auxerunt', *IV Cons.* 492f.

patriis . . . castris: Müller takes this as a reference to the *cohortes urbanae*, arguing that Stilicho must have enlisted their aid in the campaign and that they are now returning to the city. This is over-ingenious and too specific. *patriis* here is parallel to *indigenas* (8) and means no more than 'Roman' or 'national': Quirinus is uniting the People of Rome with the Roman (i.e. Imperial) army in the universal patriotic rejoicing of the day.

10. Augusta . . . suffragia: the senses 'imperial suffrage' (Platnauer, i.e. voting for the Emperor) and 'venerable elections' are both present here. The adjective is the first of several etymologically related words that emphasize the idea of renewal and growth under the favour of Heaven (*inaugurat* 12; *Augusti* 17; *auget* 24: cf. the *auspicia* that underlie *auibus* 12). The link between these words was understood in antiquity and is explained at length by Ovid at *Fast.* 1. 609ff. 'sancta uocant augusta patres, augusta uocantur | templa sacerdotum rite dicata manu; | huius et augurium dependet origine uerbi, | et quodcumque sua Iuppiter auget ope. | augeat imperium nostri ducis, augeat annos, | protegat et uestras querna corona fores, | auspicibusque deis tanti cognominis heres | omine suscipiat, quo pater, orbis onus.' For the *figura etymologica* compare Enn. *Ann.* 155 Skutsch 'augusto augurio'. See further Skutsch on Enn. *Ann.* 73 'auspicio augurioque', Fordyce on Virg. *A.* 7. 153 'augusta ad moenia' (Servius explains *augusta* ad loc. as 'augurio consecrata'). *suffragia* is too technical-sounding a word to be common in poetry, but cf. Ov. *Fast.* 5. 633, Luc. 5. 393, Sil. 15. 734. Its sense here is that of *OLD* s.v. 2, 'the action of voting' or more generally 'elections'.

11f. A year inaugurated in Rome itself can be expected to be an *annus mirabilis*. The idea of renewal is continued in the allusion to the famous augury of the twelve vultures seen by Romulus at the founding of Rome. Ennius (*Ann.* 72 ff. Skutsch) has Romulus receive this augury from a position on the Aventine, but the commoner version placed him on the Palatine (*mons Euandrius, Romanis auibus*). By Claudian's time there was a well-established belief that the twelve vultures foretold twelve *saecula* of existence for the city (Censorinus, *De Die Natali* 17. 15 where Varro is said to have recorded this interpretation, which he attributes to Vettius). Claudian claims that Alaric's invasion led to fearful, if premature, speculation that the twelve *saecula* had expired and Rome was doomed (*Get.* 265 f.). Against such a background of apocalyptic terror disproved by the victory at Pollentia Claudian may be hinting that Honorius' sixth consulship will be marked by a similar augury renewing the one received by Romulus. Cf. the twelve vultures said to have appeared to Augustus when he took the auspices in his first consular year (Suet. *Aug.* 95, 'ut Romulo'), and also *IV Cons.* 141 ff. 'quae tunc documenta futuri! | quae uoces auium! quanti per inane uolatus!', at the birth of Honorius.

11. mons Euandrius: the Palatine, where tradition asserted that Evander and his Arcadians had built Pallanteum, the first settlement on the site of Rome (Liv. 1. 7. 3, Virg. *A.* 8. 51 ff., with Fordyce ad loc.: note 644 *Pallanteus apex*) and where Evander entertained Aeneas as his guest in his humble hut (*A.* 8. 359 ff.). The phrase is one of several links this passage has with Statius' poem on the seventeenth consulship of Domitian: *Silu.* 4. 1. 7 f. 'plusque ante alias Euandrius arces | collis ouet'. *Euandrius* first appears at Virg. *A.* 10. 394: cf. also Sil. 7. 18 'regna Euandria' (i.e. Rome), 13. 816, Prud. *C. Symm.* 1. 550 'Euandria curia'. The use of an adjective formed from a proper name in place of the genitive is a feature of high poetry from Homer on: see Löfstedt, *Syntactica*, i. 107–24 Austin on Virg. *A.* 2. 543, Fordyce on *A.* 7. 1, Nisbet–Hubbard on Hor. *Carm.* 1. 3. 36, Harrison on Virg. *A.* 10. 156 'Aeneia puppis'. Note also *Iuleos* (116), *Diomedeis* (479). The general effect here is to evoke 'associations of venerable antiquity' (Coleman on Stat. *Silu.* 4. 1. 7 f.).

12. The wording is broadly similar to Pacatus' address to Theodosius, *Pan. Theod.* 3. 1 'det igitur mihi sermonis huius auspicium ille felicitatis publicae auspex dies qui te primus inaugurauit imperio'.

auibus: = *auspiciis*, as often: e.g. Cic. *Leg.* 3. 9 'isque (dictator) aue sinistra dictus', Hor. *Carm.* 1. 15. 5 'mala ducis aui domum', with Nisbet–Hubbard ad loc., Prop. 4. 1. 40, Ov. *Met.* 15. 640 'ite bonis auibus', *Stil.* 2. 364; also *III Cons.* 8 f. 'secundis | alitibus'. See also Jebb on Soph. *OT* 52 for the similar use of ὄρνις.

Thybris: for the Greek form see Williams on Virg. *A.* 3. 500.

Claudian shows an overwhelming preference for it (18 ×, including 365, 425, 486, 520, 641). By contrast substantival *Tiberinus* is found only at *Prob.* 209.

inaugurat: another word far too technical-sounding to be much used in high poetry, though cf. Pl. *As.* 259. One can also speak of the consul, rather than the year, being inaugurated: Amp. 19. 11 'Scipio Nasica: qui, cum (L. A. Holford-Strevens, *Gnomon*, 67 (1995), 601) non rite inauguratus consul uideretur, consulatu se abdicauit'.

13–15. A development of the idea introduced at *IV Cons.* 619ff. 'prospera Romuleis sperantur tempora rebus | in nomen uentura tuum. praemissa futuris | dant exempla fidem: quotiens te cursibus anni | praefecit, totiens accessit laurea patri', and esp. 638ff. 'sed patriis olim fueras successibus auctor, | nunc eris ipse tuis. semper uenere triumphi | cum trabeis sequiturque tuos uictoria fasces.' In particular, the audience could recall the defeat of Gildo during Honorius' fourth consulship (398) and, of course, the victory at Pollentia during his fifth (402).

13f. quamquam . . . dederint: the subjunctive with *quamquam* in clauses of fact had become regular by the time of Tacitus. Woodcock (245) suggests this was done 'on the analogy of the subjunctive in generalizing clauses after *quisquis* etc.', but the regular use of the subjunctive with *quamuis* seems a more likely cause (cf. LHS ii. 602).

13. cognominis: *cognomen* rather than plain *nomen* is commonly found in contexts of aetiological and similar matters to convey the sense 'significant name' or ἔτυμον/αἴτιον: see Fordyce on Virg. *A.* 7. 671 'Tiburti dictam cognomine gentem' and cf. *A.* 1. 530, 8. 330ff., Prop. 4. 4. 93 'a duce Tarpeia mons est cognomen adeptus', Luc. 4. 656, *Eutr.* 2. 243, *Get.* 555. For the *consul ordinarius* 'giving his name' to the year see further 17 *numine* n.

14. inoffensum . . . successibus omen: Platnauer's translation ('rich in omens of success') fudges the difficulties of this phrase and fails to account adequately for *inoffensum*. Artaud, digesting earlier commentators' suggestions, offers two alternative interpretations. The first is that the phrase is equivalent to 'non turbatum ab euentu', but *inoffensum*, with its strong physical sense of 'not stumbled over', seems to require something with a sharper focus than *turbatum*. More significantly, parallels for *successus* in the neutral sense of 'event, occurrence' are hard to come by, the implication regularly being 'success in an undertaking' or 'successful outcome' (*OLD* s.v.). More promising is Artaud's second suggestion '(the years named by Honorius) habuerunt successus non offensos, sed respondentes ominibus, seu auspiciis felicibus, seu felicitati speratae', which takes *inoffensum* as a transferred usage from *successibus*. This is clearly roughly what Claudian means to say—all the years in which Honorius has held the consulship have been marked by favourable omens, and the omens have been fulfilled by the successes that followed—but still leaves *inoffensum* rather colourless. The answer is perhaps to take this as a compressed reference to the old superstition about stumbling in doorways being an omen of ill fortune: the years have all given an omen for success (taking *successibus* as a 'dative of the end aimed at', Woodcock 67) which has 'not been stumbled over' and thus invalidated. For *inoffensum* see further Harrison on Virg. *A.* 10. 292, McKeown on Ov. *Am.* 1. 6. 8 (Amor) 'inoffensos derigit ille pedes'.

15. secures: bound with the *fasces* and so part of the magistrate's emblems of power: see Ogilvie on Liv. 1. 7–2. 2, 1. 8. 2. Metonymical or symbolic applications of the term appear frequently in poetry: e.g. Virg. *A.* 6. 819f. (Brutus) 'consulis imperium hic primus saeuasque securis | accipiet', Hor. *Carm.* 3. 2. 19f., Prop. 1. 6. 19, 3. 11. 47, *III Cons.* 6 'Latiae redeant ad signa secures', *Theod.* 338, *Stil.* 3. 201, *VI Cons.* 647.

16f. Take *promittitur* closely with *felix* in the next line: this year 'promises to be blessed' beyond all others (*ante omnes*) as a result of its wondrous beginning (*miro . . . ortu*, ablative of cause). Cf. Florus 1. 1 (1. 16) 'clarum fore uisa circa caput flamma promiserat', 2. 17 (4. 7) 'meliora . . . omnia aues uictimaeque promiserant'. Alternatively one could understand e.g. *praestare* with *ante omnes* and punctuate with a comma after *ortu*.

17. numine: both Rome and the Emperor are divine, and the year is thus doubly blessed by the protective influence of Heaven. The beneficent influence of Honorius' divine presence appears again at 365 and 611f. For the *numen* of the living Emperor cf. Vitr. 1. *pr.* 1 'diuina tua mens et numen, imperator Caesar', Luc. 1. 63, *III Cons.* 20f. (Honorius' birth) 'numen confessa . . . | Meroe'.

The alternative reading *nomine* may at first sight seem attractive, because, in the *fasti*, the year bore the name of its consuls: see 13, 659f. *magno sextus tamen iste superbit | nomine*, Prob. 204, 267 'o consanguineis felix auctoribus annus', *Stil.* 2. 474, Luc. 5. 5. But though the year will be entered in the *fasti* under the name of the Augustus, it will not bear the name of Rome ('*urbis et* Augusti'). *numine* also provides a neat introduction to the concept of the Emperor as a star (18–25) and to the comparison with Apollo (25–38). Note further the ring-composition with 656 *ceu numen adorent* (sc. 'hunc annum anni omnes'). For confusion of *numen* and *nomen* in the manuscripts cf. 365 *uicino numine* n.

felix: *felicitas* is a regular slogan of late Imperial propaganda, and innumerable coins proclaim the advent or assurance of *felicitas Romanorum* or *temporum felicitas* under the legitimate rule of the Emperor: see MacCormack 32f., 191, 218. Most significant here, however, are a number of coins bearing the legend vrbs roma felix and the names of Arcadius, Honorius and Theodosius II, an issue almost certainly connected with Honorius' present visit: see Alan Cameron, *HSChP* 73 (1969), 258. Alaric, on the other hand, was only *felix* until he made the mistake of invading Italy (278). Note the same insistence on this theme at the end of the poem; 640 (Janus) *nouum fastis aperit felicibus annum.* The year 395, after the defeat of Eugenius' usurpation, is similarly welcomed with the words 'uotis communibus felix annus aperitur' at *C. Th.* 7. 24. 1. Cf. further *Stil.* 3. 51 'o felix, seruata uocat quem Roma parentem!', *Get.* 636 (Pollentia) 'felicibus apta triumphis': for *felix* of years cf. Tib. 2. 5. 82, *Ciris* 27, *Culex* 40, *Prob.* 267.

18–25. Claudian appears to mean that, just as astrological lore maintains that benevolent stars are at their most influential for the good when they are at the zenith (20f. *summo . . . cardine* n.), so too the omens for Italy are most propitious when Honorius, the Empire's own star, returns to his proper position, Rome. The same essential idea probably informs Lucan's infamous praise of Nero, in which the Emperor is imagined, after the model of Virg. *G.* 1. 24ff., undergoing καταστερισμός and being asked to shine down on Rome directly: Luc. 1. 53ff. 'sed neque in Arctoo sedem tibi legeris orbe | nec polus auersi calidus qua uergitur Austri, | unde tuam uideas obliquo sidere Romam'. In fact, the standard view was that it was from its ὕψωμα (*altitudo*, 'exaltation') that a planet exercised this power. Perhaps Claudian has confused, or attempted to conflate, the passage of Lucan just cited with another from the same book, so that *summo . . . cardine* might be seen as a mistaken variation on the *summo . . . caelo* of Luc. 1. 651; for the ambiguity of this phrase see Housman, edn. of Lucan, p. 326. Some heavenly bodies, principally Jupiter, Venus, and Mercury, were regarded by astrologers as generally bestowing the benefits of prosperity and peace when in the ascendant, but others, notably Saturn and Mars, were held to be harbingers of evils such as disease, famine, and war. Lucan also exploits this set of categories at length in a speech attributed to the astrologer Nigidius Figulus at the beginning of the Civil War (Luc. 1. 639ff., esp. 660ff.). See also Firmicius Junior 2. 3 'altitudines . . . in opportunis geniturae locis homines faciunt beatos . . . hac ex causa Babylonii ea signa in quibus stellae exaltantur, domicilia earum esse uoluerunt'. The simile naturally implies that Honorius too is a 'health-giving star': cf. Amm.

Marc. 21. 10. 2 (Julian in Illyricum, AD 361) 'per alias quoque ciuitates ut sidus salutare susciperetur', 22. 9. 14 (Julian's *aduentus* in Antioch, AD 362).

Astrology as a 'science' might be regarded as the natural child of astronomy: both originated in ancient Mesopotamia (cf. 18 *Babylonia cura* n.) and spread from there into the Graeco-Roman world largely through the intermediary of Hellenistic Egypt. It seems to have established itself in Rome in the 2nd c. BC, where it aroused the hostility of conservatives such as Cato. Indeed, Valerius Maximus (1. 3. 3) records the expulsion of astrologers by law from the city in 139 BC. It gradually gained a following, however, even with such usually pragmatic-minded men as Vitruvius (9. 6. 2), and certain individuals, notably Tiberius' court astrologer Thrasyllus, came to wield enormous influence. More rationalist spirits remained staunchly opposed, most notably the Elder Pliny (*Nat.* 2. 23) and Juvenal, who inveighs with scathing sarcasm against the credulity of women devotees (6. 553 ff.). By Claudian's time, the Emperors had long been associated with the cult of the *Sol Inuictus* (cf. 23 *imperii sidus* n.), and this must have gone some considerable way towards countering the general hostility of the Church to the practice of astrology as an affront to divine providence. Franz Cumont, *Astrology and Religion among the Greeks and Romans* (1912: repr. New York, 1960), remains a useful guide. See also Elizabeth Rawson, *Intellectual Life in the Late Roman Republic* (Baltimore, 1985), 306 ff.

For Claudian's similes see the full discussions in C. Günther, *De Claudii Claudiani Comparationibus* (diss. Erlangen, 1894) and P. Christiansen, *The Use of Images by Claudius Claudianus* (The Hague, 1969); also Gruzelier, p. xxiii. In general he tends to work with established material, drawn especially from nature and mythology. There are, however, a notably high proportion dealing with stars and ships, from which some scholars have been tempted to suggest that he is drawing directly on personal experience from a life largely spent in port cities (e.g. Günther, 37). In the present poem note 25–34, 132–40, 259–64, 324–30, 333–50, 470–90, and 523–8. The most striking are probably those comparing Alaric to a crippled pirate-ship (132–40) and to a distraught bee-keeper (259–64).

18. stellas . . . salubres: for both the language and the flattery cf. Hor. *S.* 1. 7. 24 f. (Persius) 'solem Asiae Brutum appellat, stellasque salubris | appellat comites'; also Luc. 1. 661 f. 'Venerisque salubre | sidus'.

Babylonia cura: for the Babylonian origins of astrology see in particular Cumont, op. cit. 18–25 n., pp. 3 ff. and Vitruvius 9. 2. 1, 8. 1 (on Berosus). Astrologers were most commonly called *Chaldaei*: Cic.

Mur. 25 'a quibus . . . dies tamquam a Chaldaeis petebatur', Juv. 6. 553, *Ruf.* 1. 148 (with Levy, who cites Hsch. s.v. Χαλδαῖοι· γένος μάγων πάντα γιγνωσκόντων), *IV Cons.* 147: cf. 348 *Chaldaea mago . . . carmina ritu.* Cf. also Lucr. 5. 727 'Babylonica Chaldaeum doctrina', Hor. *Carm.* 1. 11. 2 f., and, for Claudian's phrase here, above all Luc. 6. 428 f. 'quis . . . Assyria scrutetur sidera cura'. At Honorius' birth 'inspectis Babylonius inhorruit astris' (*IV Cons.* 146). Occasionally Claudian's native Egypt is spoken of as the home of astronomy and/or astrology: see esp. *Theod.* 126 ff. (Iustitia finds Mallius Theodorus calculating the movements of the stars) 'inuenit aetherios signantem puluere cursus, | quos pia sollicito deprendit pollice Memphis'.

Müller glosses *cura* here as *studium, ars*: see *TLL* iv. 1462. 44 ff. and cf. *Get.* 121 'Paeoniae . . . sollertia curae', of medicine. *cura* is a reasonable word to use of a system of knowledge requiring long training and great precision and skill: the development of this sense can be discerned in such passages as Cic. *Div.* 1. 93 'etenim Aegyptii et Babylonii . . . omnem curam in siderum cognitione posuerunt'.

19. spondet: cf. Virg. *A.* 12. 637, Ov. *Ib.* 213 f. 'nec quicquam placidum spondentia Martis | sidera', Suet. *Otho* 4. 1, *Eutr.* 2. 57, *Get.* 267 f. 'solus erat Stilicho, qui desperantibus augur | sponderet meliora manu'.

20. The effect of the alliteration of *c* and *l* is hard to pin-point, but must be deliberate, especially given the similar context of *pr.* 16 *circumfusi sacra corona chori.* Is it too fanciful to think of the hard glittering of the stars? At any rate, it draws the audience's attention through emphasis.

caelicolae . . . celsa tenent: cf. Apul. *Pl.* 1. 11 'astra . . . ceteraque numina, quos caelicolas nominamus'. Though the word is rarely applied to stars, it is intelligible readily enough, especially since, of course, it is so commonly used of Jupiter, Mars, etc. in their anthropomorphic guise. The general phrasing here is close to Virg. *A.* 6. 787 'omnis caelicolas, omnis supera alta tenentis'.

20 f. summo . . . | cardine: i.e. the zenith. See *OLD* s.v. *cardo* 4 b, citing Luc. 9. 528 f. 'hic quoque nil obstat Phoebo, cum cardine summo | stat librata dies', Stat. *Theb.* 2. 236 'supero . . . cardine lapsae.' See also 96 n.

21. humili statione: *humili* is in contrast with both *summo cardine* and *sublimis* (22): for the contrast cf. Sen. *Nat.* 1. 3. 11 '(imago solis) numquam non aduersa soli est sublimis aut humilis.' Though the stars and planets are in constant motion, at any one moment they appear to the naked eye to be stationary, hence *statio* is used of the position of a star in the sky: Lucr. 4. 391 ff. 'sidera cessare aetheriis adfixa cauernis | cuncta uidentur, et assiduo sunt omnia motu, | solque pari ratione manere et luna uidentur | in statione', Plin. *Nat.* 2. 61, 70 '(sc. stellae errantes) existimantur stare, unde et nomen accepit statio'. For this quasi-technical sense of *statio* cf. Vitr. 9. 1. 6, Ov. *Met.* 2. 115 'Lucifer . . . caeli statione nouissimus exit', Plin. *Nat.* 2. 59, 61.

retundunt: metaphorically 'blunt', i.e. by widening the angle: the idea and the language parallel Luc. 1. 54f. 'nec polus auersi calidus qua uergitur Austri, | unde tuam uideas *obliquo sidere* Romam.' Though *retundo* is unusual in such contexts, light, and therefore vision, are often spoken of in terms of 'sharpness' (hence *acies*) or 'bluntness', e.g. Cic. *Fin.* 4. 65 'hebes acies est cuipiam oculorum', *Tusc.* 3. 33 'hebetem facit aciem ad miserias contemplandas', Lucr. 4. 359, Plin. *Nat.* 2. 150. Claudian himself provides an example at 51f. *acies* . . . . | *circumfuso trepidans obtunditur auro*, though there the sense of the verb is rather more specialized. Cf. also Lucr. 4. 355 'angulus obtusus quia longe cernitur omnis', Agen. *agrim.* p. 31 'anguli, non tantum recti uerum etiam hebetes aut acuti'. *retundo* can also be used metaphorically to mean 'weaken' as at Sen. *Con.* 10 *pr.* 16 'diligentiam, qua uires ingenii sui ex industria retundit', a sense also appropriate here where the beneficent power of the stars is imagined as being enfeebled by their position. *recondunt* has sufficient manuscript authority to warrant some consideration. This is especially so, given that citing *obtunditur* (52) in defence of *retundunt* here might rebound upon us: the objection could be made that one had arisen from the other. None the less *retundunt* seems on balance to offer preferable sense: when a star is in *humili statione* its rays are not *recti* as they strike the earth, but *retunsi/obtunsi*, 'blunted': they are not, however, entirely 'hidden'.

22. Signifer: the Zodiac: see Pease on Cic. *ND* 2. 53 'signiferum orbem', and cf. Cic. *Arat.* 317ff. 'Zodiacum hunc Graeci uocitant nostrique Latini | orbem signiferum perhibebunt nomine uero: | nam gerit hic uoluens bis sex ardentia signa'. For *Signifer* as a substantive cf. e.g. Sen. *Nat.* 7. 18, 24, Plin. *Nat.* 2. 30, 38, *Prob.* 241, *Ruf.* 1. 365, *Stil.* 1. 145, *Rapt.* 1. 102. Müller ingeniously interprets *Signifer* here as a flattering reference with double sense to Stilicho as both the 'standard-bearer' of Rome (because he leads the Imperial army) and as the Zodiac which has brought the 'star of the Empire' (= Honorius) to its proper place (= Rome).

23. imperii sidus: the image of the divine ruler as a star, and especially as the sun, was of immemorial antiquity and came to Roman political thought and panegyrical writing through the Hellenistic world from the ruler-cults of the ancient Near East. An early Hellenistic example is Hermocles' hymn to Demeter (11f. Powell). In the hot-house atmosphere of Ptolemaic Alexandrian encomium even a lock of hair could become a star if it came from the head of a Queen (Call. *Aet.* fr. 110 Pfeiffer: Catul. 66). The popular belief that the murdered Julius Caesar had risen to Heaven in the form of the *sidus Iulium*, confirmed by his formal deification by the Senate, gave an unstoppable impetus to the employment of such imagery, which is regularly applied to all the Emperors who follow: among countless possible examples see e.g. Virg. *A.* 8. 680f., Prop. 4. 6. 59, Ov. *Met.* 15. 843ff. (Julius); Virg. *G.* 1. 24ff., Hor. *Carm.* 4. 2. 46f., Man. 1. 384f. (Augustus); Man. 4. 763ff. (Tiberius); Luc. 1. 45ff., *Buc. Eins.* 1. 22ff. (Nero); Stat. *Silu.* 1. 1. 94ff., 4. 1. 3f., 4. 2. 42 (and Coleman ad loc.), Mart. 9. 101. 22 (the Flavians, esp. Domitian). For its use in the context of an *aduentus* cf. esp. Suet. *Cal.* 13 'densissimo et laetissimo obuiorum agmine incessit, super fausta nomina "sidus" et "pullum" et "pupum" et "alumnum" appellantium'. In Claudian's poetry the star imagery is used most frequently of Theodosius: see 101ff. nn., and cf. *Ruf.* 2. 1ff. 'iam post edomitas Alpes defensaque regna | Hesperiae merita conplexus sede parentem | auctior adiecto fulgebat sidere mundus', *IV Cons.* 428f., *Gild.* 253, and the lavish description of Theodosius' καταστερισμός at *III Cons.* 162ff., with its close links to the proems of both Virgil's *Georgics* and Lucan's *De Bello Ciuili*. See also *III Cons.* 131f. (Theodosius with the infant Honorius) 'quis non Luciferum roseo cum Sole uideri | credidit?', with which compare Virg. *A.* 8. 587 ff. Note, however, that Claudian had promised the same fate to patrons who were private citizens, the young sons of Probus, a pair presented as a second Castor and Pollux (*Prob.* 240ff.): so too Ov. *Pont.* 3. 3. 2 'o sidus Fabiae, Maxime, gentis'. Here it is worth remembering that in poetry the beautiful and the young had long been 'stars', and that the imagery is thus doubly appropriate to the teenage Emperor: note e.g. Call. *Aet.* 4 fr. 67. 5ff. Pf., esp. 8 (Acontius and Cydippe) καλοὶ νησάων ἀστέρες ἀμφότεροι, Mus. 22. Note also *Theod.* 266 'sidereusque gener', *VI Cons.* 539 'principis et solis radiis'.

By Late Antiquity such language was so regular a part of Imperial encomium that Menander Rhetor specifically instructs the orator to make use of it (378. 11f.=p. 94 Russell–Wilson) ὥσπερ ἡλίου φαιδρά τις ἀκτὶς ἄνωθεν ἡμῖν ὀφθεῖσα, 381. 12=p. 100 ἀστέρα φανότατον ὀνομάζοντες), stressing its value as a means of expressing public joy at a grandee's arrival. For Menander it is thus particularly appropriate in an ἐπιβατήριος (cf. MacCormack 20f.), but it is naturally not out of place in other Imperial panegyrics, and so, for example, Corippus' panegyric on Justin is saturated with it (e.g. 1. 353f., 2. 148ff., 4. 99ff., 251ff.). The association of many 3rd- and 4th-c. Emperors with sun-worshipping cults such as that of the *Sol Inuictus* will no doubt have helped the spread of such topoi. See further Cumont, *Astrology and Religion* (18–25 n.), 20 f., 54 ff., MacCormack 45 ff., Christiansen 28 ff.

For the phrase *imperii sidus* cf. especially *IV Cons.* 182 (at Honorius' being created Augustus) 'imperii lux illa fuit', Cor. *Laud. Iust.* 1. 353 'decus imperii'.

propria . . . sede locauit: answering in advance, as it were, Roma's question to Honorius at 407 f. *quem, precor, ad finem laribus seiuncta potestas | exulat imperiumque suis a sedibus errat?* Although *sedes* is used of the position of a star in the sky often enough (Ov. *Met.* 15. 839, Luc. 1. 53, *Ruf.* 1. 365, 2. 2), here it is equally appropriate to the Imperial residence on the Palatine. For the line-ending cf. Virg. *A.* 2. 525 'sacra longaeuum in sede locauit', Cor. *Laud. Iust. pr.* 20 'summaque in sede locauit'. Müller sees *propria* as being equivalent to *sua*, a common late Latin usage (see 81 *propria* n.). The distinction is often very fine, but the 'true', classical sense is perhaps more suited to the context: the Zodiac places the star of Empire back in its own, 'appropriate' position, the one where it 'properly belongs'.

24. auget: with overtones of 'blessing' as well as 'increasing': cf. Tac. *Ann.* 2. 14 'auctus omine', and see 10 *Augusta . . . suffragia*, 660 *auctor* nn.

surgunt: like plants, growing from the fruitful soil of Rome.

25–38. *As at Delphi the oracle exultantly springs back into life when Apollo returns from the land of the Hyperboreans, so the majesty of the Palatine too is enhanced by the return of Honorius.*

25–9. The Hyperboreans were believed to live in Scythia, beyond the lands of the one-eyed Arimaspians and the griffins (Hdt. 4. 13), and no doubt featured prominently in Aristeas' lost epic, the *Arimaspea*. Theirs was a life of joyous feasting, free from sickness, old age, toil and war (Pind. *Pyth.* 10. 29 ff.). See in general *Der Kleine Pauly* ii. 1274. 40 ff., J. D. P. Bolton, *Aristeas of Proconnesus* (Oxford, 1962), index s.v. Hyperboreans. They have a very well-attested mythological connection with Apollo, who was believed to possess a great temple in their mysterious northern homeland, in which it was his custom to spend the winter. This link with Apollo is perhaps best known through Herodotus' account of the mysterious offerings sent to Delos, and of Hyperoche and Laodice, two Hyperborean maidens commemorated there in rites of mourning (4. 32 ff.): the custom also appears in the *Aetia* of Callimachus, for which see Bolton, op. cit. 23. Delphi was similarly, if more loosely, associated with them from very early times, and Himerius (*Or.* 48. 10 f.) gives a prose summary of a paean by Alcaeus which bears a strong resemblance to the present passage. It

relates how Apollo, soon after his birth, was sent by Zeus to the land
of the Hyperboreans on a chariot drawn by swans, and lived there for
a whole year, dispensing justice (cf. 36f.n.). The Delphians learned of
this and sang paeans and songs to attract the young god: Apollo
ordered the swans to take him to Delphi, and on his arrival in mid-
summer he was joyfully greeted by singing nightingales and by
Castalia flowing with silver stream while Enipeus rose in flood to meet
him. Further traces of this tradition appear at Apollonius Rhodius, at
2. 674f., where the Argonauts see the god on his way from Lycia to the
Hyperboreans, and 4. 611f., where a picturesque aetiology for amber
attributes to the Celts the belief that it came from the tears shed by
Apollo when he retreated to the land of the Hyperboreans in sorrow
at the death of his son by Coronis (contrast 164n.). See further Pind.
P. 10., 42ff., Diod. Sic. 2. 47, Cic. *ND* 3. 57, and Pausanias 10. 5. 7–9,
who mentions a hymn by one Boeo, a woman of Delphi, recording
the very foundation of the oracle by τοὺς ἀφικομένους ἐξ Ὑπερ-
βορέων.

Claudian's comparison continues the idea of Honorius as the
sun (22–4), and does further honour to Rome and the Palatine as a
place sacred to the gods and as a source of *oracula*: moreover both
Honorius and Apollo have come from the north (land of the
Hyperboreans/Ravenna). Like Alcaeus Claudian stresses the joy of
nature at the god's return. These myths connecting Apollo with the
Hyperboreans seem to have been much in Claudian's mind at this
time, and have left their mark on *Stil*. 3. 256 'Hyperboreis Delos
praelata pruinis' and more particularly 3. 58ff. 'quae numine tanto |
litora fatidicas attollunt Delia laurus, | uenturi quotiens adfulsit
Apollinis arcus?', where the same ideas of return and of epiphany
appear, almost as if in a kind of preparatory sketch for the present
lines.

25. **pulcher Apollo:** subtly echoed at 455f. g*elida cum pulcher ab Arcto* |
aduentat Stilicho, allowing the attentive reader there to put Claudian's
real patron on an equal footing with both Emperor and sun-god. For
the attribute applied to Apollo cf. Virg. *A*. 3. 119 (but see Servius ad
loc.), Calp. *Ecl*. 4. 57, and see G. Wissowa, *Religion und Kultus der Römer*
(Munich, 1912; repr. 1971), 294n. 6. Note also *Fesc*. 1. 1 'princeps
corusco sidere pulchrior'.

26. **lustrat . . . aras:** with *aras* the primary sense of the verb is that
Apollo ritually 'moves in procession around' his shrine in the land of
the Hyperboreans and so 'purifies' it, but as sun-god he also 'casts
light' over it. The latter, metaphorical sense seems in any case to have
developed from the application to the sun of the idea of a purificatory

procession moving over a given area: cf. Cic. *Arat.* 92 'Delphinus iacet haud nimio lustratu' nitore', *Rep.* 6. 17, Lucr. 5. 693, 6. 737 'radiis sol omnia lustrans', Virg. *A.* 4. 6 'postera Phoebea lustrabat lampade terras', with Austin ad loc., Ov. *Met.* 5. 464, *Rapt.* 2. *pr.* 48, *Rapt.* 3. 316 with Gruzelier.

The sense of the sun travelling which is thus often present in *lustro*, the description of Delphi as 'lying idle' (*cessantibus*, 26), and the insistence in the Alcaeus poem discussed above that Apollo's return from the land of the Hyperboreans takes place in summer, naturally lead one to think that Claudian is talking about the change in the seasons: it is winter when Apollo leaves Delphi, summer when he returns. This indeed may be the fundamental idea behind the whole connection between Apollo and the Hyperboreans, who are thus conceived in terms analogous to standard descriptions of the Antipodeans. If so, the image is a wholly poetic one, since of course the sun in reality moves (or rather, appears to move) north in summer from the Equator towards the tropic of Cancer, bringing summer to Delphi and Scythia at the same time. This line must in any case be considered in combination with Roma's appeal to Honorius to return to the City, which is the centre of the world (407 ff.). She advances the argument that the whole world may be safely ruled from there just as Phoebus lights all things without ever deviating from his central pathway through the sky: 411 f. *medium non deserit umquam | caeli Phoebus iter, radiis tamen omnia lustrans.* Whether in Delphi or Scythia, then, Apollo presumably never moves out of the 'medium caeli iter'. But as the lines that precede this comparison reminded us, a star or the sun is at its most beneficent when shining from *directly* above, hence the joy of Delphi at Apollo's return to the very centre and the parallel effect on the Palatine of the presence of Honorius.

Delphis cessantibus: in the absence of the god, Delphi lacks his literal inspiration and so can give no oracles: it is thus 'idle' or 'on holiday', or perhaps might be thought of as 'lying fallow' (*OLD* s.v. 4c). Cf. also Prop. 3. 13. 47f. 'at nunc desertis cessant sacraria lucis: | aurum omnes uicta iam pietate colunt', Ov. *Met.* 8. 277 f., of shrines neglected by impious humans.

In reality the oracle at Delphi had fallen into disuse centuries before Claudian's day. Cicero notes that by his time it gave no true oracles, and had not done so for a long time (*Diu.* 1. 37 f., 2. 117): he speculates on the possibility that the power of the shrine's divine exhalations may have simply dried up like a river. The *locus classicus* on this subject, however, is Plut. *De Defectu Oraculorum* 414A–C. Note also Lucan's sardonic account of Appius' consultation of the oracle: 5. 64 ff., especially 68 ff. 'finemque expromere rerum | sollicitat superos multosque obducta per annos | Delphica fatidici reserat penetralia Phoebi': when the Sibyl fakes inspiration Lucan comments 'sensit tripodas *cessare* . . . Appius' (5. 157 f.). See in general H. W. Parke and D. E. Wormell, *The Delphic Oracle* (Oxford, 1956), i. 287 ff., Pease on Cic. *Diu.* 1. 38; also Gruzelier on *Rapt.* 2. 246. If the reasons for the obsolescence of the most famous and prestigious oracle in the ancient world made a lively subject for contentious speculation in the times of Cicero and Lucan, by the fifth century an extra edge had entered the debate with the advent of Christianity. A tradition developed that maintained that the oracles had been rendered obsolescent by the fulfilment of history through the birth of Christ: e.g. Prud. *Apoth.* 435 ff. 'ex quo mortalem praestrinxit Spiritus aluum . . . atque hominem de uirginitate creauit, | Delphica damnatis tacuerunt sortibus antra, | non tripodas cortina regit, non spumat anhelus | fata Sibyllinis fanaticus edita libris. | perdidit insanos mendax Dodona uapores, | mortua iam mutae lugent oracula Cumae, | nec responsa refert Libycis in Syrtibus Hammon', Milton, *On The Morning of Christ's Nativity* 173 f. 'The oracles are dumb, | No voice or hideous hum | Runs through the arched roof in words deceiving. | Apollo from his shrine | Can no more divine, | With hollow shriek the steep of Delphos leaving.' Ammianus Marcellinus claims that, only about forty years before this poem was written, Julian had considered reviving Delphi (22. 12. 8). It is thus possible to read Claudian's exuberant picture of the reawakening of the Delphic shrine here as a contribution to the religious polemic of his day. Even more suggestive is Claudian's claim that at the birth of Honorius the oracles were in fact revived: *IV Cons.* 143 f. 'tibi corniger Hammon | et dudum taciti rupere silentia Delphi'. See further 30–4 n., and note also *III Cons.* 117 f. (at the *aduentus* of Honorius) 'celsaque Dodone stupuit rursusque locutae | in te Chaoniae mouerunt carmina quercus.' Elsewhere Claudian imagines Delphi falling silent in mourning for the abducted Proserpina (*Rapt.* 2. 246), a conceit borrowed from Statius' account of Apollo's grief at the swallowing of his favourite seer Amphiaraus by the earth during the Theban War (*Theb.* 9. 513, 657 f.).

27. Castaliae . . . undae: the *fons Castalius* at the foot of Mt Parnassus, famous for its prophetic and inspirational power: cf. Stat. *Theb.* 8. 175 f. 'hoc antra lacusque | Castalii tripodumque fides?', *Ruf.* 2. *pr.* 7 f. 'nullus Castalios latices et praescia fati | flumina polluto barbarus ore bibit', *c.m.* 3. 1 f. Propertius speaks in similar terms of Hippocrene, which inspired Ennius to write epic (3. 3. 6) and which, when he drinks from its lower and calmer reaches, inspires his own love-elegy

(3. 3. 32 f., 51 f.). For the collocation *Castaliae undae* cf. Stat. *Silu.* 5. 5. 2 'Castaliae uocalibus undis', Sid. *Carm.* 22. 227.

communibus: 'ordinary', and 'shared by all': the word is balanced by *uili* in 28. Normally everything Castalia 'breathes' is poetry because 'uerba negant communia Musae' (*c.m.* 3. 3). Claudian may have in mind the famous distinction that Callimachean poetics drew between the mighty but filthy river Euphrates and the pure stream from which the Melissae carried water to Demeter (*H.* 2. 108 ff.).

28. discrepat: a rare word in poetry, but cf. Virg. *A.* 10. 434 'nec multum discrepat aetas', Ov. *Fast.* 6. 572. The metaphor is properly a musical one (see Brink on Hor. *Ep.* 2. 2. 194), which gives added point in a reference to a tree associated with the god of song.

laurus: normally the bay is a tree apart, 'uenturi praescia' (*Rapt.* 2. 109). For its being sacred to Apollo see esp. F. Williams, *Callimachus: Hymn to Apollo* (Oxford, 1978), 16. Note Prop. 3. 3. 13 'Castalia . . . ex arbore'.

29. antraque maesta silent: the *Castalium antrum* (Ov. *Met.* 3. 14) inside which the Pythia sat on a tripod and supposedly inhaled the mountain's inspirational fumes. Here it is silent (i.e. gives no oracles) and is sorrowful at the absence of the god: for the language cf. Stat. *Theb.* 9. 657 f. (Apollo of Delphi grieving for the death of Amphiaraus) 'lugentia cernis | antra, soror, mutasque domos.' The comparison that informs the following lines allows us to apply *maesta* to the Palatine before Honorius' return, and the joy seen in *exultat* (36) to Delphi's reawakening in ll. 30-4.

inconsultique recessus: *inconsulti* here has its proper passive sense ('which no one has consulted') also seen at e.g. Liv. 36. 36. 2 'inconsulto senatu', Suet. *Tib.* 52. 2 'quod . . . Alexandream . . . inconsulto se adisset'. Claudian is perhaps thinking of Virg. *A.* 3. 452 'inconsulti abeunt sedemque odere Sibyllae', where the sense ('without receiving advice') is far rarer: see Williams ad loc.

The oracle is generally spoken of as being a retreat, a secluded place where the god lies hidden: cf. Luc. 5. 84 ff. '(Apollo) sacris se condidit antris . . . quis latet hic superum?', and (with conscious word-play) Stat. *Theb.* 1. 509 'salue prisca fides tripodum obscurique recessus.' The meaning of *recessus* need not be fixed more precisely, but Claudian is no doubt thinking primarily of the depths of the Pythia's cave itself: cf. such phrases as Virg. *A.* 8. 193 'hic spelunca fuit uasto summota recessu', Ov. *Met.* 10. 691 f., 11. 592 f., Luc. 5. 183 'in Euboico uates Cumana recessu', *c.m.* 3. 2 'quidquid fatidico mugit cortina recessu'. Alternatively one could take the phrase as a reference to the groves around the cave: cf. Ov. *Met.* 3. 157 'in extremo est antrum nemorale recessu', *Fast.* 6. 755f., and esp. Luc. 5. 125 'Castalios circum latices nemorumque recessus'.

30–4. The description of Delphi springing back into life at the return of Apollo is based on the standard language of epiphanies: see N. J. Richardson, *The Homeric Hymn to Demeter* (Oxford, 1974), 208f., 252. Among many possible examples cf. especially Call. *H.* 2. 1ff., Virg. *A.* 3. 90ff. (Delos) 'tremere omnia uisa repente, | liminaque laurusque dei, totusque moueri | mons circum et mugire adytis cortina reclusis', Ov. *Met.* 15. 634ff. (Delphi) 'et locus et laurus et, quas habet ipse pharetras, | intremuere simul, cortinaque reddidit imo | hanc adyto uocem pauefactaque pectora mouit', *IV Cons.* 143f. (cit. on 26 *Delphis cessantibus*), *Theod.* 272f. (at the news of Theodorus' consulship) 'concinuit felix Helicon fluxitque Aganippe | largior et docti riserunt floribus amnes', *Stil.* 2. 276f., *Rapt.* 1. 7ff., Nonn. *D.* 13. 131ff. The most common emotions aroused by the epiphany of a god are awe and fear, but here the keynote is one of joyful renewal.

30. frenis grypa iugalem: the griffin is a mythical winged animal with the body of a lion and the head of an eagle. Though griffins of various kinds appear regularly in ancient Egyptian and Mesopotamian art and are clearly of eastern origin, the Greeks and Romans thought of them as living in Scythia: according to Herodotus the *Arimaspea* of Aristeas placed them further north than the one-eyed Arimaspians, with the Hyperboreans beyond them in their turn (4. 13: see 25–9n.). They were imagined as guarding hoards of gold which they had dug up, but which the Arimaspians stole from them (Hdt. 3. 116, Plin. *Nat.* 33. 66): Herodotus was sceptical about one-eyed men, Pliny equally so about griffins (*Nat.* 10. 136 'grypas . . . fabulosos reor'). This tradition was clearly known to Claudian, as can be seen from *c.m.* 31. 8 (gifts given at the wedding of Orpheus and Eurydice) 'grypes Hyperborei pondera fulua soli'. For the connection between griffins and the Hyperboreans cf. also Apul. *Met.* 11. 24, Servius on Virg. *Ecl.* 8. 27. See further *Der Kleine Pauly*, ii. 876. 17ff., Bolton *Aristeas of Proconnesus* (25–9n.) index s.v. 'griffins'.

Alcaeus, in the poem discussed above (25–9n.), showed Apollo travelling to the land of the Hyperboreans and back again on a chariot drawn by swans, but Claudian picturesquely has him make use of local resources when leaving Scythia. Both Apollo and Dionysus had long been associated with griffins in art. We find one with Apollo riding on his back on the breastplate of the Prima Porta Augustus, for example: see in general E. Simon, *Latomus*, 21 (1962), 749–80, esp. 763–7. The widespread identification of Apollo with

Helios no doubt helps explain this, since griffins are a regular attribute of the sun-god in Oriental art. Philostratus (*VA* 3. 48) claims that the Indians depicted the sun-god as travelling on a chariot drawn by four yoked griffins, and his connections with the East no doubt explain why Alexander is sometimes shown ascending to Heaven by the same means (MacCormack 137). Simon (art. cit. 765) also mentions an altar of the reign of Nero, dedicated by Palmyrenes, which shows the sun-god Malakbel in a chariot drawn by four griffins. Griffins thus became associated with light, with the stars, and consequently with apotheosis. They should therefore be interpreted here as reinforcing the conceit of Honorius as a star (23n. *imperii sidus*), and as one destined to achieve immortality.

Sidonius Apollinaris takes up the cue for embellishment at *Carm.* 2. 307ff. 'nunc ades, o Paean, lauro cui grypas obuncos | docta lupata ligant quotiens per frondea lora | flectis penniferos hederis bicoloribus armos', 22. 66ff., and *Ep.* 8. 9. 5, v. 10. The 'baroque' fantasy of poets, especially post-classical, leads to extravagant pictures of gods' chariots drawn by all kinds of exotic beasts, such as sparrows, swans, and doves (Venus: Sappho fr. 1. 8ff., Prop. 3. 3. 39, Ov. *Am.* 1. 2. 23, *Ars* 3. 809f., *Met.* 10. 717ff., 14. 597, Sil. 7. 441f., Stat. *Silu.* 1. 2. 142, Apul. *Met.* 6. 6, *c.m.* 25. 104 and 31. 9, Sid. *Carm.* 11. 108ff.), hinds (Diana: *Stil.* 3. 286ff.), tigers (Bacchus: Ov. *Ars* 1. 549f., Stat. *Theb.* 4. 658, 7. 564ff.), lynxes (Bacchus: Ov. *Met.* 4. 24f.), dolphins (Thetis: Stat. *Ach.* 1. 221ff.), and serpents (Ceres: *Rapt.* 1. 181ff., where see Gruzelier).

31. Riphaeo: the standard Latin poetic spelling is at odds with the word's Greek form (e.g. Call. *Aet.* fr. 186. 9 Pf. Ῥιπαίου . . . ἀπ' οὔρεος, Ap. Rh. 4. 287): see J. B. Hall, *Claudian: De Raptu Proserpinae* (Cambridge, 1969), 29, Thomas on Virg. *G.* 3. 382, Servius on Virg. *A.* 9. 81. The Riphaean mountains were thought to be in the far north of Scythia, and so are broadly appropriate in the present context: for their association with the Hyperboreans cf. Virg. *G.* 3. 381f. 'talis Hyperboreo Septem subiecta trioni | gens effrena uirum Riphaeo tunditur Euro', 4. 517ff. More commonly, Claudian follows the usual practice of Roman poets and applies the adjective loosely to 'the north': Col. 10. 77, Sil. 11. 459, *Ruf.* 1. 242, *Eutr.* 2. 151, *III Cons.* 149, *Stil.* 1. 123f., *Rapt.* 3. 321f.

tripodas: i.e. the tripod from which the Pythia delivered her oracles. For the loose use of the plural to indicate Delphi and its power cf. Ov. *Fast.* 3. 855f. 'mittitur ad tripodas', Luc. 5. 81 'cum regna Themis tripodasque teneret', 161f., *Ruf.* 1. *pr.* 12.

axe: part of the sky and so, by extension, the region beneath. See

Smolenaars on Stat. *Theb.* 7. 7f. 'axemque niuosi | sideris', citing Luc. 3. 69 'medium . . . sub axem', Sil. 1. 657.

32f. The quadruple anaphora of *tum/tunc* is unique in Claudian's poetry (for double *tum* see e.g. *Prob.* 25, *c.m.* 26. 37f.) and helps create a tone of excitement and exuberant joy. It is to be contrasted with the similarly striking triple *tum* at 304f. *tum uis extincta Getarum*; | *tum mihi, tum letum pepigi,* where it expresses Alaric's dejection. Variation between the forms *tum* and *tunc* in the same line should raise no eyebrows; cf. e.g. Ov. *Ars* 1. 239f.

32. loqui: i.e. utter oracles: cf. Luc. 5. 82ff. 'ut uidit Paean uastos telluris hiatus | diuinam spirare fidem uentosque loquaces | exhalare solum', Stat. *Theb.* 1. 491f. 'diuina oracula Phoebi | agnoscens monitusque datos *uocalibus antris*', Sil. 15. 311: also Ov. *Met.* 13. 716, Sen. *Her. O.* 1623 f., Stat. *Silu.* 5. 5. 2 'Castaliae uocalibus undis', Nonn. *D.* 13. 133f. ἀσιγήτοιο δὲ πηγῆς | Κασταλίης λάλον οἶδμα σοφῷ πάφλαζε ῥεέθρῳ.

uiuere fontes: i.e. regain their prophetic power. For the idea of water being joyously 'alive', cf. Stat. *Silu.* 1. 2. 155 'perspicui uiuunt in marmore fontes', 1. 5. 51f. 'caerulus amnis | uiuit'. There is also wordplay on the common application of *uiuus* | *uiuere* to flowing (rather than standing) water: see Austin on Virg. *A.* 2. 719f. 'donec me flumine uiuo | abluero', Bömer on Ov. *Met.* 3. 26f. 'iubet ire ministros | et petere e uiuis libandas fontibus undas.' The latter sense is commonly found in contexts of ritual purification and of being or becoming acceptable to the gods: here the waters of Delphi are once more pure and hallowed by the presence of Apollo.

33. sacer horror aquis: an ingenious adaptation of the idea of hair bristling in awe or fear at the epiphany of a god, as at e.g. Luc. 5. 154f. 'nulloque horrore comarum | excussae laurus' (of Phemonoe shamming inspiration), *Prob.* 125f. 'conscia ter sonuit rupes et inhorruit atrum | maiestate nemus' (of an epiphany of Roma). The surface of the water 'is ruffled': cf. Virg. *A.* 3. 195 (= 5. 11) 'inhorruit unda tenebris' (as a storm rises), Luc. 5. 446 'non horrore tremit' (of a calm sea), 5. 564f. 'niger inficit horror | terga maris' (of a storm rising), Stat. *Silu.* 5. 4. 5f. Barth (1612) ad loc. points out that *horror* can also have the sense 'relligio quaedam cum timore coniuncta', and cites Luc. 3. 410 'arboribus suus horror inest'.

33f. A loud noise often marks the epiphany of a god, as at *Prob.* 125 (cit. supra in the previous note) and *Rapt.* 1. 9ff. 'iam magnus ab imis | auditur fremitus terris templumque remugit | Cecropium'. Cf. the thunderous applause that marks the appearance of the earthly god in the Circus at 617f., where too the sound echoes all around. There is added point here in that the oracle in the Pythia's cave is to be imagined as breaking into voice at Apollo's arrival: cf. Virg. *A*. 3. 92 'mugire adytis cortina reclusis', Nonn. *D*. 13. 132f. Πυθιὰς ὀμφήεσσα θεηγόρος ἔκλαγε πέτρη | καὶ τρίπος αὐτοβόητος.

34. doctae: i.e. 'inspired.' The epithet is far more commonly used of the waters of Delphi, especially Helicon, and of the poets they in their turn inspire: cf. Stat. *Silu*. 2. 7. 12 'docti . . . amnes', *Theod*. 273, *c.m*. 31. 61, Sid. *Ep*. 8. 9. 5, v. 2: also Nonn. *D*. 13. 134 σοφῷ . . . ῥεέθρῳ.

spirant: the fumes exhaled from the cave are breathed in by the Pythia, who is thus inspired: see Luc. 5. 82ff., cit. on 32 *loqui* n.

35-8. For the general idea of the Emperor's presence enhancing the sanctity of a place, amidst an atmosphere of joy and blessing as he enters upon a new consulship, Müller cites Stat. *Silu*. 4. 1. 23ff. (Janus speaking) 'aspicis ut templis alius nitor, altior aris | ignis, et ipsa meae tepeant tibi sidera brumae | moribus aequa tuis? gaudent turmaeque tribusque | purpureique patres, lucemque a consule ducit | omnis honos. quid tale precor prior annus habebat?'

35. Palatino . . . monti: see *pr*. 23 *orbis apex aequatus Olympo*n.

reuerentia: a non-classical use of the word rare even in Claudian's day, here indicating an inherent quality of the Palatine by applying in a kind of oblique or transferred sense a term normally used of the feeling it inspires. So Müller translates 'Würde, Majestät', and cites SHA *Avid. Cass*. 4. 6 'Romani imperii reuerentia': cf. *OLD* s.v. 1d 'the condition of being regarded with awe', tentatively citing Stat. *Theb*. 5. 27 'adflicto spirat reuerentia uultu'. For the phrasing cf. also Aus. *Ad Patrem* 9 Green 'tua quo reuerentia crescat'. For a Greek precedent in the use of αἰδώς see Richardson on *h. Cer*. 214f.

36. exultat: yet another detail recalling Statius' celebration of the seventeenth consulship of Domitian, *Silu*. 4. 1. 5 'exsultent leges Latiae, gaudete, curules': see Coleman ad loc., and note also *IV Cons*. 4 'exultant reduces Augusto consule fasces'. It is picked up in the description of the general public rejoicing below (547).

deo: though his poems are saturated with divine imagery and vocabulary applied to the Emperor, Claudian is rarely quite so explicit: cf., however, *III Cons. pr*. 15f. 'me . . . | audet magna suo mittere Roma deo'.

36f. potioraque Delphis . . . oracula: i.e. Imperial decrees and/or legal judgements by the Emperor. This sense is a development of the application of the word to the 'weighty' or 'majestic' pronouncements of revered men, e.g. Cic. *ND* 1. 66 'physicorum oracula', Ov. *Met*. 15. 145, Col. 11. 1. 26 'illud uerum est M. Catonis oraculum; nihil agendo homines male agere discunt'. By Claudian's time it had become a standard feature in the vocabulary of political courtesy and adulation, since it was no doubt natural enough to conceive of petitioners to the Emperor as being like petitioners at Apollo's shrine. See *TLL* ix/2. 873. 9ff., citing e.g. Symm. *Rel.* 16. 2 'sed decuit uim constitutionis sacro oraculo reseruare', 19. 10, Jord. *Get.* 153 'donationem sacro oraculo confirmatam'. Add *Theod.* 34ff. (of Imperial edicts drafted by the eloquent Mallius Theodorus) 'terris edicta daturus, | *supplicibus* responsa, uenis. *oracula regis* | eloquio creuere tuo', where the equation *edicta = oracula* is made explicit; also *Stil.* 2. 298f., *C. Th.* 8. 4. 26. Still later the word came to be used for 'papal privilege', or 'royal charter': see J. F. Niermeyer, *Mediae Latinitatis Lexicon Minus* (Leiden, 1976), s.v. 6, 7.

38. The bay is regularly associated with Apollo as an instrument of prophecy, but with the 'god' Honorius also because it is an emblem of triumph and of the victory which always accompanies his consulships (cf. 13–15 n.). Plin. *Nat.* 15. 127 observes that there are two types of laurel, the Delphic and the Cyprian, but that it is the Delphic which is appropriate to victors in the games and to triumphators. Honorius thus not only surpasses Apollo in the efficacy of his oracles, but puts the laurels of his most famous shrine to a further, and perhaps better use, to boot. See also 120, 355, *IV Cons.* 24f.

ad signa: 'for' the Imperial army standards. For *ad* and the accusative of purpose or goal, see Woodcock 6.

iubet reuirescere: cf. Ov. *Met.* 2. 407f. 'dat terrae gramina, frondes | arboribus, laesasque iubet reuirescere siluas'. The echo is not otiose: Ovid describes the restoration of the world by Jupiter after it had been almost destroyed by Phaethon, with whom Eridanus explicitly associates Alaric at 186ff. (see also 165ff.). Now, under Honorius, an earthly Jupiter as well as an earthly Apollo, the Palatine (i.e. Rome herself) orders the restoration of the Roman world.

39–52. *Nowhere is better fitted to be the home of the rulers of the whole world than the Palatine, with its view over this majestic city protected by so many gods.*

As in a number of places, De Consulatu Stilichonis offers a passage which practically functions as a kind of dress-rehearsal for the present lines: *Stil.* 3. 125ff. 'per quem (i.e. Stilichonem) fracta diu translataque paene potestas | non oblita sui seruilibus exulat aruis, | in proprium sed ducta larem uictricia reddit | fata solo fruiturque iterum, quibus haeserat olim, | auspiciis capitique errantia membra reponit.' *Stil.* 3 was also recited at Rome, in Feb. 400, and no doubt many individual senators and officials were in the audience on both occasions, but Claudian is never shy of being seen to rework the same ideas: see further

40f. se . . . aestimat n. The two passages share the idea that Rome is the true home of *potestas*, but the earlier poem's conceit of the return of proper authority from exile is also skilfully recast later in *VI Cons*. At 407f. Roma, pleading with Honorius to visit the city, asks *quem, precor, ad finem laribus seiuncta potestas | exulat imperiumque suis a sedibus errat?*, and, in a clear allusion to Stilicho's visit during his consulship in 400, receives the answer that when he could not come himself the Emperor had sent his revered father-in-law (429ff.). Note also that in both *Stil*. 3. 125ff. and *VI Cons*. 39ff. the treatment of the idea that Rome is the natural seat of power is followed by a memorable passage glorifying the city: in the first case we have the great encomium of Rome that begins 'proxime dis consul, tantae qui prospicis urbi', probably the most famous lines in the whole of Claudian, and here a shorter but magnificently evocative description of the Capitol and Forum.

The passage naturally has discernible links with the epideictic genre of encomium of lands and cities, discussed by Menander Rhetor at 344. 15ff. (pp. 28ff. Russell–Wilson; see ad loc., p. 245), and of which the best-known example is no doubt Aelius Aristides' encomium of Rome (*Or.* 14). Cameron (pp. 26f., 391) makes a very good case for the theory that Claudian wrote foundation epics and other, shorter poems on various cities in the Empire which will also have had much in common with this type of encomiastic writing. See also Nisbet–Hubbard on Hor. *Carm.* 1. 7 (esp. pp. 92, 95), Matthews, 385.

40. larem: cf. 53 *agnoscisne tuos, princeps uenerande, penates?*, 603f. *hinc te iam patriis laribus uia nomine uero | sacra refert*. At *Stil*. 3. 127 'proprium . . . larem' was used fairly loosely of Rome in general, while Ammianus Marcellinus calls Rome the 'imperii uirtutumque omnium larem' (16. 10. 13). But 40f. makes it quite clear that here, as in the two passages cited above, Claudian is thinking more precisely of the Palatine and the Domus Augustana, the Imperial palace complex. Cf. also Stat. *Silu*. 4. 2. 25f. (Domitian and the Domus Augustana) 'ille penatis | implet', *Eutr.* 2. 63 (the palace in Constantinople) 'Augustis laribus'.

40f. se . . . aestimat: Claudian frequently uses a reflexive construction for a classical passive: see Birt, p. ccxxii, and cf. 229f. *se . . . deicit*, 502 *uiuo se perforat arcu*. This would appear to be a regular trait of spoken Latin in Late Antiquity, given the strength of the construction in modern Romance languages (e.g. It. 'qui si parla inglese', Sp. 'aquí se vende vino'): see further LHS ii. 294.

aestimare appears in only one other place in Claudian's poetry, and examining the passage in question reveals something of his working methods. *Theod. pr.* 11ff. 'Iuppiter, ut perhibent, spatium cum discere uellet | naturae, regni nescius ipse sui, | armigeros utrimque duos

COMMENTARY ON LINES 40–1

aequalibus alis | misit ab Eois Occiduisque plagis. | Parnasus geminos fertur iunxisse uolatus; | contulit alternas Pythius axis aues. | princeps non aquilis terram cognoscere curat; | certius in uobis *aestimat imperium*. | hoc ego concilio collectum metior orbem; | hoc uideo coetu quidquid ubique micat.' Jupiter, on assuming the kingship of Heaven, let loose two perfectly matched eagles, which would fly at the same speed, from the eastern and western boundaries of the world: where they met each other must be the centre of the world. In the event, they crossed at Delphi. Honorius, the earthly Jupiter, has no need of such devices to measure his Empire, since he can see the world's power gathered together in the assembly of the court. On the small scale, a comparison of the use of *aestimare* in the two passages confirms that *potestas* at *VI Cons.* 40 is to be interpreted as practically equivalent to *imperium*. Of more general significance is the fact that Claudian seems to have been stimulated to talk of 'measuring power' on the Palatine here by the association in his thoughts of that idea with Delphi: these lines lead on, of course, from an extended comparison between the two places. The association may be deliberate, but it is equally possible to conceive of it as being a subconscious process here betrayed by the use of *aestimare*. In any case, the extreme flexibility of panegyric is once again evident in Claudian's easy application of the same encomiastic topos to two different subjects: in one poem the new Delphi, the new centre of the world, is Milan, and in the other Rome.

40. potestas: a usefully vague word from the poet's point of view. It may be used almost as a synonym for *imperium*, as can be seen at 407 f. and e.g. Stat. *Theb.* 5. 324 f. 'subeo—pro dira potestas!—| exsangue imperium'. It therefore often indicates Roman magistracies, especially the consulship (e.g. Luc. 5. 664, *IV Cons.* 362 'polluta potestas', of Eutropius' consulship, *Theod.* 12, 59: see further *OLD* s.v. 3). Cf. such equally nebulous, but stirring, phrases as Plin. *Pan.* 63. 2 'uidit te populus Romanus in illa uetere potestatis suae sede', *Prob.* 193 'Romana potestas', *Gild.* 44 'Latiae uires urbisque potestas'.

41. summi . . . fastigia iuris: in the context of the Palatine and the Domus Augustana this could be taken as a reference to the principate, but cf. *Stil.* 2. 313 (Roma exhorting Stilicho to assume the consulship) 'plus ideo sumenda tibi fastigia iuris': Velleius Paterculus likewise calls the consulship 'principale in re publica fastigium' (1. 11. 6). But the phrase is naturally loose enough to be used flatteringly of almost any important position which the honorand happens to have held, and the closest parallel to the present phrase is *Prob.* 58 f. 'ad summi quotiens fastigia iuris | uenerit', where it is clear from the context that the reference is to Probus' tenure of the praetorian prefectures of Italy and Illyricum.

42. attollens apicem: for *apex* applied to the roof of an imposing building cf. Mart. 8. 36. 7f. 'aethera sic intrat nitidis ut conditus astris | inferiore tonet nube serenus apex', also of the Domus Augustana (there the newly built 'Domus Flavia' of Domitian). There is a substantial element of word-play, since the palace in any case practically occupies the whole of the Palatine: for *apex* used of hills see *pr.* 23 n. *attollere apicem* | *caput*, used literally or metaphorically, is often found in contexts that have a tone of pride or majesty: e.g. Virg. *A.* 9. 682, 12. 702f. 'gaudetque niuali | uertice se attollens pater Appenninus ad auras', Liv. 6. 18. 14 'ut caput attollere Romana plebes possit', Luc. 1. 604, Stat. *Theb.* 9. 414, Sil. 13. 863, *c.m.* 27. 18f.

regia: perhaps recalling Virgil's ironic or whimsical application of the term to Evander's hut on the Palatine (*A.* 8. 363). *rex* and its cognates had by Claudian's time long since lost the pejorative associations they had held for the Romans in earlier days: cf. 64 *regale . . . culmen*, 234 *excubiis . . . regni*, 516 *regali . . . equo*, 552 *regius . . . sanguis*, 613f. *regia . . .* | *. . . purpura*, 646 *regius . . . lictor*, *IV Cons.* 124, 299f. 'conponitur orbis | regis ad exemplum', *Theod.* 35 'oracula regis', *Stil.* 3. 115. See further Levy on *Ruf.* 1. 113, Simon on *Theod.* 35 'regis': compare also Millar 613ff. That the *rostra*—the emblem of *libertas loquendi*—should be described as 'subjected to the palace' without any apparent embarrassment at the possible metaphorical interpretation shows how far we are from the days of the late Republic or the principate of Augustus.

43. tot . . . tantis: generally taken by commentators as equivalent to *tot . . . tot*: see Müller ad loc., Platnauer 'so many temples . . . so many protecting deities'. *tanti* for *tot* is found from Augustan times (e.g. Man. 5. 170 'tantos orbes', Luc. 7. 834, 9. 34 'ratibus tantis', Stat. *Theb.* 2. 495), as is *quanti* for *quot* (e.g. Prop. 4. 11. 11f. 'quid currus auorum | profuit aut famae pignora tanta meae?'). Claudian has plenty of examples of both, including ll. 227 and 631 below: see Levy on *Ruf.* 1. 224, Gruzelier on *Rapt.* 1. 28, and further *OLD* s.v. *tantus* 5, Fedeli on Prop. 1. 5. 10, LHS ii. 206f., E. Löfstedt, *Philologischer Kommentar zur Peregrinatio Aetheriae* (Oxford, 1911), 147, id., *Syntactica*, ii. 43 n. 2. Here, however, perfectly good, and indeed more forceful sense can be had if the combination of *tot* and *tanti* is respected as fully operational: Rome is guarded by 'so many' but also 'such powerful' gods (not least Jupiter Optimus Maximus Capitolinus). Cf. Caes. *Ciu.* 1. 85. 6 'tot tantasque classis', Ov. *Met.* 2. 96f., Tac. *Dial.* 8. 4, *Rapt.* 3. 92ff. 'cuius tot poenae criminis? . . . cui tanta potestas | in me saeuitiae?'

44. excubiis: the gods in their shrines keep watch over the city: their vigilance is matched by the godlike Stilicho (234 n.). Traditionally, such 'gods of the city' as Vesta (Ov. *Fast.* 6. 267 'uigil ignis') and the Lares keep watch (Ov. *Fast.* 2. 615 f. 'qui compita seruant | et uigilant nostra semper in urbe, Lares'), but Claudian is thinking of all the gods with shrines in the Forum and on the Capitol, including the mightiest. Cf. Rut. Nam. *Red.* 1. 95 f. 'confunduntque uagos delubra micantia uisus: | ipsos crediderim sic habitare deos'.

44f. It seems that Claudian is remodelling Luc. 1. 195 f. 'o magnae qui moenia prospicis urbis | Tarpeia de rupe Tonans', where the 'Thunderer' is Jupiter and *Tarpeia . . . rupe* is used by metonymy for the Capitol as a whole (see further below). These majestic lines of Lucan's form part of a general invocation of the protecting deities of the city (cf. 44 *excubiis*), and have also left their mark on *Stil.* 3. 130 'proxime dis consul, tantae qui prospicis urbi', the relationship of which to this passage has already been discussed (39–52 n.).

Claudian's words have sometimes been interpreted as referring to a relief on the temple of Jupiter Tonans depicting the Gigantomachy, but this view was vigorously opposed in an article by L. Jeep (*RhM*, NF *27* (1872), 269–77). Jeep argues, rightly, that *Tonantis* is much more likely to refer to the temple of Jupiter Optimus Maximus Capitolinus (see following n.). But Jeep also maintains that a frieze-relief is out of the question because, at a height of only about 1 m, it would not be visible to anyone looking across from the Palatine. He interprets *Gigantas* as indicating instead the colossal statues of, no doubt among others, Apollo, Hercules, and Jupiter which are known to have stood on the Capitol, probably in the *area Capitolina* near the edge of the hill (Plin. *Nat.* 34. 39–43). Seen from a distance these 'gigantic' figures would have appeared to be 'schwebend' ('floating', 'hanging': *pendentes*). This is in many ways a persuasive argument, but it is open to a number of objections. (1) Claudian is giving so imprecise a description that it would be a mistake to press him too far on any point. He is also presumably describing to the audience what they know to lie across the way on the Capitol but none of which they can, as he speaks, actually see at all since they are inside an *aula* (*pr.* 26). What they know to be there may thus be more important than what they can actually see with the naked eye, especially if the poet is selecting his details with an eye partly on symbolism; see (3) below. (2) If, as Jeep himself thinks (art. cit. 271), the doors mentioned in l. 46 are those of the temple of Jupiter Capitolinus, then the progression from *tecta* in the literal sense to a relief of the Giants just *infra*, and then to the doors below would make perfect sense. See also 46 n. (3) The repeated insistence on the

COMMENTARY ON LINE 44

traditional topos of Gigantomachy as an image for the defeat of Alaric
(see 45 *Gigantas* n.) is such that it would be very careless of Claudian to
use *Gigantas* here instead of e.g. *colossos*: it is hard to see how the word
could fail to be taken as an allusion to Gigantomachy by an audience
which had heard the preface (17 ff.). (4) Jeep's strongest point is that the
striking use of the participle makes it difficult to see how *Tarpeia pendentes rupe* could apply to a relief. Though the phrase is difficult, it is by
no means as far beyond the limits of poetic fantasy as he claims. One
could imagine that such a relief displayed the Giants as, for example,
blasted by bolts of lightning and thus 'falling': this is particularly so if
the figures were carved in high-relief on a large-scale so that they
seemed to be tumbling from the surface of the pediment or doors. The
combination of *pendentes* with *Tarpeia rupe* is decidedly daring, but not
impossibly so if Claudian is trying to give an impressionistic and
morally coloured idea of the scene: the Giants seem to be falling from
the great temple that dominates the hill above the Tarpeian Rock and
are described in a compressed way that alludes to the traditional
punishment of the enemies of Roman order. (5) As Dr Holford-
Strevens points out to me, however, the most telling objection to
Jeep's argument is the patent absurdity of employing the term *Gigantas*
to indicate statues of the gods rather than of their traditional enemies.
It is perhaps not quite beyond the realm of possibility that Claudian,
in the manner of Statius or Sidonius, might attempt to be provoca-
tively inventive in such a manner, but so extreme a case would beggar
belief: it would risk reducing to utter incomprehensibility the theme of
Gigantomachy so prominent in this poem and in *De Bello Getico*. On
balance, then, Jeep's case has some merit, but it is most likely that
Claudian is alluding to a prominent and famous work of art, one
which depicted a subject entirely appropriate to a temple of Jupiter
and easily paralleled by other sculptural works in his honour, and
at the same time one which fits in well with Claudian's own preferred panegyrical topoi. In the absence of conclusive evidence, either
textual or archaeological, certainty is, however, impossible for us,
though presumably the allusion was clear enough to the contemporary audience.

44. Tonantis: there was a temple of Jupiter Tonans in the *area
Capitolina*, built by Augustus in thanksgiving for his escape from a close
shave with lightning while on campaign in Spain (*Res Gestae* 19. 2,
Suet. *Aug.* 29), and this would have been visible from the Palatine. But,
in addition to the evidence of the imitation of Lucan cited in the previous note, it should be said that plain *Tonans* for Jupiter was so
common by Claudian's time that it would be perverse to take this as

anything other than a reference to the far larger and more important temple of Jupiter Capitolinus: cf. Jeep, art. cit. n. 272. Moreover, Claudian appears to have in mind Statius' lines ingeniously imagining the astonishment of Jupiter, from his temple on the Capitol, at finding his neighbour Domitian housed in equal splendour in the new Domus Augustana: *Silu.* 4. 2. 20ff. 'stupet hoc uicina Tonantis | regia teque pari laetantur sede locatum | numina'.

45. For the phrasing cf. Virg. *Ecl.* 1. 75f. 'non ego uos posthac . . . | dumosa pendere procul de rupe uidebo', Luc. 1. 435 'gens habitat cana pendentes rupe Cebennas'.

Tarpeia . . . rupe: such metonymical phrases for the Capitol abound in high-style verse: cf. esp. Luc. 1. 196, 3. 154 'tunc rupes Tarpeia sonat', but also Virg. *A.* 8. 652 'Tarpeiae . . . arcis', Luc. 5. 27, 306 'Tarpeiam . . . Iouis sedem', Stat. *Silu.* 5. 3. 196 'Tarpeio de monte', Sil. 12. 609 'e Tarpeio . . . uertice', 13. 1 f. 'Tarpeia . . . | culmina', *Gild.* 30, *Stil.* 1. 214: note also *Tarpeio . . . Ioui* at 375 below, Prop. 4. 1. 7 'Tarpeiusque pater nuda de rupe tonabat.' The metonymy is made clear by Virg. *A.* 8. 347 'hinc ad Tarpeiam sedem et Capitolia ducit', where see Fordyce. Similarly, Martial regularly substitutes *Tarpeius* for *Capitolinus* when talking about Domitian's Capitoline games (4. 54. 1, 9. 3. 8, 9. 40. 1: cf. Stat. *Silu.* 5. 3. 231ff.). It seems possible that the Capitol was indeed originally known as the *Mons Tarpeius*, and that it owed its name to the settlements there of the *gens Tarpeia*; the story of the virgin Tarpeia and her betrayal of the citadel to the Sabines (best known from Prop. 4. 4) has the look of 'a patent aetiological invention' (Richardson 378).

Jeep held that Claudian's phrase was not just a poetic way of indicating the Capitol in general but was precise and literal: he thus attempted (art. cit., 44 f. n.) to use Claudian's words to identify the Tarpeian Rock proper with the eastern slopes of the *Capitolium* under the temple of Jupiter Optimus Maximus. Topographers used by and large to agree that the Tarpeian Rock, from which condemned criminals were hurled to their deaths, probably was at the SW corner of the summit of the hill properly called the *Capitolium*: see S. B. Platner, *The Topography and Monuments of Ancient Rome* (Boston, 1904), 276 ff. Recently, however, F. Coarelli, *Il Foro Romano* (Rome, 1985), ii. 80 ff. has offered an attractive argument to the effect that the Tarpeian Rock was, rather, on the SE side of the Capitol's other summit, the *arx*, overlooking the Forum and forming part of a general complex of localities associated with the punishment of malefactors which included the *carcer*, the *robur*, and the *scalae Gemoniae*. This interpretation also accords better with the aetiological legend of Tarpeia, which is indisputably linked with the *arx*. This part of the hill, though further away than the *Capitolium* and the *area Capitolina*, is also clearly visible from the Palatine. Richardson, however (pp. 377f.) disputes the evidence adduced by Coarelli linking the Tarpeian Rock with the *Scalae Gemoniae*, and reasserts the old claim that the Rock was on the SW corner of the hill. He does so largely on the strength of Liv. 6. 20. 12, where it is said that Manlius Capitolinus was flung to his death from the Tarpeian Rock, and thus 'locus . . . idem in uno homine et eximiae gloriae monumentum et poenae ultimae fuit.' Taking the words *locus . . . idem* to mean 'the very spot', Richardson argues that Livy means the cliffs above the *Carmentis fanum* at the SW corner of the hill (cf. Liv. 5. 47. 1–5): others will feel that this is too literal-minded, and that Livy meant no more than, loosely, the Capitol.

At any rate, there is no real evidence elsewhere to back up Jeep's claim that Claudian is referring to the Tarpeian Rock proper *and* that this was the eastern slope of the hill, under the *area Capitolina* and directly across from the Palatine. Claudian's phrasing is surely too vague to give support to any of the theories discussed above. The only thing that need not be doubted is that choosing to talk of the 'Tarpeia rupes', whatever the precise location of that cliff-face, allows Claudian to allude to the idea of punishment; the propagandistic significance of the reference is therefore clear.

Gigantas: the battle between the gods and Giants (and/or Titans) had long been used in encomium to illustrate the victories of the rulers of antiquity over the forces of confusion and disorder, especially with reference to the defence of civilization against barbarian foes. In literature this topos goes back to Pindar's use of Zeus' defeat of Typhoeus as an image for the defeat of the Carthaginians at Cumae by Hieron of Syracuse in 474 BC (*Pyth.* 1. 13ff.), while Callimachus calls the Celts who attacked Delphi ὀψίγονοι Τιτῆνες (*H.* 4. 174): the most famous example in Latin poetry is probably Horace's application of the imagery to Actium in *Carm.* 3. 4. In art the topos left its mark most spectacularly in the sculpture of the Great Altar of Zeus at Pergamum. See Philip Hardie, *Cosmos and Imperium* (Oxford, 1986), 85–156, D. Innes, 'Gigantomachy and Natural Philosophy', *CQ* NS 29 (1979), 165–71. This line thus contributes to a pattern of allusions casting Alaric and the Goths as latter-day Giants, impiously trying to storm that other Olympus, Rome, and receiving their just punishment. See *pr.* 17ff., 185f. nn., and compare the treatment of the idea on a larger scale at *Get.* 61ff. For Claudian's fondness for the Greek accusative plural ending see Fargues on *Eutr.* 2. 468 'Cilicas'.

46. caelatasque fores: Müller suggests that we take the phrase as an expansion of the preceding lines ('dem Inhalt der Darstellung folgt associativ auch der Ort, wo sich diese befand') and imagine that the doors display scenes from a Gigantomachy. A parallel would be the doors of the temple of Palatine Apollo, which had ivory reliefs of the repulse of Brennus and the Gauls from Delphi: Prop. 2. 31. 12 ff. 'et ualuae, Libyci nobile dentis opus; | altera deiectos uertice Gallos, | altera maerebat funera Tantalidos.' If this idea is accepted, *pendentes rupe Gigantas* (45) would refer to a relief on the doors much larger and more visible than the 1-m-high frieze-relief Jeep seems to imagine, only to dismiss it: see 44 f. n.

Assuming that these are indeed the doors of the temple of Capitoline Jove, there is a bitter irony for the reader who remembers the story that Stilicho later ordered them to be stripped of their gold plate: Zosimus (5. 38. 5) gleefully records that when the workmen carried out their orders they found the inscription 'misero regi seruantur', which was taken in retrospect as foretelling Stilicho's unpleasant end. At any rate, bronze, probably covered with gold plate, seems on balance a more likely material than ivory. *caelo* properly refers to the use of the chisel, but the poets also use it of the creation of reliefs on metal surfaces: see Fordyce on Virg. *A*. 8. 701 (Mars on the shield of Aeneas) 'caelatus ferro' and cf. *VI Cons*. 167, 375 *caelata metallo*, *Rapt*. 2. 21 f. 'casside fulua | caelatum Typhona gerit' (*fulua* implies that the helmet is made of gold). For the phrasing cf. Ov. *Met*. 8. 701 f. 'aurataque tecta uidentur | caelataeque fores adopertaque marmore tellus', Stat. *Theb*. 7. 56 f. 'caelataque ferro | fragmina portarum'. Elaborate ecphraseis of engraved doors in literature can be found at Virg. *G*. 3. 26 f., *A*. 6. 20 ff. (the temple of Apollo at Cumae), Ov. *Met*. 2. 4 ff. (the palace of the Sun), V. Fl. 5. 416 ff. (Apollo's temple at Colchis), Sil. 3. 32 ff. (Hercules' temple at Gades).

46 f. mediisque uolantia signa | nubibus: the hyperbole is seen also at *Stil*. 3. 67 f. 'aequataque templa | nubibus': cf. also Stat. *Silu*. 1. 1. 32 f., 3. 4. 47 ff. (the Domus Augustana and the Palatine) 'ueterisque penates | Euandri, quos mole noua pater inclitus orbis | excolit et summis aequat Germanicus astris', Mart. 4. 64. 9 ff., 8. 36. 11 f. (the Domus Augustana) 'haec, Auguste, tamen, quae uertice sidera pulsat, | par domus est caelo', *Stil*. 3. 134 'aemula uicinis fastigia conserit astris'. Gesner explains 'statuas deorum in fastigio templorum positas ita alto loco, ut, qui de imo illas suspicerent, volare eas inter nubes putarent': cf. Prop. 2. 31. 11 (the temple of Palatine Apollo) 'Solis erat supra fastigia currus'. Statues on top of columns and, following from Stat. *Silu*. 1. 1. 32 f., colossal equestrian statues are also possibilities.

47. densum: Gesner suggests that the sense is 'obscured': 'densum aethera interpretari forte licet obscuratum, ut vix videri possit prae templis illum intercipientibus'. Note also Barth (1650 edn., p. 727): 'ut totus plenus videatur, aegre visus prae templorum tot apicibus'. For the kind of phrase Claudian could be imagined as attempting to vary see e.g. Virg. *A.* 12. 253 'aetheraque obscurant pennis'. But *stipantibus* has the effect of personifying the temples as they seem to pack the Forum in droves, leaving the sky 'crowded'. An easier example of this usage of *densus* is Stat. *Silu.* 4. 4. 14 'ardua iam densae rarescunt moenia Romae'; see Coleman ad loc.

densum here is in any case paradoxical, since air is naturally *rarus*. Cf. Ov. *Met.* 15. 250 'ignis enim densum spissatus in aera transit', where the air is called 'thick' only because it seems so by comparison with fire (*Met.* 1. 28). Similarly clouds, especially storm- or rain-clouds, are regularly 'thick', at least relatively in comparison with the 'pure' air around them, e.g. Lucr. 6. 185 'densis . . . nubibus', Virg. *G.* 1. 445, *Prob.* 45, *IV Cons.* 173 'densos . . . imbres'.

48 f. A reference to *columnae rostratae*, triumphal columns raised to celebrate naval victories and adorned with the bronze prows of captured vessels. The most famous example was undoubtedly the column of C. Duilius, commemorating his victory over a Carthaginian fleet at Mylae in 260 BC. See Richardson 97, s.v. *Columna Rostrata C. Duilii* (2), Sil. 6. 663ff. Duilius' column stood in the Forum on or near the Rostra, but Livy, for example, mentions another, erected by M. Aemilius in 254 BC, which was on the Capitol (42. 20). Note also that Virgil, with Actium in mind, promises to raise 'nauali surgentis aere columnas' (*G.* 3. 29) in the poetic temple he will build to celebrate Octavian's victories.

It might seem easiest to take *aera* as an example of the common metonymy 'bronze statues': see *OLD* s.v. 7, noting e.g. Virg. *A.* 6. 847, *Prob.* 18, *Theod.* 27, *Stil.* 2. 177: cf. also *VI Cons.* 379 f. *in aere trementem . . . Atlanta.* There would thus be bronze statues 'planted' on top of the columns, as well as bronze prows decorating the shafts. That *columnae rostratae* carried images in this way is evident from Pliny's discussion of the old custom of putting statues on top of honorary columns, during which, in a clear reference to the column of Duilius, he expressly mentions a statue erected 'C. Duilio, qui primus naualem triumphum egit de Poenis, quae est etiam nunc in foro' (*Nat.* 34. 20). Likewise, there were columns on the rostra proper which carried statues, as can be seen from a bas-relief on the Arch of Constantine in Platner (45 *Tarpeia rupe* n.), 214ff. But 'flying' statues have already been mentioned (46 f. n.), and more here would seem superfluous. In addition, Claudian probably has in mind Virg. *G.* 3. 29, where *nauali . . . aere* is a periphrasis for *rostris*. It is therefore surely best to follow the acute suggestion of Hall and take *aera* here to mean 'prows' and *numerosa puppe* as in effect repeating this, with amplification (i.e. = *numerosis rostris*): Claudian's expression could thus be paraphrased as 'plurima ex aere rostra columnis adfixa.' Cf. Barth, who glosses *aera* as 'rostra navium aerata'. For expressions of this type Hall cites Housman on *Man.* 1. 539 f. 'conuexo mundus Olympo | obtineat', where *mundus* and *Olympus* must refer to the same thing. For similar uses of pleonasm see 122 f. *Parnasia . . . Pieriis . . . fidibus chelys* n. At any rate, one thing which is quite clear is that we should discount Müller's suggestion that Claudian is in fact referring here to the rostra, since, as Platner shows, these were decorated with bronze prows only along the front of the platform proper, and not on the columns.

48. uestitis: cf. Cic. *Ver.* 4. 122 'iis autem tabulis interioris templi parietes uestiebantur', Luc. 10. 119 'ebur atria uestit', *Ruf.* 1. 339.

puppe: by metonymy practically = *rostro*, a very daring usage, perhaps designed to tease the audience. The *rostrum* was, of course, affixed to the prow of a ship, while the *puppis* is properly the stern, the opposite end. The way to understanding is smoothed by the regular metonymy of *puppis* for 'ship' (as at 497) and by, for example, the resulting apparent interchangeability of 'aeratae . . . prorae' (Virg. *A.* 10. 223) and 'aeratas . . . puppes' (Ov. *Met.* 8. 103). For such playful uses of metonymy see Housman on Luc. 7. 871 and cf. on 634 *Gortynia tecta* (of the labyrinth at Knossos). One might almost speak of the '*pars pro parte* construction'.

49. consita: 'sown' and therefore 'thickly planted'. For the literal sense see Ov. *Ep.* 5. 27 f. 'popule, uiue, precor, quae consita margine ripae | hoc . . . carmen habes', and for the poetic use e.g. Lucr. 2. 211 '(sol) lumine conserit arua', Stat. *Theb.* 8. 704 f. 'densis iam consitus hastis . . . umbo', Aus. *Mos.* 48 Green. For a rather bolder metaphorical use cf. Catul. 64. 207 f. 'caeca mentem caligine Theseus | consitus', with Fordyce ad loc.

subnixas . . . iugis inmanibus aedes: commentators have taken this as a reference to temples resting on mammoth substructures, such as those Cicero chooses to regard as 'mad' at *Mil.* 53, 85. But (*pace* Müller), the sense 'substructure' for *iugum* is hardly common: *TLL* vii/2. 644. 53 f. offers only one example of *iugum* used 'hyperbolice de saxis', namely Plin. *Nat.* 36. 2 'naues . . . marmorum *transportandum* causa fiunt, ac per fluctus . . . portantur iuga'. It is perhaps preferable to understand Claudian to mean the seven hills (*iuga* of hills: cf. 291, 519 etc., *TLL* vii/2. 644. 25 ff.) of Rome piled high with masonry; this would give more point to *naturam cumulante manu* (see below). Cf. esp. Stat. *Silu.* 4. 1. 6f. 'septemgemino iactantior aethera pulset | Roma iugo', from a poem which, as we have seen, has exercised great influence over Claudian. The hyperbole of applying *inmanibus* to the modest-sized hills of Rome is entirely in tune with *mediis . . . uolantia signa* | *nubibus* and *densum stipantibus aethera templis.* The seven hills are similarly prominent in another awed panorama of Rome (*Stil.* 3. 65f.: cf. the notes on 46f., 50f.). For *subnixus* of man-made constructions resting on hills cf. Virg. *A.* 3. 402 'parua Philoctetae subnixa Peteleia muro', Stat. *Theb.* 7. 345f. 'Hyampolin acri | subnixam scopulo'.

50. naturam cumulante manu: on the literal level, the mighty hills of Rome are 'heaped up' still higher by the works of man: this fits in well with the passage's general emphasis on towering height. In addition, there is probably a metaphorical sense of man 'putting the finishing touch to' the work of nature: cf. see 201f. *non paruum . . . cumulum* n. The triumphalist claims made by Statius about human ingenuity surpassing nature had a considerable influence on the poets of Late Antiquity: see van Dam on *Silu.* 2 *passim,* Z. Pavlovskis, *Man in an Artificial Landscape* (Leiden, 1973). For the sense of *manu* cf. 526, *c.m.* 17. 20, 26. 49 'facta manu credas' (of the perfectly shaped, but natural, 'amphitheatre' around Aponus), 51. 14 'aemula naturae parua reperta manus' (of Archimedes' sphere). The whole phrase is repeated verbatim by Merobaudes at *Pan. Aet.* 155, though he uses it of rather less august constructions, namely the fortifications of military camps.

50f. spoliis . . . micantes | innumeros arcus: cf. *Stil.* 3. 67 'indutos . . . arcus spoliis', and for the decoration of triumphal arches with military spoils or trophies, Suet. *Cl.* 1. 3, Luc. 8. 819. See also 370f. *nominis arcum . . . tui* n. Barth and Heinsius both wanted to emend to *innumeris,* in conformity with the rule that a noun should not have more than one epithet (cf. 6f. n.). As Birt (p. ccxxi) points out, however, in the application of this rule participles are discounted: cf. 167f. *fulta . . . nobilis . . . urna,* 263f. *oblita . . .* | *perfida . . . examina,* 337f. *mirata . . . Maeotia terra,* 504f. *minantes . . . cultas . . . aras,* 576f. *uibrata . . . rubra . . . serica.* See also 484f. *minacem* | *Tyrrhenam . . . manum* n.

51. stupet: works of literature in this period often comment enthusiastically on the dazzling effect of contemporary art and architecture on the eyes: see Roberts 73ff. For the verb cf. Val. Max. 5. 4. ext. 1 'haerent ac stupent hominum oculi, cum huius facti pictam imaginem uident'.

igne: of the sheen of metal also at *c.m.* 53. 77f. 'splendentior igni | aureus ardescit clipeus': cf. Virg. *A.* 10. 271 'uastos umbo uomit aureus ignis', Mart. 14. 109. 1. The word is also used often of the brilliance of gem-stones: Man. 5. 511, Petr. 55. 6. v. 13, Stat. *Theb.* 2. 276, *Stil.* 2. 92.

52. obtunditur: of the dulling or dimming of sight also at e.g. Cic. *Sen.* 83 'cui obtusior sit acies', Stat. *Theb.* 7. 372, Plin. *Nat.* 22. 142 '(lens) aciem quidem oculorum obtundit et stomachum inflat', Aur. Vict. *Caes.* 38. 8. *retundo* is similarly used at *IV Cons.* 185, *Rapt.* 2. 135: see also 21 *retundunt* n.

53–76. *Do you recognize your home, Honorius? This is the city at which you gazed in wonder when you came here as a child with your father on the occasion of his triumph, and were presented to the Senate as the Empire's new heir.*

In the summer of 383 the first major military challenge to Theodosius' rule from within the Empire appeared in the form of a usurpation by Magnus Maximus, the *comes Britanniarum.* Maximus crossed the Channel into Gaul, and, after Gratian was killed, set up court at Trier. At first an uneasy equilibrium was maintained, and since coins in Maximus' name were actually minted at Constantinople Theodosius must have in some sense accepted the newcomer's legitimacy (Timothy D. Barnes, 'Religion and Politics in the Age of Theodosius', in Hugo A. Meynell (ed.), *Grace, Politics and Desire: Essays on Augustine* (Calgary, 1990), 162 ff.; Kenneth G. Holum, *Theodosian Empresses* (Berkeley and Los Angeles, 1982), 44 ff.). The situation, however, changed dramatically in 387, when Maximus invaded Italy, part of the domains of Gratian's half-brother Valentinian II. With his redoubtable mother Justina Valentinian fled to Thessalonica, and successfully appealed to Theodosius for redress. The reasons for Theodosius' volte-face are obscure. Zosimus (4. 43) attributes it to the wiles of Justina, who inflamed his lust for her daughter Galla: more pragmatically, Theodosius may have begun to fear Maximus' growing power, and been glad of 'the opportunity to replace a formidable western Augustus with one he could readily dominate' (Holum 45 f.). At any rate, Theodosius, recently widowed by the death of the Empress Flaccilla, bound himself to Valentinian's cause by marrying Galla in Thessalonica before the year was out. After careful preparations for a campaign over the winter, he advanced through Illyricum in the summer of 388, and inflicted severe defeats on Maximus in Pannonia. Maximus' support quickly fell away, and the usurper was captured and killed at Aquileia near the end of August. Theodosius' next task was the stabilization of the western half of the Empire, and he settled in at Milan for the winter. The next year (389) he summoned his younger son Honorius, then only four years old, from Constantinople, and took him with him to Rome, where he stayed from 13 June to 1 Sept. and celebrated a triumph. This 'State Visit' to the mother city may well have been in some measure 'a romantic pilgrimage to the historic capital of the Roman empire' (Matthews 227), and the first great 'Catholic' monarch no doubt also toured the holy places. But the primary purpose of the trip will certainly have been political. It was probably in some measure a public relations exercise aimed at the conciliation of those of the senatorial aristocracy who had, with whatever degree of enthusiasm, given Maximus their support. There is good evidence that the celebrations held in various parts of the Empire to mark the defeat of Maximus were very lavish and that they were of the utmost importance as an instrument of Theodosian propaganda: see McCormick, 44f., who points out that several monuments were erected in Rome and an obelisk put up in the Hippodrome at Constantinople, while the anniversary of Maximus' defeat remained a state holiday even in the sixth century. But it seems that Theodosius had also decided to show the West that its future rulers would come from his own family: see 65f.n. It was during Theodosius' sojourn in Rome that Pacatus delivered to him the famous panegyric (= *Pan. Lat.* 2) which is the primary source for the campaign against Maximus to survive from antiquity. See further the detailed account of the campaign and the visit to Rome given at Matthews 173ff., esp. 223ff. It has most often been assumed that this was Theodosius' only visit to the capital, but see Alan Cameron, *HSCPh* 73 (1969), 247–80, where a cogent case is made for a second visit after the defeat of Eugenius and Arbogast in 394.

53–55. There is more than a passing resemblance to Sil. 6. 406 'agnoscisne diem? an teneris non haesit in annis?', where Regulus' son Serranus is asked if he remembers his father's famous embassy as a Carthaginian captive to Rome. The context of this model may help give emotive colour to *patre pio* (55).

53. princeps uenerande: again at *c.m.* 48. 1. Cf. 599n. *reuerenda . . . sacraria,* 614 *ueneratur purpura uulgus, Stil.* 2. 279 (Roma speaking) 'Stilicho . . . uenerande'. Given the insistence on Honorius' youth (*puer* 55), Claudian may be thinking of such passages as Virg. *A.* 9. 276 (Nisus to Euryalus) 'uenerande puer' and Stat. *Theb.* 12. 73f., though the sorrowful circumstances of both those passages are in contrast with the atmosphere of rejoicing here. There is an element of oxymoron, in that reverence is more properly owed to age than to youth: cf. *Stil.* 2. 71 (Stilicho and Honorius) 'ceu sanctum uenerere senem', Juv. 14. 47 'maxima debetur puero reuerentia'.

penates: see n. 40 *larem.*

54. primis . . . in annis: for the phrase cf. Ov. *Ars* 1. 181 (Gaius Caesar, another child prodigy) 'primis . . . ducem profitetur in annis', *Met.* 8.

313. The use of *in* seems to be emphatic ('while still in your youth'): see Woodcock 54 (ii). Similar too is 'primis ab annis' e.g. Virg. *A*. 2. 87, 8. 517, Stat. *Theb*. 6. 608, 8. 554, where the preposition is clearly essential to the meaning ('right from').

miratus: setting the tone for 77ff. His childlike awe is shared by older and more world-weary sophisticates: Amm. Marc. 16. 10. 13 (Constantius II in Rome 357) 'cum uenisset ad rostra . . . obstipuit', 15 'uerum cum ad Traiani forum uenisset, singularem sub omni caelo structuram, ut opinamur, etiam numinum assensione mirabilem, haerebat attonitus'. For ellipse of parts of *sum* see LHS ii. 423, Birt, p. ccxxiv: *es* is also omitted with the past participle of a deponent verb in the perfect at 186 (*adgressus*) and *Stil*. 1. 294 (*locutus*).

55. patre pio monstrante puer: recalling Virg. *A*. 1. 382 'matre dea monstrante uiam'. We are no doubt expected to remember another pious old king showing a newcomer the sights of Rome, namely Evander and Aeneas: see Virg. *A*. 8. 337 'dehinc progressus monstrat et aram . . .', 343, 345.

55 f. optimus ille | diuorum: loosely equating Theodosius with Jupiter, though the epithet is applied to other gods too, e.g. Stat. *Theb*. 1. 651 (Coroebus to Apollo) 'diuum optime'. Claudian regularly talks of Theodosius and his father as *diui*, conforming in this to pagan practice (*IV Cons*. 190, *Gild*. 215, 292, 320). See further 102 f. nn., and the description of his καταστερισμός at *III Cons*. 162 ff. Similarly Pacatus says of Theodosius that 'deum dedit Hispania quem uidemus' (*Pan. Theod*. 4. 5): see Nixon ad loc.

Claudian is, however, principally intent on implying that Theodosius surpasses even the deified Emperor Trajan, on whom the Senate had conferred the title *optimus princeps*: Plin. *Pan*. 2. 7 'iam quid tam ciuile tam senatorium, quam illud additum a nobis Optimi cognomen?'; cf. Eutropius *Breu. a. u. c*. 8. 2. 1 'rem publicam ita administrauit, ut omnibus principibus merito praeferatur, inusitatae ciuilitatis et fortitudinis', 8. 8. 2, Sid. *Carm*. 7. 116 f. Cf. 58–64, 59 *terrore remoto* nn. Theodosius, like Trajan, was of Spanish origin, and Claudian, Themistius and Aurelius Victor all claim that a blood link existed between the two: see Gualandri 52 f., Matthews 108 f., MacCormack 209, Barr on *IV Cons*. 19, but note also that Pacatus, while not directly claiming such descent for his honorand, still links the two (*Pan. Theod*. 4. 5). Note also Aur. Vict. *Epit*. 48. 8 f. 'fuit autem Theodosius moribus et corpore Traiano similis . . . mens uero prorsus similis, adeo ut nihil dici queat, quod non ex libris in istum uideatur transferri.' Other Emperors could, of course, receive similar compliments: Gaius *Inst*. 1. 102 'epistula optimi imperatoris Antonini.'

Eutropius records (8. 5. 3) that in his day Emperors were standardly acclaimed in the Senate with the ritual cry 'felicior Augusto, melior Traiano.' See further 59 *terrore remoto*, 61, 333–8 nn.

56. toto . . . aeuo: 'in all his life' (i.e. on Earth), Platnauer. Contrast the far commoner sense of the phrase, 'for all time' (e.g. Ov. *Fast.* 5. 377, *Tr.* 1. 8. 25, Luc. 6. 764; 'in totum . . . aeuum', Luc. 7. 640).

    felicius: see 17 n.

57. Romuleis . . . moenibus: cf. Sil. 11. 583 'moenia Romuleae . . . urbis.' Augustan poets are scrupulous about using this lofty-sounding adjective, redolent of tradition and antiquity, only of things directly connected with Romulus himself: see Virg. *A.* 8. 654 'Romuleo . . . culmo' with Fordyce ad loc., Ov. *Met.* 14. 845, 15. 625 'Romuleae . . . urbis.' But anything connected with Rome is, loosely, connected with the City's founder, and so in later poets *Romuleus* quickly becomes one of the standard exalted variants for *Romanus*: e.g. Sen. *Apoc.* 12. 3. v. 30, Stat. *Silu.* 1. 1. 79, Sil. 10. 279, *Prob.* 96f. 'fetus . . . Romulei', of Romulus and Remus, *IV Cons.* 619, *Gild.* 75, *Get.* 332.

    uictor: implying a triumph: cf. Pac. *Pan. Theod.* 46. 4 'uidisti, inquam, finitum ciuile bellum cui decernere posses triumphum', 47. 3. The celebration of a triumph for a victory in a civil war was a delicate matter: see 392–406 n.

58. te consorte: sc. *triumphi* (Müller): cf. 65 f. n. Cf. *IV Cons.* 204 f. (Theodosius returning with his sons from the ceremony in which Honorius was created Augustus) 'duplici fultus consorte redibat | splendebatque pio conplexus pignora curru'.

58 f. Honorius matches the virtues of the great Emperors of the past, and in so doing becomes in his turn an *exemplum* for later princes to follow.

58–64. Roman Emperors were by ancient convention expected to behave not as autocrats but as 'first citizens' in their dealings with both the Senate and the People. An excellent examination of the political significance attached to this 'play-acting' during the Principate is offered by Andrew Wallace-Hadrill, *JRS* 72 (1982), 32–48 who argues that in itself it was regarded as a virtue and a guarantee of constitutional, non-tyrannical rule. See further MacCormack 293 n. 142, Millar 368 ff. The ideal, and the rewards in popularity which observance of it could win, may be gauged from e.g. Suet. *Cl.* 12. 1–3: Claudius' scrupulous courtesy to the Senate, the consuls and the tribunes of the people 'in breui spatio tantum amoris fauorisque collegit' that, on hearing a false rumour that he had been killed in an ambush near Ostia, the people turned on the army and the Senate in fury until reassured that the Emperor was safe. Even in Claudian's time convention still permitted the Roman populace an unusual degree of liberty expressing their opinion of visiting rulers. In their turn, Emperors who failed to strike the right note could be taken as having manifested a tyrannical disposition. See further 82–7 n. Quite how outrageous the jokes at the expense of visiting rulers were we cannot be sure, though the scandalous songs sung at the triumph of Julius Caesar (Suet. *Iul.* 49, 51) may help us judge the character of the occasion. No doubt each side was expected to maintain some sense of what could and what could not be said, and Ammianus Marcellinus praises both the people and Constantius II for not lapsing into excess: (16. 10. 13) 'et saepe, cum equestres ederet ludos, dicacitate plebis oblectabatur, nec superbae nec a libertate coalita desciscentis, reuerenter modum ipse quoque debitum seruans.' In this connection, note that *alternos cum plebe iocos* (60) implies that Theodosius, showing the common touch, gave as good as he got.

Theodosius' display of *ciuilitas* on this occasion is praised by Pacatus in the closing passage of his panegyric: *Pan. Theod.* 47. 3 'ea uero quae Romae gesta sunt, qualem te Vrbi dies primus inuexerit; quis in curia fueris, quis in rostris; ut pompam praeeuntium ferculorum curru modo, modo pedibus subsecutus alterno clarus incessu nunc de bellis, nunc de superbia triumpharis; ut te omnibus principem, singulis exhibueris senatorem; ut crebro ciuilique progressu non publica tantum opera lustraueris sed priuatas quoque aedes diuinis uestigiis consecraris, remota custodia militari tutior publici amoris excubiis, horum haec linguis, horum, inquam, uoce laudentur qui de communibus gaudiis et dignius utique quae maxima et iustius poterunt praedicare quae propria sunt.' Though there must certainly have been a number of set topics so that all such descriptions will have had a similar flavour, none the less Claudian's language here is so close to that of Pacatus that it seems undeniable that he was imitating him directly: see esp. 59 *terrore remoto*, 63 *publicus hinc ardescit amor* nn. Theodosius' *ciuilitas* is another link with the 'best of Princes', Trajan, who is given similar praise in Dio (68. 7. 3) and Eutropius (*Breu. a. u. c.* 8. 2–5). The general sentiment was pithily summed up in a saying attributed to Trajan: Eutropius *Breu. a.u.c.* 8. 5. 1 'amicis enim culpantibus, quod nimium circa omnes communis esset, respondit talem se imperatorem esse priuatis, quales esse sibi imperatores priuatus optasset.' Not all Emperors, however, had the character to deal with the *libertas loquendi* of the Roman people so successfully: Diocletian even abandoned his plans to celebrate his *vicennalia* and a consulship in Rome, and set out in the cold and the rain, to the detriment of his health (Lact. *De Mortibus Persecutorum* 17. 2 f.). Most pertinently for our purposes, Honorius' next visit to Rome (407–8) ended in his losing his temper to such an extent that he stormed back off to Ravenna: for references and comment see Cameron 382 ff. See further Matthews 227 ff., and cf. 549–59 nn.

Claudian, unsurprisingly, attributes the same lack of tyrannical arrogance to the king-like Stilicho: *Stil.* 2. 160 ff. 'quin ipsa Superbia longe | discessit, uitium rebus sollemne secundis | uirtutumque ingrata comes. contingere passim | adfarique licet. non inter pocula sermo | captatur, pura sed libertate loquendi | seria quisque iocis nulla formidine miscet. | quem uidet Augusti socerum regnique parentem, | miratur conuiua parem, cum tanta potestas | ciuem lenis agat', 3. 191 ff., though there his magnificent condescension is bestowed upon the people of Milan, not Rome.

59. ciuem gereret: cf. Val. Max. 4. 1. 4, *Stil.* 2. 167 f. 'cum tanta potestas | ciuem lenis agat', and contrast SHA *Sev. Alex.* 15 'ubi Augustum agere coepit.' Theodosius practises here what he preaches to Honorius at *IV Cons.* 294 ('tu ciuem patremque geras'). For *gero* ('act like', 'play the part of') cf. Sen. *Tro.* 715 'gere captiuum' (with Fantham ad loc.), Stat. *Theb.* 9. 13; and, more generally, for the use of 'concrete for abstract' see Nisbet–Hubbard on Hor. *Carm.* 2. 18. 32.

terrore remoto: i.e. without a bodyguard. This seems to be a direct borrowing from Pacatus, *Pan. Theod.* 47. 3 'remota custodia militari tutior publici amoris excubiis' which has also left its mark on l. 63. Behind both lies, as so often, Pliny's panegyric on Trajan and its contrasting denigration of Domitian as a tyrant: *Pan.* 49. 2 f. 'quanto nunc tutior, quanto securior eadem domus, postquam erus non crudelitatis sed amoris excubiis, non solitudine et claustris, sed ciuium celebritate defenditur! ecquid ergo? discimus experimento fidissimam esse custodiam principis innocentiam ipsius. haec arx inaccessa, hoc inexpugnabile munimentum, munimento non egere. frustra se terrore succinxerit, qui saeptus caritate non fuerit; armis enim arma irritantur.' The idea that the good king is loved by his people and therefore needs no bodyguard, while the tyrant is hated and so never truly safe, is, however, a standard one. It was, for example, partly his lack of a bodyguard that distinguished the mild rule of Cypselus from the true tyranny of his son Periander; see e.g. A. Andrewes, *The Greek Tyrants* (Tiptree, 1956), 45 ff. Seneca links it closely with the exercise of *clementia* by a good prince (*Clem.* 1. 19. 6 'unum est inexpugnabile munimentum amor ciuium'), and it also features prominently in the formal debate on kingship in the Pseudo-Senecan *Octauia*: 456 f. Cf. further Plin. *Ep.* 8. 24. 6, Themistius, *Or.* 1. 10 d, *IV. Cons.* 281 f. 'non sic excubiae, non circumstantia pila | quam tutatur amor.' Theodosius' conduct in Rome is mirrored by that of Stilicho at *Stil.* 3.

220 ff. 'sed uerus patriae consul cessantibus armis | contentus lictore uenit nec inutile quaerit | ferri praesidium solo munitus amore.' It also corresponds once again to that of Trajan; Dio 68. 7. 3 καὶ πολλάκις καὶ τέταρτος ᾠχεῖτο, ἔς τε τὰς οἰκίας αὐτῶν καὶ ἄνευ γε φρουρᾶς ἔστιν ὧν ἐσιὼν εὐθυμεῖτο. In ch. 17 of *Il Principe* Machiavelli dissents from the traditional view by arguing that for the wise prince fear is better, so long as he also strives to avoid hatred.

60. dilecta: i.e. by the people: this is a right they cherish. Note the oxymoron with *iurgia* (61).

61. Cf. Pacatus, *Pan. Theod.* 47. 3 'priuatas quoque aedes diuinis uestigiis consecraris', and also the praise of Trajan as recorded in Dio and Eutropius (cit. 58–64 n.). Given the insistence on the importance of the Palatine in these early parts of the poem it is highly likely that Claudian also had in mind Evander's words encouraging Aeneas to visit his humble hut: Virg. *A.* 8. 362 f. 'ut uentum ad sedes, "haec" inquit "limina uictor | Alcides subiit, haec illum regia cepit. | aude, hospes, contemnere opes et te quoque dignum | finge deo, rebusque ueni non asper egenis."'

There ought to be some point to the distinction between *patricias* and *priuatas*, but Platnauer's interpretation ('the homes of the poor' and 'the palaces of the noble') seems unlikely: *priuatus* hardly means 'poor', and it is in any case far from easy to imagine that Theodosius unbent so far as to make house calls in the Subura. Since Claudian often uses *patricius* with the sense 'of a senator' (599 n.), the meaning is probably that he visited the homes both of leading senators and of important individuals who did not hold that or any other rank. By Claudian's time, however, *priuatus* had lost its classical sense ('one not holding a magistracy') and had come to mean no more than 'subject', 'not connected with the Emperor (and his family)': see 654 *priuati . . . anni* n. It is thus just about possible to maintain that no real distinction is being made and that the two epithets serve no function other than variation of diction.

62. deposito . . . fastu: cf. *Nupt.* 198 'laxet terribiles maiestas regia fastus', *Stil.* 3. 118 f. 'posito iam purpura fastu | de se iudicium non indignatur haberi', *Theod.* 247.

63. publicus hinc ardescit amor: another verbal echo of Pacatus: see 59 *terrore remoto* n. Phrasing and content are also similar to *IV Cons.* 120 f. (Theodosius) 'hinc amor, hinc ualidum deuoto milite robur, | hinc natis mansura fides' and *Stil.* 2. 173 ff. The cynic might recall Tacitus' remark 'breues et infaustos populi Romani amores' (*Ann.* 2. 41).

64. inclinat populo: the image is of the Emperor bowing his head to the people, the reverse of the usual practice: cf. 614 *ueneratur purpura*

COMMENTARY ON LINES 64-5f.

uulgus n. For the phrasing cf. Aug. *Conf.* 3. 5 'inclinare ceruicem ad eius gressus'.

regale . . . culmen: cf. Amm. Marc. 15. 5. 16 (Silvanus assumes the purple at Cologne, 355) 'ad culmen imperiale surrexit', 15. 5. 17, 21. 16. 11, Orosius 7. 37. 1 'regale fastigium', and see further *TLL* iv. 1294. 20 ff. *culmen* of 'power', 'rank' etc. is especially common in later Latin: see Serv. on Virg. *A.* 2. 290 'a culmine uel a dignitate sua', *TLL* iv. 1293. 14 ff., and cf. 41 *summi . . . fastigia iuris* n. For *regale* cf. 42 *regia* n.

modestia: not so much 'modesty' as 'restraint', 'moderation': see Cic. *Tusc.* 3. 16, where *modestia* is one of several Latin words put forward as an equivalent of σωφροσύνη. Cf. also Pl. *Bac.* 613 'sine modo et modestia sum', Sal. *Cat.* 11. 4 'neque modum neque modestiam uictores habere'.

65. rudem uitae: picking up *puer* (55) and picked up in turn by *paruum* (67). Honorius, born on 9 Sept. 384, was not yet quite 5 years old. The rather mannered genitive is perhaps, as Müller implies, modelled on Hor. *Carm.* 1. 22. 1 'integer uitae' ('*uita* would have been more normal', Nisbet–Hubbard ad loc.: cf. also Stat. *Theb.* 1. 415 'integer annorum'), and it is possible that Valerius Flaccus wrote 'aeui rudis' at 1. 771. But for the genitive used with *rudis* to indicate the area in which experience is lacking see *OLD* s.v. 6a, citing e.g. Cic. *Ver.* 2. 17 'tametsi non prouinciae rudis et tiro', Hor. *Carm.* 3. 2. 9, Stat. *Theb.* 3. 24, 4. 247 'rudis armorum'. *rudis* is used regularly to stress the Emperor's extreme youth: cf. *III Cons.* 85, *Gild.* 302, *Nupt.* 2.

65 f. It is possible to take *socium sumebat honorum* as meaning no more than that Theodosius allowed Honorius to participate with him in the celebration of his triumph (cf. 67 f.), perhaps, for example, by having him ride with him in the triumphal chariot. See 67 *pupureo fotum gremio*, 579 *curru . . . uectus eodem* nn. But the remark that Honorius did not yet wear the diadem seems to hint at something more pointed. It is highly likely that on this occasion Theodosius raised Honorius to the rank of Caesar, thus designating him future Emperor of the West. Alan Cameron (*HSCPh* 73 (1969), 260 n. 25) combines the evidence of this passage with a statement by Theophanes to the effect that during the 389 visit to Rome Theodosius made Honorius βασιλεύς. Since Honorius was not created Augustus until 23 January 393 this cannot be literally true, but Cameron argues that Theophanes' only mistake is to have confused the titles of Augustus and Caesar. That there was a preliminary period in which, in accordance with the usual practice, Honorius held the rank of Caesar is clearly indicated by *IV Cons.* 169 f. 'nec dilatus honos: mutatus principe Caesar | protinus aequaris fratri', of Honorius' elevation to the purple. Moreover, it seems highly improbable that Theodosius would have summoned Honorius all the way from Constantinople merely to enjoy the show. To this it should be added that ll. 73–6 are most effectively interpreted as referring to a formal presentation of the boy to the Senate for their official confirmation of his new office. That Valentinian II, technically the senior Augustus, was sent off to Gaul and not permitted to attend the ceremonies must surely (despite the caution of Matthews 227n. 3) have been a deliberate indication that Theodosius intended the future to rest in the hands of his sons. See further McCormick 121f., who points also to the issue of bronze coins from the Roman mint carrying the slogan 'The Hope of the State', a formula regularly used of heirs to the throne, and which may be linked to this very occasion.

quamuis diademate necdum | cingebare comas: the *diadema* was not a crown of metal, but a strip of cloth, usually white but often purple or with purple ornamentation, bound around the head. It was believed to have been invented by Dionysus, and came to the Roman world from the Persian kings through the intermediaries of Alexander and his successors. See Weinstock 333ff. for the antipathy felt towards it as a symbol in Republican Rome. It was very slow indeed to establish itself as a regular part of the regalia of Roman Emperors; Diocletian is shown wearing it on coins, but it was probably Constantine who established it as a regular part of the Imperial insignia. See further Millar 612f. By the time of Constantius II the convention seems to have been that the diadem was specifically the emblem of an Augustus, while Caesars wore laurel wreaths: see *RE* v. 303ff., MacCormack 189, 194, 201. Note also *IV Cons.* 165ff.

The use of the indicative with *quamuis*, by analogy with *quamquam*, is found as early as Lucretius (*DRN* 4. 426 'porticus aequali quamuis est denique ductu') and is fairly common by Claudian's time. See LHS ii. 604, Woodcock 249 and cf. 538 *quamuis . . . foedauerat, Get.* 129. See also 13f. *quamquam . . . dederint* n.

For **diademate . . . cingebare comas** cf. Luc. 5. 60 'cingere Pellaeo pressos diademate crines', *III Cons.* 83f. 'ille (sc. Theodosius) . . . rerum . . . tibi commendat habenas | et sacro meritos ornat diademate crines'; also Sid. *Carm.* 2. 4f.

In verse Latin verbs of putting on or removing clothing, weapons etc. (*induo, exuo, cingo*) frequently take a direct object when they are passive in form. Such verbs should thus be seen as having a middle force in their passive form which is broadly analogous to the Greek construction: though this is apparently a feature of the native language, poets will no doubt have been influenced in their use of it by the frequent appearance of such constructions in their Greek models. See LHS ii. 36f., Williams on Stat. *Theb.* 10. 641 'exuitur uultus', Skutsch on Enn. *Ann.* 519 'succincti corda machaeris', and the lucid classification of the different types of the so-called Greek accusative in appendix D (pp. 290f.) of S. J. Harrison's commentary on Virgil, *Aeneid* 10 (Oxford, 1991). Cf. Ov. *Am.* 3. 9. 61f. 'hedera iuuenalia cinctus | tempora', Stat. *Theb.* 4. 41 'contentus ferro cingi latus', Sil. 13. 366, *Rapt.* 3. 377 'cincta sinus'. By contrast, the 'normal' construction can be seen at e.g. Virg. *A.* 8. 274 'cingite fronde comas', Hor. *Carm.* 3. 30. 15f. 'mihi Delphica | lauro cinge uolens, Melpomene, comam'.

66. socium . . . honorum: cf. *Ruf.* 2. 383 (Rufinus urging Arcadius to raise him to the purple) 'participem sceptri, socium declaret honoris'. The point is driven home by the double *tecum* (72f.).

67. purpureo fotum gremio: a protective as well as an affectionate gesture. Similar phrases abound: cf. Virg. *A.* 1. 718 'gremio fouet inscia Dido', V. Fl. 1. 355f., Stat. *Theb.* 1. 61, *Silu.* 1. 2. 109f., 260f., 2. 7. 36ff., *Prob.* 143f. (Roma speaking) 'pignora cara Probi, festa quos luce creatos, | ipsa meo foui gremio', *Ruf.* 1. 92f., *IV Cons.* 159f., *Nupt.* 42, Sid. *Carm.* 23. 204ff. The wording and situation are especially close to *III Cons.* 128f. (Theodosius and Honorius after the victory at the Frigidus) 'cum tu genitoris amico | exceptus gremio mediam ueherere per urbem', i.e. in a chariot. In both these passages there is a pointed juxtaposition of the affectionate gesture with the majesty intimated by the Imperial purple. Note also Suet. *Cl.* 27. 2 'Britannicum . . . natum sibi paruulum etiam tum, et militi pro contione manibus suis gestans et plebi per spectacula gremio aut ante se retinens assidue commendabat faustisque ominibus cum adclamantium turba prosequebatur.'

67 f. paruumque triumphis | imbuit: the martial precocity of Honorius is a recurring theme of Claudian's panegyrics: compare for example *III Cons.* 22 ff. 'reptasti per scuta puer, regumque recentes | exuuiae tibi ludus erant'. An early example of the encomiastic repertoire developed, probably, by Hellenistic court poets, to cope with the difficulties presented by youthful honorands can be found in Ovid's praise of Gaius Caesar, *Ars* 1. 181ff. 'ultor adest primisque ducem profitetur in annis | bellaque non puero tractat agenda puer. | parcite natales timidi numerare deorum: | Caesaribus uirtus contigit ante diem. | ingenium caeleste suis uelocius annis | surgit et ignauae fert male damna morae: | paruus erat manibusque duos Tirynthius angues | pressit et in cunis iam Ioue dignus erat.' Gaius, however, had at least reached the formal age of manhood, but panegyrists praising infant consuls and Caesars will have faced still more taxing problems.

One hopes that on this occasion the infant Honorius behaved better than Jovian's son Varronianus when he was installed with his father as consul: Amm. Marc. 25. 10. 11 'consulatum iniit adhibito in societatem trabeae Varroniano filio suo, admodum paruulo, cuius uagitus, pertinaciter reluctantis ne in curuli sella ueheretur ex more, id quod mox accidit portendebat'.

For the metaphorical use of *imbuo* cf. Vitr. 1. 1. 18 'ut architectus his litteris imbutus haec nisus sum scribere', Sen. *Dial.* 12. 17. 4 'utinam . . . uoluisset te praeceptis sapientiae erudiri potius quam inbui', Tac. *Hist.* 3. 15.

68. praeludere: Theodosius' great victory over Maximus is here made merely to set the scene for the crushing of Alaric. *praeludo* is a word little used in verse, and so it is all the likelier that Claudian is thinking of Statius' flattery of Domitian, *Ach.* 1. 19 'magnusque tibi praeludit Achilles'. Note also Prud. *Ham.* 723f.

69. linguis uariae gentes: a clear allusion to Virgil's description of Augustus' triumph as depicted on the shield of Aeneas: *A.* 8. 722f. 'incedunt uictae longo ordine gentes | quam uariae linguis, habitu tam uestis et armis.' Pollentia is thus raised to the same status as Actium in the catalogue of Roman victories. Note also Luc. 3. 288ff.

69f. That ambassadors from various foreign states were present at so important an event seems likely enough, but this Persian embassy is not otherwise attested (*pace* Platnauer ad loc., Themistius *Or.* 19. 227 is not helpful here). In a treaty negotiated by Stilicho in 387, the Eastern Empire and Sapor III had partitioned Armenia and established peace with Persia, thus freeing Theodosius for the coming war with Maximus (Bury i. 94). Claudian's language (see the next note) implies that the Persians came to Rome on this occasion to sue for peace, but this is no doubt merely conventional flattery. See further 71f., 415f. nn.

missique rogatum | foedera: 'sent to sue for peace' rather than 'sent to solicit alliance' (Platnauer): cf. Liv. 4. 30. 1 'Aequorum legati foedus ab senatu cum petissent et pro foedere deditio ostentaretur, indutias annorum octo impetrauerunt.' For the slightly archaic construction (supine of purpose with a verb of motion) cf. Caes. *Gal.* 1. 11. 2 'legatos ad Caesarem mittunt rogatum auxilium'.

70. Persarum proceres: cf. *Stil.* 1. 54f. (the young Stilicho at the Court of Sapor III) 'stupuere seueri | Parthorum proceres'. Roman poets had long used *Parthi* and *Persae* interchangeably (see Nisbet–Hubbard on Hor. *Carm.* 1. 2. 22), and by Claudian's time many prose authors too do not trouble to make any consistent distinction: see J. W. Eadie, *The Breviarium of Festus* (London, 1967), 84. Though *Persae* had, since the overthrow of the Parthian Empire by the Sassanid dynasty in 226, been technically more correct, the aim of literary authors, in any case, is usually to evoke the glories of the past rather than to aim at unfailing accuracy. So, for example, Libanius in a matter of a few lines speaks of Julian's campaigns against τὸν Μῆδον (following good classical usage) and the Πέρσας (*Or.* 12. 76, 78). See further 123 *arma Getarum*, 415 *Medus et Indus* nn.

71. hac . . . domo: see 40 *larem* n., 53.

71 f. The Persian ambassadors go down on one knee and bow their heads, a posture indicating homage and subjection; see C. Sittl, *Die Gebärden der Griechen und Römer* (Leipzig, 1890; repr. Hildesheim and New York, 1970), 156. The description given here corresponds well to a scene on the NW side of the base of the obelisk of Theodosius in the Hippodrome at Constantinople, where Persians are shown, along with German barbarians, venerating the enthroned figures of Valentinian II, Theodosius, and his sons (MacCormack 56 and pl. 17). This scene, though set at Constantinople rather than Rome, also belongs to the year 389. It is likely that Claudian had seen the obelisk on a visit to Constantinople before he went to make his career in the West, though we should probably discount Birt's suggestion that Claudian was in fact the author of the inscription on it: see Cameron 27 f. In any case, the iconography is very conventional, appearing again on the column base of Arcadius and the Barberini Diptych (MacCormack 56 with pls. 21 and 22: cf. also p. 66 for the influence of such scenes on Christian art).

The tiara was an oriental head-dress, conical in shape, and often made of felt and highly decorated. Like the diadem (65 n.) it was especially associated with the Persians: see *RE* suppl. xiv. 786. 58 ff., Fordyce on Virg. *A.* 7. 247. It had strings or straps under the chin, as can be seen both from its depiction in art and from e.g. V. Fl. 6. 700 (a Parthian ambassador at the court of Aeetes) 'subligat extrema patrium ceruice tiaran'. Here the tiaras are not removed: rather, they are held in place by the straps but 'lowered' as the ambassadors bow their heads. This is confirmed by comparison with Sid. *Carm.* 2. 50 f. 'interea te Susa tremunt ac supplice cultu | *flectit* Achaemenius lunatum Persa tiaran.' Contrast the action of Tiridates of Armenia when offering homage to Nero: Tac. *Ann.* 15. 29 'sublatum capiti diadema imagini subiecit'.

posito . . . genu: cf. Ov. *Fast.* 2. 438, 6. 447 f. 'dubitare uidebat | et pauidas posito procubuisse genu', *Met.* 6. 346, Curt. 8. 7. 13 'tu Macedonas uoluisti genua tibi ponere uenerarique te ut deum', Sen. *Suas.* 1. 2 'quae tam ferae gentes fuerunt quae non Alexandrum posito genu adorarint?', Petr. 73. 2.

72f. To mark the event Theodosius distributed the usual *congiarium* to the people, who no doubt presented themselves by tribe (*tribus*). Cf. Mart. 8. 15. 4 'ditant Latias tertia dona tribus', Plin. *Pan.* 25. 2 'locupletatas tribus datumque congiarium populo', Cor. *Laud. Iust.* 2. 350f., 4. 188ff. See further 603–10n. for the *sparsio*. For the extremely rare compound *praelargus* cf. Pers. 1. 14 'pulmo . . . praelargus'.

73f. fulgentia . . . delubra: a reference to the marble facings and/or gilded tiles of the Senate House: cf. Sil. 3. 667 'fulgentia templa', 12. 85f., Rut. Nam. *Red.* 1. 95 'delubra micantia'. The Senate could only be assembled in a consecrated place, but *delubra* also helps continue the conceit of the Senate as an assembly of gods: cf. *pr.* 24 *turba uerenda, deos,* 599 *reuerenda . . . sacraria* nn.

74. trabeatus: Theodosius was not consul in 389, so we should probably take this as a reference to the *toga picta* and as an indication of his status as *uictor.* See 4 *trabeis* n. For the adjective cf. Ov. *Met.* 14. 828, *Fast.* 1. 37, *Eutr.* 1. 9, *Theod.* 338, *Stil.* 2. 370.

    adit: probably, as Müller says, a contracted perfect (with long *i*) rather than a present, to conform with *uocauit* (72) and *adsuesceret* (76). Müller compares a contracted *subit* at *Get.* 354 (between *repressit* and *iacuit*), as opposed to *subiit* at *Eutr.* 1. 186.

75f. Though the principle of heredity was generally accepted, the Roman monarchy technically remained elective, and tradition required that the accession of an Augustus be confirmed by the Senate and by the acclamation of the Roman People and the army: see MacCormack 33f., Bury i. 5ff. We should therefore take *Romano puerum . . . offerre fauori* to mean that Theodosius likewise presented Honorius to the Senate and People for formal ratification of his new position as Caesar and heir. Cf. the scene described at Amm. Marc. 15. 8. 3ff., where Constantius II presents Julian to the army and, holding him by the right hand, delivers a speech asking the troops to confirm him as Caesar: note especially 15. 8. 8 'Iulianum . . . in Caesaris adhibere potestatem exopto, coeptis (si uidentur utilia) etiam uestra consensione firmandis.' In the next line, however, Claudian speaks of this event more as if Theodosius' primary intention was that the visit to the Senate should form part of Honorius' apprenticeship in his new constitutional position (*imperio . . . adsuesceret*: cf. his initiation into the conduct of triumphs and the reception of ambassadors, 67–72).

76. adsuesceret: cf. *IV Cons.* 399f. (Theodosius instructing the young Honorius in kingship) 'antiquos euolue duces, adsuesce futurae | militiae'. For *adsuesco* with the dative cf. also Hor. *S.* 2. 2. 109, Virg. *A.* 6. 832 (a striking inversion) 'ne tanta animis adsuescite bella'.

77-100. *Since then your love for Rome grew stronger even as you grew older, and, preferring to rule over free men, you willingly conceded the Eastern Empire to your brother. Fortune intervened by inspiring Eugenius to rebel: after defeating him your father summoned you from Constantinople and, when he himself rose to Heaven, Serena delivered you to the safe-keeping of Stilicho.*

After the visit to Rome in 389 both Theodosius and Honorius returned to Constantinople, leaving the West under the formal authority of Valentinian II. On 15 May 392 the body of this unfortunate prince was found hanging in his palace at Vienne. His Frankish general Arbogast gave out the explanation of suicide, one that some modern authorities (Matthews 238) are prepared to believe: Theodosius was not. Arbogast's overtures of peace were refused and he was forced into open revolt. As a barbarian, he could not claim the purple for himself, and so provided a veneer of respectability for his actions by proclaiming Eugenius, a former teacher of rhetoric, Augustus at Lyon on 22 Aug. An offer from the usurper to share the consulship for 393 was rejected by Theodosius, who made clear his determination to crush the revolt by conferring the title of Augustus on his younger son in Jan. 393. Eugenius' consulship was not recognized in the East, nor Honorius' new rank in the West. By April Eugenius was in Rome, where his legitimacy was accepted. Though himself a Christian, he attempted to reconcile the Roman aristocracy by permitting a substantial revival of state paganism spearheaded by the vigorous Praetorian Prefect of Italy, Nicomachus Flavianus. Theodosius marched against the usurpers in the summer of the next year, and engaged their armies in a two-day battle at the river Frigidus near Aquileia (5-6 Sept. 394). The first day was inconclusive, but on the second, in what was hailed by both pagan and Christian sources as sign of divine favour, the Eastern armies were greatly aided by the strong Bora wind, which blew straight into the faces of Eugenius' troops and blinded them. Arbogast killed himself: Eugenius was taken and executed. Though Claudian is careful never to say so explicitly, Alaric commanded Gothic auxiliaries on Theodosius' side, and so he and Stilicho were on this occasion allies (Zosimus 4. 57, Socrates 7. 10). See further Matthews 238 ff.

Soon after the battle at the Frigidus, Theodosius took up residence at Milan and summoned Honorius to the West. The young Augustus was escorted by Serena, his adoptive sister and wife of Stilicho, as well, probably, as his half-sister Galla Placidia. But before their arrival, Theodosius had suddenly fallen ill. He died on 17 Jan. 395. Honorius was in time for the funeral (Ambrose, *De Obitu Theodosii* 3, 34). There can be no doubt that, since the dynasty of Valentinian I was now extinct, Theodosius' intention was to establish his younger son as permanent ruler of the West, thus securing for his own family the loyalty of an area that must have seemed all too prone to challenge his rule when it was exercised from distant Constantinople. This must be why Arcadius was not summoned too: his place was in the East and he was not needed here. Zosimus (4. 59. 1 f.) records that Theodosius appointed the 10-year-old Honorius ruler of Gaul, Spain, Italy, and Africa, with Stilicho as his regent. Presumably the intention was for Stilicho to take his cues on policy and crucial decisions from Constantinople. Theodosius' premature death meant that in effect he answered to no one.

77–80. On this first visit to Rome love for the City put down roots which reached into the very marrows of Honorius' bones, and, as he grew older, they also grew ever firmer. This striking metaphor powerfully conflates and develops two separate Virgilian passages. Commentators regularly compare *concreta radice* to Virg. *G.* 2. 317f. 'nec semine iacto | concretam patitur radicem adfigere terrae', where Virgil is speaking of the manner in which Boreas (i.e. winter) impedes the successful planting of vines. In that passage, *concretam* is usually interpreted as having its commonest meaning 'frozen, congealed', and so, in his edition of the *Georgics* (Cambridge, 1988) Richard F. Thomas explains that 'the root is frozen along with the soil, and therefore does not take.' Clearly, that cannot be what Claudian means here, since the roots of Honorius' love for Rome most assuredly 'take' and flourish. As R. A. B. Mynors points out in his own commentary (Oxford, 1990), it is also possible to take Virgil's *concretam* proleptically, so that Boreas is said not to allow the root to fix onto the earth and 'grow into it', a usage which foreshadows that of *A.* 6. 738 and 746. Mynors then rightly quotes our present passage and observes that Claudian must have understood Virgil in this way. But more must be said here. Claudian's interpretation of *G.* 2. 318 has obviously been strongly influenced by precisely those lines of *Aeneid* 6 to which Mynors briefly alludes. This is confirmed not just by the reappearance there of *concretus*, but also by the use in both passages of *penitus* (78) and, far more significantly, the much rarer word *inolesco* (78): Virg. *A.* 6. 735 ff. 'quin et supremo cum lumine uita reliquit, | non tamen omne malum miseris nec funditus omnes | corporeae excedunt pestes, *penitus*que necesse est | multa diu *concreta* modis *inolescere* miris. | ergo exercentur poenis . . . (745f.) donec longa dies perfecto temporis orbe | *concretam* exemit labem'. In the passage from the *Aeneid* Anchises is explaining to Aeneas that souls long hardened in sin, so that the taint of corporality has become 'in-grown', must be purified by purgatorial treatments until this stain of corruption ('concretam . . . labem') is removed. As Austin remarks ad loc., *inolescere* repeats the idea contained in *concreta*, and the latter word is glossed by Servius as meaning 'coniuncta et conglutinata'. Claudian has thus conflated two Virgilian models, and, moreover, has developed the metaphorical idea of 'rooting' while also reversing (one might almost say 'redeeming') the sense of the more striking and significant Virgilian passage. Here it is not sinfulness that has grown deep into the fibres of Honorius' body and decisively shaped his whole character, but the noble virtue of *pietas* towards holy Rome.

A more straightforward adaptation of the passage from *Aeneid* 6 can be found at *Ruf.* 2. 504 f. (Minos in the underworld preparing to pass judgement on the soul of Rufinus) 'en pectus inustae | deformant maculae uitiisque inoleuit imago | nec sese commissa tegunt.' Note also Prud. *Ham.* 828 'perpetuis scelerum poenis inolescere uermes'.

78. totis . . . medullis: regularly the seat of powerful emotions in Roman poetry: see *TLL* viii. 1. 600. 21 ff., *OLD* s.v. *medulla* 2b. The emotion in question is most often sexual love (e.g. Catul. 45. 16 'ignis mollibus ardet in medullis', Virg. *A.* 4. 66, *Nupt.* 7 f.), but for the application of the same language to the noblest and purest of passions cf. *Ap.* 5. 40 'Musaea tuis insedit cura medullis', Aug. *Conf.* 7. 1 'totis medullis credebam'.

inoleuit: an extremely rare word in Latin poetry. In addition to the passages discussed above (77–80 n.) cf. Virg. *G.* 2. 77, Sil. 8. 581. At *G.* 2. 77, where the context is one of grafting (or more properly 'budding'), Servius glosses *inolescere* as being equivalent to συμφύειν. Austin on *A.* 6. 738 cites Plato, *R.* 609 A and *Ti.* 42 A for the use of the metaphor with reference to character in Greek. In Latin cf. Gel. 12. 1. 20 'in moribus inolescendis magnam fere partem ingenium altricis et natura lactis tenet', 12. 5. 7 'natura . . . induit nobis inoleuitque . . . amorem nostri et caritatem', Aus. *Grat. Act.* 80 Green 'tu Gratiano humanarum rerum domino eiusmodi semina nostri amoris inolesti'. (Note, however, that both Gellius and Ausonius use the verb as a transitive.)

79. tenero . . . ab ungue: it should be stressed from the very beginning that the essential meaning of this phrase in the present context is entirely unproblematic. Honorius' love for Rome was conceived in his earliest youth and has stayed with him ever since: the sense, then, is much the same as e.g. *a prima infantia*. It is also clear that there existed, at least in Late Antiquity, a Greek saying, ἐξ ἁπαλῶν ὀνύχων, which meant 'from the time when the fingernails were soft', i.e. 'from one's earliest youth.' Copious parallels, both Greek and Latin, are collected by Alan Cameron at *CQ*, NS 15 (1965), 80ff. Cf. esp. Cic. *Fam.* 1. 6. 2 '"a teneris", ut Graeci dicunt, "unguiculis" es cognitus', where Cicero seems to have this semi-proverbial phrase in mind ('ut Graeci dicunt'), and see further below. For similar phrases cf. also Virg. *G.* 3. 74 'iam inde a teneris', Stat. *Silu.* 2. 3. 37 'a tenero', Vitr. 1. 1. 12 'qui a teneris aetatibus . . . instruuntur', Apul. *Mun.* 38, and see 54 *primis . . . in annis* n.

Commentators, however, long ago realized that Claudian also has in mind Hor. *Carm.* 3. 6. 21ff. 'motus doceri gaudet Ionicos | matura uirgo et fingitur artibus | iam nunc et incestos amores | *de tenero* meditatur *ungui*: | mox iuniores quaerit adulteros | inter mariti uina.' Just as in l. 77f. Claudian reversed the thrust of his Virgilian original to draw a contrast between the 'ingrown' wickedness of the souls undergoing purification in the underworld on the one hand and the *princeps* with his deeply ingrained love for Rome on the other (77–80n.), so too there is a clear contrast between the degenerate Roman woman of Horace's poem longing for illicit affairs (*incestos amores*) even from her earliest youth and Honorius' long-standing pure love for the mother city (*dilectae . . . urbis . . . amor* 79f.). The meaning of the phrase in Horace, however, is much disputed. Porphyrio ad loc. explicitly comments 'hoc prouerbium de Graeco est, quod dicunt ἐξ ἁπαλῶν ὀνύχων; significant a prima infantia', an interpretation confirmed by Acron ('ab initio, ab immatura et prima aetate'). Consider also Automedon, *AP* 5. 129. 2 (a dancing girl, apparently trained to dance lasciviously 'from the tips of her fingers', i.e. her earliest youth) ἐξ ἁπαλῶν κινυμένην ὀνύχων. But there is also another, less well-attested Greek phrase, ἐξ ὀνύχων, which means 'to one's fingertips', i.e. 'totally' (*penitus*). In Latin one can cite Pl. *Ep.* 623 'usque ab unguiculo ad capillum summumst festiuissuma', and esp. Apul. *Met.* 10. 22 'ex unguiculis perpruriscens': in the latter passage the lascivious matron longs for Lucius in his ass-shape with every particle of her body, a context perhaps implying that Apuleius has Horace in mind and interpreted *de tenero . . . ungui* as = *penitus*. For a defence of Porphyrio's interpretation, see Alan Cameron, art. cit., and for some of the linguistic and stylistic arguments against see Gordon Williams, *The Third Book of Horace's Odes* (Oxford, 1969), 66f. Those who agree with Williams that Horace's *de tenero . . . ungui* means *penitus* are practically obliged also to accept his suggestion (p. 67) that Claudian 'was . . . relying on this misinterpretation of Horace, *Odes* iii. 6. 24, which commentaries on the *Odes* will have fixed by his time.' The

COMMENTARY ON LINES 79–81

authority of the interpretation advanced by the commentators, however, rests wholly on the existence of the phrase ἐξ ἁπαλῶν ὀνύχων,
and it is hard to see how a native speaker of Greek could be taken in
by appeals to such a phrase if it did not in fact enjoy some currency:
moreover, Cicero *Fam.* 1. 6. 2 shows quite clearly that it did ('ut Graeci
dicunt'), even if undisputed instances of it before Claudian's, let alone
Horace's, time are lacking. The authority of Claudian, both a native
Greek speaker and, apart possibly from Apuleius, the only surviving
classical author whose interpretation of the Horatian line is extant,
should be considered decisive.

This, naturally, can only be the case if we accept that the reading
tenero . . . ab ungue itself genuinely belongs in Claudian's own text. The
cautious-minded would point out that it is attested in only two major
manuscripts, and ask whether it is probable that *teneris . . . ab annis*, if
considered to be a gloss, could have established itself in the text so
early. The answer must be that such a process is inherently more
likely than that an ingenious scribe with a good command of Greek,
or a good knowledge of Horace, or both, should have replaced a
standard tag with a rare Hellenism, while also contriving to incorpo-
rate into a patriotic text about Rome an allusion that so powerfully
reverses the thrust of one of Horace's 'Roman Odes'.

79 f. conceptus . . . tecum creuit amor: 'non adeo tamen, quin
Ravennae considere praeferret', as Barth rather acidly puts it. Cf.
Virg. *Ecl.* 10. 73 'Gallo, cuius amor tantum mihi crescit in horas', Ov.
Met. 4. 60 'tempore creuit amor', *Pont.* 4. 6. 24, Stat. *Theb.* 3. 553,
Juv. 14. 139. For *concipio* with *amor* cf. Ov. *Met.* 10. 249 (Pygmalion)
'operisque sui concepit amorem', Fronto 4. 4–6 van den Hout[2]; also
Ov. *Met.* 7. 17 'excute uirgineo conceptas pectore flammas.' The idea
that Honorius is motivated by a deep personal love for Rome is also
found in the non-literary evidence: *CIL* vi. 1195 records the dedication
of a statue of bronze and silver by the *populus Romanus* to Honorius 'pro
singulari eius circa se amore adque prouidentia'.

80. reuersum: i.e. to Constantinople, either immediately after the visit
to Rome in 389, or with his father in 391.

81. propria: = *sua*, as often in late Latin: see LHS ii. 179c, and cf. 467
propriae . . . salutis.

propria nutritor Bosporos arce: i.e. Constantinople, and
perhaps more precisely the Great Palace. For the phrasing cf. *Ruf.* 1.
172ff. 'Eoas . . . ad arces, . . . celsa qua Bosporos urbe | splendet'. The
New Rome was formally laid out on its own seven hills, the palace
occupying most of the 'first hill' (including the site of the acropolis of
old Byzantion) and stretching down to the shoreline, hence *arce*; see

Bury 78. Honorius was born there on 9 Sept. 384, and so the city
on the Bosporus is his *nutritor*. cf. *IV Cons.* 128 f. 'te gaudet alumno |
Bosporos', 130 'nutrix Aurora tibi'. *nutritor* has the flavour of an
epic catalogue (cf. 106 *nutrierat* n.), but it is hard to provide a direct
parallel for its application to a place as someone's home or native
land: *Rapt.* 3. 373 'Apollinei nemoris nutritor Orontes' is clearly not
the same.

82–7. Whenever Theodosius would playfully ask Honorius which part
of the Empire he wanted for his share of the Imperial inheritance,
he always willingly conceded the East to his brother and chose for
himself the West, a country of free men who would brook no tyrant.
This was a game Theodosius played again and again (*quotiens* 82),
repeatedly testing Honorius' resolve; he was only teasing (*alludens* 83),
and never seriously intended to deprive Arcadius of the wealthier part
of the Empire that was his by right (*sortem . . . paratam* 84). Every time
Honorius' resolve remained constant (*remittebas* 85).

Claudian has often been portrayed as a spirited defender of the
rights and pre-eminence of Rome over the 'upstart' Constantinople,
but Cameron, 366 ff., rightly points out that his criticisms of the East
are largely limited to *Eutr.* 2 and *Stil.* 1–3: they must therefore reflect,
not his personal opinions, but the political tension existing in the last
quarter of 399 and early 400 between Stilicho and the Eastern court
which had formally declared him *hostis publicus*. If relations between
Stilicho and the East were still strained in 403–4, then one might be
inclined to detect a shade of hostility in the words that Claudian
attributes to Honorius (85 ff.). But the stance taken there is based in
any case on the old cultural prejudice that contrasted Roman *libertas*
(cf. 58–64 n.) with the servility of Easterners living under absolute
monarchs: for example, to convey the devotion of the bees to their
'king' Virgil declares 'regem non sic Aegyptus et ingens | Lydia nec
populi Parthorum aut Medus Hydaspes | obseruant' (*G.* 4. 210 ff.). For
the uses to which the idea could be put in encomiastic writing see
Mart. 10. 72. 5 ff. The opinion expressed by Honorius here corresponds closely with the admonition given him by his father in
another imagined scene between the two, where Theodosius instructs
his son in the duties of kingship as exercised in the freedom-loving
West: *IV Cons.* 214 ff. 'si tibi Parthorum solium Fortuna dedisset, | care
puer, terrisque procul uenerandus Eois | barbarus Arsacio con-
surgeret ore tiaras, | sufficeret sublime genus luxuque fluentem |
deside nobilitas posset te sola tueri. | altera Romanae longe rectoribus
aulae | condicio. uirtute decet, non sanguine niti', 257 ff., 306 ff. 'non
tibi tradidimus dociles seruire Sabaeos, | Armeniae dominum non te

praefecimus orae. | non damus Assyriam, tenuit quae femina, gentem: | Romani, qui cuncta diu rexere, regendi, | qui nec Tarquinii fastus nec iura tulere | Caesaris.' Honorius and Theodosius are thus of one mind, and the son's wishes correspond perfectly with his father's plans for him.

82 f. quotiens . . . dedisset: the subjunctive is commonly used with *quotiens*, especially in poetry, from Virg. *A.* 3. 581 on: see LHS ii. 606. In general Claudian prefers the indicative, but cf. *Ruf.* 2.75, *III Cons.* 25.

82. moenia: not mere poetic variation, since the word effectively reduces the choice between the two halves of the Empire to one between Rome and New Rome.

83. alludens: see Fordyce on Virg. *A.* 7. 117, citing Cic. *de Or.* 1. 240, Suet. *Iul.* 22. Naturally enough, the verb can also be used of malicious mockery: Ter. *Eu.* 424 f. 'forte habui scortum: coepit ad id adludere | et me inridere', Sen. *Thy.* 157, *Ruf.* 2. 328, with Levy ad loc.

regni pro parte: for *regnum* = *imperium* cf. 234, *IV Cons.* 379, *Stil.* 2. 166, *Get.* 103, 332, 436, and cf. 42 *regia* n.

84. diuitis Aurorae: the wealth of the East was legendary: cf. Ov. *Am.* 3. 6. 39 'diues . . . Nilus', Vell. 2. 117. 2 '(Syriam) diuitem', Plin. *Nat.* 6. 111 'ipsa Persis . . . etiam in luxum diues'. Poetic convention in any case matches the economic realities of the late fourth and early fifth centuries, when, despite the fabulous riches of the Western senatorial aristocracy, the Eastern provinces were by far the richest sources of Imperial revenue. Precise figures are notoriously difficult to establish, but see e.g. A. H. M. Jones, *The Decline of the Ancient World* (Harlow and New York, 1966), 178 f.

85. remittebas: = *concedebas*; see *OLD* s.v. 12, citing e.g. Cic. *Phil.* 8. 27 'Galliam . . . togatam remitto, comatam postulo'.

uolentes: an echo of Virgil's description of Octavian's campaigns in the East: *G.* 4. 560 ff. 'Caesar dum . . . uictor . . . uolentis | per populos dat iura'. Cf. also Sal. *Iug.* 102. 6 'melius uisum amicos quam seruos quaerere, tutiusque rati uolentibus quam coactis imperitare', Liv. 3. 40. 4, Luc. 2. 314 f. 'ad iuga cur faciles populi, cur saeua uolentes | regna pati pereunt?' It is a regular topos of panegyric that subject peoples feel εὔνοια towards their ruler (see Nisbet–Hubbard on Hor. *Carm.* 1. 12. 57 *laetum*), but here Claudian ingeniously expresses it with a slightly negative *color* so as to compliment the Romans on their traditional *libertas*.

86. Assyrios: the Eastern Empire at this time included the upper reaches of the Tigris and Euphrates, and thus enclosed a part of the old heartland of the ancient Assyrian empire. But in Roman poetry the distinction between Assyria and the contemporary provinces of

Syria and the Levant is in any case rarely maintained: consider e.g.
Hor. *Carm.* 3. 4. 32 'litoris Assyrii', Sen. *Her. O.* 553 (Jupiter and the
Phoenician princess Europa) 'taurus puellae uector Assyriae', Sil. 13.
886 (Antiochus II of Syria) 'Assyrio . . . regi', and cf. Justin 1. 2. 13
'Assyrii, qui postea Syria dicti sunt'. Conversely, the word could be
applied to the Persians, who occupied most of the territory formerly
subject to the Assyrians (Luc. 8. 427, *Stil.* 1. 51f.). Traditional Roman
prejudice saw the Assyrians as particularly effeminate and servile
because they had once been ruled by a woman, Queen Semiramis:
Suet. *Iul.* 22, *IV Cons.* 308, *Eutr.* 1. 339ff. Egypt (*Pharium . . . Nilum*, 86)
may be singled out here for the same reason, because its men were
once the willing slaves of Cleopatra: the two queens are used by
Propertius as *exempla* to excuse his own humiliating subjection to a
domina at 3. 11.

Pharium: = 'Egyptian', properly a metonymy, from the island of
Pharos with its famous lighthouse at the entrance to the harbour of
Alexandria. It appears in poetry from Augustan times, especially in
connection with the cult of Isis (e.g. Tib. 1. 3. 32, Ov. *Pont.* 1. 1. 38),
and is especially common in Lucan (no fewer than 37 times), the *Siluae*
of Statius, and Claudian (e.g. *Nupt.* 50, *Gild.* 57, *c.m.* 27. 73).

cum Tigride Nilum: as often, the whole country is represented
by its chief river: cf. 148 *Eridanus* n.

87. contingat . . . Roma: for the use of a substantival subject cf. Ov.
Am. 3. 2. 9 'hoc mihi contingat', *Met.* 15. 441ff. 'ibis . . . donec
Troiaeque tibique | externum patria contingat amicius aruum.'
Much more common is the impersonal construction with a dative and
an infinitive, e.g. Ov. *Am.* 2. 10. 35 'at mihi contingat Veneris
languescere motu', V. Fl. 7. 537, Stat. *Ach.* 1. 321f., *Ruf.* 2. 315f. (with
mihi understood from the previous sentence) 'contingat in uno |
priuati fugisse modum crimenque tyranni.'

uota fefellit: cf. Ov. *Pont.* 2. 9. 29 'uana laborantis si fallat uota
coloni', Hyg. *Fab.* 89. 1.

88–91. In confronting Theodosius with another usurper in the person of
Eugenius Fortuna might seem to have been motivated by malice, but
in fact her purpose was a benevolent one: to bring Honorius back to
the West. When combined with the account of Honorius' visit after
the defeat of Maximus (53–76), the implication of *nouum . . . tyrannum*
(88) must surely be that Fortuna's reasoning was as follows: since the
rise of one usurper had persuaded Theodosius to bring Honorius to
Rome, a deliberate recreation of the same circumstances could be
relied on to achieve the same effect. For the role of Fortuna in this
poem cf. 1 *Fortunae Reduci* n. Claudian offers an extended, if highly

schematic, comparison of the characters of Maximus and Eugenius at *IV Cons.* 70 ff.

88. molita: 'ließ erstehen' (Müller) and 'set up' (Platnauer) are not really strong enough: *molior* always implies great effort and deliberation. The phrase could be seen as a variant on 'noua moliri' for 'to revolt', 'to cause sedition': cf. *IV Cons.* 78 (Maximus) 'hic noua moliri praeceps'. It is very rare for *molior* to govern a personal accusative, but cf. Sil. 1. 644 f. 'exciuit Calpen et mersos Syrtis harenis | molitur populos', Stat. *Ach.* 1. 18 f. 'te . . . | molimur', Tac. *Ann.* 12. 22 'molitur crimina et accusatorem'. For the phrasing cf. also Paul. *Orat.* 2 Malcovati 'ne quid mali fortuna moliretur'.

tyrannum: = 'usurper', a common usage in this period, in both Greek and Latin. Any bad king is a 'tyrant', and all unlawful rulers are by definition 'bad'. Cf. 398, *Prob.* 108, *Gild.* 6, *IV Cons.* 72, *Stil.* 1. 140 (Eugenius) 'caesi post bella tyranni', *Get.* 284 (Max. and Eug.) 'geminis clades repetita tyrannis', Prud. *C. Symm.* 1. 410 (Max. and Eug.: cf. Alan Cameron, *HSCPh* 73 (1969), 256 f. Cameron's arguments are confirmed by the imitation of Claudian's repeated use of the phrase *gemini tyranni*), Ambrose, *De Obit. Theod.* 56 (Eug. and Arbogast) 'Italia . . . a tyrannis iterum liberata': also Julian, *Or.* 1. 1, Zosimus 5. 38. 2 τὴν Εὐγενίου . . . τυραννίδα.

89. Latium: Müller understands Claudian to be referring by metonymy to the whole of the Western, Latin-speaking half of the Empire. This would be a reasonable enough poetic extension of the word's range: cf. e.g. Luc. 1. 253 (Ariminum) 'Latii . . . claustra', which Duff's Loeb edition translates as 'the gates of Italy'. Furthermore, in an enumeration of the different parts of the Western Empire at *Stil.* 1. 18 ff. Claudian seems to use *Latium* as a variant for *Italia*: 'quod floret Latium, Latio quod reddita seruit | Africa, uicinum quod nescit Hiberia Maurum, | tuta quod inbellem miratur Gallia Rhenum etc.' *Latium*, moreover, is apparently used with this sense at 130 and 351 below. None the less, in a passage so insistent as this one on the close link between the young Emperor and Rome, it might be better to take the word literally: cf. 22 *Latiae . . . aulae* n.

belloque secundo: a pun: the war was both 'the second' against a Western usurper and also 'favourable' in its outcome. Far commoner in epic is the phrase *Marte secundo*, with its stronger flavour of personification: e.g. Virg. *A.* 10. 21 f., 12. 497, Luc. 4. 388, 6. 4, 9. 596, 10. 531 f., V. Fl. 6. 602, Stat. *Theb.* 12. 717.

90. protinus . . . uelox accitus: the long passage at *III Cons.* 111 ff. describing Honorius' route begins similarly: 'nec mora: Bistoniis alacer consurgis ab oris'. The lines just before that passage make the sequence of events clear: after the battle at the Frigidus (*III Cons.* 87 ff.) Arbogast commits suicide (ibid. 102 ff.) and then Theodosius summons Honorius, delaying his own ascent to heaven 'dum tibi pacatum praesenti traderet orbem' (ibid. 110). Thus *receptam* (91) precedes *accitus* (90); 'summoned [from the East] . . . you took up the burden of Hesperia, recovered for a second time'.

Eoa . . . ab aula: contrast *Latiae . . . aulae* (22), and cf. *Ruf.* 1. 172, *Gild.* 226 'urbi . . . Eoae', *Get.* 517 'regni . . . fauor . . . Eoi'.

91. suscipis: with a hint of metaphor: either the Imperial authority is seen as a burden to be shouldered, or else Honorius must take up the reins of power. Cf. *Theod.* 198 'suscepit habenas' as Mallius Theodorus takes up the four reins of Iustitia's chariot, one each to control Italy, Africa, Illyria, and the islands.

Hesperiam: Müller takes this as a reference to the whole West, as *Aurora* refers to the East (84). But *Hesperia* in poetry normally means Italy, and that would suit the passage's insistence on the close association of the Emperor with Italy and Rome itself (cf. 89 *Latium* n.). The audience of 404 is also surely expected to reflect that when Honorius arrived as Augustus Italy had been *bis receptam*, but now they have recently seen it delivered a third time, and by the Emperor's own actions this time rather than by his father's. *Hesperia* for 'the western land' (usually Italy, sometimes Spain) is probably a Hellenistic coinage (Ap. Rh. 3. 311), and is found in Roman poetry from Ennius on: see Skutsch on Enn. *Ann.* 20, Austin on Virg. *A.* 2. 781. Here it could perhaps be felt to contribute to the process of elevating Stilicho's victories over Alaric in the defence of Italy to epic status: cf. 202 f. *rebus . . . Ausoniis* n.

patrio . . . Marte: compare e.g. Virg. *Ecl.* 4. 17 'patriis uirtutibus', *IV Cons.* 638 'patriis olim fueras successibus auctor'. The phrase is a highly poetic variant for 'patriis bellis.' For the use of the attributive adjective in the place of the genitive see 11 *mons Euandrius* n. The standard metonymy (*Mars* = *bellum*) is especially common in Claudian: cf. 210, 283, 307, 624, and see further Bömer on Ov. *Met.* 12. 379.

bis . . . receptam: i.e. from Maximus and from Eugenius: cf. *IV Cons.* 71 (the West) 'bis possessa manu, bis parta periclis.' For *recipio* of taking back lost territory cf. Cic. *de Orat.* 2. 273 'numquam ego (Tarentum) recepissem, nisi tu perdidisses', Liv. 6. 10. 6. It appears most commonly in Claudian's works in the context of the recovery of Africa from the rebellious Gildo (*Gild.* 334, 458, *Stil.* 1. 378, 2. 385, *Get. pr.* 5).

92–8. Serena was the daughter of Theodosius' brother Honorius, and on her father's death was formally adopted by her Imperial uncle (*c.m.*

30. 104ff.). Theodosius gave her in marriage to the up-and-coming young general Stilicho in 384, as a reward, according to Claudian (*c.m.* 30. 177ff.: cf. *Stil.* 1. 69ff.), for his great military successes. She bore him two daughters, Maria and Thermantia, as well as a son, Eucherius (for whom see 552n.). Claudian assures us that she took the place of his dead mother in Honorius' heart: see 94 *materna . . . mente*n. In 398 Stilicho tightened his links with the Imperial family by arranging the marriage of Maria and her uncle and first cousin once removed Honorius, a wedding celebrated by Claudian in both the *Epithalamium de Nuptiis Honorii Augusti* and the *Fescennina*. Here, in the winter of 394–5, Honorius is thus Serena's *futurum . . . generum* (94f.). In Claudian's poems Serena is thus variously portrayed as Honorius' sister, second mother, and mother-in-law, depending on which is most effective for the rhetorical point he wishes to make. Early in 408, after Maria's premature death, Serena's efforts resulted in a second marriage, this time between Honorius and Thermantia (Zosimus 5. 28).

History has encumbered Serena with a reputation for extreme anti-pagan sentiment ('Serena was one of the bigots', Cameron 190). But this lays very heavy emphasis on a story of doubtful validity in which it is claimed that she profaned a cult statue of Rhea in the temple of the Magna Mater by stealing a necklace from it. Zosimus (5. 38) claims that this incident took place during Theodosius' visit to Rome after the defeat of Eugenius, i.e. in 394, but this does not square with Claudian's evidence here, that she escorted Honorius that winter from Constantinople to Milan, arriving, it seems, after the Emperor's death (95–8). The story, moreover, is suspiciously like the one told of Stilicho's impiety in stripping the doors of the temple of Capitoline Jove (see 46 *caelatasque fores* n.). Her religious principles, at any rate, do not seem to have hindered her much from forming a close link with the apparently pagan Claudian, and she was sufficiently solicitous of his personal well-being to find him a bride (*c.m.* 31). He honours her with a fine encomium in which the only mention of her piety is short and hardly a document of Catholic orthodoxy (*c.m.* 30. 223f. 'numinibus uotisque uacas et supplice crine | uerris humum').

The fall of Stilicho in 408 left her in an exposed position. The reappearance of Alaric on Italian soil in the summer of that same year found her trapped within the walls of Rome, and, no doubt as a result of the persistent rumours of collusion between her disgraced husband and the Gothic king, she was accused of planning to betray the city. Her accusers may have included her own kinswoman, Theodosius' daughter Galla Placidia. She was executed by strangling on the order of the Senate, a 'cruel act, which was based on the merest, and perhaps unfounded suspicion' (Bury i. 175). This shameful tale of panic and credulity draws the full weight of Gibbon's scorn (*The Decline and Fall of the Roman Empire*, ch. 31). Zosimus, at least, acquits her of treacherous intentions, only to account for the Senate's action by calling it revenge for the supposed profanation of the temple of the Magna Mater (5. 38). See further Cameron 57f., 190, 406ff., Matthews 108, 111, 248, 258, 287.

92. per Illyricas urbes: see *III Cons.* 111ff. for a long passage describing the route in detail, esp. 119f. 'Illyrici legitur plaga litoris; arua teruntur | Dalmatiae'.

93. ire . . . deterrita: with a 'verb of hindering' such as *deterreo* one would normally expect a subordinate clause introduced by *quominus*, or, more rarely, *ne*: see Woodcock, 150, 184 and consider e.g. Pl. *Truc.* 929 'hau ferro deterrere potes, hunc ne amem', Cic. *Tusc.* 1. 91 'non deterret sapientem mors . . . quominus rei publicae suisque consulat', Tac. *Hist.* 4. 71. The use of the passive and infinitive, perhaps under the influence of that construction with *ueto* and *prohibeo*, is neater and more concise, and so presumably had particular advantages for poets. But it also appears in prose: the *OLD* cites Cic. *Ver.* 14 'nefarias eius libidines commemorare pudore deterreor', Hirt. *Gal.* 8. 41. 3 'non deterrentur tamen milites nostri uineas proferre'.

nullo . . . casu: probably no more than a vague reference to the usual dangers to the safety and health of travellers during long journeys, especially in winter. Cf. e.g. *IV Cons.* 434ff., *Stil.* 2. 409ff.

94. materna . . . mente: Honorius' mother, the Empress Aelia Flaccilla, died when he was in his infancy. Though Serena was probably only about eight years older than Honorius, she was technically his closest senior female relative. Claudian has Honorius refer to her as a second mother to him, dearer even than Flaccilla: *Nupt.* 39ff. 'o patrui germen, cui nominis heres, | successi, sublime decus torrentis Hiberi | stirpe soror, pietate parens, tibi creditus infans | inque tuo creui gremio, partuque remoto | tu potius Flaccilla mihi'. Similarly (and predictably) Stilicho is said to have taken the place of a father to both Honorius and Arcadius when Theodosius died (*III Cons.* 151ff., *Gild.* 301ff., *Stil.* 2. 50ff.). For the phrasing here compare Ter. *Hau.* 637 'animu' maternus', Ov. *Met.* 8. 499 'mens ubi materna est?', *c.m.* 47. 14 'maternis studiis': also Ov. *Fast.* 1. 534 'mente paterna'.

95 f. Claudian records Theodosius' death in terms of a divine soul leaving the world of earthly corruption to return to its home in Heaven. Cf. the account of Theodosius' καταστερισμός at *III Cons.* 162ff. 'nec plura locutus, | sicut erat, liquido signauit tramite nubes |

ingrediturque globum Lunae limenque relinquit | Arcados et Veneris clementes aduolat auras'; also *IV Cons.* 428ff., *VI Cons.* 102f. The philosophical idea that the soul is divine in origin and returns to Heaven after it is set free from the prison of the body has a long history, going back at least till the fifth century BC. It was easily adapted to ruler-cult, since 'kings are from Zeus' and are thus closer to their divine source than ordinary mortals. See Nisbet–Hubbard on Hor. *Carm.* 1. 2. 45 (to Augustus) 'serus in caelum redeas', citing Plut. *fort. Alex.* 330 D., Man. 1. 799f. 'descendit caelo caelumque replebit, | quod reget, Augustus' and 4. 57 (Caesar) 'caelo genitus caeloque receptus', Vell. 2. 123. 2. By Claudian's time it was especially associated with Neoplatonic thought, and, though easily adapted to Christian doctrine as a metaphor, seems still to have been a concept with a strongly pagan flavour. See MacCormack 136ff., citing an oracle said to have been given to Julian: ἥξεις δ' αἰθερίου φάεος πατρώιον αὐλὴν | ἔνθεν ἀποπλαγχθεὶς μεροπήιον ἐς δέμας ἦλθες (Eunapius, frg. 26). See further MacCormack 145ff. for a discussion of how Ambrose presents an alternative, Christian picture of the reception of Theodosius' soul into Heaven.

95f. supernas ... plagas: cf. Virg. *A.* 1. 394 'aetheria ... plaga', 9. 638, Stat. *Theb.* 10. 635f. 'caelestibus ... plagas.' For such language applied to apotheosis cf. Ov. *Pont.* 4. 13. 25f. 'nam patris Augusti docui mortale fuisse | corpus, in aetherias numen abisse domos', and see further Nisbet–Hubbard on Hor. *Carm.* 1. 28. 5 'aerias temptasse domos'.

96. illo sub cardine rerum: a *cardo* is a hinge, and so metaphorically a 'crucial juncture' or 'critical time.' Cf. Virg. *A.* 1. 672 'haud tanto cessabit cardine rerum', where Servius cites the proverbial phrase 'res in cardine est', and also Sen. *Ben.* 4. 22. 1 'in illo tamen cardine (i.e. death) positi abire e rebus humanis quam gratissimi uolumus', V. Fl. 5. 19f., Sil. 9. 140 'cardine uitae', Stat. *Theb.* 10. 853 'fatorum in cardine summo'.

The end of a reign was no doubt always a critical time, but Theodosius' sudden death left the Empire in particularly awkward circumstances. Neither of the reigning Augusti was as yet capable of assuming personal control of affairs of state: feelings of hostility between the Western and Eastern contingents of the army, which had fought each other at the Frigidus, were still strong: religious tension was in the air now that the pagan revival sponsored by Nicomachus Flavianus was being undone; and there were severe military problems to be faced in the form of a Gothic revolt under Alaric in Moesia, and of Hunnic and Marcomannic invasions in the East. Claudian makes Theodosius' ghost admit the gravity of the situation at *Gild.* 292ff.

'cum diuus abirem, | res incompositas (fateor) tumidasque reliqui . . .'.
See also 582 *confusa dubiis formidine rebus* n. The underlying implication
in ll. 96–100 must surely be that a less scrupulous and less loyal
general than Stilicho would have been severely tempted to brush aside
all feelings of obligation—of *pietas* and *fides*—to a 10-year-old boy, and
make an attempt on the throne himself.

97 f. sedula seruatum . . . pignus | restituit: Honorius' own person
is a pledge of Serena's *fides* to the legitimate authority constituted
by the House of Theodosius. The language used alludes to the terminology of safeguarding and faithfully returning valuables entrusted to
one's care. This passage prepares the longer and more explicit one at
577 ff., in which the faithfulness of Serena and Stilicho in keeping
Honorius safe until he reaches the age of manhood and can assume
his Imperial duties is fully rewarded by their seeing him celebrate his
triumph over Alaric in the Eternal City: see 583, 585 *depositum seruasse,*
fides nn. For the phrasing here cf. also *Rapt.* 1. 179 f. (Ceres entrusting
Proserpina to the care of Sicily) 'hic ubi seruandum mater fidissima
pignus | abdidit.' To *sedula* cf. *c.m.* 30. 232 ff., where Serena is said to
be *sedula* in sending Stilicho warnings about the treacherous intentions
of Rufinus.

97. per tot discrimina: recalling Virg. *A.* 1. 204 f. (Aeneas speaking)
'per uarios casus, per tot discrimina rerum | tendimus in Latium', and
thus associating Honorius' journey through adversity to Italy with that
of the father of the Roman people himself.

98. sceptris patrui castrisque mariti: note the nicely balanced
homoeoteleuton (*-is, -i, -is, -i*), perhaps intended to suggest linguis-
tically the atmosphere of harmony that pervades this exemplary
family. Stilicho at this point had under his command the unified
armies of both the Western and the Eastern Empires; his title in
inscriptions (*CIL* vi. 1730 and 1731) is usually given as *magister equitum*
peditumque or *magister utriusque militiae*. Stilicho is often spoken of as the
last great defender of the West against the barbarians, but for a
strongly negative assessment of his generalship see Cameron 54 ff.,
pointing out that after Theodosius' death Stilicho, at least in person,
'did not win a single decisive victory until Faesulae in 406'.

99. certauit pietate domus: cf. *c.m.* 46. 11 f. 'at tibi diuersis, princeps
altissime, certant | obsequiis soceri', though there the context is the
far less elevated one of giving gifts. As might be expected, the
members of this family regularly display towards each other this most
Roman of all the virtues throughout Claudian's poetry: cf. e.g. *Gild.*
301 f., *Stil.* 1. 116 f., 208, and see esp. *VI Cons.* 94 *materna . . . mente,* 434
f., 467 f., 555, 586 *Pietas, fouisse propinquum* nn.

99 f. fidae . . . coniugis: the commonest praise given to dutiful wives, especially in their epitaphs: among countless possible examples cf. Cic. *Sest.* 49 'fidissima coniuge', Sil. 3. 133, Dessau, *Inscr. Lat. Sel.* 7472. 4 f. 'coniunxs, una meo praedita amans animo | fido fida uiro ueixsit studio parili'.

100. Stilichonis: the true hero of the vast bulk of Claudian's work is explicitly named for the first time in this poem. The orthography of Stilicho's name in Latin has caused some difference of opinion. The unaspirated form Stilico (from the Vandal 'Stelika' or 'Stilika'), instances of which are found here and there in numerous MSS, has been defended by some authors on philological grounds, but as Birt (p. ccx) declared a century ago, 'non agitur de veritate, sed de Romana consuetudine scribendi.' Formal public inscriptions put up at the time show the aspirated form (*CIL* vi. 1188, 1189, 1730), and so it is best to deduce that Stilicho himself preferred this spelling for public use. That Claudian would have gone against Stilicho's wishes in such a matter is practically inconceivable. Note also that in Greek the form Στελίχων is regular. See Fargues on *Eutr.* 1. 378, Schroff on *Get. pr.* 18. Cameron, p. xiii, prefers the unaspirated form, but does so 'for reasons which [he] can no longer recall and would not care to justify.' His claim that 'both forms are found in official Latin inscriptions' is not verified, and his reference to Birt ('cf. Birt, p. ccx') misleading: Birt emphatically draws a distinction between the public monuments with the aspirated form on the one hand, and the inscriptions on bronze plates (*CIL* vi. 1733 and 1734) that show the unaspirated form on the other; nothing indicates that the latter are public monuments. That some fluctuation in spelling occurred from time to time, at the very least as a result of ignorance and error, is probable, and what is almost certainly the sarcophagus of Maria twice bears the form *Stelicho* (Dessau, *Inscr. Lat. Sel.* 800).

cura: fulfilling the charge laid on him by Theodosius on his death-bed, 'tu curis succede meis, tu pignora solus | nostra foue' (*III Cons.* 152 f.). Cf. also *Stil.* 2. 78 f. 'fratrem leuior nec cura tuetur | Arcadium', *VI Cons.* 233.

101–21. *In Heaven Theodosius rejoices to see his son exact from Gildo and Alaric vengeance for their perfidy. Honorius surpasses both Orestes and Augustus in his pietas.*

Honorius' revenge on Alaric is, of course, the campaign of Pollentia and Verona which provides the principal theme of the poem. The revenge on Gildo is an allusion to the events of 397–8, when Gildo, now *magister utriusque militiae* in Africa (Matthews 245), opened negotiations with Eutropius to transfer his territory from the authority of the Western Court to Constantinople. This move was a serious blow to Stilicho's prestige, and also represented a major threat to the security of the West, since Rome, now deprived of her traditional corn-supplies from Egypt, was almost wholly dependent on African grain. Stilicho revived an ancient right of the Senate, and had that august body declare Gildo *hostis publicus* by *senatusconsultum*, thus adroitly deflecting the violent anger of the populace from the Court to the senators (*Stil.* 1. 325 ff.: see Introd. pp. xlviii–xlix with nn. 106 and 107.). An expedition, under the leadership of Gildo's own brother Mascezel, was dispatched from Pisa in Nov. 397 and defeated Gildo at the river Ardalio in a matter of a few weeks after its arrival in Feb. 398. Gildo was taken prisoner as he fled towards the sea, and died at Tabraca at the end of July the same year, though it is not entirely clear whether he was executed or succeeded in committing suicide (*Eutr.* 1. 410 f., *Eutr. pr.* 2. 69 ff.). The principal ancient sources for these events are Zosimus 5. 11 and Claudian's own *De Bello Gildonico*, recited in Milan in the spring of 398 (cf. *VI Cons.* 122 f.). The fullest and most incisive examination of Claudian's poem and the historical data that underlie it remains Cameron 93–123, but see also Matthews 272 f., Liebeschuetz 91, 98.

Honorius thus completes the task which death had prevented Theodosius from undertaking himself (*Gild.* 253 ff., cit. on 112 *suppliciis fruitur*). Claudian portrays the war against Gildo as part of an inherited and destined struggle between the house of Theodosius and the family of Gildo, since it was Honorius' grandfather, Theodosius *comes*, who crushed the revolt of Gildo's brother Firmus against Valentinian I some twenty years before: *Gild.* 330 ff., esp. 341 'hoc generi fatale tuo.' See further Amm. Marc. 29. 5. 1 ff., Cameron 94, 107 f.

101. felix ille . . . qui: a standard formula of μακαρισμός, equivalent to ὄλβιος (μάκαρ, μακάριος) ὅστις. See Mynors on Virg. *G.* 2. 490 'felix qui potuit rerum cognoscere causas' for parallels in Greek literature and for the suggestion that it may have its origins in the Mystery cults. The Virgilian example is by far the most famous occurrence in Latin, and is imitated by Claudian in a poem which similarly exalts the values of life in the country: *c.m.* 20. 1 'felix qui propriis aeuum transegit in aruis'. Among many other examples, both serious and ironic, note Prop. 1. 12. 15, Ov. *Pont.* 2. 2. 91 f., Luc. 4. 393 f. 'felix qui potuit mundi nutante ruina | quo iaceat iam scire loco', V. Fl. 5. 383 f., Stat. *Theb.* 11. 36 f. and Venini ad loc., Claud. *Prob.* 204, *Ruf.* 2. 264 f., *Get.* 590 ff. 'felix Elysiisque plagis et carmine dignus, | qui male suspectam nobis inpensius arsit | uel leto purgare fidem'. The most famous

linguistic variant on the phrase must be the Beatitudes: Vulg. *Matt.*
5. 3ff. 'beati pauperes spiritu . . . beati mites . . . beati qui lugent . . .'.
See further Nisbet–Hubbard on Hor. *Carm.* 1. 13. 17, citing *Od.* 5. 306
ff., Virg. *A.* 1. 94ff., Prop. 3. 12. 15, [Tib.] 3. 3. 25f.

Here, however, the phrase has particular significance because of
the importance of *felicitas* as a slogan of Imperial propaganda and
ideology at the time: see MacCormack 32f., 191, 218 for its frequent
appearance on contemporary coins. The insistence on the 'blessed-
ness of the times' is all the greater for the very insecurity that characterized them, and Claudian accordingly exclaims at the felicity of both
the Empire and the City under the guardianship of Stilicho and
Honorius, and that of these rulers themselves: see 17 *felix* n., and cf.
Stil. 2. 77f. 'principe tu felix genero: felicior ille | te socero', 3. 51 'o
felix, seruata uocat quem Roma parentem!' And in a passage describing the κατατερισμός of Theodosius which is very close to this one in
both sentiments and language Claudian apostrophizes the deified
Emperor in the following terms: *III Cons.* 178ff. 'fortunate parens,
primos cum detegis ortus, | aspicis Arcadium; cum te procliuior urges,
| occiduum uisus remoratur Honorius ignem'. The worldliness of the
values implied in the kind of thinking seen in the present passage is
attacked by Augustine at *Ciu. Dei* 5. 24 'neque enim nos Christianos
quosdam imperatores ideo felices dicimus quia uel diutius imperarunt
uel imperantes filios morte placida reliquerunt, uel hostes rei publicae
domuerunt uel inimicos ciues aduersus se insurgentes et cauere et
opprimere potuerunt . . .'. Given that the well-known denunciation of
Claudian as being 'a Christi nomine alienus' follows shortly after this
(5. 26), perhaps Augustine actually has one or both of these particular
passages in mind. Note also Prud. *C. Symm.* 1. 36f. 'felix nostrae res
publica Romae | iustitia regnante uiget', where Theodosius is viewed
as a Christian philosopher-king.

securus: recalling two predictions of his ascent attributed to
Theodosius himself, one to Stilicho on his death-bed at *III Cons.* 158f.
'iamiam securus ad astra | te custode ferar', and another to his sons
at *IV Cons.* 394f. 'tunc ego securus fati laetusque laborum | discedam,
uobis utrumque regentibus axem.' *securitas* similarly characterizes the
benefits of Honorius' and Stilicho's rule on earth: see e.g. *Eutr.* 1. 393,
Get. 51 'securas iam Roma leuat tranquillior arces'.

Olympum: = *caelum*: see below, 169 n. The ascent of Theodosius
to Heaven as a star is recounted in full at *III Cons.* 162ff.: cf. also *IV
Cons.* 428ff. and see below 103 *creuisse* n. Κατατερισμός of emperors
had been a part of Roman panegyrical writing since Virgil's extravagant praises of Octavian at *G.* 1. 24ff.: cf. also Ov. *Met.* 15. 848ff., Luc.

1. 45ff., 9. 11ff. For the development of the imagery and its adaptation to Christian thought see MacCormack 91 ff., esp. 145ff.

102f. The idea that an Imperial father looks down from Heaven with joy at the deeds of a son which enhance his own is very close to *Pan. Lat.* 12. 24. 4–25. 1 Mynors (to Constantine) 'sed etiam recentissima et pulcherrima diui patris tui facta superasti . . . ipsum, inquam, diuum Constantium iam primis imperii tui lustris rerum gestarum laude cumulasti. inuitus hoc forte accipis, imperator, sed ille dum dicimus gaudet e caelo, et iam pridem uocatus ad sidera adhuc crescit in filio et gloriarum tuarum gradibus adscendit.'

102. ab aethere cernit: similar phrases at Ov. *Met.* 2. 178f., 4. 623f., 10. 719ff., Luc. 7. 447f., Stat. *Theb.* 6. 356f., 10. 73f. For the epic conceit of the gods looking down from heaven at the deeds of men, see Griffin 82, 179ff. In Homer the emphasis is sometimes on Zeus as the protector of justice, but often simply on the pleasure the gods take in the spectacle of human warfare, while remaining unaffected by the sufferings it entails on the mortal plane. In Latin epic, however, the gods show a keener interest in the welfare of humanity, and so, for example, Jupiter's first appearance in the *Aeneid* reveals him gazing down in anxiety at the troubles of the Trojans in the storm off the coast of Africa (*A.* 1. 223ff.).

103. creuisse: the idea and the wording are close to *Pan. Lat.* 12. 25. 1 Mynors, cit. 102f.n.: note esp. 'crescit in filio'. But perhaps both authors are drawing on Ovid's description of the ascent of Julius Caesar to Heaven as a star and his joy at seeing himself surpassed by his adoptive son, Augustus: *Met.* 15. 848ff. 'luna uolat altius illa | flammiferumque trahens spatioso limite crinem | stella micat natique uidens bene facta fatetur | esse suis maiora et uinci gaudet ab illo.' Note in particular how *gaudet* seems to be picked up by *laetus*, *uidens* by *cernit*, and *facta* by *factis*. The model is adapted, however, to stress the *pietas* of Honorius, whose deeds are not said to eclipse those of his father, but rather to enhance their glory. It may not be strictly speaking impious for a son to surpass his father, but *pietas* requires modesty (cf. 'inuitus hoc forte accipis', *Pan. Lat.* 12. 25. 1): Claudian is discreet and tactful. The allusion here to Augustus prepares the explicit comparison between the two in 116–18. There is a more straightforward adaptation of the same Ovidian passage at *IV Cons.* 428ff. For thought and phrasing cf. also *Stil.* 2. 64f., 3. 91 (Rome, through the deeds of Stilicho) 'seque etiam creuisse uidet.'

104. Maurusius Atlans: the use of Atlas as a metonymy for Africa was no doubt greatly encouraged by Virgil's famous description of the anthropomorphic mountain at *A.* 4. 246ff. At 379f. an image of Atlas is said to have been prepared to be carried in the triumphal procession to celebrate Gildo's defeat. Cf. also *Stil.* 1. 248f. 'mouerat omnes | Maurorum Gildo populos, quibus inminet Atlans'.

Both *Maurusius* and *Maurus* are frequently used to mean by extension no more than 'African'. *Maurusius* is far less common, though Silius naturally finds it useful on occasion as a means for varying his diction in his long epic on the 'African' wars against Carthage (e.g. 10. 401, 11. 412). Claudian's choice here may have been influenced by Virg. *A.* 4. 206f. 'Maurusia . . . gens', shortly before the description of Atlas. See also 122 *captum . . . Maurum* n.

105. furias: cf. *Gild.* 332 'progenies uaesana Iubae'. Madness characterizes all the enemies of Rome, including Alaric (185f., 206 *furorem* nn., 405) and Eugenius (*IV Cons.* 360 'furiis praedonis acerbi').

Alaricum: Alaric is never explicitly named in the works of Claudian outside *VI Cons.* and *Get.*, and the bold use of his name in these later poems could be taken not only as proof of his own greater status as an opponent of Rome and invader of Italy in 402–4, but also as a clear indication of how decisive Claudian believed Pollentia and Verona were: perhaps now that Alaric seems to have been decisively defeated he can be named in all security.

barbara Peuce: the name of the largest and most famous of the six mouths of the Danube and also of an island in the mouth of the river itself (Plin. *Nat.* 4. 79, Mela 2. 98). Poets associated it with the νόστος of the Argo (e.g. Ap. Rh. 4. 309ff.) and Valerius Flaccus makes it the site of the wedding of Jason and Medea (8. 217ff.). Martial talks of 'Geticam Peucen' (7. 84. 3) and this will have aided Claudian in making a link between the island and the Goths (see further 123 *arma Getarum* n.). But the choice of epithet here most strongly recalls Luc. 3. 200ff. '*barbara* Cone, | Sarmaticas ubi perdit aquas sparsamque profundo | multifidi *Peucen* unum caput adluit Histri'. Claudian's verbal dependency on the literary tradition is such that, *pace* Barr on *IV Cons.* 630, we cannot simply assume that Peuce was literally 'the birth-place of Alaric.' The lower Danube was, however, the most recent 'home' of the Goths, hence Claudian speaks of Alaric swearing to destroy Rome by the 'patrii numen . . . Histri' (*Get.* 81: cf. Prud. *C. Symm.* 2. 697). For Gothic culture in the Danube area see Wolfram 89ff. Cf. also 220 *saeuum . . . Histrum* n.

106. nutrierat: the use of the verb with a personified river, country or city to identify a hero's origins is a common feature of epic, especially catalogues: cf. Stat. *Theb.* 4. 178f. 'quos fertilis Amphigenia | planaque Messene montosaque nutrit Ithome', 7. 273, Sil. 4. 344f. 'Collinum . . . uiridi quem Fucinus antro | nutrierat', 8. 580: cf. also Virg. *A.* 7. 684f.

'quos diues Anagnia pascis, | quos Amasene pater'. See 81 *propria nutritor Bosporos arce* n.

saepe: a frustratingly vague claim which cannot be pressed too far. For Alaric's repeated breaches of faith with the Roman authorities, however, see Cameron 158. Cameron also suggests the intriguing possibility that Gildo was disloyal to Theodosius during the revolt of Maximus in 387–8 (p. 104, esp. n. 1), and that *saepe* alludes to that incident. Certainly, Africa supported Maximus on that occasion, and much will depend on how one interprets Claudian's assertion at *Gild.* 153 ff. that by 397 Gildo had 'oppressed' Africa for twelve years ('bis senas . . . hiemes'), i.e. been appointed *comes Africae* in 385. See further Matthews 179 n. 5 and S. I. Oost, *CP* 57 (1962), 27–30.

106 f. profana | mente: the collocation is, perhaps surprisingly, rather rare, but cf. Ov. *Met.* 2. 833, and also *Ruf.* 1. 75 f. 'animi . . . profanus | error'. *profana* implies the breaking of oaths of loyalty to Theodosius: cf. *Gild.* 323 f., *Stil.* 1. 271 ff. 'quamuis obstreperet pietas, his ille regendae | transtulerat nomen Libyae *scelerique profano* | fallax legitimam regni praetenderat umbram', *Get.* 102.

107 f. The incident referred to here is so obscure as to make any detailed reconstruction of the facts quite impossible. Even if, as seems likely, *Get.* 524 'tot Augustos Hebro qui teste fugaui' alludes to the same events (see Liebeschuetz 51 n. 26), this still vaguer formulation does nothing to lighten our darkness. The most promising evidence from an historical source can be found in Zosimus' account (4. 45. 3, 48–9) of the activities of some of the barbarians in the Eastern army during the campaign against Maximus in 388–91. Zosimus tells us that when Theodosius was on the point of setting out for Italy in 388, a rumour reached him that the troops in question had been bribed by Maximus. On learning that they were under suspicion the barbarians fled into the marshes of Macedonia, probably in the region of the Axios (Vardar). They were pursued and largely, but clearly not entirely, wiped out: after Theodosius continued on his way they profited from his absence to make regular raids in Macedonia and Thessaly. On his return in 391 Theodosius was obliged to hunt them down in the marshes before he could make his way back to Constantinople. Some considerable success was marred by an incident in which the Roman army was caught off-guard by a night attack during which the life of the Emperor himself was threatened, and the situation was only saved by the quick thinking and resolute action of Promotus. Scholars reasonably assume that the barbarians were Goths, or mainly Goths, and also, on the strength of what Claudian says here, suggest that Alaric was one of their leaders. If this is so, then we have in these lines the earliest attested appearance of Alaric on the stage of history (Wolfram 136, Liebeschuetz 54, and, most convincingly of all, Heather 183 ff.). It is also usually assumed that Claudian's conflict on the Hebrus belongs to the circumstances of 391 (e.g. Cameron 158; also perhaps Heather 184, though this is not quite clear), no doubt because the far greater attention given by Zosimus to the later campaign seems to square better with an incident as important as the one the poet must have in mind. A further possibility is that the 'hold up' on the Hebrus and the night attack on the Roman camp may be one and the same, as Wolfram appears to believe and as Liebeschuetz tentatively suggests (54 n. 43). Claudian's wording, however, is a major obstacle to a date of 391 for the encounter he is alluding to. As Liebeschuetz observes (51 n. 26), by far the most natural way of taking *Thracum uenientem e finibus* is as meaning that Theodosius was coming *from* Thrace (through Macedonia, presumably) on his way *to* Italy, and this would imply a date in 388 when the barbarians first fled to the marshes and were pursued by Theodosius. Two considerations strengthen this possibility. First, *clausit* must mean that in some way Alaric impeded Theodosius' advance, and though Zosimus' narrative at 4. 45. 3 is very concise, what is clear is that Theodosius thought that he had to deal with the deserters first before he proceeded to Italy. Zosimus makes no direct mention of the campaign; indeed, far from implying any initial victories for the barbarians, he says only that they fled into the woods and marshes and had to be hunted down there. But his sketchy narrative does leave some room for an incident in which the Emperor may have been 'hemmed in' by the waters of the Hebrus and prevented, at least for a time, from continuing his advance. Secondly, and more importantly, if Alaric is to be imagined as having impeded Theodosius' march towards Italy, then the treacherous actions of Alaric and Gildo would neatly parallel each other: Alaric obstructed Theodosius' campaign against the usurper Maximus in 388 and Gildo, by failing to provide support, obstructed the campaign against the usurper Eugenius in 394. One last word of caution: nothing in Zosimus' narrative can be said to match Claudian's statement with the slightest degree of precision, nor does he once mention either Alaric or the Hebrus. Claudian seems to assume that the event was well enough known for a brief allusion to it to be comprehensible to his audience, and in that case one might reasonably have expected Zosimus to be more explicit.

107 f. uenientem . . . Hebri clausit aquis: the reading *ueniens e* is easily disposed of, since (1) *clausit* needs an object, and (2), whereas *ueniens* would describe the actions of Alaric, the rhetorical balance of the sentence requires that the two present participles (*uenientem/uocantis*) both refer to the same individual, i.e. Theodosius. Rather more difficult is the choice between *aquis* and *aquas*, since both would yield good sense, and in fact end up meaning much the same thing. *aquis* is neater, attested by the better manuscripts and does not necessitate the adoption of Heinsius' conjecture *uenienti*: for similar phrases see below, 108 *clausit aquis* n. Moreover, *uenienti* would necessitate a strong elision of the kind that Claudian is usually at pains to avoid: see Introd. § 5. On the other hand, the context, which seems to have Theodosius held up at the river, is similar to that in other passages where *claudo* governs a direct object and the person obstructed is in the dative: cf. Ov. *Fast.* 1. 272 'clauderet ut Tatio feruidus umor iter', Stat. *Silu.* 3. 2. 143, *Stil.* 2. 211 'aut totum oppositi claudunt fugientibus aequor'. Since there is so little in it and the situation described cannot be reconstructed in such a way as to have any decisive weight, it seems best to stick with a perfectly intelligible reading that needs no alteration or supplementation from scholarly ingenuity.

108. Hebri: the Maritsa, one of the principal rivers of Thrace (Plin. *Nat.* 4. 40, Mela 2. 17). Poets (e.g. Virg. *A.* 1. 317 'uolucrem . . . Hebrum', Ov. *Ep.* 2. 114 'admissas exigit Hebrus aquas') often represent the Hebrus as a river notable for the speed of its course, and so Claudian will no doubt have imagined it as presenting a formidable barrier. See further Nisbet–Hubbard on Hor. *Carm.* 1. 25. 20 (pp. 300f.).

    clausit aquis: cf. Virg. *A.* 8. 473 'hinc Tusco claudimur amni', Ov. *Met.* 8. 185 'clausus erat pelago'; also Luc. 2. 433 'cum Scyllaeis clauditur aquis', with Fantham ad loc.

108–10: Claudian claims that in 394 Gildo ignored an explicit summons from Theodosius to send troops to aid him in the suppression of the revolt of Eugenius and Arbogast and illegally 'seized' Africa as if it were a private estate. This passage must be examined in tandem with *Gild.* 235 ff., where the ghost of Theodosius appears to Arcadius in a dream and recalls the events of 394 in an attempt to encourage his elder son to support Honorius in his campaign against Gildo. In the earlier poem it is also said that, while peoples at the very edges of the Empire, including Armenians, Geloni and Goths, all contributed troops, 'solus at hic non puppe data, non milite misso | subsedit fluitante fide' (*Gild.* 246f.). Theodosius adds that he would have been less aggrieved to see Gildo in open revolt, but the wily African bided his time, intending to throw in his lot with whichever side would prove victorious (*Gild.* 247 ff.). It is best to assume, therefore, that Gildo did not openly oppose the will of Theodosius in 394, but that six years after the composition of *De Bello Gildonico* Claudian was content to exaggerate Gildo's alleged disloyalty in order to maximize the achievement and glory of Honorius. He presumably was counting on his audience's not being able to remember with any certainty the details either of the events of 394 or of his own earlier account of them. See in general Cameron 103ff., Olechowska 133f.

Since Claudian clearly distorts the facts and interprets all Gildo's actions in the light of his final, disastrous defection from the Western Court in 397, there are good grounds to be suspicious of virtually all the accusations of treachery which he levels against him. Indeed, Matthews argues that Gildo's loyalty to the house of Theodosius was exemplary, pointing out, for example, that he was 'an old client' of the family (p. 179) and linked to it by ties of kinship, since his daughter Salvina was married to one Nebridius, a nephew of the empress Flaccilla (pp. 109f., 272; Jer. *Ep.* 79. 2). Furthermore, Zosimus' narrative (5. 11. 1f.) implies that negotiations between Gildo and Constantinople for the transference of Africa from the authority of the West to the East began after the Eastern Empire, at Eutropius' instigation, had declared Stilicho *hostis publicus*. In these circumstances it is easy to argue that 'Gildo was "constitutionally" quite correct in supporting Arcadius rather than Honorius' (Matthews 272 n. 7), since Arcadius was the senior Augustus. None the less, it is difficult to see how Claudian could have expected to persuade anyone of the veracity of his accusations if they had no kernel of truth at all, unless indeed by constant repetition of this tale Stilicho's government had already altered people's memories. Matthews dismisses the evidence of *Gild.* 241ff. in the following terms: '(Claudian rebukes Gildo) for not openly declaring himself against Eugenius, and withholding supplies from Rome . . . but there is no reason to doubt that, in 393 and 394, his attitude was authorized by the legitimate emperor. As he had in 388, Theodosius was going to advance by the land route through Illyricum against an enemy marching out from north Italy. With the loyalty of Africa secure, there was no immediate purpose to be served by starving out Rome' (p. 245). But it seems that Matthews has misread *Gild.* 241ff., or else has possibly been duped into attacking a man of straw by the confident assertion of O. Seeck (*Geschichte des Untergangs der antiken Welt* (Berlin, 1913; repr. Darmstadt, 1966), v. 283) that Gildo 'unterstützte diesen (i.e. Eugenius) ebenso durch Kornzufuhren, wie er es bei Maximus getan hatte', just before turning to the question of Theodosius' call for Gildo to supply troops. In plain fact, though Gildo did cut the corn supplies to Rome in 397, with serious consequences for Stilicho's régime (see above 101–21 n.), there is no mention, either at *Gild.* 235ff. or in the present passage, of Theodosius requiring any similar action in 387–8. Instead, Gildo is accused *only* of failing to send troops for use against the usurper. Cutting the food-supply of Rome no doubt was, as Matthews argues, unnecessary, but the contribution of troops would have been a perfectly reasonable request for the Emperor to make: Claudian's evidence on this score should not be made to appear weaker than it is by reference to wholly chimerical designs on the food-supply to the City. Perhaps Gildo stalled, pleading in his justification that with the enemy so close at hand (cf. *proxima bella* 109) he could spare no men, though such a supposition need by no means necessarily imply the cynical motive which Claudian chooses to impute to him.

108f. Contrast the *pietas* of Honorius himself at 429ff. *sed nec post Libyam* . . . | . . . *patriae mandata uocantis | spreuimus.*

109. respuit: this rather violent sense of *respuo* is totally avoided by Virgil and sparingly used in other authors (Liv. 42. 14. 2, Ov. *Ibis* 166, V. Fl. 5. 321f. 'sin uero preces et dicta superbus | respuerit'), but Claudian seems to have a liking for it, using it no fewer than nine times. Cf. esp. *Gild.* 30, 277, *Stil.* 2. 43, 181, 283. A similarly forceful metaphor can be found applied to Gildo's later rejection of the authority of Honorius at *Gild.* 256f. 'germani nunc usque tui responsa colebat: | en iterum calcat'.

auxiliis: perhaps literally 'auxiliary contingents' (*OLD* s.v. 5), but the looser sense of 'reinforcements' (as at e.g. Virg. *A.* 8. 8) is more in keeping with the dignity of traditional heroic verse. The same ambiguity can be seen at e.g. Luc. 7. 548f. 'non illic regum auxiliis collecta iuuentus | bella gerit'.

proxima: i.e. Gildo had no excuse based on logistical difficulty for his failure to contribute troops, a state of affairs all the more shameful when we remember the poet's claim at *Gild.* 243ff. that support came to the Emperer from as far away as Armenia and Lake Maeotis.

110. abiurata . . . possederat arua: compare the complaints of the goddess Africa at *Gild.* 157ff., of similar actions attributed to him in 397: 'priuato iure tenemur | exigui specie fundi. quod Nilus et Atlans | dissidet, occiduis quod Gadibus arida Barce | quodque Paraetonio secedit litore Tinge, | hoc sibi transcribit proprium. pars tertia mundi | unius praedonis ager.' *abiurata* implies that through his disloyalty he had lost all title to rule over the land, *possederat* that his continued exercise of authority amounted to an illegal seizure of it as private property. *abiuro* is rare in Latin verse, and may have been thought too technical to be entirely suitable to high literature, but cf. Virg. *A.* 8. 263, Stat. *Theb.* 6. 151. *arua* is surely pointed here, given the threat posed by illegal occupation of the African cornfields to the food-supply of Italy: cf. *Gild.* 75 'Romuleas uendit segetes et possidet arua.' For the tense of *possederat* (pluperfect for aorist, a common usage in Late Antiquity, but one normally avoided by Claudian) see Birt, p. ccxxiii.

palam: Gildo was brazen-faced in his disloyalty. Platnauer prints *palam* but seems to be translating *olim* ('the fields . . . he had long forsworn'), or perhaps thinking of πάλαι.

111. meritam . . . iram: cf. Virg. *A.* 8. 501 'merita accendit Mezentius ira', where the context is similarly presented as one of resistance to tyranny. Cf. also Ov. *Pont.* 1. 1. 49 'nec quia uel merui uel sensi principis iram'.

112. suppliciis fruitur: the most neutral way of interpreting this statement is to take it as meaning that Theodosius is glad to see justice done at last. But the phrase may leave the modern reader uncomfortable, to say the least, especially since elsewhere Claudian seems to espouse the standard doctrine that to take pleasure in the bloody punishment of wrongdoers is a mark of savagery inimical to the teachings of the divine Clementia: contrast *Stil.* 2. 14 f. (Stilicho taught by Clementia) 'haec docet ut poenis hominum uel sanguine pasci | turpe ferumque putes', and see also *Theod.* 224 f. 'qui fruitur poena, ferus est, legumque uidetur | uindictam praestare sibi.' However, in all these places Claudian is responsive, not to his personal opinions (whatever they were), but to the needs of his case. The most famous exposition of the standard doctrine in Roman moral writing can be found at Sen. *Cl.* 1. 25. 1 f. 'crudelitas minime humanum malum est indignumque tam miti animo; ferina ista rabies est sanguine gaudere ac uulneribus et abiecto homine in siluestre animal transire.' Note also Sen. *Ben.* 7. 19. 8. More disturbing still, almost the same phrase is used of the bloodthirsty Rufinus at *Ruf.* 1. 234 f., though there Claudian inserts the damning epithet *crudelibus*. For the phrasing note also Mart. 8. 30. 3 f. (Scaevola) 'aspicis ut teneat flammas poenaque fruatur | fortis et attonito regnet in igne manus.'

In the event, it may be that neither Gildo nor Alaric was actually executed by the Imperial authorities: the former possibly took his own life and the latter was lucky enough to escape (223 ff. n.). At *Gild.* 253 ff., however, Claudian attributes to Theodosius the intention to inflict upon Gildo the same brutal punishment which Mettus suffered at the hands of Tullus: 'o si non cupidis essem praereptus ab astris! | exemplum sequerer Tulli laniandaque dumis | inpia diuersis aptarem membra quadrigis' (cf. Virg. *A.* 8. 642 ff.). Gildo, then, like Mettus, is an oath-breaker and guilty of *perfidia*, that is, guilty of violating that very *pietas* which is here vindicated by Honorius: note *inpia* at *Gild.*

255, and cf. Virgil's exclamation 'at tu dictis, Albane, maneres!', *IV Cons.* 402 'perfidiam damnas? Metti satiabere poenis.' Theodosius' apparently unholy glee should therefore be interpreted as delight at the righteous punishment of an exceptionally heinous crime.

natoque ultore: cf. *Gild.* 402 ff. 'te prodita iura, | te pater ultorem, te nudi puluere manes, | te pietas polluta rogat', though there the reference is not to Theodosius but to Mascezel, whose children Gildo is said to have killed and flung out without burial (*Gild.* 389 ff.). Cf. also *Stil.* 1. 326 'exercitus . . . ultor'. *ultore* prepares the comparison with Orestes (cf. Aesch. *Ag.* 1280 ἥξει γὰρ ἡμῶν ἄλλος αὖ τιμάορος) and Augustus (cf. the Temple of Mars Ultor).

113-21. A carefully constructed sequence, three lines apiece being given to the manner in which Orestes, Augustus, and Honorius all avenged their fathers. In the cases of Orestes and Augustus a first line records the act of vengeance, but is then undercut by *sed* in the second line as Claudian goes on to show how their *pietas* towards their fathers was marred by a dreadful failure to show the same virtue towards others who had a similar claim on it. In the case of Honorius, however, the second line introduces a clause which, far from being adversative, indicates how the Emperor's single action (*isdemque tropaeis*) brought him a double crown of victory and virtue. See further Michael Dewar, *CQ*, NS 39 (1990), 580-2. Tonio Hölscher has kindly drawn my attention to his article 'Augustus and Orestes' in S. Jakobielski and Zs. Kiss (eds.), *Études consacrées à Anna Sadurska* (Travaux du Centre d'archéologie méditerranéenne de L'Académie Polonaise des Sciences, 30 = Etudes et travaux, 15; Warsaw, 1990), 164-8. Dr Hölscher produces convincing artistic evidence that in the early stages of his political career Octavian actively promoted ideological comparisons between himself and Orestes; the supposed bones of the hero were also brought to Rome and reburied near the temple of Saturn in the Forum Romanum. This would serve to confirm my view that Virgil is suggesting a link between the two at *G.* 1. 511 ff. (*CQ*, NS 38 (1989), 563-5), but makes it much less likely that Virgil's contemporaries would have considered the parallel critical of Augustus.

113-15. Orestes avenged his father, but he also contaminated *pietas* with sin by slaying Aegisthus' mistress and accomplice, his own mother Clytemnestra. Claudian here takes the standard view of Orestes' action, but to point more strongly the contrast between Orestes' deeds and the unambiguous rightness of Honorius' action he suppresses all mention of Orestes' final acquittal as recorded in the *Eumenides* of Aeschylus. Cf. these lines to Ovid's record of a similar case, Alcmaeon's killing of his own mother Eriphyle in vengeance for the death of his father Amphiaraus: *Met.* 9. 407f. 'ultusque parenté parentem | natus erit facto pius et sceleratus eodem'.

113. Thyestiaden: Aegisthus, son of Agamemnon's brother Thyestes: cf. *Od.* 4. 518 Θυεστιάδης Αἴγισθος, Ov. *Ars* 2. 407f. 'inde Thyestiaden animo thalamoque recepit | et male peccantem Tyndaris ulta uirum'.

Thyestiaden poenas exegit: the phrase *poenas exigo* is a very common one (Ov. *Ep.* 7. 97, *Met.* 4. 190, 8. 125, *Fast.* 4. 230, *Ciris* 74, Sil. 7. 280, 9. 433); note also the variant *supplicium/-a exigo* found in e.g. Seneca (*Phoen.* 539, *Phaed.* 706) and Statius (*Theb.* 11. 167f.). The normal construction, however, requires *a* (or more rarely *de*) with the ablative of the person on whom vengeance is taken: e.g. Ov. *Tr.* 5. 8. 9 'exigit a dignis ultrix Rhamnusia poenas', Sen. *Ben.* 5. 7. 2, Luc. 7. 771 'exigit a meritis tristes uictoria poenas', 8. 21f.; Ov. *Met.* 8. 531f. 'de matre manus . . . | exegit poenas', Suet. *Iul.* 69. None the less, the manuscripts of Claudian here offer a choice between a double accusative (*Thyestiaden poenas*) and the combination of the accusative with what should no doubt be seen as a dative of disadvantage standing in for the ablative of separation (*Thyestiadae poenas*). Much the same situation obtains at *Get.* 194f. 'tandem supplicium cunctis pro montibus Alpes | exegere Getas *or* Getis', though there the accusative *Getas* has far less impressive manuscript support than *Thyestiaden* does here. At any rate it would appear that Claudian was experimenting with the phrase at this stage of his career, though deciding what he wrote is not easy. Heinsius preferred the dative, and pointed to Ov. *Fast.* 4. 230, where he read '*huic* poenas exigit ira deae', but editors of the *Fasti* tend to prefer the alternative reading *hinc*. Early commentators refer to Sen. *Her. O.* 970, where manuscripts divide between 'exigat poenas sibi' and 'exigam poenas tibi', but this passage is not useful here, because in either case the dative would have a different sense ('exact punishment on his own | your behalf', not 'from himself | you'). On the other hand, neither is there a conclusive example of the double accusative with *exigo* before Claudian's time. Clearly relevant for our purposes, however, is the use of the passive of *exigo* with the person from whom money is demanded, a construction which is the subject of a brief discussion by Aulus Gellius (15. 14). Gellius cites two examples from early Latin, one from a speech of Q. Caecilius Metellus Numidicus ('socios ad senatum questum flentes uenisse, sese pecunias maximas exactos esse' = *orat.* 5 Malcovati), and one from Caecilius ('ego illud minus nihilo exigor portorium' = 92 Ribbeck | 88 Warmington). Gellius considers this 'noue dictum' and thinks it is an imitation of the Greek idiom seen in εἰσεπράξατό με ἀργύριον, which, he says, is the same as 'exegit me pecuniam.' In this he seems to be in error. The double accusative is familiar in Latin from verbs of related meaning (*rogo, posco*) and, as can be seen from *TLL* v/2. 1458. 24ff., the use of the double accusative with the passive of *exigo* is also attested in a fairly wide range of prose texts from the fourth century and later, and is even something of a mannerism in legal language: consider e.g. *C. Th.* 6. 35. 1 'ut qui haec contempserit . . . poenas debitas exigatur'. None the less, the present case is not quite parallel to these examples. Claudian uses the double accusative in combination with the active verb (*exegit*), and the whole construction, whether active or passive, is not often found in literary works. Note, however, that the *TLL* loc. cit. offers one example from the Vulgate (*Job* 11. 6 'minora exigaris ab eo (sc. Deo) quam meretur iniquitas tua') and two from the 6th c.: Cassiod. *Hist. Eccl.* 6. 32. 5 'sed pro his impietatibus uesanisque praesumptionibus non post multum poenas exacti sunt', 6. 45. 3 (of Julian the Apostate) 'ferus sacrae uineae deuastator poenas exactus est uastationis suae'. But if ancient scholarship held that the construction was a Graecism of venerable antiquity, then that will no doubt have been adequate to absolve it of any perceived stain of prosaicness in the eyes of a bookish poet whose native language was Greek in any case. See also *OLD* s.v. *exigo* 8 for the suggestion that the passages discussed by Gellius should be thought of as examples of the passive combined with that consciously poetic feature, the 'retained' accusative (see 153 *resoluta comam* n.). On balance, then, it seems best to accept the double accusative, and see it as a deliberate 'Graecism'. See further 510 *uoce . . . maiore* n. for the importance of ancient scholarship, even where mistaken, in deciding what Claudian actually wrote.

114. mixtum pietate nefas: as Müller remarks, one might more logically expect e.g. 'mixta scelere pietas', but the phrase as it stands serves to throw special emphasis on the surprise element *nefas*. For other striking examples of hypallage in Claudian see Birt, p. ccxxv.

dubitandaque: the gerundive of the verb is sometimes used for *dubius*, especially in hexameter verse, where the three shorts of the adjective cannot be easily accommodated. See *TLL* v/1. 2102. 75ff., and cf. Virg. *A.* 3. 170, Ov. *Pont.* 2. 4. 2, Luc. 4. 60, *IV Cons.* 185, *Gild.* 102.

115. materno . . . crimine: = 'crimine in matrem commisso'.

laudem cum crimine pensat: commentators compare Plin. *Nat.* 9. 79 'crimina una laude pensat', Quint. *Inst.* 2. 12. 5 'id et raro prouenit et cetera uitia non pensat.' More important is the clear echo of Ov. *Met.* 13. 192 'laudem ut cum sanguine penset', of Agamemnon's sacrifice of Iphigenia at Aulis, where Odysseus balances that barbaric action with the glory won by the leader of the expedition against Troy in defence of his brother's honour. Claudian must have expected those who recognized the allusion to reflect that father and son are alike, since, just as Orestes was *pius* towards his father but failed to show the same virtue towards his mother, so too Agamemnon displayed exemplary *pietas* towards Menelaus but a hideous lack of it towards his daughter.

116–18. The first avowed political goal of the young Augustus (Octavian) was to take revenge on the murderers of his adoptive father Julius Caesar, that is, the *soi-disant* 'tyrannicides'. This he achieved at the battle of Philippi in 42 BC, afterwards commemorating his own *pietas* in the construction of the temple of Mars Ultor, vowed on the field of victory and completed in 2 BC (*Res Gestae* 2, 21. 1: cf. Hor. *Carm.* 1. 2. 43f. 'patiens uocari | Caesaris ultor', Ov. *Fast.* 3. 705ff.). Both contemporaries and posterity were in some cases sceptical about the sincerity of this filial piety, preferring to see in it a cynical motive for the power-games of war and politics against dangerous rivals. The most cogent exposition of this doubt regarding his motives is found in Tacitus' famous summing up of popular reactions to his death: *Ann.* 1. 9 'hi pietate erga parentem et necessitudine rei publicae, in qua nullus tunc legibus locus, ad arma ciuilia actum', 10 'dicebatur contra: pietatem erga parentem et tempora rei publicae obtentui sumpta . . .' Dio has Tiberius in his *laudatio* defend Augustus' conduct in his youth along the lines indicated by Tacitus above (56. 37. 3, 38. 1). The consensus among later authors, however, is that though Augustus' principate was on balance a credit to him, he had begun very badly indeed with a great number of acts of bloodthirsty savagery in the civil wars and the proscriptions: see Sen. *Clem.* 1. 11. 2 'ego uero clementiam non uoco lassam crudelitatem', Stat. *Silu.* 4. 1. 32 'coepit sero mereri'. Hostility to Augustus reappears at *Gild.* 49f. 'postquam iura ferox in se communia Caesar | transtulit', where 'Caesar' is 'Augustus' and the influence of Tacitus is dominant (Cameron 336). Claudian in his turn seems to have exercised some influence over Cor. *Laud. Iust.* 3. 26f. 'supremum patri talem celebrauit honorem | Augusto melior Iustinus Caesare princeps' (where see Averil Cameron's n.), and possibly Sid. *Carm.* 7. 93 'trux Auguste'. The still fiercer opposition of Prudentius (*C. Symm.* 1. 245ff.), on the other hand, is motivated by Augustus' deification and by his lamentable sexual mores as seen in his marrying Livia when she was pregnant by another man.

116. pauit . . . sanguine manes: taken with *parentans* (118) this implies that Augustus shed the blood of Caesar's murderers as a kind of *parentalia* offering to the spirit of his adoptive father. For the idea cf. Cic. *Pis.* 16 'a me quidem poenas expetistis quibus coniuratorum

manis mortuorum expiaretis', and for the phrasing cf. Ov. *Am.* 3. 8. 10
'sanguine pastus eques', Luc. 1. 39 'Poeni saturentur sanguine manes'
(i.e. of the Romans killed at Pharsalus) 9. 151f., Sil. 15. 517f. Claudian
may well have in mind the old calumny that, at the end of the siege of
Perusia, Augustus sacrificed three hundred prisoners of equestrian and
senatorial rank to Caesar's ghost on the Ides of March (Suet. *Aug.* 15).
Contrast *IV Cons.* 93ff., where Theodosius' elimination of Maximus
and Eugenius is presented as a worthy sacrifice to the aggrieved spirits
of Gratian and Valentinian II: 'solacia caesis | fratribus haec ultor
tribuit. necis auctor uterque | labitur; Augustas par uictima mitigat
umbras. | has dedit inferias tumulis, iuuenumque duorum | purpureos
merito placauit sanguine Manes.' Note especially the difference in
tone between the neutral *placauit* and the hint of bloodthirstiness
in *pauit*, as well as the explicit condemnation of the slain usurpers in
merito ... sanguine as against the more non-committal *inuiso sanguine* here.

Iuleos: for the use of an attributive adjective derived from a
personal name in the place of the genitive see 11 *mons Euandrius* n.
Iuleus is a relatively rare and intensely poetic form, found also at Prop.
4. 6. 17, Ov. *Fast.* 4. 124, *Pont.* 2. 5. 49, Luc. 1. 197, 9. 995.

inuiso sanguine: recalling the single-minded patriotism of the
Roman army at Pollentia as it drives home its advantage over the
Goths (*Get.* 604ff.).

117. praeconia: rare in high verse; Ovid is fond of the word, for
example, but all but one (*Met.* 12. 573) of its thirteen appearances in his
poetry are in the elegiacs. Cf. Luc. 1. 472 'falsa . . . praeconia', Stat.
Theb. 2. 176, *Stil.* 2. 185.

118. ciuili strage: perhaps implying the act of a tyrant: cf. Plin. *Pan.*
48. 3 (of Domitian) 'nunc se ad clarissimorum ciuium strages
caedesque proferret.' Stilicho, on the other hand, is praised because in
his case 'non ulla nocendi | tela nec infecti iugulis ciuilibus enses'
(*Nupt.* 328f.).

parentans: a semi-technical word, and so very rare in verse, but
cf. Ov. *Am.* 1. 13. 3f. 'sic Memnonis umbris | annua sollemni caede
parentet auis'.

119. Müller compares Cic. *Red. Pop.* 16 (of Pompey) 'causamque meam
cum communi salute coniunxit.' Plain *res* (singular or plural) for *res
publica* goes back to the beginnings of Latin epic: Enn. *Ann.* 363
Skutsch 'unus homo nobis cunctando restituit rem', Virg. *A.* 1. 278 'his
ego nec metas rerum nec tempora pono'. *salus rerum* is a phrase used
in poetry to honour various individuals, such as Augustus (Ov. *Tr.* 2.
574 'o pater, o patriae cura salusque tuae!'), Domitian (Mart. 5. 1. 7)
and the infant son of Hannibal (Sil. 4. 815f.). But as well as contrast-

ing the noble patriotism of Honorius with the slaughter of fellow-citizens by Augustus, Claudian is also recalling Lucan's impassioned outburst after his own description of Sulla's carnage during the civil war with Marius: 2. 221 f. 'hisne salus rerum, felix his Sulla uocari. | his meruit tumulum medio sibi tollere Campo?' See also MacCormack, pls. 47, 51, 59, 60 for coins of Constantine and Galla Placidia bearing the slogan *salus rei publicae*.

120. duplicat: reminiscent of the magnificent peroration of *De Bello Getico*, and the wish that a single trophy mark the spot where both the Cimbri and the Goths were annihilated: 644 'duplices signet titulos, commune tropaeum'.

isdemque tropaeis: to Honorius' blameless victory contrast 394 f. *eadem sed causa tropaei, | ciuilis dissensus, erat.*

122–6. *I have sung in the past of the defeats of Gildo and of the Goths: now it is my Muse's delight to sing of the sacred ceremonies of your* aduentus.

Claudian now moves from describing the consular ceremonies proper, and from the reminiscences they provoke of Honorius' earlier dealings with Rome, to an epic-style account of the aftermath of Pollentia and of the Emperor's ceremonial triumphal *aduentus* into the City. That the generic status of the poem is thus about to be raised by the use of exalted heroic narrative is signalled by Claudian's deliberately drawing a parallel between the present poem and two earlier compositions that were formally not panegyrics but epics, even if neither in the end exceeded the length of a single book. The unfinished *De Bello Gildonico* was recited in Milan in the spring of 398 (*iam pridem* 122), though in fact the completed portion extends only as far as the sailing of the Imperial fleet, and does not record Gildo's actual capture and death (*captum . . . Maurum* 122). The victory over Alaric at Pollentia is the theme of *De Bello Getico*, delivered in Rome, in the presence of Stilicho (*apud socerum* 124), some eighteen months before the present poem (*nuper* 124: for the chronology see the Introd. Sect 3, pp. xxxi–xliv). Now (*nunc* 125) Claudian takes up the story at the point where he had on that occasion left it, with Alaric painfully retreating from the disaster inflicted upon him on the fields of Pollentia.

This bridge-passage fulfils the function of an epic invocation of the Muses, though their co-operation in this glorious undertaking is simply assumed rather than requested (*libet edere Musis* 125). The technique of using a delayed invocation followed by a narrative which explains the present circumstances being celebrated by the poet already appears in Claudian's earliest extant panegyric (*Prob.* 55 ff.). The language used in these lines is especially close to two passages of Statius concerning proposed epic-style encomium of the deeds of Domitian: *Theb.* 1. 32 ff. 'tempus erit, cum Pierio tua fortior oestro | facta canam: nunc tendo chelyn satis arma referre | Aonia', and *Silu.* 1. 2. 180f. (to Stella) 'Dacasque . . . | exuuias laurosque dabit celebrare recentes.' In his turn, Claudian is remodelled by Sidonius: *Carm.* 22. 12 'ergo age, Pierias, Erato, mihi percute chordas'.

122. captum . . . Maurum: see 101–21 n. *Maurus* is used regularly of Gildo (*Gild.* 70, 338), whose domains included the old kingdom of Mauretania: cf. 104 *Maurusius Atlans* n. Ammianus records that his father Nubel belonged to an African tribe, the Iubaleni (29. 5. 44).

122 f. Parnasia . . . Pieriis . . . fidibus chelys: the instrumental ablative is in effect a pleonasm, though perhaps one could argue that it stresses the physical action involved. Structures of this kind are fairly common in some classical authors, especially Propertius, but they appear with great frequency in the poetry of Late Antiquity. See Housman on *Man.* 1. 539, D. R. Shackleton Bailey, *Propertiana* (Cambridge, 1956), 33 f. (who regards them as indicative of 'verbal indiscipline'), Nisbet–Hubbard on Hor. *Carm.* 2. 3. 12, and L. A. Holford-Strevens, *Aulus Gellius* (London, 1988), 140 n. 78. It is hard to see why a distinction should be made between a 'Parnassian' lyre and its 'Pierian' strings, but the general effect is to associate Claudian's poetry with both Apollo and the Muses. Similarly, a Muse asked for inspiration at *Prob.* 71 is addressed as 'Parnasia'. For similar phrases cf. also Sen. *Her. O.* 1033 f. 'aptans Pieriam chelyn | Orpheus', Sil. 11. 415 'Pieria . . . lyra'.

captum . . . Maurum . . . egit: 'sang of how the Moor was taken.' For the *ab urbe condita* construction see *pr.* 17 *uictusque Typhoeus* n. *egit* probably = *cecinit*: cf. V. Fl. 4. 87 (Orpheus) 'agit . . . medicabile carmen'. Varro makes the distinction between dramatic poets who 'make' (we should say 'write') plays and actors who 'act' them (*L.* 6. 77 'poeta facit fabulam, et non agit, contra actor agit et non facit'), and *ago* is a natural word to use of actors delivering verse, with all the appropriate gestures, on stage, e.g. Cic. *de Orat.* 3. 102 'numquam agit hunc uersum Roscius eo gestu quo potest . . .'. Since oratory too is a kind of dramatic art, *ago* is also found in contexts involving emotional performance: e.g. Cic. *de Orat.* 3. 214 (after quoting from a speech of Gaius Gracchus) 'quae sic ab illo acta esse constabat oculis, uoce, gestu, inimici ut lacrimas tenere non possent.' Claudian will no doubt, like an orator, have made full use of the expressive qualities of both his voice and his eyes; *ago* thus seems a reasonable enough word to use here.

Alternatively, Barth suggested that the sense is *captum Maurum egit* 'velut in triumphum'. The case for this can be strengthened by taking the expression as an example of the poet being said actually to do what his poem records: see e.g. Virg. *Ecl.* 6. 62f. (Silenus) 'tum Phaethontiadas musco circumdat amarae | corticis atque solo proceras erigit alnos', with Servius ad loc., 'mira autem est canentis laus ut quasi non factam rem cantare sed ipse eam cantando facere uideatur'.

arma Getarum: Claudian regularly uses the noun *Getae* (roughly 'Thracians') and adjective *Geticus* for the Goths: see Levy on *Ruf.* 1. 308, Schroff on *Get. pr.* 6. The Goths had long been settled in Thrace (Wolfram 117ff.), and it was the custom, especially in poetry and in prose that aimed at sublimity, to give tribes inhabiting northern regions the names assigned to the earlier inhabitants in classical works such as Herodotus' account of Scythia (4. 1–117; Γέται, 4. 93ff.) in order to enhance the dignity and solemnity of the work: see A. Cameron, *Agathias* (Oxford, 1990), 82f. As Wolfram points out (pp. 28f.), Jerome observes that the use of *Getae* for the Goths was well-established practice by his time. Examples include Julian *Or.* 1. 9 D, Themistius *Or.* 8. 110 C, 13. 166 C, 13. 179 C: cf. also Rut. Nam. *Red.* 1. 40, and Σκύθαι at Themistius *Or.* 16. 210 d. *arma Getarum* is thus a nobler-sounding variant for *De Bello Getico* (itself a more dignified version of *De Bello Gothico*) etc. (e.g. 384, 490), alluding as it does to such lofty formulations as *arma uirumque cano*.

The identification of the Goths with the Thracians has the further poetic and propagandistic advantage of allowing Claudian to attribute to the enemy negative qualities regularly associated in classical poetry with the inhabitants of this region. Since Homer, Thrace had been linked with Ares in his bloodiest aspect (*Il.* 13. 301, *Od.* 8. 361, Virg. *G.* 4. 462, *A.* 3. 35, Stat. *Theb.* 7. 34ff.) and the Thracians were therefore traditionally seen as savage and warlike: see Hor. *Carm.* 2. 16. 5 'bello furiosa Thrace', Ov. *Tr.* 5. 3. 22 'Marticolam . . . Geten', *Pont.* 1. 8. 6. Hand in hand with this ferocity went cruelty, which is prominent in such myths as those of Diomedes' man-eating horses (e.g. Ov. *Met.* 9. 194ff., Stat. *Theb.* 6. 348ff.), the slaughter of Orpheus by the Ciconian women (Virg. *G.* 4. 520ff., Ov. *Met.* 11. 1ff., Sil. 11. 475f.), and Tereus, characterized by Ovid as a 'barbarus' and 'crudelis' whose rape of Philomela is partly inspired by racial ancestry (*Met.* 6. 424ff., 460 'flagrat uitio gentisque suoque'). The association of the Goths, as latter-day 'Getae', with Mars also appears in Jordanes (*Get.* 41), who cites *A.* 3. 35, and Sidonius (*Carm.* 7. 502).

124. apud socerum: at a recitation, it seems, probably held in the library of the temple of Palatine Apollo: see *pr.* 23 *orbis apex aequatus*

Olympo n. For *apud* with this sense in the context of public oratory or literary performances cf. Cic. *Inu.* 2. 134 'apud populum haec et per populum agi conuenire', Liv. 3. 10. 3, Ov. *Met.* 12. 163.

plectro celebrata recenti: recalling *Get.* 635 'o celebranda mihi cunctis Pollentia saeclis'. Cf. also Ov. *Pont.* 4. 8. 87 'unde tuas possim laudes celebrare recentes', Stat. *Silu.* 1. 2. 180 f. cit. 122–6 n., 4. 2. 7 'qua celebrem mea uota lyra'. It is best to take *recenti* as reinforcing *nuper. De Bello Getico* was delivered not long after Pollentia and before the later battle of Verona, only some eighteen months before the present poem: see Introd. Sect. 3.

125. aduentus . . . sacra tui: the Emperor is an earthly deity and his arrival is thus a kind of divine epiphany. For the language used cf. *III Cons.* 121 f. (Honorius' arrival in Italy) 'oppida . . . | aduentu sacrata tuo', Lucr. 1. 6 f. (Venus), Virg. *A.* 8. 201 with Fordyce ad loc., and in particular *A.* 6. 798 f. 'huius (i.e. Augusti) in aduentum iam nunc et Caspia regna | responsis horrent diuum'. For the ceremonial character of an Imperial *aduentus* see MacCormack 17 f., Introd. Sect. 2.

sacra: the use of the noun implies, correctly enough, a formalized set of rituals modelled on divine cult: compare *sacra* of the consular ceremonies at *IV Cons.* 577. *sacer* is applied to reigning Emperors and things associated with them as early as the Augustan period (Vitr. 1 *pr.* 1 'diuina tua mens et numen, imperator Caesar', Ov. *Fast.* 6. 810 'sacra . . . domo'), but both Augustus and Tiberius discouraged the use of such adulatory terminology: see e.g. Suet. *Tib.* 27 'alium dicentem sacras eius occupationes . . . uerba mutare et . . . pro sacris laboriosas dicere coegit', Tac. *Ann.* 2. 87 with Goodyear ad loc. It was not until the reign of Domitian that *sacer, sacratus*, etc. with the sense 'Imperial' became both standard and generally unobjectionable: see Coleman on Stat. *Silu.* 4. *pr.* 6 'sacratissimis . . . epulis', and cf. *Silu.* 3. 3. 64 ff., 4. 2. 5, 5. 1. 190 f. 'sacri . . . uultus | Caesaris', 5. 2. 177, Mart. 7. 99. 4 'sacra Caesaris aure', Sil. 3. 620. Under the autocracy of the Late Empire everything related to the Emperor or his family is by its very nature 'holy', including the doors of his palace (*Ruf.* 2. 142), his sleep (*Eutr.* 1. 418; discussed by Alan Cameron at *CQ*, NS 18 (1968), 402), the wounds he inflicts when hunting (*Fesc.* 1. 14), his wife (Cor. *Laud. Iust.* 1. 248), and even his feet (Cor. *Laud. Iust.* 1. 158 'diuinis . . . plantis', 197 'sacro pede'). The titles given Imperial officials—*praepositus sacri cubiculi, quaestor sacri palatii, comes sacrarum largitionum*—show how uncontroversial such language had become. See further Millar 73, 79, 539, Levy on *Ruf.* 1. *pr.* 16 'sacra caterua'. Significantly, this Imperial language is also used of Stilicho ('os sacrum', *Stil.* 3. 11).

126. patratis . . . bellis: 'now that wars are ended': the ablative absolute explains why this song is one in which Claudian and the Muses rejoice. *bellum/-a patrare* seems to be a collocation more commonly found in historical writing than in poetry (e.g. Sal. *Iug.* 75. 2, Tac. *Ann.* 2. 26, 3. 47; but cf. *Gild.* 273 f.). Quintilian (*Inst.* 8. 3. 44) is censorious of those who, in his day, amuse themselves by interpreting it obscenely (as = e.g. *pedicare formosum*).

127–45. *Alaric and his army, like a pirate ship crippled in a foolhardy attack on a powerful ship of war, retreat in disarray and terror back along the way they came.*

Claudian now begins the narrative of those parts of the first Gothic invasion of Italy not covered in *De Bello Getico*, starting with the movement of Alaric's army after the check received at Pollentia on Easter Day (6 Apr.) 402. This narrative covers the retreat from Pollentia (127–200), the battle of Verona and Alaric's attempt to break westwards into Gaul (201–32), Stilicho's thwarting of this plan and Alaric's final expulsion from Italy back into Illyricum (232–330), and a flashback to the siege of Milan (441–90). For an attempt to construct a coherent account of the chronology of the campaign from this extremely tendentious and elliptical account see Introd., Sect. 3.

127. Pollentini: though named by Pliny (*Nat.* 3. 49) as one of the many 'noble towns' in the Po valley, Pollentia (modern Pollenza) had played only a small part in history before 402. It was involved in the fighting that followed Caesar's assassination and the defeat of Hirtius and Pansa (43 BC), and Cicero wrote a letter from there (*Fam.* 11. 13) reporting on the campaign against Antony. Its principal claim to celebrity in earlier times was the production of high-quality dark wool (Col. 7. 2. 4, Sil. 8. 597, Mart. 14. 157). For the use of the adjective in verse Claudian could have appealed to the authority of Statius (*Silu.* 2. 6. 63); cf. Prud. *C. Symm.* 2. 720.

tenuatus: i.e. 'weakened', or, to use the English idiom, 'with his ranks thinned'. Professor Nisbet compares the English idiom 'cut down to size', which well conveys the general sense but is, of course, not in the appropriate register. *tenuo* is frequently used of the wasting effects of hunger or love, but no parallel is at hand for this very striking use of the word to describe the losses suffered by Alaric at Pollentia. Cameron (182 f.) is properly sceptical about the claims of Claudian and Prudentius (*C. Symm.* 2. 715 ff.) on the subject of Gothic losses; so too is Heather (209), who points out that the Goths were still strong enough to contemplate forcing their way over the Alps into Gaul (229 ff.). See further 210–28, 281–5 nn.

funere: also metaphorically of a disastrous battle at *Get.* 387 'et Trebiam saeuo geminassent funere Cannae'.

128 f. A brief allusion to the rationale already given at length elsewhere (*Get.* 95 ff.) for Alaric's not being hunted down and slain after the supposedly overwhelming victory at Pollentia: pragmatic considerations demanded that he be allowed to retreat unharmed, in case, in desperate straits, he should try to destroy the still-exposed city of Rome. For a full discussion of the situation that perhaps motivated such claims on the part of Stilicho see Cameron 181 ff., Introd. Sect. 3, and cf. 291 ff. n. It seems clear that this explanation was not universally accepted, and suspicions of treachery and collusion on Stilicho's part were rife, among both Christians and pagans, long after 402. Consider Orosius 7. 37. 1–2 'barbaras gentes . . . hic (sc. Stilicho) fouit. taceo de Alarico rege cum Gothis suis saepe uicto, saepe concluso semperque dimisso', Jerome, *Ep.* 123. 17 'quod non uitio principum, qui uel religiosissimi sunt, sed scelere semibarbari accidit proditoris', Rut. Nam. *Red.* 2. 41 ff., Introd. Sect. 4.

128 f. concessa . . . luce: the verb practically asserts that Alaric begged for his life. It is a boon which he at any rate comes to regret: 316 *quid moror inuisam lucem?*

128. rerum . . . usus: 'policy' (Platnauer); we might say 'the way of the world', or even '*Realpolitik*'. Cf. Cic. *de Orat.* 2. 204 'docuit enim iam nos longa uita ususque rerum maximarum', *Balb.* 60; note also Ov. *Ep.* 17. 145 f.

129. tot amissis sociis: Platnauer takes this to refer to desertions from Alaric's army in the wake of Pollentia, and in this is followed by Liebeschuetz (75 f., esp. 76 n. 226). That Alaric suffered from some desertions after Pollentia is highly probable (see *Get.* 88 f. 'desertus ab omni | gente sua manibusque redit truncatus et armis'), and more direct evidence is offered for such a situation in the aftermath of Verona at 250 ff. and 309 ff. But here *una* makes it necessary to take *tot amissis sociis* closely with *omnibus . . . direptis opibus*, and so it is preferable to understand both, clearly parallel, constructions as explaining *tenuatus*. The capture of the Gothic camp at Pollentia, and with it of a huge quantity of booty, is described at *Get.* 604 ff. A coherent narrative thus emerges, in which Alaric, weakened by casualties and by the loss of supplies but still possessing sizeable forces, slowly retreated, but was defeated at Verona and prevented from breaking through into Gaul (229 ff.); at this point those who had survived the disaster at Pollentia began to desert him in droves. This gives additional point to Alaric's wish (310 ff.) that he had lost *all* his men at Pollentia (*utinam cunctos licuisset perdere bello*, 310) rather than see them desert him.

Finally, though *amitto* is an admittedly rather colourless word, it is so frequently used of the loss of troops, comrades etc. through death (*OLD* s.v. 10 a), that this seems the most natural way to take it here also. Cf. e.g. Virg. *A.* 1. 217 (of comrades feared drowned) 'amissos longo socios sermone requirunt', Ov. *Met.* 14. 242.

130. direptis: cf. 263 *raptas mellis opes.*

Latio discedere iussus: here it seems easiest to take *Latio* as a variant for *Italia*, but it might be regarded as a way of stressing the danger that Latium proper, and Rome, were in: see 89 *Latium* n. *iussus* is, to say the least, putting it rather strongly, but clearly Alaric and Stilicho reached some kind of an agreement: see 204 *pacta mouet* n.

131. reuolutus: one might think of the wheel of Fortuna (e.g. Luc. 8. 701 ff.), but the verb is more suggestive of Sisyphus rolling his rock to the top of the hill, only to see it tumble back down again (*Culex* 243 'saxum procul aduerso qui monte *reuoluit*'). It is commoner to find such verbs as *deicio* in the context of an abrupt fall from glory: e.g. *Eutr.* 2. *pr.* 5f. 'culmine deiectum uitae Fortuna priori | reddidit insano iam satiata ioco', and also Sil. 17. 143 'ex alto deiectus culmine regni'. Also relevant is the moralizing idea that Fortune raises up the wicked only so that their fall may be the more spectacular. See *Ruf.* 1. 21 ff. 'iam non ad culmina rerum | iniustos creuisse queror; tolluntur in altum | ut lapsu grauiore ruant', where Levy quotes [Sen.] *Oct.* 379f. 'alte extulisti, grauius ut ruerem edita | receptus arce', Lucian, *Cont.* 14, Minuc. Fel. *Octauius* 37. 7. The 'reversal of fortune' motif is developed at greater length at 141 ff. and 154 ff., but see esp. 139 *ludibrium pelagi . . . iactatur* n.

132. turpe retexit iter: the gods are thus shown to be deaf to Alaric's prayers: *Get.* 528f. 'non ita di Getici faxint Manesque parentum | ut mea conuerso relegam uestigia cursu.' For the verb, with its vivid metaphor of 'unravelling' or 'unweaving', cf. Virg. *A.* 12. 763f. 'quinque orbis explent cursu totidemque retexunt | huc illuc', Ov. *Met.* 15. 249 'inde retro redeunt, idemque retexitur ordo'. Retreating is no doubt in itself unheroic (e.g. Ov. *Pont.* 2. 6. 21 'turpe referre pedem, nec passu stare tenaci', Stat. *Theb.* 12. 176) but *turpe* here refers not only to the general ignominy of Alaric's defeat but also to the shattered state of his army, which the simile will illustrate. Contrast the reaction of the Romans to the news of Alaric's invasion, when their panic inspired them to flight until they were checked by the exhortations of Stilicho: *Get.* 296 ff. 'quid turpes iam mente fugas, quid Gallica rura | respicitis Latioque libet post terga relicto | longinquum profugis Ararim praecingere castris?' The boot is now firmly on the other foot.

132–40. The enemy is compared to a pirate ship, shattered by a disastrous engagement with a stout trireme which it had foolishly mistaken for easy prey. The pirate ship corresponds to the Gothic host, the trireme to the Imperial army, and the sea-battle to Pollentia: the emphasis is on the desolation of the ship as it limps away from its defeat (cf. *turpe retexit iter*). Claudian passes from the description of the pirate ship, already laden with the plunder of many victims and arrogantly falling upon the trireme, straight to a description of the woeful state to which it has been reduced by the battle. The engagement itself is thus entirely elided to enhance the effect of the 'before and after' contrast. In tone and in the point it makes about hubris this simile has much in common with *Get.* 500 ff., where the old Goth warns Alaric against arrogant recklessness: 'his claustris euade, precor, dumque agmina longe, | dum licet, Hesperiis praeceps elabere terris, | ne noua praedari cupiens et parta reponas | pastorique lupus scelerum delicta priorum | intra saepta luas.' Alaric has disastrously failed to take this sage advice.

Since no direct model in extant Latin poetry can be traced for this vivid and dramatic image, it has won Claudian some rather extravagant praise for originality and power of observation. Müller in particular enthuses about his 'genaue Kenntnis' of seafaring and claims that 'die Eigenartigkeit des Vergleiches beweist die Anschauungskraft und Originalität des Dichters'. A more realistic assessment of Claudian's *doctrina* in general can be found at Cameron 305 ff., but it is perhaps more important here to realize that, despite the lack of an identifiable model to adapt, this simile is none the less thoroughly dependent on the literary tradition. Claudian has in fact given a twist to the old metaphor of the Ship of State, in which the leader is portrayed as a helmsman who guides it safely through political storms. This image can of course be traced back to Alcaeus, and features regularly in both Greek and Latin poetry, as well as philosophical, oratorical, and historical works: see the introductory note by Nisbet and Hubbard to Hor. *Carm.* 1. 14 (pp. 179 ff.). Claudian too has a lively but fairly straightforward and conventional example at *Stil.* 1. 281 ff., and note also Themistius, *Or.* 15. 194 D–195 C. This very traditional and easily recognizable motif provides Claudian with the basic framework of reference for the present simile, as is made still clearer by the close relationship it has with Hor. *Carm.* 1. 14, the best-known and most influential example of the extended metaphor in Latin literature. Horace's description of the ship labouring at sea in a terrible storm corresponds in a number of details to Claudian's picture of the ruined pirate vessel: to *Carm.* 1. 14. 3 ff. 'nonne uides ut

| *nudum remigio* latus, | et malus celeri *saucius* Africo, | *antemnaeque* gemant', 9 'non tibi sunt integra lintea', and 15f. 'tu, nisi ûentis | debes *ludibrium*, caue' compare *uiduataque caesis remigiis* (136f.), *antemnis saucia fractis* (138), *scissis uelorum . . . alis* (137), and *ludibrium pelagi* (139). In such similes the political dangers afflicting the city are figured as a terrible storm which wreaks havoc on, and perhaps nearly sinks, the Ship of State, but Claudian has changed both the situation and the emphasis of the image. Here there are two ships, representing the Roman and Gothic armies (and hence the Roman state and the whole Gothic tribe); there is no storm, but instead a sea-battle which is similarly destructive; the ship representing the Roman state, however, is an impregnable trireme which apparently suffers no serious damage; and it is the ship threatening the trireme that is almost destroyed. If the audience is normally expected to identify with the ship as it is tossed on the turbulent sea, and to feel fear and anxiety for it in its perils, the usual effect is thus reversed: the audience are on the side of the Roman trireme which, with Stilicho as helmsman, comes through unscathed, and they can take delight in seeing the other ship, the enemy's, almost sent to the bottom of the sea. Contrast the residual nobility in ill-fortune of Shakespeare's Coriolanus, to whom Aufidius says 'Thou hast a grim appearance, and thy face | Bears a command in't; though thy tackle's torn, | Thou show'st a noble vessel' (*Cor.* 4. 5. 60 ff.).

In addition, Claudian is drawing on a long tradition of political invective whereby an orator or writer characterizes his opponent as a brigand or, somewhat more rarely, a pirate preying on the state for his own private gain. Thus Cicero calls Verres both 'pirata nefarius' (*Ver.* 1. 154) and 'praedo' (*Ver.* 2. 184), and Pliny, referring to Domitian, compliments Trajan on having snatched Rome out of 'praedonis auidissimi faucibus' (*Pan.* 1. 94. 3). Claudian could also have found such imagery in Pacatus (*Pan. Theod.* 26), who calls Maximus 'noster ille pirata', and claims that his palace was so crammed with his ill-gotten gains that 'cuiuis . . . intuenti non illud imperatoris domicilium sed latronis receptaculum uideretur'. That this is part of the stock terminology of political abuse can be seen from Claudian's also applying the word *praedo* to all Stilicho's other principal foes, including Rufinus (*Ruf.* 1. 305: cf. Symm. *Ep.* 6. 14. 1), Gildo (*Gild.* 162, *Stil.* 1. 358), and Eugenius (*IV Cons.* 360). Note also that, in a sermon probably delivered in August 402, John Chrysostom refers to Alaric as τὸν λῃστήν (*PG* 59. 500). Particularly relevant, however, is Cicero's violent denunciation of Clodius at *Dom.* 24: 'quid tandem? si, quae tum in illis rei publicae tenebris caecisque nubibus et procellis, cum senatum a gubernaculis deiecisses, populum e naui exturbasses, ipse archipirata cum grege praedonum impurissimo plenissimis uelis nauigares: si, quae tum promulgasti, constituisti, promisisti, uendidisti, perferre potuisses, ecqui locus orbi terrarum uacuus extraordinariis fascibus atque imperio Clodiano fuisset?' Here Cicero presents Clodius as both an 'archpirate' and as one who has usurped the Ship of State by force, removing the Senate from its proper place at the helm and throwing the People overboard. It would no doubt be going too far categorically to claim this passage for Claudian's inspiration, but the combination of the two motifs is striking and strengthens the possibility that, far from having sprung wholly from Claudian's own imagination, the present simile is reworking a passage from a work no longer extant.

Brigands and pirates did in fact present an extremely serious danger to travellers beyond the confines of literary propaganda: see Ramsay MacMullen, *Enemies of the Roman Order* (Cambridge, Mass., 1966), 192ff., 255ff. Panegyrists accordingly shower lavish praise on Constantine and Julian for the successful suppression of literal pirates (*Pan. Lat.* Mynors 3. 4, 8. 6, 10. 12, 11. 7).

132f. piratica puppis . . . cunctis infensa fretis: the spluttering alliteration of *piratica puppis* gets the simile off to a resoundingly indignant start. For the phrasing cf. Sal. *Hist.* 2. 90 'piratica nauigia', Liv. 34. 32. 18 'mare . . . infestum nauibus piraticis', Mela 2. 5 'Achilles infesta classe mare Ponticum ingressus'. *cunctis* is pointed: the pirate has no civilized values, and regards all as his natural prey; cf. Cic. *Off.* 3. 107 'pirata non est ex perduellium numero definitus, sed communis hostis omnium'.

133f. Claudian frequently refers to the Goths under Alaric as plundering far and wide (440f. *populator Achiuae | Bistoniaeque plagae* n.), and *multas . . . diu . . . carinas* is thus not a piece of padding but designed to help establish a close correspondence between the Gothic host and the pirate ship. Likewise, the ship is 'crammed with the wealth won by crime', just as the Gothic camp captured after Pollentia was found to contain, as Claudian claims, the accumulated spoils of thirty years' worth of depredations since Adrianople (*Get.* 623ff.). A more sympathetic view of the Gothic plundering of Greece is offered by Liebeschuetz 56ff.; see also Wolfram 155f.

133f. scelerum . . . referta/diuitiis: Cicero similarly talks of Verres' 'uillae . . . spoliis ornatae refertaeque' (*Ver.* 5. 127). Cf. also Cic. *Man.* 55 'Delus . . . referta diuitiis'.

135. incidit in: since Alaric deliberately attacked the Romans the sense 'falls upon' seems preferable in the context to 'falls in with'

(Platnauer): cf. Liv. 8. 8. 13 'triarii . . . iam nulla spe post relicta, in hostem incidebant', Vell. 2. 112. 5.

bellatricem . . . triremim: cf. Stat. *Theb.* 7. 57 'bellatricesque carinae' (where see Smolenaars), Amm. Marc. 23. 3. 9. Since the trireme represents the Roman state, perhaps Claudian is also thinking of such phrases as 'bellatrix Roma' (Ov. *Tr.* 2. 321).

136. de more: far commoner than *in morem* (6n.): cf. Virg. *A.* 3. 369, 4. 57, Ov. *Met.* 7. 606, Stat. *Theb.* 4. 465, 12. 62, *Prob.* 159, 255, *Ruf.* 1. 345, *Eutr.* 2. 280, etc.

putat: Barth objected vigorously to *putat* on the grounds of common sense: 'An ergo illi tam experti rerum maritimarum, ut sunt omnes piratae, non agnoverint bellicam trirerim?' The whole point, however, is that common sense does not enter into Alaric's reasoning because he is in the grip of utter hubris. The pirates recognize that their target is a great and warlike trireme, but are so blind that they think that they can treat it in the same manner that they treat lesser prey ('dum praedam *de more* putat'). The suddenness with which Nemesis accordingly strikes the pirate-ship, and hence Alaric, is emphasized by the sharp break after the verb, followed by the description of the ruined ship.

136-40: a lurid description of the severely damaged ship. In addition to the passage's reliance on Horace (132-40n.), many of the details can be paralleled from poetic accounts of storms, especially if not exclusively, in epic: examples from e.g. Virg. *A.* 1, Ov. *Met.* 11, Luc. 5, and V. Fl. 1 appear in the following notes. Such descriptions are often very highly-wrought, prompting Juvenal's scathing observation 'omnia fiunt | talia, tam grauiter, si quando poetica surgit | tempestas' (12. 22ff.). See in general M. P. O. Morford, *The Poet Lucan* (Oxford, 1967), 20ff.

136. uiduata: balanced by *orba* (138), as *debilis* (137) is by *saucia* (138). Two words indicating deprivation thus appear in an *abab* pattern with two indicating weakness and wounding: the result is a highly stylized personification of the ship, which in turn aids the reader in interpreting it as an image for Alaric and the Gothic army. Any inclination towards sympathy receives a check in the reminder that this is a form of punishment (140). For the verb cf. Virg. *A.* 8. 571 'tam multis uiduasset ciuibus urbem'.

136 f. caesis | remigiis: cf. Hor. *Carm.* 1. 14. 4 'nudum remigio latus', which may indicate only that the ship's bank of oars has been lost: cf. V. Fl. 1. 618 'excussi manibus remi', from another storm-scene. Here, however, *caesis* makes it clear that the oarsmen themselves have been killed, thus setting up a close correspondence between the simile and the detail of *tot amissis sociis* (129) in the narrative. For *remigium* with the sense 'crew of rowers' see *OLD* s.v. 2, citing e.g. Virg. *A*. 3. 471 'remigium supplet', 8. 80, Liv. 21. 22. 4: add e.g. Liv. 26. 39, 33. 48, Tac. *Ann*. 14. 39 'paucas naues in litore remigiumque in iis amiserat.' In addition to the fact that *remigiis* has the support of the Horatian 'model', the reading *remigibus* found in the vast bulk of the manuscripts might be thought to have the look of a scribal 'correction'. On the other hand it must be conceded that the use of the plural of *remigium* with this sense appears to be otherwise unattested: sticking with *remigibus* will therefore seem the safest course to some, but I wonder whether we should perhaps read *caeso remigio*.

137. scissis uelorum debilis alis: corresponding to 'non tibi sunt integra lintea' at Hor. *Carm*. 1. 14. 9. Since sails are exposed to the winds they are conventionally the first victims of a sea-storm: Pl. *Trin*. 837 'scindere uela', Luc. 5. 594 ff. 'auolsit laceros percussa puppe rudentis | turbo rapax fragilemque super uolitantia malum | uela tulit', V. Fl. 1. 620 f. The *ala* is the 'reef', a part of the sail that billows in a favourable wind so that the ship seems to fly like a bird with out-stretched 'wings': see *OLD* s.v. 3, Williams on Virg. *A*. 3. 520. This bird, however, will fly no more. For *debilis* Claudian may be directly indebted to Virg. *A*. 5. 271 (a ship damaged in a race) 'amissis remis atque ordine debilis uno'.

138. orba gubernaclis: storms, literal or metaphorical, regularly deprive ships of either their helmsman or the helm by which they steer: here it is the helm, because Alaric is alive, but no longer able to control his ship. For the loss of the helmsman see e.g. *Od*. 12. 411 ff., *Eutr*. 2. 423 f. 'sic orba magistro | fertur in abruptum casu, non sidere puppis'; and for the loss of the helm, at least by the rightful helmsman, see e.g. Cic. *Sest*. 46 'hanc rei publicae nauem, ereptis senatui guber-naculis, fluitantem in alto', Liv. 27. 48. 11. In a remarkable variant on the motif at *A*. 6. 347 ff. Virgil has Palinurus tell how he was swept overboard with the helm still in his hands. For the phrasing cf. Ov. *Met*. 13. 195 'orba suis essent etiam nunc lintea uentis', Sil. 14. 407 'orba gubernacli . . . munera'.

antemnis saucia fractis: masts and the yard-arm etc. attached to them are commonly smashed or over-toppled by storm-winds: Claudian is closest, once more, to Horace (*Carm*. 1. 14. 5 f. 'malus celeri saucius Africo, | antemnaeque gemant'), but cf. also *Od*. 12. 409 ff. ἱστοῦ δὲ προτόνους ἔρρηξ' ἀνέμοιο θύελλα | ἀμφοτέρους, ἱστὸς δ'ὀπίσω πέσεν, ὅπλα τε πάντα | εἰς ἄντλον κατέχυνθ', Ap. Rh. 2. 1108, Pl. *Trin*. 836 f. 'procellae infensae frangere malum, | ruere antemnas', Ov. *Met*. 11. 489. 'The yard (*antemna*) was the name of the crosspiece fixed across the mast to which the sail was attached; sometimes it would consist of two pieces joined at the centre, and therefore the plural *antemnae* is commonly used' (Williams on Virg. *A.* 3. 549: see further Fordyce on Catul. 64. 234, Nisbet–Hubbard on Hor. *Carm.* 1. 14. 6, Bömer on Ov. *Met.* 11. 483). For *saucia* applied to inanimate objects cf. Prop. 1. 16. 5 (a door) 'saucia rixis', Ov. *Met.* 10. 372f. 'securi | saucia trabs ingens'. For the 'wounding' of ships Nisbet–Hubbard on Hor. *Carm.* 1. 14. 5 quote Liv. 37. 24. 8 'multis ictibus uulnerata nauis erat', and the common use of τιτρώσκω in Greek.

139. ludibrium pelagi . . . iactatur: from Hor. *Carm.* 1. 14. 15f. 'tu, nisi uentis | debes ludibrium, caue.' As Nisbet–Hubbard ad loc. point out, however, the sense there is 'mockery', whereas Claudian means 'plaything'. It seems that Horace has been mediated through Lucan's chilling description of the headless corpse of Pompey tossed upon the waters just off the Egyptian coast: 8. 698f. 'truncusque uadosis | huc illuc iactatur aquis' and 710 'ludibrium pelagi': cf. also Luc. 9. 14. The allusion could be interpreted as importing an element of pathos rather than triumph, but more important is the great stress laid by Lucan on the idea that Pompey, formerly Fortuna's favourite, has now been abandoned by her: 8. 712ff., 729ff., 793ff. The allusion thus strengthens the general implication of the passage that Alaric, like Pompey a darling of Fortuna, has now been completely deserted by her and reduced, in effect, to utter destruction: cf. 131 *immensi revoluto culmine fati*, where *fati* effectively = *fortuna*. Lucan's memorable lines on Pompey's corpse also leave their mark on Sil. 6. 524 and Prud. *Pe.* 5. 441ff.; cf. further *Get.* 109f.

140. uastato . . . profundo: *uasto* is, of course, more often used of devastating the land (*Gild.* 81, *Stil.* 1. 107), but note the word-play on such standard phrases as Catul. 64. 127 'pelagi uastos . . . aestus', Virg. *A.* 2. 780 'uastum maris aequor', Sen. *Med.* 318f. 'uasto | . . . ponto'. There is thus an epigrammatic feel to the phrase; what is usually 'waste' in any case is 'laid waste'.

poenas luitura: picking up *poenas exegit* 113.

141. minas retro flectebat: possibly another allusion associating Alaric with the defeated Hannibal: Hor. *Carm.* 4. 8. 16 'reiectaeque retrorsum Hannibalis minae'. For *flecto retro* cf. *Dirae* 67, Ov. *Met.* 3. 187 f., 10. 51, and esp. Liv. 22. 20. 10 'flexa retro classis'.

142. Italiam fugiens: another tendentious claim: cf. 320 *instante fugam Stilichone*.

142f. The noun to be supplied seems to be *uia*, though this is not easy, and one might reasonably suspect corruption. Müller compares Ov. *Ep.* 18. 121f. (Leander to Hero) 'ad te uia prona uidetur; | a te cum redeo, cliuus inertis aquae.' Given the comparison drawn between Alaric and Phaethon at 186f. perhaps Claudian also has in mind Ov. *Met.* 2. 67 (Apollo to Phaethon) 'ultima prona uia est': for the headstrong boy it proved, instead, to be *difficilis* and *dura*. These lines and the following two together have a satirical edge, reminiscent of Juvenal's caustic treatment of the reversal of fortune suffered by Xerxes at Salamis (10. 173 ff.: compare also l. 140 with Juv. 10. 187 'has totiens optata exegit gloria poenas').

143. iam difficilis, iam dura: the combination of the anaphora of *iam*, the alliteration of the initial dental and the asyndeton helps create a tone of triumphant excitement. *dura* is a stronger word than *difficilis*, so there is also a crescendo effect in the progression from *prona* to the end of the line.

144. clausa putat sibi cuncta pauor: the historical Alaric perhaps had good cause to fear being trapped and hemmed in by Stilicho's troops, having experienced such a dangerous situation when blockaded on Mt. Pholoe in Arcadia in 397. Claudian even claims at *Get.* 469 ff. that such fears, along with regret that they ever invaded Italy at all, afflicted the Goths *before* Pollentia: note esp. *Get.* 474 f. 'cinctaque fluminibus crebris ac moenibus arua, | seque uelut clausum laqueis'. But also operative here is the commonplace idea that fear feeds on itself, making the dangers faced seem even worse than in reality they are. The most explicit and extensive use of this idea is Statius' account of Pavor, who, as one of Mars' retinue, terrifies the Argives into thinking a cloud of dust marks the arrival of the Theban army: see esp. *Theb.* 7. 112 ff. 'bonus omnia credi | auctor et horrificis lymphare incursibus urbes. | si geminos soles ruituraque suadeat astra, | aut nutare solum aut ueteres descendere siluas, | a! miseri uidisse putant', and cf. also Luc. 7. 172 f., Sil. 4. 8 f., 6. 556 f., *Get.* 227 ff. 'utque est ingenioque loquax et plurima fingi | permittens credique timor . . .'.

   retroque relictos: the near-pleonasm has a slightly archaic flavour. For similar combinations cf. Caes. *Gal.* 4. 4 'rursus reuerterunt', Cic. *Rosc.* 41, Lucr. 4. 310, Virg. *G.* 1. 200 'retro . . . referri', *A.* 2. 169, 9. 797 f., 11. 627 f. 'rapidus retro atque aestu reuoluta resorbens | saxa fugit', Ov. *Met.* 15. 249, Apul. *Met.* 4. 18 'rursumque . . . recurrentes'. Contrast 461 f. *plurima retro* | . . . *liquerat arma*, where the use of the simple form of the verb weakens the effect.

145. Rivers could provide a serious obstacle to a retreating army, blocking its path or forcing the troops into a dangerously exposed position as they all attempt at once to cross a single bridge while the enemy harries them from behind. One might, for example, consider the disaster suffered by the defeated Athenians at the Assinaros on the retreat from Syracuse (Thuc. 7. 84). But the rivers of northern Italy are mentioned here primarily in order to allow the following excursus, in which the river-god Eridanus (= Po), symbolizing Italy herself, jeers at the humiliated Alaric and explicitly points the moral of the tale. There is at any rate no good reason to claim that the Gothic host's retreat was hampered by flooding: see 193–200 n.

temnebat: for the vivid use of the imperfect for the pluperfect see Birt, p. ccxxiii and cf. *Stil.* 3. 331, *Get.* 83 ff.

exhorruit: no doubt the perfect of *exhorresco* rather than of *exhorreo*, which is securely attested only at Col. 10. 154. This vivid compound is none the less fairly rare, but cf. Virg. *A.* 7. 265, Ov. *Met.* 4. 135, V. Fl. 7. 286, 527, Sil. 3. 146, 427, 10. 107, Stat. *Theb.* 4. 698, *Eutr.* 1. 317.

146–77. *As he ponders the will of the gods in his cavern-home Eridanus is informed of the Goths' ignominious retreat by one of his daughters, the nymphs. He rises majestically from his waters to see for himself.*

This section could be seen as a digression from the battle-narrative of the aftermath of Verona, especially if we remember the explicit advice of Menander Rhetor 374. 6 ff. (p. 86 Russell–Wilson) in his discussion of what the orator should say in the 'deeds in war' portion of the βασιλικὸς λόγος: ἐνταῦθα καιρὸν ἕξεις καὶ ἀνεῖναι κατὰ μέσον τὸν λόγον . . . καὶ φωνὴν καθάπερ ἐν δράματι ἢ χώρᾳ ἢ ποταμῷ περιτιθέναι. Menander goes on to quote the example of Scamander addressing Achilles in *Iliad* 21: this dramatic account lies behind Statius' picture of Ismenos at *Theb.* 9. 404 ff., a passage to which Claudian here is indebted in his turn (see 146 *uitreis . . . antris*, 152 f. nn.). Menander stresses the function of such descriptions as 'relaxation' from the drier portions of the narrative, but Claudian's magnificent ecphrasis of the river-god also serves to reinforce the propaganda of the poem. Eridanus is dressed in a *palla* that illustrates the tale of Phaethon's hubris, and Phaethon's driving the chariot of the sun is explicitly presented by the god as an analogy for Alaric's assault on the god-guarded city of Rome: see 165 f., 168–77, 184–6 nn.

146. undosa . . . domo: cf. Virg. *G.* 4. 363 'domum . . . et umida regna' (of Cyrene), Sil. 5. 21, Stat. *Ach.* 1. 27 f. (Thetis) 'undosis turba comitante sororum | prosiluit thalamis'. The adjective ending -*osus* is useful for translating Greek adjectives in -όεις, -ήεις and -ώδης: see Williams on Virg. *A.* 3. 705, 5. 352, Brink on Hor. *Ep.* 2. 1. 70, Palmer, p. 102, A. Ernout, *Les Adjectifs latins en* -osus *et* -ulentus (Paris, 1949). *undosus* is first attested at Virg. *A.* 3. 693. Cf. also Aus. *Ep.* 13 Green, *Nupt.* 145 (Triton) 'undosi . . . crines', *Get.* 48.

uitreis . . . antris: expanding and clarifying *undosa . . . domo.*
Underwater caves are the traditional dwelling-places of river-gods
and sea divinities: see esp. Ov. *Met.* 1. 574ff. (of Peneus) 'haec domus,
haec sedes, haec sunt penetralia magni | amnis, in his residens facto
de cautibus antro', and cf. also *Met.* 1. 583, V. Fl. 5. 209, 6. 565, Sil. 4.
344, Stat. *Theb.* 4. 108, 9. 404, *Silu.* 1. 2. 264, 1. 3. 70, 3. 1. 144, *Prob.*
209f. 'accepit sonitus curuis Tiberinus in antris, | ima ualle sedens',
Sid. *Carm.* 2. 332. The cave is 'glassy': cf. Stat. *Silu.* 3. 2. 16 'uitreis
spumosae Doridos antris', Sil. 8. 191, *Fesc.* 2. 34f. 'sub uitreis Oceanus
| luxurietur antris', and the similar phrases at Virg. *G.* 4. 350f.
'uitreisque sedilibus omnes | obstipuere', Sil. 7. 413, Sid. *Carm.* 2. 320.
Both the cave and the epithet trace their ancestry to Homer's
ἀργύφεον . . . σπέος where Thetis sits with the nymphs (*Il.* 18. 50).
Given Homer's epithet ('silver-shining') the emphasis is perhaps on
translucency: cf. Call. fr. 238 Pf. ὑάλοιο φαάντερος οὐρανὸς, *AP* 5. 48.
1, Hor. *Carm.* 3. 13. 1 'splendidior uitro', Ov. *Met.* 13. 791, Apul. *Met.*
5. 1 'fontem uitreo latice perlucidum'. Ancient glass, however, was also
sea-green in colour: see Nisbet–Hubbard on Hor. *Carm.* 1. 17. 20 and
cf. Aus. *Mos.* 418f. Green 'caeruleos nunc, Rhene, sinus hyaloque
uirentem | pande peplum'. For *uitreus* of the sea, rivers and their
inhabitants cf. also Hor. *Carm.* 4. 2. 3f. 'uitreo . . . ponto', Mart. 6. 68.
7, Stat. *Theb.* 9. 352, *Silu.* 1. 5. 16, *CIL* ix. 4756 'Tybris . . . uitreus', Aus.
Mos. 28, 55, 179 Green, *Prob.* 225, *Nupt.* 128, *c.m.* 26. 32, *Rapt.* 1. 269f.,
2. 53f.

147f. Eridanus' anxious care for Italy aligns him with the Jupiter of the
Aeneid (*A.* 1. 227 'illum talis iactantem pectore curas') and, on the
human plane, with heroes such as Aeneas (*A.* 1. 305, 8. 19), Cato (Luc.
2. 239ff.) and Silius' Scipio (*Pun.* 15. 18f.): cf. also Lucan's ironic application of the traditional phraseology to Caesar at 1. 272, and Cor. *Ioh.*
7. 20f. 'dux . . . | . . . innumeras uoluens sub pectore curas.' This
ἐπιμέλεια is a standard attribute of the good king or leader, and can
be traced back to Homer (*Il.* 2. 60ff.): see F. Cairns, *Virgil's Augustan
Epic* (Cambridge, 1989), 20. In Claudian's panegyrics such continual
curae are the common lot of Stilicho and mark his greatness: *Ruf. pr.* 2.
13, *Ruf.* 2. 4f., *Get.* 360ff., *VI Cons.* 100, 232ff.

147. rerum ignarus: cf. Virg. *A.* 8. 730, 10. 666.

    ingentes . . . curas: a standard, rather archaic-sounding phrase.
See Skutsch on Enn. *Ann.* 133, and cf. Sal. *Cat.* 46. 2 'at illum ingens
cura atque laetitia simul occupauere', Stat. *Theb.* 3. 721, Cor. *Ioh.* 6.
362.

148. pater: a regular honorific title of river-gods, who are usually conceived of as old, as at Virg. *A.* 8. 31f. 'deus . . . Tiberinus . . . senior'.

It is applied to Eridanus also at Sil. 4. 690f. and 12. 217. The same honorific intent can be seen in e.g. Virg. *G.* 1. 482 'rex Eridanus'; cf. Jord. *Get.* 150 'ipse Padus, quem Italiae soli fluuiorum regem dicunt, cognomento Eridanus'. Since, however, the title *pater* is especially associated in Latin verse with Tiber (Enn. *Ann.* 26 Skutsch, Virg. *G.* 4. 369, *A.* 10. 421, *Epic. Drus.* 221, Stat. *Silu.* 1. 6. 100; *genitor* at Virg. *A.* 8. 72), perhaps Eridanus could be said to be in some measure usurping Tiber's role as chief river and symbol of Italy: contrast *Get.* 578 'patrem clipeis defendite Thybrim'.

Eridanus: properly a river of Greek poetic fantasy located in the far west and associated with amber. Its mythical status was recognized by Herodotus (3. 15) and Strabo (5. 1. 9 τὸν Ἠριδανὸν τὸν μηδαμοῦ γῆς ὄντα). Aeschylus apparently identified it with the Rhône (Plin. *Nat.* 37. 32), but poets eventually settled down to an identification with the Po, following the lead of Pherecydes (Hyg. *Fab.* 154. 2). The other appearance of the river-god in Claudian's works is at *III Cons.* 122f., where he does homage to the young Emperor as he comes to take up the rule of the West.

Along with the Alps, the Po is the natural barrier protecting Italy. Hence Alaric boasts 'fregi Alpes galeisque Padum uictricibus hausi' (*Get.* 532), and his flight back over the river marks Stilicho's victory (302f. below). Since the battle of Pollentia was fought some 2 km below the estuary of the Stura di Demonte (Wolfram 151), a little poetic licence allows Claudian to represent the Po as the defender of Italy and avenger of his brother rivers: cf. 212 *belli medio Padus arbiter ibat* n., *Get.* 194ff. 'tandem supplicium cunctis pro montibus Alpes | exegere Getis (Getas?); tandem tot flumina uictor | uindicat Eridanus'. In general Italy is symbolized by her rivers in this poem: cf. 144f., 193ff., 495ff.

149. imperium: recalling Jupiter's promise at Virg. *A.* 1. 279 'imperium sine fine dedi.' Stilicho and Eridanus thus take their place in history as instruments of Rome's destiny. This poem celebrates the return of *imperium* to Rome itself (23, 408, 591).

150. uitae Romana quies: = 'tuta uita sub imperio Romano' (Barth), the epithet *Romana* also colouring *imperium* and *leges*. As Müller points out, apart from short incursions by the Marcomanni in the time of Marcus Aurelius (339–50n.), Italy had been spared foreign invasion under the Empire. *quies* is indistinguishable here from *pax* (*OLD* s.v. *quies* 6), as can be seen from Caes. *Ciu.* 3. 57. 4 'quietem Italiae, pacem prouinciarum, salutem' and Liv. 2. 15. 5 'seu bello opus est seu quiete'. Tertullus' praise of Felix at Acts 24. 2 πολλῆς εἰρήνης τυγχάνοντες διὰ σοῦ is translated in the King James version as 'seeing that by thee we enjoy great quietness.' Stilicho's tireless devotion guarantees the continuance of this peace: *Get.* 360ff. 'illi sub niuibus somni curaeque laborque | peruigil hanc requiem terris, haec otia rebus | insperata dabant'. Note also *placidis* 159.

151. ad . . . damnaret: the construction is first attested in prose authors of the early Empire: Tac. *Ann.* 6. 38 'ad supplicium damnatus', 16. 21, Plin. *Ep.* 10. 32.

    priscos pecudum . . . ritus: i.e. reduce mankind to the sorry state of the creature fashioned without any divine spark by Epimetheus: *Eutr.* 2. 496ff., esp. 499ff. 'hi *pecudum ritu* non inpendentia uitant | nec res ante uident, accepta clade queruntur | et seri transacta gemunt.' The underlying idea is that the end of Roman rule would be the end of civilization and law, because the barbarians are no better than animals: cf. Ammianus Marcellinus' description of the Huns, 'inconsultorum animalium ritu, quid honestum inhonestumue sit, penitus ignorantes' (31. 2. 11). Claudian may also have in mind Lucretius' famous description of the life of primitive humanity who 'multaque per caelum solis uoluentia lustra | uulgiuago uitam tractabant *more ferarum*' (5. 931f.): in particular contrast 149 with Lucr. 5. 958f. 'neque ullis | moribus inter se scibant nec legibus uti.' A very close parallel is found in 'Sulpicia's' lament on the state of the Republic in the time of Domitian, from a work nearly contemporary with Claudian, the *Epigrammata Bobiensia* (37. 12ff. = Baehrens, *PLM* v. 94): 'dic mihi, Calliope: quidnam pater ille deorum | cogitat? an terras ad patria saecula mutat | quasque dedit quondam, morientibus eripit artes? | nosque iubet tacitos et iam rationis egentes, | non aliter primo quam cum surreximus aruo, | glandibus et purae rursus procumbere lymphae? | an reliquas terras conseruat amicus et urbes, | sed genus Ausonium Romulique exturbat alumnos?' Claudian also probably has in mind Ovid's account of the gods listening to Jupiter's denunciation of Lycaon and the general wickedness of humanity: 'quae sit terrae mortalibus orbae | forma futura rogant, quis sit laturus in aras | tura, ferisne paret populandas tradere terras' (*Met.* 1. 247 ff.). For the phrasing cf. also Ov. *Met.* 15. 222 (a child) 'mox quadrupes rituque tulit sua membra ferarum'.

    ritus has given some difficulty. *P* has *rictus* in the margin (corrected to *ritus*) and another possibility is *uictus* (Heinsii Iunianus). Indeed, if *pecudum . . . uictus* is understood to mean that Jupiter is considering whether to condemn humanity once more to live on primitive foods like animals, it can be supported by reference to *Epig. Bob.* 37. 17 cit. supra, as also to *Theod.* 190f. (to Iustitia) 'tu prima hominem siluestribus antris | elicis et foedo deterres saecula uictu'.

Alternatively, it might be taken to mean something like 'to be eaten by wild beasts', in which case one might compare Lucr. 5. 990 ff. 'unus enim tum quisque magis deprensus eorum | pabula uiua feris praebebat'. But *ritus*, in addition to enjoying overwhelming manuscript support, makes excellent sense, and is strongly defended by the parallel at *Eutr.* 2. 499. Cf. also Ov. *Met.* 15. 93 (of cannibalism) 'ritusque referre Cyclopum', *Rapt.* 3. 41 ff. 'quid mentem traxisse polo, quid profuit altum | erexisse caput, pecudum si more pererrant | auia, si frangunt communia pabula glandes?', Prud. *C. Symm.* 1. 80, 455 ff. (Theodosius to Roma) 'at te, quae domitis leges ac iura dedisti | gentibus, instituens, magnus qua tenditur orbis, | armorum morumque feros mansuescere ritus'. Moreover, the general contrast Claudian is making between barbarism and civilized life seems better served by the wider implications of *ritus* than the narrower focus of *uictus*. For *pecudes* not of livestock, but of beasts as opposed to human beings cf. Lucr. 1. 116, Virg. *A.* 1. 743 'unde hominum genus et pecudes', 8. 27.

saecula: Platnauer translates 'future ages': see *OLD* s.v. 8, citing Catul. 95. 6 'Smyrnam cana diu saecula peruoluent', Petr. 88. 2, Sil. 2. 511 'extendam leti decus atque in saecula mittam'. There could even be said to be overtones of the sense 'for ever', as in the Christian phrase 'in saecula saeculorum': cf. Aus. *Eph.* 3. 83 Green 'in saecula regnans'. Müller, however, prefers to understand the word as meaning in effect 'mankind': this usage would recall in particular Lucretius' phrase 'mortalia saecula' which clearly refers to succeeding generations of human beings at *DRN* 5. 1169, 1238. Claudian must certainly have the Lucretian phrase in mind in his description of the dead in Hades at *Ruf.* 2. 473 f. 'huc post emeritam mortalia saecula uitam | deueniunt': cf. also possibly *IV Cons.* 99, Levy on *Ruf.* 2. 208. Here we would thus have a neat and clear contrast between human beings and the animals to whose state they may be reduced (*saecula | pecudum ritus*). Moreover one could even imagine a philosophically minded Eridanus ruminating in quasi-Lucretian language on the grim possibility that the gods intend to reverse the long process of humanity's rise to civilization recounted in *DRN* 5.

In all truth, however, the sense 'age' for *saeculum* is in any case a development from its core-meaning 'body of individuals born at a particular time, generation' (*OLD* s.v. 1). Ambiguity is thus often present. At Virg. *G.* 1. 468, for example, we find 'impiaque aeternam timuerunt saecula noctem', which combines the idea of a generation of sinners with that of the present age as the Hesiodic Age of Iron (see Thomas ad loc.). Since it is clear that Eridanus is thinking about the future of the human race and of civilization, 'future generations' or 'generations to come' would provide an acceptable compromise in English.

152f. Claudian may be thinking of the nymph Cymodocea explaining the portent of the ships to Aeneas at Virg. *A.* 10. 225ff. But the primary model is clearly Stat. *Theb.* 9. 416ff. (Ismenos is informed of the slaughter of his grandson) 'obuia cognatos gemitus casumque nepotis | *Nympharum* docet *una patrem* monstratque cruentum | auctorem dextramque premit'. In Statius, however, the nymph's words are not directly reported, and the tidings she brings are private and evil, not public and joyous.

152. talia . . . secum mouet: for *moueo* of turning something over in one's mind the *OLD* s.v. 19 cites Sal. *Cat.* 31. 4 'at Catilinae crudelis animus eadem illa mouebat', Virg. *A.* 10. 890 (see Harrison ad loc.), Hor. *Carm.* 3. 4. 68.

153. Naiadum: not distinguished from *Nymphas* at 158. These are no doubt the same as those who bury Phaethon on Eridanus' banks at Ov. *Met.* 2. 325ff.

resoluta comam: cf. Tib. 1. 3. 31 'resoluta comas', Sil. 8. 130. In this construction, the active form of the sentence is replaced by the passive one, but the accusative of the direct object of the active verb is 'retained'; thus 'Naias resoluit comam' becomes 'Naias resoluta comam'. Examples of this, the 'retained' accusative after a past participle with passive sense, are limited to verse texts when they first begin to appear in Latin, and so it seems likely that the construction is a conscious imitation of Greek poetic syntax. Its wide acceptance, however, may have been facilitated in part by the use of the direct object with a verb with 'middle' voice (discussed at 65f. *diademate . . . | cingebare comas* n.), from which it is none the less to be clearly distinguished. Skutsch, on Enn. *Ann.* 310 'perculsi pectora Poeni', convincingly argues that the construction was 'probably pioneered by Ennius, though the earliest undoubted occurrences are in Lucretius (1. 13 'perculsae corda tua ui', 5. 1223) and Catullus (64. 207f. 'caeca mentem caligine Theseus | consitus'). Cf. further 378 *Palladiaque comas innexus harundine Triton*, and see Fordyce on Catul. 64. 64f. 'contecta . . . pectus . . . uincta papillas', Austin on Virg. *A.* 2. 57 'manus . . . reuinctum', Williams on *A.* 3. 65 'crinem . . . solutae' and 5. 135, LHS ii. 37, Löfstedt ii. 421, KS i. 288ff., S. J. Harrison, *Vergil. Aeneid 10* (Oxford, 1991), appendix D (pp. 290f.). Claudian is fond of using it in descriptions of hair, e.g. *Prob.* 3, *Ruf.* 1. 378f. 'debellatasque draconum | tonsa comas', *Eutr.* 2. 528 'redimita comam', *Stil.* 3. 303 'sparsa comam', *VI Cons.* 378, *c.m.* 25. 28 'turbata comas, intecta papillas', *Rapt.* 1. 55, 3. 177. Here the unbound hair probably indicates that until

Stilicho's victory the nymph had been grieving: see *OLD* s.v. *soluo* 6b, and cf. Catul. 64. 349f., Virg. *A.* 11. 35 'et maestum Iliades crinem de more solutae', Liv. 24. 26. 2, Ov. *Fast.* 4. 854.

154–8. For speeches in Claudian see Fargues on *Eutr.* 1. 391 and 2. 534. The proportion in the mythological epics (46%) is particularly high. Much of the weight is accounted for by the long set speeches, such as Roma's *suasoria* (361–425) and Honorius' reply (427–93).

154. en: see *pr.* 23f.n.

non qualem: recalling Aeneas' pitiful exclamation on seeing the ghost of the disfigured Hector: *A.* 2. 274f. 'ei mihi, qualis erat, quantum mutatus ab illo | Hectore qui redit exuuias indutus Achilli'. Cf. also Ov. *Met.* 6. 273 'heu quantum haec Niobe Niobe distabat ab illa', V. Fl. 4. 398, Stat. *Theb.* 7. 706, *Gild.* 19f., *Rapt.* 3. 84ff. (Proserpina seen by Demeter in a dream) 'non qualem Siculis olim mandauerat aruis | nec qualem roseis nuper conuallibus Aetnae | suspexere deae'. Here, however, the tone is not one of lamentation but joy at the humiliation of an arrogant boaster. The idea is repeated, with greater economy, from *Get.* 79ff. 'quantumque priori | dissimilis, qui cuncta sibi cessura ruenti | pollicitus patrii numen iurauerat Histri | non nisi calcatis loricam ponere rostris'.

ouantem: the true triumph belongs to Honorius (553 *fratri . . . ouanti*).

155. uidimus: echoing Alaric's retort to the old Goth at *Get.* 524ff. 'anne . . . | te patiar suadente fugam, cum cesserit omnis | obsequiis natura meis? subsidere nostris | sub pedibus montes, arescere uidimus amnes.' But now nature—the land of Italy—takes her revenge: see 148 *Eridanus* n.

156. percensere . . . iuuabit: the sense of 'counting' can also be seen at Stat. *Theb.* 4. 576 (Niobe) 'tumido percenset funera luctu' ('proud in her grief counts o'er the bodies', Mozley): cf. also *c.m.* 25. 87f. 'cuneosque recenset | dispositos'. The Naiad invites her father to conduct a 'review' of Alaric's army, so diminished that it is no longer an *exercitus*, but only a mere *manus*. We perhaps recall Xerxes reviewing his troops (Hdt. 7. 100ff.). For the phrasing cf. Prud. *Apoth.* 596 'percensere libet'.

156f. Ammianus Marcellinus, on the subject of the Theruingian Goths transported to Thrace by Valens, refers to 'innumerae gentium multitudines' (31. 4. 8) and says that the Roman officials in charge could not count them ('numerum eius comprehendere calculo saepe temptantes, conquieuisse frustratos', 31.4. 6, quoting Virg. *G.* 2. 105f.). Obviously no precise numbers can be produced and due allowance must be made for exaggeration; Wolfram's estimate is about 100,000 people (p. 153). For Claudian's hyperbole on the Goths' losses see 127 *tenuatus*, 129 *tot amissis sociis*, 210-28, 281-5 nn.

157. reliquias . . . breues: *reliquiae* is common of the survivors of an event, especially a war: cf. Virg. *A.* 1. 30 'Troas, reliquias Danaum atque immitis Achilli', Liv. 25. 5. 10 'Cannensis reliquiae cladis hic exercitus erat', Sen. *Suas.* 5. 5, Sil. 10. 416. For the prosody (first syllable long, as required by the metre) see Austin on *A.* 1. 30, and cf. Lucr. 1. 1109, 3. 656, 6. 825. For *breuis* applied to amounts, weights and numbers see *OLD* s.v. 3, and *TLL* ii. 2184. 31 ff., quoting Hor. *Carm.* 4. 13. 22 f. 'Cinarae breuis | annos fata dederunt', V. Fl. 6. 571, Quint. *Inst.* 1. 10. 43 'breuioribus numeris', Ps. 104. 12 Vulg.

iam desine: balanced by *iam redde* (158). Cf. *Rapt.* 2. 277 f. 'desine funestis animum, Proserpina, curis | et uano uexare metu'.

157 f. maesta | fronte: Eridanus has furrowed his brow in anxious thought.

158. Nymphas . . . sorores: from the Virgilian line-ending (*G.* 2. 494, 4. 382). These are all Eridanus' daughters: cf. *patrem* (153) and e.g. *Prob.* 263 'Nymphae patris (sc. Tiberis) praecepta secutae'.

choris iam redde: the Naiad, her joyous message delivered, asks that Eridanus allow her sisters to return to the dancing that is their usual pursuit in times of peace and happiness: cf. e.g. Virg. *G.* 4. 532 f. 'Nymphae, | cum quibus illa choros lucis agitabat in altis', *A.* 1. 499 f.

Heinsius suggested the emendation *i redde*, no doubt suspecting dittography from *iam desine* (157): for comparison he pointed to *Rapt.* 1. 92 f. 'i celer et proscinde Notos et iussa superbo | redde Ioui', Ov. *Fast.* 6. 594. But the anaphora of *iam* in a context of celebration is perfectly acceptable: *Prob.* 250 ff. 'iam profluat ebrius amnis | mutatis in uina uadis; iam sponte per agros | sudent inriguae spirantia balsama uenae.' Moreover the nymph's words are echoed by Roma at 405. In any case, *i* with an imperative is normally hostile or scornful in tone: see 227 f. *i . . . i* n.

159-68. Descriptions of river-gods are extremely common in ancient poetry, and no doubt owe much to the equally abundant representations in art: see in general Roscher i. 1487 ff. Cephisus, for example, can be seen reclining on the frieze from the west pediment of the Parthenon, and Call. *H.* 4. 77 f. speaks of Ismenos and Asopus in anthropomorphic terms (Ἰσμηνοῦ χέρα πατρός, Ἀσωπὸς βαρύγοννος). The classical purist Horace may be attacking Furius Bibaculus for including a fantastic and 'tasteless' epiphany of a river-god in his epic: see *S.* 1. 10. 36 f. 'turgidus Alpinus iugulat dum Memnona dumque | defingit Rheni luteum caput', discussed by Courtney, *FLP*, pp. 197 f. Such depictions none the less quickly established themselves as part of the paraphernalia of epic poetry and were apparently particularly congenial to Roman taste in the Imperial era. In art one can cite Danube, up to his shoulders in his own waters, on Trajan's column (E. Nash, *A Pictorial Dictionary of Ancient Rome* (London, 1968), i. 286; P. M. Monti, *La Colonna Traiana* (Rome, 1980), 23), Euphrates and Tigris on the same Emperor's arch at Benevento (C. Pietrangeli, *L'Arc de Trajan à Benevento* (Paris, 1943), pl. xix), the recumbent Nile in the Braccio Nuovo of the Vatican (A. Malraux and A. Parrot, *Hellenistic Art* (London, 1973), 310), the great effigies of Nile and Tigris from the Baths of Constantine (Nash, op. cit., ii. 446-7, figs. 1248f.), and Tiber on the Arch of Constantine (Roscher i. 1489f.). In poetry particularly striking examples are Virg. *A.* 8. 31ff. (Tiber), *Epic. Drus.* 221ff. (Tiber), Sil. 4. 659ff. (Trebia), Stat. *Theb.* 9. 404ff. (Ismenos), *Silu.* 4. 3. 67ff. (Volturnus), *Prob.* 209ff. (Tiber), Sid. *Carm.* 2. 332ff. (Tiber). Certain features thus became standard, such as the god's advanced age (148 *pater* n.), his horns (161 *aurea . . . cornua* n.), the reeds in his hair (162-4n.) and his urn (168 *urna* n.).

159 f. caput . . . sublime . . . extulit: recalling esp. Virg. *A.* 1. 126f. (Neptune) 'et alto | prospiciens summa placidum caput extulit unda.' River- and sea-gods are frequently described majestically raising their heads above their waters in order to intervene in human affairs: this is the aquatic equivalent of the descent of an Olympian god to earth. Cf. Catul. 64. 14f. 'emersere freti candenti e gurgite uultus | aequoreae monstrum Nereides admirantes', Virg. *G.* 4. 352, *Epic. Drus.* 221f., Ov. *Fast.* 5. 637 'Thybris harundiferum medio caput extulit alueo', *Met.* 2. 270f., 5. 487f., Sen. *Ag.* 554, Sil. 4. 659f., 7. 254f. 'ut cum turbatis placidum caput extulit undis | Neptunus', Stat. *Theb.* 9. 408ff., *Silu.* 4. 3. 67ff., Aus. *Epigr.* 3. 2 Green, *c.m.* 22. 57f. Such sights are awe-inspiring: Stat. *Theb.* 9. 411ff. 'illum (sc. Ismenon) per ripas . . . ora exertantem siluae fluuiique minores | mirantur: tantus tumido de gurgite surgit', *Eutr.* 2. 164f. 'cornua cana gelu mirantibus extulit undis | Hebrus'. A symbolic significance is also present here. Eridanus can now hold his head high, and is *erectior* (193) as he summons the other rivers of Italy, who, in turn *frondentibus umida ripis | colla leuant* (194f.). The Goths, by way of contrast, retreat *deiecta ceruice* (179).

159. dixerat: a regular speech formula (= ὣς φάτο), though the perfect tense is commoner. Cf. *Ruf.* 1. 162, and see in general Pease on Virg. *A.* 4. 30 'sic effata.'

placidis: cf. *pacata . . . prata* (198f.) and see 150n.

fluentis: found only here and at *Prob.* 236 in Claudian, though the word is a favourite with Ausonius (e.g. *Mos.* 349, 419 Green) and his pupil Paulinus of Nola (e.g. *Carm.* 15. 39, 21. 783, 815). In using the plural Claudian shows his allegiance to the classical tradition, as seen at e.g. Lucr. 5. 949, Virg. *G.* 4. 369, *A.* 4. 143. For the singular see e.g. Apul. *Met.* 6. 12, 18 'pigrum fluentum', *Soc.* 19, Aus. *Mos.* 419 Green, Paul. Nol. *Carm.* 21. 715.

160. totis . . . ripis: probably best seen as a local ablative: cf. Virg. *Ecl.* 1. 11 f. 'undique totis | usque adeo turbatur agris', *G.* 4. 527 'Eurydicen toto referebant flumine ripae', Ov. *Am.* 2. 8. 16.

  spargentia: the verb is often used of light, especially in descriptions of dawn: Lucr. 2. 144 'primum aurora nouo cum spargit lumine terras', Virg. *A.* 4. 584, 12. 113 f., Ov. *Met.* 14. 416, Julius Montanus fr. 1. 2 Büchner 'spargere <se> rubicunda dies', Sil. 5. 55 f., *Prob.* 3 (to Sol) 'sparge diem'.

161. aurea . . . cornua: the association of rivers with bulls is explained by Porphyrion on Hor. *Carm.* 4. 14. 25 'sic tauriformis uoluitur Aufidus: omnium fluminum genii taurino uultu etiam cum cornibus pinguntur propter impetus et fremitus ipsarum aquarum.' Note also *Il.* 21. 237 (Scamander) μεμυκὼς ἠύτε ταῦρος. See the long list of examples at *TLL* iv. 966. 70 ff., and compare e.g. Virg. *A.* 8. 77 (Tiber) 'corniger', Ov. *Met.* 8. 734, 9. 1 ff., V. Fl. 1. 106, Stat. *Theb.* 7. 66, 9. 420, *Prob.* 220 f., *IV Cons.* 652, *Nupt.* 51, *Eutr.* 2. 164, *Stil.* 1. 220 f., 3. 24, *Get.* 603. Eridanus' horns are golden, one of several marks of the kingly status he enjoys among river-gods (cf. *non . . . vulgaris* 162). Claudian's authority here is Virg. *G.* 4. 371 f. 'gemina auratus taurino cornua uultu | Eridanus'. Similarly, the Rhine has golden horns at Mart. 10. 7. 6.

  roranti . . . uultu: i.e. streaming with water. Cf. Soph. *Trach.* 13 f., *Incert.* 36 Büchner (= *Incert.* 5 Courtney) 'te (tu, *Courtney*), Neptune pater, cui tempora cana crepanti | cincta salo resonant, magnus cui perpete mento | profluit oceanus et flumina crinibus errant', Ov. *Met.* 1. 266, 5. 487 f., Stat. *Theb.* 9. 415 (Ismenos) 'pectora caeruleae riuis manantia barbae', *Prob.* 220 ff. (Tiber) 'taurina leuantur | cornua temporibus raucos sudantia riuos; | destillant per pectus aquae; frons hispida manat | imbribus; in liquidos fontes se barba repectit', Sid. *Carm.* 2. 335 ff.

162–4. Common-or-garden river-gods have crowns of reeds or sedge in their hair, since such plants grow on their banks (Virg. *Ecl.* 7. 12 f. 'hic uiridis tenera praetexit harundine ripas | Mincius'; hence *A.* 10. 205 f. 'uelatus harundine glauca | Mincius', Ov. *Met.* 13. 894, *Rapt.* 2. 136 etc.). With his crown of amber-dripping poplar branches (see further 164 n.) Eridanus thus outranks even the Tiber (Virg. *A.* 8. 34 'crinis umbrosa tegebat harundo', Ov. *Fast.* 5. 637, *Epic. Drus.* 223, *Prob.* 217, Rut. Nam. *Red.* 1. 151, Sid. *Carm.* 2. 333 f.), the Euphrates (Ov. *Ars* 1.

223), the Achelous (Ov. *Met.* 9. 3) and the Rhine (Ov. *Tr.* 4. 2. 41, *Pont.* 3. 4. 107f.). Contrast also Triton at 378 below and Charon (*Rapt.* 2. 359): see further Coleman on Stat. *Silu.* 4. 3. 68f. 'crinem mollibus impeditus uluis | Volturnus'. Reeds are cheap and provide protection for the lowly: Aus. *Ep.* 13. 6 Green (a thatched hovel) 'uilis harundineis cohibet quem pergula tectis'. Note also the oxymoron *uulgaris . . . honos*.

162. harundine: see Fordyce on Virg. *A.* 8. 34 for the standard use of the collective singular with the names of plants, etc.

163. honos: see *OLD* s.v. 2d ('[concr.] a thing which confers honour or distinction') and cf. Stat. *Theb.* 2. 99f. (Laius' ghost) 'glaucaeque innexus oliuae | uittarum prouenit honos'. *honos* is also used of garlands etc. adorning the hair at Virg. *Ecl.* 10. 24f. 'agresti capitis Siluanus honore, | florentis ferulas et grandia lilia quassans', Ov. *Ars* 3. 392.

umbrauere: i.e. provided protection from the sun: cf. Virg. *A.* 6. 772 'umbrata gerunt ciuili tempora quercu', V. Fl. 4. 137f. 'umbrata . . . | tempora . . . galero', Stat. *Theb.* 6. 554, *Gild.* 444; also Virg. *A.* 8. 34 (Tiber) 'crinis umbrosa tegebat harundo', *Prob.* 217ff. (Tiber) 'uertice luxuriat toto crinalis harundo, | quam neque fas Zephyris frangi nec sole perustam | aestiuo candore mori'. *umbro* is a rather learned word, first attested at Lucr. 2. 628 in verse: see Korn on V. Fl. 4. 137f. Virgil, for example, only has it twice (*A.* 3. 508, 6. 772), but Claudian rather affects it (6×).

164. For the general role played by the Heliades in the myth of Phaethon see 165f., 172f. nn. The principal tradition asserted that the daughters of the Sun so grieved for their brother when, struck by Jupiter's lightning, he fell into the Eridanus that they were turned into poplar-trees: from these their tears dripped in the form of amber. This version is possibly as old as Hesiod, if we can trust Hyg. *Fab.* 154 (= Hesiod fr. 311 Merkelbach–West) 'harum lacrimae, ut Hesiodus indicat, in electrum sunt duratae', but James Diggle is profoundly sceptical (*Euripides: Phaethon* (Cambridge, 1970), 15–27). At any rate it is already bound up with the Phaethon myth in the Athenian tragedies, if not in the *Heliades* of Aeschylus, then certainly in Euripides: *Hipp.* 738ff. ἔνθα πορφύρεον σταλάσ | σουσ' εἰς οἶδμα τάλαιναι | κόραι Φαέθοντος οἴκτῳ δακρύων | τὰς ἠλεκτροφαεῖς αὐγάς (cf. Sen. *Her. O.* 187ff.). The pathos naturally appealed to Hellenistic poets and their Roman imitators: see, in particular Ap. Rh. 4. 603ff. ἀμφὶ δὲ κοῦραι | Ἡλιάδες ταναῇσιν ἐελμέναι αἰγείροισιν, | μύρονται κινυρὸν μέλεαι γόον. ἐκ δὲ φαεινὰς | ἠλέκτρου λιβάδας βλεφάρων προχέουσιν ἔραζε κτλ. (these are then dried by the sun and swept along by Eridanus). Among Roman poets this version was no doubt followed by Varro of

Atax (cf. fr. 10 Büchner), and allusion is made to it by Cicero (*Arat.* 145 f.), Catullus (64. 290f.) and Virgil (*A.* 10. 190: see also Servius ad loc.). For poets of the Imperial period it will have been practically cast in stone by what became the *locus classicus*, Ov. *Met.* 2. 340 ff. (where see Bömer), esp. 364 ff. 'inde fluunt lacrimae, stillataque sole rigescunt | de ramis electra nouis, quae lucidus amnis | excipit et nuribus mittit gestanda Latinis.' Cf. further Ov. *Am.* 3. 12. 37, *Met.* 10. 262 f. 'ab arbore lapsas | Heliadum lacrimas', *Culex* 127 ff., Germ. *Arat.* 365 f., Luc. 2. 410 ff., V. Fl. 5. 429, Stat. *Theb.* 12. 413 ff., *Silu.* 5. 3. 86, Mart. 9. 128. 6, Juv. 5. 37 f., *III Cons.* 124 f. 'et Phaethonteas solitae deflere ruinas | roscida frondosae reuocant electra sorores', *c.m.* 31. 11 f.: also Nonn. *D.* 2. 152 ff., 11. 32 ff., 324, 15. 381 f., 38. 90 ff. Learned variants of the myths attribute the tears of amber to Apollo grieving for his son by Coronis (Ap. Rh. 4. 611 ff.), or assert that the Heliades were turned into alders (Virg. *Ecl.* 6. 62 f.). Ancient scholarship, however, was aware that the identification of the Eridanus with the Po—which does not produce amber—was false: see 148 *Eridanus* n. Even poets off duty could afford to have a laugh at the extravagance of the myth: Sid. *Ep.* 1. 5. 3 'in Eridanum breui delatus cantatas saepe comissaliter nobis Phaethontiadas et commenticias arborei metalli lacrimas risi.'

fluunt . . . capillis: for the ablative of separation with *fluo* see Trump 18 f., and cf. Ov. *Met.* 1. 266 'canis fluit unda capillis', Stat. *Theb.* 6. 934, *pr. Nupt.* 8.

165. palla: in the Imperial period the *palla* usually took the form of a large rectangular cloak for outdoor wear, often richly decorated and generally having numerous pleats. It was usually worn across the breast and over the left shoulder, leaving the right arm free: see e.g. the description of the one worn by Isis in Lucius' vision (Apul. *Met.* 11. 3). Serena wears one on the Diptych of Stilicho (e.g. plate on Cameron, p. ii), but has apparently let one of the folds slip a little, displaying her jewelled girdle and collar to the best advantage. Eridanus seems to be wearing his over *both* shoulders (*per latos umeros*), perhaps for extra warmth and protection. The use of the *palla* in daily life was largely restricted to women and non-Roman males, but river-gods, even Italian ones, are Greek in appearance in both art and literature. Eridanus could have rebutted charges of unmanly dress by pointing to the *pallae* worn by both gods (e.g. Boreas at Ov. *Met.* 6. 705, Apollo at Ov. *Met.* 11. 166, Mercury at Stat. *Theb.* 7. 39) and great heroes (e.g. Jason at V. Fl. 3. 718, Polynices at Stat. *Theb.* 12. 312). Similar cloaks are worn by Tiber at, probably, Virg. *A.* 8. 33 f. 'eum tenuis glauco uelabat amictu | carbasus', and certainly, *Prob.* 224 'palla graues umeros uelat' and Sid. *Carm.* 5. 28.

Eridanus' cloak is decorated with a representation of Phaethon in the Sun-god's chariot: ll. 165 f. thus sketch a brief ecphrasis which can trace its ancestry to the lengthy description of Jason's mantle at Ap. Rh. 1. 721 ff. Cf. also the *palla* given by Aeneas to Dido at Virg. *A.* 1. 648, which is '*signis* auroque rigentem', though the nature of the *signa* is not specified. As is well known, an ecphrasis in an ancient literary text is rarely merely decorative, but instead often carries a considerable significance in that it invites a symbolic reading with important implications for the interpretation of the main narrative. The most discussed example in Roman literature is the depiction of the tale of Theseus and Ariadne on the coverlet at Catullus 64. 47 ff., though ecphrasis is frequently used in much the same way in prose texts, above all novels. See S. Bartsch, *Decoding The Ancient Novel* (Princeton, 1989), 36 ff., Andrew Laird, *JRS* 83 (1993), 18–30, esp. p. 18 nn. 5 and 6, D. P. Fowler, *JRS* 81 (1991), 25–35. What perhaps makes Eridanus' cloak different is that its subject carries an intensely *political* significance (165 f. n.). In this it is best compared to the consular robe made for Stilicho by Minerva (*Stil.* 2. 339 ff.), which depicts the Empress Maria giving birth, Stilicho training the young Emperor-to-be in the military arts, and the wedding of Stilicho's son Eucherius. The child is Stilicho's hoped-for grandson, and Eucherius' bashful bride must be Galla Placidia, Honorius' sister: in short, 'this description of Stilico's consular robe is the most blatant expression of Stilico's dynastic ambitions in all Claudian's work' (Cameron 154; cf. pp. 47–9). Cf. also the funeral vestment made by Sophia for Justinian's lying-in-state, Cor. *Laud. Iust.* 1. 274 ff. It depicts the 'Iustinianorum series . . . tota laborum' (1. 277) and prominently features the prostration of the defeated Vandal king Gelimer in AD 534 (1. 285 f.: see Averil Cameron, comm., pp. 140 ff.). Such literary garments, and their propagandistic purposes, had their counterparts in real life: see Aus. *Grat. Act.* 53 Green for a consular robe sent to Ausonius by Gratian and on which 'diuus Constantius parens noster intextus est.' Private citizens may also have used this method of self-aggrandizement, if we can admit a basis in reality for Aus. *Epigr.* 26 Green, in which a pretentious nobody claims descent from Mars, Romulus and Remus and (7 ff.) 'hos ille Serum ueste contexi iubet, | hos caelat argento graui, | ceris inurens ianuarum limina | et atriorum pegmata'. For the passion for richly ornamented textiles in Late Antiquity see A. Grabar, *Byzantium* (London, 1966), 323 ff., Roberts, pp. 111 ff., and see further 561 n.

palla tegit: cf. Symm. *Ep.* 1. 1. 2 v. 1 'Attica palla tegit socerum, toga picta parentem.'

latos umeros: cf. Virg. *A.* 9. 725 'latis umeris'.

165f. Discussions of the history of the myth of Phaethon and its treatment in literature can be found at Diggle, op. cit. (164n.), 3–32, and Georg Knaack's article at Roscher iii. 2. 2175–202. For its appearances in Latin literature see the authors cited at 164n., adding Lucr. 5. 396ff., Man. 4. 834ff. The earliest form of the myth and its significance are hard to establish, but it seems most likely that it was originally a tale of hubris punished: see Hyg. *Fab.* 152 A 'Phaethon Solis et Clymenes filius cum *clam* patris currum conscendisset et altius a terra esset elatus, prae timore decidit in flumen Eridanum. hunc Iuppiter cum fulmine percussisset, omnia ardere coeperunt . . . at sorores Phaethontis quod equos *iniussu patris* iunxerant, in arbores populos commutatae sunt.' See further Diggle, op. cit. 22. This version is reflected in Hor. *Carm.* 4. 11. 25ff. 'terret ambustus Phaethon auaras | spes, et exemplum graue praebet ales | Pegasus terrenum equitem grauatus | Bellerophonten, | semper ut te digna sequare et ultra | quam licet sperare nefas putando | disparem uites.' Cf. also Sen. *Med.* 599ff., where Jason's hubris in crossing the sea (already demonstrated in the choral ode at 301ff.) is compared to Phaethon's and both are seen as acting in violent conflict with the order of the universe ('sancta | foedera mundi'). That Claudian intends a moral significance here is made explicit by Eridanus' words to Alaric at 186–92: Alaric's desire to take Rome is as much a violation of the divine order as Phaethon's unauthorized and destructive chariot-ride, and so, like Phaethon, he receives his punishment by the banks of the Po. Claudian had already used the myth with the same intent at *IV Cons.* 62ff. (Theodosius checking the invasion of the Goths after the catastrophe at Adrianople is compared to Phoebus taking control of the chariot from Phaethon) 'uelut ordine rupto | cum procul insanae traherent Phaethonta quadrigae | saeuiretque dies terramque et stagna propinqui | haurirent radii, solito cum murmure toruus | Sol occurrit equis; qui postquam rursus eriles | agnouere sonos, rediit meliore magistro | machina concentusque poli, currusque recepit | imperium flammaeque modum.' In all this Claudian is most probably drawing on a well-established tradition of using the myth for explicit political comment in prose panegyric: see *Pan. Lat.* 7. 12. 1ff. Mynors (to Maximian and Constantine), esp. 7. 12. 3 'solus hoc, ut dicitur, potuit deus ille, cuius dona sunt quod uiuimus et uidemus, ut habenas male creditas et currum deuio rectore turbatum reciperet rursumque dirigeret. cuius simile tu, imperator, etiam facile fecisti', Sid. *Carm.* 7. 403ff.

The original moral content was obscured from at least the Hellenistic period by a layer of sentimentality, which also laid much of the stress on the pitiful fate of the Heliades: see 164 n. Thus Ovid's account (*Met.* 1. 750–2. 380) portrays Phaethon as merely a reckless young man whose openly made request is unwillingly granted by Apollo with tragic results, and the Heliades' transformation as the effect of grief, not divine punishment. Statius goes even further than Ovid, attributing the boy's death to the will of Fate (*Theb.* 6. 325 'iuuenem durae prohibebant discere Parcae'). This pathetic treatment is predominant in Roman poetry, and underlies 164 and perhaps also the personal grief of Eridanus (186f., *meus . . . Phaethon*); the reader, however, is not compelled to press the analogy so far as to take it as implying pity for Alaric.

165. curruque paterno: cf. Ov. *Met.* 2. 47 'currus rogat ille paternos', 2. 327; also 2. 182 'equos . . . paternos'. For the chariot of the sun-god, first attested at Mimnermus 10. 9f. D, see Diggle on Eur. *Phaethon* 2.

166. glaucos . . . amictus: recalling the apparel of Tiber (Virg. *A.* 8. 33f., cit. 165n.), the nymph Juturna (*A.* 12. 885 'caput glauco contexit amictu') and the Anio (Stat. *Silu.* 1. 3. 71). *glaucus* is used regularly of the sea, of rivers, and of their inhabitants from Lucr. 1. 719 'glaucis . . . undis' on: see *TLL* vi. 2. 2039. 40ff., and cf. *Prob.* 214 (Tiber) 'glauca . . . lumina', *c.m.* 26. 36, *Rapt.* 1. 103f.

incendit: probably a reference to gold thread: cf. *Rapt.* 1. 254 (Proserpina's tapestry) 'stellas accendit in auro'; also Virg. *A.* 1. 648 'pallam . . . auro . . . rigentem', Stat. *Theb.* 7. 38f. 'aurea . . . palla', Aus. *Grat. Act.* 53 Green, *IV Cons.* 587. Alternatively, the reference may possibly be to the bright sheen of purple, as at Ap. Rh. 1. 725ff.: cf. Quint. *Inst.* 8. 5. 28 'ut adferunt lumen clauus et purpurae loco insertae'. For *incendo* cf. Virg. *A.* 5. 87f. 'auro | squamam incendebat fulgor'. Here there is also a pun, since the real Phaethon set the world alight, as at e.g. Ov. *Met.* 2. 227f. 'tum uero Phaethon cunctis e partibus orbem | adspicit *accensum*'. Perhaps the gold thread should be imagined as representing the flames that envelop the boy as he plummets to the Earth.

167. fultaque sub gremio . . . nobilis . . . urna: for the participle and adjective qualifying the same noun see 50f.n. In both art and literature river-gods regularly appear with an urn, the symbolic source of their waters; cf. esp. Virg. *A.* 7. 792 '*caelataque* amnem fundens pater Inachus *urna*', also V. Fl. 1. 219, Sil. 1. 407, Stat. *Theb.* 2. 217f., 6. 275, 9. 410, *Prob.* 213 (Tiber) 'Nymphis urnam commendat erilem', *Ruf.* 1. 133, Sid. *Carm.* 2. 2. 339f. When they recline they rest upon it (Stat. *Theb.* 2. 218 'in laeuum prona nixus sedet Inachus urna', and so in statuary), but Eridanus must be standing up, or at least partially raised out of the water (see 159f. *caput . . . sublime . . . extulit*, 193 *erectior* nn.).

Müller therefore takes *gremio* as referring to the region of the hips; one could imagine the urn as resting on the god's hip, while he keeps his hand either around it or else underneath the base. But, as Müller acknowledges, such a sense for *gremium* is 'singulär': furthermore, the stance implied would suit *fulta* well, but leave *sub* unexplained. In fact, *sub* is distinctly odd, though Claudian may have in mind the Greek phrase ὑπὸ κόλπου. See Gow on Theoc. 16. 16, where an explanation is given in terms of the custom of pulling a fold of the chiton through one's belt to make a kind of pocket (e.g. Hdt. 6. 125. 3). If the urn were in such a fold it would be both 'supported' by the garment and the belt, and in a sense 'under' them. At any rate *sub* seems to imply some kind of protective gesture; whether the base of the urn is within such a fold or is resting against the god's lower body outside his clothing, it seems to be supported in a protective embrace or clasp and so 'rests deep in his bosom'. There is thus no need to emend *fulta*. The river-god does not yet know that the threat to Italy and to his own waters has been removed (contrast 145 *quos modo temnebat . . . amnes* and the Naiad's news at 154 ff.): it is therefore natural enough that he should seek to protect the urn which, by poetic convention, is their source. For similarly defensive gestures one might perhaps compare Petr. 123, vv. 226 f. 'ille penates | occulat gremio', Stat. *Theb.* 1. 121 f. 'genetrix . . . gremio . . . Palaemona pressit.' One last possibility would be to follow Barth and interpret the phrase as an example of tmesis (= *suffulta gremio*).

caelatis: linking the artistic commemoration of the hubristic tale of Phaethon with two thematically related works of art, the Gigantomachy on the doors of the temple of Jupiter (46 n.) and the planned representation of the fleet that defeated Gildo (*caelata metallo | classis* 375 f.).

167 f. fulta . . . nobilis . . . urna: see 50 f. n.

168–77. Claudian decides to have his cake and eat it, and the participants in the Phaethon myth undergo both metamorphosis and κατασterισμός. Here a sentimental line is taken, Apollo, the grieving father, being made responsible for placing the protagonists in heaven as stars: contrast Nonnus *D.* 38. 424 ff., where this action is attributed to the more impartial Zeus. Claudian has a passion for star-lore: see J. C. Rolfe, *TAPhA* 50 (1919), 147 ff., W. H. Semple, *CQ* 31 (1937), 161–9 and 33 (1939), 1–8. Claudian's knowledge is usually remarkably accurate: see Cameron 343. In the present passage, however, he seems to be drawing on very obscure traditions, or inventing, or simply making errors (172 *Auriga*, 172 f., 173 *Cycni* nn.).

The reader receives an explicit interpretation of the relevance of the Phaethon myth to Alaric's position in the words of Eridanus (185 ff.), and his jeers naturally do not include any reference to κατα-στερισμός. Alaric and Phaethon are alike in their hubris (cf. 165 f. n.), but there will be no glory among the stars to compensate the Gothic leader for his destruction. This piece of astronomical fantasy can thus be said to have extended the range of the political significance of the iconography of the *palla*, and to have been in effect developed for its own sake, rather in the manner of a Homeric simile.

169. argumenta: the primary sense 'proofs' is uppermost here: cf. *Eutr.* 2. 77 f. 'maneant inmota precamur | certaque perpetui sint argumenta pudoris.' But since what Apollo has placed in heaven is also represented on the urn, the use of the word as a technical term for the subject of a work of art (and hence the work itself) adds another layer of meaning. See Fordyce on Virg. *A.* 7. 789–91 'at leuem clipeum sublatis cornibus Io | auro insignibat, iam saetis obsita, iam bos, | argumentum ingens', citing Cic. *Verr.* 4. 124, Ov. *Met.* 6. 69, 13. 683 f. (a goblet) 'fabricauerat Alcon . . . et longo caelauerat argumento.' Add Aus. *Grat. Act.* 54 Green 'Constantius in argumento uestis intexitur'.

Titan: i.e. Helios, son of the Titan Hyperion (Hes. *Th.* 374), though the antonomasia is also used of Apollo without further identification at Empedocles 38. 4, and is common in Latin high poetry. Cf. Cic. *Arat.* 343 'nam semper signum exoriens Titan trahit unum', Virg. *A.* 4. 118 f. 'ubi primos crastinus ortus | extulerit Titan' with Austin ad loc., *Prob.* 94, *Ruf.* 2. 338, *Nupt.* 114, *Stil.* 2. 451, *c.m.* 27. 90, 28. 33, *Rapt.* 2. 49. See further Korn on V. Fl. 4. 91 'Titania'.

signauit: of καταστερισμός also at *Nupt.* 271 f. 'si Bacchus amator | dotali potuit caelum signare Corona'. There is also an element of word-play, since *signum* often means 'constellation' or 'star' (*OLD* s.v. 13).

Olympo: cf. V. Fl. 1. 4 (Argo catasterized) 'flammifero tandem consedit Olympo.' Homer scrupulously distinguishes Olympus from 'heaven' or 'the sky' (*Il.* 5. 749 f., 15. 192 f.), but the conflation of the two can already be seen in the Attic oath οὐ τὸν Ὄλυμπον (Soph. *OT* 1088) and is very common in high Latin poetry from Virg. *G.* 1. 450 on: note *VI Cons.* 101, 351.

170. mutatum . . . plumis et fronde: it is easiest to take this as a picturesque use of the instrumental ablative: cf. Ov. *Am.* 2. 19. 29 'mutatam cornibus (i.e. 'into a cow') Io'. More learnedly, one might see it as an example of metonymy (*plumis et fronde = cycno et arbore*) combined with the construction whereby *muto* + ablative = 'to transform into'. This construction is explained by J. Strand, *Notes on Valerius*

Flaccus' Argonautica (Studia Graeca et Latina Gothoburgensia 31; Göteborg, 1972), 46 f. Strand begins with Ov. *Met.* 11. 741 f. 'ambo | alite mutantur' where 'there can be no doubt whatever that *alite* must be rendered "into a bird", the ablative thus expressing the resulting form': see further *OLD* s.v. *muto* 12b, adding Sen. *Apoc.* 4. 1, v. 8. The first attested example seems to be Lucr. 1. 802 'alias aliis rebus mutarier omnis', but the construction is a particular favourite of Ovid's, e.g. *Met.* 4. 396 f. 'quae modo fila fuerunt, | palmite mutantur', 6. 115, 9. 81, 12. 34. See further 209 *mutauit sanguine* n. Note also the plain use of *in* with the accusative, and to Ov. *Met.* 11. 741 f. cit. supra contrast esp. Hor. *Carm.* 2. 20. 10 'album mutor in alitem', Ov. *Met.* 8. 150. It is no doubt of phrases such as this that Gruzelier is thinking when she praises Claudian for his 'felicitous brevity' (p. xxiii).

senem: Cycnus, king of Liguria, transformed into a swan as he grieved for his kinsman Phaethon: see Hyg. *Fab.* 154. 5, Ov. *Met.* 2. 367 ff., and cf. 173 *sodalis* n. That Cycnus is an old man is an idea suggested by the swan's white feathers and presumably not found in versions of the myth which imagine him as a lover: cf. Virg. *A.* 10. 192 'canentem molli pluma duxisse senectam', with Harrison ad loc., Ov. *Met.* 2. 373 f.

171. fluuium: Claudian displays his ingenuity, and plays with the literary and mythological tradition by wittily representing the earth-bound Eridanus as carrying an artistic representation of his alternative celestial self. Eridanus became the constellation *Flumen* (*Amnis*, Ποταμός), flowing in the Southern hemisphere under the feet of Orion (175–7). See Arat. *Phaen.* 358 ff., Cic. *Arat.* 145 ff., Germ. *Arat.* 362 ff., Nonn. *D.* 38. 429 ff., καὶ ποταμὸς πυρίκαυτος ἀνήλυθεν εἰς πόλον ἄστρων | Ζηνὸς ἐπαινήσαντος, ἐν ἀστερόεντι δὲ κύκλῳ | Ἠριδανοῦ πυρόεντος ἑλίσσεται ἀγκύλον ὕδωρ.

qui: the relative pronoun is often postponed for metrical convenience or to throw extra emphasis on the preceding word: examples are found as early as Ennius (*Ann.* 522 Skutsch). See further Williams on Virg. *A.* 3. 25, 37, 5. 5, 22, and cf. ll. 477, 507, 610 below.

uulnera lauit: struck by Jupiter's thunderbolt, Phaethon fell into the Eridanus, setting the river alight (Ap. Rh. 4. 595 f., Varro of Atax fr. 10 Büchner, Luc. 2. 415): Eridanus is thus the 'Phaethontius amnis' at Sil. 7. 149 (cf. 17. 496 f.). The conceit of having Eridanus wash the boy's wounds before his burial comes from Ov. *Met.* 2. 323 f. 'quem . . . excipit Eridanus fumantiaque abluit ora.' For the idea cf. Stat. *Theb.* 9. 428 (Ismenos, of Bacchus) 'hac . . . flagrantem Bromium restinximus unda', 12. 413 f. 'sic Hyperionium tepido Phaethonta sorores | fumantem lauere Pado.' Grislier is Valerius Flaccus' description of Phaethon's fall into the river: 5. 430 'ater et Eridani trepidum globus ibat in amnem'.

anheli: i.e. still on fire: cf. Ap. Rh. 4. 598 ἡμιδαὴς Φαέθων, Stat. *Theb.* 12. 413 f. For the sense of *anhelus* cf. Stat. *Theb.* 4. 681 'anhela dies', Sil. 5. 513 f.

172. stat: for the regular initial position of *stat* and similar forms see van Dam on Stat. *Silu.* 2. 5. 11.

Auriga: the Charioteer (Ἡνίοχος). The identity of the charioteer was disputed in antiquity: see *RE* viii. 281. 47 ff. (Pfuhl). The prime candidates were Erichthonius, the inventor of the *quadriga* (Virg. *G.* 3. 113 f.) and Myrtilos, the charioteer of Oenomaus murdered by Pelops: Germ. *Arat.* 157 ff. 'est autem Aurigae facies, siue Atthide terra | natus Ericthonius, qui primus sub iuga duxit | quadrupedes, seu Myrtoas demersus in undas | Myrtilos.' Erichthonius' claim is recorded at Eratosthenes *Cat.* 13 (p. 98 Robert) and probably Man. 1. 361 ff., Myrtilos' at Hyg. *Astron.* 2. 13, *Fab.* 224, Eratosthenes, *Cat.* 13 (p. 104 Robert): on balance Germanicus seems to favour Myrtilos (*Arat.* 181 ff.). Less favoured candidates include Bellerophon and an obscure Argive called Trochilos. The identification with Phaethon seems suspiciously late, and may even be Claudian's invention, unless Nonnus (*D.* 38. 424 ff.) and he are drawing on the same lost source. *Auriga* lies in the northern hemisphere, and so *gelidis . . . plagis* is intended to make a pointed contrast with *anheli* (171): Phaethon has cooled off.

172 f. *fratris* and *germanae* make it clear that Claudian identifies the Hyades with the Heliades. The Hyades were the daughters of Atlas by Aithra; their rising and setting alike were marked by rain (Hes. *Op.* 615, Gel. 13. 9. 4), hence they are 'the Rainers' (from ὕειν; cf. Virg. *A.* 1. 744 'pluuiasque Hyadas', Ov. *Fast.* 5. 166). Their name was sometimes derived from ὗς (hence the Latin *suculae*: Cic. *ND* 2. 111, Man. 5. 125 ff., Gel. 13. 9. 4), or from a brother, Hyas, no doubt invented to supply this need (Bömer on Ov. *Fast.* 4. 169). Claudian may well be innovating here, since he seems to be alone in identifying them with the Heliades. Gundel (*RE* viii. 2622. 65 ff.) suggests that he may have had an Alexandrian model. Alternatively, it is possible that he was either inspired or misled by the similarity between the myth of the Heliades and Ovid's account of the καταστερισμός of the Hyades as a reward for their *pietas* on the death of their brother when hunting: Ov. *Fast.* 5. 167 ff.

172 f. uestigia . . . seruant: the Hyades shine upon the forehead of the Bull, the one on the tip of the Bull's left horn being just under the

COMMENTARY ON LINES 172–5

Charioteer's right foot (Arat. *Phaen.* 174ff., Germ. *Arat.* 178ff.). For the phrasing cf. Virg. *A.* 2. 711 'longe seruet uestigia coniunx', Sil. 6. 565 'seruat . . . gradus'.

173. Cycni: the Swan or Bird (Ὄρνις, *Avis*). The two main candidates for identification with this constellation are a son of Phoebus (e.g. Antoninus Liberalis 12) and the swan whose form Jupiter assumed to ravish Leda (e.g. Man. 1. 337ff., 5. 25). See Germ. *Arat.* 275ff., with Gain ad loc. Only Claudian identifies the Swan with the Cycnus of the Phaethon myth; cf. 172 *Auriga* n. and see *RE* xi. 2441. 50ff.

    sodalis: recalling Ov. *Met.* 2. 367ff. 'Cycnus, | qui tibi materno quamuis a sanguine iunctus, | mente tamen, Phaethon, propior fuit.' Behind both passages lies a Hellenistic tradition of an erotic connection: see Phanocles fr. 6 Powell and Virg. *A.* 10. 189ff. 'namque ferunt luctu Cycnum Phaethontis *amati*, | populeas inter frondes umbramque sororum | dum canit et maestum Musa solatur *amorem*, | canentem molli pluma duxisse senectam'. Here *sodalis* also refers to Cycnus' location near Auriga in heaven: cf. *III Cons.* 173f. where Claudian asks, of the deified Theodosius, 'quibus esse sodalis | dignetur stellis', and also Nonn. *D.* 38. 402 γείτονι Κύκνῳ.

174. lacteus . . . circulus: the 'Milky Way' was normally imagined as a circle or belt: cf. Arat. *Phaen.* 474 εὐρέι κύκλῳ, Cic. *Arat.* 248f. 'candentem . . . Circum: | Lacteus hic nimio fulgens candore notatur', Plin. *Nat.* 2. 91, 18. 280. The alternative idea of a 'way' or 'path' is first attested at Ov. *Met.* 1. 168f. 'est uia sublimis, caelo manifesta sereno; | lactea nomen habet, candore notabilis ipso': see Bömer ad loc. and cf. Germ. *Arat.* 457, Aus. *Eph.* 3. 38f.

    Ancient mythology and science offered a variety of ways in which to explain the Milky Way and its origins. These are conveniently summarized by Manilius (1. 684ff., esp. 1. 718ff.) and discussed by the Loeb editor, G. P. Goold (Cambridge, Mass. and London, 1977), p. xxxv. The most relevant for Claudian is the Pythagorean account, which held that it marked the disastrous passage taken by Phaethon in his father's chariot (Man. 1. 735ff.).

    extentas . . . alas: cf. Arat. *Phaen.* 280 τὰ δεξιὰ πείρατα τείνων, Man. 1. 341 (Cycnus) 'nunc quoque diductas uolitat stellatus in alas.'

175. stelliger: picked up by *sidereo*, 177. Cf. Arat. *Phaen.* 358 Ποταμοῦ . . . ἀστερόεντος, Nonn. *D.* 38. 430. The form *stelliger* enjoys superior manuscript backing and is in general much commoner (e.g. Cic. *Arat.* 238, Sen. *Her. O.* 1344, 1907, Sil. 2. 289, 13. 863, Stat. *Theb.* 12. 565). *stellifer*, however, may be right: cf. Cic. *Rep.* 6. 18 'summus ille stellifer cursus' (a popular text in Claudian's time) and Cor. *Ioh.* 1. 232 'stelliferas . . . undas'.

sinuatis flexibus errans: probably a conscious refashioning of Aus. *Mos.* 285 f. Green 'quas medius dirimit sinuosis flexibus errans | amnis'. There is, however, no need to accept Heinsius' conjecture *sinuosis*: this is imitation with variation, in accordance with standard classical practice. Behind both passages lies Sil. 15. 621 f. 'qua curuatas sinuosis flexibus amnis | obliquat ripas'. Similar phrases are widely used of earthly rivers (e.g. Virg. *G.* 3. 14 f. 'tardis ingens ubi flexibus errat | Mincius', Plin. *Nat.* 5. 113 (Maeander) 'sinuosis flexibus': see also 635 n.), and for their application to the constellation cf. *Phaen.* 634 καμπαὶ . . . Ποταμοῖο, Man. 1. 440, 5. 14 'Fluminaque errantis late sinuantia flexus', Germ. *Arat.* 374, Nonn. *D.* 38. 431.

176. Noti convexa: the Southern hemisphere: contrast *III Cons.* 170 'Arctoa . . . convexa'. See Levy on *Ruf.* 2. 244 'calcare Notum' for the extent to which the stereotypical use of the name of the wind for the region had gone. This particular usage is first attested at Calp. *Ecl.* 1. 74 f. 'quaecumque Notum gens ima iacentem | erectumue colit Borean'. It appears to be an extension of the well-established use of *Boreas* and *Eurus* seen at e.g. Virg. *G.* 3. 278, Hor. *Carm.* 3. 24. 38, Ov. *Met.* 13. 727, Luc. 8. 812 f., Stat. *Theb.* 3. 288. For *convexa* of the sky cf. 542 below, and Cic. *Arat.* 314 'convexum caeli' ('conixum caelo' Buescu; 'conixum caeli' Soubiran), Virg. *A.* 4. 451, 6. 241, Sen. *Thy.* 993, with Tarrant ad loc.

176 f. Homer records that Artemis slew Orion as a punishment for a presumptuous liaison with Eos (*Od.* 5. 121 ff.). The commoner version is that she did so because he attempted to rape either herself or her companion Otis: Call. *H.* 3. 264 f., Hor. *Carm.* 3. 4. 70 ff., Servius on *A.* 1. 535, Apollod. 1. 4. 5 with Frazer. A more detailed account given by Aratus (*Phaen.* 634 ff.: followed by Cic. *Arat.* 418 ff., Germ. *Arat.* 644 ff.) asserts that while hunting on Chios in the service of King Oenopion he laid hands on Artemis' robe.

176. gladioque tremendum: cf. Arat. *Phaen.* 588 ξίφεός γε μὲν ἴφι πεποιθώς, Germ. *Arat.* 601 f., *III Cons.* 171 'succinctus Orion'. His sword is composed of three stars: Man. 1. 391 'tribus obliquis demissus ducitur ensis'. In Nonnus' version of the Phaethon story, Lucifer warns the boy as he careers out of control to watch out μὴ θρασὺς Ὠρίων σε κατακτείνειε μαχαίρῃ (*D.* 38. 336), and before very long Orion is described drawing his sword (ξίφος) to do precisely that (38. 398 f.). Orion is no doubt also fearsome because he is a giant: Arat. *Phaen.* 636, 639, Cic. *Arat.* 433, Germ. *Arat.* 655, Man. 1. 387 ff., 5. 12 'Orion, magni pars maxima caeli', 5. 58, Ov. *Fast.* 5. 537 'creuerat immensum', Avienus 1170. The lofty adjective *tremendus* is discussed by Korn on V. Fl. 4. 232 (Pollux) 'nec fronte trucem nec mole tremendum'. It does not appear to be used with the ablative before Valerius: cf. V. Fl. 6. 175f., *Stil.* 3. 317f. Cf. also *manu metuendus* 216.

177. The four-word hexameter is discussed by S. E. Bassett at *CP* 14 (1919), 216–33, by Mayer on Luc. 8. 407, and by Courtney on Cinna fr. 1. 2 (*FLP*, pp. 214f.). Though found fairly frequently in Homer ('four in every 250 verses', by Bassett's calculation, e.g. *Il.* 2. 92, 18. 355) and still commoner in later Greek epic, in Latin poetry it seems generally to be an ornament of style used only sparingly and for special effect: Virgil can offer only a handful of examples (*Ecl.* 5. 73, *A.* 3. 517, 549, 4. 542, 7. 410, 8. 158). Such lines, however, are abundant in Claudian, even appearing in little 'clusters' (e.g. *IV Cons.* 98, 106, 117; *Stil.* 2. 87 and 90). He particularly likes their majestic, 'summing-up' effect: cf. 421 *tranquillique Pii bellatoresque Seueri*, 505 *Appenninigenis cultas pastoribus aras*, *Stil.* 1. 217, 2. 361, *Get.* 429. He can even boast a *three*-word hexameter at *IV Cons.* 560 'Bellerophonteas indignaretur habenas': cf. *Il.* 2. 706, 11. 427, 15. 678, *Od.* 10. 137, Hes. *Op.* 383, Lucr. 3. 907 (with Kenney ad loc.), Sid. *Carm.* 2. 204 and 507, 5. 184 and 455, 7. 536. See further Simon on *Theod.* 293 'amphitheatrali faueat Latonia pompae', Gruzelier on *Rapt.* 1. 104, Michael Dewar, *Hermes*, 122 (1994), 122–5.

The four-word hexameter also often has a spondaic fifth foot, as it does here: cf. Call. *H.* 3. 171 ἀγχόθι πηγάων Αἰγυπτίου Ἰνωποῖο, Catul. 64. 15, Luc. 6. 386, *Rapt.* 1. 104 'Neptunum gremio conplectitur Amphitrite'. Note the self-conscious artistry of *Alcestis Barcinonensis* 69 Marcovich 'cedunt labuntur moriuntur contumulantur', where each word of the four-word hexameter is one syllable longer than the previous one. Spondaic lines in general are rare in Claudian, but cf. *Nupt.* 175, *Get.* 337, *c.m.* 4. 1. A still further refinement in this line is the use of a four-syllable word to cover two whole feet: this practice is castigated as *praemolle* by Quintilian (*Inst.* 9. 4. 65), who in fact gives as one of his examples of this the line-ending *Orione*. The same combination of precious features can be found twice in a very short space in Virgil: *A.* 3. 517 'armatumque auro circumspicit Oriona', 3. 549 'cornua uelatarum obuertimus antemnarum'. All in all, a metrical *tour de force*.

subterluit: the word is alien to the classical period, so perhaps Claudian is upgrading the apparently rather prosaic *subluo* (e.g. Caes. *Gal.* 7. 69. 2, *Ciu.* 3. 97. 4 'hunc montem flumen subluebat', Curt. 9. 6. 20) by analogy with *subterlabor*, seen at e.g. Virg. *Ecl.* 10. 4, *G.* 2. 157 'flumina . . . antiquos subterlabentia muros', and esp. Aus. *Mos.* 22 Green 'subterlabentis tacito rumore Mosellae', a line with which this one may be intended to compete. Note also *Mos.* 454f. Green 'addam urbes, tacito quas subterlaberis alueo, | moeniaque antiquis te prospectantia muris'. At *c.m.* 26. 61 he has *subtermeo*, a verb almost as rare, though cf. Plin. *Nat.* 2. 214 'subtermeare sidera'.

Oriona: the full Greek prosody (’Ωρίωνα), for which see Nisbet–Hubbard on Hor. *Carm.* 1. 28. 21, Bömer on Ov. *Fast.* 5. 493.

178–200. *Eridanus jeers at Alaric's failure to make good his hubristic boasts, and summons the other river-gods of northern Italy to join him in witnessing the Goths' retreat.*

The dominant tone is one of triumph and joyful celebration at the utter defeat of the Goths and at the restoration of peace in the countryside of the Po valley. The symbolism of the *palla* with its representation of the death of Phaethon is made explicit by Eridanus himself (186–92: see 165 f. n.). Through allusions to, primarily, the *Punica* of Silius Italicus and to Livy Alaric is associated with an earlier impious violator of the sanctity of Italian soil: see 182–4, 184–6 nn., and further, 300 f. nn.

178. hoc . . . effulgens habitu: cf. Sil. 3. 694 f. 'ante aras stat ueste sacerdos | effulgens niuea'. The primary reference here is presumably to the gold thread in the *palla* (166 *incendit* n.), enhanced by the blaze of gold from his horns (160 f.). Cf. further Virg. *A.* 5. 132 f. 'auro | ductores longe effulgent ostroque decori', Ov. *Met.* 6. 566 f., Sil. 16. 576 'effulgens Laelius ostro'. This linguistic detail helps draw a parallel between the audience that watches Alaric's retreat and the spectators at Honorius' triumphant *aduentus* (546 *altas effulgere matribus aedes*).

prospexit: recalling the river-god Tiber watching the inauguration of the brother-consuls from the Isola Tiberina in a similarly joyful frame of mind: *Prob.* 230 'hic stetit et subitum prospexit ab aggere uotum'.

179. deiecta ceruice: in humilation and defeat, as if ready for the yoke: cf. *IV Cons.* 445 'attonitos reges humili ceruice', and contrast 229 f., where Alaric has not yet been utterly humbled. For Claudian, heads held high may be a mark of just pride in the truly virtuous (*Ruf.* 1. 52 f. 'Concordia, Virtus, | cumque Fide Pietas alta ceruice uagantur'), but are more usually an indication of hubris: *Ruf.* 2. 294 (Ruf.) 'magna ceruice triumphat', 2. 446 f., *Get.* 628 (Alaric's wife) 'Romanas . . . alta famulas ceruice petebat.' For this use of *deicio*, much rarer than e.g. *oculos/uultum deicio*, cf. Col. 6. 14. 3 'si ceruix mota et deiecta est', Ov. *Met.* 12. 255; also *subiecta ceruice* at Ov. *Pont.* 1. 1. 33, Stat. *Theb.* 10. 380.

180 f. sicine . . . sic . . . ?: for the structure cf. Sil. 9. 157 ff. 'sicine te nobis, genitor, Fortuna reducit | in patriam? sic te nato natumque parenti | impia restituit?', *Rapt.* 2. 251 f. 'sic me crudelibus umbris |

tradere, sic toto placuit depellere mundo?' *sicine* ('is this how . . . ?') has something of a colloquial tone, and in earlier Latin literature its appearances are largely limited to the lower genres, esp. comedy (Pl. *As.* 127, *Pseud.* 320, *Rud.* 884) and elegy (Catul. 77. 3, Prop. 2. 15. 8), or to the stylistically ambiguous sub-genre of the epyllion (Catul. 64. 132). Its standing rose in the poetry of the early Empire, and we find it once in the tragedies of Seneca (*Phaed.* 864) and occasionally in epic (Luc. 8. 331 'sicine Thessalicae mentem fregere ruinae?', Sil. 5. 107, 9. 25f. 'sicine, sic . . . grates pretiumque rependis, | Paule, tui capitis?). See further Fordyce on Catul. 77. 3, and the judicious note by Mayer at Luc. 8. 331. The tone is usually one of incredulous reproach, perhaps bitter or disillusioned: Eridanus expresses shocked disbelief at the folly of the Goth's hubristic undertaking.

180 f. mutatis . . . | consiliis: cf. Cic. *Att.* 3. 13 'mutaui consilium', Stat. *Theb.* 7. 559f. Given the explicit comparison with Phaethon drawn shortly below, perhaps Claudian is thinking of Sol's appeal to his son: Ov. *Met.* 2. 145f. 'si mutabile pectus | est tibi, consiliis, non curribus utere nostris!' Phaethon does not change his plan, with disastrous result: Alaric, equally disastrously, changes his too late.

181. iam paenitet: Platnauer understands this as sarcastic, and translates 'Art wearied so soon of the coasts of Italy?', an interpretation supported by the more explicit authorial statement concerning the Goths' feelings at *Get.* 476f. 'nimium prono feruore petitae | iam *piget* Italiae'. Moreover, such a sense for *paenitet* provides a neat balance with *mutatis . . . consiliis*, and for the sense one might also compare e.g. Sal. *Hist.* 1, fr. 68 Maurenbrecher 'Lepidum paenitentem consili'. Alternatively one might understand e.g. 'sic te iam paenitet Italiam inuasisse?'; the invasion of Italy, after all, is a crime (191) for which even Alaric might just possibly be thought to feel some genuine remorse: cf. Ov. *Met.* 10. 460f. (Myrrha) 'ausi | paenitet', Stat. *Theb.* 3. 22 'iam pudet incepti, iam paenitet'.

182–4. A recurring theme of *De Bello Getico* and, to a lesser extent, of *VI Cons.*, is the presentation of Alaric as a second Hannibal, bent upon the capture of Rome itself: both, of course, invaded the usually impregnable land of Italy, and directly threatened, or seemed to threaten, the City. The parallel is, however, rarely made explicit, except *ex inverso* when Stilicho is said, as a result of his victory at Pollentia, to combine in one man the qualities of all three Roman generals responsible for Hannibal's downfall, namely Fabius, Marcellus, and Scipio (*Get.* 138ff.). Instead, the figure of Hannibal is mainly kept before the eyes of the attentive and well-read audience through a number of allusions to the presentation of Hannibal in both the historical (or more usually, the rhetorical) and poetic traditions, not least the text of the *Punica* of Silius Italicus. For example, Claudian claims that Alaric, like the Hannibal of legend, swore an oath to destroy Rome (*Get.* 79 ff.), an assertion which almost certainly has no basis in fact whatsoever, but is inspired by Claudian's chosen literary exemplars alone. See in general Gualandri 61 ff., Introd. p. xxxi, Michael Dewar, *Mnemosyne*, 4th ser., 47 (1994), 349-72.

Eridanus' words in the present passage offer an especially subtle example of the intertextual techniques employed by Claudian. In Silius' account of the speech of encouragement delivered to his troops by Hannibal just before the battle of Cannae, the Carthaginian general refers to the symbolic humiliation of Eridanus: 'pater ipse superbus aquarum | Ausonidum Eridanus captiuo defluit alueo' (9. 187f.). He also promises his men that, after the Romans have been crushed, he will settle those who wish it on farms here in Italy, even on the banks of the Tiber: 'seu Laurens tibi, Sigeo sulcata colono, | arridet tellus, seu sunt Byzacia cordi | rura magis, centum Cereri fruticantia culmis, | electos optare dabo inter praemia campos. | addam etiam, flaua Thybris quas irrigat unda, | captiuis late gregibus depascere ripas' (9. 203 ff.). Claudian's text reverses the situation envisaged there by having Eridanus rise majestically from his supposedly humbled waters and asking Alaric why he is not now feeding his horse on Tiber's banks or ploughing the fields of Italy, as he said he would: the boasts which are here flung back in Alaric's face are in fact those of his *alter ego* Hannibal. See further 184-6, 239 f., 344-6 nn.

182. cornipedem: originally used only as an adjective (Virg. *A.* 6. 591 'cornipedum . . . equorum', 7. 779, Ov. *Ars.* 1. 280, *Fast.* 2. 361), but found as a substantive from the time of Seneca (*Phaed.* 809 'si dorso libeat cornipedis uehi', Luc. 4. 762, Sil. 2. 72, 4. 231, Stat. *Theb.* 4. 271, 9. 693, 874, etc.). In Claudian the word is invariably a substantive: e.g. *Prob.* 82, *Ruf.* 1. 311, 2. 180, *Stil.* 1. 357, *VI Cons.* 570, *Get.* 217, *Rapt.* 2. 224.

Thybrino gramine pascis: while the Greek form of the noun *Thybris* commonly appears in verse (see 12 n.), the adjective is extremely rare: compare, however, Virg. *A.* 12. 35 'Thybrina fluenta', *c.m.* 30. 16 f. 'per undas . . . Thybrinas'. For the phrasing cf. also V. Fl. 2. 487 f. 'iam cui candentes uotiuo in gramine pascit | cornipedes genitor'.

183. ut rebare: cf. Virg. *A.* 10. 608, *Ruf.* 1. 358, and also Stat. *Theb.* 7. 196 'ut rere'. The verb has a rather archaic colour; see Fordyce on Virg. *A.* 7. 437.

tuum: Burman's *tuo* ('on Tiber's grass, which, as you thought, was yours') is very attractive, and may well be right.

183 f. Barth (1650 edition) thought this was a reference to the custom of ploughing over the ruins of a destroyed city to mark its utter eradication as a place of human habitation: 'urbibus dirutis, quae in collibus olim sitae. non enim tam de cultu agrorum, quam eversione civitatum loqui poëtam existimo.' But in addition to stretching *collibus* rather further than is comfortable, this does not take into account the imitation of Sil. 9. 203 ff. (cit. supra, 182–6 n.). At *Get.* 504 ff. Claudian also makes the old Goth in the council ask Alaric 'quid palmitis uber Etrusci, | quid mihi nescio quam proprio cum Thybride Romam | semper in ore geris?' This surely implies that Alaric had frequently spoken of the glories of Rome and the fruitfulness of the vineyards of Tuscany in one breath, with the likely implication that he intended settlement on such rich land. For the use of the plough to prepare hillsides for the cultivation of the vine see Virg. *G.* 2. 188 ff., 289.

Claudian's claim that the Goths intended to find farm-land in Italy on which to establish permanent homes may well be no more than propaganda designed to augment the outrage and the danger from which Stilicho has saved Italy. In addition to the fact that these lines seem to have originated in Silius, they are not supported by an examination of Alaric's policy in his subsequent dealings with the Imperial administration. The issue of land for settlement does not, for example, appear to have been raised in the negotiations between Alaric and Ravenna in the winter of 408/9 (Liebeschuetz 69 ff.), and indeed, up until the sack of Rome in 410, the Goths' campaigning 'seems to have been extraordinarily aimless' (ibid. 72). Not until 414 was a deal struck by which the Goths would receive land for farming in Gaul in return for military service against the Vandals in Spain (Liebeschuetz 73 f.). They would eventually be permanently settled in Aquitaine in 418. See further Wolfram 156, Liebeschuetz 83 f.

183. figis aratrum: the simple form of the verb should probably be understood as doing duty for *defigo* on the analogy of Virg. *G.* 3. 519 'opere in medio defixa reliquit aratra.' Cf. the description of Delos at Sen. *Ag.* 372 f. 'nunc iam stabilis *fixa* terras | radice tenet' with Stat. *Theb.* 7. 182 f. 'potuit Latonia frater | saxa . . . *defigere* Delon'.

184–6. Eridanus' passionate outburst contains a clear adaptation of the authorial curse pronounced on the ghosts of Eteocles and Polynices at the climax of Statius' epic: *Theb.* 11. 574 f. 'ite truces animae funestaque Tartara leto | polluite et *cunctas Erebi* consumite *poenas!*' Alaric's monstrous impiety thus puts him on a level with the greatest sinners of myth and history. The audience might also think of Virgil's Sibyl

cataloguing the torments of the underworld at *A*. 6. 562 ff., especially
since 185 f. is close in both thought and expression to *A*. 6. 582 ff. 'hic
et Aloidas geminos immania uidi | corpora, qui manibus magnum
rescindere caelum | adgressi superisque Iouem detrudere regnis'.

The idea that attacking Rome is an action parallel in its madness
and impiety to the assault of the Giants on Olympus similarly features
in the old Goth's warning to Alaric at the council: *Get*. 506 ff. 'referunt
si uera parentes, | hanc urbem insano nullus qui Marte petiuit | lae-
tatus uiolasse redit; nec numina sedem | destituunt: iactata procul
dicuntur in hostem | fulmina diuinique uolant pro moenibus ignes, |
seu caelum seu Roma tonat.' At the bottom of the hair-raising stories
supposedly handed down among the Goths is the traditional picture
of Hannibal being driven from the walls of Rome by the thunderbolts
of Capitoline Jupiter: see Sil. 12. 703 ff., esp. 719 ff. 'sed enim aspice,
quantus | aegida commoueat nimbos flammasque uomentem |
Iuppiter et quantis pascat ferus ignibus iras . . .'. In particular,
Claudian in the present passage surely has in mind Silius' Juno, who
at this critical moment dissuades Hannibal from continuing his hope-
less attack on the City by comparing it to the Gigantomachy: 'cede
deis tandem et Titania desine bella' (12. 725). For Alaric as a second
Hannibal see above 182–4 n. For the motif of the Gigantomachy see
pr. 17 f., 45 *Gigantas* nn. Like any opposition to the just rule of the
Olympians their action is conventionally 'mad': cf. *Get*. 72, *III Cons*.
161 'furor Enceladi'. Madness also characterizes Hannibal in his
assault on Rome (Sil. 12. 703 'quo ruis, o uecors?', *Get*. 143 'furentem')
as well as other barbarian invaders of Italy (*Gild*. 126 'Senonum
furiis', *Get*. 292 'Teutonico . . . furori', 647). See further 105 *furias*, 206
furorem nn.

185. urbem . . . deorum: for the idea of Rome as a city protected by
the many gods who live there see 43 *tot . . . tantis*, 44 *excubiis* nn., and
cf. *Get*. 52 f. 'certa secundis | fide deis', Rut. Nam. *Red*. 1. 48 ff.

    temptare: cf. Luc. 3. 316 'aut si terrigenae temptarent astra
gigantes'.

186. adgressus: cf. Virg. *A*. 6. 584, cit. 184–6 n., and for the omission
of *es* see 54 *miratus* n.

    inprobe: cf. *Get*. 72 f. (of the Giants) 'inproba numquam | spes
laetata diu'.

186 f. nec te . . . terruit exemplo Phaethon: recalling, and incredu-
lously reversing, Hor. *Carm*. 4. 11. 25 ff. '*terret* ambustus *Phaethon* auaras
| spes, et *exemplum* graue praebet ales | Pegasus terrenum equitem
grauatus | Bellerophonten.' *terruit* in effect = *deterruit*. For Phaethon's
hubris see 165 f. n.

187 f. fulmina praeceps | in nostris efflauit aquis: for Phaethon's
fall into the Eridanus after being struck by Jupiter's thunderbolt see
Ov. *Met.* 2. 31 ff., and cf. 171 *uulnera lauit* n. The bold idea of Phaethon
'gasping out' the thunderbolt that brought him crashing down in
flames has caused some difficulty. Birt judged *fulmina* 'vix sanum', and
suggested reading *fulmine praeceps . . . efflauit*. He explained *fulmine
praeceps* as meaning 'fulmine Iouis deiectus', and presumably either
understood *efflauit* as an intransitive usage ('breathed his last',
'expired'; cf. Stat. *Theb.* 9. 899 'efflantia . . . ora') or else thought the
object (sc. *animam*: see *OLD* s.v. *efflo* 1b) had to be supplied. This interpretation is accepted by the compilers of the *TLL* (v/2. 190. 58 ff.), but
in fact the transmitted text is effectively guaranteed by the adaptation
of Stat. *Theb.* 11. 2 f., where Capaneus, struck by a thunderbolt hurled
at him by Jupiter as he challenged the god while scaling the walls of
Thebes, 'exspirauit . . . receptum | fulmen' ('cum anima amisit siue
efflauit', Lactantius ad loc.). The Statian passage itself presents an
intensification of the language used by Virgil to describe how Ajax too
was struck by a thunderbolt in punishment for his sins, in a storm off
Euboea on the voyage home from Troy: *A.* 1. 44 f. 'illum exspirantem
transfixo pectore flammas | turbine corripuit' (paraphrased by
Williams ad loc. as 'and as Ajax's breath turned to fire from his
pierced lungs she snatched him up in a whirlwind'). Capaneus and
Phaethon, then, are both to be imagined as consumed with fire and
belching out flames with their dying breath. For the general picture cf.
also Germ. *Arat.* 363 ff. 'Amnem qui Phaethonta suas defleuit ad
undas, . . . uulnere reddentem flammas Iouis'. For *efflo* of breathing
out fire cf. also Virg. *A.* 7. 785 f. 'Chimaeram . . . efflantem faucibus
ignis', Ov. *Met.* 7. 104. More ominous and significant is Ovid's use of
the verb to describe the horses of Sol's chariot in the unheeded
warning which Sol gives Phaethon at *Met.* 2. 84 ff. 'nec tibi quadri-
pedes animosos ignibus illis, | quos in pectore habent, quos ore et
naribus efflant, | in promptu regere est': cf. also Virg. *A.* 12. 114 f.,
Prob. 4 f. 'iugales | efflantes roseum . . . ignem'.

188–90. Sol stressed that his spirited horses needed to be kept firmly in
rein: Ov. *Met.* 2. 127 f. 'parce, puer, stimulis et fortius utere loris! |
sponte sua properant, labor est inhibere uolentes'.

188 f. flammea caeli . . . frena: compare esp. V. Fl. 3. 400 f. (the land
of the Cimmerians) 'quo *flammea* numquam | Sol *iuga* . . . mittit', and
also Luc. 1. 48 'flammigeros Phoebi . . . currus', 2. 413 'succendit
Phaethon flagrantibus aethera loris', Sil. 1. 210, 5. 55.

189. terrenis: contrasting sharply with *caeli* (188). Cf. Ov. *Met.* 2. 56
'sors tua mortalis, non est mortale quod optas'.

meditatur: balanced by, and nearly synonymous with, *sperat* (190), as the *TLL* sees (viii/1. 577. 62). The sense is practically the same as *consilium capere*, as the *TLL* (ibid. 52ff.), once again rightly observes, comparing Virg. *A.* 1. 673f. 'cingere flamma | reginam meditor', Prop. 3. 4. 1 'arma deus Caesar dites meditatur ad Indos (sc. ferre)', Suet. *Nero* 35. 2, *Eutr.* 2. *pr.* 7 'scindere nunc alia meditatur ligna securi', Prud. *Ham.* 174.

190. diem . . . diffundere: cf. Lucr. 1. 9 'placatumque nitet diffuso lumine caelum', 3. 22. The force of the prefix is appropriate to the sun pouring out its rays in all directions, but *infundo* and *effundo* are commoner: Virg. *A.* 9. 461 'iam sole infuso, iam rebus luce retectis', Sen. *Ep.* 82. 14 'dies . . . lucem infundit', *Phaed.* 154. See also 160 *spargentia* n.

uultu: the idea of the sun as the 'face' of the sun-god is well-known: e.g. Virg. *G.* 1. 452, Ov. *Fast.* 2. 786 'condere iam uoltus sole parante suos.' But Phaethon has only the face of a mortal, and it is folly for him to expect (*sperat*) to be able to illuminate the whole world with it. The audience may also recall how, in Ovid's account, Sol hid his face in mourning for the doomed boy (*Met.* 2. 329ff.).

191. bacchatur: practically = *furit*: cf. Cic. *har. resp.* 39 'cum sacra ludosque conturbas . . . tum baccharis, tum furis', Cor. *Ioh.* 6. 301 'miles bacchatur anhelans', and see further *TLL* ii. 1663. 78ff. ('insanire in uniuersum'). Claudian will also no doubt have been influenced by the frequent use of the word in epic to describe the impious actions of the Furies: Virg. *A.* 10. 41 'Allecto medias Italum bacchata per urbes', Stat. *Theb.* 7. 466f., *Ruf.* 1. 82 (Megaera) 'haec Agamemnonios inter bacchata penates', 368.

192. adspirat Romae spoliis: another echo of Silius' Hannibal: at *Punica* 6. 604f. Jupiter says of Hannibal 'Tarpeium accedere collem | murisque aspirare ueto.' See above 182–4, 184–6nn. The construction with the dative is a poeticism first attested in Virgil: *A.* 12. 352 'nec equis aspirat Achilli', Sil. 5. 442, *Eutr.* 1. 464 'adspirant trabeis'. See further Trump 10. Note the prose construction with the preposition: e.g. Cic. *Ver.* 1. 142 'quisquam ad meam pecuniam me inuito adspirat, quisquam accedit?', Liv. 4. 35. 6 'ad spem consulatus . . . adspirare', Gel. 10. 3. 15.

193–200. Eridanus (Po) summons the other river-gods of northern Italy to witness Alaric's humiliating retreat: like their chief, they raise their heads above their waters and taunt the Goth (*insultant profugo* 198) who had previously scorned them (*temnebat* 145).

The ancients had severely limited access to even the most rudimentary maps. Geographical knowledge was therefore mainly obtained from verbal records, primarily such topographies as Strabo and Pomponius Mela. In such works rivers, as significant features of the landscape, are given considerable prominence, and are used as the basis for the organization of ethnographic material. Epic catalogues of rivers, though naturally less detailed and thorough, originally fulfilled a similar practical purpose in addition to providing poetic ornamentation: the earliest extant example is probably the mini-catalogue of the streams that flow from Mt. Ida at *Il.* 12. 18 ff. Both literary and scientific interest in them received a great boost in the Hellenistic period from Callimachus' Περὶ ποταμῶν, and elaborate catalogues or descriptions of individual rivers proliferate in Apollonius Rhodius and Roman epic. A particularly impressive example, undoubtedly well known to Claudian, is Lucan's description of Italy (2. 392-438), in which rivers are the main organizing principle; see Fantham's introductory note ad loc. (pp. 152 ff.), from which much of the information given above is derived.

Patriotic Roman sources counted the Po as one of the great rivers of the world, comparable in volume and number of tributaries, if not in length, to the Nile and the Danube, and also high in its literary status because of its association with the myth of Phaethon. See Mela 2. 62 f., Plin. *Nat.* 3. 117 'nullo amnium claritate inferior, Graecis dictus Eridanus ac poena Phaethontis inlustratus', 119, Luc. 2. 408 ff. 'quoque magis nullum tellus se soluit in amnem' etc., with Fantham's notes ad loc. Here he is the prince of all the rivers of northern Italy, summoning his lesser brethren to do his bidding. Of the five mentioned by name, only three (Ticino, Adda, Mincio) are actually tributaries of the Po, but all are presented here as subordinates. The order in which they are presented moves from west to east, except that the Mincio and the Adige have been reversed. The literary preoccupations of the passage emerge still more clearly when it is realized that almost exactly the same sequence of events appears in Claudian's earliest extant work, the *Panegyricus Dictus Probino et Olybrio Consulibus*. There Tiber, like Eridanus, is first found in his cave (*Prob.* 209 f.: *VI Cons.* 146), when his attention is alerted to something happening above the surface (Tiber hears a noise (*Prob.* 209-11): Eridanus receives his information from a Naiad (*VI Cons.* 152-8), having been so far *rerum ignarus*). Both gods go to see for themselves and are made the subject of a lavish description (*Prob.* 211-25; *VI Cons.* 159-77). Both then see a joyful sight, in Tiber's case the celebrations for the joint consulship of the young brothers and in Eridanus' the retreat of Alaric (*Prob.* 226-35; *VI Cons.* 178 f.). Each reacts with a triumphant speech (*Prob.* 236-62; *VI Cons.* 180-92) which ends with the issuing of a summons to other Italian rivers to come and join in the celebration (reported directly at *Prob.* 253–62, indirectly at *VI Cons.* 193 f.). The dominating emotion in both passages is joy, and both also convey a sense of majesty and patriotic feeling.

The dangers of attempting to press such a literary narrative too far can be seen in Birt's use of, in particular, the shallow soil of l. 197 to dig the foundations for a mighty edifice of theory concerning the chronology of the entire campaign against Alaric (pp. lii, liv). From this mention of the Timavo Birt concludes that Alaric, after Pollentia, retreated without further conflict as far as Istria: he then argues that there would not have been enough time left for him to change his plans and retrace his steps as far as Verona to fight a battle there in the summer of 402 (see 215 *aestiuo*n.). From this he is driven to conclude that Alaric must have remained in the neighbourhood of Aquileia over the winter and that the battle of Verona was the climax of a second invasion of Italy in the summer of 403. As Müller observes (pp. 17 f.), this painfully literalistic reasoning takes no account at all of the literary motivation of the scene: *all* the rivers of the area are summoned to celebrate the freedom of Italy and to witness Alaric as he is still in the process of retracing his steps through the area of the Po basin. If there is any particular point to the presence of Timavo among their number it is that he has special reason to be glad of Alaric's humiliation (see 197 n.). Nor is Birt's reasoning even completely consistent by its own lights, since, if these lines were a faultless factual record of the path taken by Alaric on his retreat, then the Mincio should have been mentioned before the Adige (cf. Müller 17). And we should add that Birt seems totally unaware of the passage's close correspondence with *Prob.* 209–62 and all that it implies for the primacy of literary motivation in the construction of these lines. Finally, Birt's interpretation also does considerable violence to a perfectly coherent and unbroken narrative by forcing us to assume the passing of an entire unrecorded year between ll. 200 and 201. It is, in short, an argument unsustainable on historical grounds, and wholly inadmissable on literary ones. See further Introd., Sect. 3. Still more naïve an inference is drawn from these lines by Liebeschuetz, who assumes that Alaric's retreat was 'hindered by floods' (p. 63 n. 118, citing '*VI Cons.* 193 ff., but no other evidence). The same literalist logic would presumably require us to interpret *Prob.* 253 ff. as a record of widespread flooding throughout the Italian peninsula on 1 January 395 and of a soggy interruption to the celebrations in honour of the young Anicii.

193. erectior: Eridanus only raised his head (and shoulders?) above his waters at 159f. for a preliminary look, but, having witnessed the truth of the nymph's tale, he now rises further out to summon his brother-rivers to see the spectacle of the retreating Goths. Müller assumes that so far he had been in a half-lying, half-sitting position, but this does not necessarily follow. In art river-gods at rest are indeed shown in such a position, and that is no doubt how we should picture Eridanus when we first encounter him in his cave (146: cf. Ov. *Met.* 1. 475 (Peneus) 'in his residens facto de cautibus antro'). But since he must presumably have had to stand up in order to leave his cave and move out into midstream, he is surely imagined as already upright, if mostly submerged, at 159f. Here we should perhaps picture him raising his whole chest and upper body above the waters, like the figure of the Danube on Trajan's Column (for references see 159–68n.) or the Nereides who rise above the surface of the sea to inspect the Argo (Catul. 64. 14, 18 'nutricum tenus exstantes e gurgite cano'). But Claudian's wording is in any case too vague to make certainty attainable.

194. magna uoce ciet: i.e. by name: 255f. *nomina . . . ciet, Eutr.* 2. 514f. For the collocation cf. Lucr. 4. 575f. 'palantis comites . . . quaerimus et magna dispersos uoce ciemus', Virg. *A.* 3. 68.

194f. umida . . . colla leuant: see 159f. *caput . . . sublime . . . extulit,* 161 *roranti . . . uultu* nn., and for the phrasing cf. esp. Stat. *Silu.* 4. 3. 67ff. 'at flauum caput umidumque late | crinem mollibus impeditus uluis | Vulturnus leuat ora'; also Stat. *Theb.* 9. 408f. 'leuat aspera musco | colla'.

195. pulcher Ticinus: the Ticino flows south from Lago Maggiore (Lacus Verbannus) to enter the Po not far downstream from Pavia. For the epithet cf. Virg. *G.* 2. 137 'pulcher Ganges', *III Cons.* 116 'pulcher Enipeus'. In choosing it Claudian may perhaps have been influenced by the fine description of the river's idyllic calm at Sil. 4. 82 ff. 'caeruleas Ticinus aquas et stagna uadoso | perspicuus seruat turbari nescia fundo | ac nitidum uiridi lente trahit amne liquorem . . . .' But Ticinus' historical associations as the site of Hannibal's first victory in Italy are no doubt significant too: see 182–4n.

195–7. The central portion of the catalogue shows a very close correspondence, in both the order of the rivers and the choice of the epithets attached to them, with Sid. *Ep.* 1. 5. 4 'uluosum Lambrum caerulum Adduam, uelocem Athesim pigrum Mincium . . . inspexi'. In this letter Sidonius answers his friend Heronius' inquiry about his visit to northern Italy, including 'quos . . . fluuios . . . poetarum carminibus inlustres' (1. 5. 1) he saw there; the literary impulse behind his selection of individual details is thus pretty much acknowledged from the beginning. The direct influence of Claudian is surely indisputable, unless one cares to argue from Sidonius' inclusion of the 'sedgy Lambrus' that both poets are drawing on the same lost literary source. Cf. also 494–522 n. However that may be, it should be noted that Sidonius' claim to be giving an eye-witness account of what he saw on his travels is in effect the same as Ausonius' at *Mos.* 1 ff.: in both authors autopsy is controlled and mediated by literary reference.

195. Addua: the course of the Adda extends from Lago di Como (Lacus Larius) to the Po, which it enters a little above Cremona. It passes close by Milan: cf. 456–69, where it witnesses the heroism of Stilicho.

196. caerulus: a difficult adjective apparently used of a rather wide range of predominantly subdued colours, from dark blue or blue-green to a kind of glossy mix of blue and black. It can, however, also be used of the lighter grey-green of the olive (Lucr. 5. 1373 f. 'olearum | caerula . . . plaga', Man. 5. 260). See J. André, *Étude sur les termes de couleur dans la langue latine* (Et. et Comm. 7; Paris, 1949), 162–71, Servius on Virg. *A.* 3. 64 and 7. 198, Austin on *A.* 2. 381 and 6. 410, Fordyce on *A.* 7. 346. It is regularly applied to the sea, rivers and the divinities who dwell in them. See *TLL* iii. 104. 40 ff., *OLD* s.v. 3, Fordyce on Virg. *A.* 8. 64 'caeruleus Thybris', and cf. *Prob.* 214 ff. (Tiber) 'glauca nitent hirsuto lumina uultu | caeruleis infecta notis, reddentia patrem | Oceanum'.

196 f. uelox Athesis tardusque meatu | Mincius: the Adige flows from the Tridentine Alps, turns eastwards at Verona, and empties into the northern Adriatic. As a mountain river it is swift-flowing: cf. Virg. *G.* 4. 344 'uelox Arethusa' (the nymph is swift because her stream is), Luc. 1. 433 'Rhodanus . . . uelocibus undis', 2. 405. Elsewhere Virgil speaks of the 'Athesim . . . amoenum' (*A.* 9. 680), but the river will be rather less attractive when reddened by the gore from the Goths slaughtered at the battle of Verona (208 f.). The Mincio rises from the Lago di Garda (Lacus Benacus: Virg. *A.* 10. 205 f.) and, before emptying into the Po, flows through Mantua. The influence of Mantua's most famous son can be felt in Claudian's wording here: see Virg. *G.* 3. 14 f. 'tardis ingens ubi flexibus errat | Mincius et tenera praetexit harundine ripas.'

Claudian also pairs the Adige and the Mincio in two marriage-songs, where we find the same stylized contrast between the violent speed of the Adige with its roaring waters and the gentle meandering of the quiet Mincio: see *Fesc.* 2. 11 ff. 'Athesis strepat choreis | calamisque flexuosus | leue Mincius susurret' and *c.m.* 25. 105 ff.

'uolucres, quaecumque frementem | permulcent Athesim cantu . . . |
. . . quas excipit amne quieto | Mincius'.

197. The Timavo flows into the Gulf of Trieste not far from Aquileia. It
was thus the first major river Alaric crossed as he invaded Italy, and is
now the last he sees as he returns to Illyricum. Here the god presumably will rejoice to see vengeance taken on Alaric for the dishonour
done to his waters (*Get.* 562f. 'deploratum . . . Timauo | uulnus'). The
river was regarded as a major geographical phenomenon in antiquity,
and is discussed with respect by Strabo (5. 1. 8), who relies on the evidence of Polybius and Posidonius. It apparently flowed underground
for a considerable distance (Plin. *Nat.* 2. 225), then re-emerged in a
number of streams not far from the sea. These streams, most of which
were saline, formed a kind of lagoon, the *lacus Timaui* (Liv. 41. 1. 2):
Strabo says that the 'seven springs' ran directly into the sea, 'in a deep
and wide river', and the local inhabitants seem to have referred to the
river itself at this stage of its course as a 'sea' (Austin on Virg. *A.* 1. 246:
'the important thing is that *mare* means the river itself, not the actual
sea'). For poets this provided the fine paradox of the Timavo's
'springs' being in effect indistinguishable from its 'mouth(s)': see in
particular Virg. *A.* 1. 244 ff. 'fontem . . . Timaui, | unde per ora nouem
uasto cum murmure montis | it mare proruptum et pelago premit
arua sonanti', with Austin ad loc. The above description does not
correspond to the modern coastline, which has probably been greatly
altered by silting.

nouem . . . ora: for the nine 'mouths' of the Timavo Claudian is
primarily dependent on the authority of Virgil (*A.* 1. 245), though cf.
also Mela 2. 61 'interfluit Timauus nouem capitibus exsurgens, uno
ostio emissus.' The number, though, is a poetic approximation with a
whiff of mystery and magic to it: Strabo (5. 1. 8) and Martial (4. 25. 6)
assign seven. See further Austin on Virg. *A.* 1. 245, and cf. also *III Cons.*
120 'Phrygii numerantur stagna Timaui.'

consurgens: 'swelling up', because this is an underground river
rising to the surface. The prefix may also help suggest the majestic
gathering of a mighty flood: compare Luc. 10. 287 (Nile) 'medio consurgis ab axe'.

198-200. With the restoration of peace the river-gods invite the cattle to
return to graze upon their peaceful banks, and recall the deities of the
countryside, Pan, the Dryads, and the Fauns. These lines hint at the
restoration of a pastoral world, with its traditional pursuits of hus-
bandry and love-making.

198. insultant . . . profugo: prose authors prefer to use *in* with the
accusative, but for the poetic construction with the dative cf. Virg. *A.*

8. 570 'huic capiti insultans', 12. 339, Ov. *Tr.* 2. 571 'insultasse iacenti', Stat. *Theb.* 1. 78, 10. 451, *Ruf.* 1. 55 f. 'ipsa mihi . . . Iustitia insultat', *IV Cons.* 112, *Rapt.* 3. 328.

pacata: the meadows now share the serenity of Eridanus' own stream (*placidis . . . fluentis* 159).

198 f. laetum . . . pecus: cf. Virg. *G.* 1. 423 'laetae pecudes'. Claudian has in mind a scene of rustic peace depicted on the shield of Hannibal at Sil. 2. 441 f. 'it liber campi pastor, cui fine sine ullo | inuetitum saltus penetrat pecus' (itself drawn from *Il.* 18. 574 f.). That scene could be read symbolically, as indicating the peace of Italy which Hannibal will shatter: the damage is 'now' repaired through the expulsion from Italy of Hannibal's literary avatar.

199. Pana Lycaeum: cf. Virg. *A.* 8. 344 'Panos de more Lycaei', Liv. 1. 5. 2 'nudi iuuenes Lycaeum Pana uenerantes', Calp. *Ecl.* 4. 132 f., V. Fl. 6. 533. Mt. Lycaeus in Arcadia was sacred to Pan, who had a temple on its summit (Paus. 8. 38. 5). See further Pind. fr. 100 b, Theoc. *Id.* 1. 123 f. ὦ Πὰν Πάν, εἴτ' ἐσσὶ κατ' ὤρεα μακρὰ Λυκαίω, | εἴτε τύγ' ἀμφιπολεῖς μέγα Μαίναλον, Virg. *G.* 1. 16 ff., Hor. *Carm.* 1. 17. 1 f. with Nisbet–Hubbard ad loc., Ov. *Met.* 1. 698 f.

200. Dryadas . . . et, rustica numina, Faunos: Dryads are properly tree-nymphs. Now that peace has returned, these much put-upon creatures will no doubt soon be once again fighting off (whether in earnest or in sham) the attentions of Pan and the Fauns, a notably amorous crew of divinities. Among many possible examples of their exhausting routine see Mart. 9. 61. 13 f. 'dumque fugit solos nocturnum Pana per agros, | saepe sub hac latuit rustica fronde Dryas', and esp. *c.m.* 25. 17 ff. 'defendunt alii lucum Dryadasque procaces | spectandi cupidas et *rustica numina* pellunt | siluestresque deos, longeque tuentibus antrum | flammea lasciuis intendunt spicula Faunis'. The native Italian forest-god Faunus was part man and part wolf, his name being cognate with θώς and θαῦνον(?); hence his association with the Lupercalia at Ov. *Fast.* 5. 101. Sometimes he is assimilated in literature to Pan, but alternatively he may, as is the case here, be multiplied into a number of minor rural deities: see Fordyce on Virg. *A.* 7. 47 ff.

Claudian is making his contribution to a long line of mini-catalogues of rustic divinities neatly rounded off by a phrase in apposition. Cf. Virg. *G.* 1. 10 f. 'et uos, agrestum *praesentia numina, Fauni,* | (ferte simul Faunique pedem Dryadesque puellae)', Ov. *Met.* 1. 192 f. 'sunt mihi semidei, sunt *rustica numina, Nymphae* | Faunique Satyrique et monticolae Siluani', 6. 392, *Fast.* 6. 323 'conuocat et Satyros et, *rustica numina, Nymphas*', Stat. *Theb.* 4. 684, Aus. *Mos.* 177 Green.

201–9. *Verona has put the finishing touch to the work of Pollentia and Hasta.*

For the dating and significance of the battle of Verona, and its relationship with the better-attested battle of Pollentia, see Introd. n., Sect. 3.

201. The apostrophe of a place, the litotes, the phrasing (*tu quoque*—καὶ σύ) and the jubilant tone irresistibly recall Matt. 2: 6 (from Micah 5: 2) καὶ σύ, Βηθλεέμ, γῆ Ἰούδα, οὐδαμῶς ἐλαχίστη εἶ ἐν τοῖς ἡγεμόσιν Ἰούδα. For Claudian's acquaintance with scripture see Cameron 217f. Apostrophe can serve any of a number of different purposes, ranging from the pragmatic function of being metrically convenient or conferring stylistic variation to the communication of deep emotion and the creation of an impression of personal involvement. See Norden on Virg. *A.* 6. 14ff., Austin on Virg. *A.* 1. 555, LHS ii. 836f.

201 f. non paruum . . . cumulum: 'no small addition'. Contrast Cic. *Att.* 16. 3. 3, *Fam.* 13. 62 'ita magnum beneficium tuum magno cumulo auxeris.' The sense—with litotes—is fairly close to 'the finishing touch' or 'consummation' (*OLD* s.v. 4), though in many examples the connotations are profoundly negative, e.g. Ov. *Met.* 11. 205f. 'et addit, | perfidiae cumulum, falsis periuria verbis', *Pont.* 4. 12. 38, Sen. *Phaed.* 1119 'equidem malorum maximum hunc cumulum reor'.

201. Getico: see 123 *arma Getarum* n.

202. Pollentia: see 127 *Pollentini* n. Given the unmistakable word-play in *Hastae* (203n.), we should think of *polleo* here. Pollentia would thus be the place where Alaric came face to face with the true 'power' of Rome.

202 f. rebus . . . Ausoniis: a more elevated version of Hor. *Ep.* 2. 1. 2 (to Augustus) 'res Italas armis tuteris'. Cf. *IV. Cons.* 619 'Romuleis . . . rebus', *c.m.* 30. 63 'Latiis . . . rebus', *VI Cons.* 418 *Romanis rebus*, and contrast *Eutr.* 1. 154 'rebus Eois' for the Eastern Empire. The Ausones were a people of ancient Italy, and *Ausonia* and the adjective *Ausonius* are found in learned Hellenistic poetry: see Gow–Page 2. 23f., citing Call. fr. 238. 28 Pfeiffer Ἀυσόν[ι]ον κατὰ π[όντον, Ap. Rh. 4. 553, 590. Both noun and adjective become common in Augustan poetry, and are especially frequent in the patriotic epics of Virgil and Silius. Claudian uses the word here to raise the tone in his stirring account of the defence of Italy against a new Hannibal: cf. 273, *Get.* 386 'cum ferus Ausonias perfringeret Hannibal arces', and the similar use of *Hesperia* (91 n.).

203. moenia uindicis Hastae: the modern Asti, which stands at the confluence of the Tanaro and the Stura, some 30 km NE of Pollentia. *Hasta* is clearly the classical spelling, transmitted by virtually all the MSS. Birt defends it by reference to Plin. *Nat.* 3. 49, Liv. 39. 21 and

CIL v, p. 857. There is surely an element of word-play here (Alaric is defeated by 'an avenging spear'), while *uindicis* helps personify Hasta as Verona was personified by apostrophe.

Most historians assume from this phrase that a separate engagement took place at Hasta (Crees 165, Döpp 213) or (inspired by *moenia*) that the town was unsuccessfully attacked or besieged (Bury 161, Matthews 274, Wolfram 151). But no other source mentions this engagement, and given the proximity of Hasta to Pollentia, it is at least possible that the phrase is a rhetorical expansion and reduplication of *Pollentia*. Another possibility is that, when defeat at Pollentia was imminent, some of the Gothic cavalry fled back towards Hasta but found the gates shut against them. Thus the final slaughter of Pollentia would have taken place under 'the walls of avenging Hasta.' For this intriguing suggestion, which would neatly answer the problems posed by the vagueness of Claudian's phrasing, I am indebted to my colleague Dr John Vanderspoel.

204. hic: picking up *Verona* (201).

rursus dum: as Birt and Koch saw, *dum* is postponed (cf. 151, 171 n.) and *rursus* is to be taken with *movet*. The effect is, of course, to emphasize the repeated treachery of Alaric. For the implications of *rursus* see 106 *saepe* n.

pacta mouet: scholars, led on by the assumptions of anti-Stilichonian writers such as Orosius (7. 37. 2 cit. 128 f. n.), have often suspected that Stilicho had a long-standing arrangement with Alaric, and in 395, 397, and 402, let him off the hook with the intention of later using him to further his own designs. Cameron (pp. 157 f., 185) convincingly argues that this is a retrojection of the situation of 405, when Stilicho persuaded Honorius to enlist Alaric's aid in his plan to coerce the Eastern Empire into ceding eastern Illyricum to the Western Court. The precise nature of the *pacta* concerned here cannot be established beyond all doubt, but Cameron may well be right in his supposition that it 'was no more than a safe-conduct out of Italy' back into Illyricum worked out after the stalemate of Pollentia (p. 185). Stilicho no doubt simply did not have the resources to crush him completely, and will have been relieved to see him go back to Illyricum, where he would be once more the Eastern Empire's problem and not his (p. 185: see further Introd. p. xxxvi). Alaric may, however, have also been offered something more tangible, and presumably will have at the very least wanted to have his wife and children, captured at Pollentia, returned to him (243, *Get.* 623 ff.: cf. Seeck, v. 574 n. 7). Furthermore, the possibility that there was indeed some kind of anti-Eastern compact, perhaps involving official jurisdiction over

Illyricum, cannot be totally ruled out, though here one is reduced to mere speculation. At any rate, it seems clear that, whatever concessions the Romans may have made, Alaric agreed to leave Italy: see further Liebeschuetz 63, esp. n. 117, citing *Get.* 144 'uicitque manu uictumque relegat'.

Exactly how the Goths broke this agreement is also obscure. Possibly they launched a direct attack on the city of Verona itself, but one might have expected so gross an example of Gothic perfidy to leave some record in the chroniclers, as well as to have been given rather larger billing by Claudian. A much smaller incident would have been sufficient to scupper the agreement, and so Cameron's assumption (loc. cit.) that the Goths stopped to loot is an attractive one: furthermore, it is neatly consistent with Claudian's describing Alaric as being in desperate straits (204f., esp. *damnis . . . coactus*). Hall (*Philologus*, 132 (1988), 256f.) adds a refinement to this theory by suggesting that it was perhaps not Alaric's doing, but that of 'disgruntled hotheads who were disillusioned by the débâcle for which they held Alaric personally responsible.' See also Wolfram, p. 152, and 229–37 n. For Claudian's explanation of the 'clemency' shown Alaric after Pollentia see Introd. p. xlii and 128 f. n.

pacta movet is rather an unusual phrase, and one would more naturally have expected e.g. *rumpo (Eutr.* 2. 213), *frango* (Sil. 13. 286f.) or *resigno* (Sil. 4. 788). There is, however, a striking near-parallel at Liv. 35. 33. 4 'quotiens ab iis fides mota foederis esset'. Note also Ov. *Fast.* 4. 204 'acceptam parce mouere fidem', and see *OLD* s.v. *moueo* 9 'to interfere with, disturb, violate'. Heinsius' *nouat* is thus unnecessary, and would serve only to turn a strikingly associative phrase into the dull and prosaic.

damnis: i.e. those suffered at Pollentia: see 127 *tenuatus* n.

205. This is only one of a number of systematic allusions linking the battle of Verona with Pharsalus, as recounted in Lucan. When Pompey, against his better judgement, is persuaded to give battle by Cicero and his supporters Lucan's Caesar spots his chance to end the war with a single trial of fortune, and eagerly seizes the opportunity offered: *De Bello Ciuili* 7. 237 ff. 'conspicit in planos hostem descendere campos, | oblatumque uidet uotis sibi mille petitum | tempus, in extremos quo mitteret omnia casus.' Caesar's motivation is split in Claudian's text between the two protagonists, the trial of fortune being attributed to Alaric here, and the eagerness to fight to Stilicho at 210f. (see ad loc.). What in Lucan's narrative is a successful stroke of initiative and daring that reveals Caesar's military brilliance thus becomes a mere act of desperation on Alaric's part, and one doomed to failure (206f.). Caesar's initiative and speed of action, on the other hand, are transferred to Stilicho.

extremo . . . casu: i.e. by one last trial of the hazards of war. *casus* in this sense (*OLD* s.v. 8b) is especially found in the historians and in historical epic: cf. Cic. *Sest.* 12 'homini . . . nimium communem Martem belli casumque metuenti', Liv. 4. 27. 6, Luc. 9. 84 'tu pete bellorum casus'.

praesentia: the neuter plural used as a substantive has rather a prosaic feel (e.g. Cic. *Fam.* 2. 8. 1, *ND* 1. 23) and is rare in poetry except that which aims at a colloquial tone (Hor. *Ep.* 1. 17. 24). Its appearance here is licensed by its frequent use in history, e.g. Liv. 24. 23. 5 'id tutissimum ex praesentibus uidebatur', Tac. *Ann.* 1. 30.

206. furorem: thematically linking Alaric once more both with the insane rebellion of the Giants and with all the other enemies of Rome defeated by Stilicho (*pr.* 17f., 105 *furias*, 185f. nn.).

207–9. The triumphant apostrophe of Verona ends on a high note with the corpses of the Goths feeding carrion birds and fish. This grisly end is the traditional fate of many heroes in epic from the opening lines of Homer on: *Il.* 1. 3ff. πολλὰς δ'ἰφθίμους ψυχὰς Ἄϊδι προΐαψεν | ἡρώων, αὐτοὺς δὲ ἑλώρια τεῦχε κύνεσσιν | οἰωνοῖσί τε πᾶσι. The poignant contrast between the prowess of the hero in life and his present degraded and helpless state, with the denial of burial, is frequently a powerful source of pathos: see Griffin 115ff. and cf. further *Il.* 11. 816 ff., 13. 831f., 16. 836, 22. 42, 81. Griffin 115 n. 25, quotes Deut. 28: 26 'And your dead men shall be food to the birds of the sky and to the beasts of the earth' and I Sam. 17: 44.

207. loco: Verona may be a different place, but the result will be the same as at Pollentia, since that is what destiny requires. Birt's *dolo* would simplify needlessly.

208. diras: because defiled by human flesh (see Servius on Virg. *A.* 8. 235 'dirarum . . . uolucrum', offering the explanation 'quae humanis cadaueribus uescebantur': also Lactantius on Stat. *Theb.* 9. 28). *dirae uolucres* seems the more usual collocation, e.g. Luc. 1. 558, Stat. *Theb.* 2. 522, 3. 510, Sil. 13. 597. Note also Virg. *A.* 3. 241, 262 'siue deae seu sint dirae obscenaeque uolucres,' of the Harpies. Vultures are the most frequently specified type of carrion-bird in epic: e.g. *Il.* 4. 237 τῶν ἦ τοι αὐτῶν τέρενα χρόα γῦπες ἔδονται, 16. 836, 22. 42, Enn. *Ann.* 125 Skutsch 'uolturus . . . miserum mandebat homonem': cf. also *Ibis* 167. But given the north Italian setting and Claudian's explicit association of Pollentia with Marius' defeat of the Cimbri (*Get.* 640ff.), possibly he has in mind Juv. 8. 251f. 'postquam ad Cimbros stragemque uolabant | qui numquam attigerant maiora cadauera corui'.

pauit: cf. Luc. 4. 809f. 'Libycas, en, nobile corpus, | pascit aues nullo contectus Curio busto,' Sil. 13. 597, *Ruf.* 2. 451 'nudus pascit aues'.

208 f. For the Athesis (Adige) see 195–7, 196f. n. Its speed, expressed here by the swift dactylic rhythm, serves to sweep the Goths' corpses down into the sea. Epic rivers rolling corpses down to the sea trace their ancestry to Homer's Scamander: *Il.* 21. 124f. ἀλλὰ Σκάμανδρος | οἴσει δινήεις εἴσω ἁλὸς εὐρέα κόλπον. Cf. also Stat. *Theb.* 9. 358f., Sil. 4. 633 f. (Thelgon, killed by Scipio) 'turgentia membra | Eridano Trebia, Eridanus dedit aequoris undis.' Once in the sea, the corpses are eaten by fish and denied burial for ever, as Achilles tells Lycaon (*Il.* 21. 125 f.). Contrast also the related theme of the river so choked by corpses that its flow is impeded: *Il.* 21. 218ff., Virg. *A.* 5. 806ff., Sil. 1. 47f., 4. 662ff., Stat. *Theb.* 9. 436f., Sid. *Ep.* 1. 5. 7, Nonnus *D.* 36. 200f. (of Lethe!). Claudian explores this grisly idea in greater detail at *III Cons.* 99ff. 'Frigidus amnis | mutatis fumauit aquis turbaque cadentum | staret, ni rapidus iuuisset flumina sanguis' and *Stil.* 1. 185ff. 'plurima Parrhasius tunc inter corpora Ladon | haesit et Alpheus Geticis angustus aceruis | tardior ad Siculos etiamnunc pergit amores.' See also *IV Cons.* 628ff., where Barr quotes the prescriptions given by Menander at 374. 11ff. (p. 86 Russell–Wilson) ὅταν εἴπωμεν . . . ὅτι ἐστενοχωρεῖτο τοῖς τῶν πεσόντων σώμασιν. In prose panegyrics we find, for example, *Pan. Lat.* 4. 30. 1 Mynors 'non commemorabo hic tectas continuis stragibus ripas, non oppletum aceruis corporum Tiberim et inter congestas alte cadauerum moles aegro nisu ac uix eluctantibus gurgitibus exeuntem'.

208. corpora uoluens: the phrasing is Virgilian: cf. *A.* 1. 100f. 'ubi tot Simois correpta sub undis | scuta uirum galeasque et fortia corpora uoluit,' 8. 539.

209. Ionios . . . fluctus: those turned by Arrius into 'Hionios' (Catul. 84. 11f.); cf. also Stat. *Theb.* 3. 23, 4. 105, *Silu.* 1. 3. 68. Even by the notoriously vague standards observed by Roman poets in matters of geography applying the phrase to the northern Adriatic seems unusually lax. A less likely alternative would be to see this as a spectacular piece of hyperbole by which the whole Adriatic as far as the Ionian coasts of Epirus and Calabria is turned red by blood.

mutauit sanguine: this is a repeat performance of Stilicho's earlier slaughter of the Goths in Thrace: *Stil.* 1. 131ff. 'uos, Haemi gelidae ualles, quas saepe cruentis | stragibus aequauit Stilicho, uos, Thracia, testor, | flumina, quae largo mutastis sanguine fluctus.' The note of triumph here corrects Horace's pessimism about the decline of Roman manhood, *Carm.* 3. 6. 33f. 'non his iuuentus orta parentibus |

infecit aequor sanguine Punico'. For the sense and construction see *OLD* s.v. *muto* 11, and cf. Luc. 7. 537 'non alio mutentur sanguine fontes', Stat. *Theb.* 9. 257f. 'crasso vada mutat uterque | sanguine'. See also 170 *mutatum . . . plumis et fronde* n.

210–28. *Stilicho gladly seized the chance to do battle presented to him by Alaric's treachery, and was an example to his men at Verona. The hot-headed action of the Alan auxiliaries let Alaric escape once more, but this is no cause for regret: he will serve as a living trophy of Roman victory.*

As we have seen (Introd., pp. xxxvi, 128f.n.), Claudian offered as an explanation for Alaric's escape from Pollentia, and as an excuse for the pact Stilicho subsequently arranged with him (204 *pacta mouet* n.), an overriding concern for the safety of Rome: Alaric was allowed to retreat unharried in case, in a frenzy of despair, he should try to involve the City in his own ruin (*Get.* 95 ff.). The text of *VI Cons.* is so constructed that the wisdom of the policy defined in *De Bello Getico* will be directly confirmed from the horse's mouth at 290–7, but in the following passage Claudian adds futher justification in the authorial voice. Once Alaric was beyond the Po and Rome out of danger, Stilicho joyfully took advantage of the opportunity to destroy him offered by the Visigoth's violation of the pact (210–15). If Alaric had not proved perfidious, then Claudian's hero would no doubt have kept the bargain and let him leave without further harm, but Alaric's record (106 *saepe*, 204 *rursus dum* nn.) made a confrontation such as Verona the nearest thing to a sure bet. Alaric's complaint that the whole arrangement was in fact a cunning ruse to entice him back across the Po (300–4) functions not as a denigration of Stilicho's character on the grounds of insincerity but as a validation of his astute generalship.

This same military acumen is seen at Verona in Stilicho's use of barbarian auxiliaries against a barbarian enemy, a 'double profit' to the Romans: compare *astu* (219) to *insidiis* and *arte* (300). But hot-headed barbarians have their drawbacks, and it is the reckless courage and over-eagerness of the Alan auxiliaries that Claudian blames for Alaric's second escape from the clutches of the Romans (223–6). It might be argued that the use of barbarians was thus an error of judgement on Stilicho's part, but Claudian naturally presents both matters in the light most favourable to his honorand. In any case, now that Alaric has supposedly been rendered totally harmless, his escape is presented as having no significance: he can be simply dismissed with contemptuous scorn (227–8).

This passage, and the preceding lines that record in vague terms the vast carnage of the Gothic host, are the only contemporary account of the battle of Verona remaining to us: see further Cameron 182ff., esp. p. 185. Just as Claudian's account of Stilicho's motives and of the bungled attempt to take Alaric alive should be treated with caution, so too his claim of huge losses on the Gothic side cannot be trusted entirely. The difficulties involved in evaluating Claudian's evidence may be gauged by comparing the divergent natures of his statements concerning the size of the Gothic losses at Pollentia. In *De Bello Getico* Claudian speaks of the Gothic host as having been practically decimated at Pollentia (33 f. 'caesa Getarum | agmina', 78 'rarum referens inglorius agmen'), but something of a climbdown can be found in *VI Cons.*, where the same battle is said to have caused large but not utterly disastrous losses to Alaric (127 *tenuatus*, 129 *tot amissis sociis*, 281–5 nn). Practically all that can be firmly established about the battle of Verona is that the success of the Imperial army was sufficient to drive Alaric from Italy and to end the campaign.

210f. Stilicho's eagerness in seizing the opportunity to fight at Verona recalls the reaction of Caesar to Pompey's offer of battle at Pharsalus: Luc. 7. 238f. '*oblatum*que uidet *uotis* sibi *mille* petitum | tempus, in extremos quo mitteret omnia casus.' For both generals the coming conflict is a chance to decide things once and for all, a chance they joyfully take and which results in a decisive victory. The comparison with Lucan's cynical and power-crazed anti-hero might be thought unflattering to Stilicho, but the reworking of Lucan's text should rather be said to proceed *ex inverso*: Verona is as momentous a victory as Pharsalus, but is even greater in that the earlier battle was presented as a disaster for the Republic, while this one is the salvation of the Empire. These lines, at any rate, form part of a network of allusions to Lucan's account of Pharsalus, whereby Alaric in his turn is associated both with the defeated Pompey (139 *ludibrium pelagi . . . iactatur* n.) and with Pompey's successor Cato (259–64 n.). For the wording used here cf. also Liv. 35. 12. 17, Tac. *Ann.* 2. 42 'struxit . . . causas aut forte oblatas arripuit', Jer. *Ep.* 65. 11, Orosius 3. 22. 3 'tam feliciter confecit bellum quam constanter arripuit'.

210. uiolato foedere: picking up *pacta mouet* (204). The collocation is a fairly standard one: cf. Lucr. 5. 1155 'uiolat factis communia foedera pacis', Tib. 1. 9. 2 'foedera per diuos, clam uiolanda, dabas', Liv. 8. 7. 5, 28. 44. 7, Sil. 15. 279. Cf. also Caes. *Ciu.* 2. 15. 1 'indutiis . . . per scelus uiolatis', Sil. 17. 349 'fractis foederibus'.

211. omnibus adripuit uotis: best interpreted as a conflation of 'omnibus adpetiuit uotis' and 'omnibus adripuit uiribus.' Alternatively, given the model in Lucan, we might perhaps supply e.g.

'quem petierat', understanding 'the opportunity for battle which was the object of all his prayers'.

211 f. Roma periclo | iam procul: so fulfilling the poet's prayer at *Get.* 100 ff. 'procul arceat altus | Iuppiter, ut delubra Numae sedemque Quirini | barbaries oculis saltem temerare profanis | possit et arcanum tanti deprendere regni'.

212. belli medio Padus arbiter ibat: commentators rightly point to Hor. *Carm.* 3. 20. 11 'arbiter pugnae', but for the phrasing cf. also Ov. *Fast.* 3. 73 (of Mars) 'arbiter armorum', *Eutr.* 1. 241, and esp. Sen. *Tro.* 1068 ff. 'est una magna turris e Troia super, | assueta Priamo, cuius e fastigio | summisque pinnis *arbiter belli* sedens | *regebat acies*', where Priam does not merely observe the battle, but controls the troops. The phrase here should therefore be taken to mean that the river in a sense controls the outcome of the battle, rather than merely witnessing it (*pace* Platnauer, 'and Padus flowed between, witnessing the strife'). This is not easy to reconcile with Eridanus' apparent ignorance at 147, but perhaps the use of the non-poetic name here helps signal a formal distinction between the river-god and his waters: Statius seems to make a similar distinction in his treatment of the Ismenos (see Dewar on *Theb.* 9. 344 f.). *medio* is a substantive (in the plain local ablative), on the analogy of such usages with e.g. *dubius*: see *TLL* v/1. 2120. 70, and note e.g. Ov. *Am.* 2. 13. 2 'in dubio uitae', Luc. 9. 304, Stat. *Theb.* 9. 493 'undarum ac terrae dubio'. Barth's emendation *medius belli* (supported by Burman, who cites Luc. 4. 18 and 33 'medius tutam castris dirimebat Ilerdam') should thus be rejected. The sense of *medio* is 'between the battle and Rome', expanding *Roma periclo | iam procul.*

Commentators have succumbed to the temptation to use this line to reconstruct the topography of the battle. Müller, for example, glosses *medio* with the words 'inter Gotos et Romanos', an interpretation which can be supported by the occasional use of *arbiter* to designate natural dividing features in landscape, as at e.g. Sen. *Phaed.* 528 f. 'nullus in campo sacer | diuisit agros arbiter populis lapis', Stat. *Theb.* 6. 352 f., Tert. *Pall.* 2 'amnis finium arbiter.' But such interpretations *au pied de la lettre* must be avoided: Verona is a long way north of the Po, and these lines cannot be easily harmonized with the rhetorical picture of the Adige filled with corpses (207–9). In short, if the battle was literally fought over and in the waters of a river, then it will have been not the Po but the Adige. The Po's involvement is perhaps better seen as a looser, more emotional one: cf. *Get.* 195 f. 'tandem tot flumina uictor | uindicat Eridanus'.

213 f. opportunam . . . perfidiam: formally an oxymoron, and so perhaps stressing the ingenuity and resourcefulness of Stilicho in a situation that would reduce others to despair.

213. motu . . . rebelli: the adjective helps draw out what the noun in any case commonly implies: cf. Caes. *Gal.* 5. 5. 4 'motum Galliae uerebatur', Liv. 25. 16. 10 'qui ad Poenum in illo communi Italiae motu descissent', *Stil.* 1. 148, *c.m.* 30. 235. See also 204 *pacta mouet* n.

strepuisse: cf. e.g. Sil. 15. 515 'non tanto strepuere metu primordia belli'. The verb is properly speaking transferred from the blare of trumpets that conventionally signals the onset of battle or beginning of a campaign: Virg. *A.* 8. 1 f. 'ut belli signum Laurenti Turnus ab arce | extulit et rauco strepuerunt cornua cantu', V. Fl. 6. 28, Stat. *Theb.* 4. 95.

214 f. Stilicho is in general presented as the 'uiuida Martis imago' (*Get.* 468), regularly setting his men an example in military endurance. The fullest development of this in Claudian's work is *Get.* 348 ff., where he is seen in the Alps, enduring extreme cold and spare meals, sleeping rough in shepherds' huts with his shield for a pillow, and so on. Such encomium of endurance in a general is frequent in Latin poets and historians, but the passage in question seems to draw directly on Livy's famous description of Hannibal's character (21. 4, esp. 21. 4. 5 'nullo labore aut corpus fatigari aut animus uinci poterat'). Theodosius is shown attempting to instil a similar power to inspire the troops in Honorius at *IV Cons.* 349 ff.: 'nunc eques in medias equitum te consere turmas; | nunc pedes adsistas pediti. tum promptius ibunt | te socio, tum conspicuus gratusque geretur | sub te teste labor'.

215. The ability to endure the heat and dust of high summer regularly marks both the good general or soldier and the good athlete: cf. the examples listed by Nisbet–Hubbard on Hor. *Carm.* 1. 8. 4 'patiens pulueris atque solis', esp. Sen. *Ep.* 80. 3 'si corpus perduci exercitatione ad hanc *patientiam* potest qua et pugnos pariter et calces non unius hominis ferat, qua *solem ardentissimum in feruentissimo puluere sustinens* aliquis et sanguine suo madens diem ducat . . .'. Add Stat. *Theb.* 6. 870 f., *Stil.* 1. 350 'solibus effetos mersurus puluere Gallos'. Stilicho can put up with both severe cold (*Get.* 348 ff.) and severe heat, a quality he shares with Hannibal (Liv. 21. 4. 6 'caloris ac frigoris patientia par', Sil. 1. 255 f.). The young Achilles and the young Honorius both receive training in this heroic endurance: compare Stat. *Ach.* 2. 107 f. 'durataque multo | sole geluque cutis' with *III Cons.* 42 ff. 'sed noua per duros instruxit membra labores | et cruda teneras exercuit indole uires | frigora saeua pati, grauibus non cedere nimbis, | aestiuum tolerare iubar'.

The line as transmitted has given a great deal of trouble on the grounds of logic: the sun can heat the sand of the arena or the dust of the battlefield (e.g. Curt. 7. 5. 3 'harenas uapor aestiui solis accendit'), but how can the dust 'heat', or 'inflame', the sun? Heinsius suggested reading *aestiuos accenso puluere soles*, which would certainly remove the problem but is open to the charges of simplification and prosification. Birt, on the other hand, printed the received text, but (p. ccxxv) took it as a kind of hypallage, with reversal of sense (presumably = 'the dust inflamed by the summer sun': cf. 114 *mixtum pietate nefas* n.). Müller was rightly sceptical of Birt's hypallage because it involves such a striking and abrupt reversal of cause and effect, and therefore also accepted the transmitted text but interpreted *aestiuo puluere* as a local ablative (= 'suns aflame in the dust of summer battle'). But given the word-order, with *aestiuo puluere* coming in so close after the past participle and enclosed by *accensos . . . soles*, it is surely far more reasonable to take the ablative as one of instrument. The idea that the sun, or rather the heat of the sun, is 'inflamed' by the dust should be seen as a kind of deliberately paradoxical reversal of the more commonplace idea of the sun heating up the dust. The sun's heat is made to *seem* worse by its being combined with dust, and so, perhaps, with thirst and hot sweat: *accensos* is thus subjectively equivalent to *auctos*, despite Müller's scorn of the idea. Cf. V. Fl. 7. 645 f. 'qualis Getico de puluere Mauors | intrat equis uritque grauem sudoribus Hebrum', Stat. *Theb.* 1. 422f. (at the Olympic games) 'crudis . . . uirum sudoribus ardet | puluis'.

aestiuo: an important clue for the dating of the battle of Verona: cf. *anni . . . uapore* (241), and see Introd., Sect. 3. Though *aestiuus sol* is the common collocation (Virg. *G.* 4. 28, Curt. 7. 5. 3, Stat. *Silu.* 4. 4. 19), *aestiuus puluer* is easy enough to understand and is, furthermore, attested at *Copa* 5 'quid iuuat aestiuo defessum puluere abesse?'

216–20. Claudian's insistence on Stilicho's direct personal involvement at Verona is matched by Prudentius' claims with regard to Pollentia: *C. Symm.* 2. 743f. 'at noster Stilicho congressus comminus ipsa | ex acie ferrata uirum dare terga coegit'.

216. manu metuendus: for the use with the ablative of the object causing the fear cf. Hor. *Carm.* 1. 12. 23f. 'metuende certa | Phoebe sagitta', V. Fl. 8. 218 (Hister) 'ripa semper metuendus utraque'. See also 176 *gladioque tremendum* n.

216f. Stilicho reveals the same capacity for quick action in the account of Pollentia at *Get.* 596f. It is a quality shared by Theodosius: *IV Cons.* 101ff. 'nuntius ipse sui longas incognitus egit | praeuento rumore uias, inopinus utrumque | perculit'. For the idea and phrasing cf. also *Stil.* 3. 64f. 'his, Stilicho, cunctis inopina reluxit | te uictore salus.'

Note further 'inopino Marte' (Ov. *Pont.* 1. 8. 15) and 'bella inopina' (Sil. 10. 187).

218–20. It had been common practice for over three centuries to put barbarian auxiliaries in the more dangerous positions, or else to use them first in any battle, so as to save Roman lives. The policy was followed by Agricola at Mons Graupius: 'instinctos ruentesque ita disposuit, ut peditum auxilia, quae octo milium erant, mediam aciem firmarent, equitum tria milia cornibus adfunderentur. legiones pro uallo stetere, ingens uictoriae decus citra Romanum sanguinem bellandi, et auxilium, si pellerentur' (Tac. *Agr.* 35. 2; see Ogilvie ad loc., citing also *Hist.* 5. 16. 1 and *Get.* 579ff. as well as the evidence of the reliefs on Trajan's Column). Here the strategy is not strictly speaking the same, since the auxiliaries are not said to be used first, but rather are brought on to bear the brunt of the action when the regular Roman troops are under pressure (*fesso si deficit agmine miles*). None the less, the reasoning is much the same; barbarians are expendable. If Heather is right in suspecting that Theodosius deliberately put the Goths in the most exposed part of his line at the Frigidus (pp. 199, 223), then in this as in so many other matters Stilicho might even be said to be continuing Theodosius' policy.

Wishing self-destructive dissension on your enemies is natural enough: see e.g. Hor. *Carm.* 3. 8. 19f. 'Medus infestus sibi luctuosis | dissidet armis'. In particular, Claudian's glee at seeing barbarians destroy each other to Rome's benefit is matched closely elsewhere in the pages of Tacitus, where a catastrophic battle between German tribes far beyond the boundaries of the Empire is seen as a heaven-sent gladiatorial show for a Roman audience: 'super sexaginta milia non armis telisque Romanis sed, quod magnificentius est, oblectationi oculisque ceciderunt. maneat, quaeso, duretque gentibus, si non amor nostri, at certe odium sui, quando urgentibus imperii fatis nihil iam praestare fortuna maius potest quam hostium discordiam' (*Germ.* 33). This chilling passage should by itself serve as a useful check on those inclined to censure Claudian here for particularly rabid anti-barbarianism and callous racism, but, as Cameron argues at greater length (pp. 366ff.), not only is Claudian less violently anti-barbarian than many of his contemporaries, he is also in fact trying to reconcile two apparently contradictory facts of political life. Stilicho continued the Theodosian policy of employing barbarian mercenaries and of reaching an accommodation with unassimilated peoples, but many within the Empire whose support he also needed were hostile in the extreme to any apparently barbarophile action. As always, Claudian is concerned less with expressing his own opinion or prejudice than with 'writing to a brief' to persuade a particular audience. Here he is reassuring the anti-barbarian Senate that Stilicho is not a 'genuine barbarophile', but is at pains to spare Roman lives. The savagery of contemporary opposition to the growing importance of barbarian elements in Roman politics and society can be sensed from the invective at Synesius, *De Regno* 22A–26C: see Alan Cameron and Jacqueline Long, *Barbarians and Politics at the Court of Arcadius* (Berkeley and Los Angeles, 1993), 109 ff. Still clearer is the conviction of many that Stilicho was indeed a secret barbarophile bent on opening the Empire to ruination by his kinsmen: e.g. Orosius 7. 37. 1 'barbaras gentes . . . hic fouit', Rut. Nam. *Red.* 2. 41 ff., esp. 46 'immisit Latiae barbara tela neci.' Contrast on the other hand the distaste of Orosius for the use of Goths, and others, to destroy each other: 7. 37. 3 'taceo de ipsorum inter se barbarorum crebris dilacerationibus, cum se inuicem Gothorum cunei duo, deinde Alani atque Huni uariis caedibus populabantur'. This comment follows directly after Orosius' expression of horror at the violation of the Easter feast under Saul the Alan at Pollentia, and is thus most naturally taken as referring to that battle rather than Verona; it is, however, at least possible that he is reacting to what Claudian says here.

Claudian also has in mind Pompey's proposal to use the Parthians against Caesar in order to reverse the disaster at Pharsalus and so perhaps save the Republic: Luc. 8. 322 ff. 'Roma, faue coeptis; quid enim tibi laetius umquam | praestiterint superi, quam, si ciuilia Partho | milite bella geras, tantam consumere gentem | et nostris miscere malis? cum Caesaris arma | concurrent Medis, aut me fortuna necesse est | uindicet aut Crassos.' Stilicho, however, outdoes Pompey in both patriotism and *Realpolitik*; Pompey's proposal would still have resulted in the deaths of Romans, albeit impious ones, but Stilicho's action is a surefire way of maximizing the good of the Empire (*duplici lucro* 221). Note also Luc. 7. 233 f. A final point worth making is that it would be something of a misnomer to call Stilicho's frugality 'Machiavellian', since in ch. 13 of *Il Principe* Machiavelli is at pains to advise against the use of mercenaries in any circumstances.

218. miles: collective singular, and standard for 'regular troops' as opposed to auxiliaries. The *auxilia* are clearly cavalry, so we can also see here something of the standard contrast between *milites* (= *pedites*) and *equites* (e.g. Caes. *Gal.* 5. 10. 1, Liv. 22. 37. 7).

219. auxiliis: see 109 *auxiliis* n. These are, at least mainly, the Alans (cf. 224). They were a nomadic people whose earliest traceable homeland was in the area of the Sea of Azov, and whom Ammianus identifies with the Massagetae of classical times (22. 8. 31, 23. 5. 16). They had long been troublesome to the Romans: if Luc. 8. 133 is to be believed, Pompey fought against them, and certainly there were Alan attacks on Roman Armenia in Domitian's time. They took part in the general migrations of barbarian peoples west and south in the fourth century, so Roman sources from the reign of Theodosius on (e.g. Pac. *Pan. Theod.* 32. 4) regularly associate them with the Goths and Huns. Ammianus offers an extensive ethnographic account of them at 31. 2. 16 ff. Gratian was the first Roman Emperor to enlist their services, and so trusted and rewarded them that he aroused the hostility of the regular troops (Zosimus 4. 35. 2 f.). See further *RE* i. 1282. 1 ff., Wolfram 19 f., 92.

damni securus: a variant on the epic idea of a warrior raging in battle regardless of his *own* wounds, e.g. Luc. 1. 212 'per ferrum tanti securus uolneris exit.' Here the profligate recklessness is paradoxically laudable: contrast *Eutr.* 2. 52 'ruit in uetitum damni secura libido'.

astu: cf. *insidiis* and *arte* at 300. This quality may not seem to some modern readers wholly consistent with the praise showered on Stilicho for his *fides* at e.g. *Stil.* 2. 30 ff., but it is one that standardly enhances the effectiveness of a general, and in Roman eyes untrustworthy and savage barbarians no doubt deserved no better. Contrast the terms in which Stilicho's relief of Milan is compared with the actions of Diomedes and Ulysses in the *Doloneia* (470–93 n.).

220. debilitat: a slightly prosaic word appearing in only a few scattered places in verse, but cf. Lucr. 6. 1150, Hor. *Carm.* 1. 11. 5, Ov. *Met.* 13. 112, *Tr.* 2. 334, *c.m.* 40. 12.

saeuum . . . Histrum: cf. Ov. *Pont.* 3. 3. 26 'barbarus Hister', 4. 2. 38, V. Fl. 8. 219 'in freta per saeuos Hister descendit alumnos'. Here, however, the adjective is not otiose, but justificatory: see further 105 *barbara Peuce,* 648 *triumphati . . . Histri* nn. For the dramatic metonymy (of the river for the people who dwell on its banks) cf. *Gild.* 312 f. 'quae gens, quis Rhenus et Hister | uos . . . tulisset?', *Nupt.* 277 ff.

cognatis uiribus: a condensation of *uiribus cognatae gentis*: for similar phrases cf. Virg. *A.* 3. 502 'cognatas urbes', Man. 1. 906 'cognata . . . bella', V. Fl. 5. 538. This is the same language of civil war that is designed to unsettle the reader when it is used of Roman fighting Roman in Lucan: 1. 4 'cognatas . . . acies', 4. 554 'cognato tantos inplerunt sanguine sulcos'; cf. *Stil.* 1. 322, and see further 401 n.

221. duplici lucro: for the idea cf. Cic. *Phil.* 13. 40 'quibus, utri nostrum ceciderint, lucro futurum est', and for the phrase cf. Prop. 3. 1. 22 'duplici faenore'.

222. As Dr Holford-Strevens points out to me, this line should be seen as a deliberate and pointed variation of Pacatus, *Pan. Theod.* 46. 2 (addressed to Roma) 'praeter stragem militum tibi utraque parte pereuntium'. In Pacatus the context is civil war, and *tibi* is a dative of disadvantage recording Rome's loss. Claudian ingeniously reverses the thrust of Pacatus' words, since his *nobis* is dative of advantage, and celebrates Rome's double profit in this war against a foreign enemy. See also 403–6 and esp. 405 f. n.

barbariem: the collective is common (*Gild.* 432, *Theod.* 250, *IV Cons.* 49, *Get.* 102), and here balances *miles* (218).

223–8. Jeep thought these lines suspiciously similar to the account of the Alan Saul's reckless conduct at the battle of Pollentia (see 224 n.), and therefore suggested that they are an interpolation. But not only do they provide a stirring rhetorical climax to a description of the battle of Verona that would otherwise be very brief indeed, they also deal fairly convincingly with a subject that his audience must surely have expected Claudian to address, namely how it was that Alaric, yet again, managed to escape the clutches of the Romans. Moreover, as F. Baehrens points out (*Quaestiones Claudianae* (Münster, 1885), 20 f.), in ll. 210–22 the text concerns itself with Stilicho, while the *ingenium atrox* of 229 must be Alaric's. Unannounced changes of subject are not uncommon in Latin epic (see Mayer on Luc. 8. 68, Dewar on Stat. *Theb.* 9. 683), but this would be a particularly abrupt example. Lines 223–8, then, are apposite in their current position and easy enough to reconcile with *Get.* 580 ff., while they also provide an effective bridge between 222 and 229. Their removal would leave a gaping wound in the text.

223. caperet: one would expect *cepisset*, to balance *dedisset* and *turbasset*. For the use of the imperfect subjunctive in past unreal conditions in general see S. A. Handford, *The Latin Subjunctive* (London, 1947), 124, Woodcock 199. Such imperfects are often explained as expressing 'a supposed state, or continuous action', but Woodcock shows that 'the sense "was destined to", "was likely to", can usually still be seen.' This seems to be the case here: Alaric 'was doomed' to be captured, but bad luck got in the way.

leto . . . dedisset: a lofty phrase redolent of archaic ceremony. Varro (*L.* 7. 42) informs us that the formula 'ollus leto datus est' was pronounced at funerals, and the phrase is found in epic and tragedy from the earliest times: Enn. *trag.* 283 f. Jocelyn 'quorum liberi leto dati | sunt in bello', Pac. *trag.* 145 Warmington, Virg. *A.* 5. 806 'milia multa daret leto', 11. 172, Ov. *Met.* 1. 670, 3. 547, 5. 479, Luc. 9. 732, Sil. 4. 109, 343, 10. 132, Juv. 10. 119. Alaric's death would have been a solemn execution.

224. Hot-headed action on the part of the Alan auxiliaries is blamed for creating a confusion that allowed Alaric to slip through the net. Cf. the account of Pollentia given at *Get.* 580ff., where the Alan general (named as Saul by Orosius, 7. 37. 2), is said to have gone into battle with particular zeal as a result of his eagerness to disprove Roman suspicions of treachery on his part. Though Claudian extols his courage ('animis ingentibus', *Get.* 584), he also reveals that his death threw the Alans into a panic that would have degenerated into a rout if Stilicho had not come to the rescue with regular troops. See further Cameron 181, 375ff. In this description of Verona, then, *Alani* cannot refer to Saul, who died at Pollentia, but should be taken as another collective singular (cf. *miles*, 118, and *barbariem*, 222). Thoughtless battle-lust (*calor incauti . . . Alani*) is now presented as a racial characteristic of the whole tribe and not just a personal trait of Saul. For the frighteningly warlike nature attributed to the Alani cf. Luc. 8. 223 'duros aeterni Martis Alanos', *Ruf.* 2. 271, *Stil.* 1. 109 'terrisonus stridor uenientis Alani'. Claudian has been influenced here by the kind of racial theories expressed by Vitruvius, who argues quite confidently that cold climates slow the thought-processes. Vitruvius claims that the inhabitants of the northern regions are accordingly brave, but rush into battle without any real strategy, and that their efforts therefore come to nothing (*De Architectura* 6. 1. 9f.). Cf. also Arist. *Eth. Nic.* 1115 b 28ff. for the rashness of the Celts.

224. calor: i.e. 'battle-spirit': cf. Luc. 2. 324f. 'iuuenisque calorem | excitat in nimios belli ciuilis amores', 7. 103, Stat. *Ach.* 1. 881f. 'calor . . . Martius'.

male festinatus: to be taken closely together. Haste to join battle can be a sign of good morale (e.g. *Gild.* 420, *IV Cons.* 370ff.), but here its effects border on the disastrous.

225f. anhelum | uerbere cogis equum: cf. Luc. 4. 759 '(equi) uerberibus stimulisque coacti', Sil. 16. 383f. 'fumantes uerbere cogi | assiduo uiolenter equos': also Sil. 4. 18f. 'domitat pars uerbere anhelum | cornipedem'.

226. nec te uitasse dolemus: *uitasse* is best taken as an absolute usage: see *OLD* s.v. 1a, citing Cic. *de Orat.* 3. 200 'ut, quemadmodum qui utuntur armis aut palaestra, non solum sibi uitandi aut feriendi rationem esse habendam putet, sed . . .', Stat. *Theb.* 6. 861 'uitantia crura lacessit' (cf. also 11. 687 'intrepidusque secet non euitantia colla'). Alternatively, Müller translates 'wir bedauern nicht, dich gemieden zu haben' (= 'nec dolemus quod [nos] te uitauimus'), and compares 427, where *numquam . . . uoluisse dolebis* clearly = 'numquam dolebis quod uoluisti', and *Rapt.* 3. 112. But such an interpretation would yield the sense 'we are not sorry to have kept out of your way', implying precisely the kind of deliberate failure to engage with the enemy that Stilicho's opponents suspected and that Claudian is at pains to deny. Yet another, but much harder course, would be to take *uitasse* as transitive and supply e.g. *uindictam | poenam*, or perhaps *manus nostras* on the model of *Ruf.* 2. 308 f. 'quisnam conatus adire | has iactat uitasse manus?'

227 f. i . . . i: the imperative of *eo* is regularly used to signify contemptuous dismissal, either on its own (and perhaps doubled, as here) or in combination with *nunc*. The most famous example in Latin poetry must be Dido's scathing words to Aeneas, 'i, sequere Italiam uentis' (Virg. *A.* 4. 381), which Quintilian classifies as a form of εἰρωνεία (*Inst.* 9. 2. 48). Pease's typically full and useful note ad loc. offers a host of examples, ancient and modern, from both verse and prose: note esp. Virg. *A.* 7. 425 f. 'i nunc, ingratis offer te, inrise, periclis; | Tyrrhenas, i, sterne, acies' (and see further Fordyce ad loc.), 9. 634, Ov. *Ars* 2. 635, Sil. 4. 787 ff., 10. 62 'i, demens, i, carpe fugam', 11. 96, Stat. *Theb.* 10. 713 f. 'i, proelia misce, | i Danaas acies mediosque per obuius enses', Plin. *Ep.* 4. 27. 4, Juv. 10. 166, *Ruf.* 2. 301 f. 'i nunc, exitium nobis meditare remotus | incassum'. Note, however, that double *i* can also indicate pride, as in Deiphobus' words to Aeneas, 'i decus, i nostrum' (Virg. *A.* 6. 546): cf. V. Fl. 2. 422, Sil. 3. 116, 10. 572.

genti reliquus tantisque superstes . . . populis: Claudian may be directly indebted to Aus. *Epit.* 15. 1 Green (Astyanax) 'flos Asiae tantaque unus de gente superstes'. *reliquus* was originally tetrasyllabic, thus posing a problem for poets writing in hexameters on account of its string of four naturally short syllables. Lucretius' solution to the problem was to accept it as a tetrasyllable but artificially lengthen the first syllable (e.g. 2. 955, 3. 648); Augustan poets, however, seem to have objected to this, and avoid the word entirely. The solution that finally won general acceptance was to treat the word as a trisyllable, a prosody which is first attested in Persius and then crops up in a few scattered places in Flavian poetry (Sil. 10. 373, Stat. *Theb.* 1. 302, *Silu.* 3. 2. 81).

Manuscripts divide between *genti* and *gentis*, neither enjoying clear authority. One would normally expect *reliquus* to take a genitive (e.g. Tac. *Ann.* 11. 16 'uno reliquo stirpis regiae', *Eutr.* 1. 280 'inguinis . . . reliquum') or else be followed by *ex/de* and the ablative. In defence of the dative Birt points to Stat. *Theb.* 10. 238 f. 'gentique superstes | sanguis', presumably believing that Claudian has appropriated Statius' wording and not troubled himself about the resulting irregularity of construction. This is no doubt possible, but it seems more likely that the expected form *gentis* has been attracted into the dative to provide a balance with *tantisque superstes . . . populis*. For the regular construction of *superstes* with the dative see (in addition to Stat. *Theb.* 10. 238f.) Prud. *Per.* 4. 115f. 'sola tu morti propriae superstes | uiuis in orbe'. Moreover, it could be said that *gentis* has the look of a correction. The converse problem appears in a crux at Stat. *Theb.* 11. 155f. 'extremus socium gentis- *or* gentique superstes | Argolicae'. Hall ad loc. prints *gentis*, thus producing a neatly balanced pair of phrases with the genitive.

tantis: perhaps = *tot*: see 43n. For the numbers of the Gothic host see 156f. n.

228. i, nostrum uiue tropaeum: cf. *Eutr.* 2. *pr.* 47 'uiue pudor fatis', and note also Luc. 8. 17f. 'cladisque suae uix ipse fidelis | auctor erat' for a similar conceit. According to Claudian, Alaric would have preferred a glorious death in battle to this living disgrace (291–7), so his escape in effect becomes an index of Roman success: cf. *Get.* 93f. 'quae uindicta prior quam cum formido superbos | flectit et adsuetum spoliis adfligit egestas?' Related to this idea is the concept of the tyrant sparing his victims' lives, but only for his own cynical political purposes or his own malignant pleasure: see e.g. Sen. *Ag.* 994f., *Thy.* 246ff., and Claudian's own denunciation of Rufinus' cruelty in this respect at *Ruf.* 1. 236ff. The *locus classicus* for this in epic is Caesar's cynical *clementia* in reprieving Domitius: Luc. 2. 507ff., esp. 512ff. '"uiue, licet nolis, et nostro munere", dixit | "cerne diem. uictis iam spes bona partibus esto | exemplumque mei"', where see Fantham's notes. Besides varying the idea that it is more of a punishment to spare the victim's life than to take it, the presentation of Alaric as a 'living trophy' also corresponds to Caesar's identifying Domitius as a living embodiment of his clemency ('exemplumque mei'). Cf. also Stat. *Theb.* 9. 294f. (Hippomedon maliciously sparing only one of two twin brothers) '"uiue superstes" ait "diraeque ad moenia Thebes | solus abi miseros non decepture parentes."' Stilicho, however, is not to be seen as a tyrant here, for the simple reason that Alaric is only receiving the punishment due to his shocking impiety in attacking divine Rome: cf. 112 *suppliciis fruitur* n. Moreover, what may seem like special pleading on Claudian's part is in fact wholly in conformity with the more generally applicable instructions give by Menander Rhetor regarding encomium of the Emperor's virtues as displayed in war, in particular 'humanity' (φιλανθρωπία: here, apparently = *clementia*), which is regarded as one facet of the cardinal virtue of 'justice' (δικαιοσύνη). See Menander Rhetor 375. 1ff. p. 88 Russell–Wilson ἐνταῦθα στήσας φιλανθρωπίᾳ τὰς πράξεις ἀνῆκε συγχωρήσας τὸ λείψανον τοῦ γένους σώζεσθαι, ἅμα μὲν ἵνα μνημεῖον τοῦ πάθους τοῦ γεγονότος σώζηται τὸ λειπόμενον, ἅμα δὲ ἵνα καὶ τὴν φιλανθρωπίαν ἐνδείξηται. Here, as so often, the praise that Menander recommends for the encomiast of an Emperor is transferred to Stilicho.

229–37. *Still undaunted, Alaric tried to break through over the Alps into Gaul, but Stilicho's foresight frustrated his purposes.*

In Claudian's account Alaric's morale was still not wholly crushed by his supposedly decisive defeat at Verona. Rather than retreat back to Illyricum, he now tried to break through the mountains into Gaul, but was prevented from achieving this by the foresight of Stilicho. The language used is too vague to admit of any real certainty, but a reasonable deduction is that Alaric hoped to make his way over the Alps by such a route as the Brenner Pass, only to find it unexpectedly blocked by Roman garrisons, or else was outmanœuvred as Catiline was by Metellus Celer (230–3 n.). Claudian presents this plan for a westwards trek as a last-ditch attempt to save something from an expedition whose original goal was the capture of Rome, but Wolfram (p. 152) suggests that it may have been planned even before Verona. Similarly, Heather (p. 208) argues that obtaining land for settlement was probably the Goths' aim all along and that Alaric's object in the siege of Milan may have been to force Honorius into making concessions of this kind; prevented from settling in Italy, the Goths might well in such circumstances have thought that their best course was to continue west. Note also Jord., *Get.* 153 'cui (sc. Honorio) ad postremum sententia sedit, quatenus prouincias longe positas, id est Gallias Spaniasque . . . Halaricus sua cum gente sibi tamquam lares proprias uindicaret'. At any rate, Gaul is a recurring possibility, and would at a later date become a relatively attractive alternative to a Roman Court feeling the pressure of Alaric's presence on Italian soil: it was in Aquitaine that, after 418, the Goths were to make their permanent home.

229–35. For the scansion of these lines see Introd. Sect. 6.

229. non tamen: highly emphatic: cf. 244, *c.m.* 30. 33, *Rapt.* 3. 357.

ingenium . . . atrox: the adjective implies stubbornness as well as fierceness. Claudian is thus indulging in clever oxymoron at *c.m.* 22. 13 'manibus Hectoreis atrox ignouit Achilles' and *Rapt.* 1. 68 'animusque relanguit atrox | quamuis indocilis flecti.' For the collocation cf. Liv. 7. 4. 3 (L. Manlius Imperiosus) 'inuisum ipsum ingenium atrox', and also Hor. *Carm.* 2. 1. 24 'atrocem animum Catonis'.

229 f. se . . . deicit: the reflexive for the passive: cf. 40 f. *se . . . aestimat* n. His men were already *deiecta ceruice* after Pollentia (179), but Alaric is

made of sterner stuff. He is thus perhaps all the more a fitting
opponent for Stilicho, of whom Claudian says 'frons . . . non deiecta
malis, mixta sed nobilis ira' (*Get.* 375 f.).

230–3. The situation and language are very similar to Sal. *Cat.* 57. 1 ff.
'reliquos Catilina per montis asperos magnis itineribus in agrum
Pistoriensem abducit eo consilio, uti per tramites occulte perfugeret in
Galliam Transalpinam. at Q. Metellus Celer cum tribus legionibus in
agro Piceno praesidebat . . . igitur ubi iter eius ex perfugis cognouit,
castra propere mouit ac sub ipsis radicibus montium consedit, qua illi
descensus erat in Galliam properanti.' For Claudian's knowledge of
Sallust see Cameron 334 ff.

230. occulto . . . tramite: we remember Ephialtes guiding the Persians
at Thermopylae (Hdt. 7. 213), but if there were any Roman traitors at
work, Claudian says not a word of their disgrace. Contrast the success
of the barbarian invaders at *Ruf.* 2. 28 ff. 'alii per Caspia claustra |
Armeniasque niues inopino tramite ducti | inuadunt Orientis opes.'
For the phrase compare Virg. *A.* 3. 695 'occultas . . . uias', 9. 383 'rara
per occultos lucebat semita callis', Ov. *Fast.* 3. 240.

231. Cf. Virg. *A.* 9. 512 f. 'si qua | possent tectam aciem perrumpere'.
  subitas: adverbial. See the useful note by van Dam at Stat. *Silu.* 2.
1. 137 f. 'subitas inimica leuauit | Parca manus.' As van Dam shows,
the adverbial use of the adjective, as well as being metrically convenient, was attractive to poets who 'wanted to concretize or depict
someone or something rather than to use the abstract adverb.' The
use of *subitus* in this way is especially common: cf. 346 *subitis fluxere
uaporibus*, 535 *erexit subitas turres*, *Gild.* 366 'subitae collo sonuere
catenae', *Nupt.* 188, *Rapt.* 2. 188 'apparet subitus caelo timor'.

232. Raetos Gallosque: i.e. *through* Raetia *into* Gaul. Since Stilicho had
campaigned in Raetia the previous winter (*Get.* 321 ff.), he had something of an advantage.

232–7. The superhuman *consilium* and *uigilantia* of Stilicho are regular
themes of Claudian's panegyric. Cf. esp. *Stil.* 1. 309 ff. 'quot nube
soporis | immunes oculi per tot discurrere partes, | tot loca sufficerent
et tam longinqua tueri? | Argum fama canit centeno lumine cinctum
| corporis excubiis unam seruasse iuuencam!', *Get.* 360 ff. It is a
quality he shares with his wife Serena: *c.m.* 30. 228 ff. 'uigili tu prospicis
omnia sensu . . .'. Such *uigilantia*, of course, is a virtue regularly
attributed to great or charismatic generals, and as Livy (21. 6 f.) and
Silius (1. 246) concede it to Hannibal so Sallust also grants that
Catiline possessed it (*Cat.* 5: cf. Cic. *Cat.* 1. 26). See in general
Woodman on Vell. 2. 79. 1 'M. Agrippa, uirtutis nobilissimae, labore
uigilia periculo inuictus'. For the theme of *uigilantia* in encomiastic

poetry see Michael Dewar, *Mnemosyne*, 4th ser., 46 (1993), 211–23; to the examples cited there add Virg. *A.* 10. 217 with Harrison ad loc., *Eleg. Maec.* 1. 14 'Romanae tu uigil urbis eras.' Claudian also adapts the topos for ironic or obscene effect at *Gild.* 449 f. and *Eutr.* 1. 362 f.

233. cura ducis: *cura* for the well-being of both Honorius and the Empire in general could be said to be the single most distinguishing characteristic of Stilicho in Claudian's portrayal of him: cf. 100 *cura* n. It takes precedence over all more purely personal loyalties: *Stil.* 1. 121 f. 'patris stimulos ignesque mariti | uicit cura ducis.'

diuinum . . . pectus: the truly superhuman intelligence of a seer, gifted with the power to divine the future: cf. Enn. *Ann.* 15 f. Skutsch 'Anchises . . . Venus quem pulcra dearum | fari donauit, diuinum pectus habere', Catul. 64. 382 f. 'talia praefantes . . . | carmina diuino cecinerunt pectore Parcae', Lucr. 1. 731, Petr. 7. 2. The sense of *diuinum* is 'inspired', 'prescient', 'prophetic': see further *OLD* s.v. 6, and cf. Shakespeare, *Hamlet* 1. 5. 40 'O my prophetic soul!' For *pectus* as the seat of intelligence see *pr.* 2 *pectore sopito* n.

234. excubiis: either a plain ablative (= 'on sentry duty') or, just possibly, a dative of purpose, explaining and expanding *uigilantia*: 'unsleeping so as to keep watch over the Empire.' Heinsius suggests reading *excubias*, in apposition to *lumina*.

uigilantia lumina: Ovid uses the phrase twice, but of literal lamps (*Ep.* 18. 31, 19. 35). Truer parallels are Stat. *Theb.* 5. 212 'oculis uigilantibus' and *Silu.* 1. 4. 119 'nunc aure uigil, nunc lumine'.

regni: = *imperii*; see 83 *regni pro parte* n.

235. consilium: another of the qualities that regularly distinguish Stilicho in Claudian's encomia: cf. *Nupt.* 313 f., *Gild.* 318 f. 'noui consilium, noui Stilichonis in omnes | aequalem casus animum'. He combines it with military skill, producing a perfect blend: *Theod.* 162 f. 'similem (sc. Stilichoni) quae protulit aetas | consilio uel Marte uirum?' In this we can perhaps discern the beginnings of the medieval distinction between two forms of feudal service to a lord, equally valid and equally desirable, i.e. *commilitium* and *consilium*. Consider the famous characterization of Charlemagne's great vassals at *Chanson de Roland* 1093 f. 'Rollant est proz e Oliver est sage, | Ambedui unt merveillus vasselage.'

236. nec potuit texisse suum: for the phrasing cf. Virg. *A.* 4. 477 'consilium uultu tegit'. Birt, p. ccxxv, claims we should supply *cui* to balance *cuius* (235), and for further examples of such ellipsis in Claudian he points to *Get.* 35, 483. But *nec cui* is not possible in Latin relative clauses.

237. nosse prior: an epexegetic ('explanatory') infinitive after the Greek model, defining the sphere or purpose of the adjective which governs it. See Austin on Virg. *A.* 4. 564 'certa mori', Woodcock 26. Cf. *Stil.* 1. 65 f. 'quis Stilichone prior ferro penetrare leones | comminus aut longe uirgatas figere tigres?'

    celeri . . . sensu: cf. Vell. 2. 118. 2 'iuuenis genere nobilis, manu fortis, sensu celer, ultra barbarum promptus ingenio', *Eutr.* 1. 361 'celeri degustat singula sensu': also *c.m.* 30. 228. This is a variant of the common collocation *celeris mens*: e.g. Cic. *Orat.* 200 'mens . . . qua nihil est celerius', Ov. *Rem.* 89, *Pan. Lat.* Mynors 11. 8. 5 'cum nihil sit animo uelocius': see further *TLL* iii/1. 750. 71 ff. and cf. also Virg. *A.* 4. 285 (= 8. 20) 'animum nunc huc celerem nunc diuidit illuc'.

    dolis occurrere: cf. Virg. *A.* 1. 682 'ne qua scire dolos mediusue occurrere possit'.

238–64. *Hemmed in on a single hillside, the Goths are afflicted by hunger and disease, and begin to desert in droves. Alaric proves unable to prevent them, just as an old bee-keeper is powerless to stop his bees from swarming and abandoning their hives.*

That Alaric's retreat across the Alps was gruelling, and that defeat was followed by substantial defections from the Gothic host, is not inherently improbable. Wolfram, for example, takes Claudian's evidence largely at face value (p. 152). On the other hand, Claudian is the only extant source for the situation described in these lines, and so his account must be treated with still greater allowance for exaggeration than usual: it may be nothing more than a poetic fantasy from beginning to end, as the great speech of despair for which it provides the opportunity (274–319) most certainly is. The cynic will point to the very close similarities between the situation in these lines and that in which Alaric found himself when he was enclosed by Stilicho's troops on Mt Pholoe in Arcadia in 397. Compare Zosimus 5. 7, *IV Cons.* 459 ff., esp. 478 ff. 'quorum turbae spatium uix praebuit orbis, | *uno colle* latent. sitiens inclusaque uallo | ereptas quaesiuit aquas, quas hostibus ante | contiguas alio Stilicho deflexerat actu | mirantemque nouas ignota per auia ualles | iusserat auerso fluuium migrare meatu'. See further Fargues 117.

This passage is remarkable for its reliance on elements of diction more generally found in prose literature, especially history. Consider e.g. *probra* (242), *subiugat* (249), *transfuga* (250), *inque dies* (251), *deditio* (252), *discedere* (253), *deplorat* (264), and see the notes *ad locc.* The proliferation of such terms can hardly be accidental, and it seems that Claudian is deliberately trying to give the impression of honest and accurate reporting. This is all the more effective in setting the stage for what must be the poem's most conscious distortion of the 'facts', the great lament of Alaric (274-319).

238. omnibus . . . coeptis: his original intention to take Rome, his last military gamble at Verona, and finally his unsuccessful attempt to break through into Gaul (229-37).

uno: not, as Müller tentatively suggests, an example of a Late Latin indefinite article, but pointed: their numbers are now so reduced (cf. 129 *tot amissis sociis* n., 156f., 207-9) that they can all be accommodated on a single hillside; cf. *IV Cons.* 478f. (cit. 238-64n.).

239. frondes . . . depastus amaras: and not, that is, on the lush grass of Tiber's banks, as Alaric apparently promised his men (182-4n.). For the phrasing cf. Calvus fr. 9 Büchner 'herbis pasceris amaris', Virg. *Ecl.* 6. 62f., Ov. *Met.* 1. 632 'frondibus arboreis et amara pascitur herba'. Cf. also Lucan's description of an army in similarly desperate straits, 4. 410ff. 'non pabula tellus | pascendis summittit equis, non proserit ullam | flaua Ceres segetem; spoliarat gramine campum | miles et attonso miseris iam dentibus aruo | castrorum siccas de caespite uolserat herbas'.

240. arboreo: adjective for genitive, as often in poetry: see Löfstedt, *Syntactica*, i. 107ff. Thomas on Virg. *G.* 1. 55 'arborei fetus' points out that not only are adjectives in *-eus* apparently deemed more poetic, they are often metrically convenient. Here the genitive plural form *arborum* would be hard to fit into a hexameter.

figat . . . morsus: a poetic version of *(in-)figere dentes* (Tib. 1. 2. 18, Ov. *Met.* 3. 84, Curt. 9. 1. 33): cf. Nem. *Cyneg.* 214 'insanos cogens infigere morsus': also Luc. 3. 699.

sonipes: established as a substantive from the archaic period (Acc. *trag.* 657 Warmington = *Theb.* 400 Dangel 'quadripedantum sonipedum', Lucil. 507), and no doubt so used by Ennius in the *Annales*, though the earliest extant appearances in epic are in Virgil (*A.* 4. 135, 11. 600). Cf. 344, and, for the collective singular, *Ruf.* 2. 35 'proterit inbellem sonipes hostilis Oronten.' For the 'hollow noise' which would have been made by an unshod horse see Austin on Virg. *A.* 4. 135.

241f. Disease afflicts the Goths, caused by their tainted food and by the heat of the season. We are now in late summer or early autumn (cf. 215n.), traditionally the unhealthiest time of year in Italy. Cf. Virgil's description of the onset of the Noric plague, esp. *G.* 3. 479 'totoque autumni incanduit aestu': Thomas ad loc. compares Hor. *S.* 2. 6. 18f. 'plumbeus Auster | autumnusque grauis, Libitinae quaestus acerbae.' Plague was generally conceived as being air-borne: cf. Ov. *Met.* 7. 528f. (the plague at Aegina) 'principio caelum spissa caligine terras |

pressit et ignauos inclusit nubibus aestus', 532, *Ruf.* 1. 301 ff., *Gild.* 514 f. Lucretius attempts a scientific explanation at 6. 1090 ff.

taetris collecta cibis . . . lues: cf. Sen. *Ep.* 5. 4 'cibis . . . taetris et horridis.' For *colligo* of sickness etc. see *TLL* iii/2. 1614. 44 ff., citing e.g. [Quint.] *Decl.* 17. 15 'collecta de calamitatibus . . . infirmitas', Amm. Marc. 21. 16. 5 'ut raros colligeret morbos'; note also Cic. *Brut.* 283 'metuensque ne uitiosum (sc. sanguinem) colligeret'.

241. anni . . . uapore: for similar phrases cf. Sen. *Phaed.* 765 'aestatis calidae . . . uapor', *c.m.* 28. 17 'loca continuo solis damnata uapore'; also Sen. *Nat.* 4b. 13. 3 'contra anni feruorem', Stat. *Silu.* 3. 1. 135 f.

242f. The Roman army (*miles* is collective singular, as at 218) taunt Alaric and humiliate him by displaying to him his children, captured when the Gothic camp was stormed at Pollentia. Their taunts are the equivalent on the human plane of those of Eridanus and his brother rivers (180–200). Note also Claudian's authorial scorn at *Get.* 83 ff. 'qui foeda parabat | Romanas ad stupra nurus, sua pignora uidit | coniugibus permixta trahi'. Seeck (v. 574) argues that it is unlikely that Alaric's kin were at this point still in Roman hands, but that they must have been returned with the conclusion of the *pacta* mentioned in 204. If so, Claudian is presumably letting his imagination prevail over hard fact for poetic effect, or else was simply misinformed. On the other hand, it may be that Alaric was not to have his kin returned to him until *after* he was safely out of Italy. See further 204 *pacta mouet* n.

probra . . . | ingerat: a common enough phrase in prose writing, implying a great deal (*ingero:* 'heaps') of vigorous abuse: cf. Liv. 2. 45. 10, 45. 36. 8, Tac. *Hist.* 3. 31; also *Ann.* 1. 39 'ingerunt contumelias'. Contrast Apul. *Met.* 5. 6 'ingerens uerba mulcentia'. *probrum*, however, is very rare in the high style of verse, being wholly avoided by Virgil, Lucan, and Statius, and appearing only once each in Ovid's *Metamorphoses* (10. 695) and Silius (2. 505). Exchanges of insults are a standard feature of ancient battle-narrative, discussed by Ward Parks, *Verbal Dueling in Heroic Narrative: The Homeric and Old English Traditions* (Princeton, 1990), but are not always mere ritual or figments: where the position of both sides is more suited to defence than attack, each will wish to provoke the other into giving battle (Plut. *Mar.* 33. 4). In the present case, where Alaric has not been completely destroyed, the Roman soldiers are not simply jeering at a defeated foe, but attempting, as vv. 244–8 make clear, to provoke him into action that will result in his annihilation; but he knows this and therefore in his heart accepts that he is beaten.

244–8. *non tamen* is highly emphatic (cf. 229 n.). Not even such horrific circumstances, in which a man might try any course of action, however desperate, can persuade Alaric once again to risk battle with an enemy who has so comprehensively proved his superiority: sickness (*morbi tabes*), hunger (*fames*), and grief (*luctus*) are not enough to overcome fear of Stilicho (*pallor*). All four, personified, accompany Alaric with shrieks as he flees from the soil of Italy at 321–3. The contention that Alaric will never again threaten Roman society is, of course, ironic to modern readers in the light of the events of 410. It is, however, worth bearing in mind that Alaric did in fact not present any serious threat to the Western Empire until after Stilicho's death in 408.

244 f. aut morbi tabes aut . . . fames: a regular pair: cf. Virg. *G.* 4. 318 'morboque fameque', Ov. *Met.* 13. 52. *morbi tabes* implies a slow-acting wasting sickness: cf. Plin. *Nat.* 2. 156 'ne . . . fames . . . lenta nos consumeret tabe', Tac. *Ann.* 1. 53 'inopia ac tabe longa peremit'.

omne periclum | docta subire fames: hunger conventionally will drive men to try any wicked or desperate action. Cf. Virg. *A.* 6. 276 'malesuada Fames', Stat. *Theb.* 10. 44 'nil non ausa fames', and the whole tale of the utter shamelessness to which Erysicthon's insatiable hunger reduces him at Ov. *Met.* 8. 843ff.

The epexegetic infinitive (cf. 237 *nosse prior* n.) with *doctus* steadily gains currency in verse from the Augustan period on, and generally displaces the older constructions with *ad* or *in*. Cf. Lucr. 5. 961 'ualere et uiuere doctus', Hor. *Carm.* 1. 29. 9, Luc. 1. 601, Sil. 1. 412ff., Stat. *Silu.* 5. 2. 72, *Ruf.* 1. 104f. 'quam fallere mentes | doctus et unanimos odiis turbare sodales!', *Eutr.* 2. *pr.* 68. See further Trump 30.

245. praedae luctus ademptae: the thirty years' worth of booty lost to the Romans at Pollentia (*Get.* 604ff.: see 129 *tot amissis sociis*, 130 *direptis* n.).

246. dictis . . . procacibus: the *probra* of l. 242. Cf. Catul. 61. 119f. 'procax | Fescennina iocatio', Sal. *Cat.* 25. 5, Liv. 42. 54. 1 'probris quoque in ipsum Macedonasque procacibus iaculati sunt': given the thrust of these examples, the taunts imagined as being flung at Alaric must include at least some that are sexual in nature. The rather odd use of the dative after *irae* is no doubt the result of influence from the construction with *iratus*, and provides a concise expression welcome in verse: contrast e.g. Liv. 25. 15. 7 'mouit eos non Tarentinorum magis defectio . . . quam ira in Romanos'.

247 f. The heavy alliteration of *t* and *c* in these lines is particularly striking, and may be intended to convey a sense of hesitation and fear on Alaric's part. For the phrasing cf. Virg. *A.* 9. 42 'neu struere auderent aciem neu credere campo'.

248 f. The idea that victory only becomes 'real' when the defeated party acknowledges that he has been beaten can be traced in Roman epic as far back as Enn. *Ann.* 513 Skutsch 'qui uincit non est uictor nisi uictus fatetur.' Skutsch's note ad loc. offers a number of parallels, but cf. esp. Caes. *Ciu.* 1. 84. 5 'itaque se uictos confiteri', Liv. 42. 47. 8 'eius demum animum in perpetuum uinci cui confessio expressa sit se neque arte neque casu, sed collatis comminus uiribus, iusto ac pio esse bello superatum', Luc. 3. 234, 6. 142 f. Claudian, however, goes a little further by stressing that Alaric is now totally demoralized and admits this defeat even to himself (*animo quoque*).

249. subiugat: the metaphorical sense is one to which modern English speakers are entirely accustomed, but the *OLD* offers only one parallel, Amp. *Lib. Mem.* 32. 5 'omnia terra atque mari Romanis subiugauit.' It was in fact quite frequent by Claudian's time: Lewis and Short cite Ps.-Ascon. on Cic. *Ver.* 1. 21, Lact. *Mort. Pers.* 34 'multi periculo subiugati . . . sunt.' These examples might seem to suggest that the word was largely confined to the realm of prose, but it also appears four times in the poems of Prudentius (*Per.* 10. 419 'subiugatis hostibus' and 777, *Cath.* 7. 11, *Apoth. pr.* 31).

250-3. Numerous individuals had already deserted, thus weakening the strength of the Gothic host (note the tense of *coeperat*), but this process now gathers speed enormously as whole troops of infantry and cavalry abandon Alaric. Historians tend to take Claudian's statement here pretty much at face value, though no doubt most would agree that considerable allowance must be made for hyperbole (e.g. Liebeschuetz 63, Heather 313 f.).

250. frequens rarum: such juxtapositions are common in Latin poetry: Müller compares Hor. *S.* 2. 4. 77 'angustoque uagos piscis urgere catino', *Ars* 465 f. (Empedocles) 'ardentem frigidus Aetnam | insiluit.' *rarum* may be taken to mean that, after Verona, the Gothic host was already much depleted before even the individual desertions began: this squares well with the scenes of carnage described at 207-9. Alternatively, we could understand *rarum* as being used proleptically, in which case the striking juxtaposition with *frequens* would stress the effect the desertions have on Alaric's army. But Claudian's regular use of hyperbole in any case makes him unreliable: already after Pollentia but before Verona he speaks of Alaric 'rarum referens inglorius agmen' out of Italy (*Get.* 78 f.). For *rarus* of an army whose ranks have been 'thinned' cf. also Virg. *A.* 9. 508, Stat. *Theb.* 4. 82, 6. 132, Tac. *Hist.* 3. 25, 4. 35.

decerpere: i.e. 'reduce', 'diminish', possibly to be interpreted as implying a gradual process. For this rare sense *TLL* v/1. 158. 77 ff. cites this passage and Iuuenc. 4. 134 f. 'decerpere tempus | et numerum . . . breuiare dierum'.

transfuga: another rather prosaic word avoided by classical epic poets, except for Lucan who uses it in order to shock (5. 346 'transfuga uilis', 8. 335 (of Pompey) 'transfuga mundi', where see Mayer). Note also Hor. *Carm.* 3. 16. 22ff. 'nil cupientium | nudus castra peto et transfuga diuitum | partis linquere gestio'. Claudian has it again with its literal sense at *Gild.* 261 and metaphorically at *Eutr.* 1. 15 (of the Nile: cf. Stat. *Silu.* 1. 2. 203).

251. in . . . dies: 'as the days went by' (*OLD* s.v. *dies* 3b); see further KS i. 565 and Nisbet–Hubbard on Hor. *Carm.* 2. 13. 14 'in horas.' Contrast Caes. *Gal.* 3. 23. 7 'in dies hostium numerum augeri'.

decrescere: cf. Stat. *Theb.* 10. 4 'immeritas ferro decrescere gentes'.

252. deditio paucis occulta parari: *paucis* = 'by a few', i.e. presumably 'at any one time', since all together these desertions added up to a large number (*frequens*). Note the sharp contrast with *totae* (253). The dative of agent is a Graecism, well established in verse in passive constructions, esp. with past participles: see Fordyce on Virg. *A.* 7. 411 f. 'locus Ardea quondam | dictus auis', Harrison on Virg. *A.* 10. 6 f. 'sententia uobis | uersa retro', and LHS ii. 96–8. *deditio* is another relatively unpoetic word, whose appearances are primarily in historical authors. *occulta* implies treachery (cf. *Stil.* 1. 113 'occultus proditor') and contrasts with *palam* (253).

253–6. These four lines are identical in metrical structure (DSDS or DSDD with heavy caesuras in the second and fourth feet, and a light trochaic caesura in the third). See Introd. Sect. 5, Birt, p. ccxii, Cameron 289, Gruzelier, p. xxviii. Cameron points out that this procedure often results in 'a certain jerkiness, involving, as it tends to do, coincidence of verse ictus and word accent in the middle of the line followed by conflict in the fourth foot'.

253. Claudian may mean that both 'troops of infantry' (*cunei*) and 'cavalry squadrons' (*turmae*) alike abandoned Alaric. But this might be over-ingenious: Statius seems to make no distinction when he says 'turma subit cuneumque replent' (*Theb.* 9. 123), and by Claudian's time the phrase *cuneus equitum* had become standard in the real Roman army (Kromayer–Veith 579).

discedere: = 'desert', another largely prosaic usage: cf. Caes. *Gal.* 5. 56. 3 'Caesaris secutum fidem ab eo non discessisse', Liv. 25. 20. 4 'ducis ab signis discessit'. Lucan's Caesar, however, dismisses his mutineers with the contemptuous words 'discedite castris' (5. 357); cf. also *Rapt.* 3. 313 'ei mihi, discedunt omnes'.

254–9. Alaric first attempts to impose discipline by shouting and forcefulness, moves on to emotional appeals to their former loyalty and the labours they have endured with him, and finally climaxes in a dramatic gesture beseeching them to end his life. All is in vain, and his spirit is finally broken. The passage is reminiscent of Aeneas' unsuccessful attempt to prevent the Trojans from rushing into battle when Juturna violates the truce at Virg. *A.* 12. 311ff.: 'at pius Aeneas dextram tendebat inermem | nudato capite atque suos clamore uocabat: | 'quo ruitis? quaeue ista repens discordia surgit? | o cohibete iras . . .'.

254. uano: the text, as it were, sabotages Alaric's attempts to impose discipline even before it reveals exactly what they are. *uano* is picked up by *frustra* (257), the two words thus providing a frame that resoundingly indicates the uselessness of all Alaric's efforts that lie between. For the collocation with *clamore* cf. V. Fl. 3. 128 'saepe sibi uano Thamyrim clamore petebat'. The general phrasing also recalls V. Fl. 5. 678f. 'nec uana retentet | spes Minyas'.

retentat: perhaps implying repeated attempts and shouts, though it is true that the use of vivid frequentatives for simple verbs, always common in ordinary speech, becomes, through 'linguistic attrition', steadily more common in late Latin: see Palmer 77, 169. For Claudian's fondness for frequentatives see Birt, p. ccxxii.

255f. nomina supplex . . . ciet: by calling upon individuals by name Alaric tries to appeal to the personal bond between himself and his men. My colleague Dr John Vanderspoel points out that Claudian may have in mind the particularly close bond of the clan-group (*kuni*) in the formation of the Gothic army, for which see Wolfram 96ff. *supplex*, combined with *precibus fletuque* (256), robs Alaric of his dignity. We should probably even picture him on his knees: cf. esp. Tac. *Ann.* 1. 21 (mutinous legionaries being hauled off to punishment) 'prensare circumstantium genua, ciere modo nomina singulorum, modo centuriam quisque cuius manipularis erat', Virg. *A.* 12. 758f. (Turnus appealing for aid to his comrades) 'ille simul fugiens Rutulos simul increpat omnis | nomine quemque uocans', *IV Cons.* 448f. In happier times a good general might be expected to know the names of his men, at least those of the officers, and to call upon them individually to encourage them in battle. Tradition ascribed this ability in particular to Cyrus (Xen. *Cyr.* 5. 3. 46ff.), though whereas Xenophon, with greater plausibility, claims that Cyrus learnt the names of all those to whom he had to give orders directly, later authors apparently imagine him knowing the names of each and every one of his men (Val. Max. 8. 7. ext. 16, Plin. *Nat.* 7. 88, Quint. *Inst.* 11. 2. 50). Note also Caes. *Gal.* 2. 25. 2 'centurionibus . . . nominatim appellatis reliquos cohortatus milites signa inferre et manipulos laxare iussit',

Sal. *Cat.* 59. 5 'ipse equo circumiens unum quemque nominans appel-
lat, hortatur', Virg. *A.* 11. 730f. His ability to do this marks Stilicho as
an effective and caring commander: *Stil.* 2. 153ff. 'mensaeque adhibes
et nomine quemque | conpellas, clari sub te quod gesserat olim |
admonitum facti.' Conversely, the technique is as fruitless for Rufinus
as it is here for Alaric (*Ruf.* 2. 369). *nomen | nomina ciere* and similar
phrases had long been part and parcel of the language of both poetry
and history: e.g. Acc. *inc.* 37f. Warmington = 704f. Dangel, Virg. *A.*
3. 68, Liv. 35. 38. 12, Ov. *Fast.* 4. 484, Luc. 4. 177, V. Fl. 4. 648f., Sil.
1. 454f., 3. 437f., Stat. *Theb.* 6. 460f., Suet. *Nero* 46. 2, Apul. *Mun.* 37,
Eutr. 2. 514f.

256. cum precibus fletuque: cf. Virg. *A.* 3. 598f. 'mox sese ad litora
praeceps | cum fletu precibusque tulit'; also *c.m.* 22. 50 'quod si nec
precibus fletu nec frangeris ullo'.

256f. ueterumque laborum | admonet: a variation on the regular
topos of comradeship whereby a leader recalls previous difficulties
which he and his men have shared in order to encourage them to
endure still more: note esp. Hor. *Carm.* 1. 7. 30f. (Teucer) 'o fortes
peioraque passi | mecum saepe uiri', and Virg. *A.* 1. 198f. (Aeneas) 'o
socii (neque enim ignari sumus ante malorum), | o passi grauiora,
dabit deus his quoque finem', Luc. 1. 299f.: cf. also, of similar action
in happier circumstances, *Stil.* 2. 154f., cit. 255f.n. Whereas Teucer
and Aeneas may be presumed to be successful in heartening their
men, Alaric clearly does not restore their lost confidence in himself,
and in any case cuts a sorry figure, his being a pathetic appeal to
their loyalty rather than the words of a strong man firm in the face of
adversity.

257. frustra iugulum parcentibus offert: Alaric's last dramatic stab
at heroism is frustrated by either his men's pity or their contempt. He
is thus denied the kind of glory that Vulteius and his comrades achieve
in their suicide pact at Luc. 4. 529ff. Not only have Alaric's men
no intention of dying with him or for him, they seem not to share
the respect and concern for their leader's dignity that characterize
Vulteius' subordinates. Contrast Luc. 4. 540f. 'primus dux ipse
carinae | Vulteius iugulo poscens iam fata retecto | "ecquis" ait
"iuuenum est, cuius sit dextra cruore | digna meo" . . . (544f.) nec
plura locuto | uiscera non unus iam dudum transigit ensis'. The
phrase *iugulum offerre* is a more vivid variant of the commoner *iugulum
dare* (e.g. Cic. *Tusc.* 2. 33 'si nudus es, da iugulum', Ov. *Pont.* 2. 9. 31):
cf. Tac. *Hist.* 1. 41 'plures obtulisse ultro percussoribus iugulum'.

258. defixoque malis animo: at last: contrast 229f. *defigo* implies an
absolute absence of motion, and so is commonly used of characters

being 'paralysed' by fear, sorrow, or similar emotions: cf. Virg. *A.* 7. 249f. 'talibus Ilionei dictis defixa Latinus | obtutu tenet ora soloque immobilis haeret', Liv. 1. 29. 3 'silentium triste ac tacita maestitia ita defixit omnium animos', 7. 10. 12, 21. 33. 3 'utraque simul obiecta res oculis animisque immobiles parumper eos defixit', V. Fl. 4. 226 (with Korn ad loc.), 7. 81f., 8. 369, Sil. 9. 253, Apul. *Met.* 2. 7.

258f. His troops are Alaric's strength, his very limbs and hands without which he cannot continue to fight. For the idea compare e.g. Cic. *Att.* 8. 1. 1 'nec sum miratus eum qui caput ipsum reliquisset reliquis membris non parcere'. This strength he now feels ebbing away; cf. Stat. *Theb.* 9. 853 'iam uires paulatim abscedere sentit'. Note the highly emphatic anaphora of *sua* and *suas.*

259–64. Alaric is like a bee-keeper who, for all his recourse to the traditional remedy of clashing cymbals, proves unable to prevent his bees from swarming and abandoning him. It has long been recognized that Claudian here is reworking *in extenso* the simile found at Luc. 9. 283ff. There the news of Pompey's death provokes mutiny and mass desertion in the ranks of the Republicans in Africa until their commander Cato delivers a powerful speech that shames them into recovering their sense of duty: 'dixit, et omnes | haud aliter medio reuocauit ab aequore puppes | quam, simul *effetas linquunt examina ceras* | atque *oblita faui* non miscent nexibus alas | sed sibi quaeque uolat nec iam degustat amarum | desidiosa thymum, *Phrygii sonus* increpat *aeris,* | attonitae posuere fugam studiumque laboris | floriferi repetunt et sparsi mellis amorem: | gaudet *in Hyblaeo* securus *gramine pastor* | diuitias seruasse casae. sic uoce Catonis | inculcata uiris iusti patientia Martis'. In particular, with the italicized phrases cf. *relictis . . . fauis* (261f.), *uacuis examina ceris* (264), *Cybeleia . . . aera* (259f.) and *tinnitu* (261), and *Hyblaeus . . . senex* (260). Note that Claudian's reworking is tighter and more compressed than its model, ruthlessly excising the picturesque pastoral details Lucan gives in his description of the bees first in flight and then returning to the work they love.

The broad situation is identical—in the aftermath of a disastrous battle a general tries to halt desertions from his army, just as a bee-keeper tries to prevent his bees from swarming—and so too is the method used in the simile to restrain the bees. The real thrust of the reworking of Lucan, however, is to draw out the contrast in stature between Cato and Alaric. Cato's speech is a majestic and scathing denunciation of the weakness of his men's loyalty to the cause for which they are fighting, and his personal force of character and stern, unbending sense of duty are successful in halting the desertions: in Lucan, the bee-keeper is thus correspondingly successful in preserving his hive. Alaric, on the other hand, cuts a very sorry figure, not upbraiding his men from a position of strength but wheedling and cajoling (254–9), and all to no effect: thus the bee-keeper of Claudian's simile proves unable to restrain the bees, and so is ruined and loses his livelihood (263f.: contrast 'diuitias seruasse casae', Luc. 9. 292). This imitation by reversal is strengthened by the significant alteration of certain details in the model. In particular, Lucan's *pastor* is replaced by an ineffective old man (*senex* 260), a change which diminishes Alaric's stature still further, while Claudian's simile also lays great emphasis on the futility of the bee-keeper's actions (*sonituque exhaustus inani* 263; *deplorat* 264). Lucan's simile is rounded off by a resounding coda (9. 292f.) that loftily records the restoration of quasi-Stoic virtue ('iusti patientia Martis'), but Claudian's ends with the unedifying spectacle of the bee-keeper weeping. Moreover, whereas in Lucan Cato's powerful speech precedes the simile, the one attributed to Alaric comes *after* the corresponding lines, and serves not as a means to re-establish the Gothic leader's authority, but rather as a confession that he has lost it completely and as a lament (cued by *deplorat* in the simile, 264) for the utter ruination of all his hopes. This simile is the climax, and most extensive example, of a large-scale series of imitations of Lucan's account of the events leading up to, and following on, the battle of Pharsalus. See 210f. n. Within this frame of reference Alaric is both a failed Cato and a failed Caesar.

Claudian offers some other striking bee similes. The shades of his victims in the underworld gather around the newly arrived ghost of Rufinus just as bees rise to do battle with the *pastor* who has come to rob their hive (*Ruf.* 2. 460ff., drawing on Virg. *A.* 12. 587ff. and Stat. *Theb.* 10. 574ff.), while Honorius is honoured by his subjects just as the bee-king is thronged around by his devoted swarm (*IV Cons.* 380ff., inspired by Virg. *G.* 4. 210ff., and Xen. *Cyr.* 5. 1. 24). See further Christiansen 82, Gruzelier on *Rapt.* 2. 124ff.

259–61. Making a great deal of noise, with cymbals, crockery, or stones, or by the clapping of hands, was the procedure recommended in agricultural treatises both for attracting a swarm to settle in your hive and for stopping it from leaving. See in general Mynors on Virg. *G.* 4. 64. Ancient authorities differed in their explanations for the efficacy of this procedure, some maintaining that the bees were attracted by the noise and found it pleasurable (Plato, *Lg.* 8. 843D, Arist. 627A15, Plin. *Nat.* 11. 68), others that it served to immobilize them with fear (Var. *R.* 3. 16. 7, Col. 9. 8. 10, 9. 12. 2). Although Claudian's language shows some similarity to that of Pliny and Columella, it is, unsurprisingly, most strongly reminiscent of Virgil's fourth *Georgic*: 4. 64ff.

'tinnitusque cie et Matris quate cymbala circum . . .'. Cf. also Ov. *Fast.*
3. 741 ff.

259 f. Cybeleia . . . aera: cymbals were regularly used in the cult of the
Magna Mater, and so in verse are frequently called *Cybeleia, Corybantia,
Phrygia,* etc. See Bailey on Lucr. 2. 618 f. 'tympana tenta tonant palmis
et cymbala circum | concaua, raucisonoque minantur cornua cantu',
and cf. also Catul. 63. 19 ff., Virg. *G.* 4. 64, *A.* 3. 111, *IV Cons.* 149 f.

260. Hyblaeus: Megara Hyblaea on the southern slopes of Mt Etna
was conventionally celebrated in ancient verse for its flowers and
therefore for its honey: see Strabo 6. 2. 2, Plin. *Nat.* 11. 32, and cf. Virg.
Ecl. 1. 54 'Hyblaeis apibus florem depasta salicti', Ov. *Ars* 2. 517, Sil.
14. 26, Stat. *Silu.* 2. 1. 48 'Hyblaeis . . . fauis', 3. 2. 118, Mart. 9. 26. 4,
Fesc. 4. 7 ff., *Rapt.* 2. 125. If Claudian's old bee-keeper had not been
Hyblaean, then it is a pretty safe bet that he would have been from
Hymettos in Attica: Mart. 7. 88. 8 'pascat et Hybla meas, pascat
Hymettos apes', 11. 42. 3 'mella iubes Hyblaea tibi uel Hymetta nasci'.

    senex: a detail not strictly relevant to Alaric, though it helps
establish him as pathetic and helpless in his defeat. Claudian perhaps
wants us to recall Virgil's 'Corycium . . . senem', who kept bees as well
as growing flowers and vegetables for his living (*G.* 4. 127, 139 ff.).

261. tinnitu: regular of the clanging or clashing of cymbals: Catul. 64.
262 'aut tereti tinnitus aere ciebant', Virg. *G.* 4. 64, Ov. *Met.* 6. 589
'nocte sonat Rhodope tinnitibus aeris acuti', 14. 536, *Fast.* 4. 184, Sil.
17. 18.

262. desciuere: compare *perfida* (264). The worlds of the narrative and
the simile interpenetrate each other: Alaric's men are compared to
bees swarming, but the bees themselves, in abandoning the old man
to ruin and poverty, metaphorically 'desert' him and are 'traitors'.
There was a well-established tradition of speaking about bees in
anthropomorphic terms, but note in particular the extended use of
military diction to describe the activities of the bees at Virg. *G.* 4. 67
ff., Stat. *Theb.* 10. 574 ff., *Ruf.* 2. 460 ff., *Rapt* 2. 125 f. *descisco* is a
decidedly unepic word, and so is grimly appropriate to a decidedly
unheroic act. It is common enough of deserting or defecting from an
allegiance in political language, but is rarely found in verse. Virgil and
Ovid avoid it entirely, and it is used only once each, for special effect,
by Lucan (2. 727 f. 'lassata triumphis | desciuit Fortuna tuis', where see
Fantham) and Statius (*Theb.* 2. 311 f. 'respiciens descisse deos trepi-
doque tumultu | dilapsos comites'). Cf. also Lucr. 1. 103, *Eutr.* 2. 237.

    sonitu . . . inani: corresponding to *uano . . . clamore* (254) in the
narrative, and perhaps also recalling Alaric's *minas . . . inanes* (141). For
similar collocations see Cic. *de Orat.* 1. 51 'uerborum . . . sonitus

inanis'; also Prop. 2. 16. 37 'fremitu . . . inani', V. Fl. 2. 33 'gemitu . . . inani', *IV Cons.* 279 f. 'inanes | . . . strepitus', *Stil.* 3. 28, *Rapt.* 2. 249 'questus . . . inanes'.

263. raptas mellis opes: cf. 130 *direptis* n. It would be tempting to see the honey as corresponding to the booty Alaric has lost, but that was taken from him by the Roman army during the storming of the camp at Pollentia, not by his men as they deserted. But the honey was the old bee-keeper's livelihood and he is now presumably destitute: so too, without his men and the booty he could win in future campaigns with their aid, Alaric is ruined.

263 f. oblita . . . perfida: see 50 f. *spoliis . . . micantes | innumeros arcus* n.

263. latebrae: most probably the inner recesses of the hive, unless Claudian has in mind the natural hives described by Virgil, *G.* 4. 42 ff. 'saepe etiam effossis, si uera est fama, latebris | sub terra fouere larem, penitusque repertae | pumicibusque cauis exesaeque arboris antro'.

264. perfida: see 262 *desciuere* n.

deplorat: the simple form *ploro* was considered acceptable in lyric and elegiac metres, but not really appropriate to epic, and among the major epic poets only Statius seems happy to admit it into his verse (*Theb.* 1. 44, 3. 579, 4. 461, 8. 196, *Ach.* 1. 241); see Axelson 28 f. The compound will surely have been open to similar objections on the grounds of stylistic decorum, and is avoided by Virgil and Valerius Flaccus, even if it had the authority of Ovid (*Met.* 1. 272, 5. 63, 13. 481) and appears in scattered places in post-Augustan epic and other hexameter poetry (Luc. 6. 788, Petr. 123, v. 195, *Eutr.* 1. 292, *Get.* 562). Its use here in connection with Alaric does not contribute to his dignity.

uacuis . . . ceris: an ablative of attendant circumstances, explaining why the bee-keeper is weeping. *cerae* is a regular metonymy for the hive, e.g. Virg. *G.* 4. 57, 162, Ov. *Fast.* 4. 546. Note also Ov. *Met.* 9. 522 'dextra tenet ferrum, uacuam tenet altera ceram' (of a wax tablet).

265–73. *Alaric, overcome by the contrast between his former triumphs and his present state of utter ruination, breaks into lament.*

Authorial comment had already pointed to the striking reversal in Alaric's fortunes at 141–5, a theme taken up by the Naiad in her speech to Eridanus (154–7) and one with which Eridanus himself taunted the humiliated Goth at 180–4. Now Alaric himself finally realizes the truth of his present plight.

265 f. At the back of Claudian's phrasing here lie Virgil's words introducing another highly-wrought speech of lamentation: *A.* 11. 151

(Evander over the corpse of Pallas) 'uia uix tandem uoci laxata dolore est'. Cf. also Stat. *Theb.* 5. 606 f. 'tandem laxata dolori | uox inuenit iter, gemitusque in uerba soluti', [Quint.] *Decl.* 9. 7. Claudian has kept the idea of grief first preventing and then yielding to impassioned speech, but replaced Virgil's 'loosening a pathway for the voice' with the somewhat more concrete image of 'loosening the reins' (or, to be more accurate, 'bit') on the voice (or, as we might say, the tongue): cf. Eur. *Bacch.* 386, Plin. *Pan.* 66. 5 'obsaepta diutina seruitute ora reseramus, frenatamque tot malis linguam resoluimus', *Rapt.* 3. 179 f. 'postquam suspiria tandem | laxauit frenosque dolor', and also such less explicit examples as Ov. *Met.* 3. 261 'linguam ad iurgia soluit', Luc. 1. 472, *Eutr.* 2. 254. Also present, perhaps, are traces of the still commoner idea of 'giving free rein' to a powerful passion seen at e.g. Luc. 7. 124 f. 'frenosque furentibus ira | laxat', Sid. *Ep.* 4. 11. 7, Milt. *Sam. Ag.* 1578 'yet ere I give the reins to grief'. But the idea of the 'pathway of the voice', in any case, still lies half-concealed in *praeclusae*.

265. praeclusae uoci: a regular collocation; Liv. 33. 13. 5 'omnibus praeclusisse uocem uidebatur', Ov. *Met.* 2. 658, Phaed. 1. 2. 26, 1. 23. 5 f., Stat. *Silu.* 2. 4. 3 'quis tam subito praeclusit murmura fato?'

265 f. laxata remisit | frena: a striking tautology. For *frena/habenas laxo* vel. sim. cf. Cic. *Amic.* 45, Virg. *A.* 1. 63, Curt. 4. 9. 24, V. Fl. 2. 35, Sil. 4. 210, 9. 657, Sid. *Carm.* 22. 7, and for *frena remitto* cf. Cic. *Amic.* 45, Ov. *Met.* 2. 185 f. and 191, 6. 228, *Tr.* 1. 4. 14, *Pont.* 4. 2. 23, Stat. *Theb.* 7. 819. Elsewhere Claudian prefers *frena (re-)soluo: Ruf.* 2. 22, *Nupt.* 330, *Rapt.* 2. 318.

266 f. notas oculis umentibus Alpes | aspicit: compare esp. Luc. 4. 522 f. 'ante ducis uoces oculis umentibus omnes | aspicerent', and also Tib. 1. 9. 38 'umentes . . . genas', Ov. *Met.* 11. 464, 14. 734, Luc. 5. 737, Stat. *Silu.* 5. 3. 32, *Pan. Lat.* 5. 9. 5 Mynors 'uidimus misericordiam tuam umentibus oculis eminentem'. Alaric's tears here correspond to *deplorat* in the simile (264). The Alps are *notas* because he had seen them already on his way into Italy: his tears, however, are not inspired by fondness, but by the knowledge that the resighting of the Alps is the marker of his failure.

267. diuerso stamine fati: the triumphant march of the Goths into Italy and their ignominious retreat back out of it were both fated, but the Parcae spun these contrasting destinies on different threads. The manuscripts read *diuersi*, but the epithet surely reads more smoothly with *stamine* ('a different thread of fate'): cf. *Ruf.* 1. 176 f. 'ductusque maligno | stamine fatorum'. The use of *fortunatos* in the next line implies that Claudian is not troubling to distinguish between *fatum* and *fortuna*.

268. reuoluit: of recalling and pondering the past also at e.g. Virg. *A.* 2. 101f. 'sed quid ego haec autem nequiquam ingrata reuoluo | quidue moror?', Luc. 8. 316f. 'cuncta reuoluens | uitae fata meae', Stat. *Theb.* 8. 227f., *Eutr.* 1. 474. The image is of the unrolling of a papyrus-roll; in the context of fate cf. also Virg. *A.* 1. 262 'longius et uoluens fatorum arcana mouebo', though there it is the future, and not the past, that is at issue.

269. solo . . . murmure: the mere rumour of Alaric's arrival was sufficient to bring the enemy to his knees. In Alaric's case this power has proved deceptive, but with Stilicho it is a constant: *Eutr.* 2. 504f., *Stil.* 1. 188ff. 'miramur rapidis hostem succumbere bellis, | cum solo terrore ruat? (*Heinsius*; ruant *codd.*) num classica Francis | intulimus? iacuere tamen', *Get.* 421f. For murmur of a rumour cf. Prop. 2. 5. 29, 'quamuis contemnas murmura famae', Juv. 10. 88f. 'hi sermones | tunc de Seiano, secreta haec murmura uolgi'.

tum: contrasting sharply with *nunc* (271).

270. For the hyperbole Müller compares Hor. *Carm.* 4. 6. 6ff. 'filius quamuis Thetidis marinae | Dardanas turris quateret tremenda | cuspide pugnax': add Ov. *Met.* 2. 767f. 'postes extrema cuspide pulsat. | concussae patuere fores', Sil. 4. 513 'clausas pulsari cuspide portas', 12. 565f., 17. 196, *c.m.* 29. 22 'Mauors, sanguinea qui cuspide uerberat urbes'. If *moenia* is taken literally, then we should understand this as a reference to the Goths' storming all the towns that they came upon as they descended from the Alps: cf. *Get.* 213ff. 'nonne uidebantur, quamuis adamante rigentes, | turribus inualidis fragiles procumbere muri | ferrataeque Getis ultro se pandere portae?' Müller, however, points to the balance with *scopulos* (271) and prefers to interpret *moenia* here as referring to blockading forts in the Alpine passes, all of which proved to be totally ineffective in preventing the Gothic advance; he might also have quoted in support *Get.* 532 'fregi Alpes'. The striking parallel with *Get.* 213ff., however, is compelling, and there towns and cities are surely meant, especially since Claudian goes on to talk of the ensuing panic and intention of the court to abandon Milan itself. Moreover, *moenia* seems rather too grand a word for the walls of mere forts, while *scopulos* makes perfect sense if we think of Alaric mocking at the great barrier of the Alps for being unable to prevent him from bursting through and overrunning the cities of the Veneto that lay below them. See further 271f.n. Another attractive possibility might be to see *moenia* as picking up *notas . . . Alpes* (266) and thus referring metaphorically to the whole Alpine range. The idea that the Alps are the 'citadel' or, more usually, the 'walls of Italy' is an old and well-established one, dating back at least to Polybius 3. 54. 2 ὥστε . . .

ἀκροπόλεως φαίνεσθαι διάθεσιν ἔχειν τὰς Ἄλπεις τῆς ὅλης. Consider also Cic. *Prou.* 34, *Pis.* 81 'Alpium uallum' with Nisbet ad loc., *Phil.* 5. 37, Liv. 21. 35. 8f. 'militibus Italiam ostentat subiectosque Alpinis montibus circumpadanos campos, moeniaque eos tum transcendere non Italiae modo sed etiam urbis Romanae', *Pan. Lat.* 11. 2. 4 Mynors. See also 272 *pulsato* n.

leuiter: reinforcing the sense of *protento . . . conto*, since the *contus* itself is light (see the next note). The adverb thus also reinforces the strict grammatical parallelism between that phrase and *solo . . . murmure* (two ablatives indicating the instrument with which the war was carried on). This power too is quasi-divine, since gods do all things easily and quickly; see Nisbet–Hubbard on Hor. *Carm.* 1. 12. 31, West on Hes. *Op.* 5. Cf. Ov. *Met.* 8. 619 'quidquid superi uoluere, peractum est', noting *peragens* in 269. So hackneyed is the idea that Petronius (*Sat.* 76) puts the proverb 'cito fit, quod di uolunt' into the mouth of Trimalchio.

conto: a long, light cavalry lance, usually fitted with an iron point. It was traditionally associated with the Sarmatians (V. Fl. 6. 162, Stat. *Ach.* 2. 132f., Sil. 15. 684f., Tac. *Ann.* 6. 35, *Stil.* 1. 111), but later with all northern barbarians who fought on horseback. By Claudian's time it was also regularly used in the Imperial army: see e.g. *III Cons.* 137.

271f. Müller takes *scopulos* as meaning the cliffs on which his 'barrier forts' stood (270 n.), but the reference is to the Alps in general, as the correspondence with *monti* (272) shows. Alaric 'mocked' the Alps by crossing them, and so they here rejoice at the sight of his humiliation, a sight 'owed' to them as the punishment for his hubris. Cf. 144f. *retroque relictos | quos modo temnebat, rediens exhorruit amnes* and the jeering of the river-gods of the Po valley at Alaric's shameful retreat (195–8); also *Get.* 194ff.

271. desolatus: common in contexts of bereavement and therefore on epitaphs (see van Dam on Stat. *Silu.* 2. 1. 233), but rare in epic. Alaric is emotively said to have been 'left in loneliness', with the implication that *all* his troops are dead (129 *tot amissis sociis* n., 207–9) or, the next thing to it, have deserted (250–5). This could be seen as an ingenious twist on the idea of the death of a commander leaving the grief-stricken army 'desolate': Virg. *A.* 11. 870 'disiectique duces desolatique manipli', Stat. *Theb.* 9. 672f. 'desolatum . . . magistro | agmen', 10. 180f. Note also Luc. 4. 700f. 'nocturnaque munera ualli | desolata fuga', in the context of desertion.

expes: a word generally used rather sparingly, and carrying extra weight from its being often combined with others expressing destitution: Acc. *trag.* 407 Warmington = *Med.* 492 Dangel 'exul inter hostes

expes expers desertus uagus', Ov. *Ep*. 6. 162, *Met*. 14. 217 'solus inops
expes leto poenaeque relictus'.

272. debita . . . reddit spectacula: the sight of his humiliation is
a debt which Alaric now repays to the mountains he had himself
humiliated. For the phrasing cf. Nep. *Reg*. 1. 5 'morbo naturae
debitum reddiderunt', Virg. *A*. 2. 537f. 'praemia reddant | debita',
Ov. *Tr*. 2. 160 'reddatur gratae debitus urbis amor', *Fast*. 4. 898.

pulsato: the verb is very commonly used of 'assailing', or 'batter-
ing' the gates or walls of a city: among many possible examples cf.
Virg. *A*. 12. 706 'imos pulsabant ariete muros', Vitr. 10. 13. 1 'summum
murum continenter pulsantes summos lapidum ordines deiciebant',
Ov. *Pont*. 3. 1. 25, Luc. 5. 529ff., Stat. *Theb*. 8. 348f., 11. 257. Silius in
particular uses such phrases of Hannibal's literal and metaphorical
assault on the walls of Rome and other Italian cities: 1. 270 'extremis
pulsat Capitolia terris', 4. 513, 6. 642f. 'exuta spe moenia Romae |
pulsandi', 12. 40, 565f., 16. 695f., 17. 300f. 'pulsantem te . . . | moenia
sublimis Capuae'. This is surely significant in the light of Claudian's
portrayal of Alaric as a second Hannibal (182–4, 184–6nn.). It is even
conceivable that Claudian is playing on the idea of the Alps them-
selves as 'caelum | pulsantes . . . scopulos' at Sil. 12. 71f. Elsewhere
characters as various as Alaric, Hannibal, and Theodosius are
regularly spoken of as having 'broken' (*Get*. 532) or 'burst' through
(*ruptas . . . Alpes*, 442; *Ruf*. 2. 389, *Gild*. 82f., *IV Cons*. 637, *Get*. 547) the
barrier of the Alps.

monti: the collective singular for the whole range, as often: cf. e.g.
Mela 2. 58 'iugo Appennini montis', *Ruf*. 2. 32f. 'nec se defendit iniquo
| monte Cilix', *Eutr*. 2. 468. See further 286 *Appenninum* n.

273. Looking upwards during prayer is naturally common enough, but
for epic characters raising their eyes heavenwards as a prelude to
the utterance of lamentations that denounce the gods' injustice cf. in
particular Virg. *A*. 9. 480 (Euryalus' mother) 'caelum dehinc questibus
implet', *Rapt*. 2. 249 (Proserpina during the Rape) 'questus ad nubila
rumpit inanes'.

Ausonium: the highly poetic adjective patriotically puts the focus
once more on Italy as an ancient land associated with heroic deeds
and divine favour: cf. 202f. *rebus . . . Ausoniis* n.

274–319. *Alaric's lament and acknowledgement of his utter defeat.*

Alaric implores the land of Italy, as if she were a goddess, to exact no
greater penalty than the total reversal of his fortunes which he has
already suffered (274–80). He regrets that he did not immediately press

onwards to Rome after Pollentia, thus depriving himself of a glorious death in battle, within sight of Rome (280–97). But concern for his kin led him to make his disastrous pact with Stilicho, who thus tricked him into crossing back over the Po, where he then destroyed his forces (297–309). Now Alaric has been totally abandoned by all his remaining troops, and there is no land where he will be safe from hearing the victorious names of Stilicho and Italy assailing his ears (310–19).

This is the first of the three great speeches that dominate the central portion of the poem, the others being Roma's *suasoria* encouraging Honorius to visit the City (361–425) and the young Emperor's reply (427–93). Alaric's speech is formally a lament, as is signalled by the repeated use of *heu* (274, 300). It could be said to be essentially tragic in nature, in that he admits that it is the weaknesses in his own character that have led to his nemesis (305, 307f. *capiorque uicissim | fraudibus ipse meis*). Its primary purpose in the narrative, however, is to provide, from the horse's mouth, a full justification for the wisdom of Stilicho's policy of *clementia* and for his having made his pact with Alaric after Pollentia: see Introd., Sect. 4, 204 *pacta mouet* n. The implication that it was Stilicho's deliberate intention all along first to lure Alaric safely over the Po, and then deliver the fatal blow (210–28 n.) is now dramatically confirmed by Alaric's realization that it is his own treachery that has led him into Stilicho's snare (300–8). Of this cunning 'plan' there is not the slightest hint in *De Bello Getico*; that is, before the battle of Verona was fought and won. See further Cameron 184f., Fargues 118.

274. heu . . . heu: setting the tone for the whole lament, and picked up at 300, where the repetition helps articulate the essentially bipartite structure of the speech. Double *heu* is rather rarer than might be thought, and is thus highly emphatic. Cf. Virg. *Ecl.* 2. 58 'heu heu, quid uolui misero mihi?', Hor. *Carm.* 4. 6. 17, *Rapt.* 3. 97f.

regio funesta Getis: contrast *Get.* 170f. (the Goths) 'Histrum transuecta semel uestigia fixit | Threicio funesta solo': their arrival in Italy has the reverse effect. Alaric begins with the calamities of his entire people, but then swiftly turns his attention to his own misfortunes (*mihi*, 275).

274f. sinistris | auguriis: Alaric's invasion was heralded by many grim auguries, but these in retrospect seem to have been intended for the Goths rather than the Romans: see *Get.* 228ff., and note esp. 229 'tum monstra deum monitusque sinistri'. For similar phrases cf. Virg. *A.* 11. 347 'ob auspicium infaustum moresque sinistros', Ov. *Ep.* 2. 115, 13. 49 'di, precor, a nobis omen remouete sinistrum', Luc. 4. 194, V. Fl. 3. 121, Juv. 10. 129; *Rapt.* 3. 125f. 'triste . . . augurium'. If *sinistris* is taken literally, Claudian is following the Greek custom in divination;

in traditional Roman practice omens that fell on the left were considered lucky.

275. calcata: recalling his arrogant boast 'non nisi calcatis loricam ponere rostris' (*Get.* 82).

275 f. satiare nocentum | cladibus: for the appeal to a god for clemency compare e.g. Ov. *Met.* 6. 280 ff. (Niobe) '"pascere, crudelis, nostro, Latona, dolore, | pascere" ait "satiaque meo tua pectora luctu!"'; and for the idea and wording cf. also Cic. *Q. fr.* 1. 3. 4, Liv. 8. 20. 10 'apud satiatos iam suppliciis nocentium', Apul. *Met.* 11. 1 'fato scilicet iam meis tot tantisque cladibus satiato'. At *Ruf.* 2. 206 ff. Stilicho passionately addresses 'numina Romanis necdum satiata ruinis', and at *Gild.* 36 ff. Roma invokes Jupiter's pity with the words 'satiauimus iram | si qua fuit; lugenda Getis et flenda Suebis | hausimus': Alaric's prayers fall upon deaf ears, but theirs, naturally, do not.

276. inflectere: cf. esp. Jupiter's appeal to Juno to desist from persecuting the Trojans: Virg. *A.* 12. 800 'desine iam tandem precibusque inflectere nostris'. For *inflecto* with the sense 'move (to pity)', 'win over' cf. also Sen. *Phaed.* 416 'inflecte mentem', with Coffey–Mayer ad loc., Stat. *Theb.* 8. 715 'ibat enim magnum lacrimis inflectere patrem', 8. 758, *IV Cons.* 300, *c.m.* 31. 45 'inflexit soceros', Sid. *Ep.* 1. 7. 11.

277. en ego . . . ferebar: the dominant note is one of wistful pride in something now lost: cf. Ov. *Ep.* 6. 113 f. 'si te nobilitas generosaque nomina tangunt—| en, ego Minoo nata Thoante feror!', and esp. *Rapt.* 3. 412 f. 'quam nuper sublimis eram quantisque procorum | cingebar studiis!' Similar too is Ov. *Tr.* 2. 118 'grande . . . toto nomen ab orbe fero'. For the passive of *fero* in such contexts cf. Virg. *A.* 12. 235 'uiuusque per ora feretur', and see *TLL* vi/1. 550. 13 ff.

278. ante tuum . . . aditum: = 'before I came to you.' For this strikingly compressed expression Müller judiciously cites Macr. *Sat.* 1. 2. 1 'temptanti mihi, Postumiane, aditus tuos et mollissima consultandi tempora', Dictys Cret. 6. 15 'patrio aditu prohibitus.' In those examples, however, the use of the adjective is a reasonably natural development from the use of the genitive with *aditus* (= 'access' to a person's notice) seen at e.g. Cic. *Cat.* 3. 16 'omnium aditus tenebat', Virg. *A.* 4. 423 'uiri mollis aditus'. Here the 'person' is a country, and the sense of *aditus* is perfectly literal. For the sense compare the old Goth's observation in the council of war that 'numquam Mauors adeo constrinxit in artum | res, Alarice, tuas' in the thirty years between their crossing the Danube and their coming to Italy (*Get.* 491 f.).

legibus exul: cf. Lucilius 1088 Marx (= 1017 Warmington) 'legibus exlex'. Alaric is now as destitute and as much cut off from his native society as a condemned criminal exiled by law for his crimes; alternatively, it may be that he has so longed for Italy that in leaving her now he actually feels like an exile from his own country.

279. addictus . . . reus: his crimes are hubris against heaven and rebellion against the legitimate rule of Honorius. Cf. Eridanus' words at 191f., esp. *simili bacchatur crimine.*

flatu propiore sequentum: note the comparative: his pursuers are getting nearer. The language is reminiscent of that used to describe athletic competition, both chariot- and foot-races. Cf. *Il.* 23. 380f. πνοιῇ δ' Εὐμήλοιο μετάφρενον εὐρέε τ' ὤμω | θέρμετ', Soph. *El.* 718f., Virg. *G.* 3. 111 'umescunt spumis flatuque sequentum', *A.* 5. 167f., Stat. *Theb.* 6. 603ff. (the foot-race) 'quem deinde gradu premit horridus Idas | inspiratque umero, flatuque et pectoris umbra | terga premit.' Ovid cheekily transfers this language of noble endeavour to amorous pursuit: *Met.* 1. 541f. (Apollo and Daphne) 'tergoque fugacis | inminet et crinem sparsum ceruicibus adflat', 5. 616f.

280f. Müller cites Virg. *A.* 2. 361f. 'quis cladem illius noctis, quis funera fando | explicet?', presumably for the anaphora and the aporia. More apposite is Virg. *A.* 4. 371 'quae quibus anteferam?', where Servius gives this kind of rhetorical question the designation 'amphibolia', and explains that it suggests that 'omnia et paria et magna sunt.' Quintilian, however, uses the same term of something quite different, namely ambiguity of various types, especially word-play and punning (*Inst.* 3. 6. 88, 7. 9. 1ff.). Note also *Od.* 9. 14 τί πρῶτόν τοι ἔπειτα, τί δ' ὑστάτιον καταλέξω;, Eur. *El.* 907f. τίν' ἀρχὴν πρῶτά σ' ἐξείπω κακῶν, | ποίας τελευτάς; τίνα μέσον τάξω λόγον;, Virg. *A.* 4. 284 'quae prima exordia sumat?'

281–5. After Pollentia Alaric still had powerful forces at his disposal. The admission of this fact here acts as a corrective to the exaggeration in Claudian's earlier claims of vast carnage among the Goths in that battle: see 210–28 n. That his cavalry was largely intact must have left Alaric still dangerous indeed, since the Romans were dependent on the unreliable Alans (224 n.).

282. captae . . . opes: for the despoiling of the Gothic camp see 129 *tot amissis sociis* n.

cruciastis: of mental torment also at e.g. Hor. *S.* 1. 10. 78f. 'aut cruciet quod | uellicet absentem Demetrius', Prop. 2. 25. 40: see *OLD* s.v. 3, and cf. Catul. 85. 2 'sed fieri sentio et excrucior'. Though common in comedy and the letters of Cicero, and to a lesser extent in elegy, *crucio* was clearly not generally considered appropriate to the higher genres: Virgil, Lucan, and the Flavian epic poets avoid it entirely, but cf. Ov. *Met.* 2. 651, 3. 694, 9. 292, [Sen.] *Oct.* 940. There may thus be extra point in Statius' talking of his 'Thebais multa cruciata lima' in the lighter genre of the *Siluae* (4. 7. 26).

282 f. aspera fati | sors: for the collocation cf. Stat. *Theb.* 1. 196 'aspera sors', and also Ov. *Pont.* 3. 6. 14 'aspera fata', Stat. *Theb.* 1. 173 f. '"hancne Ogygiis", ait, "aspera rebus | fata tulere uicem . . . ?"' Note also the regular phrase *res asperae* of adversity (Cic. *de Orat.* 2. 346, Liv. 25. 38. 18; cf. *Get.* 116 'uel laeta uel aspera rerum').

283. tulerit: concessive subjunctive: the losses at Pollentia he could bear, and attribute calmly to the vicissitudes of war.

Martisque uices: cf. Sil. 3. 13 'belli . . . uices', Stat. *Theb.* 4. 620, 9. 78, 566, 11. 40 'quas uoluis, Gradiue, uices?', 12. 552.

283 f. non funditus armis | concideram: combining echoes of Virg. *A.* 11. 413 'funditus occidimus' and Luc. 8. 266 f. (Pompey after Pharsalus) 'non omnis in aruis | Emathiis cecidi'.

284. stipatus: perhaps to be taken absolutely, with reference to infantry so that Alaric claims that Pollentia left him 'with [plenty of] troops still at [his] back, with [his] cavalry intact' (Platnauer), i.e. still perfectly capable of conducting an effective campaign with both principal types of forces. But the past participle would then be left uncomfortably high and dry without an ablative, so alternatively we could see *equitum . . . cateruis* as being governed by both *stipatus* and *integer.* Cf. also e.g. Luc. 7. 492 'Pompei densis acies stipata cateruis', *Rapt.* 2. 55 f. 'comitantur euntem | Naides et socia stipant utrimque caterua'.

285. integer: the whole phrase = *cateruis equitum integris,* but the poetic construction lays the emphasis on Alaric himself and on his ability to continue fighting. The sense of *integer* is 'unaffected by any losses': see *OLD* s.v. 9, and cf. Caes. *Ciu.* 2. 5. 2 'quos integros superauissent ut uictos contemnerent', Tac. *Hist.* 3. 56 'integro exercitus sui robore'.

ad montes . . . cessi: see Introd., p. xl, 229–37 n.

reliquo cum robore: cf. Sil. 10. 373 'reliquo cum milite'. For the prosody of *reliquus* see 227 n.

286 f. These lines recall Luc. 6. 15 ff. 'hoc iter aequoreo praecepit limite Magnus, | quemque uocat collem Taulantias incola Petram | insedit castris'.

286. Appenninum: the singular is commonly used when the entire range is being collectively indicated. Cf. Mela 2. 58, Plin. *Nat.* 3. 48, Luc. 2. 396, Pers. 1. 95 (= Nero fr. 4. 3 Büchner), *IV Cons.* 106, *Stil.* 2. 273, 3. 307. Note also *ab Alpe* at *Gild.* 82, *Stil.* 3. 285, and see 272 *monti* n.

perhibent: cf. Enn. *Ann.* 20 Skutsch 'est locus Hesperiam quam mortales perhibebant'.

286–90. Geographical digressions are part and parcel of both epic and historical writing; Claudian offers more extensive and more elaborate examples in the form of descriptions of Phrygia (*Eutr.* 2. 237–73), Raetia (*Get.* 329–48), and Sicily (*Rapt.* 1. 142–59, where see Gruzelier's helpful note). See further Richard F. Thomas, *Lands and Peoples in Roman Poetry* (Camb. Phil. Soc. Suppl. 7: 1982), esp. ch. 1. Even at only five lines, however, this one is already open to the charge of dramatic implausibility in its present context. But then, dramatic plausibility is not Claudian's aim in this entirely fictional speech; his mind remains fixed on the senatorial audience of his poem, and it is to their clear understanding of the situation, and of its panegyrical significance, that all his efforts are directed.

For his description of the Apennines Claudian takes his cue from Lucan's majestic description of the whole of Italy at *De Bello Ciuili* 2. 392–438, esp. 396 ff. 'umbrosis mediam qua collibus Appenninus | erigit Italiam nulloque a uertice tellus | altius intumuit propiusque accessit Olympo. | *mons inter geminas medius se porrigit undas* | inferni superique maris, collesque coercent | hinc Tyrrhena uado frangentes aequora Pisae, | illinc Dalmaticis obnoxia fluctibus Ancon', and 431 ff. 'piniferis *amplexus* rupibus *omnis* | *indigenas Latii populos*, non deserit ante | Hesperiam, quam cum Scyllaeis clauditur undis, | extenditque suas in templa Lacinia rupes, | longior Italia, donec confinia pontus | solueret incumbens terrasque repelleret aequor, | at postquam. *gemino tellus elisa profundo est,* | extremi colles *Siculo* cessere *Peloro.*' In particular, to the italicized portions, cf. *porrectus* (287), *populos complectitur omnes* | *Italiae* (288 f.), *geminumque latus stringentia . . . utraque . . . discriminat aequora* (289 f.), and *Siculum . . . ad usque Pelorum* (287). Claudian's much-compressed account omits most of the lavish detail of his model, especially the insistence on the great height of the range with which Lucan begins his exhaustive description. Claudian emphasizes instead the idea of the mountain chain dividing the Tyrrhenian and Adriatic seas, and, more particularly, the fact that it extends the whole length of the peninsula from Liguria to the straits of Messina. In this he is also close to the brief formulation of Pliny, *Nat.* 3. 48 'Appenninus mons Italiae amplissimus perpetuis iugis ab Alpibus tendens ad Siculum fretum'. In Claudian, however, this geographical fact is given special point: the Apennines thus formed a kind of high road, and if Alaric had kept a straight course along the range (*continuum . . . per iuga . . . cursum*, 291), it would have taken him directly to Rome. That he instead allowed himself to be tricked by Stilicho into crossing back over the Po is thus all the more reprehensible in his own eyes.

The same passage of Lucan also seems to have left its mark on *VI Cons.* 494 ff. See in general Fantham's note ad loc. (pp. 152–6) for an excellent discussion of the usefulness of verbal topographies for the Romans, to whom maps were unknown and few of whom (in Claudian's time as well as Lucan's) had first-hand experience of travelling the whole length of Italy.

287. Siculum . . . Pelorum: Cape Pelorus is the promontory forming the NE corner of Sicily, facing across to Scylla on the Calabrian coast: Plin. *Nat.* 3. 73 'duo aduersa promuntoria, ex Italia Caenus, e Sicilia Pelorum; xii stadiorum interuallo'. It was traditionally said to have been named after a helmsman of Hannibal's buried there (Sall. *Hist.* 4, fr. 29 Maurenbrecher = Serv. on Virg. *A.* 3. 411, Mela 2. 116) in an aetiology parallel to, and perhaps inspired by, those concerning Capes Misenus and Palinurus (see Austin on Virg. *A.* 6. 156–82, 162, 337–83). Cf. Virg. *A* 3. 411 'angusti . . . claustra Pelori', Ov. *Met.* 15. 706 'Siculi . . . angusta Pelori', Sen. *Med.* 350, Luc. 2. 438, Sil. 4. 494, Stat. *Silu.* 1. 3. 33 'Sicanium . . . Pelorum', *Rapt.* 1. 151 f., 3. 255.

porrectus: passive with 'middle' sense (= 'extending'), as at Virg. *G.* 3. 351 'medium Rhodope porrecta sub axem', Sil. 1. 130. At *Rapt.* 1. 153 'in medio scopulis se porrigit Aetna perustis' the reflexive stands in for the passive: see 40 *se . . . aestimat* n. and contrast Stat. *Theb.* 1. 330 f. 'Cithaeron | porrigitur.' The choice of verb has been influenced by Luc. 2. 399 f., cit. 286–90 n., though there the emphasis is on height: cf. also Luc. 6. 576 'qua iuga deuexus Pharsalica porrigit Haemus'.

288. finibus ab Ligurum: for the poetic placement of a preposition between a noun and either an attributive adjective or an attributive genitive see KS i. 587 f.

conplectitur: from Luc. 2. 431 f., cit. 286–90 n. *amplector* and *complector* are frequently used in geographical descriptions, though more usually of the 'all-embracing' sea or sky. Cf. e.g. Catul. 64. 30 'Oceanus . . . mari totum qui amplectitur orbem', Liv. 21. 30. 2 'omnes gentesque et terrae quas duo diuersa maria amplectantur', Plin. *Nat.* 5. 41, V. Fl. 1. 195, Stat. *Theb.* 5. 288 f., Tac. *Ger.* 1. 1 'cetera Oceanus ambit, latos sinus et insularum inmensa spatia complectens'.

289. Luc. 2. 399 ff. has also served as the model both for these lines and for a passsage in Claudian's contemporary, Rutilius Namatianus: *Red.* 2. 27 ff. 'diuersas medius mons obliquatur in undas, | qua fert atque refert Phoebus uterque diem: | urget Dalmaticos eoo uertice fluctus | caerulaque occiduis frangit Etrusca iugis'. Cf. also Ov. *Met.* 14. 6 f. (the straits of Messina) 'nauifragumque fretum, gemino quod litore pressum | Ausoniae Siculaeque tenet confinia terrae'.

geminum . . . latus: the 'twin coasts' of Italy are washed by the Adriatic and Tyrrhenian Seas (*utraque . . . aequora*, 290). For *latus* with the sense 'coast' cf. Virg. *A.* 3. 417f. 'uenit medio ui pontus et undis | Hesperium Siculo latus abscidit', Luc. 1. 547, 2. 613f. 'hinc latus angustum iam se cogentis in artum | Hesperiae'. This should perhaps be seen as a poetic extension of *latus* to indicate the sides of a ditch, and thus the deep bank of a river: see *OLD* s.v. 6c, citing Ov. *Fast.* 1. 501 'fluminis illa latus'. Since the emphasis in such contexts is on verticality, the use of *latus* for *litus* | *ora* will have been made all the easier by the frequent application of the word to the 'side' of a mountain, and hence a sea-cliff: see e.g. Pers. 6. 7f. 'hibernatque meum mare, qua latus ingens | dant scopuli et multa litus se ualle receptat'.

stringentia: extended from the common use of the verb to describe rivers 'grazing' their banks, as at Virg. *A.* 8. 62f. 'ego sum pleno quem flumine cernis | stringentem ripas', Stat. *Theb.* 1. 39f. 'arentes adsuetum stringere ripas | . . . Ismenon'. Cf. also Lucr. 5. 256 'ripas radentia flumina', Aus. *Mos.* 460 Green.

290. perpetuo . . . tractu: cf. Mela 2. 58 'perpetuo iugo Appennini montis', Plin. *Nat.* 3. 48 'Appenninus mons . . . perpetuis iugis ab Alpibus tendens', Curt. 3. 4. 6. *perpetuo* is balanced by *continuum* in the next line; an 'uninterrupted course along the unbroken chain of peaks' would have brought Alaric to the gates of Rome.

291. haec: clearly superior to *huc*, providing as it does the necessary balance to *iuga*, as well as neatly resuming the narrative after the digression of 286–90. If accepted, *huc* would have to mean something like 'in this direction' (= *hac*), a sense for which parallels are lacking. Between *haec* and *huc* there probably lies an intermediate corruption *hac*.

292–7. Alaric's own words confirm the wisdom of Stilicho's policy: see 274–319 n. With 292–4 cf. esp. *Get.* 96ff. 'tua cura coegit | inclusis aperire fugam, *ne peior in arto* | *saeuiret rabies uenturae conscia mortis*; | nec tanti nomen stirpemque abolere Getarum, | ut propius peterere, fuit'; and to 295 compare *Get.* 100ff. 'procul arceat altus | Iuppiter, ut delubra Numae sedemque Quirini | barbaries oculis saltem temerare profanis | possit et arcanum tanti deprendere regni.' Stilicho's policy is thus entirely vindicated, and Alaric's intentions correspondingly frustrated. In the Council of the Goths in *De Bello Getico* he had declared his intention to 'do or die', that is, to possess Italy either as victor or in burial: *Get.* 530f. 'hanc ego uel uictor regno uel morte tenebo | uictus humum.' Instead, he has been forced into an ignominious retreat, and so has achieved neither. For Claudian's original audience in Jan. 404, these lines may have been sufficiently pointed by dint of their intertextuality with the earlier poem. Later readers, however, will remember not only the sack of Rome in 410, but also Alaric's death at Consentia (Cosenza) in Bruttium, and his subsequent burial in the bed of the river Basentus, and for them the irony is rich indeed.

293 f. The desire to go down while causing as much damage as possible to the enemy is a mark of the old-fashioned epic hero: in slaying as many of his foes as he can the doomed hero paradoxically avenges his own death in advance ('solacia leti'), and descends to the underworld escorted by his victims. Consider for example Aeneas' reaction in similarly desperate straits: Virg. *A.* 2. 668 ff. 'arma, uiri, ferte arma; uocat lux ultima uictos. | reddite me Danais; sinite instaurata reuisam | proelia. numquam omnes hodie moriemur inulti.' But in Alaric the instinct is perverted and becomes a mark of hubris and Giant-like *furor*, since what he wants to burn around him is the divinely protected land of Italy: cf. 184–6 n.

Given the many links between *VI Cons.* and Lucan's account of the battle of Pharsalus (see 210 f., 259–64 nn.), we should even compare his reaction directly and unfavourably with Pompey's paradoxically heroic victory over this instinct at Pharsalus: Luc. 7. 654 ff. 'nec, sicut mos est miseris, trahere omnia secum | mersa iuuat gentesque suae miscere ruinae: | ut Latiae post se uiuat pars maxima turbae, | sustinuit dignos etiamnunc credere uotis | caelicolas uouitque, sui solacia casus. | "parcite," ait "superi, cunctas prosternere gentes. | stante potest mundo Romaque superstite Magnus | esse miser."' This passage of Lucan had already been reworked more thoroughly by Claudian in his account of the downfall of Rufinus. See *Ruf.* 2. 17 ff. 'quid restat nisi cuncta nouo confundere luctu | insontesque meae populos miscere ruinae? | euerso iuuat orbe mori: solacia leto | exitium commune dabit nec territus ante | discedam: cum luce simul linquenda potestas', and see Levy's note ad loc., citing R. T. Bruère, *CP* 59 (1964), 231. Also to the point in the present context is *Stil.* 1. 333 ff., where Claudian attributes Stilicho's unwillingness to command a vast expeditionary fleet against Gildo to his caution and his desire not to panic the rebel into flight or the destruction of the towns of Africa. See esp. *Stil.* 1. 335 ff. 'consilio stetit ira minor, ne territus ille | te duce suspecto Martis grauiore paratu | aut in harenosos aestus zonamque rubentem | tenderet aut solis fugiens transiret in ortus | missurusue sibi certae solacia mortis | oppida dirueret flammis. res mira relatu, | ne timeare times et, quem uindicta manebat, | desperare uetas.' The same policy is accordingly said to have saved Carthage in 400 (*Stil.* 1. 343) and to have saved Rome in 402 and 404. The repeated use of this topos thus strongly suggests what the cynic might well have suspected in any case, namely that the claims advanced for Stilicho's motivation in sealing the controversial *pacta* with Alaric at *Get.* 95 ff. are no more than fictions invented after the fact.

293. uoluissem: obviously right, since the whole point is that it was only a matter of choice. Conversely, *ualuissem* would fly in the face of the whole argument of 281–6.

294. omnibus . . . perustis: apparently not including Rome, since in the next line he only envisages dying closer to, and within sight of, the City. If we combine this with the reference to *cultas segetes* in l. 296 we may discern a significant piece of propaganda. The City itself, protected by walls recently refurbished at Honorius' command (Introd. Sect. 3), would have been safe from capture, but Alaric could have advanced through Italy as far as Rome, burning and pillaging the countryside as he went. He would thus have destroyed the estates of the senators, and burned their harvests: *cultas* is pointed because, if Verona took place in the late summer or early autumn (215 *aestiuo* n.), the fields would have been full of standing corn. Claudian simultaneously gives Stilicho the credit for a successful defence of Rome itself, and, through his plan of diverting Alaric back over the Po, the glory of having saved the senators' estates. Stilicho's controversial *pacta* with Alaric after Pollentia are thus presented in the best possible light to those who were no doubt most hostile to them. For the phrasing compare also Liv. 24. 20. 4 'perusti late agri'.

oppeterem: a high poeticism, found only here in Claudian. Standard usage required *oppetere mortem* vel sim., as at Enn. *scen.* 170, 210 Warmington = *trag.* 183, 323 Jocelyn, *Rhet. Her.* 4. 27, Cic. *Tusc.* 1. 116, Liv. 28. 19. 11. The absolute use seems to have been pioneered by the Augustan poets (Virg. *A.* 1. 96, 11. 268, 12. 640: cf. V. Fl. 1. 554, Sil. 4. 508, 10. 39); they were then followed by such anti-classicizing prose authors as Tacitus (*Ann.* 2. 24. 2, 4. 50. 3). For the use of the imperfect subjunctive in the place of the pluperfect see 223 *caperet* n.

fama maiore: reflecting, no doubt, that 'stat sua cuique dies, breue et inreparabile tempus | omnibus est uitae; sed famam extendere factis, | hoc uirtutis opus' (Virg. *A.* 10. 467 ff.). As it is, all that Alaric has to show for his Italian adventure is shame and a disgraceful retreat (e.g. *turpe retexit iter*, 132).

297. damnosa: sparingly used in high verse, but cf. Ov. *Met.* 8. 215, 10. 707, 11. 376, Luc. 9. 316, *IV Cons.* 334; also Stat. *Silu.* 1. 4. 7, *c.m.* 49. 24. For adjectives ending in *-osus* see 146 *undosa . . . domo* n.

297f. Alaric's wife and children, as well as a vast amount of booty supposedly collected over thirty years of pillaging, were captured by the Romans when they stormed the Gothic camp at Pollentia (*Get.*

604–34, esp. 625 ff.). The sense and plural form of *nurus* may cause some difficulty. The literal meaning 'daughters-in-law' is not very appropriate here, not just because Alaric hardly seems to have been old enough to have married sons, but also because it would be relatively anti-climactic after *pignora*. Far more likely is the poetic use of *nurus* for 'young women', especially married ones; this is particularly so because of *caras* (a regular epithet for wives, e.g. Virg. *A.* 4. 91, 8. 377, Ov. *Tr.* 5. 14. 2). For *nurus* with this sense see Löfstedt, *Syntactica*, i. 69, Austin on Virg. *A.* 2. 501, Gruzelier on *Rapt.* 2. 312. This interpretation is confirmed by Claudian's own earlier moralizing on this subject: 'qui foeda parabat | Romanas ad stupra nurus, sua pignora uidit | coniugibus permixta trahi' (*Get.* 83 ff.). Alaric, that is, planned to dishonour the young *matronae* of Rome (*nurus*), but in the event it was his own wives who were carried into captivity, along with his children: *pignora . . . carasque nurus* here correspond to *sua pignora . . . coniugibus permixta* in the earlier passage. There remains the difficulty of the plural form. Tacitus tells us that the pagan Germans were usually monogamous but might take additional wives for political and dynastic reasons (*Germ.* 18. 1: see Anderson ad loc., and also E. A. Thompson, *The Early Germans* (Oxford, 1965), 59): an attested case is that of Ariovistus (Caes. *Gal.* 1. 53. 4). None the less, Alaric, as an Arian Christian, should not be found practising polygamy. In the account of the capture of the camp Claudian concentrates on a single wife: 'pulsaret . . . tuas ululatus coniugis aures' (*Get.* 625). It is therefore best to take *coniugibus* and *nurus* as referring inclusively to a single 'wife' in the proper sense and to a number of 'concubines'. See further Schroff on *Get.* 85.

298. Romanus: collective singular, unless we take it as a pointed reference to the 'barbarian' Stilicho. For the collective singular, particularly of 'the enemy', cf. Eng. 'the Hun', 'the Boche', and see LHS ii. 13 f., KS i. 6, Löfstedt, *Syntactica*, i. 12 ff., Nisbet–Hubbard on Hor. *Carm.* 1. 19. 12. Note esp. Var. *R.* 1. 2. 2, where 'Romanus sedendo uincit' is said to be a 'uetus prouerbium'.

299. exertum: i.e. free of hindrances. This is a very striking extension of the usual application of the word to descriptions of characters who keep their breast or arms bare in order to allow greater freedom of movement in battle or in the hunt: Virg. *A.* 11. 649 (the Amazon-like Camilla) 'unum exserta latus pugnae', Stat. *Ach.* 1. 346, *Prob.* 87 (Roma) 'dextrum nuda latus, niueos exerta lacertos', *Rapt.* 3. 377. Claudian will perhaps have been encouraged in his daring by the example of Statius: cf. *Theb.* 7. 609 'fugit exsertos Iocasta per hostes' ('already in battle trim', Mozley), *Silu.* 5. 2. 39. For such transferred usages see further *TLL* v/2. 1859. 49 ff. ('i.q. expeditus, intentus, in alqd . . . attentus, promptus'), citing e.g. Apul. *Met.* 2. 30 'cum . . . custos hic sagacissimus exertam . . . teneret uigiliam', Pacatus, *Pan. Theod.* 35. 1, Ven. Fort. *Carm.* 7. 17. 11 'prouidus, exsertus, uigilans'.

succinctior: *succinctus* properly means 'girt up', i.e. with the skirts raised and belted so as to remove all impediment to swift movement, especially running: see e.g. Ov. *Met.* 3. 156 'succinctae . . . Dianae' (i.e. for the hunt), Stat. *Theb.* 3. 426f. 'Fama . . . uanos rerum succincta tumultus | anteuolat currum.' See also 380 *succinctae . . . cohortes* n. As in the case of *exertum*, here too we have an extension of the word from its usual province of dress so that it is applied to a general state of readiness which is perhaps primarily mental. Müller compares Amm. Marc. 31. 8. 10 'cum promptis accinctis ad proelium'. The emphasis is thus on the greater speed with which, if he had only seized his chance, Alaric could have descended upon Rome.

300. insidiis . . . circumdedit arte: Stilicho's cunning in luring Alaric back over the Po. Here the action is seen from Alaric's point of view: for a more positive view of cunning as a military virtue see 219 *astu* n. For the phrasing cf. Hirt. *Gal.* 8. 18. 1 'uelut indagine hunc (sc. campum) insidiis circumdederunt', Sil. 7. 134, 11. 590 'occulto circumdamur astu', 12. 477. But above all, in this line and at 307f. (*capiorque uicissim | fraudibus ipse meis*), Claudian seems once more to have Hannibal in mind: Liv. 21. 34. 1 (Hannibal) 'ibi non bello aperto, sed suis artibus, fraude et insidiis, est prope cicumuentus'. Most of Claudian's 'Hannibalic' allusions, however, are to the text of Silius Italicus: see 182–4, 184–6 nn.

301. fatalis semper Stilicho: Stilicho has always brought Alaric disaster. Cf. the old Goth's warning to Alaric at the Council: *Get.* 511 ff. 'si temnis Olympum, | a magno Stilichone caue, qui semper iniquos | Fortuna famulante premit.' It may not be accidental that Livy calls Hannibal's conqueror Scipio 'fatalis dux huiusce belli' (22. 53. 6). Note also *Prob.* 149 'Gallis . . . genus fatale Camillos'.

parcere fingit: the reflexive pronoun is also omitted at *Eutr.* 2. 306f. 'ignorare tamen fingit regnique ruinas | dissimulat.' Such omissions are very common in *oratio obliqua* in cases where they can easily be supplied from the context: see KS i. 700f.

302. rettudit: more vivid than the *rettulit* ('he brought back', i.e. 'reverted to' his old hostile attitude) accepted by Birt and Müller. Alaric was lulled into a false sense of security by Stilicho's plan and this 'blunted' or 'took the edge off' his hostility and battle-readiness. Cf. Ter. *Hau.* 945f. 'eius animum . . . retundam redigam', Liv. 33. 36. 11 'quorum cum primus secundusque impetus rettudisset inferentem

se ferociter hostem', Sil. 8. 319 'belli feruore retuso'. For the underlying idea see e.g. Tac. *Hist.* 2. 32 'multa bella impetu ualida per
taedia et moras euanuisse'.

302f. remenso . . . Pado: for the past participle of compounds of
metior used with passive force see Austin on Virg. *A.* 2. 181 'pelago . . .
remenso', and cf. also *A.* 3. 143f., V. Fl. 2. 501, 3. 227 'fluuiis et nocte
remensa', *c.m.* 31. 13 'Nilo . . . remenso'.

303f. foedera saeuo | deteriora iugo: the *pacta* of 204. The yoke is
that of slavery, expressing Alaric's view of Roman rule. Cf. Luc. 2.
314f. 'ad iuga cur faciles populi, cur saeua uolentes | regna pati
pereunt?', *Ruf.* 2. 88f. 'quonam usque feremus | exitiale iugum?', *c.m.*
18. 6 'duro . . . iugo'.

304f. For the triple anaphora of *tum* see 32f. n.

304. uis extincta Getarum: recalling the words of the old Goth to
Alaric at the Council, with reference to the earlier confrontation with
Stilicho in Arcadia: *Get.* 516f. 'extinctusque fores, ni te sub nomine
legum | proditio regnique fauor texisset Eoi.' Stilicho, then, has now
completed the task that Rufinus' treachery prevented him from finishing up in 397. Cf. also *Stil.* 1. 109ff., esp. 112 (of the Goths, among
other tribes) 'extinctique forent penitus'.

305. letum pepigi: an emotionally compressed and paradoxical way of
saying that in agreeing to Stilicho's pact Alaric essentially agreed to
his own destruction. Here Alaric recalls Turnus on his way to the fatal
duel with Aeneas: Virg. *A.* 12. 49 'letum . . . sinas pro laude pacisci'.
The allusion might be thought to give Alaric some aura of pathos and
tragedy, but note that his bargain brings him no *laus*, only shame and
humiliation. For the phrasing compare also Virg. *A.* 5. 230 'uitamque
uolunt pro laude pacisci', Stat. *Theb.* 1. 319 'hac aeuum cupiat pro luce
pacisci'.

305f. uiolentior armis . . . clementia: a powerful oxymoron.
Contrast e.g. Stat. *Theb.* 12. 482 'mitis . . . Clementia'. Alaric retro-
spectively validates Claudian's claim that 'magis ex aliis fluxit clemen-
tia causis, | consulitur dum, Roma, tibi' (*Get.* 95f.). See also 340 *clemens
Marce* n.

307. Mars grauior sub pace latet: cf. Cic. *Phil.* 12. 17 'quoniam sub
nomine pacis bellum lateret'. *grauiore* should be read as meaning that
concealed beneath the surface of this peace lay Verona, a more disastrous battle than Pollentia: see 281-5n. and cf. *Stil.* 1. 335f. (of Gildo
similarly being tricked into thinking himself safe) 'ne territus ille |
te duce suspecto Martis grauiore paratu'. For the phrasing cf. also Ov.
Fast. 1. 277 (to Janus) 'at cur pace lates', Stat. *Ach* 1. 816f. 'Lycomedis
regia . . . tranquilla sub pace silet.'

307 f. The idea has a proverbial feel. Cf. Liv. 21. 34. 1, cit. 300 n., Eccles. 10. 8 'He that diggeth a pit shall fall into it.' A. Otto, *Die Sprichwörter und sprichwörtlichen Redensarten der Römer* (Leipzig, 1890; repr. Hildesheim, 1962), 187 s.v. *laqueus*, cites Ov. *Ars* 1. 646 'in laqueos, quos posuere, cadant', *Rem.* 502; add Pl. *Cas.* 113 'proin tu te in laqueum induas', Cic. *Ver.* 2. 101. Claudian offers an extensive passage moralizing on this theme at *Eutr.* 1. 157ff.: 'quam bene dispositum terris, ut dignus iniqui | fructus consilii primis auctoribus instet . . . .' Alaric, it seems, accepted the *pacta* offered him by Stilicho after Pollentia while fully intending to renege on it when it suited his convenience, but in the event he found he was outmanœuvred: cf. 213f. *iamque opportunam motu strepuisse rebelli | gaudet perfidiam*, 230–7.

308. fraudibus: stronger and considerably more unambiguous than e.g. *arte* (300) in its negative connotations. By contrast, Stilicho's character is marked by a lack of *fraus* both in his dealings with other Romans (*Stil.* 2. 32ff.) and on the battlefield (477f.). But see 219 *astu* n. and note also that Theodosius' instructions to the young Honorius concerning warfare include the recommendation that he learn 'quae fraudi commoda uallis' (*IV Cons.* 327).

308 f. For the phrasing cf. Ov. *Tr.* 5. 2. 41 'quo ferar? unde petam lassis solacia rebus?'

309. socius suspectior hoste: since so many have proved to be traitors, why should he trust those that are left? Cf. 250–5, 262 *desciuere* n., and 264 *perfida . . . examina*. The collective singular *socius* is used to give balance with *hoste*. For the line-ending cf. also Stat. *Theb.* 7. 220 'ueniet suspectior aetas'.

310–14. It would have been better if all his men had died in battle, for then they would have perished while still 'his' (i.e. still loyal to him), and so they would have remained his for ever. Utter but still honourable defeat would thus have been far preferable to the disgrace and humiliation of desertion. Alaric essentially draws a contrast between the loss of his men in battle on the one hand and the loss of them through breach of faith on the other. Related to this, if not quite the same, is the idea that a chief's men are dishonoured if they survive his death on the field, part of the warrior code of northern barbarians that impressed a number of Roman writers: see Tac. *Germ.* 14. 1 'iam uero infame in omnem uitam ac probrosum superstitem principi suo ex acie recessisse; illum defendere tueri, sua quoque fortia facta gloriae eius adsignare praecipuum sacramentum est: principes pro uictoria pugnant, comites pro principe' with Henderson ad loc., and Amm. Marc. 16. 12. 60. At any rate, though Alaric is here concerned principally with his own woes and humiliation, *laesa fides* is naturally a condemnation of his men as well: they should have stayed at their leader's side whatever his circumstances.

310. atque utinam: the more highly emotional tone of *o utinam* might seem particularly appropriate as Alaric reaches the climax of his lament. Moreover, *o utinam* (first attested at Tib. 1. 3. 2 'o utinam memores ipse cohorsque mei', where see Kirby Flower Smith) is no stranger to epic, and is found at e.g. Ov. *Met.* 1. 363, 3. 467, Luc. 2. 306, 4. 509, 8. 88, V. Fl. 7. 135. Here, however, there is very little in it from the point of view either of meaning or manuscript tradition, and so it is probably best to be guided by Claudian's usage elsewhere; he has *atque utinam* three times (*Ruf.* 1. 367, *Gild.* 157, *c.m.* 31. 49), but no sure examples of *o utinam*. For *utinam* combined with *licere* cf. Ov. *Met.* 2. 51f., 10. 202f. 'atque utinam merito uitam tecumue liceret | reddere', Luc. 2. 306.

311. duro . . . certamine: cf. Virg. *A.* 9. 725f. 'multosque suorum | moenibus exclusos duro in certamine linquit': also Cic. fr. 30. 7 Büchner 'graue certamen belli', Virg. *A.* 10. 146. Note that while Virgil uses the preposition, Claudian has the plain ablative of place: cf. 580 *urbe*.

311f. numquam | desinit esse meus: cf. *Eleg. Maec.* 2. 20 'nec tibi qui moritur desinit esse tuus'.

312. melius mucrone perirent: one would expect *perissent* (and *abstulisset* in 313) but the change of tense turns a reflection on a particular event in the past into a moral generalization. The sense of *melius* is 'to better purpose, effect etc.': i.e. 'it would be better that they should die by the sword.' This is the so-called 'adverb of judgement', which 'comment[s] on the choice made, not on the manner of choosing' (Brink on Hor. *Ars* 40). See further LHS ii. 827, KS 1. 795, Nisbet–Hubbard on Hor. *Carm.* 1. 2. 22 (ferrum) 'quo graues Persae melius perirent', and cf. Prop. 3. 11. 37 'issent Phlegraeo melius tibi funera campo', Ov. *Ep.* 6. 93, Stat. *Theb.* 3. 351f. 'melius legatus adissem | Sauromatas', 9. 387, 441, *Gild.* 149f. 'melius deserta iacebo | uomeris inpatiens'.

313. luctu leuiore: cf. Cic. *Fam.* 4. 6. 1 'ea scripsisti, quae leuare luctum possent', Ov. *Met.* 5. 21 'luctuque leuabere nostro'.

314f. clientum . . . comites . . . propinqui: Claudian may be drawing some distinction between mere 'retainers' and more intimate and higher-ranking 'comrades' or 'companions', before rising to the still closer bond that should exist between 'kinsmen'. On the other hand, it is just as likely that he is simply varying his vocabulary. Trying to make these Latin terms square precisely with particular sections of Gothic society is in any case a futile exercise. *cliens* is commonly found loosely designating the vassals or dependants of barbarian princes; see *OLD* s.v. 3 citing Caes. *Gal.* 1. 4. 2 'Orgetorix . . . omnis clientis obaeratosque suos . . . eodem conduxit', Tac. *Ag.* 12. 1 'honestior auriga, clientes propugnant'; add Tac. *Ann.* 1. 57, 'ereptus Segestes magna cum propinquorum et clientium manu', 2. 45. For *comites* in similar circumstances see Tac. *Germ.* 14 and Amm. Marc. 16. 12. 60, cit. 310–14n.

314–19. The speech ends with a highly-wrought and emotional expression of aporia. A brief question (314f.) is followed by a perfectly balanced statement (315) with the structure *abab* (alternating verb forms with substantives), which is made still tighter by asyndeton, the use of assonance (*o, e*), and the fact that all four words are trisyllabic. Three rhetorical questions forming tricolon abundans and bound together by anaphora (*qua/quae*) then bring the speech to its despairing conclusion.

A strong note of pathos is reinforced by echoes of two of the most emotional passages of the *Aeneid*. In particular, we recall Dido's mixture of pleading and reproach in her first speech to Aeneas in the 'quarrel scene': Virg. *A.* 4. 320f. 'te propter Libycae gentes Nomadumque tyranni | odere, infensi Tyrii', 325f. 'quid moror? an mea Pygmalion dum moenia frater | destruat aut captam ducat Gaetulus Iarbas?' But note the changes: *offensi*, rather than *infensi*, perhaps implies an admission that Alaric has in some sense wronged his companions, while Claudian's lines contain no equivalent of *te propter*; it is not for another's sake that Alaric has alienated himself from those who should be closest to him, but solely out of his own crazed obsession with sacking Rome. Alaric also recalls Evander's words at the funeral of Pallas: *A.* 11. 177ff. 'quod uitam moror inuisam Pallante perempto | dextera causa tua est, Turnum gnatoque patrique | quam debere uides'. Both Evander and Alaric are prostrated by their losses and find life hateful, but Evander, in his desire to see vengeance taken, at least still has a reason for living.

315. For the language used cf. also *Ruf.* 1. 106ff. 'talem progenies hominum si prisca tulisset, | Pirithoum fugeret Theseus, offensus Oresten | desereret Pylades, odisset Castora Pollux'.

316. quid moror inuisam lucem?: in addition to Virg. *A.* 11. 177 (cit. 314–19n.) cf. Virg. *A.* 2. 647f. (Anchises) 'iam pridem inuisus diuis et inutilis annos | demoror', 4. 631 (Dido) 'inuisam quaerens quam primum abrumpere lucem', Ov. *Met.* 13. 517. Note also Lucr. 3. 79f.

316–19. These lines are best seen as offering a variant on the situation, particularly associated with tragedy but also found often enough in epic and oratory, in which a character in desperate straits deliberates on where to take refuge or whom to turn to for help, only to rule out all the possibilities one by one. The most famous examples are Eur. *Med.* 502ff. (Medea) νῦν ποῖ τράπωμαι; κτλ., Catul. 64. 177ff. (Ariadne), and Virg. *A.* 4. 534ff. (Dido); cf. also Soph. *Aj.* 457ff., Cic. *de Orat.* 3. 214 (a fragment from a speech of Gaius Gracchus = fr. 61 Malcovati). Here Alaric does not present himself with even the most tenuous of possibilities, an indication of the utter hopelessness of his situation. The answer which the reader is no doubt expected to provide on his behalf is 'nowhere', for the whole world resounds with the glory of Stilicho.

316. qua sede recondam: implying a wish for both safety and seclusion. Cf. Virg. *A.* 1. 680f. (Venus and Ascanius) 'hunc ego sopitum somno super alta Cythera | aut super Idalium sacrata sede recondam', 7. 774f. But closest to Claudian is Stat. *Theb.* 11. 729f., where Antigone promises Creon that she will remove Oedipus from the world of men and take him where he can hide his shame and where he will not be importunate to anyone: 'coetibus abducam solaque in sede recondam. | exul erit'. For verbs beginning in *re-* (cf. *requiram*, 317) see *pr.* 3 *reponit* n.

317. naufragii fragmenta mei: a well-established metaphor for ruin and disaster, whether public (as at e.g. Cic. *Dom.* 129 'in illo rei publicae naufragio', *IV Cons.* 61f. (Theodosius) 'certaque leuasset | naufragium commune manu') or personal (e.g. Catul. 68. 3, Ov. *Tr.* 1. 6. 8 'naufragii tabulas qui petiere mei', *Pont.* 2. 6. 11ff., 2. 9. 9, *Ibis* 18, *Eutr.* 2. *pr.* 72 'naufragio Cyprus sit memoranda tuo').

318. quaeue: *-ue* here practically = *et*. Both *-ue* and *aut* are commonly used to link a series of questions in a very weak manner, with the result that the sense of any real alternative is lost: see LHS ii. 498f. and cf. Austin on Virg. *A.* 2. 520.

318f. The speech ends with its focus, as at the beginning, on the holy land of Italy, and also on her great defender, Stilicho. The adjective *potens* here recalls Virgil's description of Hesperia as 'terra antiqua, potens armis atque ubere glaebae' (*A.* 1. 531, 3. 164): cf. also *Eutr.* 2. 527 'tendit ad Italiam supplex Aurora potentem'. It is easiest to understand *nimium* as meaning that Italy is 'too powerful' for Alaric, or any other invader, to defeat her; such a reading makes Alaric's last words a dramatic admission of utter defeat and thus entirely appropriate to the propagandistic intentions of the poem.

320–30. *Pursued by Stilicho, Alaric finally flees from Italy, while a hellish troupe of personified evils accompanies him. Italy is purified of the pollution of his presence as a sick man's body is purified by a priest with sulphur and incantations.*

320. haec memorans: one of Virgil's speech formulae which did not manage to establish itself firmly in epic diction: cf. *A.* 5. 641, 743, 10. 680; also 'sic memorans' at *A.* 6. 699, 9. 250, Sil. 5. 603.

fugam . . . tetendit: cf. Virg. *A.* 9. 781 'quo deinde fugam, quo tenditis?' and see in general *OLD* s.v. *tendo* 7.

321. expertas: = 'which he had experienced before', i.e. at Pollentia and Verona, experiences the terrified Alaric has no desire to repeat: cf. 244–8 n. For past participles of deponent verbs used with passive force see LHS ii. 139, and for such uses of *expertus* cf. Cato, *Agr.* 157. 10 'cito sanum facies hac cura: expertum hoc est', Acc. *Inc.* 41 Warmington = *Inc.* 715 Dangel, Stat. *Theb.* 8. 535 'expertae iam non uenit obuius hastae', Tac. *Ann.* 12. 2. Contrast the true deponent at 435.

aquilas: by metonymy for *legiones*. This usage is far rarer in Latin than the regular use of 'the Eagles' in English might lead one to expect, but cf. *B. Hisp.* 30. 1 'erat acies XIII aquilis constituta', Juv. 14. 197, *Ruf.* 2. 238 'concordes aquilas'. There is also a certain touch of anachronism here, since by Claudian's time the regular emblem of Roman armies was the Oriental dragon standard: see 566–8 n.

321–3. Though abstract personifications had played a part in Greek poetry since Hesiod, they are far more frequent in Latin literature, perhaps largely because the Romans were in any case much more inclined to honour abstract deities: see e.g. Austin on Virg. *A.* 6. 273 ff., Hollis on Ov. *Met.* 8. 801 ff., Dewar on Stat. *Theb.* 9. 32 'Fama'. That they are found in abundance in Ovid and Statius must have especially encouraged Claudian: see Levy on *Ruf.* 1. 29 ff., and cf. *Prob.* 1. 77 ff., *Nupt.* 78 ff., *Theod.* 166 ff., *Stil.* 2. 100 ff. Alaric's flight from Italy is accompanied by Pallor, Fames, Luctus, and Morbi, all of which evils were shown afflicting his own army at 239 ff., esp. 244–8. These afflictions correspond to the *dira numina* purged from the patient's body at 327 f.; the evils which Alaric had hoped to inflict on Italy he now, as he flees, takes with him. Claudian has in mind above all the personified evils shown clustering around the entrance to the underworld at Virg. *A.* 6. 273 ff.: 'uestibulum ante ipsum primisque in faucibus Orci | *Luctus* et ultrices posuere cubilia Curae, | *pallentes*que habitant *Morbi* tristisque Senectus, | et Metus et *malesuada Fames* ac turpis Egestas, | terribiles uisu formae, Letumque Labosque; | tum consanguineus Leti Sopor et mala mentis | Gaudia, mortiferumque aduerso in limine Bellum, | ferreique Eumenidum thalami et Discordia demens | uipereum crinem uittis innexa cruentis.' For precise echoes of Ovid's description of the retinue of Tisiphone see 321 *comitatur euntem* n. Similar catalogues of hellish personifications include Sen. *Oed.* 590ff., Sil. 2. 548ff., 13. 579ff., *Ruf.* 1. 29ff. Note also Stat. *Theb.* 10. 557ff., Prud. *Ps.* 464f. Claudian may also have been influenced by such passages as *Pan. Lat.* 4. 31. 3 Mynors, where, as Constantine enters Rome in triumph, 'duci sane omnibus uidebantur subacta uitiorum agmina', among them Scelus, Perfidia, Audacia, Furor, Crudelitas, Superbia, Arrogantia, Luxuries, and Libido.

321. comitatur euntem: recalling Ov. *Met.* 4. 484f. (the grisly retinue of the Fury Tisiphone) 'Luctus comitatur euntem | et Pauor et Terror trepidoque Insania uultu': see Bömer ad loc. Similar line-endings can be found at Virg. *A.* 6. 863 'uirum qui sic comitatur euntem', Stat. *Theb.* 3. 117, *Rapt.* 2. 55.

322. Pallor et atra Fames: cf. Ov. *Met.* 8. 790f. (Scythia) 'Frigus iners illic habitant Pallorque Tremorque | et ieiuna Fames', Sil. 13. 582. Poets more usually concentrate on the power of Hunger to induce utter recklessness and desperation: Virg. *A.* 6. 276, Stat. *Theb.* 10. 44 'nil non ausa Fames', *Ruf.* 1. 31 'imperiosa Fames'; cf. 244f. *omne periclum | docta subire fames.* Pallor indicates sickness rather than fear, thus helping prepare the simile: cf. Virg. *G.* 3. 552 'pallida Tisiphone Morbos agit ante Metumque', *A.* 6. 275.

322f. saucia liuidus ora | Luctus: Grief's face is 'torn' and 'discoloured' because mourners beat their faces or tear them with their nails; cf. e.g. *Eutr.* 2. 529f. (Aurora) 'stat liuida luctu, | qualis erat, Phrygio tegeret cum Memnona busto'; also Ov. *Ep.* 20. 82 'ora . . . sint digitis liuida nostris', *c.m.* 30. 176 (Achelous) 'saucia truncato pallebant flumina cornu'. Alternatively, Luctus may rip her clothes and tear her breast in her misery: Stat. *Theb.* 3. 125f. 'sanguineo discissus amictu | Luctus atrox', *Ruf.* 1. 33 'scisso maerens uelamine Luctus'. For such ritual self-disfigurement in lamentation see Margaret Alexiou, *The Ritual Lament in Greek Tradition* (Cambridge, 1974), index s.v. 'laceration of the flesh'.

323. inferno stridentes agmine Morbi: plagues and sicknesses traditionally come in vast armies: see Nisbet–Hubbard on Hor. *Carm.* 1. 3. 30f. 'noua febrium | terris incubuit cohors', citing e.g. Aesch. *Supp.* 684 νούσων δ' ἑσμὸς, Juv. 10. 218 'circumsilit agmine facto | morborum omne genus'. Gesner explained *stridentes* as a detail transferred to the Morbi from their victims: 'signant febres, quarum frigus stridor dentium comitari solet.' But given the context Claudian is probably also thinking of the shrieking of ghosts and other denizens of the underworld, e.g. Luc. 6. 623 'feralis strideat umbra', Stat. *Theb.* 7. 770, 9. 298f., *Ruf.* 1. 126 'umbrarum tenui stridore uolantum'.

324–30. The patient's body corresponds to Italy, the priest who con-
ducts the ceremony to Stilicho, and the *dira numina* to the afflictions
which Alaric brought with him into Italy and now leads back out
again. Behind this simile lies the old idea of a city or state in political
disarray as being afflicted with disease, for which see Aesch. *Ag.* 848
ff., with Fraenkel ad loc., *Eutr.* 2. 11 ff. with Fargues, Susan Sontag,
Illness as Metaphor and AIDS and its Metaphors (New York, 1989), 76 ff.

Elsewhere in Claudian's poetry Stilicho is a doctor: *Stil.* 2. 204 f.
'solo poterit Stilichone medente | crescere Romanum uulnus tectura
cicatrix', *Get.* 120 ff. (of his *clementia* towards Alaric) 'cautius ingentes
morbos et proxima cordi | ulcera Paeoniae tractat sollertia curae |
parcendoque secat, ferro ne largius acto | inreuocandus eat sectis
uitalibus error'. Here it is the resources of magic that are brought to
bear, as the body is purified by lustration with torches smeared with
sulphur and pitch (324–6), as well as water (327), pungent herbs (327 f.),
and incantations (330) in an elaborate and complicated ritual. The
same combination of ritual elements to drive away sickness is attested,
in particular, in elegy, the clearest example being Tibullus 1. 5. 9 ff.:
'ille ego, cum tristi morbo defessa iaceres, | te dicor uotis eripuisse
meis. | ipseque te circum lustraui sulpure puro | carmine cum
magico praecinuisset anus'. Cf. also Ov. *Ars* 2. 329 f. (what to do to
show your devotion if your girlfriend should fall sick) 'et ueniat quae
lustret anus lectumque locumque, | praeferat et tremula sulpur et oua
manu'. Making a strict division between 'medicine' and 'magic' is,
however, no doubt anachronistic: as Kirby Flower Smith remarks on
the Tibullus passage cited above, the ceremony 'combines magic with
practical disinfectants', and rests primarily on the 'theory of disease as
a demon to be exorcised'. Such magic may also be used to free the
lover from the affliction of love, but its efficacy is doubtful, if the
elegists are to be believed: see Tib. 1. 2. 61 ff. (a witch) 'nempe haec
eadem se dixit amores | cantibus aut herbis soluere posse meos, | et
me lustrauit taedis, et nocte serena | concidit ad magicos hostia pulla
deos', Ov. *Rem.* 249 ff., esp. 259 f. Cf. also Virg. *A.* 4. 478 ff., 634 ff., Juv.
2. 157 f., and, a passage particularly close to the present one, Nem. *Ecl.*
4. 62 ff. 'quid prodest, quod me pagani mater Amyntae | ter uittis, ter
fronde sacra, ter ture uaporo, | incendens uiuo crepitantes sulpure
lauros, | lustrauit cineresque auersa effudit in amnem, | cum sic in
Meroen totis miser ignibus urar?'

Although the most striking extant parallels in Latin poetry for
ceremonies of this type seem to be in elegy, and are thus associated
with love, none the less the essential element of purification is appropriate to all kinds of circumstances. In epic one can point to similar

ceremonies of purification for various purposes. Examples are Ov. *Met.* 7. 261 (Medea rejuvenating Aeson, a process also involving spells and magic herbs) 'terque senem flamma, ter aqua, ter sulpure lustrat' and Stat. *Theb.* 4. 416 ff. (Tiresias preparing a necromancy) 'circumque bidentum | uisceribus laceris et odori sulpuris aura | graminibusque nouis et longo murmure purgat'. Cf. also Theocritus' epyllion, *Id.* 24. 88 ff., where Tiresias recommends a similar combination of elements (aromatic twigs, fire, sulphur, disposal of the remains while not looking back) to purify the house of Amphitryon and Alcmene after the infant Heracles kills the serpents sent to harm him by Hera.

324. sic: that what follows is a simile is clear enough from *circum membra* (326), a phrase that could have no literal application here. Moreover, as Müller saw, it was Stilicho, and not some unknown and unnamed priest who cleansed Italy of Alaric's hateful presence. *sic* is therefore necessary for the simile to have a proper introduction. *tum*, which looks like an attempt at rationalization by a scribe who has missed the point of the comparison, would merely introduce another, and rather extraneous and anti-climactic, element of narrative.

324 f. The torch (or torches, if *facem* is a collective singular) is smeared with pitch and sulphur, and so billows out large amounts of pungent, acrid smoke. Cf. esp. Ov. *Fast.* 4. 739 f. (the purification of flocks at the Parilia) 'caerulei fiant puro de sulpure fumi, | tactaque fumanti sulpure balet ouis'. As well as having a purificatory capacity, torches treated in this way would burn with greater ease; see Ov. *Met.* 3. 373 f. 'non aliter quam cum summis circumlita taedis | admotas rapiunt uiuacia sulpura flammas', V. Fl. 3. 124 f., Sil. 13. 199 'aptabat flammis ac sulpure taedas': also Sil. 1. 354 f. (a missile) 'sed cetera pingui | uncta pice atque atro circumlita sulpure fumant'.

324. lumen odorum: 'pungent light', a poetic synaesthesia. Alternatively, the adjective could be said to be transferred; contrast Stat. *Theb.* 4. 417 'odori sulpuris aura'.

325. sulpure: mentioned as a purifying agent from Homer on. It is used by Achilles to clean a cup from which he will pour a libation to Zeus (*Il.* 16. 228 f.), and by Odysseus for the still more solemn task of purifying his house after the slaughter of the suitors (*Od.* 22. 480 f., 23. 50: cf. Eur. *Hel.* 865 f., Plin. *Nat.* 35. 177). Janko, on *Il.* 16. 228–30, notes that sulphur was a holy substance, associated with the thunderbolt and etymologically connected with the gods (θέειον/θεός; Plut. *Mor.* 665 c). At the other extreme, though following the same logic, Virgil recommends its inclusion, along with pitch, in his recipe for sheep-dip (*G.* 3. 449). Note also the passages cited at 324–30 n. above, and Bömer on Ov. *Fast.* 4. 739 f., who cites Veget. *mul.* 3. 12 'suffimentorum compositio fascinum pellit, lustrat animal, fugat daemones, submouet morbos. odoris namque fumus ac spiritus per os ac nares ingrediens penetrat ad uiscerum omnes recessus ac curat saepius loca, quae potiones non potuerunt curare; sic tussis etiam in hominibus suffimentorum uapore praecipue sanatur.' See further Robert Parker, *Miasma: Pollution and Purification in Early Greek Religion* (Oxford, 1983), 215 n. 41.

   caeruleo: the adjective is transferred from the smoke: cf. Larg. 250 'sulpur nigrum', and contrast Ov. *Fast.* 4. 739 'caerulei . . . puro de sulpure fumi', Hor. *Epod.* 5. 82 'bitumen atris ignibus.' For the colour range implied by *caeruleus* see 196 n.

326. circum membra . . . purganda: i.e. the patient who is to be cleansed, as at Tib. 1. 5. 11 etc. *membra* seems to imply the purification of the whole body, with which we should compare Virg. *A.* 4. 635 'dic corpus properet fluuiali spargere lympha' and perhaps 6. 229ff., cit. 327n. On many occasions it is the head in particular that is specified as being purified, whether with sulphur (Prop. 4. 8. 86), *uerbena* (Liv. 1. 24. 6), or water (Ov. *Fast.* 4. 314f., *Pont.* 3. 2. 73).

327. rore pio spargens et . . . herbis: recalling Virg. *A.* 6. 229ff. (Corynaeus purifying the Trojans at the funeral of Misenus) 'iam ter socios pura circumtulit unda | spargens rore leui et ramo felicis oliuae'. *ros* for *aqua* is found as early as Lucretius (1. 496). Only immersion in naturally flowing streams, or purification with water drawn from them, was adequate in religious ceremonies: see Pease on Virg. *A.* 4. 635, Austin on Virg. *A.* 2. 719. Such water is usually designated *uiua* (Virg. *A.* 2. 719, Ov. *Met.* 3. 27, Sil. 8. 125 'uiuo purgor in amni') or *pura* (Virg. *A.* 6. 229, Ov. *Fast.* 4. 314) in poetry. *pio* is no doubt a conscious variant; for the transferred epithet see Catul. 68. 79 (a sacrifice) 'pium . . . cruorem', with Fordyce ad loc. For the language cf. also Ov. *Met.* 7. 189f. 'ter sumptis flumine crinem | inrorauit aquis', *Fast.* 4. 315 'ter caput inrorat'. The water could be sprinkled by hand, but in the passage of Virgil that serves as Claudian's model *rore leui et ramo felicis oliuae* is a hendiadys (= 'gentle drops from a branch of fruitful olive', Austin ad loc.). In this passage, then, *herbis* is probably a bundle of *uerbenae* used as the instrument for sprinkling the holy water: see the next note.

327 f. dira fugantibus herbis | numina: i.e. *uerbenis*. This term is used of aromatic plants employed in religious and magical ceremonies as well as those possessing medicinal qualities. Here both senses are operative, since their odour drives away the demons afflicting the body and the sickness that they cause (cf. the *lumen odorum* of the torches at 324f.). A wide range of plants fell in this category, the commonest being bay, olive, myrtle, and tamarisk. See further Nisbet–Hubbard on Hor. *Carm.* 1. 19. 14, citing Celsus 2. 33. 3; add Servius on Virg. *A.* 12. 120. For their use in magical ceremonies see e.g. Virg. *Ecl.* 8. 64 f. 'effer aquam et molli cinge haec altaria uitta | uerbenasque adole pinguis et mascula tura', 82, *Ciris* 369 f.

For *fugare* in such contexts cf. V. Fl. 4. 462, *Stil.* 2. 109 f. 'procul inportuna fugantur | numina, monstriferis quae Tartarus edidit antris', Veget. *Mul.* 3. 12 'lustrat animal, fugat daemones, submouet morbos'; also Luc. 3. 369 f. 'at enim contagia belli | dira fugant', 9. 914.

328. purificumque Iouem: = Δία καθάρσιον (Hdt. 1. 44): cf. *CIL* x. 6641 '<sacrum I>oui <Pu>rgatori'. The rarity of citations of Jupiter in this aspect, and the dearth of examples of *purificus* in classical Latin, have given rise to some manuscript confusion. *t(h)urificum* is perhaps an attempt at rationalization based on *herbis* (327), but Jupiter receives incense, he does not either 'offer' or 'make' it. *terrificumque* may be an unconscious error, but looks like either a correction of *turificum* or a guess inspired by *fugantibus* (327); at any rate it is clearly not appropriate here in the way that *purificum* is. Heinsius' *lustrificum* (with which he compares V. Fl. 3. 448 'lustrifico cantu') is not only unnecessary, but is also not very attractive after *lustralem* (324). The neologism *purificus* is a perfectly natural one, along the lines of e.g. *sacrificus, munificus*.

Triuiamque: i.e. Hecate, the chthonic deity associated with magic and spell-casting. For Triuia ('she of the crossways') see Pease on Virg. *A.* 4. 511, 609, Williams on Stat. *Theb.* 10. 366 f., and cf. *Rapt.* 1. 15 'ternis Hecate uariata figuris'.

329. trans caput auersis manibus: compare esp. Virg. *Ecl.* 8. 101 f. 'fer cineres, Amarylli, foras riuoque fluenti | transque caput iace, nec respexeris.' The aim is to avert the gaze from this most solemn and crucial part of the spell; direct witnessing of the magical activity would render it inoperative, and perhaps put the person responsible in danger. For this very common superstition see Gow on Theoc. *Id.* 24. 96, and cf. *Od.* 5. 349 f. (Ino's instructions to Odysseus regarding her magic veil) ἂψ ἀπολυσάμενος βαλέειν εἰς οἴνοπα πόντον | πολλὸν ἀπ' ἠπείρου, αὐτὸς δ' ἀπονόσφι τραπέσθαι (with Heubeck–West–Hainsworth ad loc.), Ap. Rh. 3. 1038, Virg. *A.* 6. 223 f. (the funeral of Misenus) 'subiectam more parentum | auersi tenuere facem', Ov. *Fast.* 5. 436 f. (at the Lemuria) 'uertitur et nigras accipit ante fabas, | auersusque iacit', Liv. 21. 22. 7, Plin. *Nat.* 21. 176, Nemes. *Ecl.* 4. 64.

329 f. in Austrum | secum rapturas cantata piacula taedas: a vivid way of saying that the torches are solemnly hurled away along with all the other refuse of the expiatory rite. That this is the usual practice can be seen from a number of the passages cited in the previous note; note esp. Aesch. *Ch.* 98 f. στείχω καθάρμαθ' ὥς τις ἐκπέμψας πάλιν | δικοῦσα τεῦχος ἀστρόφοισιν ὄμμασιν, where καθάρμαθ' = *piacula*. The instruments of the spell, or the débris, are more usually disposed of in running water (Theoc. *Id.* 24. 93 ff., Virg. *Ecl.* 8. 101 f., Nemes. *Ecl.* 4. 64). If there is any ritual point to the choice of the south wind, it is hard to establish exactly what it is. Müller takes *Austrum* as an example of *species pro genere*, citing Serv. on Virg. *A.* 1. 51 'figura est celebrata apud Vergilium, et est species pro genere. apud Ennium *furentibus uentis* legerat, sed quasi asperum fugit et posuit *austris* pro "uentis".' *cantata* = *incantata* ('over which spells have been chanted'), as often in verse: cf. Prop. 4. 5. 13 'audax cantatae leges imponere lunae', Ov. *Am.* 1. 14. 39 'cantatae . . . paelicis herbae', *Met.* 7. 98, Sen. *Med.* 730, Luc. 6. 767. But perhaps the south wind is named here because it was regularly identified as a source of disease, a bringer of pestilence in the heat of late summer. Consider e.g. Ov. *Met.* 7. 532 'letiferis calidi spirarunt aestibus austri', Juv. 4. 56 ff.

331–55. *Both the Senate and the People of Rome clamour to see their victorious young prince: their enthusiasm surpasses that felt in the past for the return of Trajan from his Dacian campaigns or of Marcus Aurelius from his miraculous war against the tribes of Germany.*

Honorius is compared favourably with those two of his Imperial predecessors who, more than any others, are regularly eulogized as *optimi principes*, Trajan and Marcus Aurelius. What is discernible here is therefore almost certainly not some deep personal political conviction on Claudian's part, but merely the 'standard line' of the rhetorical handbooks, florilegia, etc. from which he probably derived most of his knowledge of both Republican and earlier Imperial history. By the same token, others are standardly presented as 'tyrants': see, for example, *IV Cons.* 311 ff., where Theodosius, in his sermon on kingship, advises the young Honorius to avoid the delicta of Nero and Tiberius, and to take Trajan for his model instead. Perhaps surprisingly to modern readers, Augustus figures in Claudian's works in a less than favourable light: see above 116–19 n., Cameron 340 ff.

Claudian digressed from his main *argumentum* (Honorius' *aduentus*, his triumph, and, above all, his consulship) at l. 122, in order to tell of its genesis in the successful prosecution of the Gothic war. Now, at roughly the half-way point of the poem, he returns to it in his account of the people's desire to see their Emperor in the capital and of Roma's successful attempt to persuade him to satisfy this desire. A number of problems of structural interpretation have bedevilled study of this section of the poem, the most damaging being the various theories arguing that the whole narrative of the Verona campaign in ll. 127–330 has been inserted into the text of *VI Cons.*, either accidentally or deliberately, probably from *De Bello Getico*, or drafts from uncompleted portions of it. Birt (p. lvi) and Müller (331 *interea* n.) rightly dismiss the theory of T. G. Paul (*Quaestionum Claudianearum particula*, Progr. Grossglogau, 1857; Forts. Progr. Berlin, 1866, 6ff.) that this huge section is a mere interpolation.

Birt, who accepts the integrity of the narrative of the Verona campaign with the rest of the poem (p. lvi), also praises the structural balance of the composition, which he sees as being divided into two precisely equal halves, one dealing with Alaric (1–330), and the other with Honorius' consulship (331–660). Müller (loc. cit.) tartly points out that this is inaccurate, since ll. 53–121 were already concerned with Honorius. He might have added that the same is true of ll. 1–52, even if Honorius was not addressed directly in them, while, conversely, Alaric features prominently in a flash-back in the second, 'Honorian' half (440–90). None the less, that there is a significant break at this, the mid-way point is clear enough. The bulk of the first half narrates the past victories that gave rise to the celebrations 'now' under way (i.e. in January 404, at the time of the poem's delivery), and the bulk of the second records the resulting *aduentus* promised in ll. 125 and the celebrations that go with it. The two halves melt into one another by virtue of Claudian's deliberate conflation of the diverse celebrations of *aduentus*, triumph and consulship, all three owing their origin, political and poetic, to the same set of military events.

331–3. Similarly emotional descriptions of public enthusiasm for the *reditus* of an Emperor are as old as the Principate itself. Cf. Hor. *Carm.* 4. 5 (prayers for Augustus' return from the western provinces, *c.*13 BC), 1 ff. 'diuis orte bonis, optime Romulae | custos gentis, abes iam nimium diu; | maturum reditum pollicitus patrum | sancto concilio, redi', 9ff. 'ut mater iuuenem, quem Notus inuido | flatu Carpathii trans maris aequora | cunctantem spatio longius annuo | dulci distinet a domo, | uotis ominibusque et precibus uocat, | curuo nec faciem litore dimouet: | sic desideriis icta fidelibus | quaerit patria Caesarem', Mart. 7. 5. 1ff. (the prayers of the Senate and the People for Domitian's return from his campaigns in Pannonia, AD 92) 'si desiderium, Caesar, *populique patrumque* | respicis et Latiae gaudia uera togae, | redde deum *uotis* poscentibus', 7. 7. 6. In Claudian's own work we can compare the desire of the Romans to see Stilicho in 400: *Stil.* 3. 54f. 'cuius et aduentum crebris petiere Quirites | uocibus et genero meruit praestante senatus!' The present lines balance the welcome-scenes at 542–59. Also broadly comparable is the old practice of offering public vows for the health of the Emperor: see Weinstock 217ff.

331 f. The fire-imagery seen in *ardor* and *accendit* links the passion of the contemporary Romans with that of their ancestors in the time of Trajan (*caluisse* 334). In *VI Cons.* the same passionate heat manifests itself in the people during Theodosius' visit (63 *publicus hinc ardescit amor*: see n. ad loc.), and during Honorius' actual stay in the City (604 *flagrat studiis concordia uulgi*). Matching all this is the devotion felt by Italy for Stilicho: *Stil.* 2. 264ff. '"si uos adeo Stilichone curules | augeri *flagratis*" ait "quas sola iuuare | fama potest, quanto me dignius *incitat ardor*, | ut praesente fruar conscendentemque tribunal | prosequar atque anni pandentem claustra salutem?"'

332. cum plebe patres: = *cum senatu populoque*: cf. *Gild.* 53, *Stil.* 3. 45f., 116 'ad arbitrium plebis patrumque reducit'. Such combinations predate the Augustans: e.g. Lucil. 1229 Marx (= 1146 Warmington) 'populusque patresque', Virg. *G.* 2. 509 'plebisque patrumque', *A.* 8. 679, Ov. *Fast.* 2. 127f., 4. 293, *Tr.* 4. 2. 15: cf. also Luc. 7. 578 'in plebem uetat ire manus monstratque senatum', Tac. *Ann.* 13. 48. For *patres* (sc. *conscripti*) = *senatus* cf. 551, 589. Examples abound in the Roman epics of Lucan (e.g. 1. 488, 3. 104, 5. 8, 46) and Silius (1. 675, 6. 590, 15. 265), and no doubt had some precedent in lost works such as the *Res Romanae* of Cornelius Severus. For the topos whereby all classes express the same joy in welcoming the honorand at an *aduentus* see 543–59, 545 *una . . . turbae facies* nn.

332f. saepe negatum | . . . aduentum: his last visit had been in 389, and the last by any reigning Emperor in 394: see 53–76n. Occasions when a visit to the Capital might have seemed in order but which had been missed include Honorius' *Quinquennalia* and the victory over Gildo. Note Symm. *Ep.* 6. 52 (a letter of AD 397, expressing hope that Honorius would visit Rome the next year) 'aduentus domini et principis nostri denuo postulandus est'.

333–8. Trajan fought two major wars against the Dacians. The first (AD 101–2) forced their king Decebalus to accept a humiliating peace, and won Trajan a triumph and the title *Dacicus*, but it was the second (AD 105–6) that resulted in the storming of Decebalus' capital Sarmizegethusa and the permanent establishment of a Roman province. Claudian's insistence on the extreme north being made subject to Roman legal authority (*iura, fasces, leges, tribunal* 336–8) might thus be understood as an indication that he has the second in mind. His wording, however, shows the influence of a passage of Pliny's *Panegyricus* on Trajan that does not refer to either Dacian war, but rather to the events of 98: see 337f.n. For the public clamour for

Trajan's return from the Danube, Claudian is similarly indebted to Plin. *Pan.* 20. 1 'iam te ciuium desideria reuocabant, amoremque castrorum superabat caritas patriae', 22. For the importance of Trajan as a role-model and for his supposed blood-connection with the house of Theodosius see 55 f. *optimus ille | diuorum*, 59 *terrore remoto*, 61 nn.

333. publica uota | consensu . . . caluisse: Claudian is adapting the conclusion of Ovid's account of the young Theseus' triumphant arrival at Athens after clearing the Isthmus of its murderous brigands: *Met.* 7. 449 ff. '"pro te, fortissime, uota | publica suscipimus, Bacchi tibi sumimus haustus." | consonat adsensu populi precibusque fauentum | regia'. The network of general similarities—two heroic youths, after the performance of glorious martial exploits, arrive to popular acclaim in their ancestral capital, where, it should be added, they are to take possession of their inheritance—is surely not accidental. Ovid also lays stress on the precocity of Theseus' achievement (*Met.* 7. 448 f. 'si titulos annosque numerare uelimus, | facta prement annos'), as Claudian so often does with Honorius (67 f. *paruumque triumphis | imbuit* n.). There is, however, one significant difference: Theseus is shown already doing what Honorius has not yet done (as a grown man, at least). For the phrase *publica uota* see also Prop. 4. 6. 42, Ov. *Tr.* 2. 60, Juv. 10. 284 f. (Pompey saved from the fever contracted in Campania in 50 BC) 'multae urbes et publica uota | uicerunt', *IV Cons.* 295, and see Bömer on Ov. *Met.* 7. 449 f.

334. caluisse: perhaps transferred from the altars: see e.g. Virg. *A.* 1. 416 f. 'centumque Sabaeo | ture calent arae', Ov. *Met.* 12. 152 'calentibus aris', V. Fl. 2. 331, 8. 260, Stat. *Theb.* 7. 577 f. But, above all, it suggests popular devotion: cf. *Pan. Lat.* 5. 8. 3 Mynors (of an *aduentus* of Constantine) 'caluit in nobis ultra uires animus ad laetitiam'; also Prud. *Per.* 14. 76 'nec demorabor uota calentia'.

335. Dacica . . . cum fregerat . . . arma: cf. Sil. 15. 14 'qui fregerit arma duorum': also *IV Cons.* 318 (Trajan) 'alta . . . inuectus fractis Capitolia Dacis'.

bellipotens . . . Vlpius: Trajan's victories in Dacia and Mesopotamia took the Roman Empire to its greatest historical extent: cf. Eutropius *Breu. a.u.c.* 8. 2. 2 'Romani imperii, quod post Augustum defensum magis fuerat quam nobiliter ampliatum, fines longe lateque diffudit.' See *TLL* ii/2. 1815. 59 ff. for *bellipotens* applied to a human being, citing Enn. *Ann.* 197 f. Skutsch 'stolidum genus Aeacidarum: | Bellipotentes sunt magis quam sapientipotentes.' Claudian uses it also of the elder Theodosius (*c.m.* 30. 40) and, predictably enough, of Stilicho (*III Cons.* 144). In classical verse the title is usually given to

Mars (Virg. *A.* 11. 8, V. Fl. 1. 529, Sil. 10. 547, Stat. *Theb.* 3. 577) or
Minerva (Stat. *Theb.* 2. 715 f. 'diua ferox . . . bellipotens'; cf. also Virg.
A. 11. 483 'armipotens . . . Tritonia uirgo'). Tertullian hijacks it for the
glory of the Faith: *Adu. Marc.* 3. 14 'bellipotens et armiger Christus'.
Vlpius is Trajan's *nomen gentile*: cf. 646 *fora . . . Vlpia*.

336. indignantes . . . Arctos: i.e. the Dacians: cf. *Stil.* 1. 246 'post
domitas Arctos': also *Stil.* 1. 216 f. 'sine caede subactus | seruitio
Boreas exarmatique Triones'. Claudian is drawing on a common epic
formulation of Imperial conquest as the domination, against its will, of
unruly Nature by the civilizing force of Roman power. Cf. esp. Virg.
A. 8. 726 ff. (Augustus' conquests) 'Euphrates ibat iam mollior undis, |
extremique hominum Morini, Rhenusque bicornis, | indomitique
Dahae et pontem indignatus Araxes', V. Fl. 1. 9, Sil. 3. 616 f.
(Domitian on the Danube) 'indignantem tramittere Dardana signa, |
Sarmaticis uictor compescet sedibus Histrum'. Such formulations
originate in the use of *indignor* to express the fury of the elements, as at
Lucr. 6. 196 f. 'uenti . . . magno indignantur murmure clausi', Virg. *A.*
1. 55 f.: see *TLL* vii/1. 1186. 7 ff. The earliest example with political
connotations similarly expresses the conquest of nature, but in Italy
rather than as an element of Imperial expansion: see Virg. *G.* 2. 161 ff.
(the Portus Iulius, built by Agrippa on Lake Avernus and the Lucrine
Lake in 37 BC) 'an memorem portus Lucrinoque addita claustra |
atque indignatum magnis stridoribus aequor, | Iulia qua ponto longe
sonat unda refuso | Tyrrhenusque fretis immittitur aestus Auernis?'
Some modern critics interpret such passages as invitations to subversive readings which are thought to counteract the surface eulogies
of the text: see e.g. Thomas on *G.* 2. 161–4, David Quint, *Epic and
Empire. Politics and Generic Form from Virgil to Milton* (Princeton, 1992), 31.
Thomas, for example, believes that Virgil's language 'supports the
sense of a violent act against nature', and it is not impossible that contemporary readers found some of these model texts troubling too.
Even if that is so, however, it is extremely improbable that Claudian
read Virgil in the same way. His language is far less problematic in its
Imperial rhetoric, and if there is any subversive element in *indignantes*
at all, it is amply compensated for in *mirata* (337) and *stupuit* (338).

in iura redegerat: a poetic variant on *in potestatem redigere*, a
favourite phrase of the historians (*OLD* s.v. *redigo* 10). Cf. also *Stil.* 3. 7 f.
'conplectere dextram, | sub iuga quae Poenos iterum Romana
redegit'.

337 f. The extreme north (here Dacia is hyperbolically extended as far
as Ukraine and the Sea of Azov) is, to its own astonishment, made
subject to the authority of Roman law. The whole country practically

becomes a Roman court, fenced in with *fasces* (i.e. lictors) and with a magistrate's judgement-seat (*tribunal*) in its midst. Claudian is probably drawing upon a passage of Pliny's *Panegyricus* to Trajan in which great play is made on the fact that the Emperor's second consulship was inaugurated not in Rome, but on the very fringes of the Empire: *Pan.* 56. 3ff. 'secundum consulatum . . . gestum non in hoc urbis otio et intimo sinu pacis, sed iuxta barbaras gentes . . . .decora facies multa post saecula consulis *tribunal* uiridi caespite exstructum, nec *fascium* tantum sed pilorum signorumque honore circumdatum . . .'. Nerva adopted Trajan in October AD 97, when the latter was acting as governor of Germania Superior. The new arrangement was solemnized by their holding the consulship for AD 98 together, but Trajan did not return to Rome that winter and so could be said to have held this, his second consulship 'iuxta barbaras gentes'. The apparent influence of Pliny and the direct mention of the *fasces* (337) suggest strongly that in Claudian's text we are to imagine Trajan actually inaugurating a consulship in Dacia rather than simply enforcing Roman rule there in more general terms. This is confirmed by the link between the present passage and 645ff., discussed below. It is at any rate clear enough that though Pliny is referring to the situation of AD 98, Claudian in these lines has the Dacian wars in mind (*Dacica . . . arma*, 335). It may be, then, that he has simply misunderstood Pliny's admittedly vague language; alternatively he may be adapting it and consciously applying it to AD 101, the year in which Trajan both held his *fourth* consulship and began the first Dacian war.

Later we read that Honorius completes the celebrations for his consulship by taking his seat in the curule chair in the Forum of Trajan itself, surrounded by his lictors: 645ff. 'desuetaque *cingit* | regius auratis *fora fascibus Vlpia lictor*, | et sextas Getica praeuelans fronde secures | colla triumphati proculcat Honorius Histri.' The Forum of Trajan, with its column and its countless statues of Dacian prisoners, was the peacetime monument to Trajan's conquest of the north: his 'descendant' Honorius (cf. 55f. *optimus ille* | *diuorum* n.) symbolically makes it the site for the celebration of his own victory over northern barbarians, who, moreover, had crossed over into the Empire from what had formerly been Dacia. He thus once more unites the signs of triumph in war with those of legitimate authority in peace.

337. fasces cinxere Hypanin: for the idea cf. *Gild.* 20 'trepidos summittit fascibus Indos.' For the phrasing, in addition to 645f., cited in the previous note, cf. Stat. *Silu.* 5. 2. 166f. 'cingique superbis | fascibus et patrias dabit insedisse curules', and *Stil.* 3. 199f. 'solio seu fultus eburno | cingas iure forum': in the latter *iure* expresses the authority of the consul which is symbolized by the ring of lictors with their *fasces*. The Hypanis is the present-day Southern Bug (Pivdennyj Buh), which flows south-east through Ukraine and empties into the Black Sea. For Cornelius Gallus it marked the boundary between Europe and Asia: see Gallus fr. 1 Büchner 'uno tellures diuidit amne duas' with Courtney, *FLP*, p. 263.

338. Romanum . . . tribunal: by metonymy = 'Roman law': cf. Ov. *Am.* 1. 10. 40. The *tribunal* was the dais on which the presiding magistrate's (and hence the judge's) chair was placed. It was thus the central feature and focus of the court.

stupuit: used of nature's awe at the achievements of an Emperor also at *III Cons.* 116f. 'te pulcher Enipeus | celsaque Dodone stupuit', *Rapt.* 2. *pr.* 45 'te Libyci stupuere sinus'. Similar also are Stat. *Silu.* 4. 2. 20f. 'stupet hoc uicina Tonantis | regia', Plin. *Pan.* 14. 1 'Rhenumque et Euphraten admirationis tuae societate coniungeres'.

Maeotia terra: the area around the Sea of Azov (Lake Maeotis): see Plin. *Nat.* 2. 245, 4. 78, Mela 1. 7, and cf. Virg. *A.* 6. 799 'Maeotia tellus'.

339–50. Incursions on to Italian soil by the Quadi and Marcomanni in AD 170 endangered the very heart of the Empire (340f.). Though these invaders were successfully driven out, Marcus Aurelius pursued them into their own territory in order to secure the frontier. For a general account of Marcus' northern wars see Anthony Birley, *Marcus Aurelius. A Biography*, 2nd edn. (London, 1987), 159ff., 251f. During this campaign the Roman army witnessed two 'miracles'. The precise dates are disputed, but either both took place in 172 or else one belongs to that year and the other to 173. In the first, Heaven supposedly intervened in favour of the Romans by striking an enemy war-engine with lightning, while the second involved a spectacular rainstorm which brought timely relief to a Roman army afflicted by severe thirst and heat. For full discussions of these incidents see Birley, op. cit. 71ff. and the characteristically lucid account by R. B. Rutherford in *The Meditations of Marcus Aurelius. A Study* (Oxford, 1989), 221ff. To both of these works this note is heavily indebted.

The two events were strictly speaking separate from each other, and they were accordingly commemorated on clearly differentiated panels of Marcus' Column (Birley, op. cit., pls. 25 and 26). Most sources, however, tend to conflate them: SHA *Marc. Ant.* 24. 4 'fulmen de caelo precibus suis contra hostium machinamentum extorsit, suis pluuia impetrata cum siti laborarent', Cassius Dio 72. 14, esp. [10. 3] ἦν οὖν ὁρᾶν ἐν τῷ αὐτῷ χωρίῳ ὕδωρ τε ἅμα καὶ πῦρ ἐκ τοῦ οὐρανοῦ φερόμενα. καὶ οἱ μὲν ὑγραίνοντό τε καὶ ἔπινον, οἱ δὲ ἐπυροῦντο καὶ ἔθνῃσκον. The phrase *flammeus imber* (342) may therefore be taken as more than a metaphor, and as implying that Claudian also imagined the two miracles as being simultaneous. None the less, although in their discussions of this passage Platnauer (ii. 98), Fargues (pp. 162 f.) and Cameron (pp. 223 f.) all talk in terms of the 'rain miracle', Claudian's emphasis is very much on the thunderbolt, the heat of which is dramatically shown as scorching the enemy and melting their weapons (343–6). Since both ancient authors and modern scholars alike tend to regard the rain miracle as the more striking and the more significant, this choice of emphasis requires explanation. The lightning which actively destroys the enemy makes a neater parallel with the supposed eradication of the Gothic host at Pollentia and Verona, and allows Claudian to stress the triumphal aspects of both present and past engagements with these two sets of northern barbarians as well as the delivery of Italy from danger (341 *exuit Hesperiam . . . periclis*). Furthermore, the blasting of the Quadi with the Thunderer's lightning means that they, like Phaethon and Hannibal elsewhere in the poem, become typological models for the routing of Alaric's hubris: see 344 *ambustus sonipes*, 344–6 nn.

Divine intervention in favour of one side in a battle is, of course, a frequently recurring motif in myth and history, and such intervention is regularly attributed to the prayers of Emperors, whatever their religious affiliation. Claudian's audience would certainly remember that the victory at the Frigidus was said to have been won by Theodosius' prayers: see 351–5 n. Conversely, credit for similar success in averting the anger of Poseidon is given by pagan sources to the prayers of Julian: see MacCormack 136, Rutherford 23 n. 130. In the present passage Claudian offers two possible explanations for Heaven's intervention on the side of the Romans; it was due either to magic or to divine approval of Marcus' character (348–50). The poet explicitly states a preference for the latter (*quod reor* 349). He thus aligns himself in general terms with the standard view of Marcus as a saintly Stoic sage: SHA *Marc. Ant.* 1. 1 'Marco Antonino, in omni uita philosophanti uiro et qui sanctitate uitae omnibus principibus ante-cellit', 12. 1 ff., 15. 3, 24. 3, Cassius Dio 71. 30. 2, Eutropius *Breu. a.u.c.* 8. 11. 1 f. More particularly, he ranges himself with SHA *Marc. Ant.* 24. 4 and Themistius (*Or.* 15. 191B), who interpret the miracle as Heaven's answer to the prayers of the Emperor. Note above all Tert. *Ad Scapulam* 4. 6 'Marcus quoque Aurelius in Germanica expeditione Christianorum militum orationibus ad Deum factis imbres in siti illa impetrauit'; Tertullian is attempting a formulation that expresses the Christian view while courteously extending the credit to the pious

257

emperor. The alternative explanation discounted by Claudian, that the miracle was the work of magicians with 'Chaldaean spells', alludes to the belief held in some quarters, and given considerable prominence by Dio, that an Egyptian magician on Marcus' staff, named Arnouphis, used his arts to secure the aid of Hermes Aerios (possibly the Egyptian god Thoth-Shou). A variant version named as the magician responsible Julian the Theurgist, the author of the 'Chaldaean' oracles: see further 348 *Chaldaea mago . . . carmina ritu* n. In addition to these explanations, yet another claimed that the miracle was granted by God to the intercessions of Christian soldiers serving with Marcus in the Twelfth Legion. This tradition is an old one, and Rutherford (p. 223), points out that it is already attested in a fragment from an *Apology* addressed to Marcus by a bishop Apollinaris (*ap.* Euseb. *Hist. Eccl.* 5. 4f.). It was also supported by the existence of a letter, purporting to be from Marcus to the Senate and informing them of the army's debt to the Christians (Tertullian, *Apologeticus* 5. 6). The fullest account of the Christian version of events is given by Xiphilinus, a Byzantine monk, who interpolates it as a 'correction' into the text of Dio. Needless to say, the extant letter attributed to Marcus is a patent forgery, while Xiphilinus' account is hardly trustworthy, being both reliant on hearsay and disfigured by serious errors; most notably, Xiphilinus claims that the Twelfth Legion received its title *Fulminata* to honour the occasion, when in fact the legion had borne this name for more than a century (Birley 173). At any rate, Marcus's official propaganda on coins and on his column gave credit exclusively to pagan deities, namely Jupiter and Mercury: see Birley 172f., Rutherford 223. From this Fargues (pp. 162f.) argues that in linking the *Tonantis obsequium* with his own expressly stated opinion (*quod reor*) Claudian is striking a blow against Christian propaganda: 'on peut voir en lui un défenseur timide mais convaincu de la vieille religion nationale.' It seems unlikely, however, that a panegyric for a devout Christian prince would have been thought the appropriate place for anti-Christian polemic, and accepting that the Court was tolerant of pagans and pagan literature is not the same as thinking it ready to put up with a direct attack on its religion from its own chief spokesman. But above all, Cameron (pp. 223f.) quite rightly notes that Fargues is wrong to imply that Claudian rejects the Christian version; in fact, he simply does not mention it at all, offering instead two pagan alternatives and actually opting for the one less likely to give offence to Christians. Claudian's most natural sources for the rain and lightning miracles were pagan (e.g. Themistius), and unless the issue were a live one at the time of writing, there seems no particular reason why he should even have heard of the Christians' claims on the subject. To this we should add that he has deliberately chosen the alternative that does most credit to Marcus personally, and that can only reflect well on Honorius, who is being compared with him. See further Lellia Cracco Ruggini, *Athenaeum*, 55 (1977), 107–26, esp. 114 n. 37 for the similarities in conception between the columns of Marcus and Arcadius; and H. Z. Rubin, *Athenaeum*, 57 (1979), 357–80.

339. patriae studiis: picked up by 604 *flagrat studiis concordia uulgi.*

340 f. The Marcomanni and Quadi swept into Italy from Pannonia in AD 170, apparently putting Aquileia in serious danger. See Birley, op. cit. (339–50 n.), 161 f., citing Amm. Marc. 29. 6. 1 'Quadorum natio . . . parum nunc formidanda, sed immensum quantum antehac bellatrix et potens, ut indicant properata quondam raptim procliuia, obsessaque ab eisdem Marcomannisque Aquileia, Opitergiumque excisum, et cruenta complura perceleri acta procinctu, uix resistente perruptis Alpibus Iuliis principe Pio, quem ante docuimus, Marco.' The lightning- and rain-miracles properly belong to Marcus' later offensive deep into the enemy's home territory after they had been driven from Italy (Birley 171 f., 252). Claudian, however, compresses these two separate campaigns in such a way that the text seems to imply that the miracle he goes on to describe happened on Italian soil. This dramatically heightens the tension, and allows a closer correspondence with the salvation of Italy at Pollentia and Verona.

340. clemens Marce: the Romans had long revered *clementia* both as a cardinal virtue of philosophy and as an instrument of pragmatic politics useful for reconciling defeated enemies to their authority. From the time of Caesar it became one of the standard virtues of Roman rulers, and might be exercised not only towards foreign enemies but also towards political opponents within the state. Augustus continued his adoptive father's policy, and *clementia* is one of the virtues attributed to him on the *clupeus uirtutis*, along with *iustitia* and *pietas*. The Senate decreed the construction of a temple to the Clementia Caesaris in 43 BC; though this seems never actually to have been built, an altar was raised to the goddess in the reign of Tiberius, and Gaius Caligula celebrated an annual festival in honour of his own *clementia*. An influential philosophical and theoretical basis for the exercise of the virtue by the Emperors was later provided by the *De Clementia* which Seneca wrote for Nero. See further Weinstock 233 ff.; also R. S. Rogers, *Studies in the Reign of Tiberius* (Baltimore, 1943), 35 ff., Inez Scott Ryberg, in L. Wallach (ed.), *The Classical Tradition: Literary and Historical Studies in Honor of Harry Caplan* (New York, 1966), 235 ff. As for Marcus Aurelius, his *clementia* is praised at SHA *Marc. Ant.* 26.

10, and is commemorated in a number of coins (AD 172, 176): see Henry Cohen, *Description historique des monnaies frappées sous l'Empire romain*, iii (Paris, 1883), nos. 27, 28, 358. It is a virtue he shares with Honorius (*clemens aditu*, 550).

gentibus undique cinctam: the situation of 337–9 is inverted: now it is not the extreme north that is 'surrounded' by the symbols of Roman rule (*cinxere*), but Italy that is surrounded by northern tribes. For the phrasing cf. Sil. 15. 169 (Massilia) 'populis . . . cincta superbis'. *gentes* is used regularly of foreign peoples, whether within the Empire or beyond its boundaries: see Löfstedt, *Syntactica*, ii. 464ff., Nisbet–Hubbard on Hor. *Carm.* 1. 2. 5.

341. exuit Hesperiam paribus . . . periclis: perhaps to be seen as a development of phrases like *exuo uinclis*: Virg. *A.* 2. 153 'exutas uinclis . . . palmas', Ov. *Met.* 7. 772f., *Eutr.* 1. 137 'soluit et exuto lucratur uincula collo', *c.m.* 18. 16; cf. also Sen. *Ep.* 104. 21 'si uelis uitiis exui'. For *Hesperiam* cf. 91 n. The sense of *paribus* is 'equal to ours' (i.e. the Gothic invasion), cueing the explicit comparison that ends the section on Marcus Aurelius and evaluates the relative merits of Marcus and Honorius (351–5).

Fortuna: for the prominence of Fortuna in *VI Cons.* see 1 *Fortunae Reduci* n. Attempting to reconcile this claim with the direct intervention of the Thunderer in 343 hardly seems worthwhile: Claudian is speaking very loosely and means no more than that Marcus was 'fortunate' and 'blessed by Heaven'. One might compare Dio's self-correction in introducing the same event: 72. 14 (8. 1) πόλεμος αὐτῷ συνέστη μέγας καὶ νίκη παράδοξος εὐτυχήθη, μᾶλλον δὲ παρὰ θεοῦ ἐδωρήθη.

342. laus ibi nulla ducum: i.e. the victory was not won by military skill. If the plural has any particular significance rather than merely generalizing, the reference may be to Marcus and Pertinax: see Birley, op. cit. (339–50 n.) 173.

flammeus imber: 'a shower of flame'. Cf. Lucr. 2. 215 (lightning) 'cadit in terras uis flammea', Prud. *Ham.* 729 (the destruction of Sodom) 'flagrantemque diem crepitans incenderet imber'. Seneca the philosopher notes that lightning 'quod urit, . . . igneum magis est quam flammeum' (*Nat.* 2. 40. 1), but in his capacity as a poet he could still write 'trisulco flammeam telo facem | per pectus hoc transmitte' (*Thy.* 1089f.). For the phrase cf. also Virg. *A.* 12. 284 (weapons) 'ferreus ingruit imber', Stat. *Theb.* 4. 729f., 7. 408 (portents) 'nunc sanguineus, nunc saxeus imber', Sil. 13. 181. The choice of adjective also helps set up a correspondence with Phaethon and his attempt to control the *flammea frena* of Sol's chariot (188f.); see also the following note.

343. dorso . . . fumante: recalling descriptions of other characters blasted by Jupiter for their hubristic attacks on Heaven or Heaven's favourites. See Ov. *Met.* 2. 324 (Phaethon) 'excipit Eridanus fumantiaque abluit ora', 325f., Stat. *Theb.* 10. 936 (Capaneus) 'pectora . . . fumantia', 12. 413f. 'Phaethonta . . . | fumantem', *Rapt.* 3. 350 'ipsius Enceladi fumantia gestat opima'.

344. ambustus sonipes: cf. *Culex* 128 'ambustus Phaethon'; also Virg. *A.* 3. 578 'Enceladi semustum fulmine corpus'. For *sonipes* see 240n.

344-6. The lightning bolt melts the weapons of the enemy. Claudian is reworking Silius' description of Jupiter driving Hannibal from the very gates of Rome: 12. 622ff. 'celsus summo de culmine montis | regnator superum sublata fulmina dextra | librauit clipeoque ducis, non cedere certi, | incussit; summa *liquefacta est cuspis* in hasta, | et *fluxit,* ceu correptus fornacibus, *ensis.*' The association of the Marcomanni and the Quadi with Hannibal exaggeratedly suggests that Rome itself was in danger from them, thus making the situation square better still with the danger recently presented by the Goths and by Alaric in particular. For Alaric and Hannibal see 182–4, 184–6nn. Once more, we see that all those who attack Rome are guilty of hubris.

The language used here is also reminiscent of Lucan's description of the portents that assailed the Roman armies on their way to the battle at Pharsalus: 7. 153ff. 'totus uenientibus obstitit aether | aduersasque faces inmensoque igne columnas | et trabibus mixtis auidos typhonas aquarum | detulit atque oculos ingesto fulgure clausit; | excussit cristas galeis capulosque solutis | perfudit gladiis ereptaque pila liquauit, | aetherioque nocens fumauit sulpure ferrum'.

344f. tabescente solutus | subsedit galea: the hapless soldier collapses in agony as his helmet fuses on his head. *solutus = membra solutus,* as Müller sees, but note how the metaphor ingeniously continues the literal sense of *tabescente.* More normally found of melting snow (Lucr. 6. 964; cf. Pl. *St.* 648 'quasi nix tabescit dies') or wax (Lucr. 6. 515f., Ov. *Ars* 2. 89), *tabesco* here is used of metal to striking effect.

345. liquefactaque fulgure cuspis: in addition to Sil. 12. 625, cit. 344–6n., cf. Cic. *Catil.* 3. 19 'compluris in Capitolio res de caelo esse percussas . . . et legum aera liquefacta', Tac. *Ann.* 15. 22. 2 'gymnasium ictu fulminis conflagrauit, effigiesque in eo Neronis ad informe aes liquefacta'.

346. canduit: 'glowed white hot'. Cf. Virg. *A.* 12. 90f. 'ensem quem Dauno ignipotens deus ipse parenti | fecerat et Stygia candentem tinxerat unda', Ov. *Met.* 9. 170f. 'gelido ceu quondam lammina candens | tincta lacu', Sil. 1. 171.

subitis: adverbial: see 231 *subitas* n.

fluxere: in addition to Sil. 12. 626 'fluxit . . . ensis' cf. *Stil.* 2. 177f. 'quantis fluerent fornacibus aera | effigies ductura tuas'.

347. contenta polo: = *contenta telis caelestibus* (i.e. bolts of lightning).

348. Chaldaea mago . . . carmina ritu: a reference either to Arnouphis the Egyptian (Dio 72. 14 Ἀρνοῦφίν τινα μάγον Αἰγύπτιον) or to Julian the Theurgist, the author of the 'Chaldaean' oracles: see 339–50 n. *Chaldaea* probably indicates that Claudian is thinking of Julianus, but a degree of caution is necessary. *Chaldaeus* had long been a generic term for astronomers (e.g. Gel. 1. 9. 6: see also 18 *Babylonia cura* n.) and distinctions between *Chaldaei* and *magi* were in any case not tightly made, as can be seen from Claudian himself. Consider e.g. *Ruf.* 1. 148f. 'qua gens Chaldaea uocatis | imperet arte deis', with Levy ad loc., *Stil.* 1. 59 ff. 'penetralibus ignem | sacratum rapuere adytis *ritu*que iuuencos | *Chaldaeo* strauere *magi*'. It is thus, to say the least, perfectly possible that Claudian is thinking of the (in any case commoner) version concerning Arnouphis. See, however, the persuasive arguments of Garth Fowden, *Historia*, 36 (1987), 83–95, esp. 90–4, who suggests that by the end of the fourth century Julianus had come to usurp the place of Arnouphis in pagan versions of the rain miracle, as part of the response to Christian propaganda on the issue: 'those pagans who occupied themselves with such matters are likely to have realized that neither talk about the piety of an emperor who had not even witnessed the miracle, nor a compromise rain-god dreamed up by civil servants, were going to make much of a dent in the assiduously propagated Christian version. Something more colourful and trendy was required, and the *Chaldaioi* fitted the bill perfectly' (p. 93). On the very minor role played by magic in Claudian's work in general see Harry L. Levy, *TAPhA* 79 (1948), 87–91.

349. reor: the verb is included by Cicero in a list of words that are 'inusitata . . . prisca fere ac uetusta', and freely used by both poets and orators (*de Orat.* 3. 153). But Quintilian thought it archaic, if still *tolerabile* (*Inst.* 8. 3. 26).

Tonantis: Jupiter, most likely (44 *Tonantis* n.), though see Introd., p. xx. In any case, the traditional epithet can hardly be said to be merely decorative here.

350. obsequium: for the quasi-paradox see also Luc. 5. 293f. 'licet omne deorum | obsequium speres', Sil. 3. 506, Val. Max. 1. 8. 2 'numen ipsius dei subsecutum uerba mortalium caelesti obsequio conprobauit'. The more usual state of affairs can be seen at e.g. Plin. *Ep. Tra.* 100 'quam (sc. benignitatem) super magnas plurimasque uirtutes praecipua sanctitate obsequio deorum honore meruisti'.

Marci mores potuere mereri: for Marcus's exemplary character

see 339–50 n. The sound effects (alliteration of *m*, the jingling double
-*er*- combined with coincidence of ictus and accent in the fifth and
sixth feet) give the section on the lightning miracle a resounding,
emphatic climax. Cf. *IV Cons.* 458 'quod longis alii bellis potuere
mereri', *Get.* 90.

351–5. Heaven would have intervened to save Rome from Alaric too, if
this had been necessary, but Stilicho's military prowess was sufficent
and the gods were unwilling to rob him of the glory. The adaptability
of the panegyrist to his circumstances can be measured once more by
comparing these lines to Claudian's treatment of the 'wind miracle' at
the battle of the Frigidus (cf. 339–50 n.). This battle took place in Sept.
394, the year in which Honorius had held his second consulship.
Claudian therefore attributes Theodosius' victory to his son's auspices
and the favour he found with heaven as well as to Theodosius'
military skills: *III Cons.* 87 ff. 'uictoria uelox | auspiciis effecta tuis. pug-
nastis uterque: | tu fatis genitorque manu', 96 ff. 'o nimium dilecte
deo, cui fundit ab antris | Aeolus armatas hiemes, cui militat aether |
et coniurati ueniunt ad classica uenti.' The miracle at the Frigidus
was, naturally enough, claimed by Christians for the Faith, while the
pagan sources on the battle in effect simply ignore the phenomenon
and imply that Eugenius lost through improvidence when his army
was taken unprepared by an attack at daybreak. The sources on both
sides are neatly gathered and evaluated by F. Paschoud in his edition
of Zosimus, ii (Paris, 1979), appendix C, pp. 474–500. See further
Cameron 217, who argues that despite the pagan language Claudian
is essentially following the official version of the Christian court.
Augustine, in his discussion of the battle at *De Ciuitate Dei* 5. 26, cites a
condensed version of *III Cons.* 96 ff., apparently taking it as evidence
that even our pagan poet accepted the reality of the miracle ('unde et
poeta Claudianus, quamuis a Christi nomine alienus, in eius tamen
laudibus dixit: O nimium dilecte Deo . . .').

351. Latio: probably = 'Italy', but see also 89 *Latium* n.

   desset: < *deesset.* The contracted forms are standard in verse: e.g.
Catul. 64. 151 'quam tibi fallaci supremo in tempore dessem', Ov. *Met.*
1. 292 'derant quoque litora ponto', Juv. 3. 303, *Eutr.* 1. 243 'et sentit
iam desse uiros'.

352. Aether: i.e. 'the gods.' For the metonymy see *OLD* s.v. 1c and cf.
Virg. *A.* 9. 24 'multa deos orans, onerauitque aethera uotis', Stat.
Theb. 9. 445, *III Cons.* 97 'cui militat aether', *IV Cons.* 170 ff. 'non
certius umquam | hortati superi, nullis praesentior aether | adfuit
ominibus', *Get.* 230, *Rapt.* 3. 201, *c.m.* 17. 35.

353. titulos: 'titles to fame', and so 'glory'. Cf. e.g. Stat. *Theb.* 3. 155 f.

'uos uteri fortuna mei, qua tangere diuos | rebar et Ogygias titulis anteire parentes?', *Silu.* 2. 7. 62 'castae titulum decusque Pollae', *Get.* 29, *c.m.* 30. 33 (Claudia, Penelope) 'non tamen audebunt titulis certare Serenae'. Contrast the literal sense at 373, 654.

354f. The phrase *meruit uirtus* balances the achievement of Marcus (350), and the virtue thus belongs to Honorius. The victory is, however, also owed to the efforts of Stilicho (*soceri sudore*), and Claudian thus combines his encomium of his honorand proper with praise of the general who actually led the campaign, and who was also his own real patron. Cf. the words spoken to Stilicho by Theodosius in the death-bed scene: *III Cons.* 144 ff. 'bellipotens Stilicho, cuius mihi robur in armis, | pace probata fides—quid enim per proelia gessi | te sine? quem merui te non sudante triumphum?'

354. sudore: for *sudor* in military contexts see Nisbet–Hubbard on Hor. *Carm.* 1. 15. 9f. 'quantus . . . | sudor.' The metonymical sense ('effort', 'exertion') is particularly frequent in Statius (Dewar on *Theb.* 9. 98) and Claudian: cf. *Gild.* 334 'Libyam nostro sudore receptam', *Eutr.* 2. 395, *IV Cons.* 343, *Get.* 537 'tot galeas multo Thracum sudore paraui'. The verb is used in the same way: e.g. *Gild.* 94f. 'in Bocchi regnum sudauit uterque | Scipio', *Nupt.* 111 'quae proelia sudas?', *IV Cons.* 525, *c.m.* 47. 12. Examples of this usage are absent from Virgil and Lucan, and first appear in Flavian epic (V. Fl. 5. 668, Sil. 3. 531).

355. ambirent . . . laurum: 'compete for | dispute the crown of laurel'. For the direct accusative cf. Pl. *Am.* 69 'siue qui ambissent palmam <his> histrionibus', 74 'quasi magistratum sibi alteriue ambiuerit'.

356–425. *The goddess Roma herself leaves her shrine and upbraids Honorius for neglecting her. She recalls the disappointment she suffered when he failed to come to the City to celebrate a triumph over Gildo, and claims the right to witness his presence within her walls as he marks his present victory over the Goths.*

Roma's *querellae* belong to an old rhetorical tradition that can be traced in the extant sources as far back as Cicero's spectacular denunciation of Catiline. Such prosopopoeia is explicitly characterized as a device of the elevated style ('grande atque robustum, quod ἁδρὸν dicunt', *Inst.* 12. 10. 58–61) by Quintilian. The step from high-style oratory to epic and panegyrical poetry is thus, in terms of genre, an entirely predictable one.

In Cicero's speech the orator sought to enhance the strength of his own invective by enlisting the aid of the goddess: *Catil.* 1. 17 ff. 'nunc te patria, quae communis est parens omnium nostrum, odit ac metuit . . .

quae tecum, Catilina, sic agit et quodam modo tacita loquitur: 'nullum iam aliquot annis facinus exstitit nisi per te, nullum flagitium sine te . . . haec si tecum ita ut dixi patria loquatur, nonne impetrare debeat, etiam si uim adhibere non possit?' In addition to the basic idea of the goddess delivering a speech of recrimination or complaint, note that Claudian and Cicero also share the insistence on Roma's status as the mother of her people, and above all the assumption that her entreaties should be successful (see further 362 *uestra parens*, 427 f. nn.). Lucan is no doubt subverting these conventions when he describes the appearance of the 'patriae trepidantis imago' to Caesar as he prepares to cross the Rubicon (1. 185 ff.); there the speech of the goddess is an ineffectual two lines or so long, while Caesar's more substantial refusal to heed her appeals to his loyalty to her serves to reveal the depths of his impious megalomania. In Claudian, by contrast, Roma is motivated not by fear or by hostility to her interlocutor but by love (361), and the dutiful Honorius willingly accedes to her request. In the meantime, however, he points out that on an earlier occasion he had sent his revered father-in-law Stilicho in his place (429–35). In this way it is suggested that her complaints are unjust, but only because a degree of injustice could perhaps be thought of as typical of a doting mother.

Roma also appears in texts closer to *VI Cons.* in both time and genre. In the field of prose panegyric Claudian may well have known *Pan. Lat.* 7. 10. 5–11. 4 Mynors (AD 307), an extended prosopopoeia in which the goddess herself pleads with Maximian to resume the throne which he had abdicated in 305. There too Roma is a suppliant, but one who has a complaint to make: 'supplices tibi manus tendens uel potius queribunda clamauit' (7. 10. 5). Her opening words are likewise very similar to the beginning of the present speech: with 362 f. cf. 'quousque hoc, Maximiane, patiar me quati, te quiescere; mihi libertatem adimi, te usurpare tibi inlicitam missionem?' (7. 11. 1). See also 427 f. n. Far more famous, though not so close to Claudian in structure, is Symmachus, *Relatio* 3. 9, where Roma is summoned up to plead with Gratian and Valentinian for the restoration of her traditional cults. See also Prudentius' riposte to this scene at *C. Symm.* 2. 649–773.

Claudian's Roma is thus so firmly grounded in the rhetorical tradition that we must treat with caution the claims of some scholars that she has for the poet a singular reality all her own. E. R. Curtius, for example, calls Roma and Natura in Claudian's poems 'actual divine powers, more real than the Gods of Olympus' (*European Literature and the Latin Middle Ages*, tr. W. R. Trask (Princeton, 1953), 104), and see also F. Paschoud, *Roma Aeterna* (Bibliotheca Helvetica Romana, 7; Rome, 1967), 152. Cameron is rightly sceptical: see pp. 274 f., 364 f., esp. 364 'she appears so frequently in Claudian, not because he was obsessed with her or worshipped her, but rather because she was dramatically the most appropriate figure to exhort Stilicho to save the East from Eutropius or Africa from Gildo or (above all) to officiate in a consular panegyric'. To this it should be added that her presence also contributes a degree of sublimity and epic majesty. As a result, she plays a starring role in Claudian's work, and is outshone only by Stilicho and Honorius. We find her flying to the Frigidus to ask Theodosius to make Olybrius and Probinus consuls (*Prob.* 73 ff.), and pleading with Jupiter on Olympus for relief from the famine which afflicts her as a result of Gildo's rebellion and the cutting of the corn supplies (*Gild.* 17 ff.). At *Eutr.* 1. 371 ff. she appeals directly to Honorius for vigorous opposition to Eutropius' consulship and its pollution of the *fasces*, and at *Stil.* 2. 223 ff. she can be seen making her way to Milan to persuade Stilicho finally to accept the consulship that is his due. See further Christiansen, 49 ff. In general, scenes involving her take the form of briefly sketched tableaux that provide the setting for long speeches of exhortation or encomium; her words thus serve dramatically to give authority to the propaganda of Claudian's panegyric. The demonstrated advantages of this technique appealed also to Sidonius Apollinaris, whose panegyrics are in general so heavily indebted to Claudian. Roma is a major figure in all three of his poems in praise of Emperors (*Carm.* 2 on Anthemius, 5 on Majorian, and 7 on Avitus), and indeed the vast bulk of *Carm.* 5 and 7 especially consists of exchanges of speeches between Roma and other deities (Africa, Jupiter), extending over hundreds of lines.

The present poem offers the very minimum of descriptive detail of the goddess's appearance (*uultus* . . . *coruscos,* 359) but a full description can be found at *Prob.* 84 ff.: compare also the still more luxuriant descriptions at Sid. *Carm.* 2. 387 ff., 5. 13 ff., and see further Rut. Nam. *Red.* 1. 117 f., Cor. *Laud. Iust.* 1. 288 ff. In general she appears as a warrior maiden, much like Minerva, wearing a helmet and carrying a spear, and with her arms and her right breast bare in the manner of an Amazon. Alternatively she may be shown wearing a crown of walls and turrets in the traditional manner of deified cities in art, with a sceptre and an orb rather than a spear, and enthroned in majesty. In all this the poets are very much in agreement with the countless representations of Roma in paintings, sculpture and, above all, on coins. A full discussion can be found in C. C. Vermeule, *The Goddess Roma in the Art of the Roman Empire* (Cambridge, Mass., 1959), *passim.* See further Roscher, iv. 130 ff., J. M. Toynbee, *JRS* 37 (1947), 135–44, R. Delbrueck, *Die Consulardiptychen und verwandte Denkmäler,* 2 vols. (Berlin, 1929), nos. 16, 22 f., 32, U. Knoche, 'Die Augusteische Ausprägung der Dea Roma', *Gymnasium,* 59 (1952),

COMMENTARY ON LINES 356-8

324–49, H. Stern, *Le Calendrier de 354: Étude sur son texte et ses illustrations*, Inst. Fr. d'arch. de Beyrouth: Bibl. archéol. et hist. 55 (Paris, 1953), pl. ii. 1, MacCormack, 177f., 210 with pls. 56 and 57, pp. 213, 227f. with pl. 57, Michele Renee Salzman, *On Roman Time. The Codex-Calendar of 354 and the Rhythms of Urban Life in Late Antiquity* (Berkeley and Los Angeles, 1990), 184, 259, Fig. 2.

356f. Senatorial ambassadors, that is, had on numerous occasions appealed to the Emperor to grace the City with his presence, only to be disappointed. Müller compares *Stil.* 3. 1f. 'quem populi plausu, procerum quem uoce petebas, | aspice, Roma, uirum', though it is not, strictly speaking, clear that ambassadors are meant there.

356. proceres: i.e. senators, a natural extension of the basic meaning of the word. It can perhaps be traced to Liv. 9. 18. 7 'aduersus eum nemo ex tot proceribus Romanis uocem liberam missurus fuerit', where the context imagined seems to be of hypothetical opposition to Alexander in the Senate. Indisputable examples include Luc. 2. 279, 5. 9f. 'peregrina ac sordida sedes | Romanos cepit proceres', Stat. *Silu.* 4. 2. 32 'Romuleos proceres' with Coleman ad loc., *IV Cons.* 579, and (sarcastically, of the Senate of Constantinople) *Eutr.* 1. 471, 2. 136. In the present poem, the word certainly has this sense at 594, and probably at 556. The tone is elevated and poetic rather than official, and the term is therefore useful in epic as a way of designating various constitutional or semi-constitutional bodies in a dignified manner: Juvenal, for example, uses it of Domitian's *consilium principis* at 4. 144f. 'surgitur et misso proceres exire iubentur | consilio'.

356f. responsa . . . rettulerant: cf. Virg. *A.* 11. 226f. 'ecce super maesti magna Diomedis ab urbe | legati responsa ferunt', V. Fl. 5. 547, Sil. 11. 120f.

357f. differri . . . communes non passa preces: i.e., by extension, not enduring that the *fulfilment* of the prayers of all the citizens should be put off any longer. For the reproving tone cf. e.g. Cic. *Red. Sen.* 12 'non solum ciuium lacrimas, uerum etiam patriae preces repudiauit'.

357. urbis: Barth proposes *orbis*, but Roma is only concerned here with the City.

358. penetralibus altis: Claudian is undoubtedly thinking of the great temple of Venus and Rome (or 'Templum Vrbis') on the Velia, only a little below the spot on the Palatine where the poem was delivered. Cf. *Stil.* 2. 227f. 'conueniunt ad tecta deae, quae candida lucent | monte Palatino', Prud. *C. Symm.* 1. 218ff. This magnificent building with its double-cella was built by Hadrian and consecrated in AD 135 to Venus Felix and Roma Aeterna. After serious damage by fire in 283, it was reconstructed under Maxentius (305–11). It was not only the chief cult site of Roma in the capital, but also, at 66 m by 136 m, the largest temple in the entire city. Its vast ruins still dominate the Forum, and in Claudian's time it must have been very imposing indeed. Apollodorus, however, criticized it for being set too low and thus looking squat. See further *RE* viii A. 870. 54 ff., J. B. Ward-Perkins, *Roman Imperial Architecture* (Harmondsworth, 1970), 122 f., 421, Richardson 409 ff. For the line-ending cf. Virg. *A.* 7. 59 'laurus erat tecti medio in penetralibus altis', Stat. *Theb.* 5. 313, 10. 104.

359. prosiluit: Roma springs vigorously into action. Cf. *Ruf.* 1. 129, *Rapt.* 3. 112 f. (Ceres after her dream of Proserpina in torment) 'penetralibus amens | prosilit'.

uultus . . . coruscos: imitated by Dracontius, *Rom.* 2. 6 f. 'mater deuota coruscos | indulget uultus.' Note also Prud. *Tit. Hist.* 29 'Deus igneus ore corusco.' Shining faces or eyes are characteristic of deities (*Il.* 3. 397 (Aphrodite) ὄμματα μαρμαίροντα, Virg. *A.* 1. 228 (Venus) 'oculos . . . nitentis', Ov. *Met.* 15. 674 (Aesculapius) 'oculos circumtulit igne micantes', Sid. *Carm.* 22. 72, Boeth. *Cons. Phil.* 1. 1). This is no doubt because they signal beauty and youth; Tib. 1. 8. 31 'iuuenis, cui leuia fulgent ora', Ov. *Met.* 1. 498 f., Stat. *Theb.* 9. 701 f. 'radiis . . . trementes | dulce nitent uisus'.

palam confessa: Honorius is vouchsafed a full epiphany: compare Roma's appearance to Stilicho at *Stil.* 2. 275 ff. For the phrasing cf. Virg. *A.* 2. 591 f. 'alma parens, confessa deam qualisque uideri | caelicolis et quanta solet', Ov. *Met.* 12. 601 (Apollo) 'fassus . . . deum' with Bömer ad loc., Stat. *Theb.* 2. 122. Contrast the rather less mannered use of the plain reflexive at Ov. *Met.* 3. 1 f. 'iamque deus posita fallacis imagine tauri | se confessus erat', Stat. *Theb.* 7. 771.

360. inpulit . . . cunctantem: the participle picks up *morantis* (356). Cf. *Stil.* 2. 284 f. (Roma to Stilicho) 'quae iam causa morae? quo me cunctabere rursus | ingenio?' The primary sense of *inpulit* here is 'urged him on', i.e. to a particular action, as at Virg. *A.* 4. 22 f. 'solus hic inflexit sensus animumque labantem | inpulit.' One is also reminded in the context of the common use of the word to describe sounds 'striking' the ear: e.g. Virg. *G.* 4. 349 f. 'iterum maternas inpulit auris | luctus Aristaei', Stat. *Theb.* 5. 554 f.

querellis: picked up in her own words with *queror* (362) and in Honorius' reply (429). This is her favoured mode of rhetoric: see 356–425 n., citing *Pan. Lat.* 7. 10. 5 Mynors, and cf. *Gild.* 27 'tales orditur maesta querellas', *Stil.* 2. 278 'tum prior attonitum gratis adfata querellis'. *querella* is practically a technical term for rhetorical complaints, as can be seen at e.g. Cic. *Top.* 86 'quo ex genere sunt querellae, incitationes, miserationesque flebiles', *de Orat.* 3. 106. In certain circumstances it can also function as a legal term: see Mayer on Luc. 8. 512. For the philologist the correct spelling of the word is *querela*, this being what LHS i. 312 call a *deverbativum nomen rei actae*; but Roman grammarians regularly misinterpreted it as a diminutive form and many poets, following their lead, wrote *querella*.

361–425. The second of the three great speeches dominating the central portion of the poem. At sixty-five lines it is neatly balanced by Honorius' reply, which extends over sixty-seven (427–93). The goddess's *querellae* are intended to have an exhortatory effect, aimed as they are at securing Honorius' commitment to visit the City. This is mirrored in the structure of the speech, which falls into three sections of roughly equal length. The first records her past grievance (there was no visit and triumph to mark the defeat of Gildo: 361–83), and the second her present one (why has Honorius not yet come to celebrate a legitimate triumph for the recent victory over the Goths, and so wipe out the sorrows of the last hundred years, marked as they were only by rare visits and melancholy celebrations for civil wars?: 383–406). This second section is already moving by its end to exhortation (*restituat* 403; *iam redde . . . absolue* 405 f.); the third (407–25), conversely, begins by re-echoing the complaints that began the speech (*quem . . . ad finem* 407), picks up the *quonam usque* of 362, but goes on to give reasons that justify Honorius' presence in Rome in more general terms. The world can indeed, the goddess claims, be safely ruled from the City, as it was in the glory days under the 'adoptive' Emperors. The basic internal structure of the first two sections is effectively identical, each beginning with a brief statement (361 f.; 383) followed by a number of rhetorical questions (362–8; 384–6), and then proceeding to offer the main body of the argument. The third section, while broadly similar, is more complex; see further 407–25 n.

361. dissimulata: 'ignored'. For this sense see *TLL* v/1. 1483. 32 ff., *OLD* s.v. 3, and cf. Ov. *Pont.* 1. 2. 145 f. 'sed de me ut sileam, coniunx mea sarcina uestra est: | non potes hanc salua dissimulare fide', Petr. 103. 6, Quint. *Inst.* 5. 13. 9 'quod defendi non possit, silentio dissimulandum', Stat. *Theb.* 8. 695 f., 9. 203, 12. 287.

Müller took *dissimulata* closely with *uestra parens*, understanding it to mean that Roma's status as 'mother' had long been denied or that she had been effectively 'disowned'. This is very tempting and may indeed be right, but entails the interlacing of *dissimulata uestra parens* and *tristes in amore repulsas queror*; it therefore seems more natural to take *dissimulata diu* by itself and *uestra parens* in apposition to the implied subject *ego* of *queror*. An alternative, but much less plausible, interpretation of the participle is implied by Platnauer's translation 'too long . . .

have I, thy mother, borne in silence the hurt thy refusal to return hath done me', in which *dissimulata* governs *tristes . . . repulsas*; we should then have a rather strained example of the 'retained' accusative (see 153 *resoluta comam* n.). One might compare Ov. *Ars* 1. 689f. 'Achilles | ueste uirum longa dissimulatus erat': see Hollis ad loc. Given that this is an epiphany, it is also just possible that Claudian is thinking of such phrases as 'dissimulata deam' (Ov. *Fast.* 6. 507, Stat. *Silu.* 1. 2. 14). The sense of *dissimulare* would then be roughly 'turn a blind eye to', as at e.g. Liv. 39. 47. 9 'multa et dissimulare et obliuisci et pati praeterita senatum posse'. One last possibility is to accept this sense of *dissimulata*, but take the participle to be used absolutely with middle force (cf. Ov. *Ibis* 349f. 'quaeque sui uenerem iunxit cum fratre mariti | Locris in ancillae dissimulata nece'), *tristes in amore repulsas* being governed by *queror*.

tristes in amore repulsas: the language of elegy: 'mother' Roma sometimes sounds more like a querulous mistress, and her speech almost like a reverse παρακλαυσίθυρον as she metaphorically throws the doors open and entreats the lover to enter. For *repulsa* cf. Prop. 1. 3. 43f. 'interdum leuiter mecum deserta querebar | externo saepe in amore moras', 3. 14. 26 'longae nulla repulsa morae', Ov. *Am.* 1. 8. 76, *Met.* 3. 395. See further 365 *torquebit*, 368 *duras . . . aures* nn.

362. uestra parens: 'quia est patria parens omnium nostrum' (Cic. *de Orat.* 1. 196). Cf. 397, and see also 428 *legum . . . matri* n. Examples are legion, but note esp. Cic. *Catil.* 1. 17 (cit. 356–425n.), *Att.* 9. 9. 2, Var. *Men.* 235 'si qui patriam, maiorem parentem, extinguit, in eo est culpa', *Get.* 52 'ueneranda parens', *Stil.* 3. 175f., Prud. *C. Symm.* 1. 415f. (Theodosius to Roma) 'exue tristes, | fida parens, habitus!' Roma is, moreover, the mother of the whole world: e.g. Flor. *Epit.* 2. 6. 5, *Stil.* 3. 150ff. 'haec est in gremium uictos quae sola recepit | humanumque genus communi nomine fouit | matris, non dominae ritu', Rut. Nam. *Red.* 1. 49 (Roma, usurping the epic title of Jupiter) 'genetrix hominum genetrixque deorum'.

362–5. While the usual residence of the Court had for a number of years been Milan, in 402 Honorius moved for greater safety to Ravenna, guarded by its marshes: this is where Roma now accosts him (cf. 494 *antiquae muros egressa Rauennae*).

362. quonam usque: a regular phrase in *querellae*, found also at *Ruf.* 2. 88, *Gild.* 368, *Nupt.* 20f. 'quonam usque uerendus | cunctatur mea uota socer?', *Eutr.* 2. 391. Claudian may have acquired his fondness for it from his reading of Statius; see *Theb.* 1. 215, 9. 511f. 'quonam miseros, sator inclute diuum, | Inachidas, quonam usque premes?', *Ach.* 1. 624, 638, *Silu.* 1. 2. 162. Such phrases belong traditionally to prayers from mortals to deities: cf. e.g. Ps. 13: 1 'How long wilt thou forget me, O Lord, for ever; how long wilt thou hide thy face from me?' and see T. Jacobsen, *The Treasure of Darkness* (New York, 1976), 102 for Mesopotamian parallels. At Virg. *A.* 1. 241 'quem das finem, rex magne, laborum?' we have one god interceding to another on behalf of mortals; here the usage is even more pointed, since a mighty goddess is imploring an earthly deity for herself.

363. mea uota: concrete (= 'the thing I pray for'). Cf. Plin. *Nat.* 9. 140 'uotumque factum e uitio portentosis ingeniis', *III Cons.* 10 (of Honorius) 'spes uotumque poli'.

Ligus: collective singular, and with the inhabitant(s) doing duty for the name of the country. Cf. 193, 288, 443, though here the reference is more precise; Claudian means Milan, the seat of the Imperial court, and since AD 300 the capital of the province of Liguria (cf. *IV Cons.* 567, *Nupt.* 180, *Get.* 554). In Late Antiquity the boundaries of this province extended considerably further than the strip of coast around Genoa to which the name is now applied. Milan (*Mediolanum*) cannot be named directly in hexameter verse because of its string of three initial short syllables.

363–5. The general sense will be clearer for the reader if the word order is rearranged as follows: '(et quonam usque) Rubicon, discernens gaudia spatiis paruis, torquebit uicino numine Thybrim uetitum propinqua luce frui?' The Tiber, as so often, stands in for Rome, as perhaps the Rubicon does for Ravenna; whichever modern river the Rubicon should be identified with, it entered the sea only some 30 to 35 km south of the new capital. The point is that, though the Court and the Emperor have moved further south and closer to Rome, this near-presence is still an absence. Indeed it is a torment, because the Tiber is prevented from taking pleasure in the divine light of the Emperor's presence even though it is near (*uetitum . . . propinqua luce frui*), and the Rubicon, cutting Rome off from what would give her joy by only a small distance (*spatiis discernens gaudia paruis*), tortures her with the nearness of a godhead that is still inaccessible (*torquebit . . . uicino numine*).

364. luce: see 18–23, esp. 23 *imperii sidus* n.

spatiis discernens gaudia paruis: for *discerno* of barriers of water cf. Catul. 64. 178f. 'Idaeosne petam montes? at gurgite lato | discernens ponti truculentum diuidit aequor', Sal. *Iug.* 79. 3, *Prob.* 227f. 'urbes | discretas subeunte freto'. For the phrasing cf. also Tac. *Hist.* 4. 46 'modicis inter se spatiis discretos', *Ruf.* 2. 172 'nec multo spatii distantibus aequore uallis'. *gaudia* is concrete and refers to Honorius, so balancing *uota* (363).

365. torquebit: 'torment' with jealousy. The language recalls love elegy; Tib. 1. 4. 81 'eheu, quam Marathus lento me torquet amore', Prop. 3. 17. 11 'semper enim uacuos nox sobria torquet amantis', Ov. *Ars* 2. 124. Cf. *Stil.* 3. 4f., where, on the general's arrival in Rome, the poet declares to the City 'non dubiis ultra torquebere uotis. | totus adest oculis, aderat qui mentibus olim'.

    Rubicon: so too a palace official at Ravenna is hailed as 'Rubiconis amoeni | incola' (*c.m.* 19. 1f.). Müller suggests that Claudian is also alluding to Roma's appearance to Caesar 'parui Rubiconis ad undas' at Luc. 1. 185f.

    uicino numine: providing a far better balance with *propinqua luce* than *uicino nomine* could. Moreover, the *numina* of the Emperor and the City should be united; thanks, dramatically, to the intervention of Roma here the New Year will be *urbis et Augusti geminato numine felix* (17). See 17 *numine* n. for the divine power of the Emperor and for the manuscript confusion.

    Thybrim: see 12 *Thybris* n.

366-83. For the war against Gildo see 101-21 n. It is not inherently improbable that plans were indeed made for a triumph in Rome itself (in her capacity as τὴν μητρόπολιν τῶν τροπαίων, in the words of Themistius, *Or.* 3. 42 B), especially since the City was, through the cutting of the corn supply, put in particular danger by the war. There seems, however, to be no evidence to this effect other than what Roma is made to say here, and that could, of course, be pure fantasy. Even so, there must surely have been some kind of victory celebration at the court in Milan, as is implied by *Stil.* 1. 3ff. In Rome statues were erected in honour of both Honorius and Stilicho in the Forum, and some kind of victory monument apparently commemorated, quite untruthfully, the *concordia* of the Eastern and Western courts in the conduct of the campaign. The relevant inscriptions survive (*CIL* vi. 1187, 1730, and 31256), and, perhaps predictably enough, their language is in places close to Claudian's: see 366f. *reddita bellis | Africa*, 373 *defensam ... Libyam* nn. See further Cameron, 114f., McCormick 51, 117.

366f. These lines are picked up directly and pointedly refuted by Honorius at 429–33; far from spurning (*spreuisse | spreuimus*) her on that occasion, he did Roma the signal honour of sending her Stilicho in his place.

366f. reddita bellis | Africa: sc. *imperio, Italiae.* Cf. *Stil.* 1. 18f. 'Latio quod reddita seruit | Africa'. *CIL* vi. 1187 'senatus populusque Romanus uindicata rebellione et Africae restitutione laetus.' The phrase *Libyam recipere* is also found, in various forms, at *Stil.* 1. 378, 2. 385, *Get. pr.* 5.

367. uenturi lusit spe principis urbem: compare the scene described at *Stil.* 2. 397ff. 'quae tum Flaminiam stipabunt milia uulgi! | fallax o quotiens puluis deludet amorem | suspensum, ueniens omni dum crederis hora!' For the phrasing cf. also Virg. *A.* 1. 352 'multa malus simulans uana spe lusit *amantem*', V. Fl. 3. 555, Ov. *Fast.* 3. 685 f.

368. duras . . . aures: i.e. 'unresponsive', with an overtone of 'cruel'. We recall in particular Dido: Virg. *A.* 4. 428 'cur mea dicta negat duras demittere in auris?' The collocation may, however, be traced back to Terence if we supply *aures* at *Haut.* 402 'diu etiam duras dabit': see *TLL* v/1. 2308. 28ff. Cf. also Ov. *Pont.* 2. 8. 44 'accipe non dura supplicis aure preces', Luc. 10. 104, Sil. 6. 519; at Gel. 13. 25. 22 'durae auris hominibus' the sense is 'insensitive', 'cloth-eared'. One might also see here a kind of reversal of situations such as the παρακλαυσίθυρον, with the *dura puella* replaced by one eager to admit an *amator* who, conversely, is imagined as unwilling to visit her: contrast e.g. Tib. 2. 6. 28 'dura puella', Prop. 2. 22. 43 'aut si es dura, nega; sin es non dura, uenito!', Hor. *Carm.* 3. 7. 31 f. 'et te saepe uocanti | duram difficilis mane'.

   permouimus: cf. Cic. *Ver.* 4. 66 'ubi uidet eum nihilo magis minis quam precibus permoueri.' The compound is fairly rare in verse, but cf. Sil. 3. 53, Stat. *Theb.* 7. 501, 12. 589.

369 f. Roma claims she was already preparing a triumphal chariot for him, drawn by white horses. Though the conservatism of Latin poetry is such that the word *currus* continues to be used (377 n.), by the fourth century the *triumphator's* traditional chariot (a *quadriga*) had been replaced by the *carpentum*. This was a low-slung four-wheeled vehicle, on which the *triumphator* sat enthroned; see McCormick 87, and also fig. 1 (p. 38) where, in a panel from the Arch of Constantine, the Emperor is clearly shown entering the City on a *carpentum* drawn by four horses.

369. ast: in early Latin *ast* functions as a continuative particle, employed primarily in conditional clauses with the sense 'but if'; the Augustans, however, simply used it as an archaic alternative to *at*. It is virtually always followed by pronouns and interrogatives beginning with a vowel (*ast ego, ast ille, ast ipse, ast alius, ast ubi*), and only rarely by nouns (Virg. *A.* 10. 173 'ast Ilua', 11. 293 'ast armis'), adverbs (V. Fl. 8. 255 'ast inde', Sil. 12. 471 'ast aeque'), prepositions (Virg. *A.* 10. 743 'ast de me', V. Fl. 8. 363 'ast inter') or by an initial consonant (Virg. *A.* 10. 743, Ov. *Met.* 7. 241 'ast laeua parte', Stat. *Theb.* 2. 668 'ast tamen', Sil. 11. 190 'ast delecta'). Claudian's usage is impeccably classical, all eight of his examples being followed by *ego* (*Rapt.* 1. 109, *Gild.* 114), *ille, alius*, or *ubi*. See further F. Leo, *Senecae Tragoediae* (Berlin, 1878; repr. 1963), i. 214ff.,

A. E. Housman, *Classical Papers*, ed. J. Diggle and F. R. D. Goodyear (Cambridge, 1972) iii. 1229, Fordyce on Virg. *A.* 7. 308, Skutsch on Enn. *Ann.* 93 (arguing that Ennius pioneered this usage), Harrison on Virg. *A.* 10. 173, *LHS* ii. 489.

geminos: a decidedly unusual detail, given that four was the near-universal number, as seen regularly in both art (e.g. the Arch of Constantine, 369f. n. above) and literature (e.g. Pl. *As.* 279 'quadrigis albis', Ov. *Tr.* 4. 2. 54). Servius states bluntly 'qui autem triumphat, albis equis utitur quattuor' (on Virg. *A.* 4. 543), and Claudian is well aware of this practice (*Get.* 127, cit. 370 *electi candoris* n.).

quibus altior ires: for all to see his glory. Cf. Ov. *Tr.* 4. 2. 47f. 'hos super in curru, Caesar, uictore ueheris | purpureus populi rite per ora tui', *IV Cons.* 566ff. (a consular rather than a triumphal procession) 'cum . . . per Ligurum populos *solito conspectior ires* | atque inter niueas *alte* ueherere cohortes'. For the line-ending cf. Virg. *A.* 8. 162f. 'sed cunctis altior ibat | Anchises', *Ruf.* 2. 344.

370. electi candoris: in the Orient white horses were associated from very early times with gods and kings, especially Zeus and the Sun-god: see Weinstock, 68ff. Though it is not quite clear when such iconography entered Italy, Virgil is no doubt drawing on a very old tradition at *A.* 3. 537f. (Aeneas' first sighting of Italy) 'quattuor hic, primum omen, equos in gramine uidi | tondentis campum late, candore niuali'; on this passage Weinstock 68, comments 'an omen of the coming wars and of their successful end, but also probably of his right to a chariot.' Similarly, Suetonius records (*Aug.* 94. 6) that Augustus' father Octavius was said to have dreamed that he saw his son with the attributes of the Sun (as well as of Jupiter), namely a radiate crown and a triumphal chariot drawn by, not four, but twelve white horses (presumably one for each sign of the Zodiac). Since the *triumphator* was regarded as a manifestation of the divine power of Jupiter, it is hardly surprising that white horses came to be used to draw his chariot in the triumphal procession. The first surely attested historical instance of this practice is Caesar's quadruple triumph of 46 BC, but such texts as Pl. *As.* 279 'quadrigis albis' and Hor. *S.* 1. 7. 8 'Barros ut equis praecurreret albis' perhaps suggest that it is older still. In his own day Caesar was thought to be following the example of Camillus after the conquest of Veii in 396 BC: see in general Weinstock 71ff. Augustan authors freely project the practice back further still, Ovid to the triumph of A. Postumius Tubertus, dictator in 431 BC, over the Aequi and Volsci (*Fast.* 6. 723f.), and Propertius all the way back to Romulus (4. 1. 32). Cf. also Tib. 1. 7. 8, Ov. *Ars* 1. 214, *Pont.* 2. 8. 50, *Stil.* 2. 369f. (Mars in triumph) 'candentibus urbem | ingreditur trabeatus equis', 3.

20, *Get.* 127 (Paulus and Marius) 'qui captos niueis reges egere quadrigis.' For *candoris* see further 476 n., and, in addition to Virg. *A.* 3. 538, *Stil.* 2. 369, cf. V. Fl. 6. 206 (equorum) 'candore notato'.

370f. nominis arcum . . . tui: = 'arcum triumphalem nomini tuo dedicandum', Gesner. No such arch commemorating the defeat of Gildo is attested elsewhere, and it may very well be no more than the product of Claudian's encomiastic fantasy. Alternatively, this reference could be taken as a graceful allusion to the Arcus Arcadii Honorii et Theodosii, dedicated by the Senate in celebration of the victory, not over Gildo, but over the Goths. This arch is believed to have been the last erected in the capital in ancient times. Its precise location is obscure, but it stood very close to the Arcus Gratiani Valentiniani et Theodosii (constructed AD 379–83), which in its turn commanded the approach to the Pons Aelius (Ponte Sant'Angelo). The Arcus Arcadii Honorii et Theodosii would appear to have been still standing in the early 15th c.: see further Platner (45 *Tarpeia rupe* n.), 359, McCormick p. 118, and Richardson 23, 26. Though nothing remains of the arch itself, the inscription is preserved (*CIL* vi. 1196 = Dessau, *ILS* 798): 'imppp. clementissimis felicissimis toto orbe uictoribus, ddd. nn[n]. Arcadio Honorio Theodosio Auggg. ad perenne indicium triumpho[rum], quod Getarum nationem in omne aeuum doc[u]ere exti[ngui], arcum simulacris eorum tropaeisq. decora[tum] s. p. q. R. totius operis splendore.' The date and circumstances of the construction are not clear from this inscription, and scholars accordingly manifest a degree of confusion. Platner offers the date 403, thus implying that it commemorated the victories at Pollentia and Verona. Dessau, on the other hand, declares 'pertinet titulus ad victoriam a. 405 a Stilichone de Radagaiso reportatam', and Richardson confuses the two wars in his statement that it was 'erected by the senate after the victory of Stilicho at Pollentia in AD 405' (p. 23: for the dating of Radagaisus' defeats to 406 see Matthews 274). The language of the inscription, though conventional, is tantalizingly similar to that of *VI Cons.*, which could be taken as evidence in favour of an association with the victories over Alaric rather than that over Radagaisus: with 'ad perenne indicium triumpho[rum]' cf. *titulo . . . perenni* (373) and 'Getarum nationem in omne aeuum . . . exti[ngui]' with the whole tenor of 201 ff., 250 ff., 303 ff.

If the arch had already been finished by the time that Honorius arrived, one might have expected him to proceed in triumph under it. Claudian's description of the combined *aduentus* and triumphal procession, however, seems to envisage a descent along the Via Flaminia, then through the Campus Martius by the Via Lata to the Forum

(543 ff.: see also McCormick 86). It is not easy to see how such a route could be made to include the Arcus Arcadii Honorii et Theodosii except by means of a long detour to the west. If the arch in question did indeed commemorate Pollentia and Verona, then perhaps it was thought too difficult to stretch the route so as to include it; alternatively, it is quite possible that it was simply not yet complete.

371 f. radiante decorus . . . toga: i.e. the *toga picta*. This garment properly belonged to the *triumphator*, though its use had been extended greatly under the Empire and it was regularly worn by the Emperor on various formal occasions. By Claudian's time it was 'especially associated with the consuls, Imperial or otherwise, who [wore] it when entering office or presiding at the games' (Roberts 111). See also 4 *trabeis* n. Claudian offers two luxuriant descriptions of such garments, at *IV Cons.* 585 ff. and *Stil.* 2. 339 ff. *radiante* hints at the gold and jewels with which the *toga picta* was encrusted: cf. *Stil.* 2. 89 'gemmatas . . . togas', *VI Cons.* 561. For the phrasing cf. Ov. *Fast.* 2. 503 f. 'trabeaque decorus | Romulus'; also Sil. 2. 166 'radiantis tegmina laenae'.

373. defensam . . . Libyam: i.e. against Gildo. The phrase recalls the dedication on the base of Honorius' statue: *CIL* vi. 31256 'armipotens Libycum defendit Honorius [orbem].' Cf. also *Stil.* 3. 13 (Stilicho) 'defensor Libyae'.

titulo . . . testata perenni: the standard language used of commemorative inscriptions. Cf. esp. Cic. *Diu.* 1. 87 'clarissimis monumentis testata consignataque antiquitas', Suet. *Iul.* 54. 1, Stat. *Theb.* 6. 127 f. 'titulisque pios testantur honores | gentis quisque suae', Tac. *Ann.* 11. 10; and for the epithet Hor. *Carm.* 3. 30. 1 'monumentum aere perennius', Ov. *Fast.* 2. 265, *Ibis* 7 f. 'perennem | candoris titulum'.

374–80. Floats bearing artistic representations of the battles fought and, more particularly, of the cities, mountains, and rivers of conquered lands were regularly carried in triumphal processions. They could be very elaborate: Josephus, *BJ* 7. 132 ff., esp. 139 ff., describes tableaux three or four storeys high being carried at the Judaean triumph of Vespasian and Titus. Various materials could be used, including metal, ivory, and painted wood, hence the joke recorded at Quint. *Inst.* 6. 3. 61 'Chrysippus, cum in triumpho Caesaris eborea oppida essent translata, et post dies paucos Fabii Maximi lignea, thecas esse oppidorum Caesaris dixit.' Roma's missed triumph would have featured representations of the Roman fleet on its way to Africa, the towns of Africa, the river or lake Triton, and Mt. Atlas; the materials are conceived of as costly metals (*caelata metallo*, 375; *auratum*, 376; *aere*, 379). It would thus have been very similar to the multiple triumph which Stilicho might have celebrated, says Claudian, if he had not preferred the labour to its rewards; *Stil.* 3. 22 ff. 'hi facta metallo | oppida uel montes captiuaque flumina ferrent. | hinc Libyci fractis lugerent cornibus amnes; | inde catenato gemeret Germania Rheno'. For such *simulacra* cf. also Cic. *Pis.* 60, Liv. 26. 21. 7 'cum simulacro captarum Syracusarum' (borne in the triumph of Marcellus), 37. 59. 3, Prop. 2. 1. 31 f., Ov. *Ars* 1. 219 ff. 'atque aliqua ex illis cum regum nomina quaeret, | quae loca, qui montes quaeue ferantur aquae . . .' (esp. 223 f. 'Euphrates, praecinctus harundine frontem; | cui coma dependet caerula, Tigris erit', with which compare Triton in 378), *Pont.* 3. 4. 105 ff., Vell. 1. 9. 6, Plin. *Nat.* 5. 36, Tac. *Ann.* 2. 41 (Germanicus' German triumph, AD 17) 'uecta spolia captiui simulacra montium fluminum proeliorum', App. *BC* 2. 101. For the continuance of this custom in Late Antiquity see e.g. Pac. *Pan. Theod.* 47. 3, McCormick 87. Conversely, Sidonius imagines Bacchus leading the 'real' river-god Ganges in triumph after his Eastern victories (*Carm.* 22. 41 ff.).

374. iamque: picking up *iam molita* (371), with the anaphora stressing that preparations were well under way when Roma suffered her disappointment.

pompae simulacra futurae: cf. Sil. 7. 119 'pugnaeque agitat simulacra futurae'.

375. Tarpeio . . . Ioui: *Tarpeio = Capitolino.* See 45 *Tarpeia . . . rupe* n. and cf. Ov. *Fast.* 6. 34, *c.m.* 4. 4 'Tarpeio referunt quos pia uota Ioui.' This particular collocation is far less common in verse than *Tarpeius pater/parens* (e.g. Prop. 4. 1. 7, Sil. 4. 48, Stat. *Silu.* 4. 3. 161) and *Tarpeius Tonans* (Ov. *Pont.* 2. 2. 42, Sil. 4. 548, Mart. 9. 86. 7, *CIL* xiv. 2852).

375 f. We should probably imagine this as a representation of the Roman fleet sailing to Africa (cf. *Gild.* 504 ff.), cast in silver or bronze, with the waves picked out in gold. Claudian alludes to the battle of Actium on Aeneas' shield: Virg. *A.* 8. 675 ff. 'in medio classis aeratas, Actia bella, | cernere erat, totumque instructo Marte uideres | feruere Leucaten *auro*que effulgere *fluctus*'. The Gildonic war is thus majestically associated with the centrepiece of the *Aeneid*'s panegyric and with the defining battle of Roman history.

375. caelata metallo: for *caelo* see 46 *caelatasque fores* n. The phrasing recalls several other epic ecphraseis of artistic works: cf. Virg. *A.* 1. 640 f. 'caelataque in auro | fortia facta parentum', 8. 700 f. 'saeuit medio in certamine Mauors | caelatus ferro', 10. 499, Ov. *Met.* 5. 188 f., *Stil.* 3. 22 f.

376. auratum . . . fluctum: in addition to Virg. *A.* 8. 677, cit. 375 f.n., cf. *Rapt.* 2. 34 f. (Diana's tunic) 'motoque in stamine Delos | errat et aurato trahitur circumflua ponto', and Man. 4. 515 (Laniger/Aries) 'uitreum findens aurauit uellere pontum'.

sulcaret: a very old metaphor, deriving ultimately from the Homeric τέμνειν. See Nisbet–Hubbard on Hor. *Carm.* 1. 1. 14 'pauidus nauta secet mare', citing *Od.* 3. 174 f., Harrison on *A.* 10. 222 'innabant pariter fluctusque secabant'; add *A.* 5. 158, 10. 197, Ov. *Met.* 4. 706 f., Sil. 7. 411, 15. 239. *aro* is sometimes used in the same kind of way: see Cic. *Arat.* 373 (129) 'naues . . . rostro Neptunia prata secantes', Virg. *A.* 2. 780 'uastum maris aequor arandum' with Austin ad loc.

377. Massyla: as at e.g. *IV Cons.* 25, *Gild.* 284, and used as a poetic variant for 'African' in the same way as *Maurusius* (104 n.) and *Maurus* (122).

currus: for the *carpentum* (see 369 f. n.): cf. 396, 551, 579, Prud. *C. Symm.* 2. 731 'scande triumphalem currum'. Prose authors can be blunter: contrast Amm. Marc. 16. 10. 6 (Constantius' entry into Rome, AD 357) 'insidebat aureo solus ipse carpento'.

378. Triton was the name of both a river and a lake, or marsh, in north Africa, and it is not quite clear which Claudian means here. The general description is perhaps better suited to a river (cf. Ov. *Ars* 1. 223 'Euphrates, praecinctus harundine frontem', *Pont.* 3. 4. 107 f. 'squalidus inmissos fracta sub harundine crines | Rhenus', both of *simulacra* carried in triumphs). *Palladia*, however, alludes to a learned legend about the birth of Athena, according to which she either was born from the waters of Triton or else first alighted there after she sprang from her father's head: in the sources Claudian seems to have known best the lake, and not the river, is specified (Luc. 9. 347 ff., Sil. 3. 322 f.: cf. Mela 1. 36 'ingens palus amnem Tritona recipit, unde et Mineruae cognomen inditum est, ut incolae arbitrantur, ibi genitae'). Claudian alludes to this myth at *IV Cons.* 36 'uirgineum Tritona bibit'.

comas innexus harundine: for reeds as a characteristic of river-gods see 162–4 n. The construction ('retained' accusative after a past participle with passive sense) is discussed at 153 *resoluta comam* n. Compounds of *necto* appear frequently with this construction in poetic descriptions of hair: cf. Virg. *A.* 6. 281 'uipereum crinem uittis innexa cruentis', Ov. *Am.* 3. 1. 7, Stat. *Theb.* 2. 99 f., *Silu.* 5. 3. 115, *Stil.* 2. 228 f. (Hispania) 'glaucis . . . Mineruae | nexa comam foliis'. Cf. also Virg. *A.* 8. 277, Stat. *Theb.* 9. 419 f. (the river-god Ismenos) 'nexa uirentibus uluis | cornua'.

379. edomitis . . . aquis: for the subjection of rivers as a trope for the conquest of the countries associated with them cf. also *III Cons.* 203 'famulis Gangen pallescere ripis', *Stil.* 3. 23.

379 f. in aere trementem | . . . Atlanta: no doubt an anthropomorphic figure of the man-mountain (cf. 104 *Maurusius Atlans* n.), here shown trembling with fear. This is a deliberate paradox, since he is cast in all the solidity of bronze: cf. *c.m.* 17. 11f. (a statue of two brothers rescuing their parents from an eruption of Etna) 'perque omne metallum | fusus in attonito palluit aere tremor.' For the use of *in* with a material see *OLD* s.v. 44b, noting esp. Apul. *Met.* 3. 11 'ut in aere stet imago tua'.

380. succinctae . . . cohortes: so huge is the Atlas that whole troops of soldiers (or slaves?) are needed to carry him. The skirts of their tunics are girt up for ease of movement (cf. 299 *succinctior* n.: here the word is literal). Cf. Ov. *Fast.* 4. 413 'a boue succincti cultros remouete ministri', Luc. 1. 612; also Hor. *S.* 2. 6. 107 'ueluti succinctus cursitat hospes', Ov. *Met.* 8. 660f., Mart. 12. 24. 7.

famulum . . . Atlanta: Platnauer apparently thought that *famulum* was an 'archaic' genitive plural ('crowds of slaves with upgirt dresses'), but it is in fact an accusative, qualifying *Atlanta*: cf. *Stil.* 3. 22f. (Stil.'s triumph) 'hi famulos traherent reges', *Rapt.* 2. 13f. (Venus) 'iam Dite subacto | ingenti famulos Manes ductura triumpho'.

381-3. In 105 BC Jugurtha was betrayed to the Romans by King Bocchus of Mauretania in a deal worked out with Marius' lieutenant, Sulla; the next year he was made to march in Marius' triumph and then killed, along with his two sons, in the state prison (Sal. *Iug.* 105ff., Liv. *Epit.* 66f.). If Roma had had her way, Gildo would have suffered the same fate, but then, it is implied, Honorius' African triumph would have surpassed that of Marius because the chief prisoner would have been captured fairly and honourably in battle, and not by trickery. For Gildo's actual fate see 101-21 n. Note also *Gild.* 91ff. and see further Cameron 334f. for Claudian's familiarity with Sallust.

381. Iugurthinam: for the personal adjective used in verse cf. Ov. *Pont.* 4. 3. 45 (Marius) 'ille Iugurthino clarus Cimbroque triumpho'.

subiturus . . . poenam: a venerable phrase in the Roman legal tradition, attested in the XII Tables: Table VIII. 3 (Warmington) 'manu fustiue si os fregit <collisitue> libero CCC, si seruo CL poenam subito [sestertiorum]'.

382. praeberet . . . colla iugo: a rarer and more self-consciously poetic version of e.g. *colla summitto* (*Eutr.* 1. 42): cf. Ov. *Fast.* 4. 403 'illa iugo tauros collum praebere coegit', Luc. 1. 613 'uictum praebebat . . . collum', Sil. 7. 32, Stat. *Ach.* 1. 280.

383. non . . . dolis: this traditional 'Roman' disdain for deceit may seem out of place after the insistence on Stilicho's *astus* (219, 300 nn.), but the panegyrist makes his treatment fit the circumstances. Cf. 477-80, where Stilicho is said also to surpass Ulysses because he relies on force of arms and not *fraus*.

383. remitto: 'overlook', as at e.g. Pl. *Mos.* 1169 'remitte quaeso hanc noxiam', Prop. 2. 34. 21, Sen. *Con.* 2. 3. 1 'remisit iniuriam', *Stil.* 3. 110f. 'pietate remittat | errorem'.

384. Getici . . . belli: see 123 *arma Getarum* n. and cf. 201 *Getico . . . triumpho*, 490 *Geticis . . . bellis.* Contrast *Gothicum bellum* in a prose inscription (*ILS* 799).

    laurea: by metonymy = 'triumph', as at e.g. Ov. *Pont.* 2. 7. 67 'praestat et exulibus pacem tua laurea, Caesar', Luc. 1. 122. Müller compares Tac. *Ann.* 2. 26 'adsequi nomen imperatorium et deportare lauream'.

385. declinare: see *OLD* s.v. 5 'to turn aside in order to avoid, to dodge', citing e.g. Cic. *Planc.* 97 'urbem unam mihi amicissimam declinaui', Tac. *Ann.* 6. 15 'deuiis . . . itineribus ambiens patriam et declinans'.

385f. sedesne capacior . . . tantae laudis: Rome is the true home of glory, just as she is the true *sedes* of the Emperors (23) and of lawful authority (408). For *capax* used with reference to abstractions cf. Liv. 39. 9. 1 'urbis magnitudo capacior patientiorque talium malorum', Sen. *Oed.* 930f. 'scelerum capax | . . . Cithaeron', Sil. 6. 616f. 'laudum cladumque quieta | mente capax'. For *tantae laudis* cf. 491 n.

386–8. Honorius' own services to Rome have created a relationship of obligation, but it is not merely one in which the City is indebted to him. His virtue and conscience are under an obligation to continue to care for those whom they have saved because the benefactor is now bound by love. Seneca says something very similar in the *De Beneficiis*, though he places the emphasis on the idea that we take pleasure in adding fresh *beneficia* to old ones because virtue itself is pleasurable: *Ben.* 4. 15. 2f. 'non mentiar, si dixero neminem non amare beneficia sua, neminem non ita compositum animo, ut libentius eum uideat, in quem multa congessit, cui non causa sit iterum dandi beneficii semel dedisse. quod non accideret, nisi ipsa nos delectarent beneficia . . .'. The idea that a god who has granted a devotee one favour may be expected to grant more can be traced in literature as far back as Sappho, fr. 1.8ff.

386. benefacta: in classical verse *benefactum* functions as a useful alternative to *beneficium*, because the latter, with its run of short syllables, cannot be accommodated in dactylic metres (e.g. Catul. 76. 1, Virg. *G.* 3. 525, Prop. 2. 1. 24, Ov. *Met.* 13. 270, *Stil.* 2. 42, 3. 182).

    morantem: i.e. to visit Rome: cf. *morantis* (356) and *cunctantem* (360).

387. conueniunt: like suppliants crowding round a patron. Cf. [Quint.] *Decl.* 19. 2 'unde uos lacrimae gemitusque conueniunt', Paul. Nol. *Carm.* 15. 287 'multa Christum prece conuenienti'.

meritis . . . obnoxia uirtus: a paradox, since normally the recipient of the *beneficium* would be the one feeling the obligation: e.g. Pl. *As.* 284f. 'adeo ut aetatem ambo ambobus nobis sint obnoxii, | nostro deuincti beneficio', Liv. 35. 31. 8 'totam Graeciam beneficio libertatis obnoxiam Romanis esse.' *meritis* is dative, governed by *obnoxia*, though Platnauer apparently took it as an ablative ('constrained by its own fair deeds').

388f. 'Now for the hundredth time the sickles of summer shear the harvests of golden Gargara.' Gargara was the name of both a mountain in the Ida range in the Troad, and of a town at its foot (Plin. *Nat.* 5. 122). The area was famous for its fertility, and its very name suggests abundance (γάργαρα, 'heaps'): Virg. *G.* 1. 103 'ipsa suas mirantur Gargara messis', Ov. *Ars* 1. 57, Sen. *Phoen.* 608, Pac. *Pan. Theod.* 4. 4 'Gargara prouentu laeta triticeo', *Rapt.* 1. 208, Sid. *Carm.* 7. 146f. 'collataque semper | arida Mygdoniae damnarunt Gargara falces', 22. 174.

388. flauescentia: cf. Virg. *Ecl.* 4. 28 'flauescet campus arista', *Rapt.* 1. 188f., Paul. Nol. *Ep.* 39. 2 'de flauescentibus propinqua iam messe regionibus'; also *Eutr.* 1. 112 'flaua . . . rura'.

389. detondent: the compound is normally used of shearing hair (e.g. Pl. *Bac.* 1128, *Eutr.* 1. 383) or sheep's wool, or figuratively of stripping foliage from trees (Ov. *Fast.* 3. 237 'arboribus redeunt detonsae frigore frondes'). For the poeticism seen here cf. Enn. *Ann.* 468 Skutsch 'et detondit agros laetos', Nem. *Buc.* 1. 6f. 'dum gramina uaccae | detondent'.

390f. 'And the hundredth consul hurries on the returning ages that celebrate the games no man has seen a second time.' A *saeculum* was properly the longest possible extent of a human life, calculated by some at as much as 120 years, but generally reckoned for official purposes at a round 100 (e.g. Varro *L.* 6. 11 'saeculum spatium annorum centum uocarunt dictum a sene, quod longissimum spatium senescendorum hominum id putarunt', Censorinus, *De Die Natali* 17 'nostri maiores, quod naturale saeculum quantum esset exploratum non habebant, ciuile ad certum modulum annorum centum statuerunt'). The first celebration of the *ludi saeculares* may have been held in 348 BC, and festivals at hundred years' intervals are certainly attested for 249 BC and 149 (or perhaps 146) BC. The Civil War prevented the holding of games in 49 BC, so Augustus juggled the figures. He persuaded the *decemuiri* to declare that the period should last one hundred and ten years, and therefore celebrated his famous *ludi saeculares* in 17 BC. Claudius restored the old method of calculation and held the games in AD 47, thus making them coincide with the 800th anniversary of the foundation of the City. After that, Emperors readily switched from one system of calculation to the other, according to which would allow them to earn the glory of staging so significant and splendid a spectacle. Antoninus Pius, following Claudius' sequence and using the hundred years measure, celebrated the games in AD 147 (or rather 148? see L. A. Holford-Strevens, *Latomus* 36 (1977), 96), and so Philip the Arab again in 248 (the last attested proper celebration, marking the 1,000th anniversary of the foundation of the City). Domitian, however, had in the meantime reverted to Augustus' 110-year *saeculum* and celebrated the games in AD 88, calculating from Augustus' assumption of the *tribunicia potestas* in 23 BC. In this his lead was followed by Septimius Severus, who accordingly held the games in AD 204, i.e. 220 years after Augustus' celebration of 17 BC. By the fourth century the hundred years measure had once more become standard. None the less, Maximian took Septimius' games as his reference-point; the celebration he planned for AD 304 would have marked the centenary of Septimius' games, and thus would have conflated the two systems. Claudian is therefore probably alluding to the fact that, by this measure, AD 404, the year of Honorius' sixth consulship, should have been marked by a full-scale celebration of the *ludi saeculares*. See in general the instructive article at *RE*, 2nd ser., iA. 1695. 44 ff., esp. 1720. 21 ff.

390. spectatosque iterum nulli . . . ludos: compare Suetonius' account of the mockery that met Claudius' proclamation of the *ludi saeculares* on the restored chronology: (*Cl.* 21. 2) 'uox praeconis irrisa est inuitantis more sollemni ad *ludos, quos nec spectasset quisquam nec spectaturus esset,* cum superessent adhuc qui spectauerant, et quidam histrionum producti olim tunc quoque producerentur.' It need not be assumed that Claudian has Suetonius in mind here, since the phrase would seem to have been part of the traditional proclamation formula for the games ('more sollemni').

celebrantia: the participle ushers in a pattern of words with initial alliteration on *c* (*celebrantia, circumflexa, centenus, consul*) alternating with others (*ludos, rapit, saecula*); this is further reinforced by the internal alliteration in *spectatos, circumflexa,* and *saecula*. The clamorous quality of these lines is perhaps intended to be triumphant or majestic.

391. circumflexa: = 'ad se redeuntia', Barth. Similar phrases of the cycle of time can be found at e.g. Virg. *G.* 2. 402 'atque in se sua per uestigia uoluitur annus', *Prob.* 2 (to Sol) 'uoluis inexhausto redeuntia saecula motu', *c.m.* 27. 104f. (Phoenix) 'te saecula teste | cuncta reuoluuntur'. *circumflecto* makes few appearances in high verse, and where it is found it is usually applied to changing the course of ships in a metaphor drawn from the circus: Virg. *A.* 3. 429f. 'praestat Trinacrii metas lustrare Pachyni | cessantem, longos et circumflectere cursus', 5. 131, Jer. *Ep.* 125. 3 'regendae et circumflectendae nauis'. Here the metaphor is applied to the passage of the ages, whose cycles are like the laps of a chariot-race. For *celebrantia* and *circumflexa* qualifying the same noun see 50f. *spoliis . . . micantes | innumeros arcus* n.

rapit: a reading which has drawn some suspicion. Goodyear conjectured *aperit*, and Platnauer, though he printed *rapit*, understood it in a similar sense ('the consul has introduced the games'). But the consul is poetically imagined as responsible for the swift flow of time, which, in inaugurating the ceremony once more, he seems to 'hurry on'. For *rapio* with this sense cf. Liv. 30. 14. 2 'raptae prope inter arma nuptiae', and esp. Sil. 4. 485 'iamque dies rapti cursu nauoque labore'.

centenus: = *centesimus*. Though the distributive is regularly used in poetry for the cardinal (see Fordyce on Virg. *A.* 7. 538, LHS ii. 212f.; also 392 n., *Stil.* 1. 312 'centeno lumine' = 'centum oculis'), its substitution for the ordinal is absent from classical and rare in classicizing verse, even in Claudian's day. Cf., however, Cor. *Ioh.* 3. 15f. 'ultio . . . quae . . . Vandalicum . . . genus centeno perderet anno'. For the common use of the distributive for the ordinal in late and medieval Latin in general see Housman on Man. 4. 451.

saecula: Gesner thought the plural significant: 'plurium numero dixit, puto, ut indicaret, esse in hoc nomine relationem ad plura, quorum quisque saeculi sui certum initium et finem numerat. universim orbem centum annorum describere voluit, nihil amplius.' But, as Müller saw, the plural is used for metrical reasons: the singular *saeculum* cannot appear in a hexameter before a consonant, since it would then be a cretic. Indeed, it can only be accommodated at all by eliding the terminal *-um* before a short vowel; this was evidently considered ugly. *saecula* is thus the regular form, as is the case with e.g. *gaudia, iurgia, otia*; cf. also *pomeria* 393.

392–406. The basic nature of Roma's claims and the main thrust of the propaganda are clear enough. Only three times, asserts the goddess, has an Augustus visited the City in the last century, and on each occasion the purpose was to celebrate victories in civil wars; if Honorius comes now he will wipe out this shame because his triumph over the Goths will be a pure and wholly uncontroversial one. Two difficult questions, however, arise from this statement: (1) which three visits does Claudian mean, and (2) how do we interpret the apparent denigration of Honorius' predecessors, not least of his own father?

This passage has come under close scrutiny in recent years, most notably from Alan Cameron (*HSCPh* 73 (1969), 247–80, esp. 262–4) and T. D. Barnes (*HSCPh* 79 (1975), 325–33). It should be asserted from the beginning that, in the strictest possible terms, the claim made here by Roma is quite simply wrong. As Barnes stresses (pp. 326 f.), '[F]ive imperial visits to Rome . . . are . . . indubitably attested in the relevant hundred years, even apart from the presence there of Maximian (306–308), Maxentius (306–312), and the usurper Nepotianus (350)', though note that Claudian would indeed almost certainly have discounted not just Nepotianus, but all three as *tyranni* (398 n.). Barnes's five 'indubitably attested' Imperial visits are the following: (*a*) 312: Constantine, after the defeat of Maxentius at the Mulvian Bridge, commemorated in his triumphal arch, (*b*) 315: Constantine, for his *decennalia*, (*c*) 326: Constantine, for his *vicennalia*, (*d*) 357: Constantius, after the defeat of Magnentius, famously described by Amm. Marc. 16. 10, and (*e*) 389: Theodosius, after the defeat of Maximus. The second and third visits of Constantine, though also associated with victories over would-be usurpers (Barnes 326 with n. 9), could be said to be so minor that overlooking them would have been easy after nearly eighty years. Of the three remaining visits, Claudian can hardly be omitting (*e*), which he himself describes at 53–76 (and which he clearly thinks of in terms of a triumph; *uictor* 57: so too Pacatus, see below infra), while (*a*) and (*d*) left striking memorials, visual and literary, with which he might reasonably have been expected to be familiar. *ter* would thus at first sight seem to be easily explained. But Cameron argues very cogently for the likelihood that Theodosius made a second visit to Rome, soon after the defeat of Eugenius and Arbogast at the Frigidus, a visit which would then have to have taken place between 6 Sept. 394 and Theodosius' death on 17 January 395. In addition, Barnes offers good evidence for further Imperial visits, by Constans in 340 or 341 (pp. 327 f.) and by Gratian in 376 (pp. 328 ff.). If Constans and Gratian did indeed visit Rome as Barnes argues, it would seem that there is no reason to assume that they held triumphal celebrations. It is hardly likely that Constans celebrated the death of his brother Constantine, and though Gratian's visit might have had a political reason related to the executions of the elder Theodosius and of Maximinus (as Barnes suggests, p. 330), their deaths did not constitute the suppression of a full-scale usurpation. Thus, if Claudian even knew of them, it is possible that he might have ignored them for the sake of economy; after all, he is concerned with visits connected with victories. Nor would he feel much incentive to allude to a visit connected with the judicial murder of the present honorand's grandfather. A second visit to Rome by Theodosius after the Frigidus is, however, quite another matter. If it took place, then

Claudian must surely have known of it, since he was in Rome in time to celebrate the consulship of Olybrius and Probinus in Jan. 395, only a matter of three months at the most after Theodosius must have left the City. We are thus faced with a number of possibilities. One is Cameron's suggestion that Claudian, who probably arrived after Theodosius' departure, might 'ten years later . . . have overlooked it' (art. cit., 263), especially since it was 'very brief . . . and was not commemorated by spectacular monuments like the arch of Constantine or the obelisk of Constantius' (ibid.); this is no doubt possible, but it stretches credulity in Claudian's 'absence of mind' (ibid.) rather further than is comfortable. Alternatively, if this brief visit was not marked by any formal victory celebrations, then it would not have fitted well into Claudian's scheme and so perhaps, as a poet, he would have felt justified in tacitly passing it over. On the other hand, as Cameron more persuasively goes on to suggest (ibid. 264), Claudian possibly has both visits by Theodosius in mind, and *nostra ter* is perhaps used in preference to *tres nostra* for the very reason that the three visits were not made by three different Emperors. In this case, the inclusion of the visits of both 389 and 394 in *ter* obliges us to omit from our calculations either Constantine in 312 or Constantius in 357. Cameron (loc. cit.) argues for the omission of the latter, but given that this passage and Ammianus Marcellinus' description of Constantius' visit take a similar line on the matter of celebrating triumphs for civil wars (see below), it would surely be better to discount Constantine's visit; this is in any case so far distant as to be easily excluded if we take Claudian's 'hundred years' as a poetic round number.

An alternative possibility is to argue that Roma's wording is a little loose, and that in the general context of Imperial visits to celebrate military victories, Roma really has in mind *only* such formal visits as were marked by triumphs. This would allow us to concentrate on the attested triumphs over Maxentius, Magnentius, and Maximus; the 394 visit, even if its reality is accepted, could be ruled out here on the grounds that no formal triumph seems to have been celebrated. Some supporting evidence for this might be seen in Roma's choice of wording, if *intra pomeria* (393) is taken as a reference to the traditional privilege whereby the *triumphator* was permitted to cross the sacred boundary of the City with armed troops. Against this it should be objected that this is simply not what, on the surface, Roma says: she explictly claims only to have seen an Emperor within the *pomeria* three times in a century, and *intra pomeria* is probably no more than a poeticism for *intra muros*. Moreover, *ter*, whether it arises from hyperbolic simplification, deliberate suppression, or plain ignorance is most cogent in the speech's principal argument if taken literally and precisely; Roma's complaint is twofold, first that the Emperors, including Honorius, have neglected her shamefully, and, secondly, that when they have come to her, their visits have been connected with civil war and have thus brought her not only pleasure but also sorrow. Both deficiencies Honorius can now remedy.

If deciding exactly which three visits Claudian has in mind is difficult in the extreme, two facts, at least, can be established. First, Claudian's *ter* is inaccurate, whether we imagine that to be the result of ignorance, carelessness, or deliberate omission. Secondly, it must of necessity include at least one, and perhaps two, visits by Theodosius in the aftermath of civil war. The passage, therefore, apparently censures Theodosius, even if only discreetly and without mentioning him by name. To this extent, Claudian echoes the criticism levelled at Constantius and his 'triumphal' visit to Rome by an historian admittedly very hostile to him: 'Constantius quasi cluso Iani templo stratisque hostibus cunctis, Romam uisere gestiebat, post Magnenti exitium absque nomine ex sanguine Romano triumphaturus. nec enim gentem ullam bella cientem per se superauit, aut uictam fortitudine suorum comperit ducum, uel addidit quaedam imperio, aut usquam in necessitatibus summis primus uel inter primos est uisus, sed ut pompam nimis extentam, rigentiaque auro uexilla, et pulchritudinem stipatorum ostenderet agenti tranquillius populo, haec uel simile quicquam uidere nec speranti umquam nec optanti' (Amm. Marc. 16. 10. 1f.). The entry of Constantius into the City may have been properly speaking a ceremonial *aduentus* rather than a formal triumph, as MacCormack 41 argues, but Ammianus clearly felt that the ceremony none the less practically amounted to a triumph, and was one that did the celebrant no honour whatsoever. By the late fourth century, however, victory celebrations to commemorate the defeats of internal enemies and usurpers had in fact become extremely common, and regularly assumed a significant political role as occasions on which communities and individuals could visibly assert their loyalty to legitimate authority. See McCormick 80ff. None the less, Ammianus' view may well have been primarily one that 'in some conservative circles . . . remained fashionable' (ibid. 81). The size and strength of those conservative circles is hard to determine, but the prejudice was an old one, and its force can be felt, for example, in Septimius Severus' refusal to celebrate a triumph after the defeat of Niger (SHA *Sept. Seu.* 9 'sed triumphum respuit, ne uideretur de ciuili triumphare uictoria'). What is very likely, at least, is that such sentiments were particularly strong in Rome. In this connection it surely cannot be a coincidence that, in his panegyric on Theodosius, Pacatus goes out of his way to stress that the victory over Maximus is one whose happy outcome makes it a rare example of a civil war that actually deserved a triumph: (*Pan. Theod.* 46. 4, addressed to Roma) 'uidisti ciuile bellum hostium caede, militum pace, Italiae recuperatione, tua libertate finitum; uidisti, inquam, finitum ciuile bellum cui decernere posses triumphum': note also the use of much the same technique at *Pan. Lat.* 12. 20. 3f. Mynors. Pacatus' panegyric, we should remember, was delivered at Rome in 389, and it is quite possible that its author was smoothing ruffled conservative feathers. A panegyrist takes his material where he can find it, and Pacatus will have had to reconcile the fact of the victory celebrations with the feeling in some quarters that impropriety was being breached. Claudian is in the happier position of having for his subject a victory which, at least in this respect, was uncontroversial, and so it is perhaps not surprising that he (and Stilicho) should have taken full advantage of the circumstances in order to further the overarching policy of reconciling the Senate with the Court. We should no doubt see this less as a denigration of Theodosius—who is not named, and who in any case has had his full share of praise elsewhere—than as a further exaltation of his son. See R. B. Rutherford, *The Meditations of Marcus Aurelius: A Study* (Oxford, 1989), 113f., for some judicious remarks on the encomiastic theme whereby a predecessor is praised but still 'shown to be slightly inferior to the panegyrist's own hero'.

392. lustra . . . bis dena recensent: cf. esp. Hor. *Saec.* 21f. 'certus undenos decies per annos | orbis ut cantus referatque ludos.' This type of periphrasis, which may have a stately, almost oracular feel, regularly exhibits one or more features; (i) the use of a multiplicative phrase for a simple cardinal; (ii) the substitution, contrary to normal grammar, of either (*a*) distributive for a cardinal in a simple number or (*b*) a cardinal for a distributive in a multiplicative phrase; (iii) the calculation of time in five-year periods (*lustra*) rather than single years. Here Claudian exhibits (i) and (iii). These devices may enable poets to avoid unmetrical numbers; e.g. *Gild.* 154 'bis senas torquent hiemes' (i), for the unmetrical *duodecim*. For similar use of elaborate periphrases in designating long periods of time cf. Ov. *Ibis* 1 'tempus ad hoc lustris bis iam mihi quinque peractis' (i, ii*b*, iii), Stat. *Silu.* 3. 3. 146 'dextra bis octonis fluxerunt saecula lustris' (i, iii), and by addition rather than multiplication 5. 3. 253f. 'trinisque decem quinquennia lustris | iuncta ferens' (ii*a*, iii).

392f. recensent . . . uidi: there is good manuscript support for each of the alternative readings *recenset* and *uidit* individually, and so Birt tentatively combined them and conjectured *sibi* to replace *mihi*, thus yielding *his annis qui lustra sibi bis dena recenset,* | *nostra ter Augustos intra pomeria uidit.* As Müller points out, however, the tense-sequence *recenset* | *uidit* is an unlikely one. Moreover, the whole tenor of the passage is one of high emotion in which Roma concentrates, often in the first person, on the wrongs she has endured: *mihi*, far from requiring emendation, corroborates *uidi*. Birt also scrupulously compared Ov. *Fast.* 3. 575 'signa recensuerat bis sol sua' (= 'two years had passed'), of the sun making his way through the signs of the Zodiac. But the sense here is simply that the years are poetically made to 'count up' the total of the *lustra* which they themselves constitute ('during these years which number twice ten lustres', Platnauer).

393. pomeria: probably no more than a poeticism for *muros*, as at Juv. 9. 11 'salibus . . . intra pomeria natis'. The *pomerium*, however, marked the sacred boundary of the City, beyond which the *auspicia urbana* could not be taken (Varro, *L.* 5. 143 'qui quod erat post murum, post-moerium dictum, eo usque auspicia urbana finiuntur'). For the plural form *pomeria* cf. Luc. 1. 594, and see 391 *saecula* n.

394. temporibus uariis; eadem: note the effective juxtaposition. More striking examples in Claudian include *Ruf.* 1. 237 'parcendi rabies', *Eutr.* 2. *pr.* 44 'et te nunc inopem diues amare negat', *Theod.* 90 'dixitque tacendo', *Get.* 138 'fulmineum lento luctamine Poenum'. The phrase *temporibus uariis* also stands at the head of the line at Prud. *C. Symm.* 1. 329.

sed: for postponement of particles see in general E. Norden, *P. Vergilius Maronis Aeneis Buch VI* (Stuttgart, 1957), 402ff. Norden gives numerous examples with *sed*, including Catul. 51. 9, Hor. *Carm.* 4. 4. 33, Virg. *A.* 1. 353, 5. 320, 6. 315. At e.g. *A.* 5. 5 and Ov. *Am.* 1. 5. 14 it stands in third position. Note also LHS ii. 488. The effect is to throw a great weight of emphasis on the preceding word, here *eadem*.

395. ciuilis dissensus: for the phrasing cf. Cic. *Ver.* 1. 34 'erat tum dissensio ciuium.' Other variants used for *ciuile bellum/ciuilia bella* (*Ruf.* 2. 236, *III Cons.* 63f., *IV Cons.* 633f., *Get.* 286) include *ciuilia classica* (*Ruf.* 2. 117f.), *ciuile nefas* (*Ruf.* 2. 389) and *ciuilibus armis* (*Stil.* 2. 85). *dissensus* is preferred in hexameter verse to the less easily tractable *dissensio*, which requires either elision or correption of the terminal *o*: cf. Virg. *A.* 11. 455, Stat. *Theb.* 1. 423, 5. 148, *Ruf.* 1. 70, *Gild.* 300, *Stil.* 2. 86. For the practice of Latin poets in general, and of Claudian in particular, with regard to the corruption of terminal o see Austin on Virg. *A.* 2. 735, Dewar on Stat. *Theb.* 9. 437, Birt, p. ccxi, Gruzelier, p. xxix.

superbi: a damning word, if we include Theodosius among the culprits. Contrast Pac. *Pan. Theod.* 47. 3 'nunc de bellis, nunc de superbia triumpharis'.

396. scilicet: regularly conveying bitter scorn: see Austin on Virg. *A.* 6. 526 'scilicet id magnum sperans fore munus amanti'. Other examples in Claudian are *Gild.* 84, *c.m.* 22. 53 f. 'scilicet insignis de paupere uate triumphus! | scilicet egregiis ornabere uictor opimis!'

   Latio respersos sanguine currus: *respersus sanguine* is used with particular frequency to heighten the horror of impious acts: cf. Cic. *S. Rosc.* 68 'respersas manus sanguine paterno', Virg. *A.* 7. 547 (Allecto stirring quasi-civil war) 'Ausonio respersi sanguine Teucros', Ov. *Am.* 2. 14. 29, Stat. *Theb.* 7. 211, Sil. 11. 54, *IV Cons.* 75 f. 'domini respersus uterque | insontis iugulo.' To *Latio . . . sanguine* contrast Sen. *Clem.* 1. 26. 5 'currus barbarorum sanguine cruenti'. For *currus* see 377 n.

397. piae . . . parenti: picking up *uestra parens* (362): Roma is their mother as well as Honorius'. The collocation is surprisingly rare, but cf. Ov. *Met.* 13. 301 'pia mater', *Fast.* 4. 555, 6. 559, Stat. *Ach.* 1. 595 'piae . . . matres'.

   laetanda: for the gerundive ('to be rejoiced at') see *OLD* s.v. 1f, citing Cic. *Man.* 3 'illud in primis mihi laetandum iure esse uideo', Sal. *Iug.* 14. 22 'laetandum magis quam dolendum puto casum tuum', Stat. *Theb.* 12. 90.

398 f. periere tyranni, | sed nobis periere tamen: the vanquished may have been usurpers, but they were still Roma's sons and she feels the loss personally (*nobis* = 'to my loss'). It seems that Claudian is adapting Pacatus, *Pan. Theod.* 46. 1 f. 'ad omne ciuilis motus classicum tremescebas; quae praeter *stragem militum utraque tibi parte pereuntium* exstincta domi senatus tui lumina, suffixa pilo consulum capita, Catones in mortem coactos truncosque Cicerones et Pompeios fleueras insepultos'. No such terrors, naturally, will afflict the senate as a result of Honorius' 'pure' victory over Alaric.

   Hall prints the variant *fauere tyrannis*, | *sed nobis periere tamen.* This makes good sense if we take *natorum* (398) as referring to the unfortunate Romans who threw their lot in with the usurpers and suffered accordingly. But a number of considerations speak strongly in favour of the reading printed here. On the stylistic level, one would be loath to give up the fine epanalepsis of *periere*, combined as it also is with the very emphatic *sed . . . tamen* (for which cf. *Eutr.* 2. *pr.* 46, *Eutr.* 2. 555, *c.m.* 20. 19). Moreover, the hyperbole—Roma laments even for the usurpers themselves, not just for those whom they seduced from their proper loyalties—is also much more in keeping both with the general emotional tone of the passage and with its argument. Cf. also Hor. *Carm.* 3. 4. 73 ff. 'iniecta monstris Terra dolet suis | maeretque partus fulmine luridum | missos ad Orcum', a passage often interpreted as using Gigantomachy as a metaphor for civil war and as expressing Horace's sympathy for the defeated.

398. tyranni: = 'usurpers': see 88 *tyrannum* n.

399 f. In 46 BC Julius Caesar celebrated a quadruple triumph for his victories in Gaul, Egypt, Pontus, and Africa (Liv. *Epit.* 115), but he never commemorated his victories over Pompey and the Republicans. Cf. App. *BC* 2. 101, Florus 2. 13. 89 'Pharsalus et Thapsos et Munda nusquam; et quanto maiora erant, de quibus non triumphabat!', and note also the sentiments expressed at Val. Max. 2 Ext. 8. 7 'lugubres semper existimatae sunt uictoriae utpote non externo, sed domestico partae cruore . . . lauream nec senatus cuiquam dedit nec quisquam sibi dari desiderauit ciuitatis parte lacrimante.' Claudian may possibly have in mind Lucan's scathing reflections on Caesar's entrance into Rome after the crossing of the Rubicon: 3. 73 ff. 'pro, si remeasset in urbem | Gallorum tantum populis Arctoque subacta, | quam seriem rerum longa praemittere pompa, | quas potuit belli facies! ut uincula Rheno | Oceanoque daret, celsos ut Gallia currus | nobilis et flauis sequeretur mixta Britannis. | perdidit o qualem uincendo plura triumphum! | non illum laetis uadentem coetibus urbes | sed tacitae uidere metu'. Claudian seems to be hostile to Caesar: consider *IV Cons.* 309 ff. 'Romani . . . | qui nec Tarquinii fastus nec iura tulere | Caesaris' and compare his attitude to Augustus (116–19 n.).

400. Pharsalia: here the manuscripts are fairly evenly divided between *Pharsalia* and *Pharsalica*, but the same crux appears at *Nupt.* 291, and there 'Pharsalia rura' has considerably stronger authority.

401. socias acies cognataque signa: clearly showing the influence of Lucan's language; *De Bello Ciuili* 1. 4 ff. 'cognatas . . . acies . . . infestisque obuia signis | signa.' Cf. also Man. 1. 906 'ciuilis etiam motus cognataque bella' and see 220 *cognatis uiribus* n.

402. This *sententia* is a variation on the commonplace that in a civil war it is the winner who endures the worse fate: Cic. *Fam.* 9. 6. 3 'extremum malorum omnium esse ciuilis belli uictoriam', Luc. 4. 362 'hoc petimus, uictos ne tecum uincere cogas', 7. 706 (the poet addressing Pompey at Pharsalus) 'uincere peius erat', Tac. *Hist.* 1. 50. Intertextually the present line could be said to furnish an answer in the affirmative to the question the centurion Laelius asks Caesar at Luc. 1. 366 'usque adeo miserum est ciuili uincere bello?' The usual contrast drawn is between what is *decorum* and what is *turpe*: see e.g. Nep. *pr.* 6 'contra ea pleraque nostris moribus sunt decora, quae apud illos turpia putantur', Ov. *Met.* 9. 5 f. 'nec tam | turpe fuit uinci, quam contendisse decorum', 13. 308 f.: note also Hor. *Ep.* 1. 16. 45. For a variant on this kind of antithesis see also Sal. *Iug.* 42. 3 'sed bono uinci satius est quam malo more iniuriam uincere.' For *decorum* and a dependent infinitive cf. *Eutr.* 2. 328 'corruptas . . . dapes uariasse decorum', and see further Trump 21.

403–6. What Honorius is asked to do here is, broadly speaking, what Stilicho was said already to have achieved in his defeat of Gildo: *Stil.* 1. 384 f. 'haec omnes ueterum reuocauit adorea laurus. | restituit Stilicho cunctos tibi, Roma, triumphos.' Note also *Stil.* 1. 328 f. 'neclectum Stilicho per tot iam saecula morem | rettulit'.

403. priscum . . . morem: the old custom, that is, of celebrating triumphs over foreign foes, not other citizens. In Latin, these two words are practically made for each other: cf. Catul. 101. 7 'prisco . . . more parentum', Tac. *Dial.* 23. 3, *Stil.* 3. 14.

403 f. gloria . . . uerior: i.e. the glory won in a civil war is *not* true glory. For the collocation cf. Cic. *Pis.* 2 'mihi ista licet de me uera cum gloria praedicare', Ov. *Ep.* 17. 243, Plin. *Pan.* 16. 3 'imperatorem ueram ac solidam gloriam reportantem'.

404. fructum sincerae laudis: cf. Quint. *Inst.* 10. 7. 17 'praesenti fructu laudis'. *fructus* with metaphorical sense is especially common in Ovid (*Met.* 2. 285 f. 'hosne mihi fructus, hunc fertilitatis honorem | officiique refers?', with Bömer, *Pont.* 1. 5. 25, *Ep.* 12. 174) and Lucan (2. 190, 4. 693, 7. 32, 726 f. 'nunc tibi uera fides quaesiti, Magne, fauoris | contigit ac fructus'). Cf. 584, *Eutr.* 1. 158, *Theod.* 63, *Stil.* 3. 79. Note how *sincerae* is in effect glossed by *ab hoste*, which should also be taken as explaining *uerior. furoris externi* performs the same function for *iustis* in ll. 405 f. *laudis* picks up and reinforces Honorius' glory in saving Rome (386).

405. desuetum: passive, with the sense 'that has become unfamiliar'. See *OLD* s.v. *desuetus* 2 citing Virg. *A.* 2. 509 f. 'arma diu senior desueta trementibus aeuo | circumdat nequiquam umeris', Ov. *Tr.* 5. 7. 63, *Met.* 7. 645 f. 'uocesque hominum exaudire uidebar | iam mihi desuetas'. Cf. 645 f. *desueta . . . fora.*

iam redde: Roma echoes the Naiad who announced the good news of Alaric's defeat to Eridanus (158).

405 f. These earlier triumphs were 'guilty' because they celebrated victories won in civil wars, and Honorius is exhorted to wipe out the shameful memories associated with them by displaying the spoils taken in a 'just' war, i.e. one conducted against a foreign and hubristic enemy. The phrasing is very close to *Gild.* 429 f. (Honorius in a speech to the troops) 'iusto magnoque triumpho | ciuiles abolete notas'. Cf. also *Get.* 561 ff. 'obsessi principis armis | excusate nefas deploratumque Timauo | uulnus et Alpinum gladiis abolete pudorem'.

iustis . . . spoliis: cf. Cic. *Planc.* 89 'iustissimos omnium Metellorum et clarissimos triumphos gloria et laude superauit, quod et illos ipsos improbissimos ciuis interfici noluit et ne quis bonus interiret in eadem caede prouidit', a passage similar in wording and sentiment to the present one; and also Liv. 7. 15. 8 'nec alius post M. Furium quam C. Sulpicius iustiorem de Gallis egit triumphum', Hor. *Carm.* 1. 12. 53 f. 'Parthos . . . egerit iusto domitos triumpho'.

furoris | externi: recalling the *furorem* of Alaric at 206, as well as *Get.* 292 (Italy) 'Teutonico quondam patefacta furori'. See in general 105 *furias* n. for madness as a characteristic of Rome's enemies. Statius, by contrast, praises Domitian's mildness by saying that he was 'nec in externos facilis saeuire furores' (*Silu.* 1. 1. 26).

406. absolue: 'justify', 'wash away the guilt': cf. *c.m.* 30. 30 (Claudia) 'absoluens puppisque moras crimenque pudoris', Sil. 15. 655 f. 'heu temere abducto liquisti robore castra, | ni factum absoluit uictoria.' Perhaps, though the sense is not the same, Claudian is thinking of Luc. 2. 249 f. 'an placuit ducibus scelerum populique furentis | cladibus inmixtum ciuile absoluere bellum?'

407–25. The third section of Roma's speech generally follows the same basic structure as the first two (see 361–425 n.), but is more intricate in its variation. Instead of beginning with a brief opening statement, it plunges right into a series of three rhetorical questions (407–11), the last two of which are yoked together (*nec*, 410). The first and second of these reiterate Roma's complaint at her neglect: note how *quem . . . ad finem* (407) picks up *quonam usque* (362). The third, however, goes on to suggest a reason for it; perhaps Honorius does not believe that the world can be ruled from Rome (410 f.)? What follows is a series of refutations of this belief, starting with a cosmographical analogy (the sun, for all that it restricts itself to a central path, lights the whole world, 411 f.), and proceeding to an appeal to historical fact. The latter is expressed partly by two more rhetorical questions (was the world less firmly ruled when it was ruled from Rome?, 413–16) and partly by assertion (it was from Rome that the world was ruled in the glory days of the 'Adoptive Emperors', 417–21). Roma concludes with a direct exhortation to Honorius, urging him to follow the example of these august predecessors (422–5). The speech ends by associating the hoped-for visit to come directly with memories of Honorius' last visit, as a child, in 389, providing a neat structural link with Claudian's earlier account of this visit (54–76).

407–11. These lines emphatically recall the exaltation of Rome, and of the Palatine in particular, as the true seat of Empire at 39–41: Roma's implication that Honorius is wrong to assent to the division of *potestas* and *imperium* from their proper *sedes* is thus textually validated by Claudian's own earlier assertion. See 39–52 n., noting esp. *Stil.* 3. 125 ff. 'per quem (sc. Stilichonem) fracta diu translataque paene *potestas* | non oblita sui seruilibus *exulat* aruis, | in proprium sed ducta *larem* uictricia reddit | fata solo fruiturque iterum, quibus haeserat olim, | auspiciis capitique *errantia* membra reponit'. Panegyric is literature's most ecologically minded genre, endlessly recycling its topoi and ideas: what Stilicho was shown as already having done in 400 Honorius is now asked to accomplish some three years later.

407. quem, precor, ad finem: a regular phrase in *querellae*, indicating frustration and suffering, in a tone sometimes of anger and sometimes of humble pleading: see also 362 *quonam usque* n. and compare in particular the famous opening of First Catilinarian: Cic. *Catil.* 1. 1 'quo usque tandem abutere, Catilina, patientia nostra? quam diu etiam furor iste tuus nos eludet? quem ad finem sese effrenata iactabit audacia?' Cf. also Cic. *Ver.* 5. 75, Sil. 15. 36 'quem tandem ad finem bellando fata lacesses?', Tac. *Ann.* 14. 52, and, for similar phrases, Virg. *A.* 1. 241 'quem das finem, rex magne, laborum?', V. Fl. 4. 63 f., *c.m.* 41. 1 'quem, precor, inter nos habitura silentia finem?'

laribus: cf. *Stil.* 3. 127, cit. supra, 407–10 n., Amm. Marc. 16. 10. 13 'Romam . . . imperii uirtutumque omnium larem', and see also 40 *larem* n.

408. imperium: generally we see *abundantia* at work in these lines, as 408 repeats the ideas of 407 with a very close correspondence (*laribus/sedibus*; *potestas/imperium*; *exulat/errat*). But perhaps here the variation is slightly more pointed, with *imperium* stressing the legitimate authority of Roman magistracies, including the consulship.

409 f. All palaces take their name from the Imperial palace-complex on the Palatine. For the significance of the Palatine in the poem see *pr.* 23 *orbis apex aequatus Olympo*, 8 *natiua palatia*, 40 *larem* nn. For *cunctis tribuere . . . nomen* cf. Ov. *Met.* 6. 89 'nomina summorum sibi qui tribuere deorum', *Ap.* 5. 19 'antiquae . . . urbi proprium tribuere uocamen'.

410. neclecto squalent senio: for the language cf. Cic. *Mil.* 20 'tota ciuitas confecta senio est, squalent municipia'. The motif of 'aged Rome' is a favourite one in Late Antiquity, with the goddess frequently being shown in a state of pitiful decrepitude: for a more elaborate instance of the topos see 533–6, with the note ad loc.

411 f. The sun never strays from its central path, but it none the less illumines the whole world; so too, Roma implies, power exercised from the world's centre will still extend all over the globe. Cf. *IV Cons.*

286f. 'limite Phoebus | contentus medio', and see also 18–25 n., a passage lucidly explained by W. H. Semple at *CQ* 33 (1939), 4 f.

411 f. medium . . . caeli . . . iter: this could be taken very loosely as equivalent to *iter per medium caelum*: cf. e.g. Luc. 9. 543 'fuga signorum medio rapit omnia caelo.' Alternatively, Müller interpreted it as meaning that the sun in his journey passes through the midst of the planets. But Claudian is probably referring to the doctrine of the five zones of heaven, two frozen ones at the extremities, a central torrid one, and two temperate and inhabitable ones between: see Eratosthenes fr. 16 Powell, Virg. *G.* 1. 233ff. with Thomas ad loc., *Rapt.* 1. 259 ff. with Gruzelier. Strictly speaking, of course, the inhabitable and uninhabitable zones are on the earth, but poets apply to the heavens language appropriate to the earth beneath them: see Mynors on Virg. *G.* 1. 233. The sun's route passes through the Zodiac, extending through the three central zones, but never crossing beyond the tropics of Cancer and Capricorn into the frozen ones. All this is implied by Virgil, if we combine *G.* 1. 232 'per duodena regit mundi sol aureus astra' with 238f. 'uia secta per ambas, | obliquus qua se signorum uerteret ordo' ('and a path [the ecliptic] was cut through both [between the tropics], along which the slanting array of the constellations [the Zodiac] might revolve', Thomas: *ambas* means the two temperate zones, and for the Zodiac—and hence the sun—to pass through these, it must obviously pass through the central, torrid zone as well). Ovid is considerably clearer on this subject, when he has Sol give Phaethon his instructions for driving the chariot of the sun at *Met.* 2. 129 ff.: 'nec tibi derectos placeat uia quinque per arcus! | sectus in obliquum est lato curuamine limes, | zonarumque trium contentus fine polumque | effugit australem iunctamque aquilonibus arcton: | hac sit iter—manifesta rotae uestigia cernes'. That it is the Ovidian passage which has influenced Claudian here seems very likely, given that it has also left traces elsewhere in his poetry: cf. *Gild.* 148 f. 'crescat zona rubens; medius flagrantis Olympi | me quoque limes agat', *IV Cons.* 286f. Cf. also Ov. *Ars* 1. 329f. 'non medium rupisset iter curruque retorto | Auroram uersis Phoebus adisset equis', though there the sense is different (= 'would have broken his journey off midway'); *III Cons.* 166 'Phoebi permensus iter'. Note the comment of Barth: 'apposita comparatio. Mediam illi adsignasse ait clementiam, ne propinquior ureret, semotior a rigore non defenderet'.

412. radiis . . . omnia lustrat: for *lustro* of 'casting light' see 26 *lustrat . . . aras* n. and compare in particular Cic. fr. 6. 2 Büchner 'totum conlustrat lumine mundum', *Rep.* 6. 17, Lucr. 6. 737, Virg. *A.* 4. 607 'Sol, qui terrarum flammis opera omnia lustras'.

413–16. These two rhetorical questions essentially ask the same thing (was the world less securely ruled in the days when Rome was the capital?), but Claudian aims at stylistic balance and ποικιλία. The world is neatly divided into North and East, each being represented by a pair of rivers that form the Empire's frontier. The first pair is in the accusative, in a phrase indicating subjection (*Histrum Rhenumque tenebant*), the second in the nominative, governing a verb which, though active, also expresses subordination (*timebant Tigris et Euphrates*). The world beyond the frontiers of Rome is then represented by another pairing, this time not of rivers but of peoples (*Medus et Indus*, collective singulars). For the use of rivers to symbolize countries in the rhetoric of conquest cf. e.g. Virg. *A*. 8. 726 ff. (Augustus' triumph on the shield of Aeneas, naming *Euphrates . . . Rhenusque bicornis . . . Araxes*); Fordyce ad loc. links this poetic conceit with the custom of carrying representations of river-gods in triumphs, for which see 374–80 n. above. Cf. also Stat. *Silu*. 5. 1. 89 f. 'quid uagus Euphrates, quid ripa binominis Histri, | quid Rheni uexilla ferant', *Prob*. 160 ff. 'sic nobis Scythicus famuletur Araxes, | sic Rhenus per utrumque latus . . . sic fluat adtonitus Romana per oppida Ganges', *IV Cons*. 387 ff.

413. Histrum Rhenumque: similarly paired at Stat. *Silu*. 5. 1. 128 f., *Gild*. 312, *Nupt*. 277 ff. 'iam te uenerabitur Hister, | nomen adorabunt populi; iam Rhenus et Albis | seruiet', *Stil*. 3. 13, *Get*. 568 f.

414. nostram . . . domum: presumably the *Domus Augustana* (409 f.; 40 *larem* n.).

415. Tigris et Euphrates: for the pairing in contexts of Imperial domination cf., in addition to the passages cited at 413–16 n., Prop. 3. 4. 4 'Tigris et Euphrates sub tua iura fluent'; note also Virg. *G*. 4. 560 f., *IV Cons*. 316 f.

415 f. The Persians and the Indians supposedly sent embassies to ask for peace; given the triumphalist context we should imagine these ambassadors humbly offering tribute, and certainly not as equals. Cf. esp. *Nupt*. 224 f. 'misit Achaemenio quidquid de Tigride Medus, | cum *supplex emeret* Romanam Parthia *pacem*', *VI Cons*. 69 f. Müller points to attested Parthian embassies to Rome under Tiberius (Tac. *Ann*. 6. 31), Nero (Tac. *Ann*. 15. 24), and Vespasian (Suet. *Dom*. 2. 2), and Augustus boasted of having received embassies from India as well as many other oriental peoples (*Res Gestae* 31, Suet. *Aug*. 21. 3: see also Nisbet–Hubbard on Hor. *Carm*. 1. 12. 56, with p. xxxiv).

415. Medus et Indus: that the kingdoms of the East would be added to the Empire had been a standard theme of panegyric since the days of Augustus: see e.g. Hor. *Carm*. 1. 12. 53 ff., Virg. *A*. 6. 794 f., Prop. 2. 10. 15 f., 3. 4. 1 ff., Stat. *Silu*. 4. 1. 39 ff. with Coleman ad loc., 4. 3. 154,

Ruf. 1. 374 ff., with Levy's notes ad loc., *Gild.* 20 'trepidos summittit fascibus Indos'. In Claudian's works, the most prominent example of this theme, however, is the stirring conclusion to *De Tertio Consulatu Honorii* (201–11), in which the future conquest of the East by the Emperor and his brother Arcadius is confidently predicted; this passage, with its emphasis on the heroic precocity of the young brothers is strongly reminiscent of Ovid's praises of Gaius Caesar's Parthian campaign (*Ars* 1. 177 ff.). For the idea and for the pairing of 'Medes' and Indians note especially Hor. *Saec.* 53 ff. 'iam mari terraque manus potentis | Medus Albanasque timet securis, | iam Scythae responsa petunt superbi | nuper et Indi', *Ruf.* 1. 374 (Honorius) 'qui subiget Medos, qui cuspide proteret Indos', *Eutr.* 2. 102, *IV Cons.* 257 f. 'tu licet extremos late dominere per Indos, | te Medus, te mollis Arabs, te Seres adorent'. *Medus* = 'the Persians': see 70 *Persarum proceres* n. and cf. further Virg. *G.* 2. 136 'Medorum siluae'.

415 f. foedera . . . peteret: probably = *pacem peteret*: cf. Lucil. 729 Marx (= 737 Warmington) 'pacem cum peto', Luc. 8. 435 'ad foedus pacemque uenis?' Alternatively, we could take it as referring to a request for an alliance or *amicitia*: cf. Sil. 14. 248 f. 'Romanos Petraea duces, Romana petiuit | foedera Callipolis'; also Sil. 6. 447 f. 'non . . . complexus et sanctae foedera taedae | coniugiumue peto'. Naturally *peteret* implies subordination: contrast the manlier activity of the young Stilicho when he acted as ambassador to Persia, *Stil.* 1. 51 ff. 'uix primaeuus eras, pacis cum mitteris auctor | Assyriae; tanta foedus cum gente ferire | commissum iuueni . . .'. No doubt the Persians saw things differently.

416. hinc: i.e. from Rome. The adverb picks up *illinc* (411) and is itself picked up in emphatic anaphora by *hic* (417, 420); note also *hunc* (422).

 arce: the Palatine rather than e.g. the Capitol (409 f.). *arces* is quite commonly used of the hills of Rome: cf. 617 *septenis arcibus*, *Fesc.* 2. 19 f. 'aurea septemgeminas | Roma coronet arces', *Stil.* 3. 30 'Romanae . . . arces.' Cf. esp. Virg. *G.* 2. 172 'imbellem auertis Romanis arcibus Indum', Stat. *Silu.* 4. 1. 7 f. 'plusque ante alias Euandrius arces | collis ouet'. Statius also has 'Thybridis arces | Iliacae' and 'Ausonias . . . arces' of Rome (*Silu.* 1. 2. 144 f., 3. 4. 32).

417–21. The Empire was ruled from Rome in its Golden Age, the time of the 'Adoptive Emperors', which Gibbon famously called 'the period in the history of the world during which the condition of the human race was most happy and prosperous'. In this passage it may seem that Claudian is expressing a preference for the 'adoptive principle' over hereditary monarchy, but Cameron rightly sounds a note of scepticism (p. 378). In general, the line taken by Claudian simply reflects the reality of the manner in which his honorand happened to ascend to the purple. Thus Theodosius is praised for his election at *IV Cons.* 45 ff. in terms similar to those used here of Nerva and his successors: 'haec tamen innumeris per se quaesita tropaeis, | *non generis dono,* non ambitione potitus. | *digna legi uirtus.* ultro se purpura supplex | obtulit et solus meruit regnare rogatus': cf. also Pac. *Pan. Theod.* 7. 1 'uirtus tua meruit imperium'. And yet, only some seventy lines later Honorius is exalted for the utterly contradictory reason that he became Emperor without ever having to endure the indignity of not being of 'royal' rank: *IV Cons.* 121 ff. 'hoc nobilis ortu | nasceris aequaeua cum maiestate creatus | nullaque priuatae passus contagia sortis. | omnibus acceptis ultro te regia solum | protulit et patrio felix adolescis in ostro, | membraque uestitu numquam uiolata profano | in sacros cecidere sinus.' Note also *III Cons.* 13 ff. and see Menander Rhetor 371. 17 ff. (p. 82) Russell–Wilson. Each encomiastic statement should therefore be taken primarily in its particular context. Here the aim is to convince Honorius that the world may be safely ruled from Rome; a cogent argument for this proposition is that it was so in the days of a whole series of his predecessors who, in the traditional and rhetorical view of Roman history, were generally regarded as *optimi principes;* these Emperors were conventionally said to have been chosen for their virtue and not their lineage, and so this is the principle of accession which is praised here. Another consideration is that the Emperors in question included Trajan, the supposed ancestor of the Theodosian house. In this case, Claudian may well have been influenced by the sort of sentiments expressed on the subject by Trajan's best-known panegyrist: cf. Plin. *Pan.* 5. 1 'talem esse oportuit quem non bella ciuilia, nec armis oppressa res publica, sed pax et adoptio et tandem exorata terris numina dedissent', 6. 4 'imploratus adoptione et accitus es', 7. 6 'imperaturus omnibus eligi debet ex omnibus'. It seems, however, that not all Emperors with sons of their own would have agreed: consider e.g. SHA *Sept. Seu.* 20 'cum moreretur, laetatum, quod duos Antoninos pari imperio rei publicae relinqueret, exemplo Pii, qui Verum et Marcum Antoninos per adoptionem filios reliquit, hoc melius quod ille filios per adoptionem, hic per se genitos rectores Romanae rei publicae daret.' His biographer, however, goes on to argue against the hereditary principle at length.

The general conventionality of the virtues attributed to the 'adoptive Emperors' along with the other *boni principes* of tradition, and their ready applicability in panegyric to the reigning prince, can be sensed by a comparison with such a passage as Priscian, *Pan. Anthem.* 45 ff.

'possidet hic ueterum quidquid laudatur in ullo: | Antoninum huius
pietas, sapientia Marcum, | et mitem Neruam lenissima pectora
uincunt, | promeruitque Titus non tantum mente benigna; | gloria
magnanimi Traiani cesserit isti'.

417. mansere: = *habitauerunt*, a common late Latin usage (*TLL* viii/1.
283. 20 ff., and see Löfstedt, *Philologischer Kommentar zur Peregrinatio
Aetheriae* (43 n.), 76). It was perhaps already well established in colloquial Latin in the 1st c., but literary examples are lacking except for
Mart. 8. 14. 6 'in qua (sc. cella) nec Boreas ipse manere uelit'.

417 f. mutua uirtus | legit: cf. Plin. *Pan.* 7. 4 'nulla adoptati cum eo
qui adoptabat cognatio, nulla necessitudo, nisi quod uterque optimus
erat, dignusque alter eligi alter eligere', *IV Cons.* 47 (Theodosius)
'digna legi uirtus.' Note also Tac. *Hist.* 1. 16 'loco libertatis erit quod
eligi coepimus'.

   TLL viii/2. 1738. 18 ff. lists the present instance as an example of
mutuus used by enallage with the force of an adverb, along with Stat.
Theb. 2. 173 f. 'fixos . . . oculos per mutua paulum | ora tenent', *Theod.*
338 f. 'tradat . . . secures | mutua posteritas'. Similar language is also
used of Theodosius' selecting Stilicho as a bridegroom for Serena: *Stil.*
1. 74 'iudicium uirtutis', 76 'tu legeris'. An alternative tradition, hostile
to Hadrian as an enemy of the Senate, held that even good Emperors
could make wrong decisions in the matter of the succession, and
claimed that Trajan at least made the same mistake in his choice of
successor as Augustus had done: SHA *Sept. Seu.* 21. 3 'quid de Augusto,
qui nec adoptiuum bonum filium habuit, cum illi eligendi potestas
fuisset ex omnibus? falsus est etiam ipse Traianus in suo municipe ac
nepote deligendo'.

418. in nomen . . . adoptans: Claudian is probably recalling above all
Plin. *Pan.* 88. 5 'adoptauit te optimus princeps in suum, senatus in
Optimi nomen.' Cf. also Suet. *Iul.* 83. 2 'in ima cera Gaium Octauium
etiam in familiam nomenque adoptauit', *Tib.* 3; and for the phrasing
Sal. *Iug.* 22 'a Micipsa . . . in regnum adoptatum'. At Stat. *Theb.* 7.
259 f. 'iungunt se castris regisque in nomen adoptant | Ocalea
Medeonque' the sense is metaphorical (they 'declare for our
monarch's cause', Mozley).

   Romanis rebus: a kind of dative of 'advantage' or 'interest'. The
phrase is one of great venerability: Enn. *Ann.* 156 Skutsch, Virg. *A.* 6.
857, Tac. *Ann.* 4. 1, 16. 16.

419. iudicio: for the sentiment cf. Plin. *Pan.* 7. 7 'fecit hoc Nerva nihil
interesse arbitratus, genueris an elegeris, si perinde *sine iudicio* adopten-
tur liberi ac nascuntur; nisi quod aequiore animo ferunt homines,
quem princeps parum feliciter genuit, quam quem male elegit'.

419 f. pulchram seriem . . . proles . . . Aelia: of Nerva's adoptive 'dynasty': compare Aus. *Ordo* 27 Green 'subolis seriem', *IV Cons.* 21 'gentis seriem', *c.m.* 30. 55 f. (to Spain) 'tibi saecula debent | Traianum; series his fontibus Aelia fluxit', and contrast Luc. 8. 696 'Ptolemaeorum manes seriemque pudendam'. See further *OLD* s.v. *series* 3, citing esp. Luc. 4. 823 'Caesareae . . . domus series'. Here the use is pointed because the 'line of ancestors or descendants' is one determined by virtue rather than blood. *Aelius* is the *nomen gentile* of Hadrian, here used loosely but inaccurately of both his predecessors and successors.

420. atauum deducens . . . Neruam: by a kind of hypallage = *descendens ab atauo Nerua*, as Müller points out: cf. 114 *mixtum pietate nefas* n. As the originator of this succession of adoptive Emperors through his adoption of Trajan, Nerva is poetically seen as the 'ancestor' of the entire 'dynasty'. For *deduco* in the context of descent cf. Cic. *Phil.* 13. 27 'hominem deductum ex ultimis gentibus', Virg. *G.* 3. 122, *A.* 10. 618 'nostra deducit origine nomen', Vell. 2. 41. 1 'ab Anchise ac Venere deducens genus', Sen. *Med.* 210, Sil. 2. 49, 178, 14. 462, Aus. *Grat. Act.* 39 Green.

421. For the four-word hexameter see 177 n. Cf. in particular *Gild.* 53 'dominam plebem bellatoremque senatum', and also Sil. 1. 218 (Africa) 'altrix bellorum bellatorumque uirorum'.

tranquillique Pii: the honorific cognomen *Pius* was given to Antoninus in AD 138, and passed on to his successors. Here Antoninus' *pietas* is associated with another philosophical virtue, *tranquillitas*, which was traditionally attributed both to him (SHA *Ant. Pius* 2. 1 'placidus ingenio', 2. 7) and to his adoptive son Marcus Aurelius (*Epit. Caes.* 16. 7 'a principio uitae tranquillissimus': cf. Marc. *Med.* 9. 31), as well as to Nerva (Pac. *Pan. Theod.* 11. 6). *tranquillitas animi* was originally seen as a virtue generally characterizing the wise man (Cic. *Tusc.* 4. 8 'semper mens erit tranquilla sapientis', Sen. *De Tranquillitate Animi* passim, *Theod.* 239 ff.), especially, of course, by the Epicureans. It came in time to be especially associated with wise and beneficent rulers: Vegetius, *Epit. Rei Mil. pr.* 2 'uerum tranquillitas tua, imperator inuicte, altiori consilio, quam mens poterat terrena concipere . . .', *IV Cons.* 513 ff. (Honorius) 'quae *pietas* quantusque rigor *tranquillaque magni* | *uis animi* nulloque leuis terrore moueri | nec noua mirari facilis!'

bellatoresque Seueri: for this judgement on Septimius Severus cf. Aur. Vict. *Caes.* 20. 14 'felix ac prudens, armis praecipue; adeo ut nullo congressu nisi uictor discesserit auxeritque imperium subacto Persarum rege nomine Aggaro', *Epit. Caes.* 20. 5 'fuit bellicosissimus omnium, qui ante eum fuerunt'. *bellator* associates Severus with Mars

(Virg. *A.* 9. 721, Stat. *Theb.* 4. 356: cf. 335 *bellipotens* . . . *Vlpius* n.); cf. also *Stil.* 3. 12 (of Stilicho).

tranquilli . . . bellatores: it seems as if Antoninus Pius and Septimius Severus in particular are being set up as a more modern equivalent of 'warrior' Romulus and the 'peaceful' Numa, as seen at e.g. Liv. 1. 21. 6, *IV Cons.* 492 f. 'ceu bellatore Quirino, | ceu placido moderante Numa'. For Antoninus as a second Numa see SHA *Ant. Pius* 13. 4 'et qui rite comparetur Numae, cuius felicitatem pietatemque et securitatem caerimoniasque semper obtinuit', *Epit. Caes.* 15. 3. Septimius was said to have had a dream in which he sucked the teats of a she-wolf like Romulus and his twin (SHA *Sept. Seu.* 1. 8).

422. hunc . . . chorum: the alternative reading *hoc . . . forum* is attractive, since it seems to carry on the anaphora of adverbs of place (see 416 *hinc* n.) and because there is, as Müller (following Burman) says, a natural affinity between *forum* and *ciuis*: he compares the speech Honorius will give at the *rostra* at 587 ff. But a switch to the Roman Forum would be a little odd given that the emphasis of the adverbs of place has been on the Palatine. Moreover, it is simply most natural to look for some sort of resumptive formula that sums up the appeal to precedent in 417–21 and works it into the concluding exhortation to Honorius. *hunc ciuis dignare chorum* does this admirably, appealing to Honorius as it does to emulate the virtues of the famed *optimi principes* whose relations with the Senate were generally regarded so highly and who were thus splendid examples of *ciuilitas*. We might paraphrase this line with some such formulation as 'adde te exemplis ciuilitatis clarissimis': cf. 58 f. *cum se melioribus addens | exemplis ciuem gereret* and see the notes ad loc. As a last point, note how at the end of Honorius' reply to Roma's present speech *exere nunc doctos . . . Roma, choros* (491 f.) seems deliberately to provide a structural correspondence with this line, even if the sense of *choros* is different.

An instructive example of how political opinion and aesthetic inclination can influence even the most austere philologist is provided by Burman's additional justification of *forum*: 'et certe adulatio esset inpudentissima, si Honorius dignaretur chorum tam laudabilium Imperatorum, quibus ipse minime fuit comparandus: quamquam scio Poëtam nostrum turpiter saepe blandiri'.

ciuis dignare: in imitating the *ciuilitas* of Trajan and the other *optimi principes* Honorius will also align himself with the humility of his father, as displayed in 389: cf. 58 f. (see the previous note), and esp. 61 f. 'patriciasque domos priuataque passim | uisere deposito *dignatus* limina fastu', 559 n. For imperative forms of *dignor* politely used to request the participation or presence of the great cf. Luc. 8. 112 ff. (the citizens of Lesbos to Pompey) 'tu quoque deuotos sacro tibi foedere muros | oramus sociosque lares dignere uel una | nocte tua', Stat. *Theb.* 6. 924 ff., 12. 579 'hunc dignare triumphum', *Ach.* 1. 260, *Silu.* 3. 1. 155.

chorum: not derogatory, since it is used of the schools of philosophers and so is entirely appropriate to this dynasty of Emperors distinguished for their virtues and their devotion to philosophy. Cf. Cic. *Fin.* 1. 26 'totum Epicurum paene e philosophorum choro sustulisti', *CIL* x. 2971 'ex Epicureio gaudiuigente choro'; also Arn. *Nat.* 7. 10 'uniuersus ille doctissimorum chorus'.

423. pompam . . . priorem: Theodosius' triumph over Maximus, fifteen years before (*dudum:* 53–76 n.).

424f. In this Gothic triumph Stilicho will fill the part played by Theodosius in 389; cf. 579 f. where we see him riding in the *triumphator*'s chariot. This is only a small instance of the general theme of Stilicho fulfilling the duties of a father after Theodosius' death: see also *III Cons.* 152 f., *Stil.* 3. 122 'uerior Augusti genitor'. Note how *socero* balances *patris* just as *iuuenem* balances *tenero . . . aeuo.*

424. tenero . . . aeuo: for the collocation cf. Sil. 8. 370, Stat. *Silu.* 2. 1. 40, 2. 6. 46, Sedul. *Carm. Pasch.* 3. 327, and esp. *Get.* 493 f. (the old Goth to Alaric) 'te tenero uice patris ab aeuo | gestatum.' See also 79 *tenero . . . ab ungue* n., *Stil.* 3. 121 'teneros . . . annos'.

patris comitem susceperat: cf. 57 f. *egit* | *te consorte dies.* For *suscipio* cf. *Stil.* 3. 30 f. 'non alium certe Romanae clarius arces | suscepere ducem'.

425. te Thybris adoret: i.e. do homage to you as to a *numen* present in person, and no longer merely tantalizingly near (363–5 n.). *adoro* is standardly used in such contexts of *adulatio* from the exile poetry of Ovid on: cf. Ov. *Pont.* 2. 2. 109 'mite, sed iratum merito mihi, numen adora', 3. 1. 97, 163 'Augustum numen adora', *Tr.* 3. 8. 13, Luc. 6. 243, 10. 272, Stat. *Silu.* 4. *pr.* 6 'septimum decimum Germanici nostri consulatum adoraui' with Coleman ad loc., *III Cons.* 122 f. (at Honorius' *aduentus*) 'summissus adorat | Eridanus blandosque iubet mitescere fluctus', *Nupt.* 277 f.

426–93. *Honorius rejects Roma's complaints of neglect and tells her of Stilicho's pietas in rescuing him from the siege of Milan.*

Honorius regards Roma's complaint as unjust, because, even though he did not visit her himself after the victory over Gildo, he did send her Stilicho to celebrate his consulship. His point is that so close is the bond of kinship and *pietas* between himself and his father-in-law that Stilicho's visit was as much a mark of respect for the City as a visit from himself would have been. To illustrate both the nobility of Stilicho and his unswerving loyalty to his august son-in-law, Honorius relates Stilicho's part in relieving the siege of Milan during the recently concluded war.

In terms of structure, the speech begins with a brief but firm statement of devotion and obedience intended to reassure the goddess (427f.), followed by a rejection of the legitimacy of her *querellae* (429–35). The bulk of Honorius' reply, however, is taken up by a *probatio* designed to establish the *pietas* of Stilicho. It achieves this aim by narrating in a kind of mini-epic (see 436n.) one of Stilicho's many glorious exploits (436–90). The whole speech is thus effectively subordinated to the over-arching function of Claudian's panegyrics, the encomium of his real patron, while also providing further narrative of the events and victories which have motivated the present celebrations of 404 and the current poem. Honorius concludes with an exhortation to the goddess to lead the festivities that will honour these glorious deeds (491–3). Since he immediately sets out on his journey from Ravenna to Rome at the end of his speech (494ff.), not only does he show the loyalty and respect for Roma that he professed in his opening words, he also in effect converts his own Imperial visit to Rome, his triumph over the Goths, and his consulship into a glorification of Stilicho on equal terms with himself.

A number of verbal links help bind Honorius' reply with Roma's speech. Cf. *querellis* (429) with *queror* (362; also *querellis*, 360), *spreuimus* (431) with *spreuisse* (366), *uidistis* (433) with *uidi* (393), and *choros* (492) with *chorum* (422).

426. medio . . . sermone: implying that she had more to say but Honorius cut her off: this is, of course, at odds with the polished and resounding conclusion of her speech. Cf. Virg. *A.* 4. 277 (Mercury) 'mortalis uisus medio sermone reliquit' (and see Pease ad loc. for a long list of parallels) and V. Fl. 6. 679 ((Juno) 'haec fantem medio in sermone reliquit', where gods vanish and thus brutally break off conversations with mortals; that it is here the mortal who interrupts should therefore perhaps be taken as indicating that he is on an equal footing with the gods. Cf. also Ov. *Met.* 7. 674f., Stat. *Theb.* 2. 451f., Sil. 6. 295.

   refouit: see *OLD* s.v. 4 'to restore the spirits of, cheer up', citing Stat. *Theb.* 10. 731 'i, refoue dubium', Tac. *Hist.* 3. 58 'ipse aeger animi studiis militum et clamoribus populi arma poscentis refouebatur', *Ann.* 15. 36. For the relatively rare use of the verb with a personal object see Korn on V. Fl. 4. 280f. 'ceu Lapithas aut Paeonas . . . cum refouet'.

427f. Compliance is Roma's right: see Cic. *Catil.* 1. 19, cit. 356–425n. Honorius matches his predecessors in *pietas* towards the goddess; cf.

Pan. Lat. 7. 11. 6 Mynors (to Maximianus, after prosopopoeia of Roma) 'non potuisti resistere sanctae illius parentis imperio' and especially *Prob.* 164 f. (Theodosius reassures Roma) 'optata iubes ultroque uolentem, | diua, rogas; non haec precibus temptanda fuissent'.

427. uoluisse dolebis: for *doleo* with the perfect infinitive (= 'to regret/resent that *x* has occurred') cf. Ov. *Pont.* 1. 7. 70 'meruisse dole', Luc. 9. 1053 f., Stat. *Theb.* 10. 291 f., *Rapt.* 3. 112 'conplexu caruisse dolet'.

428. o dea: a solemn and respectful vocative sets the tone for the whole speech. Note also how the insistent vocative of *Roma* (432, 438, 492) helps emphasize the personal bond between Emperor and goddess.

    legum . . . matri: a conventional topos in contemporary encomia of Rome; cf. *Prob.* 126 f. (Theodosius to Roma) 'o numen amicum . . . et legum genetrix', *Stil.* 3. 136 f. (from the *laudes Romae*) 'armorum legumque parens, quae fundit in omnes | imperium', Rut. Nam. *Red.* 1. 77 f. Note also *Gild.* 47 f. 'domui terras hominesque reuinxi | legibus', Prud. *C. Symm.* 1. 455 f. See Cameron 354 f. and cf. 362 *uestra parens* n. Note also the pointed juxtaposition of *legum* and *fas*, human and divine law.

    occurrere: used with a personal object of contradicting someone or opposing them in debate at e.g. Cic. *Off.* 2. 7 'occurritur autem nobis, et quidem a doctis et eruditis quaerentibus', Sen. *Ep.* 116. 7 'occurres hoc loco mihi illa publica contra Stoicos uoce', Quint. *Inst.* 1. 5. 6, Suet. *Aug.* 15. 1.

429–35. Stilicho held the consulship in 400, and Claudian's panegyric on the occasion makes great play of linking it both with the downfall of Eutropius (399) and, as here, with the defeat of Gildo (summer 398). See e.g. *Stil.* 1. 1 ff., 246 ff., 3. 6 ff. 'uenerare curulem, | quae tibi restituit fasces; conplectere dextram, | sub iuga quae Poenos iterum Romana redegit'.

429. post Libyam: instances of such brachylogy can be found as early as Homer (*Il.* 18. 96 μεθ' Ἕκτορα, i.e. 'after Hector's death'), and are scattered throughout classical Latin literature: cf. Cic. *Ver.* 1. 46 'uident adhuc post legem tribuniciam (i.e. 'after the tribunician law was passed') unum senatorem uel tenuissimum esse damnatum', Hor. *Carm.* 1. 18. 5 'post uina' ('after the drinking of wine'), 3. 7. 6 'post insana Caprae sidera', Sen. *Tro.* 744 'post Troiam (sc. captam)'. But they are particularly frequent in late Latin: in Claudian's own work Müller compares *Gild.* 230 'o mihi post Alpes (sc. *transitas*) nunc primum reddite': add *Stil.* 1. 246 'post domitas Arctos', *Get.* 261 'post ruptas . . . Alpes.' See further LHS ii. 243, Housman on Luc. 5. 473, Nisbet–Hubbard on Hor. *Carm.* 1. 18. 5.

429 f. falsis ne perge querellis | incusare tuos: perhaps a deliberate conflation of two passages of Statius, *Theb.* 1. 688f. '*ne perge queri casusque priorum | adnumerare tibi*' and *Ach.* 1. 439 'geminis *incusat fata querellis*'. Also similar are Virg. *A.* 10. 94f. 'nunc sera querellis | haud iustis adsurgis et inrita iurgia iactas' and V. Fl. 8. 158 'sed quid ego quemquam immeritis incuso querellis?' Contrast [Tib.] 3. 4. 75 'ne dubita blandas adhibere querellas'. *falsis = iniustis.* Contrast Luc. 2. 44 'effundunt iustas in numina saeua querellas', Stat. *Theb.* 9. 831 'desiluit iustis commotus in arma querellis'.

429. ne perge: the use of *ne* with the plain imperative seems properly to be a colloquialism, and is avoided by classical prose authors. In verse it is first attested in relatively low genres, above all comedy (Ter. *An.* 868 'ne saeui'), but later also Catullus' lyrics (61. 193 'perge, ne remorare', 62. 59) and elegies (67. 18), and Virgil's pastoral (*Ecl.* 2. 17). It was eventually accepted in high verse with the status of an archaism: Servius, on Virg. *A.* 6. 544 'ne saeui, magna sacerdos', comments 'antique dictum est, nam nunc *ne saeuias* dicimus.' Its obvious metrical usefulness may have contributed as much to its acceptance as its presumed antiquity and its tone of forcefulness. Examples in Claudian include *Ruf.* 1. 144 'ne sperne', *IV Cons.* 319f. 'ne desine tales, | nate, sequi', *Rapt.* 1. 63, 2. 282. See further LHS ii. 340, J. Wackernagel, *Vorlesungen über Syntax*, 2nd edn. (Basle, 1926–8), i. 213ff., Ogilvie on Liv. 3. 2. 9.

430. incusare tuos: Honorius cleverly reverses the attack of *uestra parens . . . queror* (362).

430 f. patriae mandata uocantis | spreuimus: Claudian may be thinking of the vision of Roma at Luc. 1. 186ff., where the goddess is called 'patriae trepidantis imago'; Caesar's spurning her marks the beginning of the civil war. For the general phrasing cf. Sil. 17. 156 (envoys) 'qui reuocent patriaeque ferant mandata monentis', and for *mandata spernere* and similar collocations cf. Ov. *Met.* 1. 701 'precibus spretis', 8. 852, Stat. *Theb.* 9. 519f., 12. 453f. 'saeuique palam spreuisse Creontis | imperia'.

431. aduectae misso Stilichone curules: i.e. 'you celebrated the presence of a consul when Stilicho visited you (in my place).' *curulis* (= *sella curulis*) appears as a substantive from Luc. 3. 107 'uacuae . . . loco cessere curules', where, however, the sense is literal; cf. Sil. 8. 486. From the Flavian period the word is regularly used, especially in poetry, by metonymy to designate any curule magistracy, but above all the consulship. Cf. esp. Stat. *Silu.* 4. 1. 5 'exsultent leges Latiae, gaudete, curules' and 4. 1. 36f. 'totidem felix tibi Roma curules | terque quaterque dabit', from a poem whose influence on *VI Cons.* has already been seen elsewhere; also Stat. *Silu.* 3. 3. 115, 5. 2. 166f., Plin. *Pan.* 61. 7 'rursus curulis rursusque purpura', Juv. 10. 91, *Theod.* 17f., 260, *Stil.* 3. 87f. 'ipsa curulem | obtulit ultori'. A rather bolder metonymy, by which *curulis* indicates not the office but its holder, can be seen at Sil. 10. 587 'euersas bis centum in strage curules', *Stil.* 3. 6f.

432f. The word order mirrors the sense. The phrases *pro principe consul* and *generoque socer* are, as it were, internally balanced, setting Honorius and Stilicho as they do side by side. They also balance each other, in that they stand in emphatic enjambement on either side of the principal verb. The consul is thus effectively made to rank equal with the Emperor, and the father-in-law with the son-in-law; the two phrases also give equal weight to the constitutional and personal links between Honorius and Stilicho. The point is driven home explicitly by the following statement *uidistis in illo | me quoque*, with further emphatic enjambement. Sense, grammar, and word-order collude in the glorification of Stilicho, who is practically indistinguishable in status from the nominal bearer of the purple.

.**nostras tibi . . . uices . . . inpleret:** for *uices inpleo* = 'to take the place of' cf. Plin. *Nat.* 11. 140, Plin. *Ep.* 6. 6. 6 'nunc solus ante cum fratre, cuius nuper amissi ego suscipere partes, ego uicem debeo inplere', *Eutr.* 2. 454 '(terror) inpleuit . . . uicem iaculi'; also Sil. 16. 51 'caesorum inplebat solus loca'. Perhaps commoner is *uices expleo*, seen at e.g. Sen. *Her. O.* 948, Tac. *Ann.* 4. 8.

433. uidistis: addressed to Roma and, through the goddess, to her citizens.

434. sic credit pietas: sc. *mea*; = 'thus in my *pietas* do I believe'. The young Emperor's *pietas* is seen here as an innate and motivating quality with a life all of its own. We could compare Pl. *Cur.* 639f. 'O Pietas mea, | serua me, quando ego te seruaui sedulo', or Aeneas' words to Lausus at *A.* 10. 812 'fallit te incautum pietas tua'. If Claudian has the Virgilian passage in mind, one could see both a similarity and a contrast between these heroic youths: both are outstanding for their filial devotion, but Lausus' loyalty is to a monstrous tyrant of a father (*A.* 7. 653f.), Honorius' to a father-in-law whose mutual devotion is proven in the subsequent narrative (435–90). For the *pietas* of the Imperial family see 99 *certauit pietate domus* n.

434f. That after Theodosius' death Stilicho becomes a true father to Honorius (as also to Arcadius) is a regular theme of Claudian's panegyric, serving to justify the power he wields at his son-in-law's court. Cf. esp. *Gild.* 301f. (Theodosius' ghost to Arcadius) 'tunc ipse paterna | successit pietate mihi tenerumque rudemque | fouit et in ueros eduxit principis annos', *Stil.* 3. 121f. 'teneros his moribus imbuit annos, | uerior Augusti genitor'. Here an extra twist is given to this theme, in that his saving Honorius during the siege of Milan shows that Stilicho deserves to be called *parens* by the Emperor not merely by the tie of blood (*sanguine*) but through his heroism (*claris . . . factis*). Similar ideas were expressed in Claudian's comments on the succession to the throne, but in panegyric the importance attached to rival claims of blood and virtue varies in any case according to necessities imposed by the material Fate hands the poet: see 417–21 n. Cf. also *IV Cons.* 220 'uirtute decet, non sanguine niti'; this is to be contrasted with the encomium of Eucherius at l. 552 below, where the son of Stilicho and Serena, having no real achievements to his credit, is praised solely for his 'regius undique sanguis'.

434. sanguine: Stilicho and Honorius shared no ancestry, but their link by marriage can be so described in a loose way. Maria, the daughter of Stilicho and Serena, was not only Honorius' wife, but also by blood his cousin; furthermore, by virtue of Theodosius' adoption of Serena, she was also Honorius' niece.

435. claris . . . factis: his victories over Gildo and Alaric, and especially the relief of Milan. For the collocation cf. Virg. *A.* 7. 474 'claris dextera factis', Stat. *Silu.* 1. 2. 97, and also Liv. 2. 10. 6 'ambos claros genere factisque'.

436. Homer declared in the catalogue of ships that not even if he had ten tongues and ten mouths would he be able to record the names of all those who fought at Troy, were it not that the Muses aided him (*Il.* 2. 488 ff.). Disclaimers of this kind for the poet's inability to match in his verse the grandeur of his theme became one of the standard motifs of epic poetry. Ten was still the number with which Ennius felt able to gauge his own deficiencies in the first recorded appearance of the topos in Roman poetry (*Ann.* 469 f. Skutsch 'non si lingua loqui saperet quibus, ora decem sint | in me, tum ferro cor sit pectusque reuinctum'), but inflation raised this to a round hundred by the time of Hostius (fr. 3 Büchner 'non si mihi linguae | centum atque ora sient totidem uocesque liquatae'). A hundred then becomes the standard number (Virg. *G.* 2. 42 ff., *A.* 6. 625 ff., Ov. *Met.* 8. 533 ff., Sil. 4. 525 ff.; hence Pers. 5. 1 f. 'uatibus hic mos est, centum sibi poscere uoces, | centum ora et linguas optare in carmina centum'). With the passage of time, this particular currency became still further devalued, and not even a thousand voices are enough for Ovid (*Fast.* 2. 119 f.), Valerius Flaccus (6. 36 f.), and Apuleius (*Met.* 11. 25). See further *TLL* ix/2. 1078. 15. Both here and at *Prob.* 55 ff. ('non, mihi centenis pateant si uocibus ora | multifidusque ruat centum per pectora Phoebus, | acta Probi narrare queam') Claudian could therefore almost be said to be displaying a kind of classical 'restraint' in his hyperbole. He is still more modest than his predecessors in that a hundred tongues would not be sufficient for his modest talents even to 'touch upon' (*perstringere*) the events described, let alone 'tell' them comprehensively. Verbally Claudian is closest to Virgil (*G*. 2. 42 ff. 'non ego *cuncta* meis amplecti uersibus opto, | non, mihi si linguae centum sint oraque centum') and Silius (4. 525 ff. '*non*, mihi Maeoniae redeat si gloria linguae, | centenasque pater det Phoebus fundere uoces, | tot caedes proferre *queam*'). Since the topos is traditionally reserved for those parts of the epic material where the subject is so very elevated that the poet stands in special need of help from the Muses or indulgence from the audience, Honorius' narrative is thus accorded the status of a mini-epic, while Stilicho's *pietas* in his heroic raising of the siege of Milan is established as the climax of the war against Alaric.

perstringere: 'graze', and so 'to touch on' briefly in a narrative. This usage, however, is largely restricted to prose; Cic. *Phil*. 2. 47 'sed reliquum uitae cursum uidete, quem quidem celeriter perstringam', *Ver*. 4. 105, Sen. *Ben*. 7. 14. 1, Plin. *Pan*. 25. 1.

437. mundo: here = 'the Roman world', or 'the Empire', though to translate in this way would weaken the hyperbole. See *TLL* vii/2. 1638. 21 ff. citing *C. Th*. 16. 5. 18 *pr*. et 1 'quicumque sub nomine Manichaeorum mundum sollicitant, ex omni quidem orbe terrarum . . . pellantur . . . nihil ad summum his sit commune cum mundo', and Levy on *Ruf*. 1. 143 'toto dominabere mundo', 2. 212 f. Cf. also Apul. *Met*. 11. 17 'quae sub imperio mundi nostratis reguntur', *III Cons*. 63 f. 'ciuilia rursus | bella tonant dubiumque quatit discordia mundum', *Theod*. 51, *Eutr*. 1. 15. For *mundus* of 'the inhabited world' (= ἡ οἰκουμένη), a sense often hard to distinguish from the present one in panegyrical and patriotic literature, see Levy on *Ruf*. 1. 87 f.

ab: sometimes used in place of *de* or *ex* in partitive phrases. See *TLL* i/1. 13. 37 ff., citing Cic. *Inu*. 2. 5 'a multis . . . eligere . . . commodissimum quodque', Virg. *A*. 7. 152 f. 'delectos ordine ab omni . . . oratores', Paul. Nol. *Carm*. 20. 314.

438. si fama necdum patuit: a negative version of the kind of formula seen at e.g. Ov. *Pont*. 2. 9. 3 'fama loquax uestras si iam peruenit ad auris'.

438–40. Honorius insists on his reliability as an eyewitness (*docebo, subiectum oculis nostris, spectator . . . fui*) at the same time as he indicates that Stilicho's actions were motivated by his pious desire to save his Imperial son-in-law (*causa fui*).

439. subiectum nostris oculis: for the greater reliability proverbially attributed to the eyes see A. Otto, *Die Sprichwörter und sprichwörtlichen*

Redensarten der Römer (Leipzig, 1890; repr. Hildesheim, 1962), 251, and consider Hor. *Ars* 180 ff. 'segnius irritant animos demissa per aurem, | quam quae sunt oculis subiecta fidelibus et quae | ipse sibi tradit spectator', with Brink ad loc. *subicio* may be used of something that is literally before one's eyes, as is strictly speaking the case here: cf. Liv. 25. 24. 11 'ex superioribus locis urbem . . . pulcherrimam subiectam oculis uidit', 44. 3. 7. The phrase, however, is perhaps more commonly used metaphorically, particularly of literary accounts so vivid that they seem to bring the events they relate before the reader's mental vision. Müller compares Plin. *Nat.* 2. 170 'ut totum hoc . . . ceu subiectum oculis quantum sit ostendam'; add Cic. *Orat.* 139 'saepe etiam rem dicendo subiciet oculis', Vell. 2. 89. 6, and note also Cic. *de Orat.* 3. 202 'illustris explanatio rerumque quasi gerantur sub aspectum paene subiectio.' Indeed, Quintilian cleverly uses this particular metaphor in order to define the effect of metaphor (*translatio*) itself: *Inst.* 8. 6. 19 'translatio permouendis animis plerumque et signandis rebus ac sub oculos subiciendis reperta est.' The choice of phrase here, then, may perhaps function not only as a guarantee of veracity from an eyewitness, but also as an earnest of the vividness with which the event will be narrated for the benefit of Roma, and of the audience. For the importance attached to visualization in descriptions in ancient literature see further Quint. *Inst.* 4. 2. 123, 6. 2. 32, 8. 3. 65, 9. 2. 40; its continuing significance in Late Antiquity is discussed by Michael Roberts, *Poetry and the Cult of the Martyrs. The Liber Peristephanon of Prudentius* (Ann Arbor, 1993), 139 ff.

440. spectator uel causa fui: an important correction; not only did Honorius observe Stilicho's remarkable display of heroism with his own eyes, but it was *pietas* towards him that inspired it in the first place. *spectator* can have very negative undertones, implying a sadistic voyeurism akin to that of the more debased elements of the audience at the Games: see e.g. Harrison on Virg. *A.* 10. 443 'cuperem ipse parens spectator adesset', Fantham on Luc. 2. 207 f. Here, however, the dominant sense is 'eyewitness'; cf. Cic. *de Orat.* 1. 112 'mearum ineptiarum testem et spectatorem', Stat. *Silu.* 5. 3. 215 ff. 'qualis eras, Latios quotiens ego carmine patres | mulcerem felixque tui spectator adesses | muneris!'

440–69. *The siege of Milan (winter 402) and its heroic relief by Stilicho.*

The bulk of the war-narrative in *VI Cons.* is concerned with the events that took place after Pollentia, since the beginnings of the invasion and the battle itself had already been celebrated in *De Bello Getico*. In

Honorius' account, however, Roma is given a flashback to an incident from the winter between the invasion and the battle of Pollentia. Honorius tells how the Goths besieged him and the Court in Milan in the hope that, in the absence of Stilicho, they could extort favourable conditions of peace from him. Stilicho at the time was engaged in crushing a revolt in Raetia and in raising new troops with which to repel Alaric's army (cf. *Get.* 319ff.). The Goths commanded the bridge and road that led over the Adda to Milan, but Stilicho, arriving suddenly with the vanguard, forced a crossing by night and marched to the relief of the city.

The siege can be dated tentatively to late Feb. or Mar. 402. Symmachus, sent on an embassy from the Senate to the Court, was able with difficulty to reach Milan on 24 Feb., and a letter of that date to his son reveals that Stilicho was expected 'mox cum praesidiis ualentissimis adfore' (*Ep.* 7. 13). For this visit, and its possible purpose, see in general T. D. Barnes, *AJP* 97 (1976), 373–86, esp. 381–3. For the details of the relief of Milan, however, we are obliged to rely upon the present passage and on the earlier, more elliptical account of it given at *Get.* 447ff. There Claudian concentrates on describing the tension of the inhabitants of Milan, as they strain to distinguish whether the clouds they see from the walls are raised by the enemy or by their hoped-for saviour: *Get.* 455ff. 'pulueris ambiguam nubem speculamur ab altis | turribus, incerti socios adportet an hostes | ille globus'. Eventually anxiety gives way to jubilation: *Get.* 459f. 'emicuit Stilichonis apex et cognita fulsit | canities.' Although Claudian includes himself among the besieged ('speculamur'), Cameron (p. 414) has suggested that this is no more than a literary device to enhance the vividness of the narrative. Cameron is led to make this suggestion as a result of what he, in company with others, sees as an otherwise inexplicable discrepancy between *De Bello Getico* and *VI Cons*: in the earlier poem the siege is lifted by day, with the Court and the Milanese looking out upon an army that is distant but still visible, while here we are dealing with action by night (453 *nox erat*, 454f. *iam classica primos | excierant uigiles*). He therefore argues that, in *De Bello Getico*, Claudian, not having been present during the siege, used his literary imagination, but that later, 'after making inquiries, [he] discovered that unfortunately Milan had been relieved at night, [and] corrected his error in *VI Cons*.' The troubling discrepancy, however, is probably illusory. The events related in *De Bello Getico* deal with the arrival, in daylight, of Stilicho before the city wall itself, but while ll. 453ff. of the present poem must indeed refer to the early part of the night, they narrate only the forced crossing of the Adda. The river in fact flows a considerable distance to the east of the city, and, allowing time for a successful crossing and for the subsequent march to Milan, it is not too difficult to imagine that by the time Stilicho reached the gates the sun had risen. Cf. Crees 162 n. 2. Note also that the two passages have put more than one acute mind on a false trail. Birt (p. li) seemingly conflates them and misunderstands *uigiles* (455), thus making the odd claim that '*mane circa primam uigiliam* dux aduentauit'.

The formal function of Honorius' narrative in the architecture of the speech is to prove to Roma that she is unjust in her complaints of neglect. Honorius sent her Stilicho in his stead and, as the account of the heroic relief of Milan shows, such is the *pietas* of Stilicho and his son-in-law to each other that this is tantamount to Honorius' coming to the City himself. But above all, the passage serves once more to turn the focus of the panegyric from the nominal honorand to Claudian's real patron. For all that Honorius is made to claim an old-fashioned Roman virtue in his refusal to bargain for his life on shameful terms (449–52), the relief of Milan is essentially a one-man show; Stilicho, practically single-handed, surpasses even the similar achievements of both Greek and Roman antiquity as exemplified in the deeds of Diomedes in the *Doloneia* and of Horatius Cocles on the bridge.

440 f. populator Achiuae | Bistoniaeque plagae: between 395 and 397 the Goths ravaged Thrace and Achaea, despite the efforts both of Stilicho and of the Eastern court to contain them. Claudian's accounts of the destruction (*Ruf.* 2. 186 ff., *Get.* 166 ff.) have their fair share of hyperbole, but it is worth noting Zosimus' claim that the evidence of the Gothic attack was still visible in his day (5. 5. 7). Eventually Eutropius came to an accommodation with Alaric and granted him an official Roman appointment, probably that of *magister militum per Illyricum* (*Get.* 535 'at nunc Illyrici postquam mihi tradita iura'). See in general Cameron 88 ff., Alan Cameron and Long, *Barbarians and Politics* (218–20 n.), 328 ff. The present phrase is very close to the scandalized polemic of *Eutr.* 2. 214 ff. 'uastator Achiuae | gentis et Epirum nuper populatus inultam | praesidet Illyrico'. Cf. also Prop. 3. 18. 29 'hic olim ignaros luctus populauit Achiuos'. *Achiuae Bistoniaeque plagae* is a more elaborate version of the kind of poetic phrase which Korn (on V. Fl. 4. 211 'Asiae plaga') traces back to Ov. *Ep.* 12. 28 'Ponti qua plaga laeua iacet'; cf. also *Ruf.* 2. 45, *Get.* 590 'Elysiis . . . plagis', *c.m.* 31. 56.

440. populator: first attested in Ovid (*Met.* 12. 593, 13. 655), but used sparingly in verse: see also Sen. *Tro.* 26, Luc. 4. 92, 9. 441, *Ciris* 111, Stat. *Theb.* 7. 382, *Ruf.* 2. 378 (a fisherman) 'aequoreus populator'.

441. Bistoniae: the Bistones were a Thracian tribe who, in poetry, lend their name to the whole country: for them and their eponymous

founder Biston see *RE* iii. 504. 24 ff. The adjective is attested in Latin
verse at Lucr. 5. 31 'Bistonias . . . plagas'. Note also *IV Cons.* 54
'Bistonios . . . campos'.

crebris successibus amens: for the significance in Claudian's
propaganda of Alaric's 'madness' see 105 *furias*, 206 *furorem* nn. In epic,
phrases such as this one regularly indicate that a character is about to
fall into dangerous *hubris* or in some other way overreach himself
through excessive self-confidence: Alaric is riding for a fall. Cf. Virg.
A. 2. 386 'successu exsultans . . . Coroebus' (Coroebus is cut down
some forty lines later), Ov. *Met.* 12. 298f. 'adsiduae successu caedis
ouantem . . . figis', Sil. 16. 431f., Tac. *Hist.* 2. 15.

442. *spiro* may be used with the accusative to express the kind of spirit or
emotion that characterizes an individual or his actions; note esp. *OLD*
s.v. 6b 'to breathe or express the spirit of', citing Cic. *Att.* 15. 11. 1
'Martem spirare diceres', Liv. 3. 46. 2 'inquietum hominem et tri-
bunatum etiam nunc spirantem', Sil. 3. 240. Here the sense is not quite
the same, since the accusative indicates the source—the 'inspiration'—of the emotion; Alaric's present stance of threatening violence
is the result of an increase in confidence caused by his having succeeded in breaking through the barrier of the Alps. Cf. the use of the
accusative at Stat. *Silu.* 4. 6. 94f. 'Vestinus . . . quem nocte dieque |
spirat' and *Rapt.* 1. 6 'totum spirant praecordia Phoebum'. We should
therefore take *animis . . . inmanibus* as an instrumental ablative expressing the manner in which the emotion inspired reveals itself. But
Claudian will also have in mind the use of the adverbial accusative
seen in the phrase 'spirans inmane' (e.g. Virg. *A.* 7. 510; Fordyce ad loc.
suggests an origin in the Homeric μέγα πνέων). A prose author might
have written e.g. 'propter Alpes ruptas animos spirans inmanes'.

ruptas . . . Alpes: = 'the shattering of the Alps'. For the *ab urbe
condita* construction, see pr. 17 *uictusque Typhoeus* n. Alaric hopes to
emulate Hannibal (see 182–4, 184–6 nn.), and after Milan the next step
will be a march on Rome: *Gild.* 82f. 'ruptaque emissus ab Alpe |
Poenus et attonitae iam proximus Hannibal urbi', *Get.* 532f. (Alaric
boasting) 'fregi Alpes galeisque Padum uictricibus hausi: | quid
restat nisi Roma mihi?' In the event, however, 'Romula post ruptas
uirtus . . . emicat Alpes' (*Get.* 261). The fact that Silius regularly uses
such language of Hannibal in the *Punica* must have exerted some
influence on Claudian; see e.g. 5. 160 'perfractas Alpes', 11. 135, 12.
15 f. 'ille uigor, qui ruptis Alpibus arma | intulerat', also Sid. *Carm.* 2.
530f. Cf. 272 *pulsato* n. It is hard not to think of the story of Hannibal
and the vinegar: Juv. 10. 152f. 'opposuit natura Alpemque niuemque:
| diducit scopulos et *montem rumpit* aceto'.

inmanibus: implying violence and savagery: cf. Sal. *Rep.* 2. 4. 2 'animum . . . inmanem reflexit', Ov. *Met.* 8. 584 (Achelous) 'animis inmanis et undis', Tac. *Ann.* 6. 20.

443. Ligurum trepidis . . . muris: i.e. of Milan (see 363 *Ligus* n.). The inhabitants' fear is poetically transferred to the city walls; cf. esp. Sil. 14. 580 'nec mora tum trepidos hac clade irrumpere muros', and also 'trepidam . . . urbem' at Luc. 2. 160 (cf. 3. 372f., 5. 381 'trepidam . . . Romam'), *Stil.* 1. 279 and 3. 219; also *Get.* 192f. (the Goths in Greece) 'equitataque summi | culmina Taygeti trepidae uidistis, Amyclae.' The Emperor does not share their fear (449).

444f. The Goths are used to a cold northern climate, and so experience no difficulty in conducting war in conditions that are oppressive to the Romans; the implication is perhaps that an Italian winter campaign is no rougher for the Goths than a summer one in their homeland would be. The same basic idea of winter being normally favourable in war to Rome's northern enemies is ingeniously adapted by Pliny in his discussion of Trajan's winter campaigning in Dacia: *Pan.* 12. 3f. 'an audeant, qui sciant te adsedisse ferocissimis populis, eo ipso tempore *quod amicissimum illis difficillimum nobis*, cum Danubius ripas gelu iungit, duratusque glacie ingentia tergo bella transportat, cum ferae gentes non telis magis quam *suo caelo, suo sidere armantur*? . . . (sc. Romani) ultroque hiemem suam barbaris inferre gaudebant.' Cf. esp. *suo sidere armantur* and *sidere* (445). In fact, we are dealing here with something of a minor panegyrical topos, and Mamertinus praises Maximian in still more extravagant terms for a crossing of the Alps (*Pan. Lat.* 11. 9. 2f. Mynors). The fortitude of these Emperors is, predictably enough, matched by Stilicho's: *Get.* 322f. (Stilicho in Raetia) 'scandit inaccessos *brumali sidere* montes | nil hiemis caeliue memor'.

444. tutior auxilio brumae: cf. Virg. *A.* 1. 571 'auxilio tutos dimittam'.

444f. quo . . . sidere: cf. Virg. *G.* 1. 1 f. 'quo sidere terram | uertere', *IV Cons.* 424f. (a helmsman learns by experience) 'quo dextra regatur | sidere'. For *sidus* implying 'season' cf. also Virg. *G.* 1. 73, 311, 2. 1, and (with reference in particular to winter) *A.* 4. 309 'quin etiam hiberno moliri sidere classem?', Plin. *Nat.* 6. 33, Mart. 9. 13. 2, Plin. *Pan.* 12. 3. Note also 'brumali sidere' at Ov. *Pont.* 2. 4. 25 and *Get.* 322.

445. consueti . . . inclementia caeli: *inclementia* is first attested in Virgil: see Austin on *A.* 2. 602 'diuum inclementia' (and cf. Stat. *Theb.* 1. 650 'saeuo tanta *inclementia caelo*', also of Heaven's anger). The extension of such language to climate may be something of a meteorological cliché in English ('inclement weather'), but in classical Latin it always remained a conscious poeticism. It can be traced back to

Luc. 8. 365f. (the effect of climate on the character of orientals) 'quidquid ad Eoos tractus mundique teporem | ibitur, emollit gentes clementia caeli'; cf. Aus. *Ordo* 135f. (=20. 8f.) Green 'clementia caeli | mitis'. The negative noun is applied by Statius to a stormy sea at *Theb.* 5. 173 'medii inclementia ponti' (cf. *Get.* 210 'maris inclementia'). Cf. also *Pan. Lat.* 11. 9. 2 Mynors 'aduersus inclementiam locorum ac siderum uos maiestatis potentia tuebatur', Amm. Marc. 15. 4. 3, Sid. *Ep.* 2. 2. 2 (unusually, of summer heat) 'fallis clementissimo recessu inclementiam canicularem'.

446. me . . . obsidere: the emphatic positioning of the pronoun stresses the horror of Alaric's hubristic action. Cf. *Get.* 561f. (Stilicho to the troops before Pollentia) '*obsessi principis* armis | excusate *nefas*', where the emphasis is instead on the shame that the Romans should feel for having permitted this to happen.

minabatur . . . obsidere: = *minabatur se esse obsessurum.* The construction is well attested in verse from an early period, but is avoided in classical prose: see LHS ii. 357f., and cf. Pl. *Men.* 842 'minatur mihi oculos exurere', Lucr. 4. 403 'non supra sese ruere omnia tecta minari', Luc. 5. 336f., *Ruf.* 1. 298 'iugulare minatur'.

calcato . . . uallo: the Goths overran the outer defences of the city and penned the inhabitants up within the walls. Here *calcato* implies a rapid and violent advance over an obstacle; cf. Luc. 7. 332 'calcatis . . . ruunt castris' ('they tread down the fortifications and rush on' Duff), 10. 546 'obsedit muris calcantem moenia Magnum'.

447. spem uano terrore fouens: *spem* should properly be taken with *si forte.* Alaric hoped that, by filling Honorius with needless terror of capture and perhaps even death, he would be able to extort from the Court conditions favourable to himself. This fear would have been *uanus* ('needless', 'ungrounded') for the reason that Stilicho could be relied upon to save the Emperor and the city (*duce uenturo fretum,* 450). 'Empty fear(s)' is, of course, a common cliché in both Latin epic and history: e.g. Ov. *Met.* 9. 248f. 'sed enim nec pectora uano | fida metu paueant', Liv. 2. 2. 7 'exonera ciuitatem uano forsitan metu', Luc. 1. 486f., Stat. *Theb.* 7. 130, *Rapt.* 2. 278. Given the striking juxtaposition of *spem* with *uano,* however, the adjective also tends to colour this second noun: Alaric's hopes of pressurizing Honorius into dishonourable action are also 'vain', because the Emperor is too steadfast in the exercise of Roman virtue to submit. For the still commoner cliché of 'vain hopes' see e.g. Virg. *A.* 1. 352 'uana spe', Luc. 3. 134, 5. 227, *Stil.* 1. 345, *Get.* 388 'nequiquam Emathium spes uana Philippum'. Livy unites the two at 27. 26. 1 'ut . . . nec spem nec metum ex uano haberet'.

447 f. remotis | praesidiis: Stilicho and the main body of the troops, currently in Raetia.

448. urgente metu: not a contradiction of *uano terrore* if we understand everything that appears in the *si forte* clause as paraphrasing Alaric's presumed thoughts rather than representing 'reality'. Abstract nouns appear regularly as the subject of *urgueo*, as at e.g. Luc. 1. 459f. 'quos ille timorum | maximus haud urguet leti metus', *Eutr.* 1. 227 'nullum sic urget egestas', *Get.* 41f. 'tua nos urgenti dextera leto | eripuit'.

448f. qua uellet obirem | condicione fidem: the probable nature of any such conditions can only be surmised from what is known of Alaric's later bargaining terms. Useful summaries of the negotiations of AD 408–9 can be found at Matthews 288ff. and Liebeschuetz 66ff. Alaric's principal demands were for gold and silver, corn, and the control of some of the northern provinces of Italy. In 409 Jovius, Alaric's envoy to Ravenna, also demanded the Roman rank of *magister utriusque militiae* for his master: for Alaric's determination to hold an offical Roman command see Cameron 172.

obire fidem is a poeticism for *obire foedus/pacem*. Müller compares Stat. *Theb.* 11. 380 'nempe ille fidem et stata foedera rupit'; add Sen. *Thy.* 480ff. 'ante cum flammis aquae, | cum morte uita, cum mari uentus fidem | foedusque iungent'. *condicio* is alien to the diction of high poetry, its appearances in verse being usually limited to lower genres such as comedy (e.g. Pl. *Trin.* 159, *Truc.* 849), elegy (Prop. 3. 2. 22, Ov. *Tr.* 3. 14. 52), and satire (Hor. *Ep.* 1. 1. 51; cf. *Eutr.* 1. 31); also lyric (Hor. *Carm.* 1. 1. 12). Cf., however, Virg. *A.* 12. 879f. 'cur mortis adempta est | condicio?', Ov. *Met.* 10. 569, *IV Cons.* 220, 616. See also Hor. *Carm.* 3. 5. 14, discussed below at 450–2n., and Axelson, p. 103.

449–52. Honorius claims that he was not afraid, first because he knew he could rely on Stilicho, and secondly because he was inspired by the example of the Roman leaders of old who would never have yielded to dishonourable conditions solely to save their lives. Honorius in this speech is revealed as *constans* and as possessed of an old-fashioned virtue, but his words also serve to do further honour to Stilicho (he could be relied upon even in such adverse circumstances), and to Roma, mother of heroes (*tuorum, Roma, ducum*).

With the scene presented here Müller contrasts the picture of panic in the Court when it heard the news of Alaric's invasion and was set for flight until its courage was restored by a speech from Stilicho: *Get.* 296ff. 'quid turpes iam mente fugas, quid Gallica rura | respicitis Latioque libet post terga relicto | longinquum profugis Ararim praecingere castris?'. The two passages can, in a sense, be reconciled—the courage inspired by Stilicho on this occasion lived on through the winter and the siege—but in any case Honorius himself is not, of course, personally censured. However that may be, by the end of the year the Court had taken up permanent residence in Ravenna (cf. 494), a city surrounded by marshes and so safer from sudden attack and siege alike.

450–2. As a prime example of this noble ideal in the Roman literary and rhetorical tradition, Müller cites M. Atilius Regulus, and refers the reader to the discussion of the ethics involved at Cic. *Off.* 3. 99 ff. The instinct is surely right, but the passage that probably underlies these lines is Hor. *Carm.* 3. 5. 13 ff. 'hoc cauerat mens prouida Reguli | dissentientis *condicionibus* | *foedis* et exemplo trahenti | perniciem ueniens in aeuum, | si non periret immiserabilis | captiua pubes.' Note also *Gild.* 78 f. 'uoluit contempta luce reuerti | Regulus', *IV Cons.* 410 f. The continuing importance of Regulus as a model of pagan *religio* and fortitude can be gauged by the serious attention he merits in Augustine's polemics (see *Ciu. Dei* 1. 15).

450 f. memorem . . . tuorum, | Roma, ducum: Honorius thus fulfils the instructions given to him by his father at *IV Cons.* 397 ff. 'nec desinat umquam | tecum Graia loqui, tecum Romana uetustas. | *antiquos euolue duces*, adsuesce futurae | militiae, Latium retro te confer in aeuum'.

451. morte parata: cf. Luc. 8. 31 f. 'quisquamne secundis | tradere se fatis audet nisi morte parata?'

452. foedus lucis amor: perhaps a deliberate conflation of Virg. *A.* 6. 721 'quae lucis miseris tam dira cupido?' and Stat. *Theb.* 3. 370 'pro uitae foeda cupido!' But such language is, of course, very common in passages treating the theme of the heroic code of 'death before dishonour': e.g. V. Fl. 7. 493 (Medea) 'quis mihi lucis amor?', Sil. 10. 42, 517 f., Stat. *Theb.* 8. 386 f. 'pellitur et patriae et, qui mente novissimus exit, | lucis amor', 11. 182, 11. 704 f. Note also Lucr. 3. 1077 'mala nos subigit uitai tanta cupido'.

    pepigit: contrast *Stil.* 1. 210 f. (the Germans) 'illi terribiles, quibus otia uendere semper | mos erat et foeda requiem mercede pacisci'.

    dispendia famae: cf. Mela 1. 31 'quae taceri nullum rerum famaeue dispendium est.' For *dispendium* with the sense 'loss' see *TLL* v/1. 1396. 3 ff., *Theod.* 120.

453. nox erat: a frequent formula in ancient narrative, both verse and prose: cf. e.g. Hor. *Epod.* 15. 1, Virg. *A.* 3. 147, 4. 522, Ov. *Am.* 3. 5. 1, *Fast.* 2. 792, 3. 639, *Pont.* 3. 3. 5, and for copious lists of examples see Pease on Virg. *A.* 4. 522, Trump 57. It is generally used to mark the beginning or end of a narrative, or else as a formula of transition from one section of narrative to another; in modern punctuation, we should therefore indicate the beginning of a new paragraph at this line. For a detailed discussion see H. McL. Currie, *LCM* 18. 6 (June 1993), 92–5. The formula is associated with strong emotion, and especially with the creation of a tone of sorrow or despair, as seen in the most famous example in Latin literature, *A.* 4. 522 ff., where the calmness and peace of the world asleep are contrasted with the torments of Dido: see Currie p. 92. Here, however, tension and anxiety will be triumphantly overcome by joy and success.

453 f. Cf. *Get.* 44 f. 'iam non in pecorum morem formidine clausi | prospicimus saeuos campis ardentibus ignes.' The comparison of camp-fires shining in the dark around a besieged city with stars recalls the famous closing scene of the eighth book of the *Iliad*: *Il.* 8. 555 f. ὡς δ' ὅτ' ἐν οὐρανῷ ἄστρα φαεινὴν ἀμφὶ σελήνην | φαίνετ' ἀριπρεπέα, 560 f. τόσσα μεσηγὺ νεῶν ἠδὲ Ξάνθοιο ῥοάων | Τρώων καιόντων πυρὰ φαίνετο Ἰλιόθι πρό. The simile thus continues the pattern of Homeric allusion begun in l. 436, and helps prepare the extended comparison drawn between the relief of Milan and the *Doloneia* (470–83). As Stilicho's status will be enhanced by direct comparison with Diomedes, so the siege of Milan is, more subtly, associated with the greatest siege in the history of the world. This, however, is a siege that will not end in disaster.

453. stellarum more: this epic formula of comparison is considerably less common in Claudian than in many other high poets but cf. *Theod.* 320 'more auium', *Stil.* 2. 20, *c.m.* 9. 21 'Parthorum more'.

454. barbaricos . . . focos: = *barbarorum focos*; cf. *Ruf.* 1. 360 'aspice barbaricis iaceant quot moenia flammis.' *focus* can be used poetically, by extension, of all kinds of fires (see *TLL* vi/1. 990. 79 ff.), but the sense 'camp-fire' seems especially rare. Cf. Vulg. I Macc. 12. 28 'et accenderunt focos in castris suis'. Since in late Latin *focus* displaces *ignis* in ordinary usage (hence Ital. *fuoco*, Fr. *feu*, etc.), this may be a very rare example of Claudian admitting a current colloquialism into his lofty epic.

454 f. A *classicum* is any military signal given on the trumpet, and here indicates the beginning of the first watch. For the phrasing cf. Hor. *Epod.* 2. 5 'neque excitatur classico miles truci'.

455. gelida . . . ab Arcto: i.e. from Raetia (*Get.* 329 ff.).

pulcher: Stilicho's physical beauty, we are told, broke hearts when he was sent in his youth to Persia as an ambassador: *Stil.* 1. 56 f. 'defixaeque hospite pulchro | Persides arcanum suspirauere calorem'. See also 25 *pulcher Apollo* n.

456–8. The geographical realities that lie behind Claudian's description have been well explained by Müller. Claudian informs us that the

Gothic host lay between Stilicho and Milan, and controlled the bridge over the Adda. Since Milan is to the west of the river, this implies that Stilicho most probably returned from Raetia through the Brenner Pass or one of the other eastern passes (Seeck, *Geschichte* (108–10 n.), vi. 573 n. 30). Müller suggests that the Gothic garrison blocking the river was either at Pons Aureoli on the road that led from Verona to Milan through Bergamo, or else at Acerrae on the route from Verona to Milan via Cremona. Stilicho had entered Raetia via the Lago di Como (*Get.* 319 ff.). A return by the same route does not fit Claudian's description here because the obvious road to take in that area led directly from Comum to Milan without crossing the Adda at all. For the Adda see 195 n.

456. medius sed clauserat hostis: and so *medium . . . per hostem* Stilicho stoutly made his way (466). For *medius . . . hostis* cf. Virg. *A.* 2. 508 '(uidit) medium in penetralibus hostem', and see 466 n. For the postponement of *sed* see 394 n.

458. scissas spumosior incitat undas: as the waters of the Adda strike against the piles on which the bridge rests, they are 'torn' (i.e. churned up) and their course thus becomes all the more violent downstream. The effect is to heighten the atmosphere of danger and menace, thus magnifying the achievement of Stilicho in forcing a crossing. For the general idea cf. Ov. *Met.* 3. 568 ff. 'sic ego torrentem, qua nil obstabat eunti, | lenius et modico strepitu decurrere uidi; | at quacumque trabes obstructaque saxa tenebant, | *spumeus* et feruens et ab obice saeuior ibat.' Cf. also *c.m.* 26. 63 f. (the hot springs at Aponus) 'acrior interius rauci cum murmure saxi | spumeus eliso pellitur amne uapor.' When applied to rivers *scindo* more usually indicates their splitting into divergent branches, as at Ov. *Met.* 15. 739 'scinditur in geminas partes circumfluus amnis'. For *spumosus* or rivers in spate cf. Virg. *A.* 12. 524 'spumosi amnes', Ov. *Met.* 1. 570, Stat. *Silu.* 1. 3. 21, *Theod.* 237 f. 'torrentes inmane fremant lassisque minentur | pontibus; inuoluant spumoso uertice siluas'.

459–69. Stilicho was accompanied only by the vanguard. His dilemma was thus whether to wait for reinforcements and so leave Milan in danger of capture, or else to attempt to break through to the city in the face of a numerically superior enemy with a strategic advantage (457–63; see also 481 *munitior* n.). His *pietas* to Honorius won out, and considering the risk to his own life less important than the danger in which his son-in-law found himself (463–8), he boldly forced a crossing (488 f.) and cut through the enemy lines in a lightning-quick manœuvre (468 f.).

459 f. discrimina . . . adeunda: *discrimen adire* seems to be a somewhat prosaic phrase, with examples appearing in Curtius (3. 1. 10 'totis uiribus tanti belli discrimen aditurus'), Tacitus (*Hist.* 2. 52, 2. 60, 3. 80, *Ann.* 14. 7), Suetonius (*Tib.* 6, *Cal.* 4), Pliny (*Ep.* 9. 22. 3), and Ammianus Marcellinus (27. 10. 12). In verse, it is perhaps more usual to find *periculum adire*; e.g. Ter. *An.* 677 'capitis periclum adire', Ov. *Met.* 12. 161, 14. 119 'quaeque nouis essent adeunda pericula bellis'; cf. Virg. *A.* 1. 10 'tot adire labores'. The distinction, however, is by no means hard and fast; note e.g. Caes. *Ciu.* 2. 7. 1 'ad extremum uitae periculum adire cogebant', Nep. *Timol.* 5. 2 'se maximos labores summaque adisse pericula'. See further *TLL* i/1. 627. 15ff.

460. perrumperet agmen: cf. Liv. 8. 30. 6 'perrumpere non poterat hostium agmen'; also e.g. Virg *A.* 9. 513 'aciem perrumpere', Sil. 7. 705f. 'perrumpit anhelum | dictator cum caede globum'.

461. paucis comitatus: the same courage is seen at *IV Cons.* 443f. (Stilicho in Germany) 'hostiles . . . ripas | incomitatus adit.' For such phrases cf. also Virg. *A.* 10. 186 'paucis comitate Cupauo', Ov. *Fast.* 3. 603 'solo comitatus Achate'. It is impossible to tell whether the participle here is a true passive (from *comito*) or a deponent (from *comitor*) with passive sense: see KS i. 111.

461f. retro . . . liquerat: see 144 *retroque relictos* n.

462f. arma | extera: auxiliaries as opposed to regular troops (*nostras acies*, 463); cf. Caes. *Ciu.* 2. 5. 5 'uel domesticis opibus uel externis auxiliis', Ov. *Met.* 14. 454 'auget uterque suas externo robore uires'. These are most probably the new auxiliaries enrolled at the end of the successful Raetian campaign (*Get.* 400ff.).

463. uel: = 'and', as at 555. For the frequent 'unlogical' preference of Latin idiom for the disjunctive rather than the copulative see Fordyce on Catul. 45. 6f.; the path from 'if you please' to 'and' ran through such expressions as Virg. *Aen.* 6. 769f. 'pariter pietate uel armis | egregius'.

   nostras acies: the regular troops, including those who accompanied Stilicho from Milan to Raetia and those who were recalled from Britain and Germany to meet the present emergency (*Get.* 414 ff.).

463f. hoc . . . locatus | ancipiti: cf. Sen. *Phoen.* 629 'fortuna belli semper ancipiti in loco est.' The use of substantival *anceps* of situations whose outcome is in doubt (hence 'a dilemma' or just 'danger', depending on the circumstances) can be traced back to Sen. *Her. F.* 1306f. 'ut causam tuam | famamque in arto et ancipiti scias'. Cf. also Tac. *Ann.* 1. 36 'seu nihil militi siue omnia concederentur, in ancipiti res publica', 4. 73, Quint. *Inst.* 8. 2. 21 'ingeniosa haec et fortia et ex ancipiti diserta creduntur'. Goodyear (on Tac. *Ann.* 1. 36) points to the parallel with *in praecipiti*, but perhaps as influential, if not more so, is the common use of substantival *dubius* in similar phrases. Consider e.g. Sal. *Cat.* 52. 6 'libertas et anima nostra in dubio est', Ov. *Am.* 2. 13. 2, *Met.* 8. 44 f., 12. 522, Stat. *Theb.* 9. 493.

464–8. The devotion of Stilicho to Honorius (as also to Arcadius) and his habitual disregard of personal danger in their service is a recurring theme in Claudian's panegyric. Cf. esp. *IV Cons.* 434 ff. 'pro nobis nihil ille pati nullumque recusat | discrimen temptare sui, non dura uiarum, | non incerta maris: Libyae squalentis harenas | audebit superare pedes madidaque cadente | Pleiade Gaetulas intrabit nauita Syrtes', *Get.* 308 f. (Stilicho of Honorius) 'hic carior omni | luce gener'.

464 f. Note here the elaborate interlocking word-order. *socias* is separated from its noun and intrudes between *longum* and *tardum*. Two separate pairs of accusatives in the pattern *abab* are thus arranged asymmetrically around their governing verbs (*putauit, expectasse*), while *putauit*, the grammatical linchpin of the clause, is given full emphasis by a position which is practically central to the clause but also terminal in its line. For the collocation *socias . . . manus* cf. Ov. *Am.* 3. 15. 10 'cum timuit socias anxia Roma manus'.

465 f. pericula . . . pulsare: the poetic simple for the compound *propulso*: cf. Cic. *S. Rosc.* 7 'in causa Sex. Rosci periculum quod in omnis intenditur propulsetis', *Clu.* 144, Tac. *Ag.* 29. 3 'commune periculum concordia propulsandum'.

465. tendit: for *tendo* with the infinitive see Williams on Stat. *Theb.* 10. 452, Trump 28. Pointing to its position between *putauit* and *secuit*, Müller takes *tendit* as a perfect without reduplicated stem, as at *Get.* 167, and perhaps *Rapt.* 2. 37.

466. posthabitis . . . suis: balanced by *propriaeque salutis | inmemor* (467 f.). Cf. *CIL* xiii. 2027 'posthabita cura salutis'.

medium . . . per hostem: triumphantly ripping through the obstacle that seemed so daunting at 456. For the regular epic tag cf. Virg. *A.* 2. 377 'medios delapsus in hostis', 9. 799, 12. 477, Luc. 7. 365 f., 590, Sil. 4. 556, 5. 230, Stat. *Theb.* 7. 698.

467. flammatus uirtute pia: his battle courage and his devotion to his son-in-law together inspire his heroism. For the imagery and phrasing cf. esp. *Ruf.* 2. 231 'inflammata semel nescit mitescere uirtus' and also Luc. 9. 407 'incendit uirtute animos'; Virg. *A.* 3. 330 'magno flammatus amore', V. Fl. 4. 655 'flammata pudore iuuentus', Sil. 9. 110 'subita flammatus ab ira'.

propriae: = *suae*. See 81 n., and contrast *sua . . . salus* at 609.

468 f. Stilicho tears through the enemy lines with the speed of a bolt of lightning, destroying everything in his path. We may recall the battle-madness that seizes Aeneas after the brutal killing of Pallas, a savagery similarly motivated by *pietas* even if it leaves some modern readers uncomfortable: Virg. *A.* 10. 513 'proxima quaeque metit gladio'.

468. stricto . . . ferro: cf. Virg. *A.* 4. 580, 10. 715, Ov. *Ep.* 3. 145, V. Fl. 3. 425, Stat. *Theb.* 8. 140f., *Ruf.* 2. 230 (dative); *Get.* 609 'strictis . . . mucronibus', *c.m.* 29. 46.

prosternens obuia: cf. *Stil.* 2. 20 (to Stilicho) 'obuia prosternas', *Get. pr.* 6.

469. A 'golden line', triumphantly ending a section of narrative: see Gruzelier, p. xxviii, for Claudian's fondness for this figure.

fulmineo . . . cursu: cf. Sil. 12. 461f. (Hannibal is like a lioness in search of her stolen cubs) 'donec fulmineo partus uestigia cursu | colligat', 14. 446f. (fire on a ship) 'proxima cursu | fulmineo populatus'. Note also *Stil.* 1. 200 (also of Stilicho's speed in campaigning) 'fulmineum perstrinxit iter'. This is a quality he shares with other great generals, especially Caesar. See Luc. 1. 149f. 'inpellens quidquid sibi summa petenti | obstaret', followed immediately by the famous simile comparing Caesar to a bolt of lightning (1. 151–7), Florus *Epit.* 2. 13. 63 'sed hunc Caesar adgressus uno et, ut sic dixerim, non toto proelio obtriuit, more fulminis, quod uno eodemque momento uenit, percussit, abscessit.' Note also *Prob.* 73 (Theodosius) 'fulmineis inpellens uiribus hostem', *Get.* 138 (Hannibal) 'fulmineum . . . Poenum'.

secuit: of rapid, violent action also at Virg. *A.* 10. 440 (Turnus) 'uolucri curru medium secat agmen'.

470–93. *The heroism of Stilicho surpasses that of Diomedes in the* Doloneia *and of Horatius Cocles on the bridge.*

The Homeric allusions of 436 and 453f. prove to have set the scene for a considerably more extended, and more explicit, comparison between the *Iliad* and the siege of Milan. At *Il.* 10. 314ff. Dolon sets out to spy on the Greeks but is captured by Diomedes and Ulysses; he informs them that the Trojans' newly arrived Thracian allies, along with their king Rhesus, are asleep, unguarded, on the edges of the Trojan field-camp. After killing the informer, Diomedes and Ulysses proceed to the Thracian tents, wreak gruesome slaughter on the defenceless enemy, and carry off as booty the miraculous snow-white horses of Rhesus. Like the relief of Milan this incident takes place during a siege and involves a dangerous night-time raid on an enemy camp, in which individual heroism triumphs against overwhelming numbers. Certain differences are passed over in silence by the poet; for example, while Stilicho is attempting to raise a siege and is motivated, we are told, by *pietas* alone, the heroes of the action of the *Iliad* are part of the besieging army, and their primary goal is the acquisition of booty and prestige. This difference could have been exploited by Claudian to exalt his patron over the heroes of antiquity, but instead he concentrates on denigrating the achievement of the *Doloneia* by another method. He essentially gives the credit for the victory to Diomedes alone, only to undermine it by suggesting that it was not so heroic after all. In fact, it was won by trickery and deceit (*furtis* 480), since Diomedes relied on his untrustworthy comrade Ulysses (471), exploited the treachery of the cowardly Dolon (471 f.), and fought against an enemy who who had been rendered helpless by a drunken stupor (472 f.). Stilicho, by contrast, won in accordance with the true heroic code (*ecce uirum* 477), without recourse to ignominious underhand stratagems (477 f.), and against an enemy who was not only in an excellent position (*munitior* 481) but in any case far more formidable than Rhesus even if Rhesus had been on his mettle. In all this Claudian is drawing on a longstanding tradition, especially strong in Roman literature, which is hostile to Diomedes and, more particularly, to Ulysses. Both heroes were regularly attacked for their part in this and other escapades, such as the theft of the Palladium, which were thought inconsistent with the heroic, and above all the 'honest' Roman way of fighting. In the *Aeneid*, for example, Ulysses is variously called *scelerum inuentor* (2. 164), *dirus* (2. 762), *saeuus* (3. 273), *hortator scelerum* (6. 529), and *fandi fictor* (9. 602). Consider esp. the unremittingly hostile tone of *A.* 2. 163 ff. 'impius ex quo | Tydides sed enim scelerumque inuentor Vlixes | fatale adgressi sacrato auellere templo | Palladium caesis summae custodibus arcis, | corripuere sacram effigiem manibusque cruentis | uirgineas ausi diuae contingere uittas': cf. also *A.* 9. 150 ff., cit. 477–80 n., Stat. *Silu.* 5. 3. 179. Claudian's language, however, is closest to the taunts thrown at Ulysses by Ajax in the *iudicium armorum* in Ovid, *Met.* 13, though it is part of Ajax's strategy partly to exalt Diomedes in order to denigrate Ulysses: *Met.* 13. 98 ff. 'conferat his Ithacus Rhesum inbellemque Dolona | Priamidenque Helenum rapta cum Pallade captum: | *luce nihil gestum*, nihil est Diomede remoto; | si semel ista datis meritis tam uilibus arma, | diuidite, et pars sit maior Diomedis in illis. | quo tamen haec Ithaco, qui *clam*, qui semper inermis | rem gerit et *furtis* incautum decipit hostem?' In addition to the general tone and thrust of the argument, compare to the italicized words above *Ithaco* (471), *lux* (480), *palam* (478), and *furtis* (480). Cf. also Sen. *Tro.* 755 f. (Andromache to Ulysses) 'nocturne miles, fortis in pueri necem | iam solus audes aliquid et claro die', i.e. only against so easy a target as a defenceless boy will Ulysses fight without the support of Diomedes and without the protecting cover of night.

COMMENTARY ON LINES 470–93

In a second, less developed but emphatically placed comparison Stilicho is also said to have surpassed the glory of Horatius Cocles. This great Republican hero single-handedly kept at bay the army of Etruscans trying to storm the bridge over the Tiber until his companions could cut the bridge down; after this he leapt into the river, still armed, and swam to safety on the Roman bank (Liv. 2. 10). Once again, the situations are broadly comparable. In each a Roman hero, in the defence of a besieged city, displays stunning personal courage in an engagement with far superior numbers of the enemy, and swims against terrible odds and in adverse circumstances to safety over a river. The principal difference is that Cocles was himself one of the defenders of Rome already trapped in the besieged city, while Stilicho is leading his troops to the relief of the besieged inhabitants of Milan, and so for him the path led *through* the enemy to the city walls. Claudian ingeniously turns this to his advantage for a triumphant conclusion: see 489f. n.

For the modern reader it is tempting to look at this passage as offering a pair of *exempla* of which one is 'mythical' and the other, more or less, 'historical'. But for Claudian, Diomedes and Cocles were both 'historical' figures; even if the bards of old had perhaps embroidered their tales a little too much, there was no real reason to doubt the existence of either character, and their fame was preserved in much the same way in the literary–rhetorical tradition. The pairing is rather of one Greek hero and one Roman; Stilicho surpasses the greatest achievements in battle recorded by venerable antiquity in both cultures. Compare, for example, *c.m.* 30. 11 ff. where Serena surpasses Penelope and Alcestis on the one hand, and Tanaquil and Cloelia on the other, noting esp. 30. 15 ff. 'hoc Grai memorant. Latiis mouet ora Camenis | praescia fatorum Tanaquil, rediensque per undas | Cloelia Thybrinas'.

Claudian makes frequent use of Republican *exempla* throughout his works, regularly attributing to his honorands the ancient virtues traditionally associated, as if by formula, with the heroes of the past: see Cameron 337. In all this he is simply following the regular practice of Roman poets and orators trained in the schools of rhetoric and reliant less on their reading of historical authors than on such standard handbooks as Valerius Maximus' *De Factis Dictisque Memorabilibus*. Claudian's 'interest in the past is not historical at all, but rhetorical' (Cameron 337), though we should add that the impulse behind this kind of education is profoundly moral in outlook. Consider above all *IV Cons.* 396 ff., where Theodosius is imagined as giving his young son the following instructions: 'interea Musis, animus dum mollior, instes | et quae mox imitere legas; nec desinat umquam | tecum Graia loqui, tecum Romana uetustas'; Theodosius continues with a long list of Republican heroes along with the virtues they exemplify. See further H. W. Litchfield, *HSCPh* 25 (1914), 1–71, Fargues 210 and 213, Cameron 336ff., 350f.

470. Encomium frequently reaches a climax in the emphatic claim that the honorand has matched or surpassed the heroes of old in nobility, beauty, or achievements. This is regularly expressed by means of a formula of dismissal that discounts, or even denigrates as deceitful, the traditions and sources (*Vetustas, Fama, carmina, vates*) that record the glory of antiquity. The commonest such formula is *cedat/cedant*, but *tace/taceat* etc. is also well attested; *nunc* or *i nunc* may be used to render the tone more hostile or scathing. E. R. Curtius, who discusses this topos, which he calls 'outdoing', in *European Literature and the Latin Middle Ages* (trans. W. R. Trask (Princeton, 1973; in German Berne, 1948)), 162ff., traces its history in Latin literature to Statius, whose eulogistic *Siluae* offer abundant examples. These must surely have exercised great influence on his admirer Claudian, whom, in his turn, Curtius characterizes as 'a virtuoso of "outdoing"'. That Statius is largely responsible for the wide diffusion of the topos in Latin encomiastic verse need not be doubted, but in this, as in so much else, he took his cue from Ovid, and Curtius could have quoted *Pont.* 1. 3. 61ff. 'i nunc et ueterum nobis exempla uirorum, | qui forti casum mente tulere refer . . .' Cf. also Sen. *Phaed.* 741f. 'conferat nunc decus omne priscum | fama miratrix senioris aeui', Stat. *Silu.* 1. 1. 8ff. (the *equus Domitiani*) 'nunc age fama prior notum per saecula nomen | Dardanii miretur equi cui uertice sacro | Dindymon et caesis decreuit frondibus Ide . . .', 1. 1. 84ff., 1. 2. 26ff. 'cedant curaeque metusque, | cessent *mendaces* obliqui *carminis astus*, | Fama *tace*', 1. 2. 85ff., 213ff., 1. 3. 81ff., 1. 5. 22, 1. 6. 39f. 'i nunc saecula compara, Vetustas, | antiqui Iouis aureumque tempus', 2. 2. 60ff., 2. 7. 75ff., 3. 1. 142ff., 3. 4. 84ff., Pacatus, *Pan. Theod.* 17. 1 *'eat nunc sui ostentatrix uetustas* et illa innumeris litterarum uulgata monimentis iactet exempla. Pirithoi fidem praedicet et decantatum omnibus scaenis Phocaei iuuenis laudet officium . . .' (cf. 475 n.), Sid. *Carm.* 2. 149ff., 288f., 299. If Claudian has any particular passage in his predecessors in mind, it is probably Luc. 6. 48f., cit. 470 *attollant carmina uatum* n. Other examples in Claudian's own work include *Prob.* 202f. (Proba outdoes Thetis) 'taceat Nereida nuptam | Pelion', *Ruf.* 1. 283ff., *c.m.* 30. 42f. (Serena surpasses Cornelia) 'claram Scipiadum taceat Cornelia gentem | seque minus iactet Libycis dotata tropaeis'; note also *Stil.* 1. 368ff., 3. 30ff. The topos is practically tailor-made for expressing the boisterous self-confidence of the Renaissance, and, for example, is given great prominence in Camões's prologue to *Os Lusíadas*: 1. 3. 1ff. 'Cessem do sábio Grego e do Troiano | As navegações grandes que fizeram; |

Cale-se de Alexandro e de Trajano | A fama das vitórias que tiveram: | Que eu canto o peito ilustre lusitano, | A quem Neptuno e Marte obedeceram! | Cesse tudo o que a musa antigua canta, | Que outro valor mais alto se alevanta!'

470–4. Behind these lines is perceptible the clear influence of Virg. *A.* 1. 469 ff. (Aeneas sees paintings depicting scenes from the Trojan war on the walls of Juno's temple at Carthage) 'nec procul hinc *Rhesi* niueis *tentoria* uelis | agnoscit lacrimans, *primo quae prodita somno* | *Tydides* multa uastabat caede *cruentus*, | ardentisque auertit equos in castra prius quam | pabula gustassent Troiae Xanthumque bibissent'; cf. *cruentus* (478), *tentoria* (469), and, also perhaps owing its origin to this passage, *primos . . . uigiles* (454 f.). The two passages share an anti-Greek outlook, originating in different motives, but insisting on the atmosphere of treachery (*prodita, patefacta Dolonis* | *indicio*).

470. Tydiden: Diomedes, son of Tydeus. The patronymic is regular in both Homer (e.g. *Il.* 10. 363, 367) and Latin verse: e.g. Virg. *A.* 2. 164, 10. 29, Ov. *Met.* 15. 769, Stat. *Ach.* 1. 844. The triumphalist tone of *nunc . . . Tydiden attollant* is partly created by association with the use of the patronymic in phrases glorifying Diomedes, such as Virg. *A.* 1. 96 f. 'o Danaum fortissime gentis | Tydide!' and Hor. *Carm.* 1. 6. 16 'Tydiden superis parem'. *Tydiden* and *Ithaco* help reinforce the general epic character of Honorius' account of the siege of Milan.

   attollant carmina uatum: cf. esp. Luc. 6. 48 f. 'nunc uetus Iliacos attollat fabula muros | ascribatque deis'. For *attollo* of 'glorifying' in song cf. Sil. 12. 410 f. (Ennius) 'hic canet illustri primus bella Itala uersu | attolletque duces caelo', Stat. *Silu.* 5. 3. 10 f.

471. iuncto fidens Ithaco: recalling *Met.* 13. 239 f. 'at sua Tydides mecum communicat acta, | me probat et socio semper confidit Vlixe.' For the phrasing cf. also *III Cons.* 132 'iunctum Bromio radiare Tonantem'. *Ithacus* = Ulysses is found from Virg. *A.* 2. 104 on; cf. Ov. *Met.* 13. 98, 103, *Pont.* 1. 3. 33, Juv. 14. 287.

471 f. dapibusque simul religataque somno | Thracia . . . agmina: *dapibus* here implies drunkenness. There is no trace whatsoever in Homer of the idea that the Thracians are in a drunken stupor; rather, they are said to be καμάτῳ ἀδηκότες (*Il.* 10. 471), which implies a nobler cause for their profound weariness. Claudian, however, is not relying on the authority of Homer but ingeniously developing the profoundly anti-Greek line taken by Virgil (cf. 470–4 n.). In particular, the slaying of the Thracians is in some sense made to function as a prefiguration of the treacherous capture of Troy itself: Virg. *A.* 2. 265 'inuadunt urbem somno uinoque sepultam'. We also recall another instance of Ulysses' deceit: Virg. *A.* 3. 630 (Polyphemus) 'expletus dapibus uinoque sepultus'. It could be said that the Thracians are at the very least guilty of a lack of caution not unlike that against which Theodosius warns his son at *IV Cons.* 334 ff. 'multis damnosa fuere | gaudia; dispersi pereunt somnoue soluti; | saepius incautae nocuit uictoria turbae'. The image of sleep 'binding' the limbs goes back to Enn. *Ann.* 2 'somno leni placidoque reuinctus', where see Skutsch's note; cf. also Lucr. 4. 453 f. 'suaui deuinxit membra sopore | somnus', Liv. 5. 44. 7 'nisi uinctos somno uelut pecudes trucidandos tradidero', 9. 30. 9, Ov. *Met.* 11. 238, Suet. *Aug.* 16 'tam arto repente somno deuinctus'. Contrast Virg. *A.* 9. 189 f. 'somno uinoque soluti | procubuere', 9. 236, *IV Cons.* 335, *Fesc.* 1. 21 'membra somno fessa resolueris'.

religata . . . somno . . . | sopiti: not tautological: *both* the Thracian host *and* their king were deep in slumber. Homer had made the same point; *Il.* 10. 471 οἱ δ' εὗδον καμάτῳ ἀδηκότες, 474 Ῥῆσος δ' ἐν μέσῳ εὗδε.

473. The carnage is thrown into stark relief by the stately golden line. Note the subjunctives (*penetrauerit*; *rettulerit* 474), with which the author casts doubt on the veracity of the report contained in the *carmina uatum*. For the phrasing cf. Liv. 2. 12. 3 (Scaeuola) 'penetrare in hostium castra constituit'.

474. captos . . . iugales: the great prize, described by Dolon in extravagant terms: *Il.* 10. 436 τοῦ δὴ καλλίστους ἵππους ἴδον ἠδὲ μεγίστους. Substantival *iugales* for *equi* is attested in the Augustan period (Virg. *A.* 7. 280 'currum geminosque iugalis', Ov. *Met.* 5. 661), and becomes widespread in Flavian literature and thereafter.

475. The Muses had already told Hesiod at the dawn of classical literature that they were capable of recording both lies that seemed like truth, and truth itself, according to their desire: *Th.* 26 ff. ποιμένες ἄγραυλοι, κάκ' ἐλέγχεα, γαστέρες οἶον, | ἴδμεν ψεύδεα πολλὰ λέγειν ἐτύμοισιν ὁμοῖα, | ἴδμεν δ', εὖτ' ἐθέλωμεν, ἀληθέα γηρύσασθαι. That the Muses or their servants, the poets of old, exaggerate or lie, and are thus plainly untrustworthy, is thereafter frequently asserted by their successors in the craft: see e.g. Solon 21, Pind. *O.* 1. 28 f., *Carmen de Bello Actiaco* 26 f. (Courtney, *FLP*, p. 336), Stat. *Silu.* 1. 2. 27 'mendaces obliqui carminis astus', Pac. *Pan. Theod.* 17. 2 'ut haec esse uera credamus quae mendaciis uatum in plausus aptata cauearum fidem tempori debent', *Stil.* 1. 104 ff., 3. 226 ff., *Get.* 14 ff. 'licet omnia uates | *in maius celebrata ferant* ipsamque secandis | Argois trabibus iactent sudasse Mineruam', Sid. *Carm.* 2. 289 'aetas cana patrum . . . pulchro hortamine mendax'. Cf. further Luc. 9. 359 f. (on the Garden of the Hesperides) 'inuidus, annoso qui famam derogat aeuo, | qui uates ad uera uocat' with *IV Cons.* 37 f. (the elder Theodosius campaigning in Africa) 'uile uirentes | Hesperidum risit, quos ditat fabula, ramos'; contrast Plin. *Nat.* 5. 4, cit. below. Among Roman authors there is often added to this the xenophobic belief that deceitfulness is a racial characteristic of the Greeks, and that their writings, not only in poetry but also in the supposedly more truthful genres such as history, are thus full of lies: e.g. Plin. *Nat.* 5. 4 (the Garden of the Hesperides) 'minus profecto mirentur portentosa Graeciae mendacia', 8. 82, 28. 112, Juv. 10. 173 ff. 'creditur olim | uelificatus Athos et quidquid Graecia mendax | audet in historia', 14. 239 f. Ovid, like Lucan, sticks up for the poet's rights and makes a clear distinction between the expectations appropriate to the different disciplines: *Am.* 3. 12. 41 'exit in immensum fecunda licentia uatum | obligat historica nec sua uerba fide'; consider also the indulgent but knowing scepticism of Ov. *Met.* 1. 400 (Pyrrha and Deucalion making human beings from stones) 'quis hoc credat, nisi sit pro teste uetustas?' and *Fast.* 4. 203 f.

  si qua fides: a formula normally used to vouch for the speaker's veracity: see Bömer on Ov. *Fast.* 6. 715, Fantham on Luc. 2. 550. The most famous example of this usage is perhaps Aeneas' appeal to Dido in the underworld, 'si qua fides tellure sub ima est' (*A.* 6. 459). Here, however, it expresses sardonic disbelief, and undercuts the assumptions that inform traditional proud assertions of poetic power over posterity. Consider also Virg. *A.* 10. 791 ff. (the poet apostrophizes Lausus): 'hic mortis durae casum tuaque optima facta, | si qua fidem tanto est operi latura uetustas, | non equidem nec te, iuvenis memorande, silebo', where the promise of eternal fame in the poet's song is 'destabilized' by the suggestion of doubt in a cynical age (see Harrison ad loc. and also at *A.* 10. 458 n. for *si quis* introducing a pathetic 'hope against hope'). Note also Luc. 3. 406 ff. 'si qua fidem meruit superos mirata uetustas, | illis et uolucres metuunt insistere ramis | et lustris recubare ferae'. For verbal formulae used to express disbelief see Austin on Virg. *A.* 6. 173 'si credere dignum est' and T. C. W. Stinton, '"Si Credere Dignum Est": Some Expressions of Disbelief in Euripides and Others', *PCPS*, NS 22 (1976), 60–89 = *Collected Papers on Greek Tragedy* (Oxford, 1990), 236–64.

476. Claudian is adapting very closely Dolon's original description of Rhesus' horses: *Il.* 10. 437 λευκότεροι χιόνος, θείειν δ' ἀνέμοισιν ὁμοῖοι. Note, however, how much the expression has been varied to produce a dazzling *tour de force* of verbal ingenuity. In one case a noun has replaced an adjective ('whiteness' for 'whiter'), while another has been replaced by a regular Latin poetic metonym ('snow' by 'frosts') and still another, general, noun by a specific ('winds' by 'Zephyrs'). In addition, the order of comparison has been reversed (in Claudian, the speed and the Zephyrs precede the whiteness and the frosts), and Homer's pairing of a true comparative ('whiter than snow') and a statement of equivalence ('like the winds in running') has been 'surpassed' by a double claim of superiority for the horses. Cf. the similar adaptations at Virg. *A.* 12. 84 (the horses of Turnus) 'qui candore niues anteirent, cursibus auras', Sil. 13. 116 (a stag) 'quae candore niuem, candore anteiret olores'. See also 370 *electi candoris* n. For the 'whiteness' comparison note also *Nupt.* 265 f. (Maria) 'non colla pruinae . . . aequant', *c.m.* 25. 126 (Celerina) 'superatque niues ac lilia candor'; and for the 'speed of the winds' comparison note *Stil.* 3. 252 (Lycaste) 'cursu Zephyris numquam cessura Lycaste', *c.m.* 27. 21.

impetus: = 'speed'; cf. Stat. *Silu.* 4. 3. 103 f. 'tunc uelocior acriorque cursus, | tunc ipsos iuuat impetus iugales', *Stil.* 1. 200, *Rapt.* 2. 200 'impetus Austri'.

477–80. In addition to the Virgilian and Ovidian passages cited in 470–93 n. Claudian may also have in mind the sardonic boasts of Turnus: Virg. *A.* 9. 150 ff. '*tenebras* et inertia *furta* | Palladii caesis late custodibus arcis | ne timeant, nec equi caeca condemur in aluo: | *luce palam* certum est igni circumdare muros.' See further 219 *astu*, 300 *insidiis . . . circumdedit arte*, 308 *fraudibus* nn.

477. ecce uirum: highly emphatic; here, in the person of Stilicho (and, by implication, unlike in that of Diomedes) we see a 'real hero'. The use of the accusative with *ecce* is decidedly unclassical after comedy, though one might compare e.g. Virg. *Ecl.* 5. 65 f. 'en quattuor aras: | ecce duas tibi, Daphni'. In contemporary poetry, however, we find *eccum* = Italian *ecco* used absolutely: Prud. *Per.* 2. 309 'eccum talenta suscipe', 10. 1006.

taciti . . . fraude soporis: a genitive of definition. To this extent the instrumental use of *fraus* here can be compared with Virg. *A.* 9. 396 ff. 'uidet Euryalum, quem iam manus omnis | fraude loci et noctis . . . | oppressum rapit', Sil. 4. 580, 7. 279 'fraude locorum'. Sleep, like night, is usually 'silent', but here the epithet also colours *fraude*; cf. Luc. 4. 465 'Vulteius tacitas sensit sub gurgite fraudes', Stat. *Theb.* 10. 721 'fraude . . . tacita'; also V. Fl. 2. 567 'tacitos . . . dolos'.

478. palam: i.e. 'without trickery or deceit'; Stilicho attacks, not a sleeping enemy, but one who is fully prepared and at no disadvantage. Platnauer translates 'in the open light of day', an interpretation no doubt inspired by the comparison of 480 (*quantum lux tenebris*). There the balance between *lux* and *manifesta proelia* on one side and *tenebrae* and *furta* on the other might seem naturally to refer directly to the conditions of the particular engagement just fought; light is better than

darkness and open fighting is fairer than underhand combat, the argument might seem to run, and therefore Stilicho's deeds, fought as they
were in daylight and fairly, are correspondingly better than those of
Diomedes. The narrative, however, began at night (453, 454 f.), and
there has been no indication of any change in time. In any case the
initial comparison seems to have been inspired by the very fact that
the crossing of the Adda, like the *Doloneia*, took place at night. See
further 440–93 n. Line 480, then, does not refer precisely to the events
described, but offers a wider generalization, though one that we might
feel was open, in the circumstances, to the charge of having been ill-
chosen.

sibi pandit iter: a poetic version of the commoner *pandere uiam*,
which is found in verse since Virg. *A.* 12. 626 and in prose from Var.
gram. 371 'Tito Tatio <ut> Capitolinum capiat collem uiam pandere
atque aperire permissum est' (*pace* Korn on V. Fl. 4. 197, who traces it
only as far as Liv. 10. 5. 11). Cf. Sen. *Her. F.* 667 'latumque pandit
omnibus populis iter', *Laus. Pis.* 224, Sil. 2. 356, 5. 393, 14. 240, Stat.
Theb. 10. 284, Mart. 12. 98. 4.

cruentus: from Virg. *A.* 1. 471 'Tydides multa . . . caede cruentus'.
The epithet is applied in Latin verse to both Diomedes and his father
(Stat. *Theb.* 9. 1 f. 'cruenti | Tydeos'), and associates them with
Homer's Ares in his more savage aspect: *Il.* 5. 31 Ἄρες Ἄρες . . .
μιαιφόνε, 455, 844, Stat. *Theb.* 7. 264 'Mauorte cruento', 8. 231 f.

479. Diomedeis: apparently an Ovidian coinage: *Met.* 15. 806
'Diomedeos Aeneas fugerat enses'. That it was picked up by Statius
will have enhanced its authority in Claudian's eyes (*Silu.* 3. 3. 163, 5.
3. 179 'Diomedei celat penetralia furti'; cf. also Mart. 13. 93. 1, Aus.
Ecl. 17. 9). For the epic use of adjectives formed from proper names
see 11 *mons Euandrius*, 116 *Iuleos* nn.

479 f. tantum . . . quantum: Heinsius conjectured *tanto . . . quanto*, but
the substitution of the adverbial accusative for the ablative with com-
paratives is a well-attested phenomenon in post-classical Latin. See
LHS ii. 136 f. (citing earlier examples, including Liv. 5. 10. 5, V. Fl. 1.
741 ff.), and cf. *Stil.* 1. 378 ff. 'et tantum Libyam fructu maiore recepit |
quam peperit, quantum grauiorem amissa dolorem | quam necdum
quaesita mouent'.

480. manifestaque proelia furtis: the ideals and language of
the heroic code. Cf. esp. Virg. *A.* 10. 735 'haud furto melior sed fortibus armis', where Harrison cites *Il.* 7. 242 f. (Hector) ἀλλ᾽ οὐ γάρ σ᾽
ἐθέλω βαλέειν τοιοῦτον ἐόντα | λάθρῃ ὀπιπεύσας, ἀλλ᾽ ἀμφαδόν, αἴ κε
τύχωμι. Harrison, loc. cit., also quotes Ps.-Eur. *Rh.* 510 f., οὐδεὶς ἀνὴρ
εὔψυχος ἀξιοῖ λάθρᾳ | κτεῖναι τὸν ἐχθρόν, ἀλλ᾽ ἰὼν κατὰ στόμα: an

intriguing coincidence, though there is no verbal similarity with this line.

furtis has much the same sense as λάθρη in the Homeric passage quoted above, just as *palam* (478) corresponds to ἀμφαδόν. For *furtum* of military stratagems or underhand and ignoble methods of warfare see *OLD* s.v. 3b, citing Liv. 9. 31. 12 'ultimam spem furto insidiarum temptantem', Ov. *Met.* 13. 104, Sen. *Ag.* 624 Zwierlein: add Virg. *A.* 11. 515, Stat. *Theb.* 10. 253 (of a night-time attack) 'gradiens furta ad Mauortia belli.' Curtius offers a passage which, also in the context of a planned night-time raid, presents the same contrast: 4. 13. 4 'Parmenio, peritissimus inter duces artium belli, furto, non proelio opus esse censebat.' Cf. also Hor. *Carm.* 4. 6. 13 ff., Tac. *Ann.* 2. 88. 1 'responsum . . . esse non fraude neque occultis, sed palam et armatum populum Romanum hostes suos ulcisci'. In the contrast drawn between *furta* and *manifesta proelia* there is an element of word-play, since *manifestus* properly means 'caught in the act' and is more normally applied to *furtum* where that noun has its basic sense of 'theft'; see Gel. 11. 18. 11 '"manifestum" autem "furtum est," ut ait Masurius, "quod deprehenditur dum fit."'

For the phrasing here contrast Virg. *G.* 1. 465 (Sol) 'saepe monet fraudemque et operta tumescere bella', and, more particularly, Statius' adaptation of this at *Theb.* 10. 241 f. 'sed fraudem et operta paramus | proelia.' Note further Luc. 10. 345, Sil. 15. 349, Stat. *Theb.* 12. 279 'occulto . . . furto'.

481. adde quod: an argumentative formula of transition, especially appropriate to didactic (e.g. Lucr. 4. 1121; also in a learned disquisition at Luc. 10. 223) and diatribe or satirical writing (e.g. *Eutr.* 1. 187), but also found in a range of other genres (Ter. *Ph.* 168, Hor. *Carm.* 2. 8. 17, Stat. *Theb.* 7. 168, *Silu.* 1. 1. 14, and *Theod.* 144, with Simon ad loc.). Its association with polemic renders its appearance here entirely in tone with Claudian's double attack on Diomedes and the exaggerations of the *carmina uatum*, but Claudian probably has in mind, yet again, Ovid's *iudicium armorum*: *Met.* 13. 117 ff. (Ajax to Ulysses) 'adde quod iste tuus, tam raro proelia passus, | integer est clipeus'.

munitior: i.e. not just awake, but on his mettle and in a strong defensive position. For the use of the comparative cf. Sal. *Rep.* 1. 1. 5 'eo se munitiores putant, quo illei quibus imperiant nequiores fuere', Cic. *Att.* 2. 18. 3, Aus. *Technop.* 7. 8 Green.

482 f. Even if Rhesus had not been taken unawares and asleep, defeating him would still have been far less glorious than defeating Alaric. The rationale here is based on terms of race: Rhesus was a Thracian, but Alaric had already been proved superior to the latter-day

Thracians in battle (440 f. *populator* . . . | *Bistoniae* . . . *plagae*, balanced by *Thracum domitor*).

482. nec . . . fas est conponere Rhesum: for similar formulae see Virg. *G.* 4. 176 'si parua licet componere magnis', Ov. *Met.* 5. 416f. 'quodsi conponere magnis | parua mihi fas est', Stat. *Silu.* 1. 5. 61f. Note also Fordyce on Catul. 51. 2 'ille, si fas est, superare diuos'.

483. Thracum domitor: see Dewar on Stat. *Theb.* 9. 169 for nouns ending in -*tor*, and cf. Hor. *Ep.* 1. 2. 19 'domitor Troiae', Luc. 9. 1014, Sil. 15. 642, *Stil.* 3. 33 'Pellaeae domitor Paulus . . . aulae'.

483f. Given that this sentence serves as the introduction to the comparison with Cocles, perhaps Claudian is remembering Liv. 2. 10. 11 'ita sic armatus in Tiberim desiluit *multisque superincidentibus telis* incolumis ad suos tranauit'. For the phrasing cf. Virg. *G.* 3. 253f. 'non scopuli rupesque cauae atque obiecta retardant | flumina', *Gild.* 473 'nec mons aut silua retardat', *Rapt.* 2. 224.

484. obice . . . fluuii: 'the barrier presented by the river'. Cf. Virg. *A.* 10. 377 'ecce maris magna claudit nos obice pontus', Ov. *Fast.* 1. 563, Luc. 10. 246, *Gild.* 11 'obice ponti.' In a sense this is a reversal of the Goths' storming of Greece: *Get.* 184ff. 'non obice Pindi | seruati Dryopes nec nubifer Actia texit | litora Leucates'.

The verb *obicere* originates in *ob-iacere*. An intermediate form *obiicere* formerly recorded the shortening of the stressed second vowel (*a* reduced to *i*) while preserving the semi-consonantal *i*. In the classical spelling *obicere*, however, the semi-consonant is no longer recorded, but it is still pronounced. As a result, in strict classical usage the initial syllable is scanned long by dint of the combination of consonant (*b*) and semi-consonant (the unwritten *i*), but the pronunciation retains the natural short quality of the *o*. Since *obice* is derived from *obicere*, *ob* should therefore also be scanned long, but the *o* pronounced short. Confusion, unsurprisingly, crept in with time, and some post-Augustan authors scanned the first syllable short (Luc. 8. 796, Sil. 4. 24). Conversely, some Romans lengthened the vowel when pronouncing lines from earlier authors, in order to preserve the metre as they understood it, and also did as much with such similar cases as *conicere* and *subicere*. Aulus Gellius is at pains to explain the error of their ways (4. 17. 5f.). Claudian's scansion is thus impeccably classical, but how he actually pronounced the initial syllable can only be conjectured. See further Eden on Virg. *A.* 8. 227.

484f. minacem | Tyrrhenam . . . manum: this combination of words has been held to violate the usual rule that a noun may have only one epithet (see 50f. *spoliis* . . . *micantes* | *innumeros arcus*n.). Barth was much exercised about this apparent desertion of classical propriety, and conjectured *minacem | Tyrrhenum . . . manum*: 'effugies ita odiosum geminati epitheti sonum.' In this case we would understand *Tyrrhenum* as an epicizing 'syncopated' (so-called) or 'archaic' plural, on the analogy of e.g. *Danaum* (Virg. *A.* 1. 30 etc.: see Williams on Virg. *A.* 5. 174), and translate 'the threatening band of Etruscans' rather than 'the threatening Etruscan band'. As an alternative, Barth (1612) suggested reading *minacem | Tyrrhenum . . . manu*, taking *Tyrrhenum* as a collective singular (= 'exercitum Tuscum'). But against this latter conjecture it should be objected that *manu* (*a*) would weaken *clipeo* (486) and (*b*) produce a rather unattractive, and even confusing, string of clashing ablatives in *labente manu pro ponte*. The whole problem is, however, purely imaginary, since 'the truth is that any noun can have two epithets provided that one is descriptive and the other possessive' (A. E. Housman, *Classical Papers*, ed. J. Diggle and F. R. D. Goodyear (Cambridge, 1972), iii. 1120). Even then, the rule is by no means hard and fast: see further Birt, p. ccxxi, LHS ii. 160f., Harrison on Virg. *A.* 10. 391. On balance, then, though Barth's genitive plural *Tyrrhenum* is in some measure attractive, there is no compelling reason whatsoever to emend the text transmitted in the best manuscripts.

Claudian's emphasis on Cocles' having fought single-handedly against a great number of attacking Etruscans is in accord with the standard accounts. Note *IV Cons.* 405f. 'uel solus quid fortis agat, te ponte soluto | oppositus Cocles . . . docebit', and cf. also Man. 4. 32f. 'solus et oppositis clausisset Horatius armis | pontem urbemque simul', 35f. 'pendebat ab uno | Roma uiro', Sid. *Carm.* 5. 69f. For the epithet *minax* cf. also Luc. 7. 515 'turba minax', Stat. *Theb.* 1. 104; *Theb.* 12. 434 'minax globus'.

485–8. As the bridge collapses (*labente*: note the tense), Cocles leaps off and swims to safety on the side opposite to the Etruscan besiegers, inspiring wonder in Tarquin and giving Porsenna an impudent backwards look as he swims. Claudian thus follows the tradition seen at Liv. 2. 10. 11 'incolumis ad suos tranauit'. A gloomier alternative version saw his heroism end in death (e.g. Polybius 6. 55).

486. traiecit clipeo Thybrim: even in such adverse circumstances Cocles keeps to the heroic code, and returns with his shield: cf. Liv. 2. 10. 11. For the sense of *traicio* ('crossed the Tiber with his shield') see *OLD* s.v. 7, citing Virg. *A.* 6. 535f. 'roseis Aurora quadrigis | iam medium aetherio cursu traiecerat axem', Curt. 4. 1. 10, 8. 13. 23 'traicere amnem . . . parabat'. But Claudian is also punning on the commoner sense 'to traverse (with a missile)': see *OLD* s.v. 1, citing e.g. Cic. *Fin.* 4. 22 'si Hannibal ad portas uenisset murumque iaculo transiecisset.' For the Greek form *Thybris* see 12 n.

quo texerat urbem: cf. Liv. 2. 10. 9f. 'undique in unum hostem tela coniciunt. quae cum in obiecto cuncta scuto haesissent . . . ', Sid. *Carm.* 5. 69f. 'totam te pertulit uno | Coclitis in clipeo.' Note also *Gild.* 435 'clipeis tectos', and *Stil.* 3. 175 (Stilicho and Rome) 'protegis hanc clipeo, patriam'.

487f. Tarquin and Porsenna are the preferred *exempla* when panegyrists are required to speak of the delivery of Rome from tyrants; e.g. *Gild.* 123f., *Eutr.* 1. 443ff. (Roma to Honorius) 'hoc mihi Ianiculo positis Etruria castris | quaesiit et tantum fluuio Porsenna remotus? | hoc meruit uel ponte Cocles uel Mucius igne?', Sid. *Carm.* 5. 66ff. Above all, Claudian will have remembered the famous description of the defence of Roman freedom on the shield of Aeneas; Virg. *A.* 8. 646ff. 'nec non Tarquinium eiectum Porsenna iubebat | accipere ingentique urbem obsidione premebat; | *Aeneadae in ferrum pro libertate ruebant.* | illum indignanti similem similemque minanti | aspiceres, pontem auderet quia uellere Cocles | et fluuium uinclis innaret Cloelia ruptis'. As Stilicho is compared directly with Cocles, so is the defence of Milan subtly associated with the great tableau of the siege of Rome by Porsenna and Tarquin; both were moments of crisis in the defence of liberty, and both were triumphantly overcome by individual heroism. In the meantime, Alaric is put in the same category as Porsenna and Tarquin, two more assailants on Rome infamous for their pride and tyranny. This association, though far less developed, complements the 'Hannibal' motif seen elsewhere in the poem (182–4, 184–6nn.).

487. Tarquinio mirante: cf. *Eutr.* 1. 447 'attonitum tranauit Cloelia Thybrim.' Both passages have their origin in Sil. 10. 496ff. 'facta uirum sileo; rege haec et foedere et annis | et fluuio spretis, mirantem interrita Thybrim | tranauit, frangens undam puerilibus ulnis'. In *Eutr.* 1 the situation remains the same, and it is still the Tiber that feels the astonishment, but the adjective has been varied; here the adjective has been retained, but Tiber has been replaced by Tarquin and Cloelia by Cocles. See further Cameron 339. Cf. Macaulay, *Lays of Ancient Rome,* 'Horatius' 60. 8ff. 'All Rome sent forth a rapturous cry, | And even the ranks of Tuscany | Could scarce forbear to cheer', 63. 5ff. '"Heaven help him!" quoth Lars Porsena, | "And bring him safe to shore; | For such a gallant feat of arms | Was never seen before."'

superbus: impudently appropriating (and sanitizing; the sense is 'exultant' rather than 'arrogant') the epithet that belongs by right to Tarquin (Hor. *S.* 1. 6. 12f., Liv. 1. 49. 1 etc.). The effect is to express the extent to which Tarquin has been humbled by Cocles.

488. celer: not otiose, but stressing the dangers involved in Stilicho's heroic undertaking (cf. 458 *scissas spumosior incitat undas* n.).

489. sulcatus: Stilicho provides a demonstration of one of the warfare-skills which Theodosius encouraged Honorius to acquire: *IV Cons.* 347 f. 'fluuios . . . liquidos tu scinde natatu.' For the metaphor of 'ploughing' the sea see 376 *sulcaret* n. Normally applied to ships, here it indicates swimming: cf. Stat. *Theb.* 8. 230 'ingenti sulcatum Nerea tauro', *Eutr.* 2. 425 f. 'amisso pisce sodali | . . . sulcandas qui praeuius edocet undas', Sid. *Carm.* 22. 19 (Nereidum chorus) 'pontumque in flumine sulcas'.

489 f. A splendid example of the exuberant ingenuity that made Claudian's reputation in some ages, and ruined it in others. Courageous though he undoubtedly was, when Cocles swam across the river he was none the less retreating, but when Stilicho crossed the Adda he did so in order actually to engage an enemy on the further bank. For the wording, the antithesis and the line-ending cf. Luc. 4. 468 'incertus qua terga daret, qua pectora bello'.

490. pectora: for the 'poetic' plural of parts of the body see P. Maas, *Kleine Schriften* (Munich, 1973), pp. 527–85, Löfstedt, *Syntactica*, i. 27 ff., Austin on Virg. *A.* 2. 57 and 4. 673. The phrase *pectora dare* is usually associated with willing and courageous exposure to death or danger: e.g. Virg. *A.* 12. 540 f. 'dedit obuia ferro | pectora', Sil. 6. 87 f. 'dat pectora ferro | Regulus', 17. 485 'horum aduersa dedit Gradiuo (= bello) pectora uirtus'.

491–3. Honorius instructs Roma to lead out her choirs in order to celebrate Stilicho's victories. This short transitional section both concludes his own narrative and signals the beginning of the round of festivities that will now continue until the end of the poem. The celebrations for the sixth consulship, honouring Honorius, and those of triumph, also nominally celebrating the Emperor but in fact mainly glorifying Stilicho, are imperceptibly blended.

491 f. doctos tantae certamina laudis, . . . choros: Müller accepts the reading *certamine*, explaining that *tantae . . . laudis* is a genitive dependent on *doctos*, on the analogy of *peritus*, and that *certamine* is used absolutely as an equivalent for *certatim*, as at Sil. 10. 535 'funereas tum deinde pyras certamine texunt'. He might have added that, though it is rare, such a use of the genitive can be paralleled by e.g. Stat. *Theb.* 1. 398 f. 'docte futuri | Amphiarae'. This interpretation, however, does considerable violence to the flow of the rhythm. The third foot caesura after *doctos* isolates *tantae certamina/-e laudis* as a unified phrase, and it is therefore most natural to take the genitive as being governed by *certamina/-e*. This phrase is then neatly enclosed between *doctos* and *choros*, creating an elegant near-chiasmus (cf. 493 n.), with the sense 'skilled in (sc. singing, celebrating) the contest(s) of such great glory'.

The question that then remains is whether to read *certamine* or *certamina*. Either case is defensible, *certamine* as an ablative of respect (cf. Cic. *Arat.* 548 (302) 'manu doctissima Pallas') and *certamina* as a 'retained' accusative after a past participle with passive sense (see 153 *resoluta comam* n., and cf. Hor. *Carm.* 3. 8. 5 'docte sermones utriusque linguae'). But the plural is surely far more appropriate in the context: Roma is told to bring forth those of her choirs which have proven skill in hymning victories in general, so that they can celebrate this particular victory as is fitting. Cf. for the sense and wording Hor. *Saec.* 75 f. 'doctus et Phoebi chorus et Dianae | dicere laudes.' Note also *Get.* 492 f. (the old Goth to Alaric) 'per tot certamina docto | crede seni', which might be thought to offer some degree of confirmation for *certamina* here.

492. facundia pollet: cf. Sal. *Iug.* 30 'Memmi facundia clara pollensque fuit'. For *polleo* of artistic achievement note also Stat. *Silu.* 1. 2. 249 f. 'ut pollet ouanti | quisque lyra'.

493. nostrum digno sonet ore parentem: the chiasmus serves as an emphatic marker of the end of Honorius' speech. The choice of wording provides a kind of link by ring-composition with his own introduction to the speech: note *parentem* (435), and with this line and 436 cf. esp. Ov. *Met.* 8. 533 f. 'non mihi si centum deus ora sonantia linguis | ingeniumque capax totumque Helicona dedisset', Sil. 9. 342 f. (an invocation to the Muses) 'tantumne datis confidere linguae, | ut Cannas uno ore sonem?' Stilicho's mighty deeds in battle (*claris . . . factis*, 435) require that Roma's choir follow Honorius himself in employing the high style of epic, and *digno* is thus equivalent to *magno*: cf. Hor. *S.* 1. 4. 43 f. 'os | magna sonaturum', Virg. *G.* 3. 294 'magno nunc ore sonandum', Ov. *Ars* 1. 206, *Tr.* 2. 73 'te celebrant alii, quanto decet ore', *Get.* 124 'sublimi certe Curium canit ore uetustas'.

494–522. *Honorius makes his way from Ravenna along the Flaminian Way to Rome through a peaceful landscape of wonders, both natural and man-made.*

A bridge passage evocatively traces Honorius' journey from Ravenna to Rome. The Court party travels by the most obvious route, along the Via Popilia as far as Ariminum (Rimini; not directly mentioned here), and then down the Flaminian Way. Turning inland at Fanum Fortunae (Fano) they cross the Apennines through the pass at Intercisa, and then continue via Clitumnus and Narnia, finally entering the City from the north over the Mulvian Bridge. Much the same journey is traced, with even greater detail and more elaborate language, in a letter from Sidonius Apollinaris to Heronius (*Ep.* 1. 5. 5 ff.). Though there are no

334

convincingly precise verbal parallels, Sidonius probably has the present poem very much in mind, since the letter's earlier sections, on the Po valley, show striking similarities to Claudian's catalogue of rivers at 195-7 (see n. ad loc.).

These lines could be treated primarily as an excursus designed to provide variety and give pleasure in their own right, satisfying a natural curiosity about celebrated places and local wonders: note that Sidonius claims to be answering a request from Heronius himself for the description of places made famous in literature (*Ep.* 1. 5. 1). Cameron, for example, is struck by the vividness of this passage, and takes it as evidence for Claudian's residence at Ravenna and for the reasonable assumption that he accompanied the Court on this journey (pp. 414f.). See also Thomas Hodgkin, *Claudian: the Last of the Roman Poets* (London, 1875), 56f. Indeed, 'journey poems' might reasonably be regarded almost as an independent literary category, the most famous examples in Latin being Hor. *S.* 1. 5, Ov. *Tr.* 1. 10, and Rutilius Namatianus' *De Reditu Suo*. See F. Cairns, *Generic Composition in Greek and Latin Literature* (Edinburgh, 1972), 15f. and index s.v. 'travel'. Here one might also sense the influence of prescriptions on the composition of προπεμπτικά: Menander Rhetor 398. 29ff. Russell–Wilson instructs the orator to include in a προπεμπτικόν a description of the lands through which the honorand will travel.

But the present passage also fulfils the structural function of preparing the audience gradually for the great description of the *aduentus* of the Emperor into Rome. It is thus closely comparable to *III Cons.* 111–25, where we are given an account of the young Honorius' journey from Constantinople to Milan in late 394. Both passages provide a catalogue of the places passed through, embroidered by learned references and literary allusions; they use similar language (e.g. 495 *relinquit* n.); and they both stress the joy with which the Emperor is received as he travels on his way (500 *laetior* n.). Each concludes by concentrating on an act of homage involving the river associated with the city that marks the end of his journey (the Tiber and the Eridanus: see 520n.). And each is then followed directly by lavish descriptions of the thronging crowds of all ages that pour out to welcome the Emperor as he passes through the gates (523ff., 542ff., *III Cons.* 126ff.).

Most significantly, both passages have an important, and distinct, part to play in the propaganda concerns of the poem in which they are located; they are not simply duplicates of each other. In *III Cons.* the emphasis is placed on the courage of the still-unknown child-Augustus: 112f. 'inter barbaricas ausus transire cohortes | inpauido uultu'. He passes through a landscape associated with the mighty heroism of the past, and the references to Hercules' funeral pyre on Mt Oeta (114f.) and to the wedding of Peleus and Thetis (115f.) hint at the heroic feats he will accomplish in his manhood. Indeed, the grove of Dodona itself breaks its silence to prophesy his future glory (116–18). As for the present passage, it reveals to us an Italy full of wonders, both natural and man-made, an ancient land of peace and settled civilization, in the tradition of the *laudes Italiae* of Virgil (G. 2. 136–76: see Thomas's introductory note ad loc., pp. 179ff.). In particular, the port of Ravenna and the pass cut through the mountains at Intercisa correspond to the Lucrine and Julian harbours, joined by the channel cut by Agrippa (495–9; G. 2. 161–4), while the miraculous properties attributed here to the waters of the Clitumnus (508–14) confer upon Claudian's Italy the same atmosphere of mythical fantasy that is seen in Virgil's land of *uer adsiduum* and twice-yearly harvests *(G. 2. 149f.)*. In both poets, too, Italy is a land of noble rivers and ancient cities: compare *antiquae . . . Rauennae* (494), *Fano . . . uetusto* (500) with G. 2. 155ff. 'adde tot egregias urbes operumque laborem, | tot congesta manu praeruptis oppida saxis | fluminaque antiquos subter labentia muros'. All this peaceful landscape of marvels and venerable antiquity—with, we might add, all the senatorial estates that covered it—has been saved from the ravages of the Goths thanks to the victories of Pollentia and Verona, because this land of peace is also a land of warriors, ever victorious over her enemies. At the heart of Claudian's description is the Clitumnus, famous for its breed of white bulls traditionally sacrificed to Jupiter in Roman triumphs: see 506f. n., citing Virg. G. 2. 146ff. It is of course such a triumph that Honorius is even now on his way to celebrate in Rome.

494. antiquae . . . Rauennae: Honorius and the Court moved from Milan to take up permanent residence in the safer confines of Ravenna some time after the departure of Alaric from Italy. The first law issued from the city (C. Th. 7. 13. 15) is dated 6 Dec. 402. Tradition asserted that Ravenna, the capital of the province of Flaminia et Picenum, was a Thessalian colony (Strabo 5. 214, Zosimus 5. 27), though its name has an Etruscan look. Its great age, at any rate, is not in doubt: cf. Zosimus 5. 27 πόλις ἀρχαία. The epithet is one commonly applied to cities in poetry, especially epic, e.g. Carthage (Virg. A. 1. 12, *Gild.* 518), Tyre (A. 4. 670), Tiryns (Stat. *Theb.* 4. 147), Babylon (Stat. *Silu.* 3. 2. 137). But here, in addition to helping bolster the claims of the new, upstart capital to respect as a fitting seat for the Court, it serves to stress the venerable antiquity of Italy's cities, and her long history of settled and peaceful habitation which contrasts with the nomadic life of her barbarous invaders: note *Fano . . . uetusto* (500).

muros egressa: the construction with the accusative is attested since Caes. *Ciu.* 3. 52. 2 'munitiones nostras egressi': see LHS ii. 33, *OLD* s.v. *egredior* 4. Cf. Stat. *Theb.* 7. 17f. 'illi uix muros limenque egressa iuuentus | sacra colunt', *Ruf.* 2. 124 'uix Alpes egressus [transgressus *Hall*] erat', and contrast the ablative at Liv. 28. 22. 12 'ut egredi moenibus auderent', Sid. *Ep.* 1. 5. 2.

495 f. Augustus made Ravenna and Misenum the two principal military harbours of Italy (e.g. Appian, *BC* 5. 78, 80). He constructed the *fossa Augusta*, which led the southern arm of the Po, the Padusa, through the centre of the city and then down to a new harbour capable of holding some 250 ships. This harbour was called Classis, to which name the famous church of S. Apollinare in Classe bears witness; the intervening suburb, stretching over a distance of some 5 or 6 km, was known as Caesarea. See Plin. *Nat.* 3. 119, Jord. *Get.* 150, Sid. *Ep.* 1. 5. 5f., Procop. *Goth.* 1. 29. 31.

495. relinquit: cf. *III Cons.* 113f. 'linquis Rhodopeia saxa . . . iuga deseris Oetes'. The verb is reminiscent, in the context, of the language of epic catalogues, e.g. Virg. *A.* 7. 670 'tum gemini fratres Tiburtia moenia linquunt', 7. 728 'quique Cales linquunt'.

496–9. The general sense is clear enough. As the tide flows in, the sea-water (Nereus) floods into the river, carrying the ships riding upon it back upstream; then, as the tide ebbs, it carries them down again. When the sea retreats, the shore is 'laid bare' (*nudata . . . litora fluctu*), thus conforming to the territorial losses imposed upon the sea by the power of the moon as exerted in the tides (*Oceani lunaribus aemula damnis*).

There is, however, a certain difficulty in 496–8 when it comes to deciding which phrase refers to the incoming tide and which to the ebb. Usually *pronus* when applied to ships on rivers, and *secundus* when used of the direction in which a river flows, indicate a downstream movement (see below ad loc.), and *redeo* is thus a natural verb to use of rivers flowing *backwards*. It seems that this is how Sidonius interpreted Claudian's lines, which he takes as his model for an exuberant description of the waters of the Garonne being driven back by the incoming tide: *Carm.* 22. 17ff. 'uel Naidas istic, | Nereidum chorus alme, doce, cum forte *Garunna* | *huc redeunte* uenis pontumque in flumine sulcas', 105ff. 'currit in aduersum hic pontus multoque recursu | flumina quas uoluunt et spernit et expetit undas. | at cum summotus lunaribus incrementis | *ipse Garunna* suos in dorsa recolligit aestus, | *praecipiti fluctu raptim redit* atque uidetur | in fontem iam non refluus sed defluus ire.' But as Müller saw, this interpretation is at odds with the ordering of Claudian's description, which is best taken as follows. With the tide the sea intrudes upon the land (496, *aduena*; see the note ad loc.), sweeping the ships headlong (*pronas*) away from the shore: this direction is now, paradoxically, *amne secundo* (497). As the tide ebbs the river now 'returns' in its old course downstream to the sea (*nunc redeunte* 498), and the shore is exposed by the retreating sea (*nudata* 498). This interpretation of the order is backed up by the enclitic in *redeunte . . . nudataque*, which closely binds the idea of 'returning' water with the ebb. We thus have an ingenious reversal of the usual meanings associated with *pronus* and *secundus*, something which would be in conformity with much of Claudian's word-play and which would account for Sidonius' apparent misunderstanding. For Claudian's treatment of tides in general see Simon on *Theod.* 107f. 'tumidos quae luna recursus | nutriat Oceani'.

496. certis . . . legibus: the fixed 'laws of nature'; cf. esp. Sil. 14. 348f. 'nouerat atque una pelagi lunaeque labores, | et pater Oceanus qua lege effunderet aestus', Sen. *Dial.* 1. 1. 2, *Stil.* 2. 433ff. (the cave of Time) 'mansura uerendus | scribit iura senex, numeros qui diuidit astris | et cursus stabilesque moras, quibus omnia uiuunt | ac pereunt *fixis* cum *legibus*', *Ruf.* 1. 7f., Prud. *Per.* 10. 949. For the collocation with *certus* cf. Man. 1. 22, 4. 14, Ov. *Met.* 5. 530f. 'repetet Proserpina caelum, | lege tamen certa', *Fast.* 5. 65f., and see 622f. *certaque uagandi . . . lege* n.

   aduena Nereus: = 'the intruding sea'. For the idea of intrusion or transgression of proper barriers contained in *aduena* cf. V. Fl. 1. 588f. 'Libya cum rumperet aduena Calpen | Oceanus', Stat. *Theb.* 4. 239f. 'qui te, flaue, natant terris, Alphee, Sicanis | aduena', Apul. *Mun.* 34, *Rapt.* 2. 60f., 2. 222 'nostrum quid proteris aduena mundum?' Contrast Ov. *Fast.* 2. 68 'qua petit aequoreas aduena Thybris aquas.' The metonymy of *Nereus* for 'the sea' is attested in Latin poetry from Augustan times, e.g. [Tib.] 3. 7. 58 'placidum per Nerea', Ov. *Ep.* 9. 14, Sil. 14. 413f., *Ruf.* 1. 183, *Eutr.* 2. 34, *Get.* 320. Here Nereus himself is dramatically said to 'ebb and flow'; Müller compares *Dirae* 59 (Neptunus) 'atrum conuertens aestum maris undique uentis', but that is far less mannered. None the less, Claudian never attempts anything quite so daring as e.g. Luc. 2. 713 'hic primum rubuit ciuili sanguine Nereus', Stat. *Theb.* 8. 230 'ingenti sulcatum Nerea tauro'; such locutions are mocked by Persius, 1. 94 (= Nero, fr. 4. 2 Büchner) 'qui caeruleum dirimebat Nerea delphin'.

497. pronas: normally downstream, as at e.g. Virg. *G.* 1. 201ff. 'non aliter quam qui aduerso uix flumine lembum | remigiis subigit, si bracchia forte remisit, | atque illum in praeceps prono rapit alueus amni', *A.* 8. 548, Sil. 14. 190f., Stat. *Theb.* 9. 259, Tac. *Hist.* 5. 22, *Eutr.* 1. 353. But here the direction has been reversed, and the ships are being dragged *away* from the sea, though still 'downstream', i.e. with the current. Cf. *Eutr.* 1. 353 'prona petunt retro fluuii iuga'. Other poets play on the meaning of *pronus* when describing the phenomenon of witches turning rivers backwards, but do so with the help of negatives rather than by reversing the word's usual sense: see e.g. Luc. 6. 473 f. 'amnisque cucurrit | non qua pronus erat' and cf. *Ruf.* 1. 159 f. 'uersaque non prono curuaui flumina lapsu | in fontes reditura suos.' Note also Hor. *Carm.* 1. 29. 11. Claudian's daring inversion of the usual sense is in some measure prefigured by Ov. *Met.* 14. 548 'fertque rates pronas medioque sub aequore mergit', where the movement may be to the bottom of the sea but we have the same idea of ships being carried 'headlong' in an unaccustomed direction. He may also have been influenced by the frequent application of *pronus* to the sea, to indicate its flowing from the horizon down to the shore: see *OLD* s.v. 5d, citing Virg. *A.* 5. 212 'prona petit maria et pelago decurrit aperto', Luc. 4. 430.

   amne secundo: not the 'Ocean stream' (as at e.g. *Il.* 14. 245 f. ποταμοῖο ῥέεθρα | Ὠκεανοῦ, Virg. *G.* 4. 233), but the Padusa river, swollen by the tidal flood. For the paradox of the mixed waters cf. Sid. *Carm.* 22. 19 'pontum . . . in flumine sulcas.' The usual sense is 'downstream', i.e. 'to the sea', as at e.g. Virg. *G.* 3. 447 'missusque secundo fluit amni', *A.* 7. 494 f. 'fluuio cum forte secundo | deflueret', Liv. 5. 46. 8, Ov. *Pont.* 4. 15. 27. Here the ships still move with the current, but now that movement is away from the sea. Claudian may have been encouraged to make this bold experiment with traditional diction by passages where the word is applied to the tide sweeping a ship to shore, such as Ov. *Met.* 13. 630 f. 'utilibus uentis aestuque secundo | intrat Apollineam sociis comitantibus urbem'.

   Some manuscripts read *amne refuso*, others *amne retruso*, and still others *amne retuso*. Müller defends the last of these by comparing Luc. 5. 599 ff. 'iam te tollente furebat | pontus et in scopulos totas erexerat undas: | occurrit gelidus Boreas pelagusque retundit', and suggests that the reading *secundo* originates in Virg. *A.* 8. 548 f. 'pars cetera prona | fertur aqua segnisque secundo defluit amni'. But if *redeunte* does indeed refer to the river returning, with the ebb, to its natural course and once more flowing downstream to the sea, then none of these three variants could form the necessary contrast, since they would refer to the sea being 'poured', 'thrust', or 'beaten' back, i.e. to the ebbing of the tide. The most likely explanation is that the unusual sense of *secundo* has caused confusion, and all three variants are witness to mistaken attempts at emendation. Lastly, *retuso* is at least as likely to have been imported from Luc. 5. 601 as *secundo* from Virg. *A.* 8. 549.

498 f. nudataque litora fluctu | deserit: the sands are left 'bare' as the tide retreats. Cf. esp. Luc. 4. 427 f. 'tum freta seruantur, dum se declinibus undis | aestus agat, refluoque mari nudentur harenae', and also Plin. *Nat.* 36. 52 'postea reperta est (sc. harena) non minus probanda ex quodam Hadriatici maris uado, aestu nudante', Aus. *Mos.* 69 f. Green, *c.m.* 53. 64 f.

499. Oceani lunaribus aemula damnis: i.e.'matching the losses inflicted on the Ocean by the moon.' Claudian is adapting, with variation, Luc. 10. 215 ff. 'tunc Nilus fonte soluto, | exit ut Oceanus lunaribus incrementis, | iussus adest'; cf. also Sid. *Carm.* 22. 107 f., cit. 496–9 n. The idea that the phases of the moon exerted an influence on the tides was a familiar one by Claudian's day: see Caes. *Gal.* 4. 29, Luc. 1. 409 ff., esp. 414 'Tethyos unda uagae lunaribus aestuet horis', *Theod.* 107 f. For lunar influence reflected in nature, and for the wording, cf. Man. 2. 93 ff. 'sic summersa fretis, concharum et carcere clausa, | ad lunae motum uariant animalia corpus | et *tua damna, tuas imitantur, Delia, uires*', Plin. *Nat.* 2. 221. Claudian is playing on the regular use of *damna* to refer to the losses suffered by the moon as it wanes: see Hor. *Carm.* 4. 7. 13 'damna tamen celeres reparant caelestia lunae', Gel. 20. 8. 7 'contra lunae augmenta atque damna'.

500. Fanum Fortunae (Fano), famous for the great shrine of the goddess from which it took its name (Strabo 5. 2. 10), became a *colonia* under Augustus, and was formally known as *Colonia Iulia Fanestris* (e.g. Mela 2. 64). Plain *Fanum* is found to indicate the city in some authors (Caes. *Ciu.* 1. 11. 4, Sid. *Ep.* 1. 5. 7), but here the word is in any case glossed by *Fortuna*.

laetior: cf. *III Cons.* 121 f. 'gaudent Italiae sublimibus oppida muris | aduentu sacrata tuo'. To the patron goddess is attributed the joy conventionally said to be felt by the townsfolk at an Imperial *aduentus*. For rejoicing as a distinctive feature of the ἐπιβατήριος see in particular Menander Rhetor 378, 382, and 385 Russell–Wilson. Cf. e.g. Suet. *Cal.* 13 'densissimo et laetissimo obuiorum agmine incessit', Plin. *Pan.* 22. 4 'ubique par gaudium paremque clamorem', Pac. *Pan. Theod.* 37. 4, *Pan. Lat.* 8. 19. 1 Mynors 'exsultantes . . . gaudio Britanni', 11. 10. 5 'cuncta gaudio calere.' For Fortuna see also 1 *Fortunae Reduci* n.

uetusto: see 494 *antiquae . . . Rauennae* n. Cf. Luc. 4. 12 f. 'uetusta . . . Ilerda', Stat. *Silu.* 4. 5. 56 'Curibus uetustis', Tac. *Ann.* 12. 13.

501–3. The road passes high over the steep valley of the Metaurus, and through the tunnel cut by Vespasian at Intercisa (sc. *saxa*; now called the Gola di Furlò, near Calles). Though short (*c.* 37 m in length), the pass was of huge strategic importance, and was the scene of fierce fighting in the Gothic Wars (Procop. *Goth.* 2. 11. 4 ff.). See *CIL* xi. 6106,

recording the cutting of the tunnel, and Aur. Vict. *Caes.* 9. 8
(Vespasian) 'uiaeque operibus maximis munitae et cauati montes per
Flaminiam prono transgressui' (to which the gloss 'quae uulgariter
Pertunsa petra uocitatur' is added at *Epit. Caes.* 9. 10). See further *RE*
ix. 1608. 41 ff.

501. despiciturque uagus . . . Metaurus: the Metaurus, one of the
principal rivers of Umbria, flows east into the Adriatic and was noted
for its swift current (Luc. 2. 405 f. 'in laeuum cecidere latus ueloxque
Metaurus | Crustumiumque rapax', Sil. 8. 448 f., Procop. *Goth.* 2. 11.
11). Its appearance in this catalogue is motivated by considerations of
propaganda, since it was famous as the site of the defeat of Hasdrubal,
yet another unsuccessful invader of Italy whose fate Alaric has failed
to heed: Hor. *Carm.* 4. 4. 38 f. 'testis Metaurum flumen et Hasdrubal |
deuictus', Liv. 27. 47. 9, Sil. 7. 486, 15. 556 f., Sid. *Carm.* 2. 532
'improbus ut rubeat Barcina clade Metaurus', *Ep.* 1. 5. 7 (cit. 208 f. n.).
For the passive use of *despicio* in geographical descriptions cf. Luc. 5.
638 f. 'quantum Leucadio placidus de uertice pontus | despicitur'.

    praerupta ualle: note Virg. *G.* 2. 156 (the *laudes Italiae*) 'praeruptis
oppida saxis'.

502. This line is directly modelled on Statius' description of the cave of
Chiron at *Ach.* 1. 106 ff. 'domus ardua *montem* | *perforat* et longo sus-
pendit Pelion *arcu*; | pars exhausta *manu*, partem sua ruperat aetas.'
The same passage has also left its traces in *Nupt. pr.* 1 'surgeret in
thalamum ducto cum Pelion arcu'. Behind all three, however, lie, as
so often, the ingenuity and the preoccupations of Ovid: *Met.* 3. 157 ff.
'cuius in extremo est antrum nemorale recessu | *arte laboratum nulla*:
simulauerat artem | ingenio natura suo; nam *pumice uiuo* | et leuibus
tofis *natiuum* duxerat *arcum*', 11. 235 f. Ovid's cave is wholly the work of
nature, and in Chiron's cave-home nature and art share the honours;
Vespasian's tunnel, however, is celebrated as an unalloyed triumph of
human skill over nature. Or is the reflexive more than a substitute for
the passive (40 f. *se . . . aestimat* n.), hinting instead at the willing
co-operation of nature (*uiuo . . . arcu*) in the making of this miraculous
tunnel?

502 f. mons arte patens . . . arcu . . . sectae per uiscera rupis: the
image is of a sword plunging into the bowels (e.g. Prud. *Per.* 9. 60 'pro-
funda perforarat uiscera'). Cf. *c.m.* 26. 43 f. 'tunc montis secreta patent,
qui flexus in arcum | aequora pendenti margine summa ligat'. This
poem, describing the Aponus, a stream almost as much of a natural
wonder as the Clitumnus, has a number of features in common with
this passage. See also 508 f. n.

502. uiuo: i.e. 'natural'; see Austin on Virg. *A.* 1. 167 'uiuo . . . sedilia saxo', and cf. *A.* 3. 688, Ov. *Met.* 3. 159, 5. 317, *Fast.* 2. 315 (with Bömer), Tac. *Ann.* 4. 55, *Rapt.* 2. 103.

503. admisit: given that we have *recipit* and *despiciturque* in the same sentence, Müller may well be right to accept the less well-attested *admittit*. But such abrupt changes of tenses are common enough in ecphrastic passages (note that the next final verb is a perfect, *fuit*, 508), and *admittit* has something of the look of a scribal 'correction'.

per uiscera rupis: a rarer version of the commoner *uiscera montis* (Virg. *A.* 3. 575, Sil. 5. 396, *Rapt.* 1. 177) and *uiscera terrae* (Ov. *Met.* 1. 138, Stat. *Theb.* 8. 109, 9. 451, *c.m.* 29. 5). Williams on *A.* 3. 575 cites Milton, *PL* 1. 232ff. 'or the shatter'd side | Of thund'ring Etna, whose combustible | And fuell'd entrails thence conceiving Fire, | Sublim'd with Mineral fury, aid the Winds'.

504f. The shrine of Juppiter Appenninus some 15 km from Iguvium enjoyed a considerable reputation in antiquity as an oracle. Its altars are *cultas pastoribus* because they are placed so high in the mountains. See *RE* x. 1142. 34f., and note *CIL* viii. 7961, xi. 5803.

504. exuperans: with the primary sense 'rising above', as at Virg. *A.* 11. 904f. 'cum pater Aeneas saltus ingressus apertos | exsuperatque iugum', Sil. 3. 516f. 'rumpit inaccessos aditus atque ardua primus | exsuperat summaque uocat de rupe cohortes' (Hannibal crossing the Alps, also adapted at *Get.* 322, of Stilicho doing the same), Stat. *Theb.* 9. 640. But also relevant here is the sense 'passing beyond' on a journey: see Virg. *A.* 3. 697f. 'iussi numina magna loci ueneramur, et inde | exsupero praepingue solum stagnantis Helori', V. Fl. 2. 622.

saxoque minantes: *saxo* is either ablative of place ('threatening upon their rock'), or less likely ablative of separation (cf. Müller, 'vom Felsen drohend herabblickend'). *minantes* implies that the altar and the shrine loom menacingly over the pass; see Servius on Virg. *A.* 1. 162f. 'hinc atque hinc uastae rupes geminique minantur | in caelum scopuli', *OLD* s.v. *minor* 1b 'to impend (of projecting or overhanging features)', and cf. *Prob.* 228f.

505. For the four-word hexameter see 177 n.

Appenninigenis: a compound of the greatest rarity, attested only here and at Ov. *Met.* 15. 432 'Appenninigenae quae proxima Thybridis undis'. Note, however, Virg. *A.* 11. 700 (another four-word hexameter) 'Appenninicolae bellator filius Auni', Sil. 5. 626, 6. 167, Prud. *C. Symm.* 2. 521 (four-word hexameter; in competition with Claudian?) 'Appenninicolam peditem Cybeleius hostis'. For compound forms ending in *-gena*, based on Greek models and a feature of the high style of Latin verse since archaic times, see LHS i. 280f. For lines beginning with massive polysyllabic words (usually Greek) see

Simon on *Theod.* 293 'amphitheatrali faueat Latonia pompae', citing
e.g. Luc. 8. 407 'Oedipodionias infelix fabula Thebas', Stat. *Theb.* 1.
313, 486, *Eutr.* 1. 256 'Hellespontiacis legio dignissima signis', *Rapt.* 2.
66 'Thermodontiaca Tanain fregere securi', Prud. *C. Symm.* 1. 385,
Sid. *Carm.* 15. 135.

506–14. The Clitumnus is an Umbrian spring which, at Mevania, flows
into the Tinia (the modern Topino), a tributary of the Tiber. It was
one of ancient Italy's most famous beauty spots, and Pliny offers a
detailed and enthusiastic description of its glories to his friend
Romanus (*Ep.* 8. 8). In poetry, its fame was secured by the prominence given to it in the *laudes Italiae*: Virg. *G.* 2. 146ff. 'hinc albi,
Clitumne, greges et maxima taurus | uictima, saepe tuo perfusi
flumine sacro, | Romanos ad templa deum duxere triumphos'. See
also the passages cited in the next note. The best-known example of
the topos in English verse is no doubt Byron, *Childe Harold* 4. 66ff. 'But
thou, Clitumnus! in thy sweetest wave | Of the most living crystal that
was e'er | The haunt of river nymph, to gaze and lave | Her limbs
where nothing hid them, thou dost rear | Thy glassy banks whereon
the milk-white steer | Grazes'. For the spring's association with white
sacrificial bulls see further the next note, and see in general *RE* iv.
57. 5ff.

506f. Bulls that were raised on the lush grass of Mevania's wide fields
(Luc. 1. 473f. 'tauriferis ubi se Meuania campis | explicat') and drank
from the Clitumnus were traditionally prized for their distinctive and
dazzling whiteness. Since white was the appropriate colour for
offerings to sky divinities like Jupiter and Juno they were thus especially suited for sacrifice at triumphs: cf. Prop. 2. 19. 25f. 'qua formosa
suo Clitumnus flumina luco | integit, et niueos abluit unda boues',
Stat. *Silu.* 1. 4. 128ff. 'nec si uacuet Meuania ualles | aut praestent
niueos Clitumna noualia tauros | sufficiam', Juv. 12. 13f.; also Amm.
Marc. 25. 4. 17. Servius attributes to Pliny the claim that it was drinking the waters of the Clitumnus that turned the bulls white, but in fact
Pliny (*Nat.* 2. 230) has in mind the district of Falerii: see Thomas on *G.*
2. 146f. As Thomas observes, Virgil seems rather to imply that it is
swimming that causes the whiteness ('saepe tuo perfusi flumine sacro').
This is possibly what Silius and Claudian have in mind: Sil. 8. 450f.
'lauat ingentem perfundens flumine sacro | Clitumnus taurum', *c.m.*
4. 3f. 'non tales, Clitumne, lauas in gurgite tauros, | Tarpeio referunt
quos pia uota Ioui.' But they are so obviously dependent on Virgil that
their wording is hardly conclusive.

506. sacras uictoribus undas: cf. 'flumine sacro' at Virg. *G.* 2. 147,
Sil. 8. 450. *uictoribus* should probably be taken as an ethic dative ('in

the eyes of triumphators'), since the waters are properly sacred to Jupiter.

507. candida . . . armenta: cf. Ov. *Ars* 1. 290 'candidus, armenti gloria, taurus erat', *Met.* 12. 248 f. 'uelut qui candida tauri | rumpere sacrifica molitur colla securi', *Tr.* 4. 2. 5, Stat. *Theb.* 9. 334, and see further 370 *electi candoris* n.

Latiis . . . triumphis: varying Virgil's 'Romanos ad templa deum duxere triumphos' (*G.* 2. 148): cf. *Rapt.* 2. 177 f. 'et qui te, Latiis nondum praecincte tropaeis | Thybri, natat'. For *Latius = Romanus* cf. 22 *Latiae . . . aulae*, 396 *Latio . . . sanguine*, and see 89 *Latium*, 130 *Latio discedere iussus* nn.

508. uisere cura fuit: as many a tourist had done before him, including his Imperial predecessor Gaius Caligula (Suet. *Cal.* 43). But Honorius, on his way to Rome to celebrate his triumph over the Goths, might have had a more cogent reason to take a detour to a spot famous for its sacrificial animals, had he not been such a good Catholic. For the construction (*cura* with dependent infinitive) see Trump 29, and cf. Virg. *Ecl.* 8. 89 'nec sit mihi cura mederi', *G.* 1. 51 f. 'uentos et uarium caeli praediscere morem | cura sit', *A.* 1. 703 f., Tib. 1. 9. 51, Luc. 1. 639 f. 'at Figulus, cui cura deos secretaque caeli | nosse fuit', 3. 706 f., *Theod.* 176 ff.

508 f. nec te miracula fontis | praetereunt: *miracula*, the key-word to this entire passage, appears almost at its very centre. We are reminded again of Claudian's poem on the miraculous properties of the stream of Aponus: *c.m.* 26. 3 'cum tua uel mutis tribuant *miracula* uocem', 7 f. 'nonne reus Musis pariter Nymphisque tenebor, | si tacitus soli *praetereare* mihi?' The particular quality attributed to Clitumnus here is that its waters respond, in a manner reminiscent of Stoic doctrines of συμπάθεια or of the Pathetic Fallacy of the poets, to the activities, and even the character, of their human visitors. If approached gently and quietly, they themselves flow on smoothly, but if approached noisily or raucously they become agitated and turbulent; they thus mirror the emotions or state of mind of human beings. There seems to be no trace of such a *miraculum* being associated with the Clitumnus in any other ancient source, nor, as Müller points out, does anything precisely comparable appear in the catalogues of remarkable springs with unusual properties found in the Roman geographers and related works (Vitr. 8. 3, Ov. *Met.* 15. 308 ff., Plin. *Nat.* 31, Mela 1. 39). The closest parallels are: Mela 1. 39 (a spring in Cyrenaica) 'fons, quem Solis adpellant, et rupes quaedam austro sacra. haec cum hominum manu attingitur ille inmodicus exurgit harenasque quasi maria agens sic saeuit ut fluctibus', Plin. *Nat.* 31. 12

(a spring in the lands of the Tungri) 'igne admoto turbida fit ac postremo rubescit.' Müller, however, judiciously cites the Elder Pliny's own admonition to the cynical: *Nat.* 31. 21 'quod si quis fide carere ex his aliqua arbitratur, discat in nulla parte naturae maiora esse miracula.' The Younger Pliny stresses that the stream quickly turns into a river with a strong current (*Ep.* 8. 8. 3), and it is perhaps from this physical reality that a local tradition known to Claudian has grown. As for Honorius, no doubt the stream reflected the serenity and *tranquillitas* regularly attributed to Emperors in panegyric, just as the weather itself will do at 537–42 (see n. ad loc.). For Claudian's interest in the wonders of nature generally see Fargues 312ff. In *praetereunt* (= 'escape the notice of') we can perhaps discern the influence of didactic poetry on this passage: see Hollis on Ov. *Ars* 1. 75 'nec te praetereat Veneri ploratus Adonis'.

509f. si quis adiret ... si ... citasset: = 'if anyone should approach it etc.' In generalizing conditional clauses the subjunctive is regularly used with second person verbs from early times, to indicate 'that the speaker is reflecting on the matter' (Woodcock, 195). From Livy on this usage is rapidly extended to the other persons too when the generalizing clause implies an action which is repeated, as is the case here. See further Woodcock 196, citing Liv. 3. 36. 8 'si quis collegam appellasset, ab eo ad quem uenerat ita discedebat ut paeniteret non prioris decreto stetisse' and Tac. *Hist.* 2. 5 'Vespasianus, ... si res posceret, manu hostibus obniti'. The subjunctive does not in the slightest imply scepticism about the miracle on Claudian's part: 'the mood here indicates, not that the actions expressed are hypothetical, but that the speaker is practising induction upon them and arguing from the particular to the general' (Woodcock 152).

510. uoce ... maiore: since *uoce* is balanced by *gradum* the reference is almost certainly to a noisy approach—a heavy tread—rather than to loud talking. Cf. Virg. *A.* 3. 668f. 'uertimus et proni certantibus aequora remis. | sensit, et ad sonitum uocis uestigia torsit', where Servius comments 'uox enim est omne quod sonat'. Williams ad loc. disagrees with Servius, arguing that *uocis* refers to the shouts of the bo'sun keeping time. This may well be right, but it is easy to see the grounds for Servius' interpretation, and what matters here is not what Virgil meant but what Claudian probably *believed* him to have meant. The rationalizing conjectures of Heinsius (*se moxque gradu*) and Burmann (*si forte gradum*) are thus unnecessary.

   gradum ... citasset: first found in prose at Liv. 8. 6. 2 'citato gradu'. In verse the phrase is fairly rare, but a predilection for it on the part of Seneca (*Med.* 891 'effer citatum ... gradum', *Phaed.* 989, *Tro.*

999 'incitato . . . gradu', cf. *Her. O.* 513) explains its secure if minor status in the diction of the high style: cf. Luc. 6. 82, Sil. 3. 183f., 11. 64, Stat. *Theb.* 6. 587f., 10. 137f., Prud. *Per.* 5. 210. It has a literary ancestor in Catul. 63. 2 'ut nemus citato cupide pede tetigit'.

511. commixtis feruebat aquis: the waters churn (*commixtis*) and seethe (*feruebat*). For *feruo* and the related adjectives applied to turbulent water cf. Virg. *G.* 1. 327 'feruet . . . fretis spirantibus aequor', *A.* 7. 24 'uada feruida', Ov. *Met.* 3. 571, 14. 48.

512. uadis: though *uadum* properly means 'shallows' and is cognate with *uado* and Eng. 'wade', it is frequently used in verse as a general synonym for *aqua*: see Fordyce on Virg. *A.* 7. 24. It is most commonly applied to the sea, but also to rivers at e.g. Virg. *A.* 7. 242 'fontis uada sacra Numici', *Rapt.* 1. 22f. 'quos Styx liuentibus ambit | interfusa uadis'.

ut: for the use of *ut* to introduce an epexegetic clause dependent on a clause or a specific noun or neuter pronoun ('namely that', 'which is to say that'), see LHS ii. 763, citing Cic. *Att.* 11. 22. 2, Liv. 34. 9. 12, and *OLD* s.v. *ut* 39.

corporis umbras: 'reflections'. Cf. Stat. *Theb.* 9. 229, Aus. *Mos.* 223f. Green 'reddit nautales uitreo sub gurgite formas | et redigit pandas inuersi corporis umbras', *Stil.* 2. 274.

513. nouam iactantia sortem: for *sors* of 'the special law or condition governing the behaviour of a thing' see *OLD* s.v. 8c, citing e.g. Man. 2. 215 'omnia dicuntur simili sub sorte diurna', Sen. *Suas.* 3. 1, Sen. *Ag.* 407 'nam certa fari sors maris dubii uetat'.

514. humanos . . . mores: for the collocation cf. Petr. 126. 3 'ex uultu tamen hominum mores colligo'; also Stat. *Silu.* 4. 6. 89 'mores humanaque pectora.' See also Green on Aus. *Mos.* 373f. 'tantus properantibus undis | ambitus aut mores'.

515-19. Narnia (modern Narni) is an Umbrian hill-town (515 *celsa* n.) captured by the Romans and converted into a Latin colony in 299 BC. In his miniature *laudes Italiae* Claudian chooses to rank Narnia among the natural wonders of the country, concentrating on its sulphurous stream and offering a vivid description of its narrow, densely-wooded valley. An alternative might have been to put the city in the category of man-made wonders, its other principal attraction being a fine bridge built in the reign of Augustus. See *RE* xvi. 1734. 67ff.

515. celsa: perched high on its hill, like so many towns of central and southern Italy, and notorious for its inaccessibility. Cf. Sil. 8. 457f. 'duro monti per saxa recumbens | Narnia', Mart. 7. 93. 1f. 'Narnia . . . ancipiti uix adeunda iugo', Servius on Virg. *A.* 7. 517, Procop. *Goth.* 1. 17. 8 δυσπρόσοδόν τε καὶ ἄλλως ἄναντες ὂν τὸ χωρίον εἰδώς. κεῖται μὲν γὰρ ἐν ὑψηλῷ ὄρει. For *celsa* as an epithet of cities cf. Luc. 1. 198 'celsa . . . Alba', 4. 144 'celsam . . . Ilerdam', Stat. *Theb.* 1. 383, 4. 44.

patulum prospectans . . . campum: for similar language used to describe places cf. Mela 1. 89 'super angustias hinc Teos illinc Clazomenae . . . diuersis frontibus diuersa maria prospectant', Tib. 1. 7. 19f. 'utque maris uastum prospectet turribus aequor . . . Tyros', Tac. *Hist.* 3. 60, *Ann.* 14. 9.

516. regali calcatur equo: the combination of the passive with the dative of agent can be seen also at Sil. 3. 676 'calcatos . . . Ioui lucos', 11. 218, *Ruf.* 1. 375f. 'calcabitur asper | Phasis equo'. For *regali* see 42 *regia*, 64 *regale culmen* nn.

rarique coloris: see 519 *albet* n. The *albi* found in some manuscripts is clearly a gloss.

517. Both the *est* formula and the parenthetic comment on the name of a place are associated with ecphrasis; see Austin on Virg. *A.* 1. 12, 1. 109. Cf. esp. *Rapt.* 2. 112f. 'haud procul inde lacus (Pergum dixere Sicani) | panditur'.

urbi qui nominis auctor: that Narnia derived its name from the river Nar, which flowed to the north at the foot of the city, was the received wisdom in antiquity: cf. Liv. 10. 10. 5 'colonia . . . a Nare flumine Narnia appellata', Procop. *Goth.* 1. 17. 9 ποταμὸς δὲ Νάρνος τὸν τοῦ ὄρους παραρρεῖ πρόποδα, ὃς καὶ τὴν ἐπωνυμίαν τῇ πόλει παρέσχεν. Modern scholarship, however, derives it from a local people called the Nahartes (*RE* xvi. 1734. 67ff.). For the phrasing cf. Ov. *Met.* 13. 617 'praepetibus subitis nomen facit auctor'.

518. ilice sub densa: for the collective singular, the position in the line, and the word-order cf. Virg. *Ecl.* 6. 54 'ilice sub nigra'; and for the epithet, Ov. *Fast.* 2. 165 'densa niger ilice lucus'. Note also Virg. *A.* 6. 208f. 'opaca | ilice', Stat. *Theb.* 5. 600 'umbrosa . . . in ilice'.

artatus: giving, with *tortis anfractibus* (519), a vivid picture of a mountain stream winding between high banks. For *arto* applied to narrow straits or other bodies of water cf. Mela 1. 7, Sen. *Her. F.* 1210f., Luc. 5. 234 (Euripus) 'artatus rapido feruet qua gurgite pontus', *Gild.* 225 'intrantem Pontum qua Bosporos artat'. Note also Stat. *Theb.* 2. 434 'Euboicis artatas fluctibus oras'.

519. tortis anfractibus: for *anfractus* of rivers cf. Sen. *Ep.* 104. 15 'Maeander . . . implicatur crebris anfractibus', Stat. *Theb.* 4. 52 'anfractu riparum incuruus Elisson'; of valleys Virg. *A.* 11. 522 'est curuo anfractu ualles', *Prob.* 105. For *tortis* cf. Luc. 10. 290 (Nile) 'cursus in occasus flexu torquetur et ortus', Plin. *Nat.* 3. 16 'torsere se fluminum aut correxere flexus'; also Liv. 27. 47. 10 'tortuosi amnis sinus flexusque'.

347

albet: i.e. with sulphur. The sulphur-white waters of the Nar are a regular feature of Latin epic from Ennius on: see Skutsch on *Ann.* 222 'sulpureas posuit spiramina Naris ad undas', Fordyce on Virg. *A.* 7. 514ff., esp. 517 'sulpurea Nar albus aqua', Sil. 8. 451f., *Prob.* 256f. To *albet* cf. also *CIL* ix. 4756 'Nar hic fluit albus', Aus. *Technop.* 8. 10 Green; Mart. 7. 93. 1f. 'Narnia, sulpureo quam gurgite candidus amnis | circuit'. Servius on Virg. *A.* 7. 517 says that *nar* is Sabine for 'sulphur'; modern philology considers it Illyrian.

520. The same picture can be seen in reverse at *III Cons.* 122f. where the account of Honorius' *aduentus* in Italy concludes with his being welcomed with adoration by the river-god Eridanus: 'aduentu . . . tuo, summissus adorat | Eridanus blandosque iubet mitescere fluctus'. That it is here the Emperor who pays his respects indicates the unparalleled status of Rome and the Tiber; compare 612–17, where Emperor and people perform rituals of homage each to the other.

It was common practice for new arrivals to greet the local gods with prayers and sacrifice, and at Ap. Rh. 2. 1271ff., for example, we find Jason pouring into the river Phasis a libation of wine and honey to the Earth and the gods and heroes of the country. Here *salutato* must imply that Honorius prays to Tiber, but *libatis . . . lymphis* poses greater difficulties. At first sight it seems to mean that he offers the god a libation of water. Platnauer takes this to be a libation of Tiber's *own* waters ('in greeting to Father Tiber thou has poured a libation of his waters'). This is a perfectly natural way to read the Latin, but we would then have the description of a truly extraordinary ceremony, since it is hard to see why a god might be expected to take pleasure in being offered what is already his. Water is in fact offered in certain kinds of libations, particularly those made to the spirits of the dead: at *Od.* 11. 26–8 Odysseus pours out libations of honey-drink, wine, and water πᾶσιν νεκύεσσι, and Atossa offers λιβάσιν ὑδρηλαῖς παρθένου πηγῆς μέτα, as well as milk, honey, and wine, to the dead Darius at Aesch. *Pers.* 609ff. Note also Soph. *OC* 1599. But this particular type of ritual is obviously not very relevant here. More useful is the knowledge that offerings of water were made at the Eleusinian Mysteries in a rite designed to encourage rain: see Walter Burkert, *Greek Religion*, trans. John Raffan (Cambridge, Mass., 1985), 72f. Similarly Eden, on Virg. *A.* 8. 68f., points out that Servius *auctus* (on *Ecl.* 7. 21) records that offerings of water were made at the springs of the Camenae. If Claudian knew of the local rites recorded in Servius from contemporary antiquarian works, then he might be imagined here as adapting them to his own text to make a novel and inventive compliment to Rome. This is something of a stretch, however, and it might therefore seem best to agree with those earlier commentators who took *libatis* to imply that Honorius actually drank a small quantity of the Tiber's water (see *OLD* s.v. *libo* c 'to consume a little of, sip', and note e.g. Virg. *Ecl.* 5. 25 f. 'nulla neque amnem | libauit quadripes'), but here too parallels for drinking in order to pay one's respects to a river-god are lacking.

In fact, the mystery is solved if we accept that Claudian is alluding to a passage from the *Metamorphoses* of Ovid. At 1. 371 ff., after the great flood, Deucalion and Pyrrha visit the shrine of Themis to pray for guidance, but first they ritually purify themselves by sprinkling over their heads and clothing some water from the river Cephisus: 'inde ubi libatos inrorauere liquores | uestibus et capiti, flectunt uestigia sanctae | ad delubra deae'. In Ovid there is no possibility of confusion: 'libatos' means that they scooped up a little water in their hands and 'inrorauere . . . uestibus et capiti' completes the meaning by making explicit what they then did with it. The difficulty in Claudian has been caused by the extreme compression of the reworking of the earlier passage: the colourful phrase ('libatos . . . liquores') has been selected for recasting in a variant form ('libatis . . . lymphis') and the explanatory phrase showing the use to which the water was put has been suppressed altogether. Honorius, then, 'took a little' in order to cleanse himself before the prayer with which he greeted the river-god (*salutato*). For this use of *libo* note also Ov. *Ars* 1. 577 'quemcumque cibum digitis libauerit illa', where the verb is used of taking up in the hand a little food from a common dish. The allusion to Ovid's account of the end of the great flood reinforces the idea that, in driving the Goths back into Illyricum, Stilicho and Honorius have cleansed Italy and renewed her bountiful land: cf. 38 *iubet reuirescere*, 324–30 nn.

Claudian will also have expected his audience to recall Virg. *A.* 8. 68 ff., where, after a dream-vision of Tiber, Aeneas takes up the river-water in his hands and prays to the god: 'surgit et aetherii spectans orientia solis | lumina rite cauis undam de flumine palmis | sustinet ac talis effundit ad aethera uoces'. For the ritual see Fordyce and Eden ad loc. Honorius' return to Rome is thus powerfully associated with the first visit of the father of the Roman People to the divinely-appointed *sedes imperii* (39–52, 407–10 nn.).

521 f. Honorius' party enters the northern suburbs of the City along the Via Flaminia. Müller takes the words *operosaque semita uastis | molibus* closely together, and, understanding them to mean a bridge and its 'Brückenweg', suggests that the Pons Muluius is meant. This is probably right, since the phrasing implies that the *moles* actually formed part of the *semita*: Platnauer's interpretation 'and all the magnificent buildings which line the roads' should therefore be rejected. Note also Aur. Vict. *Lib. Caes.* 9. 8 'uiaeque operibus maximis munitae'. What is not at all clear is whether *arcus* forms part of the same phrase and so refers to the arches of the bridge, or is an independent item, in which case the reference would most probably be, by metonymy, to an aqueduct (see 521 *arcus* n. below). If *arcus* indicates a bridge, the Pons Muluius is indeed the most likely candidate; if an aqueduct is intended, it will be the Aqua Virgo. Overall, a tripartite structure with members of increasing length ('aqueduct', 'massive bridge', and 'all the other things found in the suburbs of a mighty city') seems to provide a more pleasing sense of progression. Note also that the great aqueducts that dominate the skyline on the Roman *campagna* would have been one of the first and most striking indications for a traveller that the City was near.

521. excipiunt: at *Stil.* 3. 9 Claudian had exhorted Roma to welcome Stilicho with the words 'excipe magnanimum pectus'.

    arcus: used of bridges at Luc. 4. 15 (the river Sicoris) 'saxeus ingenti quem pons amplectitur arcu', Stat. *Silu.* 4. 3. 70 'pontis Caesarei reclinis arcu', Sid. *Ep.* 1. 5. 3; and of aqueducts at e.g. Fron. *Aq.* 1. 15, 20 etc., Plin. *Ep.* 10. 37. 2, Juv. 3. 11 'ad ueteres arcus madidamque Capenam'. See further *TLL* ii/1. 479. 57ff.

    operosa: i.e. 'built with great labour'. Cf. Cic. *Leg.* 2. 64 'ne quis sepulchrum faceret operosius quam quod decem homines effecerint triduo', Ov. *Met.* 15. 666f. 'ad templa . . . conueniunt operosa', Tac. *Germ.* 27. 1. For adjectives ending in -*osus* see 146 *undosa domo* n.

521f. uastis | molibus: for the collocation cf. Sil. 14. 523 'uasta sed mole catenas', *Get.* 343f. 'profundae | uasta mole niues'; also Ov. *Met.* 15. 809 'molimine uasto'.

522. quidquid tantae praemittitur urbi: the passage fittingly ends with a restrained but still majestic phrase that brings before us the greatest of all Italy's marvels, Rome itself. The tone of pride and awe is enhanced for those who recall the line that begins Claudian's renowned hymn of praise to Rome: *Stil.* 3. 130ff. 'proxime dis consul, *tantae* qui prospicis *urbi*'. Note also *Stil.* 3. 69 'quantam seruaueris urbem'.

    praemittitur: the great buildings of the city are, as it were, harbingers or signs of what is still to come: for the choice of verb consider Ov. *Fast.* 3. 877, Sen. *Nat.* 2. 32. 4 'indicia uenturi ubique praemittens', Stat. *Theb.* 6. 936 'uenturi praemissa fides'.

523-42. *Rome preparing to receive Honorius is like a young bride awaiting her groom. The city's appearance has been enhanced by the magnificent restoration of her walls to meet the Gothic menace. Even the weather improves for the* aduentus *of the Emperor.*

This passage falls into three parts, the simile of 523-31, the description of the newly restored walls (531-6), and the account of the improvement in the winter weather in time for the Emperor's arrival (537-42). The motif that unites them is that of beautification: the young bride, the City itself, and even the weather are all looking their very best. This motif is continued in the following sections, where a corresponding emphasis is placed on the splendour of the appearance of the Emperor (560-4) and his retinue of cataphracts (570-7). Note how the ring-composition is marked verbally by the repetition of *ornat/ornet* (524, 576).

523-31. This simile could be seen as an adaptation and expansion of Menander Rhetor's advice on how the orator should praise a city which has no claim to antiquity: φήσεις . . . ὅτι ἀνθεῖ καθάπερ κόρη ἀκμάζουσα (355. 3 ff. Russell–Wilson). Rome, of course, is not a new city, but an ancient one rejuvenated: see further 533-6n. That the particular scene described here is best interpreted as one of the preparations for a marriage, rather than just a courtship-visit, is clear from its similarities with numerous epithalamia and epic descriptions of mothers, or more usually *pronubae* (human or divine) dressing the bride. Cf. *Nupt.* 165 ff., where the Nereids bring Maria gifts for her wedding, including *cingula* (cf. 525), a *monile* (cf. 527), and a diadem set with pearls from the Red Sea (cf. the pearl earrings of 528), and *Nupt.* 282 ff. (Venus as Maria's *pronuba*) 'dixit et ornatus, dederant quos nuper ouantes | Nereides, collo membrisque micantibus aptat. | ipsa caput distinguit acu, substringit amictus; | flammea uirgineis accommodat ipsa capillis'; also *Stil.* 1. 82 f. (Aelia Flaccilla playing the part of mother for the orphaned Serena at her wedding to Stilicho) 'inde pium matris regina gerebat | obsequium grauibus subnectens flammea gemmis', *Rapt.* 2. 322 ff. (drawing on Stat. *Theb.* 2. 227 ff.). See further Christiansen 53.

523. officiis trepidantibus: these are surely the tasks properly seen as belonging to the bride's mother, tasks which the poet then goes on to describe. Cf. *Fesc.* 3. 6 (= *c.m.* 1. 6 f.) (to Stilicho, father of the bride and spiritual father of the groom) 'patris officiis | iunge potenti pignora dextra.' *trepidantibus* is a transferred epithet expressing her agitation and excitement. Cf. *c.m.* 30. 94 ff. (at Serena's birth) 'omina non audet genetrix tam magna fateri | successusque suos arcani conscia uoti | spe trepidante tegit'; also Aus. *Ephem.* 3. 79 Green 'trepidantia uota', Maur. 38f. 'cunctis uisceribus, tamen | occultus trepidat labor.' The bride is no doubt experiencing the same emotion: *Fesc.* 4. 3 'iam nuptae trepidat sollicitus pudor'. Müller, however, understands *officiis* as an example of the abstract used for the concrete (here = *ancillis*). He compares e.g. *Eutr.* 1. 42f. 'uetustum | seruitium semperque nouum', where *seruitium* = *seruus*, and further support could be found for his interpretation in the occasional metonymical use of *officium* of servants in late antique authors (*TLL* ix/2. 522. 26ff.). In this Müller is in agreement with Burman, who compared Ov. *Pont.* 4. 4. 42 'officium populi uix capiente domo', Suet. *Iul.* 15. But in addition to the evidence presented by the parallels cited above, it should be added that the prominent intrusion of maids here would shift the focus away from the simile's protagonist, the *mater sollertior*, informing us of the maids' emotions while leaving us to guess hers from the circumstances.

ora: i.e. the whole head, including the hair (527). See *OLD* s.v. *os* 7, citing e.g. Cic. *Ver.* 4. 124 'Gorgonis os pulcherrimum cinctum anguibus reuellit atque abstulit'. Sil. 2. 202 'amputat e curru reuolutae uirginis ora'; add Virg. *A.* 8. 196f., Tac. *Ann.* 1. 61.

524. spe propiore tori: i.e. as her hopes of a good marriage for her daughter approach fulfilment. For the phrasing cf. Stat. *Theb.* 6. 442f. (Admetus in the chariot race) 'Thessalus heros | spe propiore calet'. The metonymy of *torus* for *conubium* can be traced back to Ovid (*Met.* 7. 91, *Fast.* 4. 602); examples in Claudian are particularly frequent, e.g. *Prob.* 202, *III Cons.* 116, *Fesc.* 2. 3, *Nupt.* 122, 229, *Stil.* 1. 33, 2. 76, *Rapt.* 1. 35, 130.

525f. uestesque et cingula comit | . . . manu: as Müller points out, this is a reference to the tying-on of the girdle with a particularly intractable knot known as the *nodus Herculeus*; by undoing this knot later in the bed-chamber the groom will initiate the consummation of the marriage. Cf. *Fesc.* 1. 37f. 'et seminudo pectore cingulum | forti negatum solueret Herculi' and see *RE* xvii. 807. 11ff. For *como* of arraying a bride for her wedding cf. Stat. *Silu.* 1. 2. 110ff. (Venus with Violentilla) 'nec colla genasque | comere nec pingui deducere amomo | cessauit mea, nate, manus', Tac. *Germ.* 18. 2 'noua nupta comatur'.

526. uiridique angustat iaspide pectus: Platnauer translates 'confines her breast with bands of green jasper'. This interpretation makes good sense of *angustat*, and seems to be confirmed by Jer. *Ep.* 117. 7 (censuring a woman's dress) 'papillae fasciolis conprimuntur et crispanti cingulo angustius pectus artatur'. A slender, small-breasted form was the usual Roman ideal of female beauty: see e.g. Ter. *Eun.* 313ff. 'quas matres student | demissis umeris esse, uincto pectore, ut graciliae sient. | siquaest habitior paullo pugilem esse aiunt, deducunt

cibum', Mart. 14. 134 'fascia, crescentes dominae compesce papillas, |
ut sit quod capiat nostra tegatque manus', with the note by T. J.
Leary, 'Martial's Apophoreta: An Introduction and Commentary'
(Ph.D. thesis, Cape Town, 1993). Note also Luc. 2. 364 'suppara
nudatos cingunt angusta lacertos', among the many pieces of bridal
finery Marcia lacks.

The jasper is not, in all probability, a decoration on the bands (or
'girdle'), but rather a jewelled *fibula* that holds them in place: cf. *Rapt.*
2. 40 (Diana) 'collectae tereti nodantur iaspide uestes', and Gruzelier
ad loc., noting also Virg. *A.* 4. 139, Stat. *Theb.* 9. 694 f., *Rapt.* 2. 16 f.
(Venus) 'sudata marito | fibula purpureos gemma suspendit amictus'.
Jasper enjoyed a high reputation as a gem in antiquity on account of
its rich colour (cf. 561 *uiridantia* n.), and we find it decorating Honorius'
consular robes at *IV Cons.* 591. With *uiridi* cf. Plin. *Nat.* 37. 115 'uiret et
saepe traluceta iaspis, etiam uicta multis antiquitatis gloriam retinens',
Cyprianus, *Heptateuchos E.* 1100 'iaspisque uiret' (cit. Roberts 10); con-
trast Virg. *A.* 4. 261 f. 'stellatus iaspide fulua | ensis', Luc. 10. 122, Stat.
Theb. 7. 658 f. 'fibula . . . Taenariam fulua mordebat iaspide pallam'.

527. substringitque comam gemmis: i.e. with a jewel-studded pin,
perhaps itself made of gold. Cf. Ov. *Ep.* 21. 89, *Am.* 3. 13. 25 'uirginei
crines auro gemmaque premuntur', Luc. 3. 280 ff. 'auroque ligatas |
substringens Arimaspe comas', and see Gruzelier's helpful note on
Rapt. 2. 15 f. (Venus) 'illi multifidos crinis sinuatur in orbes | Idalia
diuisus acu'. For *substringo* see also Tac. *Germ.* 38. 2 'obliquare crinem
nodoque substringere'.

527 f. colla monili | circuit: the necklace is no doubt either studded
with jewels like the hair-pin (cf. *Get.* 627 'Ausonidum gemmata
monilia matrum', *c.m.* 47. 9) or with pearls as at Virg. *A.* 1. 654 f.
'colloque monile | bacatum', Sil. 8. 134, Sid. *Carm.* 11. 84 f. The use of
circuit here, with a personal subject in the context of artistic decoration, is akin to Ov. *Met.* 6. 101 (Minerva's weaving) 'circuit extremas
oleis pacalibus oras'.

528. bacis . . . candentibus: for pearl earrings cf. Ov. *Met.* 10. 115 f.,
265 'aure leues bacae'. The famous pearl which Cleopatra supposedly
dissolved in vinegar to impress Mark Antony was set in an earring
(Plin. *Nat.* 9. 121: cf. Hor. *S.* 2. 3. 239 ff.). Both Seneca (*Ben.* 7. 9. 4, *Dial.*
12. 16. 3) and Pliny the Elder (*Nat.* 13. 91 'mensarum insania quas
feminae uiris contra margaritas regerunt') testify to the strength of the
craze for pearls among rich Roman women in their day. In Late
Antiquity, however, the elaborate Eastern-influenced Court dress of
males too was often richly decorated with pearls: see MacCormack,
plate 6, where Honorius is shown on the Diptych of Probus wearing

pearls in his ears and on a diadem. The metonymy *baca* = 'pearl' can be traced to the late Republic: *Culex* 67f. 'nec Indi | conchea baca maris pretio est', Hor. *Epod.* 8. 13f. 'nec sit marita, quae rotundioribus | onusta bacis ambulet', *S.* 2. 3. 241, Petr. 55; note also *Nupt.* 167, *IV Cons.* 592, *Stil.* 2. 88, Sid. *Carm.* 11. 85, 22. 54 'niueae . . . bacae'.

onerat: cf. Ov. *Ars* 3. 129 'aures onerate lapillis', Sen. *Phaed.* 391f. 'nec niueus lapis | deducat auris. Indici donum maris', *Dial.* 2. 14, *Ben.* 7. 9. 4, Prud. *Ham.* 270.

529. sic oculis placitura tuis: recalling other brides: Luc. 2. 337 (Marcia in mourning) 'non aliter placitura uiro', Stat. *Theb.* 12. 539 (Hippolyte) 'hosti ueniat placitura (*var.* paritura) marito'.

auctis: literally, in the first instance, as a result of the recent restoration (531–6n.); note Caes. *Ciu.* 3. 112. 9 'has munitiones insequentibus auxit diebus', Tac. *Hist.* 4. 65. But at least as important are the emotional overtones of joy and pride: cf. esp. Stat. *Silu.* 4. 1. 5ff. 'exsultent leges Latiae, gaudete, curules, | et septemgemino iactantior aethera pulset | Roma iugo', *Get.* 51 (after Pollentia) 'securas iam Roma leuat tranquillior arces.' See also 10 *Augusta . . . suffragia*, 24 *auget* nn. Rome is in any case ἐν τῇ σκοπιᾷ τῆς οἰκουμένης (Themistius, *Or.* 3. 41b): see also 42–7, *Stil.* 3. 133f.

530f. nota maior se Roma uidendam | obtulit: recalling two passages from the second book of the *Aeneid*, the epiphany of Venus (2. 589f. 'cum mihi *se*, non ante oculis tam clara, *uidendam* | *obtulit*') and the vision of Creusa (2. 773 'uisa mihi ante oculos et *nota maior* imago'). For *se offerre* of epiphany cf. Cic. *Diu.* 1. 79, Catul. 66. 52ff., Virg. *A.* 4. 556f., Ov. *Fast.* 1. 96, and for *nota maior* see Austin on *A.* 2. 773. Phrases associated in Virgil with the destruction of Troy are here adapted to record the salvation and further exaltation of Rome under Stilicho. For an example of the Christianization of such religious language see Prud. *Per.* 10. 601f. (of the Incarnation) 'hic se uidendam praestitit mortalibus, | mortale corpus sumpsit inmortalitas'.

531–6. The walls of Rome were magnificently restored in the winter of AD 401–2 against the possibility of a Gothic penetration into the very heart of Italy: see Introd., p. xxxii, and Malcolm Todd, *The Walls of Rome* (London, 1978), 58–65. Todd stresses that 'little new work was carried out on the wall, the programme being essentially one of repair and restoration' (p. 61), and Claudian's *noua* (531) is thus something of an exaggeration. The restoration, however, was in deadly earnest. The gates were narrowed and the gate-towers extensively remodelled, implying that the possibility of attack was taken very seriously. The surviving inscriptions on the gates (one of which is still *in situ* on the Porta Tiburtina) naturally attribute the restoration to Arcadius and

Honorius, but lay significant stress on the initiative of Stilicho: 'ex suggestione VC et inlustris | comitis et magistri utriusq. militiae Stilichonis' (*CIL* vi. 1188–90; Stilicho's name was obliterated after his fall in 408).

531. addebant pulchrum . . . uultum: despite the emergency, great care was taken to enhance the appearance of the walls, facings of solid stone and curtains of travertine marble being added to the gates and gate-towers. Todd (op, cit., 531–6 n., 164) points out that 'there can be little doubt that the intention was to make the city gates as handsome as possible and not merely powerful', while finding it 'extraordinary that, given the circumstances of their building, so much time and attention should have been lavished on these stones and marble facings.' Whether or not the beautification of the walls was carried out with the possibility of a future Imperial visit in mind, Honorius, in the *aduentus* described here, will have marched into the City through a splendidly refurbished Porta Flaminia adorned with statues of himself and his brother. With the confident eulogy of this renovation offered by Claudian contrast the pious scepticism of the Christian Paulinus of Nola, in a poem which can be dated to Jan. 402: *Carm.* 26. 103 ff. 'fidant legionibus illi, | perfugioque parent reparatis moenia muris, | nulla salutiferi quibus est fiducia Christi'.

With the phrasing contrast *Eutr.* 1. 120 f. 'has in fronte notas, hoc dedecus addidit oris | luxuriae Fortuna suae'. The application of *uultus* to a city's physical appearance is an easy step from the regular anthropomorphization of cities: note Stat. *Silu.* 5. 3. 104 f. 'exsere semirutos subito de puluere uultus, | Parthenope', *Gild.* 19.

533. profecit: in general compounds ending in *-ficio* are avoided in high verse: see Axelson 63 f. Ovid, however, has a dozen or so examples, and cf. *Rapt.* 3. 434.

opifex . . . timor: for *opifex* applied to abstract or non-human subjects cf. Apul. *Apol.* 14 'leuitas illa speculi fabra et splendor opifex', Gel. 12. 1. 13, *Pan. Lat.* 4. 4. 2 Mynors 'non segnis uirtutum opifex disciplina', Paul. Nol. *Ep.* 39. 2 'ipsa rerum opifex Sapientia'. Note also *c.m.* 30. 210 'iudex . . . timor'.

533–6. Here we have a minor instance of the common late antique topos of 'Rome rejuvenated', for which see Cameron 365, Curtius 104: see also 410 *neclecto squalent senio* n. Cameron traces the motif in literature back to Mart. 5. 7. 3 'taliter exuta est ueterem noua Roma senectam', pointing also to the importance of coins of the 'Roma renascens' type (Ramsay MacMullen, *Enemies of the Roman Order* (1966; repr. London and New York, 1992), 333). A far fuller exploitation of the topos can be found at *Gild.* 20 ff. where a very sorry-looking Roma with grey hair and rusted spear appeals to Jupiter for help. When the king of the gods reassures her the result is startling: (208 ff.) 'dixit et adflauit Romam meliore iuuenta. | continuo redit ille uigor seniique colorem | mutauere comae. solidatam crista resurgens | erexit galeam clipeique recanduit orbis | et leuis excussa micuit rubigine cornus.' Behind Claudian lies, in particular, the aged Roma of Symm. *Rel.* 3. 9 f. 'ad hoc ego seruata sum, ut longaeua reprehendar? . . . sera tamen et contumeliosa est emendatio senectutis', while he in his turn has served as a model for Sid. *Carm.* 7. 45 ff., 595 ff. Note also Florus praef. 8, *Get.* 51 ff., Prud. *C. Symm.* 2. 640 ff. An especially instructive comparison might be with Rut. Nam. *Red.* 1. 115 ff. 'erige crinales lauros seniumque sacrati | uerticis in uirides, Roma, refinge comas . . .', 1. 139 f. 'illud te reparat quod cetera regna resoluit: | ordo renascendi est crescere posse malis', a passage which gives us some idea of how Claudian might have treated the capture of Rome in 410 if he had lived to receive such a commission. The general adaptability of the topos of the 'age' and 'youth' of cities in panegyric may be seen from Menander Rhetor's advice that when praising a city whose neighbours are more ancient than it is itself, the orator should say αἱ μέν κεκμήκασι χρόνῳ, ἡ δ' ἀνθεῖ (350. 20 ff., p. 40 Russell–Wilson. Cf. 355; 5 ff., p. 50).

534. For the idea of peace inducing sloth and decrepitude in a usually warlike people cf. Virg. *A.* 7. 693 f. 'iam pridem resides populos desuetaque bello | agmina in arma uocat', *Eutr.* 2. 275 ff. (Phrygia ravaged by the Goths) 'securas barbarus urbes | inrupit facilesque capi. spes nulla salutis, | nulla fugae: putribus iam propugnacula saxis | longo corruerant aeuo pacisque senecta'. Under Stilicho's protection, this decay is remedied and the possibly disastrous consequences averted.

discussa: cf. Sen. *Ep.* 34. 1 'cresco et exulto et discussa senectute recalesco'. The verb is similarly applied to such abstractions as fear (Val. Max. 1. 7. 8 'metu . . . disusso', V. Fl. 4. 700, Apul. *Met.* 4. 21), anxiety (Apul. *Met.* 7. 1 'discussa sollicitudine'), and danger (Cic. *Mur.* 84 'periculum . . . consilio discutiam'). Note also Luc. 1. 119 'discussa fides', Quint. *Decl.* 254 (p. 43, l. 16 Ritter = p. 27 Winterbottom) 'seruitutem rei publicae discutere'.

535. erexit subitas turres: cf. Luc. 9. 988 'erexit subitas congestu caespitis aras', and for adverbial *subitus* see 231 *subitas* n.

535 f. Note the initial alliteration of *c*, and the manner in which it helps emphasize the quasi-chiastic word-order of *cunctosque coegit | septem continuo colles.*

coegit . . . iuuenescere: adapting Stat. *Theb.* 3. 583 f. (similarly of preparations for war) 'haerentesque situ gladios . . . adtrito cogunt iuuenescere saxo.' Note also *Stil.* 2. 201f. 'te sospite fas est | uexatum laceri corpus iuuenescere regni' and see 38 *iubet reuirescere* n. For the phrasing cf. also *Stil.* 1. 220f. 'Rhenumque minacem | cornibus infractis adeo mitescere cogis', *c.m.* 5. 2.

536. septem . . . montes: Varro tells us that Rome was originally known as 'Septimontium' *(L.* 5. 7. 41). Whatever the truth of this statement, the 'seven hills' are a poetic commonplace from the time of Augustus, first attested at Virg. *G.* 2. 534f. 'rerum facta est pulcherrima Roma, | septemque una sibi muro circumdedit arces'. See the copious list of examples given by Kirby Flower Smith in his note at Tib. 2. 5. 55f. 'carpite nunc, tauri, de septem montibus herbas | dum licet: hic magnae iam locus urbis erit.' The occurrence of numerous examples in Claudian (*Prob.* 176, *Fesc.* 1. 19f., *Gild.* 104, *Stil.* 3. 135, *VI Cons.* 617) perhaps can be attributed to the particularly common appearance of the idea in his revered Statius (*Silu.* 1. 1. 64f., 1. 2. 191, 2. 7. 45, 4. 1. 6f.). Note how a new ideological twist is given to the seven hills at *Stil.* 3. 135 (Roma) 'quae septem scopulis zonas imitatur Olympi'; for the more usual five zones see 411f. *medium . . . caeli . . . iter* n.

continuo . . . muro: i.e. in an unbroken circuit: cf. *Get.* 189f. 'duo continuo conectens aequora muro | Isthmos'.

537–42. Foul weather in the form of rain and cloud had prevailed for days before the Emperor's arrival, but his *aduentus* is greeted by a miraculous restoration of fair skies. This change is attributed partly to the gods' answering the prayers of the Emperor's loyal subjects *(fauens uotis,* 537), but more particularly to his own divine radiance *(principis et solis radiis,* 539). This topos of *adulatio* is, in Latin verse, as old as the Roman principate. Cf. esp. Hor. *Carm.* 4. 5. 5ff. (to Augustus) 'lucem redde tuae, dux bone, patriae: | instar ueris enim uultus ubi tuus | adfulsit populo, gratior it dies | et soles melius nitent', *Anth. Lat.* 250 Shackleton Bailey (attr. Virgil) 'nocte pluit tota, redeunt spectacula mane: | diuisum imperium cum Ioue, Caesar, habes', Themistius, *Or.* 5. 71 a, *IV Cons.* 170ff. (with Barr ad loc.) esp. 172ff. 'tenebris inuoluerat atra | lumen hiemps densosque Notus collegerat imbres, | sed mox, cum solita miles te uoce leuasset, | nubila dissoluit Phoebus pariterque dabantur | sceptra tibi mundoque dies', Corippus, *Laud. Iust.* 2. 91ff. 'lumen membris regalibus auxit. | haut secus ut, nubes cum se rescindere densa | coeperit, et caelum monstrauerit aethra serenum, | ardentes radios mittit iubar'. Also similar are Mart. 8. 21. 2, *Pan. Lat.* 8. 3. 1 and 11. 10. 4 Mynors. See further MacCormack 24, Ernst Doblhofer, *Die Augustuspanegyrik des Horaz in formalhistorischer Sicht* (Heidelberg, 1966), 86ff., and note Menander Rhetor 381. 16–18,

p. 100 Russell–Wilson, who at p. 286 cite Aesch. *Pers.* 300f., *Ag.* 522 (Agamemnon's return) ἥκει γὰρ ὑμῖν φῶς ἐν εὐφρόνη φέρων; note also Ar. *Eq.* 1319ff. This divine radiance and power over the weather naturally link the Emperor with, above all, Jupiter: cf. Enn. *Ann.* 446 f. Skutsch 'Iuppiter hic risit tempestatesque serenae | riserunt omnes risu Iouis omnipotentis', Virg. *A.* 1. 254f. with Austin ad loc. Linked with all this are both the traditional association of quasi-divine royalty with the sun (see 23 *imperii sidus* n.) and the attribution to Emperors of god like *serenitas* or *tranquillitas*. This latter quality was especially prized in the fourth century but was already cultivated, it seems, by Domitian: see Coleman on Stat. *Silu.* 4. 2. 41 'tranquillum uultus et maiestate serena'. The use of *serenus*, *serenitas*, etc. of Emperors is even better attested, and in particular is a regular part of Late Imperial political discourse: consider for example the frequent appearance of the term in the *Codex Theodosianus* (e.g. 1. 1. 2 'perpensas serenitatis nostrae . . . constitutiones', 15. 7. 6): note *III Cons.* 182f. 'qui mente serena | . . . regunt', *IV Cons.* 183, *Theod.* 167 'fratres . . . serenos'.

537. fauens uotis: cf. Tib. 3. 11. 9 'uotisque faueto', Ov. *Am.* 2. 13. 21 'precibusque meis faue, Ilithyia', *Tr.* 4. 2. 55, Sen. *Phaed.* 423, *Phoen.* 633.

    solitoque decentior aer: balancing *nota maior . . . Roma*, 530. *TLL* v/1. 136. 12ff. glosses *decentior* here as 'serenior' and suggests that it is a special example of *decens* with the same sense as 'pulcher, decorus'. Cf. Sen. *Phaed.* 764 'prata nouo uere decentia', and note also *Nupt.* 238 'iucundior aer'.

538. quamuis . . . foedauerat: for *foedus/foedare* of foul weather cf. Virg. *G.* 1. 323f. 'foedam glomerant tempestatem imbribus atris | collectae ex alto nubes', Tac. *Agr.* 12. 3 (the British climate) 'caelum crebris imbribus ac nebulis foedum', *Rapt.* 1. 265.

    adsiduo . . . imbre: the same collocation is found at Cic. *Att.* 13. 16. 1 'ita magnos et adsiduos imbris habebamus', Stat. *Ach.* 2. 144.

539. principis et solis radiis: see 23 *imperii sidus* n.

    detersa: the clouds are wiped away like a dirty smudge: cf. Hor. *Carm.* 1. 7. 15f. 'albus ut obscuro deterget nubila caelo | saepe Notus', where Nisbet–Hubbard cite Symm. *Ep.* 2. 83 'ut . . . nubem inuidiae superioris abstergeat'; add Ven. Fort. *Vita Mart.* 2. 40 'detersa nube' and see *TLL* v/1. 797. 16ff. For the reverse contrast Cic. *Arat.* 246 'caligans detersit sidera nubes'.

540f. turbauerat omnes | ante dies: balancing *adsiduo noctem foedauerat imbre*, 538. The persistence of the bad weather over a long period naturally heightens the 'miracle' of its sudden dispersion. Note Stat. *Theb.* 2. 250f. 'excussaque gaudia patri, | et turbata dies', 11. 130

'nunc etiam turbanda dies', though these examples are both metaphorical.

541. lunam . . . rudem: a 'young', i.e. a 'new' moon. For *rudis* applied to things rather than persons with this sense cf. Luc. 3. 193 'rudis Argo', Apul. *Met.* 11. 5 'rudem dedicantes carinam'. Müller uses this detail in an ingenious attempt to date precisely the Emperor's arrival in Rome. We know that he was still in Ravenna on 2 Oct. 403 (*C. Th.* 7. 18. 13/14), and there were new moons that fell on 2 Oct. and 31 Oct. Allowing some ten or fifteen days for the journey from Ravenna, this means that Honorius arrived in the middle of either October or November. Müller goes on to suggest that the earlier date should be seen as more probable, in order to allow Claudian sufficient time to compose his poem. This suggestion, though reasonable enough on the surface, cannot be proved, and in any case it underestimates the speed at which Claudian could compose, while also being open to the objection that much of the poem could have been prepared well in advance at Ravenna as soon as the decision to celebrate the consulship in Rome had been taken. See further Döpp 230.

madefecerat Auster: the association of the south wind with rain is regular in Latin verse; see e.g. Virg. *G.* 3. 278f. 'unde nigerrimus Auster | nascitur et pluuio contristat frigore caelum', *A.* 5. 696 'turbidus imber aqua densisque nigerrimus Austris', Luc. 9. 320, Stat. *Theb.* 5. 705, *IV Cons.* 339f. *Auster* is thus often combined with the epithets *umidus* (Virg. *G.* 1. 462, *Stil.* 2. 395), *nubilus* (Prop. 2. 16. 56, Stat. *Theb.* 11. 520), and *madidus* (*Stil.* 3. 103). See also Levy on *Ruf.* 2. 222 'madidis . . . Coris'.

542. For the language cf. *Rapt.* 2. 91 'medioque patent conuexa sereno.' The sky mirrors the *serenitas* of the Emperor: see 537–42 n. Now the Romans can enjoy such weather, in contrast to the time of the Gothic invasion itself, when bad weather was a longed-for impediment to the enemy's advance: note *Get.* 44ff., esp. 49 '(nec) coniuratum querimur splendere serenum'.

conuexa: seemingly first applied to the 'vault' of the heavens in Virgil (*A.* 4. 451), and reflecting the belief that the sky was spherical. Also found at *Ruf.* 2. 454, *Gild.* 2, *IV Cons.* 201, *Stil.* 3. 190.

543–59. *The whole of Rome from the Mulvian Bridge as far as the Palatine is filled with joyous crowds of all ages watching the* aduentus-*procession. Both Honorius and Stilicho act with commendable modesty.*

Such descriptions of the crowds pouring out to welcome the Emperor are explicitly recommended by Menander Rhetor for prominent inclu-

sion in the epilogue to an *epibaterio*. See 381. 6ff. Russell–Wilson p. 100
τοὺς δὲ ἐπιλόγους ἐργάσῃ, ὡς ἀπὸ τοῦ σκοποῦ τῆς ὑποθέσεως
†δεξιούμενος† τοὺς ὑπηκόους, οἷον ὅτι προαπηντήκαμεν δέ σοι ἅπαντες
ὁλοκλήροις τοῖς γένεσι, παῖδες, πρεσβῦται, ἄνδρες, ἱερέων γένη,
πολιτευομένων συστήματα, δῆμος περιχαρῶς δεξιούμενοι. Among the
numerous passages from Latin panegyric which are similar to the present one, Claudian seems, as so often, closest to Pliny and Pacatus. Cf.
Plin. *Pan.* 22 'ac primum qui dies ille, quo exspectatus desideratusque
urbem tuam ingressus es! . . . tu sola corporis proceritate elatior aliis et
excelsior, non de patientia nostra quendam triumphum, sed de superbia
principum egisti. ergo non aetas quemquam non ualetudo, non sexus
retardauit, quominus oculos insolito spectaculo impleret. te paruuli
noscere, ostentare iuuenes, mirari senes, aegri quoque neglecto meden-
tium imperio ad conspectum tui quasi ad salutem sanitatemque
prorepere. inde alii se satis uixisse te uiso te recepto, alii nunc magis esse
uiuendum praedicabant. feminas etiam tunc fecunditatis suae maxima
uoluptas subiit, cum cernerent cui principi ciues, cui imperatori milites
peperissent. uideres referta tecta ac laborantia, ac ne eum quidem
uacantem locum qui non nisi suspensum et instabile uestigium caperet,
oppletas undique uias angustumque tramitem relictum tibi, alacrem
hinc atque inde populum, ubique par gaudium paremque clamorem.
tam aequalis ab omnibus ex aduentu tuo laetitia percepta est, quam
omnibus uenisti'. Very similar also is Pacatus' description of Theodosius'
entry into Emona: *Pan. Theod.* 37. 3f. 'ferebant se obuiae tripudiantium
cateruae, cuncta cantu et crotalis personabant . . . quid ego referam pro
moenibus suis festum liberae nobilitatis occursum, conspicuos ueste
niuea senatores, reuerendos municipali purpura flamines, insignes
apicibus sacerdotes? quid portas uirentibus sertis coronatas? quid aulaeis
undantes plateas accensisque funalibus auctum diem? quid effusam in
publicum turbam domorum, gratulantes annis senes, pueros tibi longam
seruitutem uouentes, matres laetas uirginesque securas?' Consider also
Cic. *Pis.* 51f., *Att.* 4. 1. 5, Liv. 27. 51. 1f., 28. 9. 5, Mart. 10. 6. 6 'totaque
Flaminia Roma uidenda uia', *Pan. Lat.* 4. 31. 1ff., 5. 8. 1ff., 11. 10. 4ff., 11.
11. 3, 12. 19. 1ff. Mynors, Amm. Marc. 16. 10. 6, *III Cons.* 126ff., *Stil.* 2.
397ff., Corippus, *Laud. Iust.* 4. 206ff., with Cameron ad loc. See further
MacCormack 20ff. and, for a rich collection of parallels from the late
Republic on, T. E. V. Pearce at *CQ*, ns 20 (1970), 313ff.

Claudian's general picture, then, is very conventional in its basic composition. As with so many of his adaptations of the topoi of encomiastic
verse, what distinguishes it is the accommodation of an established
literary format to the political considerations of the moment. Here the
stress is laid on the Emperor's *ciuilitas*, as is fitting for an Imperial

panegyric set in Rome. But set into this, and as it were framed by two references to the praise and approval given to Honorius by the elders of the City for his avoidance of all tyrannical behaviour (548–51 and 557–9), is the poet's own praise for the *pietas* and self-restraint of Stilicho in his refusal to exploit the occasion for the exaltation of his son. Note that the passages from Pliny and Pacatus cited above offered Claudian good examples of how to unite the themes of triumphal *aduentus* with encomium of the Emperor's conquest of *superbia*. For Claudian this *ciuilitas* is a characteristic of the good Emperor which distinguishes him from the tyrannical usurpers of the past: those predecessors who came as *domini* must be the same *superbi* whose arrogance is censured by Roma (393–400). In Pliny too the driving impulse is provided by a deliberate contrast between the present Emperor who rules with respect for his people's ancient rights and privileges and a particular predecessor infamous for his outrageous despotic behaviour. Pacatus' praise of the modesty of Theodosius is similarly set against the hated tyranny of Maximus, particularly in the account of the Emperor's entry into Emona. Pacatus' description of Theodosius' *aduentus* at Rome is adapted still more closely in Claudian's account of the same visit of AD 389: see esp. 53–76, 58–64, 59 *terrore remoto*, 61 nn.

It seems that Honorius, coming down the Flaminian Way, crossed the Pons Muluius and entered the City through the Porta Flaminia (into the modern Piazza del Popolo); he then no doubt made his way through the Campus Martius along the Via Lata (the Corso) towards the Capitol and the Forum. For the general picture cf. *Stil.* 2. 397 ff. 'quae tum *Flaminiam* stipabunt milia uulgi! . . .' The same route had probably been taken by Constantine in 312 and by Constantius II in 357: see McCormick 86.

543 f. omne . . . quod . . . quantum: best taken as direct accusatives dependent on *replet* (545). For similar phrases cf. *Gild.* 158 ff. 'quod Nilus et Atlans | dissidet, occiduis quod Gadibus arida Barce | quodque Paraetonio secedit litore Tinge, | hoc sibi transcribit proprium', *Theod.* 56 f. Every available space is filled with people, both horizontally (from the Palatine to the Mulvian Bridge) and vertically (from the streets to the rooftops).

543. Palatino . . . colle: the heart of the City and the eventual terminus of the route (603 f.). See further *pr.* 23 *orbis apex aequatus Olympo* n.

recedit: 'stretches back'. See *OLD* s.v. *recedo* 3a ('distance covered'), and Fordyce on Catul. 64. 43 f. 'sedes, quacumque opulenta recessit | regia', citing Plin. *Ep.* 2. 17. 21 'contra parietem medium zotheca perquam eleganter recedit'. Müller, however, betrays misunderstanding of Claudian when he cites as a parallel Virg. *A.* 2. 299 f. 'quamquam secreta parentis | Anchisae domus arboribusque obtecta recessit' (cf. Stat. *Theb.* 5. 242f.), since there the point is seclusion ('distance removed'; Müller 'ist enfernt', *OLD* s.v. *recedo* 3b).

544. quantum licuit consurgere tectis: cf. Luc. 9. 461f. 'quantumque licet consurgere fumo | et uiolare diem, tantus tenet aera puluis', Stat. *Theb.* 6. 753ff. 'hic, quantum Tityos Stygiis consurgat ab aruis, | . . . tanta undique pandit | membrorum spatia'.

545. una . . . turbae facies: i.e. the crowd share the same emotion, namely joy (*exultant*, 547). Cf. e.g. Cic. *Pis.* 52 'cum senatum egressum uidi populumque uniuersum . . . quae (sc. Roma) me ita accepit ut non modo omnium generum aetatum ordinum omnes uiri ac mulieres omnis fortunae ac loci, sed etiam moenia ipsa uiderentur et tecta urbis ac templa laetari', Plin. *Pan.* 22. 4f. 'ubique par gaudium paremque clamorem', *Stil.* 3. 187f. 'publica sed numquam tanto se gratia fudit | adsensu'. See also 500 *laetior* n. For the 'harmony of the people' theme in descriptions of *aduentus* see 332 *cum plebe patres* n. and MacCormack 21: 'the enumeration serves to indicate that everyone was present, that this body of people was in a position to express that *consensus omnium* which was fundamental to most classical and late antique theories about legitimate government.' For the phrasing cf. Ov. *Ars* 2. 468, *Met.* 2. 13 'facies non omnibus una', Juv. 10. 198 'una senum facies', Prud. *Ham.* 887.

545 f. For this kind of picture cf. esp. Plin. *Pan.* 22. 4 'uideres referta tecta . . . oppletas undique uias', *Stil.* 3. 63f. 'nonne uides et plebe uias et tecta latere | matribus?'

545. undare: the metaphor can be traced to Virg. *G.* 2. 461f. 'si non ingentem foribus domus alta superbis | mane salutantum totis uomit aedibus undam'; cf. also V. Fl. 1. 539 (Scythia) 'undat equis floretque uiris', Stat. *Theb.* 2. 223f., Juv. 3. 244, *Prob.* 46 'populis undare penates'. Note also Sil. 11. 491f. (the arrival of Mago in Carthage with the news of Cannae) 'nec lentum in medios rapienda ad gaudia uulgus | procurrit fluctus'.

uideres: the second person singular attempts to involve the members of the audience in the scene personally; cf. Plin. *Pan.* 22. 4, *Ruf.* 2. 176, *IV Cons.* 445. Given the presence of *effulgere* in the next line perhaps Claudian has in mind the most illustrious ecphrasis in all Latin verse: Virg. *A.* 8. 676f. 'totumque instructo Marte uideres | feruere Leucaten auroque *effulgere fluctus*'.

546. Modesty prevents many of the womenfolk from taking to the streets, so in such scenes they are found crowding the windows and the rooftops: cf. Mart. 10. 6. 3ff. 'quando erit ille dies quo campus et arbor et omnis | lucebit Latia culta fenestra nuru? | quando morae dulces longusque a Caesare puluis | totaque Flaminia Roma uidenda uia?', *Stil.* 2. 400, 3. 63f.; also Corippus, *Laud. Iust.* 3. 47ff. (the funeral of Justinian) 'adtonitae matres resolutis crinibus ibant, ante fores aliae, tectis sublimibus illae | inplentes altas turba stipante fenestras'. Contrast *III Cons.* 126f. 'quantae spreuere pudorem | spectandi studio matres'. We are perhaps reminded here of epic teichoscopia (e.g. *Il.* 3. 130ff., 22. 460ff., Enn. *Ann.* 418 Skutsch 'matronae moeros complent spectare fauentes', and see Smolenaars on Stat. *Theb.* 7. 243 'turre procul sola'), as is only fitting for the heroic victor of a war which the poem has repeatedly associated with the Trojan war and the struggle against Hannibal: see further 564–77n. Note that *matribus* = *matronis*. For *effulgere*, a reference to the splendid dresses and perhaps also jewels which they have donned in honour of the occasion, see 178 *hoc . . . effulgens habitu* n.

547–50. In addition to the contrasting pair of *uiri* and *matres* (544f.) Claudian offers us the standard pairing of old and young: cf. Plin. *Pan.* 22. 3, *III Cons.* 127f. 'puerisque seueri | certauere senes'.

547. exultant iuuenes: picking up 36 *exultat . . . habitante deo* (of the Palatine). Cf. also *Stil.* 3. 195f. (the crowds at Stilicho's consular procession in Rome) 'exultant auidi, quocumque decorus | conspiciare loco', and see 545 *una . . . turbae facies* n.

　　aequaeui principis annis: compare *iuuenes* (547) with *iuuenem* (425).

548. temnunt prisca senes: because under Honorius' temperate rule the world is so much better than ever before: this is a variant on the 'antiquity surpassed' theme (470 n.). Here and in the next line we may perhaps detect the influence of Ov. *Ars* 3. 121f. 'prisca iuuent alios, ego me nunc denique natum | gratulor'. Claudian's *senes* are acting out of character according to the standard view of the old in ancient literature: contrast Arist. *Rhet.* 2. 13, Hor. *Ars* 173f. 'laudator temporis acti | se puero, castigator censorque minorum'.

548f. in hunc . . . gratantur durasse diem: a variant on the 'may I live to see the day' topos, for which see Virg. *Ecl.* 4. 53ff. 'o mihi tum longae maneat pars ultima uitae, | spiritus et quantum sat erit tua dicere facta . . .', with Coleman ad loc. Cf. Pacatus *Pan.* 37. 4 'gratulantes annis senes'; also Plin. *Pan.* 22. 3 'inde alii se satis uixisse te uiso te recepto, alii nunc magis esse uiuendum praedicabant'. We might also think of Simeon and the 'nunc dimittis' of Luke's Gospel (2: 28ff.). Contrast the despair of old Aletes as he faces a grim future under the tyranny of Eteocles but knows that death will soon bring him relief (Stat. *Theb.* 3. 211ff.). For the construction *sibi gratari* cf. Ov. *Pont.* 3. 3. 89 'dum sibi gratatur populus', where the context (Tiberius' German triumph of AD 13) is similar.

548. prospera fati: cf. Luc. 7. 107f. 'placet haec tam prospera rerum | tradere Fortunae', Sil. 4. 499; also 'prospera fata' (Luc. 7. 420, *Gild.* 103, *c.m.* 26. 94) and 'uersis ad prospera fatis' (Ov. *Ep.* 15. 89). In a sense the present lines fulfil the prediction of *IV Cons.* 619f. 'prospera Romuleis sperantur tempora rebus | in nomen uentura tuum'.

549. moderata: see 64 *modestia* n., and cf. Plin. *Pan.* 47. 6 (Trajan) 'principis modestiae'; also Ov. *Pont.* 3. 6. 23 'principe nec nostro deus est moderatior ullus', *Tr.* 1. 9. 25.

550. clemens aditu: such approachability is an essential part of the *ciuilitas* regarded as a mark of the good king and was considered especially necessary in Rome: see 58–64n. Pliny lays particular emphasis on the accessibility of Nerva and Trajan by contrast with the despotic isolation of Domitian: *Pan.* 47–9, esp. 47. 5 'quod enim forum, quae templa tam reserata? non Capitolium ipsaque illa adoptionis tuae sedes magis publica magis omnium. nullae obices nulli contumeliarum gradus superatisque iam mille liminibus ultra semper aliqua dura et obstantia', 48. 5 (Domitian) 'non adire quisquam non adloqui audebat, tenebras semper secretumque captantem'. Note also Auson. *Grat. Act.* 16. *clemens* here also establishes a link between Honorius and the philosopher-Emperor Marcus Aurelius (340 *clemens Marce*). Note also that Herodian claims that in approachability Marcus Aurelius surpassed all other Emperors (1. 2. 3f.).

pectore †solus†: a very tricky phrase, most probably originating in corruption. Those determined to preserve the transmitted text are obliged to resort to remarkable contortions with the word-order or with semantics in its defence. Barth and Heinsius punctuated after *pectore*, making both it and *aditu* dependant on *clemens*. Though possible, this is very artificial, does great violence to the rhythm of the line, and places a degree of emphasis on *solus* which, though by no means out of keeping with the tenor of the passage (cf. 559), still seems excessive. Using a similar tactic, one might defend the readings of the manuscripts by taking *pectore solus* closely with the next line and understanding *pectore* with *praecedere*, which would yield the sense 'he alone forbade the senators of Rome to march abreast of his chariot'. But *pectore* would then be very far from the verb it qualified, while the movement of l. 550, the anaphora of *quod*, and the taste for balance in Latin verse all make it likelier that we would read *pectore solus* (or an emendation) as a counterweight to *clemens aditu*.

Platnauer appears to employ a different approach when he translates 'so easy of access, so singular in courtesy'. Claudian is quite capable of extending the semantic range of workaday words in the interest of poetic expression, but this is rather an extreme case and, in the absence of parallels for *pectus* with such a sense this interpretation could only be accepted with great caution. Jeep struck out still more boldly on the alternative path of emendation and reordering, and suggested *quod solus habitu quod pectore clemens*. But this is a decidedly drastic measure, and there is no need to be suspicious of *aditu* at all (see the previous note); attacking what is unproblematic merely in order to accommodate what is difficult elsewhere does not, in any case, seem methodologically advisable. A more promising-looking emendation is Goodyear's *quod pectore solus | Romano*, which would lay appropriate stress on Honorius' own truly Roman—that is, not tyrannical—spirit. The point, however, is made equally well by the transmitted *Romanos* (a moderate Emperor of the Romans does not act arrogantly in his dealings with Roman senators), and though *patres* does not absolutely need an epithet (cf. 589) it reads more smoothly with one. Moreover, Goodyear's emendation, like some of the solutions proposed above, disrupts the natural movement of l. 550. In general, it seems best to follow Hall, and suppose that *solus*, wherever it has come from, has displaced another adjective such as *mitis* or *lenis* which governs *pectore* and so balances *clemens aditu*. Some support for *lenis* is perhaps to be found in *Stil.* 2. 167 f. 'cum tanta potestas | ciuem lenis agat'. Professor Nisbet has suggested another attractive possibility to me, in the form of *pectore sanctus*.

551. Either as consul or, as is the case here, as *triumphator* Honorius could have expected the honour of an escort of senators marching before his chariot. McCormick (*Eternal Victory*, 88) associates this action with Theodosius actually getting out of his carriage and walking part of the way (Pac. *Pan. Theod.* 47. 3), and interprets such behaviour as an ideological manifestation of the Emperor's triumph in ethical matters as well as in military ones. That the senators were dispensed from this duty by Honorius can only have been an act of goodwill which was initiated by Stilicho and formed part, no doubt, of his general effort to conciliate a body critical of his handling of the war against Alaric (see Introd., p. xlix, with n. 106). Honorius also addresses the Senate in accordance with ancient custom at 589 ff.

Such condescension on the part of the Emperor is not the norm, and the more usual state of affairs can probably be gauged from a description of an Imperial consulship celebrated not in the Senate's own city of Rome but at the Court in Milan: *IV Cons.* 580 ff. 'numeroso consule consul | cingeris et socios gaudes admittere patres. | inlustri te prole Tagus, te Gallia doctis | ciuibus et toto stipauit Roma senatu. | portatur iuuenum ceruicibus aurea sedes | ornatuque nouo grauior deus', with which contrast Plin. *Pan.* 22. 1 (censuring Domitian) 'nam priores inuehi et importari solebant, non dico quadriiugo curru et albentibus equis sed umeris hominum, quod adrogantius erat.' The usual scene could also be turned to propaganda advantage: *Pan. Lat.* 4. 31. 1 (Nazarius of Constantine's triumphal entry into Rome after the defeat of Maxentius) 'non agebantur quidem ante currum uincti duces sed incedebat tandem soluta nobilitas'. Maltreatment of the senators is, of course, a standard indicator of tyranny on the part of the *princeps* in Roman historical writing. Among many possible examples consider Suet. *Cal.* 26. 2 'nihilo reuerentior leniorue erga senatum, quosdam summis honoribus functos ad essedum sibi currere togatos per aliquot passuum milia et cenanti modo ad pluteum modo ad pedes stare succinctos linteo passus est'. Contrast Trajan's respect for the Senate at Plin. *Pan.* 62 f.

currum praecedere: cf. *Stil.* 2. 370 ff. (Mars' triumph) 'speciosa Quirinus | frena regit currumque patris Bellona . . . praecedit'. For *currum* see 369 f., 377 *currus* nn.

patres: sc. *conscriptos*: see 332 *cum plebe patres* n. The epithet *Romanos* is not otiose; such honour would not have been paid to the Senate of Constantinople.

552. Eucherius: the son of Stilicho and Serena, born in Rome during Theodosius' visit there in AD 389 (*Stil.* 3. 176 ff.). Cameron (p. 47) rightly argues that Eucherius was recognized at birth by Theodosius as a member of the Imperial family; this is implied by his being represented together with Arcadius and Honorius on the obelisk of Theodosius at Constantinople as well as by Claudian's account, *Stil.* 3. 177 ff. 'puerumque ferens hic regia mater | Augusto monstrauit auo: laetatus at ille | *sustulit* in Tyria reptantem ueste nepotem'. Claudian's reference to the infant crawling on purple cloth may also hint at Stilicho's son's one day being raised to the rank of co-Augustus with his cousins Arcadius and Honorius (cf. *III Cons.* 14 f., *IV Cons.* 124 f.). That Stilicho entertained such Imperial ambitions for his son was certainly the belief of some of his contemporaries: see Zosimus 5. 32. 1, Orosius 7. 37. 1 'cum alius sibi (sc. Rufinus), alius (sc. Stilicho) filio suo affectans regale fastigium', Matthews 280. Whatever the truth of that rumour, Claudian offers good evidence that Stilicho intended to tie his own family still more closely to the Theodosian dynasty by arranging a marriage between Eucherius and Honorius' half-sister Galla Placidia: see *Stil.* 2. 352 ff., and the discussion at Cameron 47 f. In any case, as a grandson of Theodosius, Eucherius would have had an excellent claim on the throne in the West if the childless Honorius had died before him. Here, however, we are informed that Stilicho insisted on a public display of 'modesty' in Eucherius' role in the ceremonies marking the Imperial visit to Rome: as a kinsman of the *triumphator*, Eucherius might have expected to ride with him in his chariot or else on a horse (see 579 *curru . . . uectus eodem* n.). This is entirely in keeping with his general policy, since he never advanced Eucherius to any rank higher than *tribunus et notarius*. Cameron 49 concludes that 'his policy with regard to Eucherius was on the one hand to foster the notion that he was a prince of the blood and destined for great things . . . but nevertheless not to give him any too flagrantly preferential treatment'. Stilicho was presumably anxious not to arouse hostility to his only son and so damage his chances, but it should also be noted that he may have preferred to wait and see his line produce an Emperor through the less controversial channel of a grandson born 'in the purple' to Honorius and Maria (*Nupt.* 340 f., *Stil.* 2. 341 ff.). See further *RE* vi. 882. 47 ff., Fargues 123, O'Flynn 59 ff.

regius undique sanguis: cf. *Fesc.* 2. 28 f., 3. 5 f. (the marriage of Honorius and Maria) 'tractus ab aula rursus in aulam | redeat sanguis'; also Hor. *Carm.* 3. 27. 65 'regius sanguis', Tac. *Hist.* 1. 14 (Piso) 'nobilis utrimque'. For *regius* see 42 *regia*, 64 *regale . . . culmen* nn. The statement that Eucherius was 'royal' on both sides of his family, which must be what *undique* means, looks like something of an exaggeration. The reference cannot be purely to Roman Imperial blood, since it was only through Serena that Eucherius could make such a claim literally. Of Stilicho's own father Claudian is almost silent, which in itself perhaps implies that he was not of particularly distinguished rank. We know little more than can be deduced from the claim of hostile sources that he was a barbarian ('Stilicho, Vandalorum inbellis auarae perfidae et dolosae gentis genere editus', Orosius 7. 38. 1; 'semibarbarus', Jerome, *Ep.* 123. 16), and held a cavalry command under Valens (*Stil.* 1. 35 ff.). None the less, his birth must have been noble, and so perhaps loosely 'royal', since in his youth Stilicho served in the *protectores*, an élite military cadre restricted to aristocratic youths: see O'Flynn 15. It was usually the Theodosian connection that Stilicho emphasized, advertising himself as 'adfinis diui Theodosii Augusti' and naming his son after one of his wife's kinsmen, namely her great-uncle, rather than his own.

553. Augusta soror: with Hall's punctuation this phrase forms part of the parenthesis that begins at *cui* (552). This flows well, provides a singular subject for the singular verb *praeberet*, and yields excellent sense: Eucherius, though 'his blood on either side [is] royal and his sister [is] the Empress', none the less performs the duty of a common soldier. The reference must therefore be to Maria, the daughter of Stilicho and Serena, and Honorius' wife. It might be objected that '*fratri* praeberet ouanti | militis obsequium' (553 f.) rules this out, but *frater* is often used of young men of much the same age, as well as of cousins on the paternal side (*OLD* s.v. 2): while Eucherius was, in law, Honorius' cousin only through his mother, by blood he was a first cousin once removed through his grandfather, Honorius the Elder, brother of Theodosius I. Furthermore, for the admittedly very rare sense 'brother-in-law' *TLL* vi. 1254. 81 f. cites Schol. Cic. Bob. *Sest.* 131, p. 139. 9 Stangl 'uel apud Clodium fratrem uel apud uxorem Clodiam'. It thus seems a perfectly natural term to apply to one who is roughly Eucherius' *aequalis*, cousin, and brother-in-law.

An alternative candidate for the *Augusta soror* might be Galla Placidia, Theodosius' daughter by his second wife Galla, herself the youngest daughter of Valentinian I. Since she was born some time between 388 and 390 she was almost exactly the same age as Eucherius. See further *RE* xx. 1910. 57 ff., Matthews 316 ff., 378 f. Eucherius is linked with her in a predicted marriage at *Stil.* 2. 354 ff.: note esp. 2. 357 'progenitam Augustis *Augustorumque sororem*', which, in the eyes of some, clinches the identification. But (*a*) 'Augustorum soror' is not the same as 'Augusta soror', (*b*) if *fratri* were taken to apply to both Eucherius and 'Augusta soror' it would thus be literal with one but not with the other, and (*c*) the singular verb *praeberet* would thus, slightly awkwardly, be governed by a plural subject. Similarly, Müller argues that Serena is meant here, because she was, by adoption, the daughter of Theodosius and therefore Honorius' sister by law as well as first cousin by blood, and because she completes the family group which is given prominence here. In addition to the arguments offered above, however, note that Claudian elsewhere in the poem prefers to portray Serena as Honorius' second mother (94 *materna . . . mente* n.), and that, while it was common for the *triumphator*'s children and younger kin to take part in the triumph, such a procession was not considered the proper place for a respectable *matrona* (579 *curru . . . uectus eodem* n.).

553 f. praeberet . . . | militis obsequium: i.e. marched before the *triumphator*'s chariot in accordance with custom (cf. 551). For the phrasing cf. *Stil.* 1. 82 f. 'pium matris regina gerebat | obsequium'.

553. ouanti: = *triumphanti* (cf. 580 *triumphantem*). This use of *ouo* for triumphs proper, in literature at least, was well established by Claudian's time: cf. Vell. 2. 96. 3 'huius uictoriae compos Nero ouans triumphauit', Petr. 123, vv. 240 f. (Pompey the Great) 'modo quem ter ouantem | Iuppiter horruerat'.

554–6. For Stilicho's praiseworthy modesty and restraint in putting his family forward cf. *Stil.* 1. 298 f. 'nec umquam | publica priuatae cesserunt commoda causae', 2. 53ff. 'nec pignora curas | plus tua quam natos dederat quos ille monendos | tutandosque tibi.' The purpose of such propaganda will no doubt have been to reassure the traditionalists that the *semibarbarus* was not getting above himself; by all accounts it seems not to have been successful. Careful thinkers might even have reflected that, in any case, this is a topos of Imperial panegyric adapted to a private citizen: cf. Pacatus, *Pan. Theod.* 16. 4 'cui cum essent domi filii, geminae illae spes oculique rei publicae, dilatis eorum magistratibus amicos consulatus ornauit', Themistius *Or.* 16. 204 c.

554 f. dura parentis | . . . pietas: associating Stilicho loosely with such outstanding exemplars of Republican virtue as Brutus (Liv. 2. 4, Virg. *A.* 6. 819 ff.) and T. Manlius Torquatus (Cic. *Off.* 3. 112, Gel. 9. 13. 20); but taking those particular analogies too far would no doubt not have been congenial to the general. Stilicho is presented as being equally puritanical with himself: *Stil.* 2. 220 f. 'mens aliorum prona fauori, | iudex dura sui'. Cf. also Cic. *Amic.* 48 'uirtutem duram et quasi ferream', Luc. 9. 444 f. 'hac ire Catonem | dura iubet uirtus', 9. 562 'durae . . . uirtutis amator', 9. 880.

555 f. Note how the alliteration (*pignora parci | neget nato | procerum . . . praestet*) helps bind the sentence together. For *uel* see 463 n. and for *procerum* 356 n. The subjunctives *neget* and *praestet* are generic, and record Stilicho's character, whereas plain indicatives might seem to refer only to the present incident.

557. cura senum: an epicizing periphrasis of the type seen in e.g. *Il.* 11. 268 μένος Ἀτρεΐδαο, though precise parallels are lacking. Birt suggested reading *curua senum* (sc. *aetas*), comparing Prop. 2. 18. 20 'ipsa anus haud longa curua futura die', Ov. *Ars* 2. 670 'curua senecta'; add [Tib.] 3. 5. 16. But an opposing pair of periphrastic phrases, each two words long (*cura senum/matura . . . aetas*) is neater than giving two epithets to *aetas* and stretching them out over nearly a whole line.

  matura . . . aetas: cf. Virg. *A.* 12. 438 'mox cum matura adoleuerit aetas', *Stil.* 1. 69 'nubilis interea maturae uirginis aetas', 2. 348, Prud. *C. Symm.* 2. 321 'maturi roboris aetas'. These are apparently not men as young as the *iuuenes aequaeui principis annis* (547) since they can, like the old men, remember visits by earlier Emperors (558 f.).

558 f. The passage ends with a succinct summing-up of its dominating theme of *ciuilitas*; Honorius distinguishes himself from his predecessors in that he comes to Rome as a fellow-citizen, and not as a tyrant. *ueteris . . . aulae* and *dominos uenisse priores* are very vague phrases, and no doubt deliberately so. They serve to throw the objects of comparison, here censured, back into the remote past, so that we think of the *superbi* of Roma's complaints (395 ff.). Claudian thus insists on drawing a distinction between Honorius and 'those who came before' while allowing us mentally to exempt Theodosius from this critical generalization. Removing Theodosius from this objectionable company is made far easier by the fact that his own *ciuilitas* has already been effusively praised in this poem (58–64). What we have in these lines is none the less a regular feature of panegyric; indeed, the contrast between the tyranny of Domitian and the constitutional rule of Trajan is the organizing principle of the whole of Pliny's *Panegyricus*. In addition to the passages cited at 58–64, 59nn. cf. esp. Plin. *Pan.* 2. 3 'nusquam ut deo, nusquam ut numini blandiamur: non enim de tyranno sed de ciue, non de domino sed de parente loquimur', 45. 3 'scis, ut sint diuersa natura dominatio et principatus, ita non aliis esse principem gratiorem, quam qui maxime dominum grauentur', 88. 1, Tac. *Ann.* 12. 6 'uidisse ipsos abripi coniuges ad libita Caesarum: procul id a praesenti modestia'. For this kind of contrast cf. also Sal. *Iug.* 85. 35. Honorius' behaviour in Rome matches that of Rome herself in her dealings with her subject peoples: *Stil.* 3. 150ff. 'haec est in gremium uictos quae sola recepit | humanumque genus communi nomine fouit, | *matris, non dominae ritu,* ciuesque uocauit | quos domuit'.

558. ueteris speciem . . . aulae: cf. *Stil.* 2. 402 (Stilicho as consul) 'antiqui species Romana senatus', *VI Cons.* 590 *ueterum . . . exempla secutus.*

    aulae: 'palace' (*pr.* 26 *aula* n.), and so here by metonymy = *imperium.*

559. dominos: in fact a regular title of Emperors in Claudian's day, in Rome just as much as at Court: the inscriptions recording the restoration of the walls, for example, are dedicated to 'impp Caess Dd Nn' (531–6n.). No bones are made at all about applying the term to Emperors in poems delivered outside Rome (*IV Cons.* 75, *Stil.* 2. 72 'dominum summissus adores'), and note also *Prob.* 76, 115 (recited in Rome in 395).

560–77. *The women of Rome gaze in wonder at the Emperor's procession with its dragon standards and cataphracts.*

Roma herself was compared to a bride waiting for her groom at 523–31, and now we see the young women of the City, both married (*nurus,* 564: see 297f.n.) and virgins (564), eagerly watching Honorius' arrival: the mature married women have already been mentioned briefly at 546 (*matribus*). The present scene concentrates primarily on the innocence of the *ignara uirgo* who asks her nurse questions about the dragon standards of the army and about the cataphracts in their heavy mail armour, questions which show her confusion about what is real and what is not. The passage could be said to highlight in a 'whimsical' way, or even in a minor comic key, the ignorance of the civilian population on the subject of military matters. But more importantly, beneath all this lies an understated erotic element. The more knowing *nurus* admire the beauty of the young Emperor, while under the modest surface of her questions we sense that the innocent girl is succumbing to a fascination with the splendour of the troops which owes its origins to nascent sexuality. Though here the war is already successfully concluded and it is a victory procession rather than a mustering of troops or an actual battle that the maiden witnesses, we should also think of epic or quasi-epic scenes of teichoscopia (cf. 546n.) which contain erotic undertones. Note for example Hor. *Carm.* 3. 2. 6ff. 'illum ex moenibus hosticis | matrona bellantis tyranni | prospiciens et adulta uirgo | suspiret, eheu, ne rudis agminum | sponsus lacessat regius asperum | tactu leonem, quem cruenta | per medias rapit ira caedis.' Especially close in basic conception is Stat. *Theb.* 7. 243ff., where, from the walls of Thebes, Argia watches the Theban troops and their allies gather, and asks her guardian Phorbas for information about the various leaders, though there any erotic element is very understated indeed. Similar situations include Scylla watching Minos from a tower on the walls of Megara (Ov. *Met.* 8. 14ff.) and Medea gazing at the figure of Jason on the battlefield and putting questions to the disguised Juno (V. Fl. 6. 575ff.). It should be stressed, however, that whereas Scylla and Medea fall in love with a foreign enemy for whom they will betray their family and their city, here the scene is wholly patriotic, and a Roman maiden is attracted by the splendour of a Roman army.

560. conspicuas tum flore genas: for the common topos of the 'flower of youth' see *TLL* vi/1. 934. 60ff., 580 *florente iuuenta* n. Given the combination with *conspicuas . . . genas*, Claudian must be thinking of the bright sheen of a youthful complexion: cf. Luc. 6. 562 'illa genae florem primaeuo corpore uolsit', Stat. *Theb.* 4. 274 'dulce rubens uiridique genas spectabilis aeuo', *Stil.* 1. 44f. 'iam tum conspicuus, iam tum uenerabilis ibas | spondebatque ducem celsi nitor igneus oris'. Alternatively, the reference may be to the appearance of down, as at Pac. *trag.* 362 Ribbeck (= 34 *inc.* Warmington) 'nunc primum opacat flora lanugo genas', Lucr. 5. 888f., Virg. *A.* 8. 160, *Prob.* 69.

  diademate crinem: for the line-ending cf. Luc. 5. 60 'cingere Pellaeo pressos diademate crinis', *III Cons.* 84 'sacro meritos ornat diademate crines.' See also 65f. *quamuis diademate necdum* | *cingebare comas* n.

561–4. Honorius' robes are magnificently decorated with emeralds. Cf. the detailed description at *IV Cons.* 585 ff. 'asperat Indus | uelamenta lapis pretiosaque fila smaragdis ducta uirent; amethystus inest et fulgor Hiberus | temperat arcanis hyacinthi caerula flammis. | nec rudis in tali suffecit gratia textu; | auget acus meritum picturatumque metallis | uiuit opus: multaque animantur iaspide cultus | et uariis spirat Nereia baca figuris. | quae tantum potuit digitis mollire rigorem | ambitiosa colus? uel cuius pectinis arte | traxerunt solidae gemmarum stamina telae? | inuia quis calidi scrutatus stagna profundi | Tethyos inuasit gremium? quis diuitis algae | germina flagrantes inter quaesiuit harenas? | quis iunxit lapides ostro? quis miscuit ignes | Sidonii rubrique maris? tribuere colorem | Phoenices, Seres subtegmina, pondus Hydaspes.' Cf. also *Prob.* 178 ff. and the splendidly ornate robe of Eridanus with illustrations of the story of Phaethon (165 *palla* n.). Though here designated *trabea* Honorius' robe is more probably the *toga picta*, confusion of terminology being common by this period: see 4 *trabeis* n. For Claudian at any rate, the garment he calls *trabea* is clearly associated with the consulship; at this point the *aduentus* procession with its triumphal imagery is merging almost imperceptibly with the ceremonies of consulship. See further McCormick 89.

561. gemmato . . . cinctu: cf. *Stil.* 2. 89 'gemmatas . . . togas'.

uiridantia: with the sheen of emeralds (563). Their colour receives high praise from Pliny: *Nat.* 37. 62 'tertia auctoritas smaragdis perhibetur pluribus de causis, quippe nullius coloris aspectus iucundior est. nihil omnino uiridius comparatum illis uiret', 37. 113. Note also Lucr. 4. 1126, *Stil.* 2. 89 f., *c.m.* 47. 8, 48. 7.

562. fortes umeros: associating Honorius with the heroes of epic; cf. Virg. *A.* 9. 364 'haec umeris nequiquam fortibus aptat', V. Fl. 1. 434, Stat. *Ach.* 1. 183; also Ov. *Am.* 2. 5. 47, *Ep.* 9. 59.

562 f. certatura Lyaeo . . . colla: a recurring comparison, linking Honorius with a god celebrated for his beauty and his youth: cf. *III Cons.* 131 f., *IV Cons.* 602 ff. (an extended comparison between Honorius in his jewelled robes of state and Bacchus), in particular 606 f. 'talis Erythraeis intextus nebrida gemmis | Liber agit currus'. The Greek cult-title *Lyaeus* is found in Roman poetry as early as Enn. *trag.* 121 Jocelyn (= 129 Warmington); cf. also Virg. *G.* 2. 229, *A.* 4. 58. The use of the dative with *certo*, which is convenient in verse, can be traced back as far as Virg. *Ecl.* 5. 8 'solus tibi certat Amyntas', where see Coleman's n. Cf. also *Ecl.* 8. 55, *G.* 2. 99, Hor. *Carm.* 2. 6. 15 f., Sen. *Her. O.* 1807, *Prob.* 201 'ceu sibi certantes', *Eutr.* 1. 349 'coruo certante ligustris', *c.m.* 30. 33.

563. Erythraeas: possibly literally from the area of the Red Sea, but in poetry *Erythraeus* often means no more than 'Eastern'. According to Pliny (*Nat.* 37. 17) the best emeralds in fact came from Scythia, while the Red Sea was much better known as a source of high-quality pearls: *Nat.* 9. 106 (margaritae) 'Indicus maxime has mittit oceanus . . . praecipue autem laudantur circa Arabiam in Persico sinu maris Rubri', [Tib.] 3. 3. 17 'in Erythraeo legitur quae litore concha', *III Cons.* 210 'uobis rubra dabunt pretiosas aequora conchas', *Nupt.* 167 f., *c.m.* 31. 14. Note also Mart. 9. 2. 9 'splendet Erythraeis perlucida moecha lapillis', *c.m.* 30. 3 f.

surgentia colla: cf. V. Fl. 2. 533 f. 'Alcides saxoque prior surgentia colla | obruit', though there the sense is more literal. Closer in idea is Stat. *Theb.* 8. 564 ff. (of the young and still growing Atys) 'triplici uelauerat ostro | surgentes etiamnunc umeros et leuia mater | pectora'. For the poetic plural *colla* see 490 *pectora* n., and cf. 648.

smaragdos: the combination of *s* with another consonant does not always result in the lengthening of a preceding short syllable, and it is only by virtue of this poetic licence that such words as *smaragdus* and *Scamander* can be accommodated in the hexameter at all. See Fordyce on Catul. 64. 357 'unda Scamandri', and cf. Ov. *Met.* 2. 24, Stat. *Theb.* 2. 276, *IV Cons.* 586, *Stil.* 2. 89, *c.m.* 47. 8, 48. 7. The orthography with *sm-* seems preferable to *zm-*; see G. P. Goold, *HSCPh* 69 (1965), 11 ('the retention of a short open syllable before *sm-* was a permissible license: its retention before *zm-* meant taking a prosodical liberty'), Courtney, *FLP* 306, 460 f.

565. cui simplex calet ore pudor: the blush conventionally hints at sexual awareness in virgins. So, for example, a maiden in Catullus lets the apple sent to her as a love-token from an admirer fall when her mother enters, and she blushes guiltily: 65. 23 f. 'atque illud prono praeceps agitur decursu, | huic manat tristi conscius ore rubor.' Among many possible examples cf. esp. Virg. *A.* 12. 64 ff. 'Lauinia . . . flagrantis perfusa genas, cui plurimum ignem | subiecit rubor et calefacta per ora cucurrit', Stat. *Theb.* 1. 536 f., 2. 230 ff., *Nupt.* 268 f., *Rapt.* 1. 272 ff. 'niueos infecit purpura uultus | per liquidas succensa genas castaeque pudoris | inluxere faces' (with Gruzelier ad loc.).

per singula cernens: in ecphrastic passages it is common enough to stress that a character in the narrative gazes at a work of art or a scene detail by detail, and *singula* therefore frequently appears in such contexts: cf. Ov. *Tr.* 3. 1. 33 'singula dum miror', Sil. 11. 261 'laetus circumfert oculos et singula discit', 13. 758, *Nupt.* 108 'dum singula cernit'. But as Hall remarks, the present phrase is 'sane mirum', since it is decidedly odd to combine *per singula* in this way with a verb of seeing that should take a direct object. Hence Burman made the ingenious conjecture *currens* (= 'percurrens singula'). No doubt the preposition is intended to stress the careful taking in of one detail after another as the eyes rove over the scene below. It seems likely, however, that Claudian's diction has been influenced by the most famous of all ecphrastic passages in Latin literature, the description of the shield of Aeneas at Virg. *A.* 8. 617f.: 'ille deae donis et tanto laetus honore | expleri nequit atque *oculos per singula uoluit*', and the adaptation of it at Sil. 2. 404f. (the shield of Hannibal) *'per singula* laetis | *lustrat* ouans *oculis* et gaudet origine regni.' Virgil breaks no rules of prose usage, while Silius' phrasing is made more acceptable by the sense of movement contained in the verb *lustro*, even if it is used there metaphorically of the process of seeing. But Claudian's phrase could be seen as a fairly easy further step for a poet to make. Given that Claudian goes on to record that the young girl asks her nurse questions as she takes in these details (*nutricem consultat anum*, 566), also relevant are Stat. *Theb.* 4. 548 'dic agedum nostramque mone per singula noctem' and Orest. *trag.* 309 'orbatum per singula quaerit Oresten' (the latter cited by Birt).

566. nutricem consultat anum: for *anus* used as an adjective in the same way as *senex* see *OLD* s.v. *anus* 2, citing Pl. *Mos.* 703 'dotatam uxorem atque anum', Catul. 9. 4, and add Pl. *Rud.* 671, Stat. *Theb.* 12. 582. *consulto* is rather rare in verse but cf. Prud. *C. Symm.* 2. 391 and 408 (both also at the head of the line).

566-8. The proper emblem of the Roman armies was the eagle, but dragon standards had also long been in use: Vegetius (2. 13) claims that the *aquila* is the standard of an entire legion, and that 'dracones etiam per singulas cohortes a draconariis feruntur ad proelium.' Kromayer–Veith 585, trace their ultimate origin to the East and their introduction in Roman warfare to Dacian auxiliaries, while Robert Grosse, *Römische Militärgeschichte* (Berlin, 1920), 231, sees their widespread use in Late Antiquity as a mark of the increasing prominence of barbarians in the Roman army. Made of purple or crimson cloth, and elongated in shape like a windsock so that the breeze could enter them by the mouth, they would flutter noisily in the wind, producing a sound which Claudian and other poets imagine as akin to a dragon or serpent's hissing. For a rather charming illustration see Daremberg–Saglio iv/2. 1321.

As in the case of the cataphracts of 569-77 (see n. ad loc.), Claudian seems to have been directly influenced by Ammianus Marcellinus' account of the *aduentus* of Constantius II in Rome in AD 357: 16. 10. 7 'eumque post antegressos multiplices alios, purpureis subtegminibus texti, circumdedere dracones, *hastarum aureis gemmatisque summitatibus illigati*, hiatu uasto perflabiles, et *ideo uelut ira perciti sibilantes*, caudarumque uolumina relinquentes in uentum.' Cf. also Nemes. *Cyn.* 84f. 'aurea purpureo longe radiantia uelo | signa micant sinuatque truces leuis aura dracones', *Ruf.* 2. 176ff. 'lateque uideres | surgere purpureis undantes anguibus hastas | serpentumque uago caelum saeuire uolatu' with Levy ad loc., *Ruf.* 2. 364f., *III Cons.* 138ff. 'hi uolucres tollunt aquilas, hi picta draconum | colla leuant, multusque tumet per nubila serpens | iratus stimulante Noto uiuitque receptis | flatibus et uario *mentitur sibila* tractu', *IV Cons.* 545, Prud. *Cath.* 5. 55f., Sid. *Carm.* 2. 232f., 5. 402ff. Note also the clever play made with this feature of Roman military life by Prudentius in his account of two Christian soldier-martyrs: *Per.* 1. 34ff. 'Caesaris uexilla linquunt, eligunt signum crucis | proque uentosis draconum, quos gerebant, palliis | praeferunt insigne lignum, quod draconem subdidit.'

566. fixa: i.e. on spear-shafts (cf. Amm. Marc. 16. 10. 7 'hastarum aureis gemmatisque summitatibus illigati', *Ruf.* 2. 176f.).

567. uentis fluitent: precise Latin parallels for the metaphor are relatively rare, but cf. Lucr. 4. 77 '(uela) per malos uulgata trabesque trementia flutant', Prop. 3. 18. 13, Ov. *Met.* 11. 470 'uela tamen spectat summo fluitantia malo', and also Tac. *Ger.* 17. 1 'ueste distinguuntur non fluitante', where the verb similarly expresses the movement of cloth.

567f. uera minentur | sibila: the answer is given at *III Cons.* 141 'uario mentitur sibila tractu' (imitated at Sid. *Carm.* 5. 404f.). Contrast Virg. *G.* 3. 421 (of real snakes) 'tollentemque minas et sibila colla tumentem'. For the transitive use of *minor* (*OLD* s.v. 2) in Claudian cf. *Rapt.* 3. 125f. 'nullusque dies non triste minatur | augurium'.

568. For the phrasing cf. Sil. 6. 197ff. (a serpent) 'tum trepidum . . . | *corripit* atque haustu sorbens et *faucibus atris* | (uidi respiciens) obscaena condidit aluo'.

569–77. Cataphracts, cavalry protected by armour-plating over the whole of their own and their horses' bodies, are first attested in the army of Antiochus: Polybius 16. 18. 6, Liv. 37. 42. 7 'cum auxiliis et cataphracto equitatu'. See also Sal. *Hist.* 4. 64ff., Prop. 3. 12. 12 'ferreus aurato neu cataphractus equo'. Like the dragon-standards (566–8n.) these particular cataphracts owe more than a little to the *aduentus* of Constantius II in Rome: Amm. Marc. 16. 10. 8 'incedebat hinc inde ordo geminus armatorum, clipeatus atque cristatus, corusco lumine radians, nitidis loricis indutus, sparsique cataphracti equites (quos clibanarios dictitant) personati thoracum muniti tegminibus, et limbis ferreis cincti, ut Praxiteles manu polita crederes simulacra, non

uiros; quos laminarum circuli tenues, apti corporis flexibus ambie-
bant, per omnia membra diducti, ut quocumque artus necessitas
commouisset, uestitus congrueret, iunctura cohaerenter aptata.' The
same passage appears also to have helped shape an earlier description
of cataphracts in Claudian's work at *Ruf.* 2. 353ff. 'equites illinc
poscentia cursum | ora reluctantur pressis sedare lupatis, | et tremu-
los umeris gaudent uibrare colores, | hinc alii saeuum cristato uertice
nutant, | quos operit formatque chalybs—coniuncta per artem |
flexilis inductis animatur lamina membris, | horribilis uisu: credas
simulacra moueri | ferrea cognatoque uiros spirare metallo. | par
uestitus equis: ferrata fronte minantur | ferratosque leuant securi
uulneris armos. | diuiso stat quisque loco, metuenda uoluptas | cer-
nenti pulcherque timor, spirisque remissis | mansuescunt uarii uento
cessante dracones.' Other similarly detailed descriptions can be found
at Julian, *Or.* 2. 57B–C and Heliodorus, *Aeth.* 9. 15. In general these
descriptions tend to lay the stress on the same features. One is that the
armour is extremely close-fitting; although in Claudian this appears
explicitly only in the passage from *In Rufinum*, in the present passage it
is what leads to the idea of the men and horses appearing actually to
be made of metal. Other features generally insisted on are the fact that
the horses are armoured in exactly the same way as the men (569 f. n.)
and that they seem more like metal statues than human beings
(572–4 n.). Note finally that, while both of Claudian's descriptions play
upon the mixed emotions of fear and pleasure in their beauty that the
cataphracts inspire (574 *gaudet metuens* n.), here the young girl's apprehension should be seen as part of her general *naïveté* and is not to be
imagined as the reaction of the rest of the audience at the procession.
By contrast, the cataphracts of *In Rufinum* are decidedly more
menacing as befits men bent upon the grisly assassination of Rufinus
which shortly follows in the narrative: see the comments of Martha
Malamud, *A Poetics of Transformation: Prudentius and Classical Mythology*
(Ithaca, 1989), 51ff. See further *RE* x. 2479. 38ff., Kromayer–Veith
139, R. Syme, *CQ* 23 (1929), 132ff. (discussing V. Fl. 6. 231ff.), Levy on
Ruf. 2. 355–62, Gualandri 60, R. M. Rattenbury, *CR* 56 (1942), 113–16,
John W. Eadie, *JRS* 57 (1967), 161–73. Magnificent and terrifying they
may have seemed, but Eadie, art. cit., argues that in Roman military
history theirs is a 'dismal record of failure'.

569. chalybe indutos: there is not much to choose between the
readings *chalybe* and *chalybem*. Both are well attested in the manuscripts, and Claudian's usage is no sure guide, since, like many
authors, he sometimes employs an ablative with *indutus* (e.g. *Stil.* 3. 67
'indutos . . . arcus spoliis') and sometimes the direct accusative

associated with 'middle' verbs (e.g. *Eutr.* 2. 183 'carbaseos induta sinus': see 65 f. *diademate . . . cingebare comas* n.). But note the ablative in 'nitidis loricis indutus' at Amm. Marc. 16. 10. 8, Claudian's 'model'. For *chalybs* = 'steel', from the name of the legendary inventors of metal-working, see Fordyce on Catul. 66. 48 and cf. Aesch. *Sept.* 728, Virg. *A.* 8. 421, *Ruf.* 2. 357 'quos operit formatque chalybs'.

569 f. The horses are as heavily protected as their riders. Cf. Sal. *Hist.* 4. 65 Maurenbrecher 'equis paria operimenta erant, <nam>que linteo ferreas laminas in modum plumae adnexuerant', V. Fl. 6. 233 f. 'riget his molli lorica catena; | id quoque tegmen equis', *Ruf.* 2. 361, Heliodorus, *Aeth.* 9. 15. 5.

569. in aere latentes: cf. Luc. 7. 499 'tuto . . . latet sub tegmine pectus', Stat. *Theb.* 11. 603 'dum tractat galeas atque ora latentia quaerit', 12. 537 f. The use of *in* rather than *sub* has the effect of stressing that the horses are totally encased within their metal coat.

570. cornipedes: see 182 *cornipedem* n.

quanam de gente: reminiscent of the Homeric formula τίς πόθεν εἰς ἀνδρῶν; πόθι τοι πόλις ἠδὲ τοκῆες (*Od.* 1. 170, 7. 238) and so strengthening the epic atmosphere. Cf. also e.g. Virg. *A.* 2. 74 f. 'hortamur fari quo sanguine cretus, | quidue ferat', Stat. *Theb.* 7. 291 (Antigone to her guardian Phorbas) 'illi autem, quanam iunguntur origine fratres?'

571. ferrati . . . uiri: cf. esp. Sal. *Hist.* 4. 64 Maurenbrecher 'equites catafracti ferrata omni specie', Prop. 3. 12. 12, Hor. *Carm.* 4. 14. 29 f. 'barbarorum . . . agmina | ferrata', Tac. *Ann.* 3. 45, Heliodorus, *Aeth.* 9. 15. 5 σιδηροῦς τις ἀνὴρ φαινόμενος, *Ruf.* 2. 361 f. See also Stat. *Theb.* 4. 204 f. 'cum tu claudare minanti | casside ferratusque sones', 7. 499, *c.m.* 30. 218 (Stilicho in a *lorica*) 'ferratum pectus'.

571 f. 'What land fashions horses born of metal?' For the phrasing cf. esp. Plin. *Nat.* 11. 181 'hoc (sc. cor) primum nascentibus formari in utero tradunt.' Müller also compares Cic. *ND* 1. 103 'igne nasci'. Note further *Ruf.* 2. 357, 2. 359 f. 'credas simulacra moueri | ferrea cognatoque uiros spirare metallo.' The verb *formo/informo* is commonly used of fashioning objects from metal, as at Virg. *A.* 8. 426, 447, *Prob.* 98 'electro Thybris, pueri formantur in auro', *III Cons.* 184 'saecula qui rursus formant meliore metallo'. Claudian's use of the word here effectively combines this with the kind of usage seen in the Pliny passage quoted above.

572–4. The idea that cataphracts seem to be statues owes as much to their immobility as to the material; Heliodorus claims that they were so heavy they could not mount their horses on their own but had to be hoisted into place (*Aeth.* 9. 15. 5). Cf. Heliodorus *Aeth.* 9. 15. 5, Julian

Or. 2. 57c αὐτοὶ δὲ ἀτεχνῶς ὥσπερ ἀνδριάντες ἐπὶ τῶν ἵππων φερόμενοι, Amm. Marc. 16. 10. 8, *Ruf.* 2. 359f. Given that the young girl imagines the possibility that they have been fashioned by Vulcan himself, perhaps, as Müller suggests, Claudian has in mind the gold automata which Homer tells us Hephaestus made as handmaids: see *Il.* 18. 417ff., with the note by Edwards ad loc. We also recall Talos, the bronze giant of Crete fashioned by Hephaestus and killed by Medea at Ap. Rh. 4. 1638ff.: see *RE* iv. 2081. 55ff. For the girl's admiring question cf. also Stat. *Silu.* 1. 1. 2ff. (the *equus Domitiani*) 'caelone peractum | fluxit opus? Siculis an conformata caminis | effigies lassum Steropen Brontenque reliquit?'

572. Lemnius auctor: Vulcan's association with Lemnos goes back to Homer, who relates how he landed there after Zeus in anger flung him out of Olympus (*Il.* 1. 590ff.). See Fordyce on Virg. *A.* 8. 454 'pater . . . Lemnius', Burkert, *Greek Religion* (520n.) 167f.: note also plain substantival *Lemnius* at Ov. *Met.* 4. 185, Stat. *Silu.* 4. 6. 49, *Nupt.* 87. *auctor* may be used of craftsmen of all kinds; for its application to sculptors cf. also Virg. *A.* 2. 150 (the Trojan Horse) 'quo molem hanc immanis equi statuere? quis auctor?', Vell. 1. 11. 4 'a Lysippo, singulari talium auctore operum', Stat. *Silu.* 4. 6. 24.

573. indidit hinnitum ferro: i.e. by divine power 'implanted in iron the power to neigh'. For the verb used of such divine action cf. Sen. *Ep.* 95. 52 (natura) 'haec nobis amorem indidit', Prud. *Per.* 13. 14, *Cath.* 11. 49ff. 'hic ille natalis dies, | quo te creator arduus | spirauit et limo indidit', *Ham.* 544f., and note also *Epig. Bob.* 12 'quid mihi propellis, uitule, ubera? uiuere maius; | indere lac fictis ars nequit uberibus', Aus. *Epigr.* 67. 1 Green 'aerea mugitum poterat dare uacca Myronis'.

573f. simulacra . . . belli | uiua: take *belli* as a kind of loose defining genitive. Since this is a full-dress parade rather than a real battle, Claudian is surely also punning on the frequent use of *simulacra belli* and similar phrases to describe sham-fights etc.: cf. Lucr. 2. 324 'belli simulacra cientes', Virg. *A.* 5. 674 'qua ludo indutus belli simulacra ciebat', Liv. 26. 51. 6, Sil. 7. 119, Stat. *Ach.* 2. 140, Gel. 6. 3. 52 'simulacris proeliorum uoluptariis', *IV Cons.* 539 'simulacra . . . Martia ludis'. See also 638 *laeta sub imagine pugnae* n.

574. gaudet metuens: cf. *Ruf.* 2. 363f. 'metuenda uoluptas | cernenti pulcherque timor', and see 569–77n. Note also Virg. *A.* 6. 733 'hinc metuunt cupiuntque, dolent gaudentque'.

574–7. Claudian frequently employs this unclassical construction whereby the accusative and infinitive of reported speech or action is replaced by a subordinate clause, introduced by *quod*, either in the indicative or the subjunctive. See Trump 36, Levy on *Ruf.* 2. 73f.

'iactabatque ultro, quod soli castra paterent | sermonumque foret uicibus permissa facultas', Fargues on *Eutr.* 1. 501 f., LHS ii. 576 ff.

574. pollice monstrat: cf. Hor. *Carm.* 4. 3. 21 f. 'totum muneris hoc tui est, | quod monstror digito praetereuntium'. The gesture was considered vulgar, or at least not appropriate to an orator, by Quintilian: *Inst.* 11. 3. 104 'auerso pollice demonstrare aliquid, receptum magis puto quam oratori decorum.' Perhaps it signifies a certain gaucheness and so confirms the girl's *naïveté*. More commonly we find the phrase *digito/ digitis (de-)monstrare*, as at e.g. Hor. *S.* 2. 8. 26, Per. 1. 28, Tac. *Dial.* 7. 4. See further Sittl, *Die Gebärden der Griechen und Römer* (71 f. n.), 51 f.

575 f. The wearing of crests, made of feathers and up to half a metre high, seems originally to have been intended to inspire fear in the enemy by increasing the apparent height of the warrior: see further Kromayer–Veith 324, 328, and cf. *Ruf.* 2. 355 'hinc alii saeuum cristato uertice nutant'. But this is parade-ground finery.

575. picturatas: a reference to the bright colours and the 'eyes' of the peacock feathers. Cf. esp. *c.m.* 31. 3 'picturataeque uolucres'. The feathers take their place in the general picture of gaiety and fine dress of both the celebrants and participants (525–8, 560–3); note also e.g. Virg. *A.* 3. 483 'picturatas auri subtemine uestis', *Ruf.* 1. 208, *IV Cons.* 590 f. (Honorius' consular robes) 'picturatumque metallis | uiuit opus'.

575 f. Iunonia . . . auis: also at Ov. *Ars* 1. 627; cf. *Eutr.* 2. 330 'sidereas Iunonis aues', and see further Gruzelier on *Rapt.* 2. 97 'uolucer . . . Iunonius'. The peacock is Juno's bird because in its tail she put the hundred eyes of Argus after he was killed by Mercury (Ov. *Met.* 1. 722 ff.): note also Ov. *Met.* 15. 385 'Iunonis uolucrem, quae cauda sidera portat', Stat. *Silu.* 2. 4. 26 'gemmata uolucris Iunonia cauda'.

576 f. As Gesner explains in his note on *Ruf.* 2. 356 below, the gilded armour rests upon a coverlet or cloth, crimson in colour and no doubt designed to prevent the metal from chafing the skin. The same phenomenon was remarked upon in Claudian's earlier description of cataphracts: *Ruf.* 2. 353 ff. (with Hall's transposition of ll. 355–6) 'equites illinc poscentia cursum | ora reluctantur pressis sedare lupatis, | et tremulos umeris gaudent uibrare colores'. There *tremulos* corresponds to our *crispentur* and *colores* could be said to be a metonymy for *rubra serica*.

576. rigidos . . . armos: presumably of the horses; contrast *umeris* of the men wearing the same gear in *Ruf.* 2. 356, and for the regular distinction see Ov. *Met.* 10. 700 (humans transformed into lions) 'ex umeris armi fiunt'. It is true that *armi* is occasionally used of human beings (e.g. Virg. *A.* 4. 11, 11. 644, Stat. *Theb.* 8. 494 f.), but there are

379

no sure examples of this elsewhere in Claudian's work, as against four of the word applied to horses (*IV Cons.* 548, *Gild.* 364, *c.m.* 47. 10, 48. 9). Moreover there seems to be a regular pattern of alternating the references to the riders with references to their horses throughout the girl's speech, and assuming this pattern is repeated in the final sentence (574–7) the horses' silk coverlets nicely balance the men's crests. For *rigidos* cf. Ov. *Tr.* 1. 4. 14 'ceruicis rigidae frena remittit equo', Stat. *Ach.* 1. 326 'colla rigentia'.

uibrata: 'shimmering', as the sun hits the cloth. Cf. Plin. *Nat.* 37. 122 '(Indica) fundit (sc. colorem) leniter blandum neque in oculos . . . uibrantem', Flor. *Epit.* 1. 46 'signa auro sericisque uexillis uibrantia'.

577. rubra . . . serica: compare the sumptuous trappings of the horse given to Honorius: *c.m.* 47. 10 'nobilis auratos iam purpura uestiat armos', 48. 8 'Tyrio dignum terga rubere toro'.

aurato: the *rubra serica* lie under the 'gilded back' so the reference is presumably to gilding on the bronze armour, and *dorso* is not precisely literal. Cf. esp. Prop. 3. 12. 12 'ferreus aurato . . . cataphractus equo', *c.m.* 47. 10 (quoted in the previous n.).

crispentur: also used of garments being ruffled in the wind at Victric. 6 'crepantis serici undae ambulantis arte crispantur', *IV Cons.* 552f. 'uestis radiato murice solem | conbibit, ingesto crispatur purpura uento', and *Rapt.* 2. 33f. (Diana) 'crispatur gemino uestis Gortynia cinctu | poplite fusa tenus' with Gruzelier ad loc.: see further *TLL* iv. 1208. 17ff.

578–602. *Stilicho receives his rightful reward for his loyal exercise of the guardianship of Honorius, whom he sees now in triumph and presiding magnificently over the Senate.*

For a discussion of the political significance of Claudian's account of the procession and of Honorius' address to the Senate see Introd., Sect. 4.

578. magnorum mercem . . . laborum: cf. Cic. *Arch.* 28, Ov. *Fast.* 6. 661 'dulcis erat mercede labor', Luc. 1. 340, 5. 331, 9. 1101. Virtue, of course, is its own reward (Sil. 13. 663 'ipsa quidem uirtus sibimet pulcherrima merces', *Theod.* 1), but Stilicho also receives the singular honour of accompanying the Emperor in the triumphal car (*curru . . . uectus eodem*). For the predominantly Late Latin use of *merx* as a synonym for *merces* (= 'reward', 'payment') see *TLL* viii/1. 852. 12ff. and cf. [Sen.] *Oct.* 600f. 'reddita et meritis meis | funesta merces', Symm. *Or.* 2. 2 'nouimus, inuicte moderator, tantis negotiis parem non esse mercedem', *Eutr.* 1. 197, *Get. pr.* 11.

Fortuna: a thematic link with Fortuna Redux (see 1 n. above). The reference here is no doubt to the traditional idea that the lives of children are fragile and subject to the power of chance: Stilicho can take pleasure in the sight of Honorius safely grown to a splendid maturity.

579. persoluit: note the force of the prefix: 'paid in full'. Cf. Stat. *Silu.* 1. 4. 38 'persoluit praemia morum'.

curru . . . uectus eodem: a rare privilege, even though Ammianus Marcellinus thinks it a mark of Constantius II's excessive pride that he never granted it to anyone at all (16. 10. 12). It was not uncommon for the small children of a *triumphator* to accompany him in the triumphal chariot, as, for example, five of Germanicus' offspring rode with him during his German triumph in AD 17 (Tac. *Ann.* 2. 41: cf. Liv. 45. 40. 8). Alternatively, they could ride on horseback in the procession: see Cic. *Mur.* 11 'cum sedere in equis triumphantium praetextati potissimum filii soleant', Suet. *Tib.* 6. 4. In Claudian's own works Arcadius and Honorius are said to have ridden with Theodosius in his chariot on their return to Constantinople after Honorius was proclaimed Augustus in 393 (*IV Cons.* 203 ff.); note also *III Cons.* 128 f. Grown adults, however, were not normally so honoured, and Tibullus imagines Messalla's father watching the progression of his son's chariot from the sidelines (2. 5. 120). See further *RE* vii/A. 508. 16 ff. for the identification of a special case (the Vestal Claudia in 143 BC) and the argument that Orosius is mistaken in his assertion (7. 9. 8) that Titus rode with Vespasian in the Judaean triumph. The privilege granted Stilicho on this occasion tacitly recognized the realities of the victory, but even so would surely have been totally unthinkable if he had not been related to the Emperor by marriage. It is, however, well worth pointing out that Stilicho could be said by some standards to have made considerable concessions to the strength of Western, and above all Roman conservatism. See McCormick 122 ff., who contrasts this passage and *Stil.* 3. 14 ff., esp. 26 ff. (Stilicho is satisfied with celebrating his triumph in men's minds) with the situation in the East; there important officials not uncommonly received honours which were strictly speaking the prerogatives of the Emperors.

580. urbe: another pointed compliment to the Romans: the triumph is celebrated not in Milan, but in Rome itself. For the plain local ablative cf. Suet. *Dom.* 1 'Domitianus natus est . . . regione urbis sexta', and see 20 f. *summo . . . cardine.*

florente iuuenta: a relatively rare version of a very old cliché, but cf. Hor. *Ars* 115, Sil. 16. 455, Aus. *Par.* 8. 11 Green. Cf. also 'flore iuuentae' at *Stil.* 2. 351 and see further 560 *conspicuas tum flore genas* n.

581–3. After the defeat of Eugenius in 394, Theodosius apparently
decided to return to the East, leaving Honorius, then only 10 years
old, in place as Augustus of the West. Although the evidence of
Zosimus (4. 59. 1) is sketchy and open to suspicion, it seems likely that
Theodosius also formally and publicly appointed Stilicho to a command over the Western armies during a visit to Rome in Oct. 394
(Alan Cameron, *HSCPh* 73 (1969), 247–80). The intention will presumably have been that Stilicho should effectively act as 'regent' for
Honorius until he came of age, though such an arrangement could
have no legal standing (Cameron 39). But there was also reportedly
another, quite separate incident in which, near to the point of death
in Jan. 395, Theodosius was said to have entrusted the guardianship
of *both* his sons to Stilicho, and to have done so in a private exchange
with no other witnesses present. The truthfulness of Stilicho's account
of this 'death-bed settlement' was, unsurprisingly, doubted at the time,
and is doubted still. Certainly, it was firmly rejected by all the
ministers of the Eastern Court, who were determined to exercise
influence over Arcadius without interference from Stilicho. Among
historical sources, Zosimus records Stilicho's version of events: 5. 4. 3
ἔλεγε γὰρ ἐπιτετράφθαι παρὰ Θεοδοσίου τελευτᾶν μέλλοντος τὰ κατ'
ἄμφω τοὺς βασιλέας ἔχειν ἐν πάσῃ φροντίδι. But he is careful to
distance himself from the claims made, as is clear from the choice of
the verb ἔλεγε, which indicates that Stilicho himself was the only
authority for them. Stilicho's claim is, it is true, repeated by Ambrose
at *De Obitu Theodosii* 5: 'gloriosius quoque in eo Theodosius, qui non
communi iure testatus est; de filiis enim nihil habebat nouum quod
conderet, quibus totum dederat, nisi *ut eos praesenti commendaret parenti*.'
Cameron 39, points out, however, that there was little Ambrose could
do unless he were simply to call Stilicho a liar and thus risk pre-
cipitating another civil war. That Theodosius truly intended Stilicho
to act as formal regent for the 18-year-old Arcadius passes belief. As
Cameron suggests (ibid.), however, there is no reason to doubt that
Theodosius on his death-bed charged his closest adult male relative to
'look after' his sons, using a general formula of the type 'commendo
tibi filios meos'. Such instructions naturally feature commonly enough
in the *mandata morituri*: cf. e.g. Ter. *An.* 282ff., *Ad.* 455ff., Prop. 4. 11.
73. See further Cameron 43.

Claudian, as the mouth-piece of Stilicho's policy, was obliged to
defend the claim to the 'double regency' as best he could. At *III Cons.*
142ff. we are given a poetic account of the scene in question, and, far
from attempting to conceal or underplay the lack of witnesses,
Claudian openly acknowledges the fact (142f. 'cunctos discedere tectis

| dux iubet'): as Cameron observes, Claudian is making the best of a bad job, and 'implying (without giving it) that Theodosius had a perfectly good reason for not wanting any witnesses' (p. 43, and see further art. cit. 275 f.). For the best part of a decade Claudian stead-fastly maintained this policy, insisting on the reality of the double regency again and again, at *Ruf.* 2. 4 ff., *IV Cons.* 432 f., *Nupt.* 307 f., *Eutr.* 2. 599 f. and, as late as 400, *Stil.* 2. 53 f. The key question about our present passage, then, is why does he now talk only of Honorius? The simple answer might be that he is concentrating on his honorand, but this concern did not prove to be an obstacle in *IV Cons.* and *Nupt.* and therefore cannot have been decisive here. On the other hand, he may have wished to simplify matters in order to bring out more neatly the implied comparison between Stilicho and Honorius on one side and Polymestor and Polydorus on the other (583 n.), but this, too, is not a very compelling consideration. Cameron (art. cit. 273 f.) initially suggested that the reference here was not to the 'death-bed settlement' at all, but to the formal announcement of 394 in Rome: *moriens* (583), however, disproves this. Cameron later went on to suggest that by 404 Stilicho had simply abandoned all hope of ever establishing a regency over Arcadius, partly because the senior Augustus was by now a very mature 26-year-old (pp. 50 f.), and partly because he realized he could not overcome the 'resolute opposition of Aurelian and his successors' (pp. 154 f.). This, though attractive, is not without its difficulties. What had changed so very much since the insistence upon the claim to authority in the East was reiterated in 400? Aurelianus and his successors, though they were emboldened by the defeat of Gainas and opposed to 'barbarian' influence, were no less hostile to Stilicho's claim than Rufinus and Eutropius. In any case, a claim to guardianship over a 26-year-old Arcadius would not be so very much stranger than one made when he was 22, or for that matter 18. Much more persuasive here is the suggestion made to me by Dr John Vanderspoel that the key element must be the recent birth of Arcadius' son, Theodosius II, and the infant's elevation as Augustus in Jan. 402: to maintain a claim to any kind of regency over a senior Augustus who had proved his manhood and was himself father to another member of the Imperial college would surely have been impossible. But if Stilicho merely wished to drop the claim, this purpose would have been better achieved by having Claudian say nothing, rather than make what amounts to a very public correction of previous policy statements. This must surely imply that Stilicho was also making a deliberate gesture of reconciliation to the Eastern court, to all intents and purposes publicly signalling his willingness to let his

claim lapse. See Liebeschuetz 61 n. 99, who points also to the shared consulship of the royal brothers in 402 and the celebration of their *concordia* in coins and on the base of Arcadius' column; also Heather 210, O'Flynn 44 ff.

581 f. illum . . . diem . . . referres | quo: similar sense and phrasing can be seen at e.g. Ov. *Tr.* 1. 3. 3 'cum repeto noctem, qua tot mihi cara reliqui', Luc. 2. 98 ff., Stat. *Theb.* 2. 309 ff. 'quippe animum subit illa dies, qua, sorte benigna | fratris, Echionia steterat priuatus in aula . . .': also Ov. *Am.* 3. 12. 1 f., Luc. 7. 354 f., Stat. *Theb.* 8. 206 f., 12. 698 f. If Claudian is directly alluding to the passage from *Thebaid* 2, then there is perhaps a contrast between the bitter scheming of the impious Polynices to replace his brother on the throne of Thebes by means of civil war and the *pietas* of Stilicho, who willingly preserved the sovereignty of the Empire for his young kinsman until he came of age, rather than usurping it for himself.

582. quo tibi: balancing *tum tibi* (578), and so strengthening the contrast between 'then' and 'now'.

confusa dubiis formidine rebus: recalling Turnus' distraught state of mind at Virg. *A.* 12. 665 'obstipuit uaria confusus imagine rerum'. For *dubiis . . . rebus* cf. Pl. *Capt.* 406, Virg. *A.* 6. 196: also Lucr. 3. 55, 1076 'in dubiis . . . periclis', Hor. *Carm.* 4. 9. 36 'temporibus dubiis'. The reference here is primarily to a world still shaken by civil war with dissension in the army not yet entirely quelled, but Müller also points to a number of situations causing concern soon after Theodosius' death, among them revolt in the Rhineland (*IV Cons.* 439 ff.), Gothic incursions into the Eastern Empire (*Ruf.* 2. 22 ff.), and the treachery of Gildo (101–21 n.). See also 96 *illo sub cardine rerum* n., citing *Gild.* 292 ff. Note how the *pietas* of Stilicho here was foreshadowed earlier in the poem by that of Serena (*VI Cons.* 96 ff.). For the phrasing cf. Luc. 2. 248 (of Cato) 'inconcussa tenens dubio uestigia mundo': cf. *III Cons.* 63 f. 'ciuilia rursus | bella tonant dubiumque quatit discordia mundum', *Gild.* 242, *Get.* 432.

583. It is true that the wording here is in line with many literary accounts of *mandata morituri* in which the dependants of the dying man are commended to the care of a trusted relative or friend: note e.g. Ter. *Ad.* 455 ff. 'in te spes omnis, Hegio, nobis sitast: | te solum habemus, tu es patronus, tu pater: | *ille tibi moriens nos commendauit senex*: | si deseris tu periimus.' Even so Claudian's narrative of the death-bed scene appears to be either a direct remodelling of Virgil's famous account of the ill-omened entrusting of the child Polydorus to Polymestor of Thrace at *A.* 3. 49 ff. 'hunc Polydorum auri quondam cum pondere magno | infelix Priamus furtim *mandarat alendum* | Threicio regi', or

an indirect one by way of Ovid's own adaptation at *Met.* 13. 430ff.
'Polymestoris illic | regia diues erat, cui te *commisit alendum* | clam,
Polydore, pater'. The most striking link between myth and recent
history to which the audience is expected to be sensitive is the obvious
fact that, whereas the impious Thracian king murdered his *depositum*
in order to possess himself of the gold that came with him, the faithful
Stilicho preserved his young charge alive and restored the entire
Empire to him on his reaching manhood (585f.). Note also that the
emphasis in the models on the secrecy in which Priam was obliged to
act by the troubled times of the Trojan war (*furtim, clam*) could be read
as hinting that a similarly good reason lay behind Theodosius' entrusting of his son, or sons, to Stilicho without witnesses (cf. 581–3, 582
confusa dubiis formidine rebus nn.). Cf. further Stat. *Theb.* 1. 581, *Ach.* 1.
650ff., *Stil.* 2. 54f. 'natos, dederat quos ille monendos tutandosque
tibi'.

infantem: Honorius (born 9 Sept. 384) was 10 years old at the
death of his father, but the use of the term here helps identify him with
the vulnerable infant Polydorus.

commisit: as he entrusted to him the governance of the whole
Empire, including, in earlier claims, the East: *Ruf.* 2. 4ff. 'iamque tuis,
Stilicho, Romana potentia curis | et rerum commissus apex, tibi
credita fratrum | utraque maiestas geminaeque exercitus aulae', *Stil.*
1. 140f.

584. uirtutes uariae: a full, Stoic-inspired catalogue of Stilicho's
virtues, including Constantia, can be found at *Stil.* 2. 100ff. Here the
emphasis, as is appropriate for the audience and the setting, is on the
traditional Roman virtues, *fides* and *pietas*.

fructus . . . receptos: for the phrasing cf. Cic. *Att.* 15. 15. 3
'quodque ex istis fructuosis rebus receptum est', *Sull.* 90. For the
metaphorical sense of *fructus* see 404 *fructum sincerae laudis* n.

585. depositum seruasse, Fides: in a world before the invention of
the safe deposit in a bank money or valuables could be left with a
friend or kinsman, whose duty it was to return them faithfully when
called upon to do so. For the sanctity of this 'pagan commandment'
see Hollis on Ov. *Ars* 1. 641 'reddite depositum', Courtney on Juv. 13.
15ff. The prohibition against keeping a *depositum* was traditionally a
severe one. His failure to observe this duty led to the destruction of
Glaucus' whole family (Hdt. 6. 86), and in murdering Polydorus in
order to seize Priam's treasure Polymestor 'fas omne abrupit', leading
to the poet's horrified outburst 'quid non mortalia cogis, | auri sacra
fames!' (Virg. *A.* 3. 55ff.). Here the *depositum* may be the whole Empire:
cf. *Stil.* 2. 58ff. 'at Stilicho non diuitias aurique relictum | pondus, sed

geminos axes tantumque reseruat | depositum teneris quantum sol
igneus ambit', where note the further reminiscence of Virg. *A.* 3. 49,
cit. 583 n. But since *depositum* is paralleled with *paruum* and *propinquum*,
the reference is best interpreted as being to Honorius himself, left to
Stilicho in sacred trust and now dutifully restored to the world. For
depositum of a person cf. Ov. *Met.* 9. 119 f. (Deianira) 'Nessoque
paranti | fallere depositum', Sen. *Tro.* 521 (Astyanax) 'sinu profundo
conde depositum meum', with Fantham, Luc. 2. 72 (Marius), also with
Fantham, Luc. 8. 190 f. (Cornelia) 'comitem pignusque recepi |
depositum', Stat. *Ach.* 1. 385, 914, *Rapt.* 3. 118 ff. (Ceres of Proserpina)
'timeo ne fama latebras | prodiderit leuiusque meum Trinacria celet
| depositum.' See further Gruzelier on the spurious lines at *Rapt.* 1.
139 f., and also 97 f. *seruatum . . . pignus | restituit* n. for a less developed
use of this idea. Naturally, *fides* is a regular attribute of Stilicho: *Gild.*
305 f. 'hunc solum memorem solumque fidelem', *Stil.* 2. 30 ff.

585 f. Constantia, paruum | praefecisse orbi: because the tempta-
tion to seize the throne himself instead was so very great. As *paruum*
implies, Stilicho could have argued that the task in hand demanded
the authority of a mature man.

586. Pietas, fouisse propinquum: recalling 'pietas sua foedera
seruet', the next after 'reddite depositum' in Ovid's pagan version of
the Ten Commandments (*Ars* 1. 641). To be more specific, Stilicho
took the place of the father whom Honorius had lost: *Gild.* 301 ff.
(Theodosius' ghost to Arcadius) 'tunc ipse paterna | successit *pietate*
mihi tenerumque rudemque | *fouit* et in ueros eduxit principis annos'.
Note also 651 f. *cuius cunabula fouit | curia* n.

587. hic est ille puer, qui: intended to provide a stirring rise in
emotion ('mirifica energia', Barth). Claudian surely expects us to
remember Aeneas' first, uplifting sight of Augustus, Virg. *A.* 6. 791 ff.
'hic uir, hic est, tibi quem promitti saepius audis, | Augustus Caesar,
diui genus, aurea condet | saecula qui rursus Latio regnata per arua
| Saturno quondam'. If so, the change to *puer* is significant, implying
that Honorius matches in his youth the achievements of the mature
Augustus (cf. 116–18 n.), and there is a suggestion that Honorius
too will introduce a new Golden Age now that Alaric has been
repelled.

In *hic* (from *hice*) the vowel is short, but in pronunciation the *c* was
often doubled and the syllable is therefore scanned long: see W.
Sidney Allen, *Vox Latina: A Guide to the Pronunciation of Classical Latin*
(Cambridge, 1965), 75 ff., and cf. *Get.* 564.

rostra Quirites: a phrase intensely redolent of Roman *libertas*
and tradition: contrast the scorn of the Senate and People of

Constantinople that colours the words 'Byzantinos proceres Graiosque Quirites' (*Eutr.* 2. 136). It was traditionally at the *rostra* that addresses were made to the people, as we can see from e.g. Cic. *Pis.* 7 'ut semper in rostris curiam, in senatu populum defenderim'. But the references here and in the next line are more specific. It was the custom in the Republic and the Early Empire for a new consul entering office formally to inaugurate his consulship by publicly taking oaths to observe the laws of the State, and then to address the first meeting of the Senate for the new year. These oaths were originally taken on the Capitol, but Claudian (and perhaps the organizers of the ceremony?) probably has in mind once again the *ciuilitas* of Trajan as glorified by Pliny: *Pan.* 65. 1 'in rostris quoque simili religione ipse te legibus subiecisti, legibus, Caesar, quas nemo principi scripsit. sed tu nihil amplius uis tibi licere quam nobis'. Claudian's words should therefore be taken to mean that Honorius did indeed address the people in the Forum first, and then the Senate (Cameron 382 f., citing Pacatus, *Pan. Theod.* 47. 3). Claudian none the less lays the emphasis on Honorius' oration to the real players (*patribus*, 589, *sub iudice* . . . *senatu*, 591), from his curule chair (*solio fultus . . . eburno*, 588) and in the presence of the statue of Victoria (597–602).

588. et: apparently marking (*pace* McCormick 88) the physical transition from the Rostra outside the Senate House into the building itself, as 597 *adfuit ipsa suis ales Victoria templis* implies. Honorius is following the example of Constantius II: Amm. Marc. 16. 10. 13 'allocutus nobilitatem in curia, populumque e tribunali'. Cf. also *Stil.* 3. 200 f. 'denso seu turbine uulgi | circumfusa tuae conscendant rostra secures', which may well refer to the delivery of a speech to the people by Stilicho on his own consulship. For such speeches see McCormick, 88 f.

solio fultus . . . eburno: the *sella curulis*, as can be seen also from *Stil.* 3. 200 f. (cit. previous n.). Cf. esp. Liv. 5. 41. 2 'qui eorum *curules* gesserant magistratus . . . *eburneis sellis* sedere', 41. 20. 1; also Ov. *Fast.* 1. 81 f. (the inauguration of a new consul) 'iamque noui praeeunt fasces, noua purpura fulget, | et noua conspicuum pondera sentit ebur', Sil. 8. 486. Livy replaces *curulis* with *eburnea*, while Claudian goes one step further and replaces *sella* with *solium*. The resulting phrase is more self-consciously poetic and also ingeniously combines the symbols both of the Republic and of royalty, since Honorius' throne recalls those of the kings of epic. Cf. Stat. *Theb.* 1. 525 f. 'iamque ipse (sc. Adrastus) superbis | fulgebat stratis solioque effultus eburno', and also the golden throne of Jupiter at Virg. *A.* 10. 116. For *fultus* see Coleman on Virg. *Ecl.* 6. 53 'latus . . . fultus hyacintho', and cf. *Rapt.*

1. 79 (Pluto) 'rudi fultus solio', Avien. *Phaen.* 188; also Virg. *A.* 1. 506 (Dido) 'solioque alte subnixa resedit'.

genitoris: stressing legitimacy: his father has preceded him in the consulship as in the purple. Is this perhaps the very throne on which Theodosius sat with the infant Honorius in 389 (cf. *cum patre sedentem,* 70)? With *solio . . . genitoris* cf. Virg. *A.* 10. 852 'solio sceptrisque paternis', Ov. *Met.* 6. 650 'solio . . . auito', *Fast.* 5. 125, V. Fl. 2. 309.

589f. gestarum . . . causas . . . rerum | euentusque: the consul's report to the Senate of his deeds, though here not his deeds *as* consul but rather the deeds (above all the victory over Alaric) which have *earned* him the consulship. Contrast the shocked tone of *Eutr.* 1. 284f. 'gestis pro talibus annum | flagitet Eutropius'. For the traditional address of the new consul to the Senate's first meeting of his year of office Müller cites Liv. 26. 26. 5 'M. Marcellus cum Idibus Martiis consulatum inisset, senatum eo die moris modo causa habuit', Ov. *Pont.* 4. 4. 35f.

res gestae are the proper stuff of epic (Lucr. 5. 1444f., Hor. *Ep.* 2. 1. 251, *Ars* 73f. 'res gestae regumque ducumque et tristia bella | quo scribi possent numero, monstrauit Homerus'), but the phrase itself may have been thought too prosaic for high verse and appears with exceeding rarity: cf., however, Virg. *A.* 9. 157. For the phrasing cf. Cic. *part.* 82 'causae rerum et euentus et consequentia requirentur', Virg. *G.* 4. 396f. 'ut omnem | expediat morbi causam euentusque secundet'. Although *euentus* is properly governed by *refert* and· *exempla* by *secutus,* perhaps Claudian has in mind Virg. *A.* 11. 758 'ducis exemplum euentumque secuti'.

589. ex ordine: for *secundum ordinem,* attested since Pl. *Rud.* 1155; cf. *Ruf.* 2. 495.

590. Honorius' respect for tradition in his dealings with the Senate and People matches that of his father, who has indeed himself become an *exemplum* of proper behaviour: *cum se melioribus addens | exemplis ciuem gereret terrore remoto* (58f.). Any address by an Emperor to the Senate is open to interpretation as an act restoring its ancient privileges and authority: consider e.g. *Pan. Lat.* 12. 20. 1 Mynors 'nam quid ego de tuis in curia sententiis atque actis loquar, quibus senatui auctoritatem pristinam reddidisti . . . ?' But here the respect shown the Senate probably carries particular political significance: see Introd., pp. xlviii–li.

591. digerit imperii . . . facta: Heinsius wanted to read *dirigit . . . fata,* both elements of which phrase have some minor manuscript support. None the less, *digerit . . . facta* is clearly more appropriate. Claudian is not making a generalizing statement about the cosmic power of the Emperor: he is recording how, in accordance with tradition, Honorius submits to the judgement of the senate (*sub iudice . . . senatu*) a report of his deeds, i.e. he gives them an account of the campaign against Alaric and of the siege of Milan, presumably covering much of the same ground as the one he gives Roma at 440–90. There is a similar crux in the text of Stat. *Silu.* 5. 1. 38 'humanos propior Iove digerit actus', where Markland defends *digerit* and cites Virg. *A.* 2. 182 'ita digerit omina Calchas'. Austin, on the Virgilian passage, comments that '*[d]igerit* implies "analysing", "arranging", and so "expounding"': here Honorius gives a full, analytical account of the war and 'expounds' its significance to the Senate. Honorius' 'State of the Nation' address, then, no doubt had the same apologetic function as *VI Cons.* itself.

sub iudice . . . senatu: the use of *sub*, rather than a plain ablative, is relatively rare, and emphasizes the degree of subjection to the authority in question. See Bömer on Ov. *Met.* 11. 156 'iudice sub Tmolo', and cf. Hor. *Ars* 78, Luc. 10. 227, Stat. *Theb.* 7. 509, Juv. 4. 12, *Nupt.* 63, *Stil.* 1. 362. The symbolic submission to the authority of the Senate and People also underlies *Stil.* 1. 239 ff. 'sub iudice nostro | regia Romanus disquirit crimina carcer . . .', and in particular 3. 99 ff. (see Introd., n. 106).

592–4. Cameron (pp. 385 f.) discerns in these lines a 'transparent ingenuity', arguing that Claudian is trying to cover up the fact that in his speech the young Emperor failed to match the high standards of oratory expected of him. But this seems excessively cynical: note that Stilicho is likewise praised for his straightforward talking at *Stil.* 2. 32 f. 'haec (sc. Fides) docuit *nullo liuescere fuco*, | numquam falsa loqui'. It could be objected that the two passages are not entirely parallel, because the context in *Stil.* 2 is not explicitly oratory but rather deceitful and hypocritical speech in general. But in any case there is a long tradition of praising plain speakers for their *sinceritas*; see e.g. Sen. *Ep.* 115. 2 'oratio cultus animi est: si circumtonsa est et *fucata* et manu facta, ostendit illum quoque non esse sincerum et habere aliquid fracti. non est ornamentum uirile concinnitas', Gel. 6. 14. 11, Min. Fel. *Octauius* 16. 6 'atque etiam, quo imperitior sermo, hoc inlustrior ratio est, quoniam non *fucatur* pompa facundiae et gratiae, sed ut est, recti regula sustinetur.' Seen in this light, Honorius' speech is being presented as one notable for its transparent truthfulness: the good old-fashioned Roman *fides* (or *fiducia*, 592) and *sinceritas* that characterize it are entirely in keeping with the audience, and also provide a link with Stilicho's *uirtutes uariae* (cf. 584 n.). Cf. *IV Cons.* 515 ff., where Claudian attributes to the boy-Emperor a restrained and learned eloquence which impresses foreign ambassadors with its *grauitas*. For the *eloquentia* traditionally expected in an Emperor see Millar 203 ff.

592. Take *uerbis* with both verbs: 'truthfulness exaggerates nothing (*nil cumulat*), and hides nothing (*nihil . . . celat*), in her words.' That is, Honorius' honest speech adds nothing, and takes nothing away: cf. Rev. 22: 18 f. Birt's emendation 'nil cumulat uerbis *quae nil* fiducia celat', though elegant, is quite unnecessary and would also utterly destroy Claudian's delicate rhetorical balance. For *cumulat* cf. 201 f. *non paruum . . . cumulum* n.

593. fucati sermonis: a further development of the standard idea (e.g. Virg. *G.* 2. 465) that the use of dyes to make something seem to be other than it is indicates corruption. In addition to the examples from Seneca and Minucius Felix quoted in 592–4 n. above cf. esp. Fronto 18. 12–19. 6 van den Hout² 'eaque delenimenta, quae mulcendis uolgi auribus conparat, ne cum multo ac magno dedecore fucata sint . . . uestem quoque lanarum <malo?> mollitia delicatam esse quam colore muliebri, filo tenui aut serico; purpuream ipsam, non luteam nec crocatam. uobis praeterea, quibus purpura et cocco uti necessarium est, eodem cultu nonnumquam oratio quoque est amicienda', i.e. the speeches of princes may be 'coloured' but not 'dyed' in 'effeminate' hues: the use of adornment is to be regulated and not allowed to undermine the masculine authority and dignity of the speech.

mens conscia laudis: i.e. mindful of the glory he has won and of the need not to disfigure it by lies or hyperbole. This phrase is but one of many variants on Virgil's famous 'mens sibi conscia recti' (*A.* 1. 604, itself adapted from Lucr. 3. 1018): for others see Ov. *Fast.* 1. 485, Sen. *Phaed.* 162, Stat. *Theb.* 6. 826, V. Fl. 3. 301, Juv. 13. 193 f., Paul. Pell. *Euch.* 51.

594. agnoscunt proceres: most simply, they 'recognize' him as one of their own: so Barth, 'unum velut ex ipsis. ait omnia ad veterem morem redacta, senatoribus jus velut conferentibus Principi.' There are two other, rather less likely, possibilities: (1) that they recognize him as a mature version of the boy who was presented to them by Theodosius in 389, and (2) that they 'recognize the truth of his account of the war (*OLD* s.v. 5, citing Cic. *Ver.* 3. 49, Stat. *Ach.* 1. 32 'agnosco monitus et Protea uera locutum'). For *proceres = senatores* see 356 n.

594–6. The normal role of the Senate is envisaged as being one of peacetime civilian administration, that of the Court as one of military defence. Now, however, the two spheres of authority have been harmoniously united by an Emperor-consul, and each body assumes the function of the other in their shared loyalty. The predominant metaphor for this unity of purpose is that of clothing. Under an *imperator* who wears the Gabine dress of a consul and senator (594n.) the military officials of the Empire don the *toga* (*ducibus* . . . *togatis* 595) and the Senate effectively becomes an army (*curia militat* 596) in the service of a Court usually associated with the *paludamentum*.

All this is a development of the traditional contrast between the military and civilian *negotia* of the Roman governing classes, rhetorically figured as the contrast between *arma* and *toga*. The best-known formulation of this opposition is probably Cicero's notorious 'cedant arma togae, concedat laurea laudi' (fr. 11 Büchner), but examples are extremely frequent: cf. Cic. *Dom.* 99 'qui consul togatus armatos uicerim', *Arch.* 27, Luc. 9. 199, *Eutr.* 2. 72f., *Stil.* 3. 215f. The present passage, however, is particularly indebted to two common rhetorical elaborations of this basic idea. One is the conceit of the law and politics as a kind of *militia* in their own right: see e.g. Ov. *Tr.* 4. 10. 18 'fortia uerbosi natus ad arma fori', *Laus. Pis.* 27f. 'licet exercere togatae | munia militiae', Stat. *Silu.* 5. 2. 108f. 'medii bellare togata | strage fori', Val. Max. 7. 7. 1, 8. 7. 5. The other is the panegyrical topos in which the honorand is praised for his excellence in both these normally opposed spheres of ability: e.g. Ov. *Met.* 15. 746f. (Caesar) 'Marte togaque | praecipuum', Sil. 6. 617 'par ingenium castrisque togaeque'. But Claudian is not influenced by literary precedent alone. By the fourth century the legal profession, as a public service, had already come to be called a *militia* in a semi-technical sense, and the use of the term was officially sanctioned by Leo in 469 (Jones, *LRE* i. 507). Indeed, though there were differences between civilian functionaries and the regular army in terms of employment, all service to the Emperor was loosely called *militia*, and the civil servant was entitled to his rations (*annona*), his uniform (*uestis*), and his badge of office, the *cingulum* (Jones, *LRE* i. 377f., 565f.). Extending this conceit to the Senate, with its ancient military pedigree, will have seemed a natural step.

Claudian had already painted a joyful picture of army and civilian authorities in harmony at Honorius' fourth consulship, celebrated in Milan in 398, in a passage which has several thematic and verbal links with this one: *IV Cons.* 5ff., cit. Introd., n. 109. There even Mars himself is encouraged to put on the *toga* and become indistinguishable from the civilians (*IV Cons.* 14ff.). Note also *Theod.* 256ff., and see further 595 *ducibus* . . . *togatis* n.

594. habituque Gabino: 'toga sic in tergum reiecta ut ima eius lacinia a tergo reuocata hominem cingat' (Servius on Virg. *A.* 7. 612). The origins and purpose of this ceremonial style of wearing the *toga* are much disputed, but Ogilvie (p. 731, on Liv. 5. 46. 2 'Gabino cinctu') convincingly argues for its origins in the traditional dress of the Gabine priests. Certainly, it was associated with religious ceremonies such as the opening of the gates of the temple of Janus (Virg. *A.* 7. 612) and the *Ambarualia* or some similar purification-ritual (Luc. 1. 596), and perhaps the aim was to keep the arms free for sacrifice. The ancients erroneously believed it was originally worn in battle, no doubt because it did not impede the sword-arm. It is also mentioned in the context of Honorius' other consulships (*III Cons.* 3, *IV Cons.* 6; cf. also *IV Cons.* 566 'Ausonio . . . succinctus amictu').

595. ducibus . . . togatis: a striking oxymoron, recalling *IV Cons.* 9f. 'togatus | miles'. Normally the generals would be wearing the *paludamentum* (596 *paludatae* n.), and perhaps Claudian is thinking of Juv. 6. 400 'paludatis ducibus'.

   circumstipata: an extremely rare compound form attested in classical Latin before Claudian only at Sil. 10. 452 'magna circumstipante caterua', and possibly Plin. *Nat.* 14. 16 (in tmesis). Cf. also *Stil.* 2. 356, Aug. *Ep.* 194. 43. For similar scenes cf. *IV Cons.* 583 'tota stipauit Roma senatu', *Stil.* 2. 397.

596. paludatae: the *paludamentum* was a soldier's cloak, fastened with a brooch, and standardly worn by generals: the tetrarchs all wear it, for example, in the famous statue-group in Piazza San Marco, and Honorius, in military garb, sports one on the Diptych of Probus (MacCormack, pls. 3, 6). It is contrasted with the *toga* by Sallust: *Hist.* 1. 87 'togam paludamento mutauit'.

   curia: by metonymy = the Senate (*OLD* s.v. 5), as at e.g. Cic. *Pis.* 7 'ut semper in rostris curiam, in senatu populum defenderim', Ov. *Fast.* 2. 127f. 'sancte pater patriae, tibi plebs, tibi curia nomen | hoc dedit', Luc. 5. 11, *Eutr.* 1. 308. Alternatively, one could understand it as a personification of the building: see Coleman on Stat. *Silu.* 4. 1. 9f. 'precibusque receptis | curia Caesareum gaudet uicisse pudorem'.

   aulae: practically a metonymy for 'courtiers', balancing *curia*; cf. *Get.* 315 'migrantisque fugam conpescuit aulae'. See also *pr.* 26 *aula* n.

597–602. Since the time of Augustus an altar of Victoria had stood in the Senate House in Rome, and, in a ceremony with its counterpart in the prayers that begin the day's business in the House of Commons, offerings were made upon it before all sessions of the Senate. A growing awareness of the incongruity between Christian Emperors and an established pagan religion culminated in Gratian's refusal (probably in 382) to accept the robes of the *pontifex maximus*, and subsequently, among other measures, to abolish state subsidies to pagan cults and order the removal of the altar of Victory from the Senate House. Pagan senators were horrified by what they saw as a shameful abandoning of those cults which they believed had given Rome her power and without which that power could not fail to be withdrawn. In 384 Symmachus, on behalf of the Senate, made his famous appeal (*Relatio* III) to Valentinian II for the restoration of the cults and of the altar, but was opposed with equal elegance and vigour by Ambrose (*Epp.* 17 and 18). The debate came to symbolize the entire struggle for the very soul of the Empire, so much so that some twenty years after their original formulation Ambrose's arguments were recast into impressive and forceful verse by Prudentius (*Contra Symmachum*, I–II). See in general Cameron 237 ff., Matthews 203 ff.

Birt thought that the description of Victoria at *Stil.* 3. 202 ff. (cit. infra) and the present passage alluded to a restoration of the altar, permitted by Stilicho but of which no other record survives (p. lviii n. 1). Cameron, however, is no doubt right to argue that these poems both refer not to the altar but to the statue of the goddess that stood above it (p. 238: cf. Matthews 204 n. 3). It was not so much the existence of representations of pagan deities as the cult attached to them that offended the sensibilities of moderate Christians, and in response to the indiscriminate destruction of statues by, in particular, fanatical Egyptian monks a law was promulgated in 399 to protect works of art in which the distinction was clearly drawn (*C. Th.* 16. 10. 18 'sicut sacrificia prohibemus, ita uolumus publicorum operum ornamenta seruari'). It seems likely, then, that the statue of Victoria was not removed along with the altar and had kept its place throughout the two decades that had passed since Gratian's formal suspension of the cult.

The tolerance of Honorius and Stilicho was none the less at variance with an old 'fundamentalist' horror of pagan art originating in the biblical prohibition against not only the worshipping but also the making of graven images. Prudentius, for example, attributes to Theodosius a long speech against pagan statues in which, it is true, the burden of his scorn falls upon the superstitious worship of mere stone and wood (*C. Symm.* 1. 415 ff.: cf. Minucius Felix, *Oct.* 22. 1 ff.). But such is the ferocity and emotional force of the attack that it comes as something of a surprise when, in language that recalls the edict of 399, Theodosius ends by calling upon the Romans to wash away the stain of impure sacrifice from works of art and to allow the 'statuas . . . puras' to stand as 'ornamenta . . . patriae' (*C. Symm.* 1. 501 ff.). Indeed, it has been argued that this section of the speech is in fact not integral to the original poetic conception: see Friedrich Solmsen, *Philologus*, 109 (1965), 310–13. It seems reasonable to assume, at any rate, that the continued presence of the statue in the Senate House will have left the more puritanical-minded among the Christians uneasy. For the pagans, on the other hand, the statue on its own will naturally not have been enough. It is known that appeals for the restoration of the altar and the cult were made by senatorial delegations to no fewer than three Emperors (Ambrose, *Ep.* 57. 4–6), and T. D. Barnes has convincingly argued that Symmachus made a second, unsuccessful, attempt to persuade the Court to relent during his embassy from the Senate to Milan during the winter of 401–2 (*AJPh* 97 (1976), 373–86, esp. 380–3). If this is so, then Symmachus will no doubt have claimed that the dangers presented by Alaric's invasion made the support of the goddess all the more essential: if Rome would not honour her, she would not protect Rome. To such fears Claudian reassuringly replies that Victoria is the 'untiring companion' of Honorius' campaigns, as the victory over Alaric proves, and that she has given a promise that she always will be (600–2). The aim is no doubt conciliatory: the altar will not be restored but respect is shown for the concerns of the pagan element in the Senate and for, in the form of her statue, the goddess herself. As Cameron reminds us, the stance taken by Claudian here must not be naïvely understood as indicating that the pagan poet is 'entering the controversy on the senatorial side' (p. 237). Whatever his personal feelings on the matter Claudian is undoubtedly expressing Stilicho's policy. Whether the respect shown Victoria was enough to win over the pagan party is highly doubtful, given the subsequent history of relations between Stilicho and the Senate, and any political benefits it did bring may have been heavily outweighed by resentment on the part of pious Catholics, whose angry dissatisfaction with Stilicho's religious policy contributed to his eventual overthrow in 408.

Romans had long been familiar with the standard outward appearance of the winged goddess Victoria (and her Greek equivalent Nike) from her statue in the forum and cult-image on the Palatine (see Liv. 29. 14. 14, Bömer on Ov. *Met.* 8. 13), but Claudian's contemporaries will have been especially so from the vast number of representations of her image on coins and diptychs: see MacCormack 71, 77, 102, 165f., 174, 189. The description given here, in its sentiments and descriptive details alike, closely corresponds to *Stil.* 3. 202ff., where the goddess throws open her shrine (i.e. the Senate House) to the new consul, and the poet invokes her protection: 'quae uero procerum uoces, quam certa fuere | gaudia, cum *totis exurgens ardua pinnis* | ipsa duci *sacras Victoria panderet aedes!* | o palma uiridi gaudens et amica tropaeis, | custos imperii uirgo, quae sola mederis | uulneribus . . . (212ff.) *adsis perpetuum Latio uotisque senatus* | *adnue, diua, tui.* Stilicho tua saepius ornet | limina *teque simul rediens in castra reducat.* | *hunc bellis comitare fauens,* hunc redde togatum | consiliis . . .'. Claudian, who delivered both poems to the same audience, surely expects them to remember the earlier occasion and see that the prayer made to Victoria there has now been answered in the spectacular defeat of Alaric. To *adsis* cf. *adfuit* (597), and to *in castra reducat* and *hunc bellis comitare* cf. *castrorum . . . comes indefessa tuorum* (600).

The kind of views expressed here are rebutted from the Christian perspective by Prudentius at *C. Symm.* 2. 17 ff. He attributes to Honorius and Arcadius the argument that in reality victory comes from human qualities such as courage and zeal for battle, 'quae si defuerint bellantibus, aurea quamuis | marmoreo in templo rutilas Victoria pinnas | explicet et multis surgat formata talentis | non aderit, uersisque offensa uidebitur hastis' (27 ff.). Victory lies in a man's own sword-arm and the omnipotence of God, 'non pexo crine uirago | nec nudo suspensa pede strophioque recincta | nec tumidas fluitante sinu uestita papillas'. Men's conception of her is the result of the deceptive power of art, especially of poetry. The Senate House should be adorned with battle trophies, not the monstrous image of some horrific cross between a woman and a vulture (59 f.). Prudentius' main target is, of course, Symmachus, and it is also true that the form of Victoria is so standardized as to make the appearance of any particular detail in two authors unreliable as evidence of imitation or influence. But given the severity of Prudentius' attack on the deceitfulness of pagan poets and the fact that 'non aderit' (*C. Symm.* 2. 30) could be taken as an explicit contradiction of Claudian's 'adsis' and 'adfuit ipsa' (*Stil.* 3. 212, *VI Cons.* 597), perhaps Prudentius is also attacking Claudian directly: compare the arguments advanced by J. Vanderspoel, *CQ*, NS 36 (1986), 244–55. For Claudian's religious beliefs see above, Introd., Sect. 1.

597. suis . . . templis: i.e. the Senate House. Cf. 'sacras . . . aedes' at *Stil.* 3. 204 and 'marmoreo in templo' at Prud. *C. Symm.* 2. 28: in the latter passage there is no ambiguity and that the Senate House is meant is clear from the very nature of the debate. Strictly speaking, decrees of the Senate could only be lawfully made 'in loco per augurem constituto, quod "templum" appellaretur' (Gel. 14. 7. 7), and, though no 'temples' in the sense of the modern English word, all successive permanent Senate Houses were ritually consecrated sacred enclosures (*templa*). Note in particular Virg. *A.* 7. 174 'hoc illis curia templum', and cf. also 73 f. *fulgentia . . . collecti . . . delubra senatus.* The Senate House is in any case regularly spoken of as 'sanctified' by the presence of the senators: e.g. Hor. *Carm.* 4. 5. 3 f. 'patrum | sancta concilio'.

598. Romanae tutela togae: for the idea and phrasing, with *tutela* in apposition and the protective presence of a statue in mind, cf. Ov. *Fast.* 1. 415 'ruber, hortorum decus et tutela, Priapus', Stat. *Silu.* 4. 6. 32f. *Romana toga* for *senatus* is a very bold metonymy, but the audience is prepared for it by the dress metaphors of 594–6: cf. *Stil.* 1. 329ff. 'ut ducibus mandarent proelia patres | decretoque togae felix legionibus iret | tessera' and note the use of *purpura* for *reges* at e.g. Luc. 7. 228.

598f. diuite pinna | . . . fouet: she spreads out her wings in a protective embrace. Cf. MacCormack, pl. 50, a *solidus* on which Victoria's wings are extended over the enthroned figures of Theodosius and Valentinian II. The adult Honorius has passed from the protection of Stilicho (*fouisse*, 586) to that of the goddess.

For Silius the goddess herself has snow-white wings (15. 99 'niueis Victoria concolor alis'), but Prudentius too testifies to the gilding of the wings on the statue: *C. Symm.* 2. 27ff. '*aurea* quamuis | . . . *rutilas* Victoria pinnas | explicet'. This detail thus helps confirm that Claudian is talking here about the statue, and not a restored altar: cf. 597–602n. For *diues* with the sense of *aureus* cf. Virg. *A.* 6. 195f. (the Golden Bough) 'diues . . . | ramus', Sen. *Her. F.* 532 (the Golden Apples of the Hesperides) 'pomis diuitibus', Luc. 9. 659. Note also the golden statue of Victoria, weighing in at 220 lb., given to the Roman People by Hiero of Syracuse in 216 BC (Liv. 22. 37. 5).

599. patricii: i.e. *patrum* (= *senatorum*). Cf. *Get. pr.* 8 'oraque patricius nostra dicauit honos' and see M. Leumann, *Glotta* 9 (1918), 129ff.

reuerenda . . . sacraria: the gerundive of *reuereor* is rare in classical poetry but cf. Ov. *Ib.* 73, V. Fl. 5. 207f. (an image of the river-god Phasis) 'reuerenda . . . | effigies', *Rapt.* 3. 11; also *pr.* 24 'turba uerenda', 53 *princeps uenerande* n. *sacraria* here continues the idea of the Senate House as a temple: cf. Virg. *A.* 12. 199 'duri sacraria Ditis', Prop. 3. 24. 19, *IV Cons.* 256, *Rapt.* 1. 266.

600. castrorum . . . comes indefessa tuorum: answering the prayer of *Stil.* 3. 213f., cit. supra at 597–60n. Claudian probably has in mind Ov. *Tr.* 2. 169f. 'sic adsueta tuis semper Victoria castris | nunc quoque se praestet notaque signa petat': Honorius thus once more matches the achievements of Augustus (cf. 103 *creuisse*, 116–18nn.). He may also be thinking of Stat. *Silu.* 4. 6. 81 (Hercules' statue grieving at being taken along on Hannibal's campaigns) 'deus castris maerens comes ire nefandis'. If so, there is a deliberate contrast between Hercules' reluctance to follow Hannibal and Victoria's willingness to accompany the conqueror of Alaric, the latter-day Hannibal (182–4n.). For *castrorum comes* cf. also Tib. 2. 6. 1f., Juv. 16. 55. The metonymy of *castra* for 'war(s)' or 'campaign(s)' can be seen also at

Prop. 3. 12. 25 'castra decem annorum', Sil. 6. 617. *indefessus* is rare in epic verse, and appears only here in the works of Claudian: cf. Virg. *A*. 11. 651, Ov. *Met.* 9. 199 with Bömer, Sil. 13. 127, 15. 576, Stat. *Silu.* 5. 2. 155 (of battle comrades) 'unanimi comes indefessus amici'.

601. nunc tandem fruitur iunctis: at first glance *uotis* looks attractive, providing a link with *Stil.* 3. 212f. 'uotisque senatus | adnue, diua, tui'. But such a link is illusory. There the goddess is asked to answer the prayers of the Senate, here she would be enjoying the fulfilment of her *own* prayers. While a goddess may be accustomed to hearing the *uota* of mortals and answering them if it pleases her, it would be strange for her to make them, nor is it easy to see who she would make them to. True, *uotis* could be taken to mean loosely 'wishes' or 'hopes' (Platnauer, 'now at last has had her wish granted'), but the incongruity is still somewhat unsettling. On the other hand, though *fruitur iunctis* is rather a difficult phrase, the sense is completed in l. 602. As Honorius will be Rome's for ever, she promises, so too will she be his. That is, she rejoices in the full spiritual union of the Emperor, who embodies the Court, and herself, the protectress of the Senate, and promises that it will endure for ever. *iunctis* thus provides the fitting climax to this whole section on the harmony between the Senate and the Court. In support of *uotis* Müller cites *CIL* vi. 5767 'hic tumulus Fructi sacer est, quem laedere noli, | hospes: sic uotis ipse fruare tuis'.

601 f. omne futurum | ... in aeuum: similar phrases at Virg. *A*. 8. 627 'haud ... uenturi ... inscius aeui', Luc. 5. 179f. 'omne futurum | nititur in lucem', 7. 390, *Ruf.* 1. 145f. 'aeuique futuri | praescius ardor inest'.

603–39. *Honorius makes his way along the Via Sacra to the Imperial residence on the Palatine, from which he salutes the people gathered in the Circus Maximus and watches the games.*

603–10. Honorius' progress along the Via Sacra is accompanied by the ecstatic approbation of the people lining the route. Their applause, Claudian assures his audience, is to be attributed to genuine gratitude at their delivery from the Gothic menace and not to the *sparsio*, the traditional scattering of coins to the populace on such occasions. Such distributions of money or, more rarely, of sweetmeats or tokens to be exchanged for other goods, which might take place during almost any kind of Imperial celebration, are attested from early in the Principate. Suetonius, for example, records that for several days in a row Gaius Caligula scattered coins to the crowds from the roof of the Basilica Iulia, though he does not explain the motive (*Cal.* 37. 1). Similarly, Stat. *Silu.* 1.

6 describes at length such distributions during the festivities arranged by Domitian for the Saturnalia: cf. also Mart. 8. 78. In time, however, the *sparsio* came to be associated above all with the inauguration of consuls, whether Emperors or subjects; indeed, by the 6th c. the technical term ὑπατείαν ῥίπτειν had firmly established itself. Cf. e.g. *Stil.* 3. 223 ff., Cor. *Laud. Iust.* 4. 9 ff. 'medioque fori, qua diuite dextra | egrediens princeps sacra trabeatus ab aula | diuitias uulgo sollemni munere donans | more niuis sparsurus erat'. Averil Cameron's detailed note on Cor. *Laud. Iust.* 4. 12 directs the reader to a wealth of useful literary and visual evidence; see also Cameron 384 f., MacCormack 37 and 183, with pl. 15 (Constantine distributing largesse on a panel from his Arch). For the largesse of Emperors in general see further R. MacMullen, *Latomus*, 21 (1962), 159–66, and Millar 133 ff.

Alan Cameron (pp. 384 f.) argues that if we read between the lines in this passage we can see that 'For whatever reason (perhaps genuine fiscal difficulties) Honorius had omitted the customary largesse— and been criticized for this omission. With characteristic ingenuity Claudian attempts, not altogether convincingly, to turn this fault into a positive virtue.' This view appears to have become the prevailing orthodoxy, and is echoed by Averil Cameron (loc. cit.) and McCormick (*Eternal Victory*, 89). Claudian's whole point, however, might seem more cogent if we assumed that the *sparsio* did indeed occur; though gold was showered upon them and they received the Emperor with joyous applause, the people's motivation was none the less genuine gratitude for a nobler and greater service, namely their deliverance from the Goths (608–10). In this reading *dispersi* (605) has its full force ('with the lure of the gold that was scattered'). It seems in any case highly surprising that there should not have been at the very least a token *sparsio* from an Emperor who was making his first visit to the capital in fifteen years. Moreover, if this essential part of the proceedings had been omitted, whether because of serious financial difficulties as a result of the war or simply through crass penny-pinching, Claudian might have done better to pass over the matter in total silence rather than both drawing attention to it here *and* reminding the audience of the 'contrasting' generosity of Theodosius in 389 (72 f.). Lastly, the sentiments expressed in these lines are plainly very conventional, and should therefore not be pressed too far: cf. *IV Cons.* 500 ff. 'munificus largi, sed non et prodigus, auri. | perdurat non empta fides nec pectora merces | alligat'.

603. After addressing the Senate in the Curia (*hinc*) Honorius proceeds to his 'home', the Imperial palace on the Palatine, along the Via Sacra and, presumably, the Cliuus Palatinus. In this he apparently follows the usual procedure for a consul: cf. Ov. *Pont.* 4. 4. 41 f. 'inde domum

repetes toto comitante senatu, | officium populi uix capiente domo'.
His route also parallels that taken at his *aduentus* in Rome by
Constantius II: Amm. Marc. 16. 10. 13 'allocutus nobilitatem in curia,
populumque e tribunali, in palatium receptus fauore multiplici'. See
further McCormick 89.

patriis laribus: the palace. Note the ring-composition with 40
larem (see n. ad loc.) and with 53 *agnoscisne tuos, princeps uenerande, penates?*
At the end of the poem the focus returns once more to the Palatine,
the very heart of the City: *pr.* 23 *orbis apex aequatus Olympo,* 8 *natiua
Palatia* nn. *patrii lares* is a fairly common collocation, whether the sense
is literal or, as here, metonymical: cf. Luc. 1. 278, Stat. *Theb.* 12. 327,
and also Juv. 12. 89 'Laribusque paternis.' Cf. also *patrii penates* (Virg.
A. 2. 717, 5. 62f., Ov. *Met.* 1. 773, Luc. 1. 353, 9. 230).

603f. nomine uero | sacra: because sanctified by the presence of the
Emperor. See 125 *sacra* n.

604. flagrat studiis concordia uulgi: cf. *Stil.* 3. 44ff., esp. 48ff.
'omnis in hoc uno uariis discordia cessit | ordinibus: laetatur eques
plauditque senator | uotaque patricio certant plebeia fauori', Cor.
Laud. Iust. 1. 295ff. 'uox ingens facta est, plausus et gaudia surgunt, |
et fragor ex imis altum petit aethera terris, | almaque discreto placuit
concordia uulgo', and see 606 *captant . . . plausus* n. For the phrasing
cf. also Cic. *de Orat.* 1. 14 'incredibili quodam nostri homines dicendi
studio flagrauerunt', *Fat.* 3, Suet. *Cal.* 15, *Stil.* 1. 55f. 'plebs pharetrata
uidendi | flagrauit studio', *Rapt.* 3. 226.

605–8. Honorius' actions are to be contrasted with the shameless and
self-serving profligacy of characters like Rufinus and Eutropius: *Ruf.* 2.
311f., *Eutr.* 2. 85ff. 'dispergere *plausum* | *empturas in uulgus opes* totosque
theatris | indulgere dies alieni prodigus auri'. The noble incorrupti-
bility of the Roman populace is typical of the whole world under the
just rule of Theodosius' sons: *III Cons.* 187f. 'non dominantur opes nec
corrumpentia sensus | dona ualent: emitur sola uirtute potestas.'
Predictably enough, the same rectitude can be found in Stilicho: *Stil.*
2. 330f. (Roma to Stil.) 'hos etiam, quamuis corrumpi munere nullo |
posse queas . . . suscipe cinctus'.

605. colligis: cf. Suet. *Cl.* 12. 3 'in breui spatio tantum amoris
fauorisque collegit'. Perhaps we should see this as a mild metaphor
from 'harvesting'; note the combination with *dispersi* and cf. e.g. Luc.
1. 606f. 'Arruns dispersos fulminis ignes | colligit'. *colligo* is commonly
used with abstract nouns, especially *ira, uires, amor:* see *TLL* iii/2. 1613.
47ff.

606–8. The conventional sentiments expressed here should be com-
pared with *Theod.* 1ff. 'ipsa quidem Virtus pretium sibi, solaque late |

Fortunae secura nitet nec fascibus ullis | erigitur plausuue petit
clarescere uulgi'.

606. captant . . . plausus: cf. Cic. *Pis.* 60 'captare plausus, uehi per
urbem, conspici uelle', Hor. *Ep.* 2. 2. 103 'cum scribo et supplex
populi suffragia capto.' The applause of the people is an essential part
of the celebrations; cf. *Stil.* 2. 174f. 'hinc nomen ubique | plausibus . . .
celebrant', 2. 403, 3. 1 and 274, Cor. *Laud. Iust.* 1. 295 (Averil Cameron
ad loc.: 'the whole poem resounds with the noise of applause'), 1. 345,
2. 359f., 3. 69, 4. 254f. 'uiso tunc consule plebes | plausibus adsurgunt,
et uoces uocibus addunt'.

607f. meritis offertur inemptus . . . fauor: cf. *Theod.* 262f. 'patuit
campus certusque merenti | stat fauor', Tac. *Hist.* 2. 60 'dedit . . .
postea consulatum Simplici innoxium et inemptum.' Contrast Tac.
Hist. 1. 17 'fauorem . . . largitione et ambitu male adquiri'.

608. pura mente: cf. Cic. *Mil.* 61 'pura mente atque integra Milonem,
nullo scelere imbutum', *IV Cons.* 256; also Lucr. 5. 18 'at bene non
poterat sine puro pectore uiui'. Note, however, that the text English-
speakers know as 'blessed are the pure in heart' (Matt. 5. 8) is rendered
by the Vulgate as 'beati mundo corde'.

609. obstringit sua quemque salus: the other, less obvious side of
the network of mutual obligation created by Honorius' salvation of
Rome is discussed at 386–8n. Here their *salus* is a gift from the
Emperor, and of course from Stilicho, to the people: note *Get.* 268,
362f. 'illae tibi, Roma, salutem | Alpinae peperere casae.' For the
phrasing compare e.g. Cic. *Clu.* 190 'ut illum confirmaret Oppianicum
accusatorem filio suo, donis, muneribus . . . obstrinxit', Plin. *Ep.* 6. 18.
1 'te gratissimo tibi munere obstringere'.

procul ambitus erret: just so, under the new Golden Age of
Honorius and Arcadius' rule, 'cumque suo demens expellitur Ambitus
auro' (*III Cons.* 186).

610. Cf. *Stil.* 3. 77f. 'nec solam populi uitam debere fatetur | armis
Roma tuis'; also Liv. 22. 30. 3, Luc. 9. 1096 'dum uitam Phario mauolt
debere clienti'.

611–39. *In the Circus Maximus the Emperor and the Imperial People perform their
reverences to each other. Chariot racing, beast hunts, and military displays entertain
the audience.*

A broad parallel for the structure of the ending of *VI Cons.* can be found
in the *Panegyric for the Consulship of Mallius Theodorus.* The earlier poem's
conclusion first gives an account of the preparations for the games given
to celebrate the inauguration of the consulship (270–332; cf. *VI Cons.*

611–39) and then moves on to a rousing *envoi* which sends the new year on its way under good auspices and with joyous predictions of future consulships for Theodorus and his son and grandsons (333–40; cf. *VI Cons.* 640–60). *De Consulatu Stilichonis* is also broadly similar, but possesses no *envoi*, and places the emphasis overwhelmingly on the *uenationes* at the expense of all other kinds of entertainment (*Stil.* 3. 223–369). What distinguishes our present passage structurally is that the description, if elliptical and weighted very heavily towards the cavalry manœuvres of 621–39, is none the less literalist in approach and vividly represents the actual content of the games. In both of the other consular panegyrics mentioned here, Claudian had instead recorded only the preparations, and done so by means of quasi-mythological fantasies. In *Theod.* we find Urania instructing the other Muses to assist in facilitating the games; Erato is to gather all the horses of Neptune for the chariot racing, for example, and Clio to ask Diana to round up animals for the beast-hunts. This last idea becomes the nucleus for the whole of the fantasy that ends *Stil.* 3, in which Diana herself gives commands to her companion nymphs to perform the same task. The poem then proceeds with a long description of their bloodless hunt in every corner of the globe as they bring in animals of all kinds. It is just possible that the difference in time-scale envisaged in the three poems reflects one in the order of service in the celebrations, i.e. that *Theod.* and *Stil.* 3 were delivered before the opening of the games and that *VI Cons.* was recited after them. But such a suggestion is unprovable, and open to the objection that poetic imagination is quite capable of using future tenses and jussive subjunctives to describe vividly something that the audience has, in real time, already witnessed.

Of these three passages, *Theod.* offers by far the most comprehensive list of public spectacles, among them not only the usual chariot-races (282–7), *uenationes* (291–310), and sham-battles (the *naumachiae* 331f.) but also lighter entertainment such as musicians, comedy, tragedy, and acrobats. *Stil.* 3 and *VI Cons.* share the chariot-races (3. 265f.; *VI Cons.* 618) and *uenationes* (3. 267–369; *VI Cons.* 618–20), but their balance is wholly different. The account in *Stil.* 3, though much the longest, is taken up almost entirely with beast-hunts; that in *VI Cons.*, though shorter than either of the other two, disposes of most of the entertainments in three lines (618–20) and then concentrates on the elaborate cavalry manœuvres of 621–39. A desire for variety is evident, but the principal reason is probably, as so often, political and panegyrical. The wide-ranging travels of Diana and her nymphs in search of fierce beasts for the amphitheatre in *Stil.* 3 take in almost every part of the Western Empire—Dalmatia, Gaul, Germany, the Alps, Spain, Corsica, and

Sardinia—and so we are given, as it were, a tour of that portion of the world eager to honour its protector Stilicho. In *VI Cons.*, the emphasis is instead on the peaceful aspects of the games; see further below.

As a result, in both *Stil.* 3 and *VI Cons.* the chariot-racing, which was in fact the central item in consular games and much the most popular and spectacular, is thus largely sidelined. In fact, Claudian here passes over the races in the most cursory manner: *nec solis hic cursus equis* (618) does little more than remind us that the races are to be assumed as a given on such occasions and that we are in the Circus Maximus, and he is almost as brief with the *uenationes* (618-20). A clearer picture of the central importance attached to chariot-racing in Late Antiquity, and especially in connection with consulships, can be obtained from numerous sources, both literary and artistic. See e.g. Sid. *Carm.* 23. 307ff., and consider especially the numerous ivory diptychs showing consuls presiding over circus races; particularly fine examples are the Lampadii diptych (*c.* AD 425; Roberts, fig. 17) and the 6th-c. diptych of Basilius, showing the consul side by side with the figure of Roma and a circus-race taking place at their feet (Peter Brown, *The World of Late Antiquity* (London, 1971), ill. 88). Other diptychs show *uenationes*: see also Roberts, figs. 20-2. The preparations were elaborate and time-consuming, the costs involved absolutely enormous (up to 4,000 lb. of gold in Rome, though expenditure was much more modest in Constantinople: see Jones, *LRE* i. 537ff., Matthews 231, 319, 384). Holding such games came to be associated with the assertion of sovereignty (see MacCormack 47, 294 n. 157), and as a result, Emperors often marked their more important *aduentus* in this way. Constantius II, for example, held equestrian games on the occasion of his visit to Rome in AD 357 (Amm. Marc. 16. 10. 13; cf. Julian ibid. 21. 10. 1f.). See in general Simon on *Theod.* 274-332 (pp. 245ff.), Alan Cameron, *Porphyrius The Charioteer* (Oxford, 1973) and *Circus Factions. Blues and Greens at Rome and Byzantium* (Oxford, 1976), McCormick 91-100, esp. p. 95 n. 70. Note also Ammianus' denunciation of the Roman *plebs*: 'eisque templum et habitaculum et contio et cupitorum spes omnis Circus est Maximus' (28. 4. 28).

Claudian lays great stress on the fact that the games given by Honorius included sham-battles but did not involve the shedding of blood (621, 637-9). It is recorded that Honorius fulfilled the desires of the vast majority of the Christian hierarchy and abolished gladiatorial combat despite its great popularity with the urban populace. Exactly when in his reign he did so is unclear, but Prudentius' *Contra Symmachum*, which can be dated to AD 402-3, contains a scathing condemnation of the practice (1. 379ff.) and concludes with a highly-charged and extremely prominent appeal to Honorius to end it (2. 1126ff. 'nullus in urbe cadat, cuius sit poena uoluptas, | nec sua uirginitas oblectet caedibus ora. | iam solis contenta feris infamis harena | nulla cruentatis homicidia ludat in armis'). Anne-Marie Palmer, *Prudentius on the Martyrs* (Oxford, 1989), 23, 216 brings Prudentius and the present passage together in order to argue that it was in 404 that Honorius banned gladiatorial games, in response to the appeal of the Christian poet. Perhaps more convincing, however, is her alternative suggestion that Prudentius' appeal is a literary conceit, in which the Emperor is asked to do what he in fact has already done or, as is generally known, already intends to do. However that may be, two things are tolerably clear from Claudian's account. First, there is no mention at all of gladiatorial games; the same silence on this matter in *Theod.* and *Stil.* 3 may even be taken as evidence that, whether or not a formal ban was in effect, no such entertainments disfigured the consular celebrations of the devout Christians Mallius Theodorus and Stilicho as early as 399 and 400. Secondly, Claudian's words cannot be used to date the decree in question, nor, *pace* Cameron 222 f., is he 'deliberately drawing attention to the bloodless character of Honorius' games' in order to 'reflect [. . .] the current Christian attitude'. Claudian is drawing a contrast, not between gladiatorial games and the 'bloodless' spectacle of the cavalry manœuvres, but between real battles and sham ones. This is the point of the remark about Janus and the closing of the Gates of War; note especially *Ianus Bella premens laeta sub imagine pugnae* and *paci* (638 f.). Under the protection of Stilicho and Honorius, the spectacle in the circus is the nearest thing to a battle that the inhabitants of Rome have witnessed in connection with the Gothic invasion. The thrust of these lines is thus entirely in keeping with the propaganda line taken throughout both this poem and *De Bello Getico*: see Introd., pp. l–li.

611–17. From the Palace the Emperor now enters the Imperial box in the Circus Maximus. In a ritual expression of the dual majesty and sovereignty of both the Emperor himself and of the Imperial People he does them reverence (612–14) and they in return acclaim him loudly (615–17). This seems to be the first recorded instance of the no doubt more developed ritual described in the 6th c. by Corippus. See *Laud. Iust.* 2. 301 ff. 'utque *salutato* tetigit subsellia *uulgo*, | auratum scandens solium sedemque paternam, | instructam plumis pulchrisque tapetibus altam, | aspexit laetos populos, uultuque modesto, | circumfusa uidens plaudentum milia, risit, | censuram seruans et plebi gaudia donans. | ut princeps solio subnixus sedit in alto, | ingens laetitiae sonuit fragor: aurea plebes | tempora principibus centenis uocibus optat. | Iustino uitam partes utraeque reclamant, | Augustae Sophiae uotis quampluribus orant. | excutiunt plausus, studiorum gaudia surgunt, | alternisque sibi respondent agmina dictis.' See Averil Cameron ad loc., esp. on 2. 301 for the further development of the ceremony. For the ideological oxymoron of the 'Imperial People' cf. Cassiodorus, *Variae* 6. 4. 6 (to a Praefectus Vrbi) 'carpento ueheris *per nobilem plebem*, publica te uota comitantur, fauores gratissimi consona tecum uoce procedunt.' The shouts of the populace (*fragor* 616) should almost certainly be taken as implying rhythmical acclamations that expressed largely conventional approbation and wishes for long life and victory, coupled with the Emperor's names and titles; in addition to Corippus, *Laud. Iust.* 2. 308–14 see ibid. 1. 358 'tu uincas, Iustine!', *IV Cons.* 174 'cum *solita* miles te uoce leuasset', the long list of acclamations offered at *C. Th. Gesta Senatus Romani de Theodosiano Publicando* 5, and the instructive examples cited by MacCormack on p. 244 and in the notes ad loc., esp. *De Caer.* 411 Λέων Αὔγουστε, σὺ νικᾷς, σὺ εὐσεβής, σὺ σεβαστός. A singularly instructive passage can be found at SHA *Sev. Alex.* 6ff., where Lampridius records the extremely elaborate exchange in which the new Emperor accepts some titles offered him by the Senate and refuses others in speeches punctuated by the recitation of long catalogues of acclamations.

acclamatio was already a part of political life in the Late Republic, though no doubt in a much less formalized fashion than in the time of Claudian: see *Der Kleine Pauly* 1. 30. 28ff. It is not clear if the acclamations recorded here were already as elaborate as those that would develop in the future, but a fairly high degree of formalization, and the use of claques, may reasonably be deduced from the comparative evidence of the period, even though it is mainly to be found in Eastern sources: see J. H. W. G. Liebeschuetz, *Antioch: City and Imperial Administration in the Later Roman Empire* (Oxford, 1972), 208ff. Such acclamations were an essential part of the interaction between rulers and ruled, a means for the people to assert their loyalty and reaffirm the legitimacy of the Emperor, or on occasion their strident disapproval of officials or policies: see Liebeschuetz, op. cit. 209 ('Acclamations had a semi-constitutional status'), MacCormack 243ff., McCormick 5, 18f., 95, 255, C. Roueché, *JRS* 74 (1984), 181–99. See also *Stil.* 3. 188ff.

611. o quantum: cf. Luc. 4. 385 'o quantum donata pace potitos', *Get.* 435 'o quantum mutata tuo fortuna regressu', *c.m.* 48. 9.

secreti: 'mysterious', Platnauer. But given the contrast with *praesens* there is also some play on the common sense of 'far removed' (*OLD* s.v. 4c); the Emperor is now at last here in person, not tormentingly distant in Ravenna (see 363–5 n.). For the Emperor's own *numen* see 17 *numine* n. and 656 *ceu numen adorent*. The two uses of the word in these closing lines of the poem thus serve structurally both to link beginning and end in ring-composition and to record the satisfaction of the complaints motivating Roma in the speech that dominated the centre of the poem.

addit: cf. Virg. *A.* 8. 301 'decus addite diuis', Stat. *Theb.* 4. 12 'timidisque etiam breuis addita uirtus'.

612. imperii praesens genius: cf. *c.m.* 31. 48 'genius regni'. This kind of phrase is perhaps best understood as a poetic variant for the *genius* of the Emperor, who is thus equated with the Empire itself: consider e.g. Stat. *Silu.* 5. 1. 74 (of Domitian) 'mitem genium domini praesentis adoras.' Note also the similar phrase 'praesens numen' (*Gild.* 308, *c.m.* 26. 70). As Müller points out, sacrifices had been offered to the *genius publicus* of the state since at least 218 BC (Liv. 21. 62. 10).

612f. quantamque rependit | maiestas alterna uicem: for the sentiment cf. esp. *Stil.* 3. 99 'maiestas augescit plena Quirini', of Stilicho's decision to let the Senate review the African magistrates. The 'majesty of the Senate and People of Rome' is a well-established concept, here strikingly adapted to the realities of a monarchy: cf. Cic. *Rab. Perd.* 20 'ut imperium populi Romani maiestasque conseruaretur', Caes. *Gal.* 7. 17. 3, Tac. *Hist.* 1. 90 'maiestatem urbis et consensum populi ac senatus', *Eutr.* 1. 424, *Theod. pr.* 7. An aura of majesty had also long been an expected qualification for the purple: note e.g. Suet. *Ves.* 7. 2 'auctoritas et quasi maiestas quaedam ut scilicet inopinato et adhuc nouo principi deerat'.

613. circi: the general trend in Late Antiquity to concentrate all secular Imperial ceremonial in the Circus or Hippodrome is discussed at McCormick 92.

613f. regia . . . purpura: compare esp. Cic. *Scaur.* 45h 'purpura regalis', Virg. *G.* 2. 495 'purpura regum'. For *regia* see 42 *regia*, 64 *regale . . . culmen*, 552 *regius . . . sanguis* nn., and for purple as the symbol of royalty see Levy on *Ruf.* 2. 346f.

The metonymical use of *purpura* is also found at e.g. Sen. *Her. O.* 647 'uigiles . . . trahit purpura noctes', Luc. 7. 228, *IV Cons.* 47, *Stil.* 3. 118f. 'posito iam purpura fastu | de se iudicium non indignatur haberi', *c.m.* 25. 78. The word may also be applied metonymically to consuls or the consulship itself: see Stat. *Silu.* 4. 1. 1 'laeta bis octonis accedit purpura fastis' and Coleman ad loc., Mart. 8. 8. 4.

614. conexum gradibus: for the local ablative cf. 580 *urbe* n., and for *conexus* of living things cf. Virg. *G.* 4. 257 (bees) 'illae pedibus conexae limina pendent'.

ueneratur purpura uulgus: it is the Emperor who is standardly *uenerandus*, as at 53: contrast e.g. Prud. *C. Symm.* 1. 191f. 'quos fabula manes | nobilitat, noster populus ueneratus adorat.' Note also 616 *plebis adoratae*, another ideological oxymoron, and for the action and its political implications regarding *concordia* and *consensus* cf. further *Ruf.* 2. 366 'Augustus ueneranda prior uexilla salutat'. Quite what is implied is not clear, though hand-gestures, some kind of ritual salutation, or perhaps even an act of obeisance such as a bow are possibilities. Cf. Suet. *Cl.* 12. 2 'eosdem spectacula edentis surgens et ipse cum cetera turba *uoce et manu* ueneratus est'.

615–17. Cf. *Stil.* 2. 403 ff. 'Pompeiana dabunt quantos proscaenia plausus! | ad caelum quotiens uallis tibi Murcia ducet | nomen Auentino Pallanteoque recussum!' Both passages appear to have been inspired by Luc. 7. 9 ff. 'nam Pompeiani uisus sibi sede theatri | innumeram effigiem Romanae cernere plebis | attollique suum laetis ad sidera nomen | uocibus et plausu cuneos certare sonantes . . .'. Lucan's lines belong to his account of the bitter-sweet dream of his former glory and happiness that visits Pompey on the eve of his utter defeat at Pharsalus, and the intertextual reminiscences here will no doubt seem ominous to some readers. But in the joyous context of Honorius' consulship and the Gothic victory Claudian's audience perhaps could be counted on to give preference to the positive aspects of the allusion: this occasion was the high point of Pompey's life when, like Honorius now, he was 'iuuenis primique aetate triumphi' (Luc. 7. 14). In his turn Claudian seems to have helped shape Corippus, *Laud. Iust.* 2. 165 f. '*intonuit* patrum subitus *fragor*, inde clientum | clamores crescunt; clamoribus adsonat *Echo*.' Note also Hor. *Carm.* 1. 20. 6 ff. 'iocosa | redderet laudes tibi Vaticanis | montis imago', Juv. 11. 197 f., Rut. Nam. *Red.* 1. 203 f.

615. cauae . . . uallis: the Circus Maximus lay in the *uallis Murcia*, between the Palatine and Aventine Hills. In epic such valleys, with their grassy slopes for seats, form natural circuses and theatres even before the application of human construction; see e.g. Virg. *A.* 5. 286 ff. 'hoc pius Aeneas misso certamine tendit | gramineum in campum, quem collibus undique curuis | cingebant siluae, mediaque in ualle theatri | circus erat', Stat. *Theb.* 6. 255 ff. For the collocation cf. Virg. *G.* 2. 391 'complentur ualles . . . cauae', Liv. 3. 8. 9, Ov. *Fast.* 6. 110, Luc. 4. 158.

615 f. Phrases of this type describing loud noise are part of the stock-in-trade of epic poets. Cf. esp. Virg. *A.* 2. 338 'sublatus ad aethera clamor', 2. 692 f., 5. 228 'resonat . . . fragoribus aether', 9. 541 'caelum tonat omne fragore', Luc. 6. 225 f., Stat. *Theb.* 3. 669 f. 'rursus fragor intonat ingens | hortantum', *Silu.* 1. 1. 64 f., Juv. 11. 197 f.

616. plebis adoratae: picking up *ueneratur purpura uulgus* (614) and also recalling, while reversing, the compliment described in *iuuenem te Thybris adoret* (425). Cf. Sal. *Iug.* 4. 3 'certe quibus maxuma industria uidetur salutare plebem et conuiuiis gratiam quaerere', Tac. *Hist.* 1. 36 'nec deerat Otho protendens manus adorare uulgum, iacere oscula et omnia seruiliter pro dominatione'.

reboat: cf. esp. Sid. *Carm.* 8. 9f. 'uel quod adhuc populo simul et plaudente senatu | ad nostrum reboat concaua Roma sophos.' For the etymologies, ancient and modern, of *reboare* see Thomas on Virg. *G.* 3. 223 'reboant siluaeque et longus Olympus.' The word is decidedly rare in the high style but cf. Lucr. 2. 28, 4. 546, V. Fl. 3. 634, Sil. 17. 251, Aus. *Ep.* 21. 21 Green, Prud. *Apoth.* 386, *Ham.* 102.

616f. Cf. esp. Pacatus, *Pan. Theod.* 46. 1 'spectabas haec e tuis collibus, Roma, et septena arce sublimis celsior gaudio ferebaris', *Prob.* 175 f. 'colles . . . canoris | plausibus inpulsi septena uoce resultant.' For the seven hills of Rome see 536 n., and for *arx* = 'hill' see 416 *arce* n.: note also Virg. *G.* 2. 535 (Roma) 'septem . . . una sibi muro circumdedit arces.' For the use of the distributive for the cardinal see 391 *centenus* n., 392 n.; cf. Stat. *Silu.* 1. 5. 23 f. 'quae Latium septenaque culmina, Nymphae, | incolitis', *Gild.* 104. The mention of Echo helps reinforce the ring-compositional structure; cf. 33.

619. arua: 'race-track', a Statian usage: see *TLL* ii/1. 734. 79 ff., citing Stat. *Silu.* 5. 3. 54 f., *Theb.* 6. 521 f. 'uolat ocior Euro, | ceu modo carceribus dimissus in arua solutis'; add *Theb.* 6. 595. This is a highly specialized development of the sense 'flat ground' (*OLD* s.v. 4), and is very far removed indeed from the primary sense of 'ploughed land'.

trabes: the word most commonly indicates timber beams or even columns when applied metonymically, but here, as Müller saw, the reference is to fences designed to protect the spectators from the lions and other dangerous wild beasts. For the staging of *uenationes* in the Circus rather than the more usual venue of an amphitheatre see Gel. 5. 14. 5 'in Circo Maximo . . . uenationis amplissimae pugna populo dabatur', J. H. Humphrey, *Roman Circuses. Arenas for Chariot Racing* (Berkeley and Los Angeles, 1986), 186, K. M. Coleman, *JRS* 80 (1990), 52.

619f. The sense of *subitae* is 'suddenly (i.e. very quickly) constructed' ('new amphitheatre', Platnauer): cf. 535 *erexit subitas turres* n. This interpretation is in effect guaranteed by *Theod.* 331 f. 'lasciui subito confligant aequore lembi | stagnaque remigibus spument inmissa canoris', of an amphitheatre adapted for *naumachiae*: see further K. M. Coleman, *JRS* 83 (1993), 48–74. An alternative, but less attractive, possibility is to take *subitae* as transferred from *aspectus*; the sight of the arena is suddenly thrust on the unfortunate lions and in an instant their blood is flowing. Cf. Virg. *A.* 11. 699 'subitoque aspectu territus haesit'.

By metonymy *harenae* has the sense of the English 'arena' (here = 'circus'), as at *Ruf.* 2. 395, *Stil.* 3. 271, 3. 316 f. 'luxuriantis harenae | delicias', *Get.* 163 f. (gladiators) 'coniurantis harenae | turba'. Müller explains the bold combination *aspectus harenae diffundit* by arguing that *harena* is the conceptual subject, and compares Mela 2. 70 'Herculaneum, Vesuuii montis adspectus': this particular parallel, however, is not very persuasive. It is true that *aspectus* is occasionally used of 'a sight' or 'something seen' (*OLD* s.v. 6 cites Stat. *Theb.* 3. 124 f. 'aspectu . . . accensa cruento | turba furit', Sil. 15. 182 'hac aspectu turbatum'), and so 'spectacle' is a possible sense. None the less, *aspectus . . . diffundit* seems very odd indeed, and it is quite likely that corruption lies at the root of our difficulties here. Professor Nisbet suggests to me that we might read *adgestus*: note that this attractive conjecture is in accord with Müller's instinct that the real subject conceptually is the arena in general.

620. Libycos . . . cruores: lions are standardly associated with north Africa, at e.g. Virg. *A.* 12. 4 ff., Ov. *Fast.* 5. 178 'Libycae . . . ferae', *Stil.* 3. 356.

aliena ualle: the *uallis Murcia*, and the artificial valley of the Circus Maximus, so far from the lions' native valleys in Africa. The pathetic detail introduces a note of melancholy. For the same feeling on a larger scale compare the magnificent simile used to describe the entrapment and slaughter of Rufinus: *Ruf.* 2. 394 ff. 'ut fera, quae nuper montes amisit auitos | altorumque exul nemorum damnatur harenae | muneribus, commota ruit; uir murmure contra | hortatur nixusque genu uenabula tendit; | illa pauet strepitus cuneosque erecta theatri | respicit et tanti miratur sibila uulgi'. The consulship, by contrast, has come home: 'natus fonte suo, quem non *aliena per arua* | induit hospes honos' (650 f.).

621–39. The centrepiece of the account of the games is an elaborate description of a formal display of cavalry manœuvres. In an effect no doubt designed to mirror the confusion of the real battlefield, the exercises executed by the cavalry involve complicated whirling formations which seem as bewildering and confused as the Labyrinth of Knossos or the winding course of the Maeander. They are, however, in fact carefully choreographed and executed in perfect time to the commands of a *magister*. The display is a sham-fight, with rhythmically performed symbolic exchanges of sword-blows; the performance is brought to a climax by the whole company sinking to its knees in an act of homage to the Emperor.

Though this is a bravura display it should not be seen simply as a kind of circus-show completely unconnected with the rigours of warfare. Such exercises served to train soldiers to maintain formation in the press of battle, to remain flexible, and to hone their skills in swordfighting; all these practical advantages are stressed at *Epit. Rei Mil.* 2. 23 by Vegetius, who comments epigrammatically that 'inexercitatus miles semper est tiro'. The adaptability of such techniques to the battlefield proper can be seen in the account given by Livy of the application of the parade-ground *testudo* exercise to a siege fought in deadly earnest: 'iuuenes etiam quidam Romani ludicro circensi ad usum belli uerso partem humillimam muri ceperunt . . . inter cetera sexageni ferme iuuenes, interdum plures apparatioribus ludis, armati inducebantur. horum inductio ex parte simulacrum decurrentis exercitus erat, ex parte elegantioris quam militaris artis propiorque gladiatorium armorum usum. cum alios decursu edidissent motus, quadrato agmine facto, scutis super capita densatis, stantibus primis, secundis summissioribus, tertiis magis et quartis, postremis etiam genu nixis, fastigatam, sicut tecta aedificiorum sunt, testudinem faciebant. hinc quinquaginta ferme pedum spatio distantes duo armati procurrebant comminatique inter se, ad ima in summam testudinem per densata scuta cum euasissent, nunc uelut propugnantes per oras extremae testudinis, nunc in media inter se concurrentes, haud secus quam stabili solo persultabant. huic testudo similis humillimae parti muri admota' (44. 9. 3ff.). See also 633 *in uarios gyros* n. Also broadly comparable to the exercises described in Claudian is the *pyrricha*, a military dance connected with training: Suetonius tells us that 'pyrricham saltauerunt Asiae Bithyniaeque principum liberi' at Caesar's Gallic triumph (*Iul.* 39. 1; cf. *Nero* 12. 1). The term was later applied to a different but similar training exercise, a kind of rhythmic marching to pipe-music (Amm. Marc. 16. 5. 10). Note also the equestrian exercises practised by the young Honorius himself at *IV Cons.* 539ff., and see further McCormick 95.

Claudian, however, is as much concerned with literary atmosphere as with military accuracy, and the most important influence on the composition of this passage is undoubtedly Virgil's description of the *lusus Troiae* as performed at the funeral games of Anchises: 'cetera Trinacriis pubes senioris Acestae | fertur equis. | excipiunt plausu pauidos gaudentque tuentes | Dardanidae, ueterumque agnoscunt ora parentum. | postquam omnem laeti consessum oculosque suorum | lustrauere in equis, signum clamore paratis | Epytides longe dedit *insonuitque flagello.* | olli *discurrere pares* atque agmina terni | *diductis soluere choris,* rursusque uocati | conuertere uias infestaque tela tulere.

| inde alios ineunt cursus aliosque recursus | aduersi spatiis, alternosque orbibus orbis | impediunt pugnaeque cient simulacra sub armis; | et nunc terga fuga nudant, nunc spicula uertunt | infensi, facta pariter nunc pace feruntur. | *ut quondam Creta fertur Labyrinthus in alta* | parietibus textum caecis iter ancipitemque | mille uiis habuisse dolum, qua signa sequendi | frangeret indeprensus et inremeabilis *error*; | haud alio Teucrum nati uestigia cursu | impediunt *texuntque fugas* et *proelia ludo,* | delphinum similes qui per maria umida nando | Carpathium Libycumque secant' (*A.* 5. 573–95). In particular, compare the portions italicized above with *insonuit . . . uerbere* (625), *discurritur ordine* (633), *pariter* (626), *choros* and *partitis . . . cateruis* (622, 632), *quos neque semiuiri Gortynia tecta iuuenci | . . . uincant* (634 f.), *errorum* (624), *textas . . . fugas* (623), and *belligeros . . . lusus* (621). Differences to note are none the less numerous. Claudian's description is in general substantially more concise, nor has he added to it a section of explicit aetiological comment as Virgil does to his account of the *lusus Troiae* (*A.* 5. 596–603). Even so, new elements are introduced, the principal ones being the account of the ritualized sword-play and the reverences paid to the Emperor (626–32). These competing impulses towards abbreviation and the inclusion of new material according to the principle of variation can be seen especially clearly in the use of similes. Claudian retains Virgil's Labyrinth simile, but substitutes the river Maeander for his dolphins; he none the less contrives to shrink eight lines (*A.* 5. 588–95) to a mere two (634 f.). The whole context of the two sets of manœuvres is also entirely different, since Virgil's forms part of the solemn ceremonies in honour of the dead Anchises while in Claudian the atmosphere is one of public rejoicing at the restoration of peace through victory. But perhaps this gap is in any case bridged by our recollection of the proud joy felt by the Trojan parents as they watch their sons perform the *lusus Troiae* (*A.* 5. 575 'gaudent'). The most important effect of this wholesale adaptation of Virgil, however, is to invest the games celebrating the defeat of Alaric with an aura of venerable antiquity. The contemporary greatness of Rome, a greatness renewed by the victories of Pollentia and Verona, is thus connected both with the remote mythological past of Rome's divinely inspired foundation and with the glories of the Age of Augustus. For a discussion of Virgil's *lusus Troiae*, the ceremony's origins, and its political significance for Romans in the time of Augustus see R. D. Williams's commentary (Oxford, 1960) ad loc. Lastly, note also that the same Virgilian passage is adapted by Silius (4. 315 ff.) and Statius (*Theb.* 6. 213 ff.: see 627 n.).

621. belligeros exercuit . . . lusus: one of several examples of

oxymoron drawing attention to the contrast between the surface confusion and the carefully choreographed discipline that lies beneath it:
cf. *armatos . . . choros* (622), *certaque uagandi . . . lege* (622f.), *pulchras errorum
artes* (624), and *docto disurritur ordine* (633). For the language cf. Cic. *Fin.*
1. 69 'ludicra exercendi aut uenandi', Liv. 5. 27. 2 'is cum in pace insti-
tuisset pueros ante urbem lusus exercendique causa producere', 44. 9.
3, *IV Cons.* 539 'simulacra . . . Martia ludis'; and contrast V. Fl. 5. 617
'belligeros . . . labores'.

   area: = 'exercise ground', as often, e.g. Hor. *Carm.* 1. 9. 18 'campus
et areae', Mart. 7. 32. 13. See further *TLL* ii/1. 497. 74ff. ('de circo, de
arena, de loco ludendi').

622. armatos . . . choros: the choice of noun is in keeping with the use
of *chorus* to indicate performers of any type (*OLD* s.v. 3b). Here, however, it also stresses the musical aspects of the display, which is a kind
of dance on horseback, performed to the sound of rhythmical sword-
blows (626–30). Claudian is following Virg. *A.* 5. 581 'diductis . . .
choris'; contrast e.g. Sil. 15. 370 'armatos in bella globos' to appreciate
the mildly oxymoronic effect.

622f. certaque uagandi . . . lege: reformulated by *pulchras errorum
artes* (624). For the paradoxical phrasing cf. esp. *Theod.* 128f. 'quam
certus in astris | error'. Contrast the more usual language of Pac.
trag. 302 Ribbeck (= 327 Warmington) 'triplici pertimefactus maerore
animi incerte errans uagat', Lucr. 3. 1052 'animi incerto fluitans
errore uagaris', Luc. 2. 12 'fors incerta uagatur', Stat. *Theb.* 10. 736.
certa . . . lege perhaps alludes to the common use of *certus* in phrases
indicating the regular movements of dance; see e.g. Hor. *Ars* 158f.
'reddere qui uoces iam scit puer et pede certo | signat humum',
Tib. 2. 1. 52 'cantauit certo rustica uerba pede', and cf. 496 *certis . . .
legibus* n.

623. textas . . . fugas . . . recursus: cf. Virg. *A.* 5. 593, Sil. 4. 319f.
'texunt alterno glomerata uolumina cursu | atque eadem refuga
cedentes arte resoluunt', *IV Cons.* 540f. In addition to the Virgilian
metaphor of weaving, the use of *recursus* suggests the ebbing of the sea;
cf. Virg. *A.* 10. 288f. 'recursus | languentis pelagi', Sen. *Dial.* 12. 20. 2
'cursusque eius alternos et recursus.' Along with *certa . . . lege* this detail
associates the cavalry display with the description of the harbour of
Ravenna (495–9).

624. pulchras errorum artes: recalling Virgil's 'inremeabilis error'
(*A.* 5. 591), from the Labyrinth simile, and so preparing the imagery of
l. 634. Cf. also Catul. 64. 115 'tecti . . . inobseruabilis error', Virg. *A.*
6. 27 'inextricabilis error', Ov. *Met.* 8. 166f., all of the Labyrinth.

   iucundaque Martis: for the use of the substantival neuter with a partitive genitive *TLL* vii/2. 593. 11 ff. cites, in addition to this passage, Hor. *Ars* 333 f. 'aut prodesse uolunt aut delectare poetae, | aut simul et iucunda et idonea dicere uitae', Mart. 12. 34. 3 f. Note also Pl. *Poen.* 206 'ludos iucundissimos'.

625. Claudian combines the reminiscence of *A.* 5. 578 f. 'signum clamore paratis | Epytides longe dedit insonuitque flagello' with another Virgilian echo, *A.* 7. 451 (Allecto) 'uerberaque insonuit'.

626. To *pariter* cf. Virg. *A.* 5. 580 'pares', and to *edunt . . . motus* cf. Liv. 44. 9. 6 'cum alios decursu edidissent motus'; also Plin. *Nat.* 11. 68 (bees) 'gyris uolatu editis', Mart. 6. 71. 1. The sound-effects of Claudian's line are as carefully orchestrated as the cavalry manœuvre itself. Note the chiastically arranged double initial alliteration (*mutatos, motus; pariter, pectora*) further enhanced by the alliteration of *t.*

627. in latus allisis clipeis: a similar action on the part of three squadrons of horsemen honours the dead Archemorus at Stat. *Theb.* 6. 217 ff. 'ter curuos egere sinus, inlisaque telis | tela sonant, quater horrendum pepulere fragorem | arma'.

627 f. clipeis . . . rursus in altum | uibratis: for such exercises cf. Veget. *Epit. Rei Milit.* 2. 23 'saltus quoque et ictus facere pariter adsuescant, insurgere tripudiantes in clipeum rursusque subsidere.' In real battle this and similar actions may be performed to intimidate the enemy: Liv. 21. 28. 1 (Gauls) 'cantuque moris sui quatientes scuta super capita uibrantesque dextris tela'.

628 f. The deep-sounding clang of the shields as they strike the soldiers' mailed sides (*graue*) is contrasted with the sharp ring of sword on sword (*acutum*). Such contrasts are ten a penny; cf. Cic. *de Orat.* 3. 216, Hor. *Ars* 348 f. 'nam neque chorda sonum reddit quem uult manus et mens, | poscentique grauem persaepe remittit acutum', Apul. *Fl.* 3 (cit. 630 *concentus* n.). For the internal adverbial accusative *graue . . . sonat* cf. Hor. *S.* 1. 8. 41 'cum . . . resonarent triste et acutum'; also Stat. *Theb.* 6. 120 f. 'cum signum luctus cornu graue mugit adunco | tibia', 6. 667. See further Trump 9 and Fargues on *Eutr.* 1. 259. The oddness here is the collocation *mucronis acutum murmur.* Although *acutus* is an appropriate word for the sound of a sword-stroke (cf. Ov. *Met.* 5. 204 'sonuit tinnitibus ensis acutis') as it is, for example, for cymbals (Hor. *Carm.* 1. 16. 7 f., Ov. *Met.* 6. 589), *murmur* is normally applied to deep, low sounds rather than high-pitched, ringing ones. Contrast Sen. *Thy.* 574 'iam silet murmur graue classicorum', Luc. 1. 209 f. (a lion) 'uasto graue murmur hiatu | infremuit', Stat. *Theb.* 9. 348. Given that both passages describe the noise of something knocking against mail-armour along with the sounds of other weapons, perhaps Claudian's unusual diction has been influenced by Stat. *Theb.* 9. 694 ff. 'tereti iuuat aurea morsu | fibula pendentis circum latera aspera cinctus, | uaginaeque sonum tremulumque audire pharetrae | *murmur*'.

629. umbonum pulsu modulante resultans: the booming sound made by the shields as they clash down on the soldiers' mailed sides sets up a kind of tempo. Müller compares *Gild.* 433f. 'fremitum raucosque repulsus | umbonum'. Note also Liv. 27. 37. 14 'uirgines sonum uocis pulsu pedum modulantes incesserunt'. For similar phrasing in descriptions of echoes cf. further Virg. *G.* 4. 49f. 'ubi concaua pulsu | saxa sonant uocisque offensa resultat imago', *Prob.* 176, *Rapt.* 3. 389f., Prud. *Ps.* 658f.

630. concentus: the rhythmical patterning of high and low notes produces a harmony: cf. Apul. *Fl.* 3 'acuto tinnitu et graui bombo, concentum musicum miscuit'.

plauditur: the manuscripts give *clauditur*. This yields good sense if we take it to mean that the blows of the swords continually complete the harmony (*concentus*) set by the reverberating shield-bosses. But if this were so, we should have to imagine that each sequence of clanging and clashing sounds forms a separate *concentus*, or else that Claudian is describing one such sequence and letting it stand for all the repetitions. Although this is perfectly possible, it does not seem well suited to the movement of the general description, which requires us to think in terms of an ongoing process. In all truth, Claudian's wording hardly admits of certainty: it is not even clear whether the shields and swords sound together or in alternation. Quite what he meant will no doubt have been obvious to the audience, most of whose members may be presumed to have witnessed the display itself.

Since, in any case, the emphasis is so very much on sound and on the creation of the *concentus*, Scaliger's brilliant conjecture is here tentatively accepted. It receives some confirmation from the possibility that Claudian has consciously modelled himself on Sil. 3. 347f. (Galician war-dances) 'pedis alterno percussa uerbere terra, | ad numerum resonas gaudentem plaudere caetras.' Note also Stat. *Theb.* 7. 133f. 'ter sustulit hastam, | ter concussit equos, clipeum ter pectore plausit'.

631. una omnis: for the juxtaposition cf. Virg. *A.* 2. 477f. 'una omnis Scyria pubes | succedunt tecto', 5. 830, 8. 105, *Ruf.* 2. 220 'his dictis omnes una fremuere manipli'.

631f. tantaeque salutant | te, princeps, galeae: for the reverse see *Ruf.* 2. 366 'Augustus ueneranda prior uexilla salutat.' As Müller (following Barth) observes, *galeae* = *milites galeati*: cf. *IV Cons.* 151f. (Honorius' birth) 'ambitur signis augustior infans, | sentit adorantes galeas.' For *tanti* = *tot* see 43n.

632f. partitis . . . cateruis | . . . discurritur: from Virg. *A.* 5. 580f. 'olli discurrere pares atque agmina terni | diductis soluere choris'. Note also Sil. 5. 30 'discretis . . . maniplis', 7. 736 'partitis . . . maniplis', *Ruf.* 2. 105.

633. in uarios . . . gyros: the connection between these exercises and the rigours of real battle can once again be seen if we compare this phrase with a passage of Tacitus on German cavalry techniques: *Germ.* 6. 2 'equi . . . nec uariare gyros in morem nostrum docentur: in rectum aut uno flexu dextros agunt, ita coniuncto orbe ut nemo posterior sit.' Cf. also Ov. *Ars* 3. 384 'in gyros ire coactus equus', Sil. 4. 18f.

docto . . . ordine: likewise reflecting a skill essential in battle, as Vegetius stresses: *Epit. Rei Milit.* 2. 23 'illud uero maius est, quod seruare ordines discunt et uexillum suum in tantis permixtionibus in ipsa prolusione comitantur nec inter doctos aliquis error existit, cum multitudinis sit confusio'.

634. semiuiri . . . iuuenci: the Minotaur, 'semibouemque uirum semiuirumque bouem' (Ov. *Ars* 2. 24). Elsewhere in Claudian *semiuir* is used only of the eunuch Eutropius (*Eutr.* 1. 171, 2. 22).

Gortynia tecta: cf. Catul. 64. 75 'attigit iniusti regis Gortynia templa', and see Fordyce ad loc. for the poetic use of *Gortynius* for 'Cretan' ('Minos' capital was at Cnossus (*Od.* 19. 178) and no stress is to be put on the adjective'). Cf. Virg. *Ecl.* 6. 60, *A.* 11. 773, Stat. *Theb.* 4. 530, *Rapt.* 2. 33, *c.m.* 9. 36.

635. For the idea of keeping the Labyrinth simile but substituting the Maeander for Virgil's dolphins Claudian is surely indebted to Ov. *Met.* 8. 159ff., where the Labyrinth is compared at considerable length to the river. Already in the fifth century Herodotus said of one tract of the Nile that it was 'as winding as the Maeander' (2. 29. 3), and with regard to the Phrygian river Strabo notes σκολιὸς ὢν εἰς ὑπερβολήν, ὥστε ἐξ ἐκείνου τὰς σκολιότητας ἁπάσας μαιάνδρους καλεῖσθαι (12. 8. 15). For examples of what Strabo means in Latin see e.g. Cic. *Pis.* 53 'quos tu maeandros . . . quae deuerticula flexionesque quaesisti?', Virg. *A.* 5. 250f. 'chlamydem auratam, quam plurima circum | purpura maeandro duplici Meliboea cucurrit', Gel. 16. 8. 17, Amm. Marc. 30. 1. 12. Descriptions of the Maeander, more often than not presented in the form of similes, abound in Latin poetry, and the subject, like Mt Etna, was 'poetarum omnium exercitatio et ludus' (Sen. *Ep.* 104. 15). See e.g. Prop. 2. 34. 35f., Ov. *Ep.* 9. 55f., *Met.* 2. 246, Sen. *Her. F.* 683ff., Sil. 7. 139f. Next to some of these, Claudian's one-line effort is decidedly small beer.

Maeandria: the adjective is very rare indeed, but cf. Prop. 2. 34. 35f. 'ut Phrygio fallax Maeandria campo | errat', Ov. *Met.* 9. 574.

flexu: see 175 *sinuatis flexibus errans,* 519 *tortis anfractibus* nn.

636. 'Flowing backwards in their separate courses the companies twist into circular formations'. *reuoluta* should possibly be seen as continuing the understated tide-metaphor of *recursus* (623). To *discreto . . . gradu* cf. Sil. 5. 30 'discretis . . . maniplis'. Alternatively, the sense might be 'with circular movements', balancing and effectively repeating *in . . . gyros* (633). For *torquentur in orbes* cf. Virg. *G.* 4. 79 (bees) 'magnum mixtae glomerantur in orbem'. Note also Ov. *Met.* 3. 41 f. (a serpent) 'ille uolubilibus squamosos nexibus orbes | torquet et inmensos saltu sinuatur in arcus'.

637-9. Janus is the guardian of peace and his introduction here primarily stresses the dominant propaganda theme of the whole description of the games: war is ended now that Alaric is gone, and the Romans will witness only these *simulacra* of battle, not the terrors of the real thing. For the ancient tradition, supposedly instituted by Numa, whereby the gates of the temple of Janus Geminus in the Forum were closed when the Roman state was at peace see R. Syme, *The Roman Revolution* (Oxford, 1939), 363 ff.; id., *AJP* 100 (1979), 189-212 = *Roman Papers,* iii (1972), 1079-97. Skutsch on Enn. *Ann.* 225 f., Ogilvie on Liv. 1. 19. 1-4, Austin on Virg. *A.* 1. 293 f., Fordyce on *A.* 7. 607 ff., Coleman on Stat. *Silu.* 4. 1. 14. Other passages in Latin poetry alluding to this custom include Luc. 1. 61 f. 'pax missa per orbem | ferrea belligeri conpescat limina Iani', Mart. 8. 66. 11 f., Stat. *Silu.* 4. 1. 13 f. As is well known, Augustus made much of the fact that he had closed these gates on no fewer than three occasions (*Res Gestae* 13), but the propaganda value of such symbolic actions was also exploited by later Emperors, particularly Domitian. In addition, however, Janus is the patron of the new year and therefore of the consulship itself. He thus provides an ingenious organic link between the end of this section and the envoi to the poem; note how he bridges the gap between lines 639 and 640 in that he is the subject of both *largitur* and *aperit.* In all this Claudian is once again taking his cue from Statius' panegyric on the seventeenth consulship of Domitian, a poem in which Janus himself pronounces encomium of the Emperor-consul and predicts numerous glorious successes for the future (*Silu.* 4. 1). For Janus as the guardian of the sanctity of the consulship and the *fasti* see also *Eutr.* 1. 319 'eunuchumque uetat fastis accedere Ianus'.

637 f. Janus firmly closes the gates of his shrine, imprisoning the personified *Bella* inside. For the basic imagery Claudian is no doubt dependent on Virg. *A.* 1. 293 ff. (a prediction of peace in the new Golden Age to come) 'dirae ferro et compagibus artis | claudentur Belli portae; Furor impius intus | saeua sedens super arma et centum uinctus aënis | post tergum nodis fremet horridus ore cruento': see both Austin and Williams ad loc. Alternatively, it may be Peace who is imagined as shut up inside the shrine, i.e. 'secured', as at Ov. *Fast.* 1. 279ff. 'ut populo reditus pateant ad bella profecto, | tota patet dempta ianua nostra sera. | pace fores obdo, ne qua discedere possit; | Caesareoque diu numine clausus ero.' In another variation on the idea, sometimes Janus seems to be thought of as a warmonger and is himself imprisoned (as in a sense his cult-image was when the gates were closed) while Peace ranges free throughout the world: Luc. 1. 61f., Stat. *Silu.* 4. 1. 13f., *Stil.* 2. 237 'Ianum pax alta ligat.' Note that Claudian's precise phrasing recalls Hor. *Ep.* 2. 1. 255 'claustraque custodem pacis cohibentia Ianum', and esp. Mart. 10. 28. 7f. (to Janus) 'at tu, sancte pater, tanto pro munere gratus, | ferrea perpetua claustra tuere sera.'

638. premens: the allusion to Jupiter's prophecy of the Golden Age is combined with one to another passage from *Aeneid* 1, Aeolus' imprisoning the winds in his rocky cavern: *A.* 1. 52ff. 'hic uasto rex Aeolus antro | luctantis uentos tempestatesque sonoras | imperio *premit* ac uinclis et carcere frenat'. Note also Stat. *Silu.* 3. 2. 45f.

laeta sub imagine pugnae: recalling Virgil's description of the *lusus Troiae* as 'pugnae . . . simulacra sub armis' (*A.* 5. 585); cf. also 573f. *simulacra belli | uiua* n. The epithet may hint at the idea that the cavalry display is in a sense a representation (*imagine*) of a war against the Goths whose conclusion has been 'successful'; for this sense of *laetus* see e.g. Sil. 10. 551 'laeti libamina belli'. But the word also plays on the idea that joy accompanies the restoration of peace through victory: see *pr.* 19f., and 198f. In addition, *laeta* sets the tone for the epilogue: see further 640 *fastis . . . felicibus* n.

639. innocuos paci largitur honores: cf. Hor. *Ep.* 2. 1. 15 'praesenti tibi maturos largimur honores', V. Fl. 2. 650, Stat. *Theb.* 1. 663f. 'tristemque uiro submissus honorem | largitur uitae', Aus. *Grat. Act.* 71 Green, *IV Cons.* 118f.

640–60. *And now begins a new year under the auspices of Victory; it surpasses all that have gone before, and is a model for all that are still to come.*

The panegyric moves with sweeping grandeur into its rousing epilogue. In ring-composition with the opening sections of the poem Claudian stresses that in the person of Honorius the consulship has returned to its proper home (649–53; cf. 11–17), but this is also united with the poem's other dominant themes of victory (645–8) and of the harmony of Court and Senate (641f.). The joyous atmosphere once more strongly recalls that of Statius' poem on the seventeenth consulship of Domitian (*Silu.* 4. 1). In Claudian this rejoicing serves to bring all the different threads together: Victory has given birth to this Imperial consulship and its celebration in the ancient capital of the Empire itself, while the rejoicing of Rome at the sight of the Emperor (643f.) melts into rejoicing at the restoration of peace through the defeat of the Goths (644–8; cf. 638 *laeta sub imagine pugnae* n.). Born under the auspices of Victory, this consulship eclipses all those that have preceded it, whether held by private citizens, by Theodosius or earlier Emperors, or by Honorius himself (654–7). And it will never be surpassed (657–60).

640f. In this, the beginning of his epilogue, Claudian seems once more to be consciously reworking the opening of Statius' consular panegyric for Domitian: *Silu.* 4. 1. 1f. 'laeta bis octonis accedit purpura fastis | Caesaris insignemque aperit Germanicus annum'. This is not, however, guaranteed since the phrasing was by now essentially traditional: cf. Ov. *Pont.* 4. 4. 23 'ergo ubi, Iane biceps, longum reseraueris annum', Plin. *Pan.* 58. 3, *PLM* v. 84. 7 Baehrens (= *Geographi Latini Minores*, ed. Riese, p. 20) (Theodosius) 'ter quinis aperit cum fascibus annum', Symm. *Ep.* 1. 13. 2, *Stil.* 2. 268, Sid. *Carm.* 2. 3. Coleman on Stat. *Silu.* 4. 1. 2 comments that 'the phrase *annum aperire* appears to have been used as a technical term referring to the cycle of the planets', and cites Virg. *G.* 1. 217f. 'candidus auratis aperit cum cornibus annum | Taurus'.

640. fastis . . . felicibus: picking up *laeta* (638) and foreshadowing *laetatur* (643), as well as echoing Stat. *Silu.* 4. 1. 1. Cf. also Stat. *Silu.* 4. 1. 20f. 'da gaudia fastis | continua'. In panegyric, of course, whoever the new consul may be, his year of office is inaugurated to universal rejoicing: cf. Stat. *Silu.* 4. 1. 5 'exsultent leges Latiae, gaudete, curules', *Prob.* 7, 267, *IV Cons.* 611f. 'auspice mox laetum sonuit clamore tribunal | te fastos ineunte quater', *Stil.* 3. 49. Hence the grim irony of Luc. 5. 382ff. (Caesar) 'populoque precanti | scilicet indulgens summo dictator honori | contigit et laetos fecit se consule fastos'.

641. ore coronatus gemino: i.e. with wreaths, presumably of victory laurel, on both his brows. Claudian is playing on the cult title *Ianus Geminus* (Var. *L.* 5. 156, Vell. 2. 38. 3, Plin. *Nat.* 33. 45). Cf. Ov. *Fast.* 1. 135, Stat. *Silu.* 4. 1. 16 'gemina . . . haec uoce profatur'.

641f. In the person of the Emperor-consul a perfect harmony is achieved between republican *libertas* (*Bruti . . . trabeas*) and monarchical rule (*sceptra Quirini*). Such sentiments recur in other passages praising both Honorius and Stilicho, and the reconciliation of Brutus, who drove out Tarquin and founded the consulship, is a regular topos expressing the constitutional nature of their rule. Note esp. *Theod.*

417

163 ff. 'nunc Brutus amaret | uiuere sub regno, tali succumberet aulae | Fabricius, cuperent ipsi seruire Catones', *Stil.* 3. 113 ff., 3. 191 f. 'macte nouis consul titulis! Mauortia plebes | te dominum Bruto non indignante fatetur', Sid. *Carm.* 7. 7 ff. Elsewhere Stilicho is associated with Brutus in his capacity as defender of the consulship against the pollution of Eutropius: *Stil.* 2. 322 'sic trabeis ultor Stilicho Brutusque repertor.' Properly speaking the *trabea* too was originally an emblem of kingship, as Claudian would no doubt have known from Virg. *A.* 7. 612 'Quirinali trabea'; cf. also Juv. 8. 259 f. (Servius Tullius) 'trabeam et diadema Quirini | et fascis meruit', Aus. *Ep.* 24. 56 f. Green. For Claudian, however, the *trabea* is primarily associated with the consulship: see 4 *trabeis* n. Cf. further Sil. 6. 103 'sceptra Quirini', *Gild.* 96 f. 'ille diu miles populus, qui praefuit orbi, | qui trabeas et sceptra dabat'.

641. Thybris: recalling both 12 *quem Thybris inaugurat, annus* and 425 *iuuenem te Thybris adoret,* and so further binding the end of the poem to both the prooemium and Roma's central speech.

643 f. The Palatine rejoices to see once more, after so long, an Imperial consul. Here we have still tighter ring-composition with the opening sections of the poem: cf. 25–38, esp. 35 f., where the Palatine revels in the Emperor's return just as Delphi does in the return of Apollo from the land of the Hyperboreans. For the Palatine as the true home of the Emperors and as the proper seat of Imperial power see *pr.* 23 *orbis apex aequatus Olympo,* 8 *natiua Palatia,* 11 *mons Euandrius,* 39–52 nn.

On the face of it *consule . . . post plurima saecula uiso* looks like a piece of particularly outrageous hyperbole; Claudian had himself celebrated the inaugurations of consuls in Rome in *Prob.* and *Stil.* 3 within the last decade. But no doubt the emphasis is on the Palatine as the home of a consul, i.e. it is *plurima saecula* since a new consul, winding his way back from the ceremonies in the Forum Romanum to his own ancestral house, ended his journey in the Palace (see 603 f. n.). Even so, *plurima* is something of an exaggeration.

644. Pallanteus apex: a learned periphrasis much like *mons Euandrius* (11 n.) in character; contrast the plainer *Palatino . . . monti* (35). According to mythological lore, Pallanteum was the name of the original settlement established on the Palatine by Evander's Arcadians (Virg. *A.* 8. 54, 341), and so it is applied as a substantive to the whole hill at *Stil.* 2. 405 'nomen Auentino Pallanteoque recussum.' The epithet, however, is of the utmost rarity, though cf. Virg. *A.* 9. 196 'moenia Pallantea'.

agnoscunt rostra curules: cf. 594 *agnoscunt proceres.* For *curules* see 431 *aduectae misso Stilichone curules,* 588 *solio fultus . . . eburno* nn.

645. auditas quondam proauis: for similar phrases, also making concise use of the dative of agent, cf. Sil. 14. 284 'spectatum proauis', Stat. *Theb.* 11. 221 'auditos proauis agnoscimus ignes'.

645–8. As Gesner remarks 'Utrum revera in foro Trajano s. Ulpio pompam ex triumphali et consulari mistam celebraverit Honorius, an ornandi modo causa hoc poeta finxerit, non liquet.' If it did indeed take place, it would seem that it featured a ritual *calcatio* of Gothic prisoners of war: see further 648 n. Whether imaginary or not, the scene described is clearly to be paralleled with the extension of Roman *imperium* into the barbarian lands of the far north under Trajan, and Honorius is thus symbolically re-enacting the conquests of his glorious 'ancestor': see 337 f. n. A passage of Sidonius may incidentally offer us a clue to another element of the ceremony Claudian has in mind: *Carm.* 2. 544 ff. 'nam modo nos iam festa uocant, et ad Vlpia poscunt | te fora, donabis quos libertate, Quirites, | quorum gaudentes exceptant uerbera malae'. The reference is to the ancient custom whereby the new consul set a number of slaves free in a public ceremony during which each slave was symbolically struck across the cheek: see R. G. Nisbet, *JRS* 8 (1918), 1–14 for this custom. Honorius had apparently performed the ceremony as part of the festivities marking his fourth consulship in AD 398 (*IV Cons.* 612 ff., with Barr ad loc.), so it is perfectly conceivable that he did so again in Rome in 404.

The Forum of Trajan would surely have been a magnificent setting for any such ceremony. Ammianus Marcellinus leaves us with a vivid record of the humbling impression it made on Constantius II in AD 357: 'uerum cum ad Traiani forum uenisset, singularem sub omni caelo structuram, ut opinamur, etiam numinum assensione mirabilem, haerebat attonitus, per giganteos contextus circumferens mentem' (16. 10. 15). It was there that Claudian's own statue was placed by order of the Senate (*Get. pr.* 7 f.; Cameron 248 f., 361, 404, 490, *CIL* vi. 1710). The same honour would later be accorded to Sidonius, as he records at *Carm.* 8. 7 f. and *Ep.* 9. 16. 3, vv. 25 ff.

645. desueta: passive: cf. 405 *desuetum* n.

646. regius . . . lictor: an oxymoron here (see 42 *regia*, 64 *regale . . . culmen* nn.), though, like the *trabea* (641 f. n.), the *fasces* and *lictores* were originally emblems of kingship: e.g. Virg. *A.* 7. 173 f. 'hic sceptra accipere et primos attollere fascis | regibus omen erat'.

auratis . . . fascibus: a step up from the usual purple bands that kept the rods of the *fasces* together (Lyd. *De Magistratibus Pop. Rom.* 1. 32 πλῆθος ἀνδρῶν ῥάβδους ἐπιφερομένων, ἐξ ὧν ἱμάντες φοινικῷ χρώματι βεβαμμένοι ἐξήρτηντο), though note that *RE* vi. 2006. 11ff. assumes that Claudian is using his poetic imagination here.

fora . . . Vlpia: cf. Sid. *Carm.* 2. 544f., 8. 8 'Vlpia . . . porticus'; also *Vlpius* (= *Traianus*) at 335, *IV Cons.* 19 'Vlpia progenies'.

647. Getica praeuelans fronde: i.e. with laurels celebrating the victory over the Goths. For the well-attested custom of intertwining the *fasces* with laurel to celebrate victories cf. *IV Cons.* 14 'laurigeras . . . secures' and see *RE* vi. 2005. 59ff. The compound *praeuelo* is also found at *Stil.* 2. 189 and *Rapt.* 2. 325. It seems to have no parallel in classical Latin, but for the general language cf. Virg. *A.* 2. 248f. 'nos delubra deum . . . festa uelamus fronde per urbem.'

648. Although 'the *calcatio* seems to have been an iconographical theme before it entered the repertory of imperial triumphal gestures' (McCormick 58 n. 76), Claudian may well be referring to a literal act of prostration and ritual trampling of Gothic captives. If so, this would apparently be the first attested example of the kind of ceremony in which, amid much pomp, Justinian demonstrated the subjection of Gelimer in the Vandal triumph of AD 534 (Cameron on Cor. *Laud. Iust. pr.* 2 'sub pedibus' and 1. 285f. nn.) as well as of usurpers on another occasion (McCormick 73) and in which Heraclius trampled Phocas (ibid. 70; cf. ibid. 57f., for the possibility that Priscus Attalus, the Visigoths' unfortunate puppet-Emperor, was humiliated in this way in 416, during triumphal celebrations likewise held in Rome). Cf. further Vulg. Deut. 33: 29 'negabunt te inimici tui, et tu eorum colla calcabis', Ps. 88: 11, 90 (91): 13, Luc. 7. 293 'calcatos . . . simul reges', *Pan. Lat.* 3. 6. 2 Mynors 'calcata regum capita superuolans', Prud. *C. Symm.* 1. 462f. 'seu debellata duorum | colla tyrannorum media calcemus in urbe', Ps. 452, Priscian, *Pan. Anast.* 171ff., Cor. *Laud. Iust.* 1. 285f. 'ipsum autem in media uictorem pinxerat aula | effera Vandalici calcantem colla tyranni', 2. 107f., *Ioh.* 1. 17, 2. 2. For coin evidence see also Henry Cohen, *Description historique des monnaies frappées sous l'Empire* (Paris, 1883; repr. Graz, 1955), i. 511, no. 503; viii. 183, no. 34.

colla: poetic plural: see 490 *pectora* n., and cf. 382, 527, 563.

triumphati . . . Histri: for the metonymy see 220 *saeuum . . . Histrum* n. Cf. *III Cons.* 25 (Theodosius) 'signa triumphato quotiens flexisset ab Histro', *IV Cons.* 317.

proculcat: a rather rare word, appearing once only in Virgil for example (*A.* 12. 534), but Claudian seems to have a fondness for it: cf. *Gild.* 31f. 'non ut proculcet Araxen | consul ouans', *IV Cons.* 472, *Get.* 607.

649. An answer is given here to the question of 11f.; the year 'inaugurated by the Palatine and the Tiber' is 'cunctis inlustrior'. For the phrasing cf. Ov. *Fast.* 1. 26 'auspice te felix totus ut annus eat', *III Cons.* 3 'festior annus eat'.

650. natus fonte suo: 'born from its own true source'. The year is born with the consulship, and so, like the consulship, it is imagined as being properly native to Rome. For idea and phrasing cf. Stat. *Silu.* 4. 1. 19 f. 'sic tempora nasci, | sic annos intrare decet'.

   aliena per arua: such as Milan, Ravenna, or Constantinople. For the collocation cf. Virg. *A.* 4. 311, 10. 78. This phrase is part of a complex of groups of alliterating words (cf. *hospes honos* 651; *cuius cunabula . . . | curia* 651 f.), which combined with anaphora (*quem, cuius, quem, quem* 650–3) and parataxis take us to a triumphant, excited pause at 653. Claudian then draws breath and soars upwards to his majestic conclusion (654–60).

651. induit hospes honos: *hospes* because 'a stranger in a strange land'. Cf. e.g. Luc. 5. 10 f. 'secretaque rerum | hospes in externis audiuit curia tectis', of the Senate in exile, and *IV Cons.* 187 f. (a star visible at noon) 'alieni temporis hospes, | ignis'. *honos* is used of the consulship (the *summus honos*) at e.g. *Eutr.* 1. 488, *Stil.* 2. 325 'instituit sublimem Brutus honorem'. For *induit* cf. *IV Cons.* 1 f. 'auspiciis iterum sese regalibus annus | induit'.

651 f. cuius cunabula fouit | curia: the consulship is the child of Victoria (*peperit* 653) and since her statue is in the Senate House, the *curia* guards the new year's cradle. Related to this are the images of Roma nurturing the young consuls (*Prob.* 143 ff. 'pignora cara Probi, festa quos luce creatos | ipsa meo foui gremio. cunabula paruis | ipsa dedi') and of Rome as the mother of the law (*Stil.* 3. 136 f. 'armorum legumque parens, quae fundit in omnes | imperium primique dedit cunabula iuris'). For the personified *curia* cf. Stat. *Silu.* 5. 2. 27 'sic te, clare puer, genitum sibi curia sensit', and for the line-ending cf. also *IV Cons.* 21 f. 'cunabula fouit | Oceanus'.

652. Quirites: i.e. Roman citizens who actually belong to Rome, the archaic word being used in triumphant and respectful emphasis, as at 587 and *Stil.* 3. 54 'aduentum . . . petiere Quirites'. Contrast the scathing oxymoron of 'Graios . . . Quirites' at *Eutr.* 2. 136; Sid. *Carm.* 2. 32 'Eoo . . . Quiriti', however, is a serious compliment.

653. domitis . . . Bellis: echoing *Ianus Bella premens* 638; cf. *Ruf.* 2. 389 'bis domitum ciuile nefas'. The phrase gives off a whiff of oxymoron, by comparison with the literal, and far more usual, *domitus bello*.

   auspex peperit Victoria: i.e. it is the victories over the Goths at Pollentia and Verona that persuaded the Emperor to assume this consulship, and so Victoria is in a sense the mother of the new year. This is an adaptation of the kind of idea seen at *IV Cons.* 619 ff., 638 ff. 'sed

patriis olim fueras successibus auctor, | nunc eris ipse tuis. semper
uenere triumphi | cum trabeis sequiturque tuos uictoria fasces'; this
time Victory precedes rather than 'follows the *fasces*'. For *auspex* of
patron or supporting deities cf. Virg. *A.* 3. 19 f. 'sacra Dionaeae matri
diuisque ferebam | auspicibus coeptorum operum', 4. 45. Cf. also *IV
Cons.* 611 f. 'auspice mox laetum sonuit clamore tribunal | te fastos ine-
unte quater.' *auspex* here prepares the triumphant last word of the
poem, *auctor*, for the etymological word-play and the ring-composition
cf. 10 *Augusta . . . suffragia*, 24 *auget* nn.

654–60. That the year to which the consular honorand gives his name
in some way surpasses all those that have gone before is an obvious
enough compliment for a panegyrist to make, and Claudian had said
much the same to his first attested patrons in Italy ten years before:
Prob. 275 ff. (addressed to the *annus*) 'omni nobilior lustro tibi gloria soli
| contigit, exactum numquam memorata per aeuum, | germanos
habuisse duces'. Here, however, the hyperbole reaches a remarkable
pitch. Claudian firmly asserts not only that the Emperor's sixth
consulship eclipses all others in the past, including his Impèrial predecessors' and his own previous five, but that it will never be equalled
by any he celebrates in Rome in the future; indeed it will be the model
for all to come. Nothing could demonstrate more clearly the huge
importance attached to the victories of Pollentia and Verona by
Claudian's patrons, but it is also fitting that Claudian's transmitted
work ends with a passage that shows him at the very height of his
rhetorical powers. Cf. the judgement of Barth, 'et ita pro tempore
etiam magnificum hoc et splendidissimum carmen seponimus': and
also that of Gesner, 'finis magnifici carminis inveniri magnificentior
an potuerit, dubito'.

654. priuati . . . anni: i.e. those in which the consul is a subject. The
application of *priuatus* to any individual other than the Emperor, indicating the extent to which the monarch had become identified with
the state, was well-established by Claudian's time. Cf. Ov. *Am.* 2. 18.
16 'sceptra . . . priuata tam cito sumpta manu', Stat. *Theb.* 2. 310, Plin.
Ep. 5. 3. 5 'si non sufficerent exempla priuata, diuum Iulium, diuum
Augustum, diuum Neruam, Tiberium Caesarem'. Claudian offers
several examples of the word used in clear contrast with the rank of
the Emperor: e.g. *Ruf.* 1. 194 f. (an oxymoron) 'populi seruire coacti |
plenaque *priuato* succumbunt oppida *regno*', *IV Cons.* 3 f. 'limina nec
passi circum priuata morari | exultant reduces Augusto consule
fasces', 123, *c.m.* 30. 37 f., 98. But see also 61 n.

titulis famulantibus: the *fasti* were headed by the name of the
consul ordinarius. Cf. *Eutr.* 1. 10 'titulumque effeminat anni' for the

sense: since Eutropius is a eunuch, his name at the head of the *fasti* renders them effeminate too, just as here the names of *priuati* on the *fasti* make them in their turn 'subject'.

655. armipotens genitor: Theodosius is thus associated with Mars: Lucr. 1. 32 f. 'Mauors | armipotens', Virg. *A.* 9. 717, Ov. *Fast.* 2. 481 (of Mars) 'pater armipotens', 5. 559, Stat. *Theb.* 3. 344, 7. 78. Note also Acc. *trag.* 127 Ribbeck (= 260 Dangel, 251 Warmington) 'Mineruae donum armipotenti.' The majestic epithet is occasionally applied to human heroes in epic, but only to the greatest, such as Achilles (Virg. *A.* 6. 839) and Paulus (Sil. 13. 711). Theodosius the Great held the consulship three times, in AD 380, 388, and 393.

retroque priores: for the adverb used as an adjective (= *prioribus*) see Birt, p. ccxxi and cf. SHA *Sev. Alex.* 35 'si quis ei recitauit Alexandri Magni laudes aut meliorum retro principum', *Eutr.* 1. 476 'retro ducibus', *CIL* viii. 6303 'principis . . . super omnes retro principes inuictissimi', *C. Th.* 9. 7. 2.

656. ceu numen adorent: the Emperor's divine power (17 n., 365, 611 etc.) is passed on to the year that bears his name, and the other years accordingly show it the same reverence that Roma had imagined Honorius receiving from the Tiber (425). Note the ring-composition with 17 (sc. *hic annus) urbis et Augusti geminato numine felix.* For the collocation cf. also Virg. *A.* 3. 437 'Iunonis magnae primum prece numen adora', Ov. *Pont.* 3. 1. 97, 163, Prud. *Tit. Hist.* 112, and see also 425 *te Thybris adoret* n.

657. quinque tui: i.e. those of AD 386, 394, 396, 398, and 402.

657f. In the event, Honorius was consul a total of thirteen times, the future consulships being held in AD 407, 409, 412, 415, 417, 418, and 422. It is not known for sure whether any of these was inaugurated in Rome, though it is possible that the seventh was; see O. Seeck, *Regesten der Kaiser und Päpste für die Jahre 311 bis 476 n. Chr.* (Stuttgart, 1919; repr. Frankfurt, 1984), who points out that Honorius is known to have been in Ravenna on 7 Dec. 406, but in Rome on 22 Feb. 407.

Wishes, assumptions, or predictions that the honorand or his sons and grandsons will celebrate more consulships are standard: cf. esp. Stat. *Silu.* 4. 1. 17 ff., esp. 35 ff. 'manet insuper ordo | longior, et totidem felix tibi Roma curules | terque quaterque dabit. mecum altera saecula condes, | et tibi longaeui renouabitur ara Tarenti', *Theod.* 336 ff. 'accipiat patris exemplum tribuatque nepoti | filius et coeptis ne desit fascibus heres. | decurrat trabeata domus tradatque secures | mutua posteritas seruatoque ordine fati | Mallia continuo numeretur consule proles.'

658f. unus in omnes | consul eas: 'and were you as sole consul to inaugurate them all'. For the striking tmesis Müller compares Ov. *Met.* 5. 668 'ibimus in poenas'. For the phrasing cf. also *IV Cons.* 612 'te fastos ineunte quater.' Although *ineo* is commonly used of taking up a magistracy (*OLD* s.v. 5), perhaps Claudian has been influenced yet again by Statius on the seventeenth consulship of Domitian: *Silu.* 4. 1. 19 ff. 'sic tempora nasci, | sic annos intrare decet. da gaudia fastis | continua'. There, however, the parallel structure with *tempora nasci* shows that Coleman is right to translate 'thus should eras be born, thus should the years make their entry'.

660. praeteritis melior, uenientibus auctor: impressively adapting and heightening the effect of yet another fairly conventional wish: cf. *IV Cons.* 619 ff., cit. 13–15 n. For *auctor* see 653 *auspex peperit Victoria* n., and cf. also *Prob.* 267 'o consanguineis felix auctoribus anne', *IV Cons.* 638.

INDEX NOMINVM ET RERVM

INDEX VERBORVM